INTERCOMMUNICATION
AMONG NATIONS
AND PEOPLES

Without communication, there is no peace.

INTERCOMMUNICATION AMONG NATIONS AND PEOPLES

edited by
MICHAEL H. PROSSER
University of Virginia

assisted by William J. Starosta

HARPER & ROW, Publishers
New York, Evanston, San Francisco, London

Under the Advisory Editorship of J. Jeffery Auer

TO MY STUDENTS

Books Edited by Michael H. Prosser

Intercommunication Among Nations and Peoples

Sow the Wind, Reap the Whirlwind: Heads of State Address the United Nations (2 Vols.)

Readings in Classical Rhetoric (with Thomas W. Benson)

An Ethic for Survival: Adlai Stevenson Speaks on International Affairs, 1936–1965

Intercommunication Among Nations and Peoples

Copyright © 1973 by Michael H. Prosser

Standard Book Number: 06-045287-0
Library of Congress Catalog Card Number: 72-82903

CONTENTS

EDITOR'S PREFACE

"Out of confrontation came communication."

Opening the debate at the twenty-fifth anniversary of the United Nations, in October 1970, Mitchell W. Sharp, Secretary of State for Canada, reminded the assembled dignitaries: "Out of confrontation came communication. . . . Nations met here, as we are meeting today, in a continuing conference. The whole concept of diplomacy went through a profound change: from narrow, formalized negotiations carried on by an elite bureaucracy, we moved to a broad interchange of ideas involving whole nations and their leaders." Walter J. Ong in The Presence of the Word argues that "without communication there is no peace," which reminds us of Camus' words: "Tragedy today is collective; the long dialogue of men must go on." Sharp concluded: "Wherever we come from, whatever our constitutional forms, whatever credentials we hold, we are all here representing people. . . . Our peoples now all know this, all around the globe. They can, via satellite and other marvels of instant communication, watch us now, all the time. They will know if we fail them, why and how."

Though Vice-President Rabamananjara of the Republic of Madagascar accused delegates assembled for the commemorative session of "talking sickness," still he recalled the proposal of St. Augustine: "It is more glorious to put down wars with words than to kill men with steel, and it is truly glorious to win peace through peace." Dialogue between nations and peoples is increasing. Sometimes it is conducted peacefully. At other times, there is truth in Vice-President Rabamananjara's statement: "Words of peace are spoken, and what we have is war."

Dialogue must occur not only between cultures but between divergent subcultures, such as American blacks and whites, to keep the channels of communication open while recognizing the very real obstacles to be encountered in maintaining this dialogue, lest blacks view themselves as victims of a cruel hoax, so that chaos rather than dialogue is the likely outcome. Similar obstacles endanger communication of subcultures of other nations. Conflict between Arab and Jewish Palestinians, Ibo Biafrans and Nigerians of other tribes, the Indo-Pakistani in Kashmir, the divided Germans, Vietnamese, and Koreans all are symptomatic of the difficulties which prevent intercommunication effectively between cultures, races, creeds, and nationalities. Still, we cannot easily afford President Tombalbaye of Chad's ultimate "despair of being a man," or Premier Khrushchev's alternative between peaceful coexistence or "coexistence at daggers drawn." While man wishes to survive, he wishes to determine the quality of his own survival. To survive, man must communicate.

In this volume, I propose to demonstrate varied aspects of intercommunication between nations and peoples, the failures inherent in such events, and their possible remedies. Seeking to discover what unites, rather than what separates, men is at best difficult. Nonetheless, it leads us to consider whether there are communication universals which transcend national and cultural boundaries. The study of intercultural and international communication is shared by the best efforts of anthropologists, political scientists, public opinion analysts, sociologists, historians, communicologists, and varied other scholars. Representing both American and foreign scholars and journals of widely diverse backgrounds, we shall search for a broader understanding of theoretical and methodological perspectives on intercommunication, attitude formation and opinion development, the communication of leadership, communciation in conflict resolution, communication as an index and agent of social change, propaganda, communication rights as aspects of freedom, and the integrative role of intercommunication. Since communication often fails, these failures, and sometimes solutions and remedies, will be studied within and between cultures throughout the volume. My own view of cautious optimism that men can communicate without resorting to the final plateau of communication, violence. is represented also by many of the writers whose essays have been collected here. This perspective offers at least a ripple of hope for the integrative function of intercommunication to which Colin Cherry, one of our earliest and foremost students of international and intercultural communication, alludes in the final essay in the volume.

I am particularly grateful to J. Jeffery Auer, Advisory Editor, for his enthusiastic recognition of the potential significance of such a volume for an interdisciplinary study of international and intercultural communication. William J. Starosta, my first graduate major in crosscultural communication, and my assistant in this endeavor, has given me considerable realistic advice and assistance. The insights provided by my former students at the State University of New York at Buffalo and Queens College of the City University of New York, and recently at Indiana University, California State College at Hayward, and Memorial University of New Foundland deserve my thanks and admiration.

Canadian Secretary of State Mitchell W. Sharp offered a stern warning to the assembled delegates at the United Nations' twenty-fifth anniversary celebration:

> Throughout the world there is deep dissatisfaction rooted, I believe, in a profound uneasiness that has seized peoples everywhere—uneasiness about a world wracked by bloody conflict, uneasiness about economic prospects, uneasiness about the quality and meaning of human life, uneasiness about the health of the air we breathe, the water we drink and the soil that gives us sustenance.
>
> . . . Dissatisfaction is most clearly to be seen among the young, the oppressed, the alienated and the poor; yet it is to be found increasingly among people in the prime of life, people who enjoy material success. It affects the leaders as well as the led.

Thus the need for renewed and constructive dialogue, reasoned discourse among and between cultures, nations, and peoples has never been more critical. If indeed we are beginning to live in a "global village," our questioning of the great constants of civilization, and relevant response to these questions must be explored and shared both internationally and crossculturally, lest the escatological doomsday prophets be proved right. Out of confrontation has come communication. Communication remains both the means and sometimes the index of the level of peaceful coexistence among nations and peoples. Failures to communicate effectively are prevalent. Nevertheless, men must communicate whether they will it or not. Silence isolates. Isolation endangers survival. The final plateau of communication is violence. Mankind deserves not merely to survive, but to share the quality of his survival peacefully and harmoniously with his fellows throughout his global village.

MICHAEL H. PROSSER

INTERCOMMUNICATION
AMONG NATIONS
AND PEOPLES

COMMUNICATION, COMMUNICATIONS, AND INTERCOMMUNICATION

COMMUNICATION AND CULTURE

Men must communicate, whether or not they will to communicate. Even contradiction implies communication. As Prime Minister Julius K. Nyerre of Tanzania says: "We believe that all mankind is one, that the psychological differences between us are unimportant in comparison with our common humanity. . . . Each one of us is part of the human species and has a part to play in the development of mankind" (Nyerre 1970: 823–834).* The humanizing feature of man is his ability to create and receive symbolic messages that help him to determine the quality of his life. Kenneth Oliver calls communication the most important business of man: "Civilization itself might well be called that state of being in which communication is achieved" (Oliver 1957: 3). Wilbur Schramm argues that although communication has no life of its own, it is something which all people do: "It is the fundamental process of society, the way that people relate to each other" (Schramm 1967: 11). The theory of Watzlawick and Beavin's argument that "in the presence of another, all behavior is communicative" rests on the assumption that communication is inevitable in social situations because all behavior, not only the use of words, is communication, which is not the same as saying that behavior is *only* communicative. Since there is no such thing as nonbehavior, it is impossible *not* to communicate (Watzlawick and Beavin 1967: 5; but for noncommunication see also Starosta in this volume). In the same sense that Schramm sees communication as having no life of its own, however, Birdwhistell thinks that an individual does not communicate but engages in or becomes part of communication: "He may move, or make noises, . . . but he does not communicate. In a parallel fashion, he may see, he may hear, smell, taste, or feel—but he does not communicate. In other words, he does not originate communication; he participates in it" (Birdwhistell 1959: 104).

Because man communicates willy-nilly, it takes almost superhuman effort to remain constantly silent or noncommunicative (see, for example, Meerloo 1967: 145–148). When the Trappists take seriously, as they have consistently since A.D. 1098, the statement "Death and life lie in the hands of the tongue" from the *Holy Rule* of St. Benedict, they use verbal communication within their monasteries only in the praise of God and in moral instruction and theological discussion. Thomas Merton has reflected: "Silence does not exist in our lives merely for its own sake. It is ordered to something else. Silence is the mother of speech. A lifetime of silence is ordered to an ultimate declaration,

* Because of the great diversity of journals from which these essays come, two general methods for reference citation are included, the one above, which is now used by the *American Anthropologist* and a growing number of journals in the social sciences, and the older pattern of notes, which many journals still adhere to. All original material in this volume consistently adheres to the above pattern.

which can be put into words, a declaration of all we have lived for. . . . We work out our salvation in silence and in hope. Silence is the strength of our interior life. Silence enters into the very core of our moral being, so that if we have no silence we have no morality" (Merton 1955: 428–429). Without some form of communication, however, the Trappists would be unable to live in the community, cooperatively interacting in order to fulfill the second aspect of the Benedictine motto, "Ora et labora" or "Pray and work." Since they live by silence, they have established an elaborate form of gestural sign language. If it seems quaint to the monastery visitor, at times it becomes absolutely hazardous when the monks misunderstand the sign language connected with a dangerous building project or electrical repairs. Additionally, traditional Benedictine hospitality is hard pressed when the visitor seeks to strike up even a brief conversation with the silent monk who has not been especially authorized to speak. Thus, recently most American Trappist monasteries have relaxed the rule of silence somewhat when verbal communication is absolutely essential and, at the same time, have isolated themselves still more from the outside world by halting the retreats for laymen that have been one of their traditional services and sources of incomes for the monasteries. In fact, some of the monks establish hermitages on the monastery property so that they will have minimal contact even with their monastic community in order to be able to devote themselves more totally to God.

Communication is a universal, transcending time and culture. Dell Hymes believes that to define communication as the whole of culture and of all behavior as culturally determined extends the meaning of either culture or communication too broadly. He agrees with the generally accepted notion that communication involves a socially shared pattern and an individual aspect of experience and capability for symbolic interpretation; but he insists that a correct understanding of culture and communication demonstrates that neither exhausts the limits of human behavior (Hymes 1967: 17–18). Alfred G. Smith assesses human communication as an ever-present set of processes: "Whenever people interact, they communicate. To live in societies and to maintain their culture they have to communicate. When people control one another, they do so primarily through communication" (Smith 1966: v). *Cybernetics*, the term coined by Norbert Weiner to explain the control of information in electronic, mechanical, and biological systems, has by current usage come to include the control of communication in societal, political, and media systems. Smith expands his concept of the relationship between communication and culture, explaining "Our perception is behavior that is learned and shared, and it is mediated by symbols. Culture is a code we learn and share, and learning and sharing require communication. And communication requires coding and symbols, which must be learned and shared. Communication and culture are inseparable" (Smith 1966: 7).

CULTURE AND THE SENSES

Culture itself affects the communicative behavior of its members. Robert T. Oliver suggests that "Mankind is separated less by language barriers (grievous though they are) than it is by cultural differences. Not only do we not speak alike, but, more importantly, we do not think alike. Every separate community has its own value system. Every culture has its own modes of thought and its own selected interest areas which constitute the subject matter it chooses to think about" (Oliver 1962: xi). Walter J. Ong would have us perceive the relation of culture to communication through man's sensorium:

> Man's sensory perceptions are abundant and overwhelming. He cannot attend to them all at once. In great part a given culture teaches him one or another way of productive specialization. It brings him to organize his sensorium by attending to some types of perception more than others, by making an issue of certain ones while relatively neglecting other ones. The sensorium is a fascinating focus for cultural studies. Given sufficient knowledge of the sensorium exploited within a specific culture, one could probably define the culture as a whole in virtually all its aspects [Ong 1967, 6].

The sense ratio and its impact on culture and communication has been variously explored by such scholars as Harold A. Innis in his *The Bias of Communication* (1951), Marshall McLuhan in his *The Gutenberg Galaxy* (1962), Henri Bergson in his *Time and Free Will: An Essay on the Immediate Data of Consciousness* (1960), Edward Sapir, *Language: An Introduction to the Study of Speech* (1921), Alfred North Whitehead in his *Modes of Thought* (1958) and his *Process and Reality: An Essay in Cosmology* (1929), John W. M. Verhaar in his *Some Relations Between Perception, Speech, and Thought: A Contribution Toward the Phenomenology of Speech* (1963), Jerome S. Bruner in his "The Course of Cognitive Growth" (1964), and Walter J. Ong in his *The Presence of the Word* (1967) and his *Ramus, Method and the Decay of Dialogue* (1958). The importance of the sensorium to culture and to communication cannot be underestimated. The sensorium itself is a universal. The sense ratio is applied differently, however, in and between cultures. Ong points out in this volume how much of the Western culture "perceives" the world with visual imagery, whereas the preliterate ancient and modern cultures tend to emphasize the oral-aural aspects of the sense ratio.

Both McLuhan in *The Gutenberg Galaxy* and Ong in *The Presence of the Word* stress that cultures historically can be divided into three stages: first, oral or oral-aural, second, script, which reached critical breakthroughs with the invention first of the alphabet and later of alphabetic movable type, and third, electronic. An understanding of these stages offers a clearer view of the relationship between communication as message and communications as media or channels. The first stage was overcome, but not supplanted by the second, and the second has been overcome by the early electronic media. Both the first and the second are again joined in the contemporary media such as television and the communication satellites. However, Ong believes that all of the stages represent aspects of man's verbalization in that they mark transformations of the word, because the word was first and still is largely concerned with the oral-aural nature of culture (Ong 1967: 17).

SOUND AND SIGHT

Because most communication is of a verbal nature, the sense of sound through verbal communication has long been recognized as a key ingredient of behavior. In the *Phaedrus*, Plato attempts to protect oral communication against that which is written, saying that "no written discourse, whether in metre or in prose, deserves to be treated very seriously," because he feared that the visual imagery created by writing would overtake the oral-aural nature of discourse in his time (Plato 1969: 258C–279C). His contemporary and rival, Isocrates, also extolled the oral method of communication:

> We are in no respect superior to other living creatures; nay, we are inferior to many in swiftness and in strength and in other resources; but because there has been implanted in us the power to persuade each other and to make clear to each other whatever we desire, not only have we escaped the life of wild beasts, but we have come together and founded cities and made laws and invented arts; and generally speaking there is no institution devised by man which the power of speech has not helped us to establish [Isocrates 1969: 253–257].

The Homeric hymns and epics of early Greece and the epics *Beowulf, Chanson de Roland*, and Froissart's *Chronicles* are all indicative of a heavy emphasis on the oral tradition, which was built upon the power of the spoken words of the bard, who was heard by generally preliterate or nonliterate peasants.

Even today in Africa, and to a lesser extent in other areas of the world, the concept of oral tradition remains of paramount importance in communicating about the present through the past. Ebiegberi Joe Alagoa calls the preservation of Africa's oral tradition the most important supplement available for studying the archaeology and history of a site such as Koumbi Saleh, the capital of the ancient kingdom of Ghana, which was located by the combined use of written records and oral traditions and investigated by the tools of the archaeologist (Alagoa 1966: 405–419). When the collector of oral data undertakes his fieldwork, he combines an approach to the three stages of cultures that Ong describes. Using an oral-aural method to record the tradition, he also applies the visual aspect of the sensorium through his attention to written records or by transcribing the sound-message into script; and, finally, by his use of advanced electronic media he preserves the oral data presented to him by his informants. Although interest in oral traditions continues today, Philip Curtin suggests that while the oral transmission of knowledge, particularly in Africa, is not on the way to complete extinction, the next two or three decades may be the last in which the present wealth of traditional history and lore will be available for the oral historian. Indeed, such writers as G. P. Murdock believe that "indigenous oral traditions are completely undependable much beyond the personal recollections of living informants" (Murdock 1959: 43). Curtin writes of him: "He was so suspicious, indeed, that he specifically declared that he would set aside all evidence based on such traditions." Curtin, however, believes the usefulness of preserving oral traditions of preliterate societies is highly valuable not only for historians but also for anthropologists, linguists, folklorists, and musicologists (Curtin, 1968: 367–385).

To be sure, as Ong suggests, memory and time as verbatim records were nonexistent in most oral-aural societies. Those Christians who hold as literally true every Biblical statement fail to understand that many books of the Old Testament were passed orally from generation to generation over a period of

1500 years before they were put into the visual form of script. Even then those who wrote down the messages were not divine recording secretaries. They made errors because of meaning changes and content changes that occurred as an elder passed on the epics of Jehovah's people to his sons. Errors in spelling, punctuation, and syntax all added to the difficulties as the Septuagint was translated into the Vulgate, and as the Vulgate was translated into the Douay-Rheims or King James versions, with translation errors taking place with each copy. The New Testament was not completed until almost A.D. 100, when the eyewitness accounts were written down by then old men.

The purpose of the Christian and Hebraic scriptures was to communicate patterns of highly moral standards of living. Surely the six hundred commandments of the Torah, if accepted literally, would make a modern Jew a frenzied neurotic. I have seen orthodox Jewish students in New York City so fearful of breaking any one of many commandments in regard to Kosher food that they hesitated to eat in public. Of course, the literalness imposed by various Western and Oriental religions is scarcely different than the minutiae of legalisms that our various governments place upon us, some of which have long since lost their meaning. Written accounts of the speeches of Thucydides, in which he represents Alexander speaking to his soldiers or Pericles giving his funeral orations, were intended to be approximately accurate rather than precisely the words which had been spoken several years before the histories were written. The blind poet Homer was probably a whole series of traveling bards, separated by time and distance, who retold and added to the heroic stories of Odysseus and the Olympian gods. This fact accounts in part for the repetition and frequent contradictions in the stories. Cicero believed in using the visual medium of script; but sometimes he commented in a letter to a friend that he couldn't write sooner because his throat was sore and he therefore couldn't say the letter that he would then put into writing.

As cultural stages overlap, time sequences and memory of specifics become more precise. Now, the electronic media can record and retrieve historical events with such precision that political analysts can predict the total vote in an American election before 1 percent of the vote is counted in many cases. Ong's essay in this volume clearly distinguishes between the dynamic and relatively unpredictable culture, an event world, which is oral-aural, and an object world, which is visually conceptualized and statistically recorded. When President Ceausescu of Romania gave his 1970 address at the United Nations, his delegation provided for live oral transmission to the Romanian radio systems as well as visual press release copies for American and Romanian newspapers. An overlapping of the three stages is evident: President Ceausescu's principal media was the oral discourse, which was supplemented by written copies and electronically transmitted to his people. Had transmission through television been feasible, no doubt he would have used this electronic medium to complete the sense ratio. That forty-two heads of state and heads of government took the time and expense to travel from their home states to the United Nations in October 1970, each to deliver a half-hour speech, suggests the importance that the oral-aural sense ratio provides even today. At the same time, the world leaders came to New York to be seen as well as to be heard, again calling upon a balance of the sense ratio of sound and sight.

TASTE

Taste, whether considered literally or metaphorically, has been little studied as a communicative aspect of the sensorium. Margaret Mead has noted: "Taste may be studied as one of the sensory modalities to which little recognition has as yet been given in the new science of semiotics" (Mead 1964). In their book, *Man, Bread and Destiny: The Story of Man and His Food*, C. C. Furnas and S. M. Furnas write: "World history could, in fact, be told almost entirely in terms of food. Some races are vigorous and aggressive, others are weak and of little consequence. The quality and quantity of the food supply have much to do with such mass characteristics" (Furnas and Furnas 1937). Ellsworth Huntington, in his *Mainsprings of Civilization*, comments:

> From the standpoint of civilization and history the most important aspects of diet are as follows: 1. The quest for food has probably been the most potent of all forces in making people work and in encouraging early inventions. 2. Agriculture, which is the main method of obtaining food, has been of paramount importance in the early development and growth of the civilized mode of life. 3. Diet, through its effect on health and vigor, is one of the main factors in determining efficiency and thus has a great effect upon character and progress.

Written in a Nazi concentration camp, H. E. Jacob's *Six Thousand Years of Bread* could have been powerfully communicative to one who was given but a little bread and water daily (Jacob 1944). Much of the eighteenth-century emphasis on taste in criticism, as exemplified in David Hume's "Of the Standard of Taste" (1757) and Hugh Blair's "Essay on Taste" (1968: 37–48), was caused in part by a society that provided plentiful riches for the discriminating palate. Jean Brillat-Savarin has argued: "The destiny of nations depends on the manner by which they are nourished" (Brillat-Savarin, cited in Henderson 1968: 3). President Tombalbaye of Chad's adoption of Daniel Rops's "the despair of being a man" stresses that much of mankind is threatened by hunger and because of widespread starvation much of Africa is "a tragic site of great suffering" (Tombalbaye 1970: 1343–1348). When Chief Leabua Jonathan, Prime Minister of tiny Lesotho, enclaved by the Republic of South Africa, proclaimed in the United Nations that "our primary task is to survive," he meant not only politically and economically but also from the point of view of having enough food for his people (Jonathan 1970: 1265–1275).

In his remarkable address to the United Nations in 1965, Pope Paul received mixed responses to his statement: "Your task is to ensure that there is enough bread on the table of mankind, and not to favor an artificial control of births, which would be irrational, in order to lessen the number of guests at the banquet of life. But it is not enough to feed the starving, each man must also be assured of a life consistent with his dignity" (Pope Paul 1970: 1051–1059). Food consistent with human dignity is a communicative aspect of a culture, especially when the affluence of one-third of the human race kills them from overeating, while two-thirds of them have discovered with Kakuzo Okakura "that nothing is real to us but hunger." The flippant statement about the 1945

San Francisco Conference to establish the United Nations, "Peace in our time can well depend on whether we soothe or insult the gastronomies of our guests" (quoted in Schlesinger 1944–1945: 215), belies the fact that world peace may be determined in part by whether the "revolutions of rising expectations" of the third-world states turn into "the revolutions of rising frustrations" because the world population has outstripped the food supply that the developed states are willing or able to assist the developing nations in obtaining.

Taste is distinct for each culture, that is it communicates the essential characteristics of the culture. As Mary C. Henderson argues: "A special kind of scientist, yet to be named, may be able eventually to solve the problem: show me what a man eats, and I will tell you where he lives, what language he speaks, what his mores are, what he works at, how he looks, and what are his general mental and physical states of health. The solution to such a problem would not be inconsiderable in terms of successful human communication" (Henderson 1970: 8). Before this problem is solved, we need to recognize that though freedom from hunger is proclaimed as a universal human birthright by the Universal Declaration of Human Rights, hunger itself is also becoming a universal and thus demands the balance of taste to the sense ratio as a first priority for swift solution.

SMELL

Like taste, the sense of smell is also a discriminatory aspect of culture. Who can forget the stench of death after he has witnessed or come to assist the victims of a Pakistani tidal wave, or a Peruvian earthquake, or a battle in a Vietnamese village? Death, too, is a universal. I am reminded of William Faulkner's As I Lay Dying in which the deceased mother's wish to be buried in a distant cemetery was honored by the family in a long, hot, and tortuous journey without the benefit of embalming. I remember, too, how one particular junior high school student warned me that his arrival in my classroom was imminent by the odor that he emitted. Daily, after the class was over, I was aware for some time that he had been present because of an unpleasant, lingering smell which upset my balance of senses and which, unfortunately, hindered my verbal communication with him because I was so distracted. Perhaps one of the reasons that the Trappists stopped having visitors at their monasteries was the frequent complaint of visitors that "an odor of sanctity" drifted from the monks' choir stalls because their rule provided for only two or three baths a week lest the monks be tempted by their own bodies. The motto, "Cleanliness is next to godliness" has generally been replaced by most Americans with "Cleanliness is godliness." This surprises and amuses not only many third-world persons but also other Westerners such as Europeans. My Japanese student relates that discussing body odor in Japan is not only not taboo, as it is among most Americans of middle or upper class origins, but a certain amount of body odor is considered communicative of a cultured person in Japan.

Two striking examples of the metaphorical use of smell as a communicative device are offered by Khrushchev during his 1960 addresses at the United Nations. In an October 1 statement about the question of seating the People's Republic of China, Khrushchev observed: "The attempts of the United States Government to resuscitate such a political corpse as Chiang Kai-shek and his putrid regime, which was repudiated by the Chinese people, merely poison the international atmosphere in the Far East. . . . The lifeless body of the Chiang Kai-shek regime must be thrown out and its place must be occupied by a living entity—the People's Republic of China" (Khrushchev 1970: 10). Concerning colonialism, he stated on October 3: "I should like to say that the representative of the United States [James J. Wadsworth], when he spoke here, was defending something which is old, rotten and already crumbling. . . . You cannot make a dead man breathe. Colonialism has lived its day. Our duty is to put away this stinking corpse as soon as possible, thereby cleansing the atmosphere and creating in the world a better life for all" (Khrushchev 1970: 547).

In a more pleasant way, the sense of smell is used to communicate dramatically at the Brooklyn Flower Garden for the Blind, where flowers and plants are arranged at approximately nose level and Braille signs at hand level. This garden is fondly called "the smelling garden" by the many people, sightless and those who see, who daily visit it. Additionally, we are all aware of the smell of an oncoming storm, or the fragrance of spring or of a summer evening. The Japanese tell time by the scent of incense burning at different times of the day. Whereas English and American foods smell generally bland, other foods, particularly Latin and Oriental dishes, have their own distinctive aromas. Ong suggests that, like taste, smell recalls memories of past events; but unlike taste and touch, which linger within time rather than progressing through it, smell loses its sensitivity to odors protracted in time. Moreover, the sense of smell lags in time for it is a less pronounced sense than the others (Ong 1957: 41).

TOUCH

Psychologists consider touch to be the most basic of the senses. According to Ong, touch—including kinesthesia (the sensation of bodily position or movement) and kinesics (body language)—helps form man's concepts of exteriority and interiority:

> We feel ourselves inside our own bodies, and the world as outside. We can feel free, not "boxed in." . . . We explore tactually the inside of a box. . . . But to explore an interior, touch must violate the interior, invade it, even break it open. Kinesthesia, it is true, gives me access to my own interior without violation—I feel myself somehow inside my own body and feel my body inside my own skin—but kinesthesia gives me direct access to nothing but myself. Other interiors are inaccessible to us (except through empathy, indirectly) [Ong 1967: 117–118].

Marjorie Latchaw and Glen Egstrom have identified the body's basic movements as bending, stretching, and twisting (Latchaw and Egstrom 1969). That these movements are communicative is clear. Although there are specialized forms of bending, stretching, and twisting that are peculiar to a specific culture, the basic movements are common across cultures. Bryant Wedge illustrates the difficulties inherent cross-culturally in kinesic communication:

> Khrushchev supplied an elegant little example of communication failure on his first visit to the United States. When he attempted to convey the greetings of a brotherly people to his American audience by his gesture of the clasped hands of friendship waved about his smiling face, he failed to take account of American conventions. Photographs of the event in our newspapers were widely captioned to suggest his gesture as that of a victorious pugilist. Khrushchev failed to communicate as he intended, and our newspapers failed to interpret his intentions correctly [Wedge 1968: 29–30].

During his 1960 visit to the United Nations, his shoe-pounding while Prime Minister Macmillan was speaking did nothing to enhance his reputation. In 1962, Ambassador Platon Morozov chided Adlai Stevenson in the Security Council: "It will become apparent that the right of veto in the Security Council is not such a bad thing but is rather a wise thing which compels even some great Powers to remain within the limits which are proper and which obliges them to keep their feet off the table whenever they put them on the table in proper American fashion." Stevenson responded as follows: "I haven't more to say, Mr. President, but before I proceed I must say that I was not aware, if I understood the representative of the Soviet Union correctly, that my shoe was on the table. [Laughter.] I wonder if he could have had me confused with someone else who still has other uses for shoes and tables. [Laughter.]" (Stevenson 1969: 476–481).

Leonard W. Doob characterizes two types of body movements that transmit information—relatively involuntary actions and voluntary actions. Relatively involuntary movement includes facial expression, eye shifting, dilation of pupils, muscle twitching, changes in breathing, tics, jerks, and scratching. These occur spontaneously and usually without the awareness of the communicator. Temporary changes in the appearance of the skin fall into the same category: flushing, pallor, sweating, drooling, rising of the hair, and so forth. Relatively voluntary movements refer to gesturing, posturing, contrived facial expression; positioning of body, movement of the limbs, spitting, nose-blowing, excreting, and sometimes scratching (Doob 1961: 68–69). Edward T. Hall calls such movements "the silent language of communication" (Hall 1959). Africans of many tribes allegedly "dance for joy and they dance for grief; they dance for love and they dance for hate; they dance to bring prosperity and they dance to avert calamity; they dance for religion and they dance to pass the time" (Gorer 1935: 289). Lord Hailey states: "In the African village singing, clapping, dancing, and drumming are not separate entities, but may be said to constitute one homogeneous art form" (Hailey 1957: 67). The messages communicated by voluntary bodily movements are often intimately linked with extremely important values of the society. In particular, there is a right and a wrong way to conduct one's body in order to demonstrate respect; but, again, that way varies and may be displayed in different social contexts:

> Ashanti of Ghana—it is insulting to use the left rather than the right hand for gesticulation. (Rattray, 1929, 164)

Chaga of Tanzania—children receiving or giving something to an older person are expected to clasp their out-stretched right hand with their left one; they must offer seats to old people who enter a hut. (Raum, 1940, 175)

Ganda of Uganda—inferior people receiving or giving something to a superior person must use both hands; if it is necessary to hold the object in one hand, then the free hand must touch the arm of the hand holding the object. (Roscoe, 1911, 44)

Luo of Kenya—while speaking, a man and his mother-in-law must turn their backs to each other. (Evans-Pritchard, 1950, 141)

Mende of Sierra Leone—anyone approaching a chief, including the younger members of his own family must bend his body, place his hands on his knees, and uncover his head. [Little, 1951: 192; cited in Doob, 1961: 72].

David Messing offers an interesting summary of the kinesic communication of the Amhara tribe of Ethiopia: "Anger is shown by the wide opening of the eyes, by biting the lower lip or finger, by a knit brow, or by 'a furious, intent stare'; melancholy by a wrinkled face; timidity and respect in the young by 'turning the eyes to the dust'; impatience by rapidly shifting the glance; and greetings or acknowledgement of superordination by rhythmic handclapping" (Messing 1957: 520–524).

THE SENSE RATIO

Since the senses are rarely isolated one from another, the concept of the sense ratio as communicative is that the senses operate on each other to communicate within or between cultures. Ong calls touch a bridge between sight and sound, since it tends to annex itself to them both. Texture can be seen and touched, but the perception of texture comes not from sight but from touch (including kinesthesia). Sight does not convey sound or smell or taste with any of the directness with which it conveys touch. Touch is associated with sound as for example when musical rhythm or even oral discourse sets off in the auditor a feeling of movement, clapping, snapping the fingers, or stamping the foot (Ong 1967: 165–166). The eating of food particularly involves several of the senses in an overlapping function. Food is seen, smelled, tasted, and touched. If we take seriously the statement of Watzlawick and Beavin that in the presence of another, all behavior is communicative, then to eat in the presence of another, as a basic example, is clearly communicative in that all the aspects of the sensorium are interacting as signs to the perceptive observer.

DEFINITIONS AND MODELS OF COMMUNICATION

To summarize the role of communication in culture, and of the relation of the sensorium in the communicative aspects of a culture, we can consider the following important definitions of communication. Gerald R. Miller states: "In the main, communication has as its central interest those behavioral situations in which a source transmits a message to a receiver(s) *with conscious intent to affect the latter's behaviors* (Miller 1966: 92). Dell Hymes objects however, "To define communication as the triggering of a response . . . is to make the term so nearly behavior and interaction in general as to lose its specific value as a scientific and moral conception" (see Hymes's essay in this volume). George Gerbner argues that to attach the criterion of intentionality to communication does not help to clarify matters: "If the interaction involves a code or representation with recognized message properties, and if the nature and role of those properties in the interaction is the focus of the study, we are inquiring into a communication act which has consequences. To reduce the range of observation to those acts, aspects, or consequences which may have been 'intended' as parts of a conscious communication effort is to place blinders on the researcher" (Gerbner 1966, 101).

I would add that it seems to me that precisely the kind of purposeful communication, or *rhetorical* communication that Miller describes does indeed occur frequently. It is demonstrated throughout this volume. My essay on the summitry of heads of state and heads of government at the United Nations demonstrates that their communication is not occurring willy-nilly but is a consciously purposeful decision to influence the attitudes and actions of leaders and people from other states, to convince their own people of the respect accorded them and their opinions, and to play an important role in the shaping of major world events which directly affect the lives of their people. Throughout this volume, essays describe purposeful rhetorical communication. For example, in all of the essays on propaganda, the intent of the mass persuaders is to plan and execute systematically a set of communication goals. In the communicative leadership of a charismatic leader, or in conflict resolution, or in the control of freedom and communication rights, planned rhetorical communication is evident. At the same time, accidental or unplanned events also occur to alter the purposeful communicative efforts which may be planned in any cultural or cross-cultural situation. I would agree then, that Miller's definition, which includes *conscious intent*, is too limiting as a definition of communication. If communication happens whether we wish it or not, conscious intent cannot always be present in all communication. In the context of a cultural setting, communication can be tested in relation to a set of twelve variables:

> The goal of the communicator depends in large part on himself and his position in the society as well as upon what he has learned about the audience in the past. The site at which an audience is located influences the kinds of basic media to be employed and may or may not require extending media. The contents of a communication are affected by all sorts of taboos or restrictions and by the mood of the audience. Whether or not changes occur in people can be traced to the way in which they perceive and react to the communication [Doob 1961: 11].

Although it is obvious that Doob perceives the communicator as goal-oriented, thus having conscious intent, it is also clear that all sorts of variables involve chance, which places the major emphasis on communication as John Weakland defines it: "an interactive, interrelational concept; its essential focus is not on the properties of single messages or single individuals, but on features characterizing the interaction of pairs or groups of actors, whatever the scope of research attention in a given instance" (Weakland 1967: 1).

Accepting the interrelationship of culture and communication, Albert E. Scheflen postulates:

> In human communication *people in social organization* perform and interpret repertoires of *coded behavior.* The people are not like simple machines capable only of transmitting bits of information in a single channel. People have learned multichanneled, highly patterned communicative behavior for multiple social roles and multiple occasions. The social organization for an interaction is not a simple alternation of speaker and listener, but involves kinship and other affiliational systems, dominance hierarchies, territorial arrangements and other abstractable dimensions [Scheflen 1967: 8].

George Gerbner defines communication as

> . . . social interaction through symbols and message systems. The production and perception of message systems cultivating stable structures of generalized images—rather than any tactic calculated to result in "desirable" (or any other) response—is at the heart of the communications transaction. Any definition or approach short-circuiting the distinguishing features of communication itself has no prospect of designating it as a recognizable field of study [Gerbner 1966: 102–103].

It should be clear, however, that while two people may communicate by chance, they don't simply socially interact and thereby effectively communicate. They interact with prescribed, coded systems through a balanced ratio of their own sensoriums, which the context of their own cultural experience provides. As the behavioral patterns in their culture are organized in predictable sequences, other members of the same culture view their behavior as acceptable and common to their own experience. Where different sense ratios are applied between cultures, and where different predictable sequences exist, it is possible, as Donald M. MacKay suggsts, for a member of one culture to develop a complex organization of sensory perceptions that are almost entirely beyond the conceptual grasp of a member of another culture. Since the same is also likely to be true in reverse, MacKay writes that "we have here a most potent and subtle source of failure of human communication" (MacKay 1964: 170). Even the basic and sensible communication model of Theodore Newcomb, A speaks to B about X, which includes A's orientation toward B as well as his orientation toward the subject X and the postulant: "The stronger the forces toward A's coorientation in respect to B and X, (a) the greater A's strain toward symmetry with B in respect to X; and (b) the greater the likelihood of increased symmetry as a consequence of one or more communicative acts" (Newcomb 1966: 65–79) fails to recognize, as John Weakland explains, that communication "always involves a multiplicity— of channels, of context and of messages. These are never absolutely separable, but interact so that, for example, messages and contexts, verbal message and vocal or facial expression, or related verbal messages are *mutually* qualifying in ways crucial to interpretation and response—and therefore to effective analysis of communication" (Weakland 1967: 2).

Taking the Newcomb model as a starting point, Bruce H. Westley and Malcolm S. MacLean attempt to develop their own conceptual model for *communications* research. They suggest two basic distinctions between face-to-face communication and mass communications:

> Face-to-face communication involves more sense modalities. It also provides immediate "feedback"—that is, information from B back to A about the change condition [sic] of B. In other words, more senses (and kinds of stimuli) can come into play in the person-person act than in any other situation. Thus B has a "cross-modality" check. He can clear impressions he gets through one sense with those he gets through another. And A has the advantage of learning B's response almost immediately—for instance, "message received."
> Mass communications, then, differ from face-to-face communications to the extent that (a) the number of modalities tends to be minimized and (b) "orientative" feedback is minimized or delayed [Westley and MacLean 1966: 81].

Although Newcomb's A and B can only be persons, Westley and MacLean make B a person, primary group, or a total social system. They add to the model C, which serves as the gatekeeper, and thus may be any of the communications media or channels that select and transmit A's message about X to B. Instead of ABX, the model becomes ABCX. Bs vary in the degree to which they share common problems that imply the necessity of attaining communication with common Xs. To distinguish between purposive and nonpurposive messages, the authors contend that "The absence of a communicator's intent to influence B transforms his act into an X. When a person says something he hopes will reach another person's ears, he is an A; but if he says it without such intent and it nevertheless is transmitted to B, his act must be conceived of as an X, the selection and transmission having been performed by a C." A critical concept for either the ABX or the ABCX model is that feedback assures the system character of the relationship. If A is to continue to communicate purposefully with B, he must have information about any changes in the condition or attitude of B attributable to his communication to B. C is equally concerned with effects on B if he is to make realistic adjustments in his role as B's agent. Westley and MacLean indicate that just as there can be purposive and nonpurposive communication from A to B, the feedback from B to A can serve the same functions. Feedback serves as the establishment of a two-way communication system, whether on a person-to-person basis, or as an aspect of the two- or multiple-step flow, or between governments and cultures. Whereas other models, such as the Lasswell model, "Who says what through what channels to whom with what effect," insist upon a purposive communicator, Westley and MacLean believe that Xs may be transmitted to Bs by way of Cs without the active presence of As. They argue that the ABCX model links the process of communication with communications as channels:

> The model is intended to be sufficiently general to treat all kinds of human communication from two-person face-to-face interaction to international and intercultural communications. It assumes that a minimum number of roles and processes are needed in any general theory of communications and attempts to isolate and tentatively define them [Westley and MacLean 1966: 80–87].

COMMUNICATIONS NETWORKS AND CHANNELS

If communication has a social interaction process orientation, *communications* can be described as the networks and channels by which communication is transmitted. Communication is transferred through space from one point to another, possibly from A to B informally, or from A to B through the selective gatekeeper, which may be any number of communications channels. Richard L. Meier indicates that communication suggests the following kinds of channels:

> a. *Face to face:* conferences, meetings, gossip, etc. b. *reading:* newspapers, magazines, books, billboards, etc. c. *man-machine:* reading instruments, gauges, microscopes, radar, etc. d. *person-person* (machine-interposed): telephone, radio, T.V., films, e. *machine-machine:* feedbacks, interlocks, automatism (Meier cited in Newmann 1966: 62).

The end points may be organized into networks and may be found in interpersonal communication, mass communication, or in intercommunication between governments and peoples. At the interpersonal level, space is seen as the study of proxemics. Just as kinesthesia or kinesics relates to the sensorium through the sense of touch, proxemics suggests the spatial and social distance between person A and person B. When person A and person B are from different cultures, their spatial relations may also affect their social distance, both as they perceive the status of each other and as they crowd or retreat from the other's protected space.

Karl Deutsch indicates that not only Americans, but also rural Asians and Africans, flock to the urban centers because in the city, within their individual limitations, they still have a wider range of human choices than in rural areas. He believes that, unfortunately, the overloading of communications networks, both human and mechanical, becomes the city's greatest disease. During the day, communications systems are overloaded to the point of complete breakdown, whereas at night they are nearly unused. Deutsch argues:

> Despite their origin, however, recurrent overloads will tend to paralyze many functions, and eventually to blight the very structure of a metropolis. It is for good reason that waiting-line theory has become a fast growing field in operations research and social science. Taken together, increasing overloads of this kind reduce or destroy many attractions of the metropolis as well as the economic value of many of the capital investments in it. . . . Cities therefore may produce a pervasive condition of communications overload. Whereas villagers thirst for gossip, city dwellers with more ample choices may crave privacy. But the internal communications overload of other people makes them less receptive to our needs (Deutsch 1966, 389–390).

Elihu Katz argues, additionally, that whereas rural sociology suggests the study of traditional values—of kinship, primary relations, Gemeinschaft—research on mass communications, on the other hand, is almost a symbol of urban society. Katz states that the two traditions of research have begun to recognize the importance of each other due, in large measure, to a revision of the image of society implicit in research on mass communications, which has assumed until recently that respondents to mass communications don't talk to each other. Rural sociologists who deal either with interpersonal communication or mass communications, in a two-step or multiple-flow process, have always accepted the fact that rural respondents talk to each other. Thus, slowly, the researcher in mass communications is beginning to study also interpersonal networks of respondents rather than to treat them as anonymous and noncommunicating individuals (Katz 1966: 551–556). In this volume, two studies by rural sociologists, van den Ban in the Netherlands, and Dasgupta in India, demonstrate the roles of both interpersonal and mass communications networks in the diffusion of innovations in rural societies.

C. R. Wright indicates that mass communications are involved with distinctive operating conditions, among which are primarily the nature of the audience, the nature of the communication experience, and the nature of the communicator. First, "mass communication is directed to a relatively large, heterogeneous and anonymous audience." Second, "mass communications may be characterized as public, rapid, and transient." And third, the communicator in mass media usually works through a complex corporate organization embodying an extensive division of labor and an accompanying degree of expense (Wright 1959: 12–15). Richard R. Fagen points out that organizations, too, can serve as communications channels, for although the mass media's primary function is always communication transmission, organizations are normally thought of in a different context. He emphasizes the following points: (1) Organizational channels of political consequence are not necessarily part of the political system in the structural sense. For example, schools and labor unions may serve as important channels of political communication but are outside of the political system as we usually think of it in America. (2) The political use of organizational channels is intermittent or partial in many instances. For example, the American labor union serves a number of purposes besides political communication. (3) Organization channels differ widely in the political communication uses which they serve, as can be seen in studying organizations in different political systems. Groups can serve the same functions as political channels. Fagen asserts that in Washington, D.C., the mass media are in a real sense the fourth branch of government, not because they keep the other three branches "honest" but because they are the key structures in the public communication network on which functionaries in the other three branches depend (Fagen 1966: 34–52).

In third-world countries there are a number of handicaps to the development of an effective communications network. S. C. Dube notes three. First, a considerable gap between the small modernizing elite and the large mass of tradition-bound people persists. Second, the traditional communication networks in these countries are still strong, and the modern media of mass communications are poorly developed. The use of the three principal media of mass communications—books, magazines, and newspapers; the radio; and television—is largely confined to the elite. In consequence, other media of communication, limited in reach and penetration, have to be pressed into service to put across innovations to the masses. Third, there is very little scientific knowledge regarding the communication situation in the underdeveloped countries. Traditional channels of communication have not been well identified, nor is there much scientific information on the "opinion leaders" who have a germinal role in the dissemination of ideas and adoption of new practices. Little is known about the importance and influence of the mass media. Additionally, the developing countries do not have a very clear image of modernity, nor have they widely used mass communications to determine their effectiveness; and developmental planners are able to utilize only limited funds for mass communications channels and networks (Dube 1967: 92–97). In fact, Harry T. Oshima insists that developing nations have no choice but to place the role of communications within the strategy of selective growth and development which their economy and national priorities dictate (Oshima 1967: 76–91).

When communications networks and channels fail, communication breakdown occurs, though it certainly occurs for other basic reasons as well. Throughout this volume, there are examples of communication breakdown, some of which are caused by role and norm conflicts. Others are the results of channel failures. If the truck carrying newspapers to the rural village breaks down, the communication, no matter how important, simply is not transmitted. More dramatically, when rebel soldiers seize a state's communications systems, a coup is likely because the head of state or head of government may be unable to persuade his people to support him by means of the normal communications media. On the international level, when diplomatic relations are broken between countries, no formal channels for continued dialogue exist. President Nixon used this situation as an excuse not to attend the funeral of President Nasser. Although his presence in Cairo might have been very dangerous for him personally, it would have offered the Arabs a symbolic gesture of reconciliation.

Alfred G. Smith writes:

When messages are transported across cultural boundaries, they are encoded in one context and decoded in another. In these intercultural situations there is little of the coorientation that is a prerequisite for communication in general. This greatly increases the possibility of misunderstanding and of unexpected reactions. This makes intercultural communication a significant illustration and testing ground for hypotheses about communication generally. Moreover, much of our communication is intercultural [Smith 1966: 565].

Without sensory context, as I have suggested, there can be no communication. If context shifts on an intercultural basis, then it is necessary for the communicator to relate to the sensory perceptions both of his own culture and of the culture of the person with whom he is communicating. Since cross-class communication, except for formalized and routinized interchange, is both difficult and rare (Schmatzman and Strauss 1966: 453; see also Gregg and McCormack 1968: 25–30), and the gap between an underdeveloped state's elite and the masses is nearly impossible to bridge (Keesing and Keesing 1966: 588–595, and Rao 1966), it is no wonder that intercommunication among nations and peoples is so difficult.

INTERCOMMUNICATION:
INTERNATIONAL AND INTERCULTURAL COMMUNICATION

The term *intercommunication* has been utilized in a contemporary sense as early as Carl Hovland's essay "Social Communication" in 1948. However, he used the term to indicate a relationship within a cultural or a single political system (Hovland 1950: 181). More recently, the term has been used to describe communication that crosses national or cultural boundaries. In his provocative statement, which has served as the impetus for my own title to this volume, Daniel Lerner says:

> The process of international development cooperation, thus conceived, is essentially a communication process. In the perceptive words of Karl Marx, the more advanced country presents to the less developed country "a picture of what it may become." . . . This is international communication on the highest level. It involves nothing less than intercommunication between countries and continents of ideas about the ends and means of social organization—the shaping and sharing of human values according to a common model that emerged in the Western past and may be transformed and improved in the Eastern future [Lerner 1967: 120].

Gerhard Maletzke distinguishes between the meanings for intercultural and international communication:

> Whereas *intercultural* communication is an exchange of meaning between *cultures*, *international* communication takes place on the level of countries or nations, which is to say across frontiers. This means: *Intercultural* and *international* communication can, on occasion, be identical; but this is not always so. Very often people who belong to a common culture are separated by a state frontier, with the effect that international communication is taking place within a single culture. And, the contrary case, humans of quite differing cultures can be united in the same state, so that within this single state intercultural communication can take place. It is thus that one tends to use the word *international* when speaking of communication on the purely political level, whereas the concept of *intercultural* communication corresponds more to sociological and anthropological realities [Maletzke 1970: 478].

Maletzke argues that a dominant factor in both international communication and the development process is the creation of images, attitudes, prejudices, and stereotypes, which develop within a given culture in reference to another. Every communicative process, whether interpersonal or founded in the mass media, which crosses national or cultural boundaries has to deal with such predispositions (Maletzke 1970: 481–482). Formal communication that takes place internationally, cross-culturally, or in a cross-class relationship, either between individuals or systems, tends to be purposive in nature, whereas informal contacts and communication in these relationships often occur by happenstance. When a head of state plans a state visit, his hosts carefully guide him, controlling to some extent both his movement and his ability to communicate. The two American visits of Nikita Khrushchev are examples. In 1959 he was prevented from visiting Disneyland for security reasons, and Ambassador Henry

Cabot Lodge's Republican Truth Squad followed him to control his communication. The next year, he was restricted to Manhattan, allegedly for security reasons but mostly to soothe Eisenhower's pique at the failure of the Paris Summit Conference. Khrushchev was largely restricted to speaking at the United Nations, which has extraterritorial status.

Totally unofficial visitors across national boundaries still have some restrictions placed on them, but generally the communication they engage in with residents includes a considerable amount of happenstance. John Bennett and Robert McKnight suggest that an international visiting experience normally includes a learning phase from the host society and its institutions and an application phase when the learner returns home (Bennett and McKnight 1966: 595). When home is in the same city or next door, or when the mass media of two adjacent cultures are interacting simultaneously, communication breakdown leads to particularly acute estrangement. Robert Browne warns of the problem in dialogue between American white and black subcultures:

> There will be little in common between the viewpoints of the two parties in the developing black-white dialogue, for the whites are likely to view the dialogue as a negotiating session in which they, the stronger party, are being forced to make begrudging concessions; whereas the blacks will view themselves as the victims of a cruel hoax in which they have too often been tricked into playing by the rules only to discover the game had been stacked against them from the beginning, so that they no longer feel bound to abide by any rules whatsoever. Under such circumstances, chaos rather than dialogue is the more likely outcome [Browne 1968: 8].

If such communication failures occur between people living in what is essentially the same cultural and national context, it is obvious that communication breakdown can happen even more easily between cultural and national groups whose total value systems have been antagonistic for hundreds of years. Remedies are not simple. Robert C. Angell offers at least a beginning set of objectives for those who seek to communicate to others their own way of life and who hope to instill a respect for their own mores and to learn to respect the mores and values of other peoples. These objectives are to create an appreciation of the common human qualities underlying cultural differences to aid an understanding of the central values of other cultures, and to instill a realization that the different value systems of the world's peoples are each compatible with the universal human qualities, even when not compatible with each other (Angell 1950: 374). Although communication and the sensorium are both universals, another way of looking at communication universals is to say that they include the finite number of communications channels and networks, of both the basic and extending media, that enable people to communicate effectively with others either in their own culture or across cultural or national boundaries. A hierarchy of priorities is needed both from the perspective of A and B as well as C in the ABCX model or, more plainly, in relation to the processes involved in empathetic communication between peoples and nations.

In this volume, we are pursuing—on a cross-disciplinary and cross-cultural basis, too, in that eleven of the essayists are non-Americans—the role of intercommunication, not only as it is utilized in Hovland's intranational sense but, most importantly, as it occurs between nations and peoples. Various researchers agree that communication serves as a significantly uniting factor both for the analyst of cross-cultural or cross-national affairs and also for the international or intercultural communicator himself. Although communications qua channels and media are not the major focus of the volume, their relationship to communication as social interaction is pervasively present. Additionally, that unhappy phenomenon, communication breakdown, is also discussed in various essays in the book. The richness of our various cultural and national heritages, and the human condition itself, simply do not permit us to choose chaos rather than dialogue. Despite contrary evidence, I believe that out of confrontation does come communication and that communication is compensatory to division. Thus, I place my lot with Camus's resolve that "tragedy today is collective; the long dialogue of men must go on."

REFERENCES CITED

ALAGOA, EGIEGBERI JOE
  1966   Oral Tradition among the Ijos of the Niger Delta. In Journal of African History. 7:405–419.
ANGELL, ROBERT C.
  1950   International Communication and the World Society. In Reader in public opinion and communication, enlarged ed. Bernard Berelson and Morris Janowitz, eds. New York.
BLAIR, HUGH
  1968   Essay on Taste. In James L. Golden and Edward P. J. Corbett. The Rhetoric of Blair, Campbell and Whately. New York.
BENNETT, JOHN W., and
RORERT K. McKNIGHT
  1966   Social norms, national imagery, and interpersonal relations. In Communication and culture: readings. Alfred G. Smith, ed. New York.
BERGSON, HENRI
  1960   Time and free will: an essay on the immediate data of consciousness. New York.
BIRDWHISTELL, RAY L.
  1959   Contribution of linguistic-kinesic studies to the understanding of schizophrenia. In Schizophrenia, an integrated approach. Alfred Auerback, ed. New York.
BROWNE, ROBERT S.
  1968   Dialogue between the races: A top priority. Today's Speech 16:5–8.
BRUNER, JEROME S.
  1964   The course of cognitive growth. American Psychologist 18:1–15.
CURTIN, PHILIP D.
  1968   Field techniques for collecting and processing oral data. Journal of African History 9:367–385.
DEUTSCH, KARL W.
  1966   On social communication and the metropolis. In Communication and culture: readings. Alfred G. Smith, ed. New York.
DOOB, LEONARD
  1961   Communication in Africa: A search for boundaries. New Haven.
DOOB, S. C.
  1967   A note on communication in economic development. In Communication and change in the developing countries. Daniel Lerner and Wilbur Schramm, eds. Foreword by Lyndon B. Johnson. Honolulu.

EVANS-PRITCHARD, E. E.
1950 Marriage customs of the Luo of Kenya. Africa 20:132–142.
FAGEN, RICHARD R.
1966 Politics and communication. Boston.
FURNAS, C. C. and
S. M. FURNAS
1937 Man, bread and destiny: the story of man and his food. New York.
GERBNER, GEORGE
1966 On defining communication: still another view. Journal of Communication 16:99–103.
GORER, GEOFFREY
1935 African dances. New York.
GREGG, RICHARD B. and
A. JACKSON McCORMACK
1968 "Whitey" goes to the ghetto: A personal chronicle of a communication experience with black youth. Today's Speech 16:25–30.
HAILEY, LORD
1957 An African survey—revised. London.
HALL, EDWARD T.
1959 The silent language. Garden City.
HENDERSON, MARY C.
1970 Food as communication in American culture. Today's Speech 18:3–8.
HOVLAND, CARL
1950 Social communication. In Reader in public opinion and communication. Enlarged ed. Bernard Berelson and Morris Janowitz, eds. New York.
HUME, DAVID
1757 Of the standard of taste. London.
HUNTINGTON, ELLSWORTH
1945 Mainsprings of civilization. New York.
HYMES, DELL
1967 The anthropology of communication. In Human communication theory: Original essays. New York.
INNIS, HAROLD A.
1951 The bias of communication. Toronto.
ISOCRATES
1969 Against the Sophists. In Readings in classical rhetoric. Thomas W. Benson and Michael H. Prosser, eds. Boston.
JACOB, H. E.
1944 Six thousand years of bread.
JONATHAN, CHIEF LEABUA
1970 Our only task is to survive. In Sow the wind, reap the whirlwind: heads of state address the United Nations. Michael H. Prosser, ed. New York.
KHRUSHCHEV, NIKITA SERGEYEVICH
1970a In Sow the wind, reap the whirlwind: heads of state address the United Nations. Michael H. Prosser, ed. New York.
1970b The seeds of truth. In Sow the wind, reap the whirlwind: heads of state address the United Nations. Michael H. Prosser, ed. New York.
LATCHAW, MARJORIE, and
GLEN EDSTROM
1969 Human movements: with concepts applied to children's movement activities. Englewood Cliffs.
LERNER, DANIEL
1967 International cooperation and communication in national development. In Communication and change in the developing countries. Daniel Lerner and Wilbur Schramm, eds. Foreword by Lyndon B. Johnson. Honolulu.

LITTLE, KENNETH L.
1951   The Mende of Sierra Leone: a West African people in transition. London.
MALETZKE, GERHARD
1970   Intercultural and international communication. In International communication: media, channels, functions. Heinze-Dietrich Fischer and John C. Merrill, eds. New York.
MACKAY, DONALD M.
1964   Communication and meaning—a functional approach. In Cross-cultural understanding: epistemology in anthropology. F.S.C. Northrop, Symposium Chairman. Helen H. Livingston, ed. New York.
MCLUHAN, MARSHALL
1962   The Gutenberg Galaxy: the making of typographic man. Toronto.
MEAD, MARGARET
1964   Food habits research problems of the 1960's. Publication 1225, National Academy of Sciences. Washington.
MEERLOO, JOOST A. M.
1967   Contributions of psychiatry to the study of communications. In Human communication theory: Original essays. Frank E. X. Dance. New York.
MERTON, THOMAS
1955   No man is an island. New York.
MESSING, SIMON DAVID
1957   The highland-plateau Amhara of Ethiopia. Unpublished Ph.D. dissertation, University of Pennsylvania.
MILLER, GERALD R.
1966   On defining communication: Another stab. Journal of Communication 16:88–98.
MURDOCK, G. P.
1959   Africa: its peoples and their culture history. New York.
NEWCOMB, THEODORE M.
1966   An approach to the study of communicative acts. In Communication and culture: readings. Alfred G. Smith, ed. New York.
NEWMAN, JOHN B.
1966   A rationale for a definition of communication. In Communication and culture: readings. Alfred G. Smith, ed. New York.
NYERRE, JULIUS K.
1970   All mankind is one. In Sow the wind, reap the whirlwind: heads of state address the United Nations. Michael H. Prosser, ed. New York.
OLIVER, KENNETH A.
1957   Our living language. Los Angeles.
OLIVER, ROBERT T.
1962   Culture and communication: The problem of penetrating national boundaries. Springfield.
ONG, WALTER J., S.J.
1958   Ramus, method and the decay of dialogue. Cambridge, Mass.
1967   The presence of the word. New Haven.
OSHIMA, HARRY T.
1967   The strategy of selective growth and the role of communications. In Communication and change in the developing countries. Daniel Lerner and Wilbur Schramm, eds. Foreword by Lyndon B. Johnson. Honolulu.
PAUL VI, POPE
1970   Never again war. In Sow the wind, reap the whirlwind: heads of state address the United Nations. Michael H. Prosser, ed. New York.
PLATO
1969   Phaedrus. In Readings in classical rhetoric. Thomas W. Benson and Michael H. Prosser, eds. Boston.

RAO, Y. V. LAKSHMANA
1966 Communication and development: a study of two villages. Minneapolis.
RATTRAY, ROBERT S.
1929 Ashanti law and constitution. Oxford.
RAUM, O. F.
1940 Chaga childhood. London.
ROSCOE, JOHN
1911 The Baganda. London.
SAPIR, EDWARD
1921 Language: an introduction to the study of speech. New York.
SCHATZMAN, LEONARD, and
ANSELM STRAUSS
1966 Social class and modes of communication. In Communication and culture:
readings. Alfred G. Smith, ed. New York.
SCHEFLEN, ALBERT E.
1967 On the structuring of human communication. The American Behavioral
Scientist April: 8–12.
SCHLESINGER, ARTHUR M.
1944–45 A dietary interpretation of American history. Proceedings of the Massa-
chusetts Historical Society. 68:215.
SCHRAMM, WILBUR
1967 Communication and change. In Communication and change in the developing
countries. Daniel Lerner and Wilbur Schramm, eds. Foreword by Lyndon B.
Johnson. Honolulu.
SMITH, ALFRED G.
1966 Communication and culture: readings. Alfred G. Smith, ed. New York.
STEVENSON, ADLAI
1969 An ethic for survival: Adlai Stevenson speaks on international affairs. Michael
H. Prosser, ed. New York.
TOMBALBAYE, FRANÇOIS
1970 The despair of being a man. In Sow the wind, reap the whirlwind: heads of
state address the United Nations. Michael H. Prosser, ed. New York.
VERHAAR, JOHN W. M., S.J.
1963 Some relations between perception, speech and thought: a contribution toward
the phenomenology of speech. Assen.
WATZLAWICK, PAUL, and
JANET BEAVIN
1967 Some formal aspects of communication. The American Behavioral Scientist
April: 4–8.
WEAKLAND, JOHN
1967 Communication and behavior—an introduction. The American Behavioral
Scientist April: 1–4.
WEDGE, BRYANT
1968 Communication analysis and comprehensive diplomacy. In International communication and the new diplomacy, by Arthur S. Hoffman, ed. Bloomington.
WESTLEY, BRUCE H., and
MALCOLM S. MACLEAN, JR.
1966 A conceptual model for communications research. In Communication and
culture: readings. Alfred G. Smith, ed. New York.
WHITEHEAD, ALFRED NORTH
1929 Process and reality: an essay in cosmology. New York.
1958 Modes of thought: six lectures delivered in Wellesley College, Massachusetts,
and two lectures in the University of Chicago. New York.
WRIGHT, C. R.
1959 Mass communication: A sociological perspective. New York.

THEORETICAL
PERSPECTIVES

Communication can be studied across and within national and cultural boundaries usefully and in a complementary fashion by varied disciplinary approaches. Sapir (1929: 166) argued long ago that linguists "must become increasingly concerned with the many anthropological, sociological, and psychological problems which invade the field of language." Hymes (1964: 2) has advanced this argument by calling for the study of the "ethnography of communication" in which researchers cannot justify taking separate results from linguistics, psychology, sociology, and ethnology to create a simple correlation about the role of communication for the individual and his society. Instead, he urges researchers to look for fresh data so that they can make a unified effort to determine how speech activities, studies of grammar, personality, religion, kinship, and society relate to the individual's and community's communicative habits. Although we can still focus on our personal disciplinary concerns, jointly considering the commonalities of the aspects of communication can lead us to understand better how cultures and peoples communicate with each other or fail to communicate.

Alfred G. Smith has attempted to draw several disparate disciplines together in his Communication and Culture. He adopts the three-fold approach to the study of communication as syntactic, semantic, and pragmatic, concepts which were first used by philosophers C. S. Peirce and C. W. Morris and later by telecommunication engineer Colin Cherry and by psychologist S. S. Stevens. Frank E. X. Dance develops this interdisciplinary attempt in his Human Communication Theory. Arthur S. Hoffman's International Communication and the New Diplomacy is a collection of essays both by professional diplomats and by scholars on the subject. In his essay in that volume, Bryant Wedge reminds those from the varied disciplines interested in the study of communication that the international communicator, whatever his profession, is not the same as the international communication analyst, whatever his discipline. One value of a volume such as the present one is that it provides the scholarship by the analyst of international and intercultural communication that is needed by the international or intercultural communicator so that he can more effectively understand his own role. Still another useful book to the study of the interdisciplinary aspects of communication is International Communication, edited by Heinz-Dietrich Fischer and John C. Merrill, in which they deal with media, channels, and functions of international communication. Pioneering efforts such as Everett Rogers' Modernization Among Peasants: The Impact of Communication, Daniel Lerner and Wilbur Schramm's Communication and Change in the Developing Countries, Richard R. Fagen's Politics and Communication, Lucian W. Pye's Communications and Political

Development, *Dean C. Barnlund's* Interpersonal Communication: Survey and Studies, *and Robert T. Oliver's* Culture and Communication *all contribute to an improved interdisciplinary understanding of the role and functions of communication between cultures and peoples.*

The essays that follow in this section provide but a few of the theories and methods available to the student of cross-cultural and international communication. Other theoretical and methodological essays are found throughout the volume, as well as case studies in which diverse theories and methods are postulated and studied. Naturally, the essayists do not agree with one another; but taken together, they represent a multidisciplinary understanding of the many-faceted aspects of human communication, both between cultures and within a single culture.

The folklorist, the oral historian, the rhetorician, the literary critic, and the anthropologist can all find significant complementary cultural interpretations on the role of the oral-aural oriented man and society vs. the visually oriented Western man and society in Walter Ong's "World as View and World as Event." *Also the author of such noted works as* Ramus, Method and the Decay of Dialogue, The Barbarian Within, *and* The Presence of the Word, *Ong considers the "world view" concept as useful for Western man but as a distorted tendency to think of all reality as visual. Preliterate man of both the earlier and contemporary periods concentrates more on a dynamic world of sound than on the static perception of a visual picture. Ong and McLuhan are in agreement that overlapping the oral-aural age and the script age, the electronic age has made a new compact with sound. In developing countries, people still receive much of their information in interpersonal spoken communication or by listening to the dominant communications medium, radio. Although Western parents decry their children's failure to read abundantly, they sometimes forget that joining sight to sound in television not only teaches vastly greater amounts of information than books can do in much longer time spans, but television actually teaches children literacy long before they are taught formally to read and write.*

In the essay "Toward Ethnographies of Communication," *Dell Hymes contends that it is not linguistics, but ethnography, not language, but communication that must provide the frame of reference within which the place of culture and society is to be described. In a section of his essay omitted from this volume, Hymes argues that the whole context of the community is essential for understanding its communicative habits as a whole, so that any given use of channel or code by an individual member of that community takes its place as but a part of the resources upon which the members of the entire community draw. The researcher must utilize wide communication studies so that he can competently concern himself with the boundaries of the community within which communication is possible. He must also understand the communicative, cultural, social, religious, and historical values and beliefs of the community as they tend to build an ethnographic construct for the members of the community. Considered cross-culturally, it is obvious that knowing and understanding the ethnographies of intercommunicating communities, societies, and cultures aids in determining causes and results of misperceptions that occur between them and in finding ways to remedy such international and intercultural problems.*

A philosopher, Garth Gillan, writes in his essay "Language, Meaning and Symbolic Presence" that a philosophy of language can be constructed with the application of de Saussur's definition of linguistics as concerned with language as a totality, as a system of signs, independent of the speech of a particular individual. In such a philosophical construct, the question of meaning assumes critical importance in determining the nature of the linguistic sign within the context of language as a social institution. Concerned as Ong is with the oral-aural man, Garth agrees with Bloomfield's dictum that the meaning of a word consists in the semantic features of the distinctive features of meaning. The spoken word is a symbolic awareness, not a symbol of something other than itself. The spoken word is the presence dwelling within the context of the whole system of signs that constitutes a basic principle of communication.

Edward T. Hall is widely recognized for his 1959 book The Silent Language and, more recently, for his studies of proxemics—the study of man's spatial relations, including kinesics and gestures. Hall and G. L. Trager developed a linguistic model for analysis of culture in which time references in the context of conversations could be labeled formal, informal, and technical. From this model they hypothesized that all culture could be viewed as communication and that all cultural events could be analyzed with the methods of linguistics. In an effort to relate linguistic and communication models, Hall currently postulates that all communication comprises three distinct phases, a beginning phase, a peak phase, and an ending phase, with most difficulties in intercultural communication arising from problems in the adumbrative phases, which begin or end the communication interaction. Thus, although the formal message itself is understood generally, misunderstandings developed in the informal phases of communication can lead to cross-cultural breakdown about the message itself.

REFERENCES CITED

BARNLUND, DEAN C., ed.
 1968   Interpersonal communication: survey and studies. New York.
DANCE, FRANK E. X., ed.
 1967   Human communication theory: original essays. New York.
FAGEN, RICHARD R.
 1966   Politics and communication. Boston.
FISCHER, HEINZ-DIETRICH, and
JOHN C. MERRILL, eds.
 1970   International communication: media, channels, functions. New York.
HALL, EDWARD T.
 1959   The silent language. Garden City.
HOFFMAN, ARTHUR S., ed.
 1968   International communication and the new diplomacy. Bloomington.
HYMES, DELL
 1964   Toward ethnographies of communication. American Anthropologist 66:1–34.

LERNER, DANIEL, and
WILBUR SCHRAMM, eds.
  1967 Communication and change in the developing countries. Foreword by Lyndon
        B. Johnson. Honolulu.
OLIVER, ROBERT T.
  1963 Culture and communication. Springfield.
PYE, LUCIAN W., ed.
  1963 Communications and political development. Princeton.
ROGERS, EVERETT M., in association with
LYNNE SVENNING
  1969 Modernization among peasants: the impact of communication. New York.
SAPIR, EDWARD
  1929 The status of linguistics as a science. Language 5:207–214.
SMITH, ALFRED G., ed.
  1966 Communication and culture: readings. New York.
WEDGE, BRYANT
  1968 Communication analysis and comprehensive diplomacy. International com-
        munication and the new diplomacy. Arthur S. Hoffman, ed. Bloomington.

WORLD AS VIEW
AND WORLD AS EVENT
Walter J. Ong, S.J.

WALTER J. ONG, S.J., *is professor of English at Saint Louis University, where he
also has a secondary appointment as professor of humanities in psychiatry in the School
of Medicine. His most recent book is* Rhetoric, Romance, and Technology
*(Cornell University Press, 1971), a collection of studies in the interaction of
expression and culture that connect with his earlier Terry Lectures at Yale University,*
The Presence of the Word *(Yale University Press, 1967). Father Ong's* Ramus,
Method and the Decay of Dialogue *(Harvard University Press, 1958), through the
study of Renaissance intellectual history, first identified some of the influences
of print on thought that have since become commonplace knowledge. He is known
also as an analyst of contemporary culture and has served as visiting professor at
New York University, the University of Chicago, the University of California,
Indiana University, and elsewhere, and as a lecturer throughout North America,
Europe, and the Middle East. He was born in Kansas City, Missouri, and received
his B.A. from Rockhurst College, Kansas City, his M.A. and S.T.L. from St.
Louis University, and his Ph.D. from Harvard. He has been a Guggenheim Fellow
and is a member of the American Academy of Arts and Sciences.*

I

This paper is addressed to the question of whether there are differences in kind between the problem of discovering the world view
of a technologized contemporary society and the problem of discovering the
world view of other societies. It appears that there may well be such differences. Our very use of the concept "world view" advertises the likelihood. This
concept is of recent formation, part of the equipment of the postromantic
historicism that, somewhat surprisingly, grows up with technological culture.
Its ready applicability to all cultures of the past or of the future can hardly
be taken for granted.

Many cultures have never generated this particular concept. I suspect that no
early culture has. In ancient Greek and Latin, for example, there appears to
be no way to express "world view" short of circumlocutions so vast as to be
surely misleading. It is a waste of time to look for an entry under "world view"
in most English-Latin word lists, and if we try for something approximating
it, such as "outlook," we find that the best Latin equivalent offered is *spes*,
hope, which is refinable into *bona spes*, good hope, and *nulla spes*, no hope.
This conjures up an atmosphere entirely different from that of "world view."
We can grope for other terms—*conspectus*, perhaps, or *contemplatio* or even
animus, opinio, sententia de mundo, consilium de orbe terrarum, or *propositum*
—but they all prove remote from our twentieth-century concept. The curious

Reproduced by permission of the American Anthropological Association from *American
Anthropologist*, Vol. 71, No. 3, 1969.

Latin word saeculum, which yields our English "secular," comes closest of all perhaps in its sense of "spirit of the age," but it lacks sufficient subjective reference: one can hardly refer to the saeculum of an individual. Ancient Greek offers theōria, but that too lacks adequate subjectivity: it suggests either abstract theorizing or a public spectacle.

"World view" is an elusive term, but when we speak of someone's world view in any of its senses, we do not mean simply the world impressing itself upon his passive receptors, sensory or intellectual. A person does not receive a world view, but rather takes or adopts one. A world view is not a datum, a donné, but something the individual himself or the culture he shares partly constructs; it is the person's way of organizing from within himself the data of actuality coming from without and from within. A world view is a world interpretation. This makes it evidently a romantic or postromantic formulation that suggests Coleridge's idea of the imagination as giving form to material otherwise disorganized.

M. H. Abrams (1953) has shown that, by and large, preromantic concepts of man hold that the art he creates imitates or mirrors nature, whereas romantic and postromantic concepts hold that it throws light onto nature, interpreting the world. This romantic concept depends, as hinted above, on technology. The reason is that it implies a degree of control over nature unknown to early man, one achieved only by the growth of technological skills and physical sciences that accelerates so remarkably during the period running from the high Middle Ages through the Enlightenment. This growth in technological skills not only vastly enlarges technological control over the external world but also enables knowledge to expand at unprecedented rates through the deveopment of writing (which needs technology for its materials) and of print, as well as through the increase of leisure time. For early man the world was something he could only participate in, not an object to be manipulated in his consciousness.

On the face of it, a concept so dated would appear probably more applicable to the cultures out of which it arose than to earlier cultures. Discovering a world view in cultures that talk of world views and in cultures that do not possess the framework for such a concept might well be undertakings differing in kind. I do not mean to suggest, however, that speaking of the world view of an early culture is illegitimate. It would be idiotic to rule that we may study a given culture only in terms the culture itself provides. That would freeze thought for good. Nevertheless, the limited distribution of the concept suggests that the term itself needs close study, especially when it is applied to cultures removed from those where it is current. Such study can become very complex, and I shall undertake it here in only a limited way, attending to some noetic implications of the term with relation to the conditions of knowledge storage and retrieval in contrasting cultures.

II

However we break it down or specify it, the term "world view" suggests some sort of major unifying perception, and it presents the unification as taking place in a visual field. "View" implies sight, directly or analogously. The concept is of a piece with many other spatially grounded metaphors we commonly avail ourselves of in treating perception and understanding: "areas" of study, "field" of investigation, "levels" of abstraction, "fronts" of knowledge, "waves" of interest, "movements" of ideas, "trains" of thought, "grounds" for analysis, and so on indefinitely. We are used to these conceptualizations by now and have found them productive, so we often forget how thoroughly metaphorical they are and how remote from actual cognitive experience. Studying anthropology or anything else gives one no experience at all of moving one's mind over an "area." We become aware in various ways of changed interests, but we do not directly experience a change of interest as a wave, whether we take a wave as visually or as kinesthetically perceived. Nor does anyone ever directly experience ideas of his as taking part in a movement. Ideas are neither moving nor static; they simply are not that sort of thing, although we can consider them analogously as one or the other.

These metaphors and others like them are useful and beyond a doubt worth keeping. Many of them have roots deep in the past. There is nothing new in taking the physical universe as somehow a model for conscious intellectual activity. The macrocosm-microcosm notion is an old one and an inevitable one. But the metaphors just noted here, including that of "world view" itself, present both macrocosm and microcosm in a distinctive fashion. In a way characteristic of modern technologized man, they take the physical world to which they relate consciousness as something visually perceived. The senses other than sight do not count here or count very little, with the exception of touch insofar as it is allied to vision in presenting extension and insofar as visual perception itself perhaps never occurs without some admixture of the tactile imagination. (Touch, as both medieval scholastics and modern psychoanalysts remind us, is the most basic sense, lying at the root of all the others.) But touch enters into these concepts of the physical world unobtrusively or even subconsciously, however really and inevitably. Essentially, when modern technological man thinks of the physical universe, he thinks of something he can visualize either in itself or in terms of visual measurements and charts. The universe for us is essentially something you can draw a picture of.

The history of this assertive and on the whole marvelously productive visualism is, in the main, fairly well known. Habitual resort to visual models or analogues is of a piece with the modern stress on "observation" (a concept referring essentially to sight; you cannot "observe" a sound or a smell but only listen to the one and sniff the other). Visualism grows to its present strength under the aegis of modern science, particularly with the application of mathematics to physics from the seventeenth century on. It has, of course, earlier roots too, which can be discerned in ancient Greece but grew much sturdier in the European Middle Ages. Elsewhere (1958) I have tried to show in some detail how medieval scholasticism, most particularly arts scholasticism rather than theological scholasticism, fostered quantification and visualization as nothing before ever had, and how scholasticism gave birth to the movement (there we are again!) known in the sixteenth and seventeenth centuries as Ramism, after Peter Ramus (1515–1572). Ramism gratified the growing desire for quantified, diagrammatic treatment of actuality. But the Ramist kind of quantification is related to actuality only obliquely at best. Instead of applying measurements to carefully observed physical phenomena, Ramists set up diagrammatic arrangements of knowledge itself in dichotomized divisions and subdivisions ad infinitum.

Nevertheless, despite the aberrancy of Ramist efforts, history from Ramus's time on shows that thinking of the universe as essentially something seen (and to a degree touched) is highly rewarding in the physical sciences. Whether it is equally rewarding in philosophy or anthropology is a question seldom, if ever, raised. Whatever the case with anthropologists, most philosophers from Locke through Kant and many down to the present day not only accept the physical universe in exclusively visualist terms but also treat understanding itself by analogy with visual knowledge to the virtual exclusion of analogies with any of the other senses (Ong 1967:66–74). The success of vision (observation) and quantification in the physical sciences has charmed the modern mind into considering its own activity as essentially like that of sight. Until the past decade or so, there was little awareness that there are any other options. Hence we are likely to take for granted that the presence of the world to man or of man to the world should be thought of in terms of a world "view."

Recent studies of oral or preliterate cultures, however, have brought out the fact that other options are indeed open. In particular, the work of psychologists and psychiatrists reported by J. C. Carothers (1959), Marvin Opler (1956), and others whom they cite, provides evidence of "auditory synthesis." There are cultures that encourage their members to think of the universe less than we do as something picturable and more than we do as a harmony, something held together as a sound or group of sounds, a symphony, is held together. Modern theological and biblical studies have made it a commonplace that the ancient Hebrew concept of knowing expressed by yadha‘ takes knowing as something like hearing—personal and communal—whereas the ancient Greek concept expressed in gignōskō takes knowing as something like seeing—impersonal, fractioning, and analytic. Leo Spitzer (1963) showed, however, that the ancient Greeks also quite commonly thought of the world as a harmony, something heard rather than something seen; the universe was something one responded to, as to a voice, not something merely to be inspected. So did many other early peoples. We are seldom aware of how strongly audile the sensibility of early man could be or that of modern, nontechnologized man often still is. Of the many rural cosmological concepts well known in nontechnologized cultures, that of the harmony of the spheres is perhaps the only one generally familiar today to technologized man, even in learned circles.

Of course, the physical universe is both seen and heard and is touched, smelled, and tasted as well. But each of the various senses has an economy of its own, and each impinges on the human life world differently, particularly with regard to awareness of interiority and exteriority.

Sight presents surfaces (it is keyed to reflected light: light coming directly from its source, such as fire, an electric lamp, the sun, rather dazzles and blinds us); smell suggests presences or absences (its association with memory is a commonplace) and is connected with the attractiveness (especially sexual) or repulsiveness of bodies which one is near or which one is seeking ("I smelled him out"): smell is a come-or-go signal. Hence "It stinks" expresses maximum rejection or repulsion: do not even go near—the farther away the better—do not even think about it. Taste above all discriminates, distinguishing what is agreeable or disagreeable for intussusception by one's own organism (food) or psyche (aesthetic taste). . . .

Sound, on the other hand, reveals the interior without the necessity of physical invasion. Thus we tap a wall to discover where it is hollow inside, or we ring a silver-colored coin to discover whether it is perhaps lead inside. To discover such things by sight, we should have to open what we examine, making the inside the outside, destroying its interiority as such. Sound reveals interiors because its nature is determined by interior relationships. The sound of a violin is determined by the interior structure of its strings, of its bridge, and of the wood in its soundboard, by the shape of the interior cavity in the body of the violin, and other interior conditions. Filled with concrete or water, the violin would sound different [Ong 1967:117–118].

Touch attests "objective reality" in the sense of something outside that is not myself.

Dr. Johnson made this clear when he undertook to refute Berkeley tactilely —once one felt contact with a stone one kicked with one's foot, idealism, Johnson thought or pretended, was doomed. His state of mind persists and no doubt will always persist. "Real as this stone," we say, feeling ourselves clutching it with our fist, in actuality or in imagination. By touch we assure ourselves that the stone is there, is objective, for, more than other senses, touch indeed attests to existence which is objective in the sense of real-but-not-me.

And yet, by the very fact that it attests the not-me more than any other sense, touch involves my own subjectivity more than any other sense. When I feel this objective something "out there," beyond the bounds of my body, I also at the same instant experience my own self. I feel other and self simultaneously [Ong 1967:169–170].

III

These examples may remind us of "worlds" we often neglect in our scientific commitment to vision. What was the "world" like to a culture that took actuality in more auditory, less visual, terms than those to which we are accustomed? Relying for support on a much longer treatment of my own (1967) that in turn draws upon the work of many others, I shall attempt a summary listing and description of four salient features. (When I say "salient features," that is, features that "stand out" or, more accurately, "leap out," I betray my own visual or visual-tactile bias. A more aural expression might be "assertive qualities.")

Dynamism

The world of a dominantly oral or oral-aural culture is dynamic and relatively unpredictable, an event-world rather than an object-world. What we are getting at here can be understood in terms of the nature of sound as compared to other sensory perceptions. Sound is of itself necessarily an event in the way in which the object of no other sense is.

Sound signals the present use of power, since sound must be in active production in order to exist at all. Other things one senses may reveal actual present use of power, as when one watches the drive of a piston in an engine. But vision can reveal also mere quiescence, as in a still-life display. Sound can induce repose, but it never reveals quiescence. It tells us that something is going on. In his *Sound and Symbol*, writing on the effect of music, Victor Zuckerkandl notes that, by contrast with vision and touch, hearing registers force, the dynamic. This can be perceived on other grounds, too. A primitive hunter can see, feel, smell, and taste an elephant when the animal is quite dead. If he hears an elephant trumpeting or merely shuffling his feet, he had better watch out. Something is going on. Force is operating [Ong 1967:112].

Moreover, voice is for man the paradigm of all sound, and to it all sound tends to be assimilated. We hear the voice of the sea, the voice of thunder, the voice of the wind, and an engine's cough. This means that the dynamism inherent in all sound tends to be assimilated to the dynamism of the human being, an unpredictable and potentially dangerous dynamism because a human being is a free, unpredictable agent.

Traditionalism

The world of a dominantly oral or oral-aural culture is traditional. Its traditionalism is closely related to the problems of acquiring, storing, and retrieving knowledge in a voice-and-ear or oral-aural economy of thought and communication, operating without the use of records.

Recent studies, many involving massive recordings of oral performances, have revealed the noetic processes of oral cultures as never before. We can only summarize here some relevant points in the new discoveries, points that will be found explicated in more detail in lengthier works (Lord 1960, Havelock 1963, Yates 1966, Ong 1958 and 1967, Chadwick and Chadwick 1932–1940).

An oral culture, we must remind ourselves, is one in which nothing can be "looked up." Words are sounds, and sounds exist only as they are going out of existence. I cannot stop a word as I can a moving picture in order to fix my attention on an immobilized part of it. There are no immobilized parts of sound. If I stop sound, I have only its opposite, silence. An oral culture is deeply aware of this evanescent quality of words. Homer expresses this awareness when he sings of "wingèd words." At the same time, oral cultures consider words more powerful than we do, probably in the last analysis because whereas we interpret movement as instability, they are keenly aware of the moment of sound as signaling use of power. Words fly, which means that they not only move but do so energetically.

How to keep knowledge stable is thus a major problem in an oral culture. We know now the general lines along which the problem is solved. Basically, the solution is to standardize utterance, making it highly "traditional." By contrast with verbal expression, which is composed in writing, oral verbalization is thematic and formulary, filled with epithets (standard, expected quali-fiers), prolific of heroic figures (fixed, "heavy," more or less symbolic individ-uals, predictable in performance, almost entirely free of any character develop-ment). When writing takes over from oral verbalization but before writing fully develops its own economy of noetics and expression, these heroic figures be-come quasiscientific abstract types (writing makes science possible). Such are the virtues and vices of medieval morality plays or the related figures of Ben Jonson's drama and eighteenth-century comedy. Stability of character helps anchor knowledge for retrieval in an oral world. If Nestor is always wise, around a story about Nestor can be clustered what Greeks knew and could later treat more scientifically as wisdom. So wily Odysseus serves to store and retrieve what was known about wiliness, Achilles what was known about brav-ery, and so on. In the interest of stabilizing knowledge, oral cultures make a great deal of commonplace statements enshrined in popular adages or proverbs and of apothegms attributed to famous persons. Oral folk want to and need to hear the treasured utterances of the past. "Tell us something from the tales of old." Highest marks are given to superlatively skilled performance of the expected, and there is little if any interest in "originality" or "creativity," such as grew up with the late typographical phenomenon called the Romantic age.

Accustomed as we are to noetic conditions, where virtually everything that men have ever known can be "looked up" on a designated page in a locatable book on a specified shelf in a library, we forget how natural and inevitable the oral exploitation of commonplace material is. In a society in which articulate utterances or statements about a subject cannot be "looked up" (although visual aides-memoire such as wampum belts or winter-count pictures may be used), even the expected is not so expected as it is for us. It is on hand only when it is being recited. And one needs to be assured that it can be retrieved by recitation on demand. Under such conditions the role of a poet in, for ex-ample, preliterate Homeric Greece, as Eric Havelock (1963) has shown in beautiful detail, is not simply that of an entertainer. The poet is also a re-caller and a repeater; if he and others like him were not around, what knowl-edge the society has would simply disappear. The orator participates in the role of the poet. He must likewise deal in the commonplace, the expected, the already known, as well as in the particular issues with which individual forensic or deliberative problems engage him.

We are now aware of just how conservative, just how fixed, just how essen-tially repetitive the poetry and the oratory of an oral society are. Homer, re-cent studies (Lord 1960 and others cited there) have shown, is made up almost completely of clichés. Everyone is familiar with his "wine-dark sea" and "rosy-fingered dawn." These are among the most heavily worked epithets. But close tabulatory study of the text shows that virtually every image in Homer, line after line, is of that sort. Epic poets sing of standard themes—the arrival of the messenger, the summoning of the council, the feast, the arming of the hero, the description of the hero's shield or sword or other armor, the journey, the challenge, the combat, the despoiling of the vanquished foe, and so on. And they sing of those themes in formulas or formulaic elements that they have accumulated by the thousands. A horse, to fabricate an English example that makes the point clear, is a "coal-black steed," a "roan-red steed," a "snow-white steed," a "fast gray mare," a "dapple-gray mount" (one extra syllable), a "dapple-gray stallion" (two extra syllables), and so on. If a rider needs a horse, the singer has a number of options he can trot out of his memory, all metrically harnessed and ready to go. And so with everything else he deals in.

That is why, as Albert B. Lord (1960), carrying on Milman Parry's work, found with oral epic singers of modern Yugoslavia, a singer can repeat an epic of an hour's duration after hearing it only once. Essentially all the singers have the same thematic and formulaic equipment—although each will have his own peculiarities in his management of it—and it is simply a matter of putting the equipment to work on a new set of characters and situations. (Of course, even today all narration is always thematic, including the most sophisticated kind of present-day historiography, for the only way to cut verbally into the unbroken web of history is to lift out certain themes; but the themes of the oral epic are much more fixed and limited in number than those of today's writers.)

Memory in an oral noetic economy is never verbatim on any appreciable scale. Lord (1960) has shown this as an indisputable fact in the case of the prodigiously skilled memory of the Yugoslavian epic singers; recordings show that they never sing any epic exactly the same way twice, despite their protestations (also recorded) that they do. I have reviewed elsewhere (1967) the evidence—or, better, the utter lack of it—that leads us to believe that no oral culture in the world achieves verbatim memory for lengthy passages of anything. But oral memory is nevertheless tenacious and accurate; it is locked in the themes and formulas. And it is extensive. Innocent hearers from chirographic and typographic cultures, who themselves generally memorize verbatim from texts, are likely to think that a person capable of reciting ex tempore thousands of lines in a highly complex meter must have memorized the material word for word. The fact is that such persons have in their store of expressions thousands upon thousands of phrases that fit into the standard metrical pattern. They are "rhapsodizers" or "stitchers," as the Greeks called them (rhaptein, 'to sew together,' from which rhapsōidein derives). It is significant that this kind of composition features complex meters but not rhyme, which would be much more unmanageable.

Even today the "feel" of an oral tradition for unchanging themes and formulas is still accessible to the post-typographic man who is familiar with the telling of fairy stories to children. Here there is no question of an original author or of originality or of telling the story each time in exactly the same words. But the story remains in its basic elements quite stable, and the audience expects the story as a whole and its formulary elements to be the same each time it is told. Anyone who in repeating the story of The Three Little Pigs to a youthful audience varies the number from three to four or seven will immediately meet with resistance from his hearers. And formulas, once uttered, are sacrosanct. I myself was pulled up by a five-year old some years ago for saying, "He huffed and he puffed, and he huffed and he puffed" instead of the expected, "He huffed and he puffed, and he puffed and he huffed."

Oratory, the other great oral art form, remained an oral improvisation or rhapsodizing ("stitching") long after the appearance of writing (Ong 1967). Cicero wrote his orations only after he had delivered them, that is, performed them. Oratory as an oral form proceeded in much the same fashion as epic, exploiting the set commonplaces or *loci communes* relentlessly, such as Cicero's "O tempora! O mores!" which was his "things-are-going-to-pot" bit, and other comparable prefabricated purple patches on dishonesty, valor, a dark night, a long time, and so on. Traffic in the commonplaces persisted as oral residue through the age of Shakespeare (who is quotable because he is made up of quotations tooled and retooled and given their final resonance by his master voice) and pretty strongly into the nineteenth century. It endures in some political oratory even today, particularly in nontechnologized cultures, where "capitalist warmongers," "colonialism," and similar themes, whatever their validity, are repeated with a persistence nauseating to technologized man but completely in accord with the older oral noetic patterns.

The noetic procedures illustrated by epic and oratory extend through the entire economy of a completely oral culture, as Havelock (1963) has pointed out. Oral Homeric Greece contrasts here with Lord's modern Yugoslavia, where oral epic poets constitute only a subculture in a society administered by literates—and a dwindling subculture, as Lord notes (1960), since growing literacy is destroying it. An oral poet must be illiterate or he will take to matching written or printed texts, thereby destroying the entire oral economy of performance. In contrast to modern Yugoslavia, Homer's Greece not only included a population of illiterate, highly skilled epic singers but also was administered from top to bottom by illiterates. In such a society the stitching or weaving of thematic and formulary elements that the epic singers practiced was a skill needed by public officials too, although not to the same specialized degree. If an official wanted to get a substantial message from Ithaca to Argos, he would have to cast it up in some mnemonic form or an illiterate messenger would never be able to deliver it.

The fixed-formula economy of an oral culture of course governs not only what it can repeat but also what it can know. Man knows what he can recall— all else is so ephemeral as to be negligible. In an oral culture this means that he knows what is cast in fixed thematic and formulary patterns. Anything else will seem unreal, nonknowledge, reprehensible, and dangerous. This is the noetic foundation for the traditionalism stemming from oral cultures. What is not traditional—cast in recognized themes and formulas—is dangerous because it is slippery and unmanageable. Oral-aural man does not like the nontraditional because, beyond his limited means of control, it advertises the tenuousness of his hold on actuality. Only when recordkeeping, first by chirography and then much more effectively by print, anchored knowledge in space for facile visual retrieval could traditionalism yield to a more flexible relationship to the world and a more flexible understanding of what the world is.

Polemicism

The world of a dominantly oral-aural culture is highly personal and polemic, at least in part because of its orality. Although this does not mean that polemic qualities in early cultures cannot also be related to other features besides orality, it is not entirely impossible that all the other features in some way or other relate significantly to orality, making it the major component in a complex of causes.

Without records, oral cultures have quite limited means of storing knowledge by categorization in what we may call scientific or highly abstract fashion. The development of bodies of knowledge of the sort we call arts and sciences has to wait on the advent of writing. Although it is fortunately out of date to say that primitive man has no idea of causality, it is true that complex chains of causality elude him. A is caused by B, B by C, and C by D, but D happens because Zeus was peeved at Athena. This means, in effect, "I pass." When divine causality is later analyzed in a sophisticated Christian tradition, it is no help at all in accounting physically for physical phenomena. It operates at another level.

The larger conceptual and verbal structures in which oral-aural man stores what he knows consist in great part of stories that turn on human action and on the interaction of man and man. Thus the Iliad and the Odyssey function not merely as entertaining stories but also as encyclopedias to an extent we often fail to appreciate. The list of the ships in the Iliad (ii. 494–875) is probably the closest thing to a national directory that an oral culture could produce. Where else would such material be verbalized? Similarly, the description of shipbuilding in the Odyssey (v. 225–261), when Odysseus is getting away from Circe, is the closest thing to a shipbuilding manual that an oral culture would know. Where else in a culture without writing would the method of building a ship be articulated? Perhaps in an oration, but orations were constructed in much the same way that epic poems were. What we find in Homer or a shipbuilding manual today would hardly be recited by a shipwright who learned and taught his trade by an apprentice system.

Whether in an epic narrative or in an oration built around some expected personal response, factual material and even technical description thus was stored and retrieved by being built into the human life world. Objects and objective fact did not inhabit an isolated section of actuality purportedly altogether screened off from contact with human "subjectivity" or personal relevance, as they do for modern technologized man. Everything was part of human activity, more or less objective and subjective simultaneously.

By the same token, in one way or another everything was caught up in the polemic of the human life struggle. The action of the heroic figures generated in an oral economy of narration would naturally at root consist of a battle between forces of good and evil. When so much of the lore of a culture was retained through narrative tales or songs about great heroes, even what would otherwise be completely neutral material thus acquired a moral flavor by association with the polemic or agonia of the hero and his adversaries. The entire world thereby tended to be polarized in terms of "good guys" and "bad guys" and later in terms of abstract personifications of virtues and vices (at least in Western European cultures around the Middle Ages, when writing was encouraging abstraction but had not yet crushed dominantly oral structures). In

the highly moral climate of heroic song the *Iliad's* catalogue of ships is thus
not merely a national directory, but, from the technically rhetorical point of
view, it is also an encomium or "praise" of the Greeks: the Greek leaders and
their followers are "good guys." Learning itself takes place in an agonistic setting under these oral-aural conditions. Puberty rites of early societies correspond in many ways to academic education in more developed cultures.
Through puberty rites the young men are initiated into the lore of the tribe,
its myths and intellectual heritage, as well as into its various skills. In this lore
objective fact and man's subjective world interpenetrate. In the process of
learning the youths are often subjected to excruciating physical torment, which
gives their new knowledge its requisite agonistic tone.

By an extension of oral practices into literate society and even for a while
into early typographical society, the agonistic element in learning is perpetu-
ated through the arts of rhetoric and dialectic, which governed all academic
practice from antiquity through the Renaissance. During that period no one
was ever formally taught neutral objectivity, although many doubtless did
achieve it in their own way. A scholar was taught to defend a stand he had
taken or to attack the stand of another; rhetorical performance and dialectical
debate governed all subjects. Truth was a human possession, to be defended
as one's own life. This long persistence of agonistic frames of reference suggests how thoroughly polemic had been oral man's life world.

More could be said about the polemic frame of mind and its connection
with an economy of scarcity, with the linguistic situation that fragmented most
of mankind into small groups hostile to outsiders, with the common acceptance
of war as the permanent state of human existence, with the incredibly harsh
punishments, including execution even for minor offenses, found in early conquest states and some other early societies, including the residually oral societies of medieval and Renaissance Europe. But enough has been retailed here
from the more substantial studies to give some indication of the noetic roots
of polemic in oral cultures.

It was against the personal world inherited from preliterate Greece that
Plato's philosophy took form, as Havelock (1963) has circumstantially shown.
Plato's expulsion of the poets from his Republic and his touting of the "ideas"
are the two sides of the same coin. His expulsion of the poets was his rejection
of the old *paideia*, in which learning was basically oral, only slightly modified
by writing; the *Iliad* and *Odyssey* were learned from a written text. The pupil
was made to identify with heroic figures in a life world in which all things,
even objective fact, were caught up. Plato's ideas launched the new world,
the opposite of the old, which his attack on the poets proscribed. The old
world had made much of man's activities and of human struggle as the focus
or axis of all reality. Where the old world had been warm and human, Plato's
"ideas" or "forms" (Greek *idéa*, "outline": a concept based on visual perception) were cold and abstract; where the old world had been mobile, event-full,
visualized as narrative is often visualized, but not visualized in explicatory,
analytic fashion. The vision of narrative was a swirl of exciting activity. In contrast, Plato's new ideas were motionless, ahistorical; where the old view had

held all knowledge in a concrete human setting, the new traced everything to the abstract, the other-worldly, the totally objective, the fixed, modeled on an immobile figure visualized on a motionless field.

Structuring of personality

In oral cultures the external world sets up and impinges on personality structures quite different from our own. The clinical studies reported by Carothers (1959) and Opler (1956) correlate definite psychological or personality structures with differences between illiteracy (studied pretty well across the globe) and literacy (as represented only by alphabetic writing, not character writing such as Chinese, which might produce a third, intermediate personality structure). The difference in psychological structures can be summarized by noting that in oral cultures schizophrenia virtually never manifests itself by delusional systematization, that is, by systematic day dreaming, by constructing a private, imaginary, unreal world in which one's problems are solved or nonexistent. When subject to the kind of strain that produces schizoid behavior, the illiterate from an oral culture (illiterates from literate cultures are not quite total illiterates, for they experience the effects of literacy vicariously) reacts, too, by losing contact with actuality. But his typical pattern is an outbreak of intense anxiety and hostility and psychic disorganization that shows itself in extreme violence toward others and sometimes toward himself; Carothers attributes the pattern to a lack of ego defenses due to tribal reliance on the group. The outbreak of anxiety and hostility is rioting, which is a regular phenomenon in many oral cultures and which is represented by the ancient Scandinavian warrior who goes berserk or the southeast Asian warrior who runs amok as well as by more recent Congolese rioters, whose behavior is interpreted by their own culture as regrettable but inevitable. The absence of schizophrenic delusional systematization appears to be the correlative of the individual's inability to isolate himself and his thought processes from the group, from the tribe, in the ways that become possible for the first time with reading. (The shift to reading, however, does not make withdrawal the only recourse of schizophrenics: in literates, too, violence can occur, perhaps as a more primitive response.) Just as physical personal privacy is at best a rare luxury in oral, tribal cultures, so psychological withdrawal is infrequent or even impossible in such cultures. Thought is not advanced by Aristotles or Einsteins or other individual discoverers but rather moves ahead with glacial slowness; everyone must advance together. We must remind ourselves that in an oral culture there is no private study. Learning is communal, unless it is achieved at the hands of that most dangerous and worst of teachers, raw experience.

IV

Script and print, with all that they entail, have transformed the oral world into the one we know today—or at least into the one we have known up to the past few years. Script, and particularly the alphabet, converted the dynamic event-world in which oral-aural man stored his knowledge into a world of static visual record. Many, perhaps even all, primitive peoples make much of sight, but the alphabet warped sound itself into a visual mold. The alphabet triumphed only slowly and never entirely, but inexorably. Print, by locking words into the same place in thousands of copies of a book and thereby making indexing and retrieving information possible to a degree utterly unknown in pretypographic manuscript culture, consolidated the work of the alphabet in reducing evanescent sound to the repose of space.

The conversion from totally oral to largely visualized vocalization took a long time, though its success was inevitable. Three thousand years and more after the invention of the first script (around 3500 B.C.) and a thousand years after the invention of the alphabet (around 1500 B.C.), classical antiquity remained largely oral. Its modes of composition were still largely based on the commonplaces and the oration, even in genres such as historiography. Its stance was polemic, its educational goal the training of the *rhetor*, the *orator*, the public speaker, outfitting him for verbal combat. The Middle Ages were far more textually oriented than antiquity and yet by our standards still impossibly oral. Their universities applied themselves to texts as man never had before, and yet the testing of intellectual achievement was never by writing but always by oral *agonia* or dialectical debate. Even the Renaissance, which culminated the medieval drive toward the written word by producing the printing press and modern textual scholarship, still felt itself committed in principle and to a surprising degree in actuality to the oratorical culture of classical antiquity. As I have undertaken to spell out in great detail (1967), all Western culture remained significantly oral until well into the Romantic age, only slowly relaxing its hold on the traditionalism and the polemicism marking oral society and personality structure.

V

In the light of the foregoing explanation, which is uncomfortably sketchy but cannot be enlarged on here, we can reflect on the applicability of the concept of world view to earlier cultures. Is an oral world unduly distorted by having appiled to it the concept of "view"? Are the very differences that mark it off from our own thereby obscured? The visual synthesis the concept endorses certainly makes the concept congenial to the psyche developed in a context of writing and print and technological design. We take very readily to synthesizing "world" as some kind of picture. But does this very type of synthesis somehow vitiate what we make of earlier man's life world?

Perhaps we cannot do otherwise. Freudians have long made the point that for thought and civilization itself to advance, man must minimize the proximity senses of touch, taste, and smell and maximize the senses of hearing and sight. The latter are more abstract in that they report on objects that can be and to a degree must be at a greater distance from the perceiver. Touch requires contact, which the eyeball cannot tolerate. Thus hearing and sight keep the individual and the object of perception nicely distinct. (Touch includes a perception of self-as-touching far more than hearing includes a sense of the self-as-hearing or sight a sense of the self-as-seeing.) Of the two, sight is the more abstract and thus the more "objective." The latter-day history of civilization has entailed a marked movement from the aural to the visual world sense.

Specialization in visually based concepts thus appears to be a sign of progress because they afford preferred information of a sort otherwise unavailable. It does not make much sense to say that we should not examine an oral culture in terms of our concept of a world view because an oral culture tended to synthesize less in terms of view and more in aural terms than we do. For the same reason, oral culture was in fact quite incapable of analyzing itself or anything else in the ways that have become feasible and even mandatory for us.

Nevertheless, we can ask whether we are not too exclusively and unreflectively exploiting visual models today to the neglect of analogs from the other senses. Insofar as understanding of the life world of a given culture requires participation in it, or a kind of empathy for it, the hypervisualism of our sensorium may to a degree disqualify us for understanding whatever unity an earlier culture may have known in its relationship to actuality.

VI

Finally, our hypervisualism may already be outmoded. It may hinder our understanding of our own life world as it is reorganizing itself today and for the immediate future. If it is true, as I have suggested elsewhere (1967; see also others there cited), that we are moving into a new era of sound, we can ask ourselves whether the term "world view" alone is adequate to conceptualize the kind of unification man of coming generations will experience or undertake to realize. The new era into which we have already entered is marked by an unprecedented augmentation of sound-communication devices. We live each succeeding day in an increasingly oral world. Telephone supplements letter-writing, radio makes voice present all over the world simultaneously, television (much more an aural device than its name suggests) does the same, rapid transportation has multiplied personal confrontation in conventions, discussion groups, and assemblies of all sorts. Sonar is even used to catch fish. As sound gains, in certain ways sight is downgraded. With radio telescopes and inter-planetary television mediated through codes of binary numbers, the use of all kinds of complex nonvisual probes in physical and chemical analysis, and other similar developments, the direct use of sight is on the wane in science. Our oralism profoundly differs from that of preliterate man, for it is programmed by means that include writing and print. But at the same time we are often more effectively oral than early man, who could not make an individual's voice heard in every quarter of the globe simultaneously.

How far does our new oralism make our culture like that of early oral-aural man, man before the advent of writing? Marshall McLuhan's statement that we live in a "global village" has become a commonplace. But it is a gnomic and paradoxical commonplace. For what is global cannot be a village, with the village's feeling of an in-group affording shelter from the larger outside world. There is no longer an outside world.

When we examine the present situation for evidence of the four features of early oral-aural culture we noted above (there are other features, of course, in addition to these), we find some striking correspondences and some striking differences. First, our present world has become an event-world to a significant, self-conscious degree. Preliterate cultures were immersed in an event-world because of their inability to structure knowledge other than around human beings. We construct an event-world self-consciously and programmatically to strengthen the human in a world filled with objective structures of the mind. And we do so, as I have attempted to show elsewhere (1962:223–229, 1967:87–110), by massive exploitation of sound.

On the other hand, our world is certainly not traditional in the way in which the old oral-aural world was. We rely on too many records and too exhaustive historical knowledge to need this sort of support. But is there some kind of new traditionalism among us? Faddism, perhaps? Are beatniks and hippies traditionalists of a new kind? Or of a reverse kind? Their drive to conformism is marked.

Further, the personal and polemic cast of preliterate oralism is represented only partially in the present situation. Personalism is indeed stressed. The protest against overmechanization is one of the many manifestations of attention to the person as such; other manifestations are the growth of counseling in all its forms, the proliferation of discussion groups of all sorts, the cult of the outsider, the study of group dynamics and group relations, and so on. Again, in contrast to earlier spontaneous or unreflective personalism, ours is reflective and programmatic. This makes it in one way less human and in another way more human. But the polemic associated with older, feudal, personalist structures is missing. Despite our much publicized strife, the irenic quest marks our age. We are still distressingly warlike, but being so troubles our collective consciences as it seldom if ever troubled the collective or even most individual consciences of earlier man. Strong in their feeling for in-groups, earlier cultures believed quite generally that war, though perhaps regrettable, was an inescapable part of life.

Finally, are we entering into the older pattern of schizoid behavior, with rioting replacing schizophrenic withdrawal? Perhaps to a degree. It is probably significant that much rioting centers in groups who are either largely illiterate in tradition or ill at ease in centers of literacy, such as universities. Elsewhere (1958, 1962) I have attempted to detail the connections the alphabet and alphabetic printing have with a sense of order. It would appear that these connections are being shaken up in our present stage of oralism.

The foregoing is no more than a sketch of the present state of oralism, but it shows that the world ahead of us, like the world of the distant past, may call for new tools of analysis. Man's experience of the "world" organizing itself today may to a significant degree elude us if we unthinkingly equate "world" with some sort of canvas spread out before us, as something of which we have primarily a "view."

The concept of world view of course need not and should not be discarded. But how can it be supplemented? We can perhaps start from a more generic concept, thinking of not merely a world view but a world sense. In fact, such a generic concept would seem to be demanded by the terms we use, or are likely to use, in analyzing various world views. Although the concept of view is visually grounded, it is also quite metaphorically interpreted, and analyses of world views do not in fact commonly restrict themselves to the use of visually grounded terms. We can analyze a world view in terms of texture, which is based patently on the sense of touch, or in terms of tonality or concordance, which refer to hearing. We might, however, gain a good deal if we reflected more on the sensory field or fields in which the various concepts we use are grounded. Perhaps it would be productive to cultivate some aurally based concepts, such as those just mentioned as well as "harmony," "cacophony," and "melody," although doing so might seem to suggest a certain affectation.

But I believe that another productive way to supplement our concept of world view is to move from the concept of world sense to the concept of world-as-presence. By presence I mean the kind of relationship that exists between persons when we say that two persons are present to one another. Presence in the full sense of the term entails more than sensation. Insofar as it is grounded in the senses, it appears to be grounded in all of them simultaneously. We speak of a "sense" of presence, rather than a sight, sound, smell, taste, or touch of presence. There is some special relationship, of course, between presence and touch; probably because with touch is associated our sense of reality and presences are eminently real, we can say that we feel someone's presence. There is also some special relationship between presence and smell, presumably because of the relationship of smell to memory. A particular odor can conjure up a presence or presences very effectively, although it may leave the impression very vague. Still, the sense of presence appears not to be founded on any one sensory field in particular.

What happens if we think of world presence or the world-as-presence rather than of the world as something viewed, something toward which we have an outlook? We do suffer some disabilities. In terms of presence we cannot achieve the precision we achieve by resort to the visual imagination for models representing the structures in consciousness. But by thinking of world-as-presence we gain in immediacy and in a certain kind of relevance.

The conditions in which we find ourselves today call for consideration of the world as a kind of presence chiefly because of what Teilhard has called quite aptly the hominization of the globe. The ambiance in which man finds himself today is made up of human beings more than ever before. For the first time in man's history the globe is pretty well covered with men all of whom are in contact with one another, at least in the large. Nature is more and more subjected to man's management and is becoming a kind of extension of humanity. Our environment is more and more a peopled environment in which things themselves exist in a context of people. This is the kind of world the concept of presence expresses. Presence applies most directly to persons. If I am in a room with a chair, a plant, a cat, and a human being, it is the human being who normally will be felt as a presence, not the other things. In the strict sense only persons are real presences. A world conceived of in terms of presence is a hominized world.

Thinking of the world as a kind of presence is, of course, not entirely new.

There is a good deal of evidence that in the past it was thought of this way after a fashion. First, as has been noted earlier, oral-aural cultures predispose man to personalize even impersonal phenomena because he has to store knowledge in narrative rather than abstract scientific categories. Secondly, as phenomenologists like to remind us, intersubjectivity is a primary mode of human experience. When I walk alone through a dark wood at night and hear what I know is the branch of one tree rubbing against another in the breeze, I cannot keep my imagination from persistently suggesting that the noise is the voice of some living being, and indeed of some person who, being otherwise unknown and of uncertain intent, may well wish to harm me. My imagination wants persons around. Every infant is initiated into an awareness of himself from the beginning in a context of persons who mediate the exterior world to him, and he can never after release himself from that context. Where persons are missing, he projects them. Animism exists in primitive cultures for a variety of reasons, no doubt, but one reason would appear to be the relative emptiness of the primitive universe. Since there are very few persons around, personal presences are projected into the otherwise empty world. Animism can persist for a while in urban populations, but it is more typically a phenomenon of loosely dispersed groups.

We no longer need animism today. The wood nymphs vanished as the woods filled with trailer camps. Water sprites have been crowded out by submarines and scuba divers. We need no longer project presences into the world, for they are already there. Besides the persons just down the street or in the next room or at our elbow, there are all the others permanently available on television. For dealing with our superpeopled environment we seem to need some attention to the notion of presence if we are to think of the world in post-Cartesian terms. We must, of course, refine our various visual models of the universe as never before. But we also need some nonvisual concepts, including even some that have not yet been born. In the present situation, this paper can pretend to be no more than maieutic.

NOTE

[1] This paper was originally prepared for and presented at Wenner-Gren Foundation Burg Wartenstein symposium no. 41, "World Views: Their Nature and Their Role in Culture," August 2–11, 1968.

REFERENCES CITED

ABRAMS, M. H.
   1953   The mirror and the lamp. New York.
CAROTHERS, J. C.
   1959   Culture, psychiatry, and the written word. Psychiatry 22:307–320.
CHADWICK, H. MUNRO, and
N. KERSHAW CHADWICK
   1932–1940   The growth of literature (3 vols.). Cambridge, Eng.
HAVELOCK, ERIC A.
   1963   Preface to Plato. Cambridge, Mass.

LORD, ALBERT B.
  1960   The singer of tales. Cambridge, Mass.
ONG, WALTER J.
  1958   Ramus, method, and the decay of dialogue. Cambridge, Mass.
  1962   The barbarian within. New York.
  1967   The presence of the word. New Haven.
OPLER, MARVIN K.
  1956   Culture, psychiatry, and human values. Springfield, Ill.
SPITZER, LEO
  1963   Classical and Christian ideas of world harmony: prolegomena to an interpreta-
         tion of the word "Stimmung."
YATES, FRANCES A.
  1966   The art of memory. Chicago.

TOWARD ETHNOGRAPHIES
OF COMMUNICATION

Dell Hymes[1]

Dell Hymes was born in Portland, Oregon, in 1927. He was educated in public schools in Portland, received his B.A. in anthropology and literature at Reed College, and his M.A. and Ph.D. in linguistics at Indiana University. Professor Hymes has taught at Harvard University, the University of California at Berkeley, and, since 1965, the University of Pennsylvania. He is a member of the graduate group of the Annenberg School of Communications. He completed field work among the Indians of Oregon, especially the Oregon Coast and Warm Springs Reservation. He was a fellow at the Center for Advanced Study in the Behavioral Sciences, ACLS, Clare Hall, Cambridge University; and he was a Guggenheim Fellow for 1969. Professor Hymes was a member of the Executive Committee of the Linguistic Society of America and a member of the Executive Board of the American Anthropological Association; he also served as the second vice-president of the American Folklore Society during 1971. Professor Hymes is editor of Language in Culture and Society (1964), Studies in Southwestern Ethnolinguistics (1967), The Use of the Computer in Anthropology (1965), and Pidginization and Creolization of Languages (1971). He is editor of the journal Language in Society and author of studies on American Indian languages and cultures, the history of anthropology and linguistics, and the relation of language to social life.

[We] cannot attempt a systematic exposition of the ethnography of communication, or of the theory it may help build.[2] Too little systematic work has been done for such an exposition to be possible. Some over-all sketch is needed, however, as an indication of relations among various lines of work that does not otherwise emerge, and of some of the specific content a systematic theory would comprise. In the sketch that follows I emphasize the needs and content of an ethnographic approach, and relations among anthropological interests. There are four aspects to be sketched, concerned, respectively, with (1) the components of communicative events, (2) the relations among components, (3) the capacity and state of components, and (4) the activity of the system so constituted. It is with respect to the third and fourth aspects that two topics prominently associated with the topic of communica-

Reproduced by permission of the American Anthropological Association from *American Anthropologist*, Vol. 66, No. 1, 1964.

Editor's Note: The first twelve pages of Hymes's essay are omitted here. His essay originally introduced a collection of essays on the ethnography of communication edited by J. J. Gumperz and Dell Hymes in the *American Anthropologist* (December 1964), pp. 1–182. Where Hymes refers specifically to the findings and theories of authors included in the collection, I have retained these references. In a few cases, comments about "the focus of these papers" make their presence in the current volume confusing and have been omitted.

tion, communication theory (in the sense of information theory), and cybernetics, find a place.

THE COMPONENTS OF COMMUNICATIVE EVENTS

The starting point is the ethnographic analysis of the communicative habits of a community in their totality, determining what count as communicative events, and as their components, and conceiving no communicative behavior as independent of the set framed by some setting or implicit question. The communicative event thus is central. (In terms of language proper, the statement means that the linguistic code is displaced by the speech act as focus of attention.)

Some frame of reference is needed for consideration of the several kinds of components co-present in a communicative event. The logic or other superiority of one classification over another is not at issue. What is at issue is the provision of a useful guide in terms of which relevant features can be discerned —a provisional phonetics, as it were, not an *a priori* phonemics, of the communicative event.

For what has to be inventoried and related in an ethnographic account, a somewhat elaborated version of factors identified in communications theory, and adapted to linguistics by Roman Jakobson (1953;1960), can serve. Briefly put, (1,2) the various kinds of participants in communicative events—senders and receivers, addressors and addressees, interpreters and spokesmen, and the like; (3) the various available channels, and their modes of use, speaking, writing, printing, drumming, blowing, whistling, singing, face and body motion as visually perceived, smelling, tasting, and tactile sensation; (4) the various codes shared by various participants, linguistic, paralinguistic, kinesic, musical, and other; (5) the settings (including other communication) in which communication is permitted, enjoined, encouraged, abridged; (6) the forms of messages, and their genres, ranging verbally from single-morpheme sentences to the patterns and diacritics of sonnets, sermons, salesmen's pitches, and any other organized routines and styles; (7) the topics and comments that a message may be about; (8) the events themselves, their kinds and characters as wholes—all these must be identified in an adequate ethnographic way.

Ethnography here is conceived in reference to the various efforts of Conklin, Frake, Goodenough, Metzger, Romney, and others to advance the techniques of ethnographic work and to conceptualize its goal, such that the structural analysis of cultural behavior generally is viewed as the development of theories adequate to concrete cases, just as the structural analysis of behavior as manifestation of a linguistic code is viewed. One way to phrase the underlying outlook is as a question of validity. Just as analysis of phonological capabilities must determine what set of phonological features is to be taken as relevant to identification and distinction of phonological sound on the part of the possessors of the capabilities in question, so analysis of cultural capabilities generally must determine what sets of features are to be taken as relevant to identification and contrast of cultural behavior on the part of the participants in same. (Sapir's "Sound Patterns in Language" [1925], seen as implying a general statement about the cultural aspect of behavior, remains classic and crucial to the development of anthropological thought in this regard, although it has taken a generation for its ethnographic import to become salient.) Another way to phrase the underlying outlook is as a question of the common element in the situation of ethnographer and person-in-the-culture. Each must formulate from finite experience theories adequate to predict and judge as appropriate or inappropriate what is in principle an infinite amount of cultural behavior. (Judgments of grammaticality are a special case.)

Mere observation, however systematic and repeated, can obviously never suffice to meet such high standards of objectivity and valdity. As Sapir once observed regarding a rule of avoidance among the Wishram Chinook:

> Incidentally there is a lesson here for the theoretical ethnologist. If the avoidance of man and woman here were known only objectively it would present a situation resembling that, say, in Melanesia. One might suppose then the explanation to be that women were set apart from the man's social fabric because of the low esteem in which they were held, or that men avoided them because of their periodic impure state. Either guess would be a shot far wide of the mark. The moral is that it is as necessary to discover what the native sentiment is as well as to record the behavior.[3]

The point is essentially the same as that of "Sound Patterns of Language," from which stems the current distinction of "etic" and "emic." An "emic" account is one in terms of features relevant in the behavior in question; an etic account, however useful as a preliminary grid and input to an emic (structural) account, and as a framework for comparing different emic accounts, lacks the emic account's validity. The point is an old one in anthropology, only made more trenchant by the clarity with which the point can be made in terms of the contrast between phonetics and phonemics. (See Pike 1954 for coinage of the terms, and conscious development of the perspective from a linguistic basis beyond linguistics, under inspiration from Sapir.) Ethnographic objectivity is intersubjective objectivity, but in the first instance, the intersubjective objectivity in question is that of the participants in the culture. No amount of acoustic apparatus and sound spectography can crack the phonemic code of a language, and a phonemic analysis, based on the intersubjective objectivity in the behavior of those who share the code, is the necessary basis for other studies, experimental and otherwise. (Cr. Hockett 1955:210–211; Lisker, Cooper, and Liberman 1962.) The same is true for the shared codes which constitute the mutual intelligibility of the rest of cultural behavior. The advantages of such an approach in providing a criterion against which to appraise participants' own explanations and conceptualizations of their behavior, their "home-made models," should be obvious, as should the advantages in providing a basis for controlled comparison, study of diffusion, and any other generalizing or analyzing approach that depends in the last analysis on the adequacy and precision of ethnographic records of cultural behavior. (Ethnographic records, of course, may be of other things: censuses, for example.)

In a discussion of genealogical method, Conklin (1964:25–26), observing that all kinship data derive from ethnographic contexts, makes explicit his assumptions regarding the nature and purpose of ethnography (citing also Goodenough 1956, and noting Frake 1962b, 1964, and a previous article of his own [1962]). The statement applies to communicative data as well as to kinship data, and can be adopted here:

An adequate ethnography is here considered to include the culturally significant arrangement of productive statements about the relevant relationships obtaining among locally defined categories and contexts (of objects and events) within a given social matrix. These nonarbitrarily ordered statements should comprise, essentially, a cultural grammar (Goodenough 1957a; Frake 1962a). In such an ethnography, the emphasis is placed on the interpretation, evaluation, and selection of alternative statements about a particular set of cultural activities within a given range of social contexts. This in turn leads to the critical examination of intracultural relations and ethno-theoretical models (Conklin 1955; Goodenough ms.). Demonstrable intracultural validity for statements of covert and abstracted relationships should be based on prior analysis of particular and generalized occurrences in the ethnographic record (Lounsbury 1955:163–164, 1956; cf. Morris 1946). Criteria for evaluating the adequacy of ethnographic statements with reference to the cultural phenomena described, include: (1) productivity (in terms of appropriate anticipation if not actual prediction); (2) replicability or testability; and (3) economy. In actual field situations, recording activities, analytic operations, and evaluative procedures (in short, the application of ethnographic technique, method, and theory) can, and I think should, be combined. The improvement and constant adjustment of field recording is, in fact, dependent upon simultaneous analysis and evaluation.

Notice that strict conception of ethnography constrains the conception of communication that is admissible. Just as what counts as phonemic feature or religious act cannot be identified in advance, so with what counts as a communicative event. There are, of course, general criteria for phonemic and for communicative status; it is a question of the phenomena by which they are satisfied in a given case. If one examines the writings of anthropologists and linguists, one finds that general conceptions of communicative status vary, sometimes in ways at variance with the conception of ethnography adopted here.

The concept of message would seem to suffice as starting point for any conception, if one grants two kinds of things. The first is that the concept of message implies the sharing (real or imputed) of (1) a code or codes in terms of which the message is intelligible to (2) participants, minimally an addressor and addressee (who may be the same person), in (3) an event constituted by its transmission and characterized by (4) a channel or channels, (5) a setting or context, (6) a definite form or shape to the message, and (7) a topic and comment, i.e., that it says something about something—in other words, that the concept of message implies the array of components previously given. The second is that what can count as instances of messages, and as instances of the components of the event constituted by the transmission of a message, must be determined in the given case along the lines of the ethnographic approach just discussed and just characterized by Conklin.

If one accepts the latter point, then some anthropological conceptions of communication must be judged to exclude too much, or to include too much, or, occasionally, both. To take first the problem of excluding too much, one cannot a priori define the sound of approaching footsteps (Sapir 1921:3) or the setting of the sun (Hockett 1958:574) as not communicative. Their status is entirely a question of their construal by a receiver. In general, no phenomenon can be defined in advance as never to be counted as constituting a message. Consider a case related by Hallowell (1964:64):

> An informant told me that many years before he was sitting in a tent one afternoon during a storm, together with an old man and his wife. There was one clap of thunder after another. Suddenly the old man turned to his wife and asked, "Did you hear what was said?" "No," she replied, "I didn't catch it." My informant, an acculturated Indian, told me he did not at first know what the old man and his wife referred to. It was, of course, the thunder. The old man thought that one of the Thunder Birds had said something to him. He was reacting to this sound in the same way as he would respond to a human being, whose words he did not understand. The casualness of the remark and even the trivial character of the anecdote demonstrate the psychological depth of the "social relations" with other-than-human beings that becomes explicit in the behavior of the Ojibwa as a consequence of the cognitive "set" induced by their culture.

There are manifold instances from cultures around the world, e.g., to take a recent report, the drinking, questioning and answering in which Amahuaca men are joined by the class of supernaturals known as yoshi associated interestingly enough with a specific form of chant and use of the vocal channel (vocal chords tightly constricted) (Carneiro 1964:8). Hallowell's account of the Objibwa concept of person shows with particular depth the implications of cultural values and world view for occurrences of communicative behavior. As indication of the contribution a conscious ethnography of communication, focused on occurrences of activity such as speech, might make to such anthropological concerns as would view, let me cite one other Ojibwa instance and Hallowell's interpolated regret: Having discussed the fact that stones are classified grammatically as animate in gender, and are conceived as potentially capable of animate behavior, especially in ceremonially-linked circumstances, Hallowell records (1964:56):

> A white trader, digging in his potato patch, unearthed a large stone similar to the one just referred to. He sent for John Duck, an Indian who was the leader of the wábano, a contemporary ceremony that is held in a structure something like that used for the Midewiwin (a major ceremony during which stones occasionally had animate properties such as movement and opening of a mouth). The trader called his attention to the stone, saying that it must belong to his pavilion. John Duck did not seem pleased at this. He bent down and spoke to the boulder in a low voice, inquiring whether it had ever been in his pavilion. According to John the stone replied in the negative.
>   It is obvious that John Duck spontaneously structured the situation in terms that are intelligible within the context of Ojibwa language and culture. . . . I regret that my field notes contain no information about the use of

direct verbal address in the other cases mentioned (movement of stone, opening of a mouth). But it may well have taken place. In the anecdote describing John Duck's behavior, however, his use of speech as a mode of communication raises the animate status of the boulder to the level of social interaction common to human beings. Simply as a matter of observation we can say that the stone was treated *as if* it were a "person," not a "thing," without inferring that objects of this class are, for the Ojibwa, necessarily conceptualized as persons.

The question of the boundaries of the speech community, and indeed, of how many speech communities within a community there are, becomes problematic from a strict ethnographic viewpoint. Ordinarily the question of the speech community of the Wishram Chinook would be discussed as a question as to whether or not the objective linguistic differences (few) between the Wishram village and that of the Wasco across the river, and perhaps those of others down the river, sufficed to constitute separate dialects, or only one. On the basis of Wishram culture, however, an ethnographic approach must recognize three speech communities within the Wishram village itself. One such community consisted of normal adults and children past babyhood; a second comprised babies, dogs, coyotes, and guardian spirits Dog and Coyote, and, possibly, old people possessing those guardian spirits; a third comprised those whose guardian spirit experience had granted them the power of being able to interpret the language of the spirits.[4]

If the strict ethnographic approach requires us to extend the concept of communication to the boundaries granted it by participants of a culture, it also makes it necessary to restrict it to those boundaries. To define communication as the triggering of a response (as Hockett [1958:573] has done, and Kluckhohn [1961:895] has accepted), is to make the term so nearly equivalent to behavior and interaction in general as to lose its specific value as a scientific and moral conception. There are many illustrations possible of actions that trigger response and are not taken as communicative by one or both participants. As an act clearly based on the triggering of response (in another or oneself), sexual intercourse would be an ideal event to test this point; what part, less than all, of triggering of response is sent or received as communication? Again, it is desirable to treat the transmission or receipt of information as not the same as, but a more general category than, communication, the latter being treated as a more specific sphere, necessarily either participated in or constituted by persons (cf. Cherry 1961:247, note). The sound of footsteps or the setting of the sun may be taken as a source of information without being taken as a message (although in either case a receiver may interpret the event as a message).

From this standpoint, genes may transmit information, but the process is communicative only from the standpoint of, and as reported by, an observer and interpreter. For the human observer to report and treat the process experienced or inferred as a communicative one is of course a right not to be challenged, for, formally, it is the same right that the ethnographer accepts when acted upon by an Ojibwa, Wishram, or other participant in a culture. The formal feature is that the evidence for the communicative event is a report by one who did not participate in it as either addressor or addressee. Such reported events (E^n, or narrated events, in Roman Jakobson's symbolization [1957] for the constituents of speech events) are common in myth, for example, and are of course of considerable importance, as when the origin of the world is so described by the ancient Hebrews, or the origin of death explained by the Wishram in a narrative culminating (as is typical for their myths) in an announcement ordaining how that aspect of cultural life is to be and what people will say in its regard.

We deal here, in short, with the fact that the communicative event is the metaphor, or perspective, basic to rendering experience intelligible. It is likely to be employed at any turn, if with varying modes of imputation of reality (believed, supposed, entertained in jest, etc.). It is this fact that underlies the apparently central role of language in cultural life. Of codes available to human beings, language, as the one more than any other capable at once of being explicitly detailed and transcendent of single contexts, is the chief beneficiary under many circumstances of the primary centrality of communication. Under some circumstances, of course, it is not.

In general, any and all of the components of a communicative event, and the occurrence of a message itself, can be imputed by one who adopts the standpoint of an addressor, addressee, or receiver as observer. One consequence is the point already made, that the ethnographic observer must do more than observe to prevent his own habits of imputation from interfering with recognition of where and what participants in another culture impute. Another consequence, since persons can impute either an addressor and intent or an addressee and attention, is to make heuristically useful for ethnographic purposes a characterization of a communicative event as one in which to the observer one at least of the participants is real.

The identification of communicative events and their components has been dwelt on . . . and is indeed seldom treated, except incidentally, in most writing relevant to ethnography. The discussion so far has been concerned with gross identification of events as such and of components individually. In point of fact, adequate determination usually will involve more than inventory of channels, setting, etc. The structures of relations among different events, and their components; the capabilities and states of the components; the activity of the system which is the event; all will be involved. Explication of genres of verbal art, once such have been identified (e.g., Ssukung Tu 1963),[5] commonly involves appeal at least to relations among components, and often to their states and activity. Such questions comprise the other aspects of the frame of reference being sketched, and to these we now turn.

RELATIONS AMONG COMPONENTS

In one sense, the focus of the present approach is on communities organized as systems of communicative events. Such an object of study can be regarded as part of, but not identical with, an ethnography as a whole.[6] One way in which to indicate that there is a system, either in the community or in the particular event, is to observe that there is not complete freedom of co-occurrence among components. Not all imaginably possible combinations of participants, channels, codes, topics, etc., can occur.

It is to the structure of relations among components that much of the surge of work in sociolinguistics is directed. The papers by Ervin-Tripp and Gumperz [in *American Anthropologist* 1964] are exemplary in this respect, and suggest the richness of the subject. Bernstein can be said to explore in depth the consequences of certain structures of relations, while labor explores correlations, and patterns of change in the correlations, between speakers, hearers, settings, and features of the code, correlations and changes that can be of considerable consequence. All the papers [in the original collection] exemplify such relations to some extent, including that by Ferguson, which is concerned primarily with a marginal part of the code component. (Notice that focus on relations among components more readily invites description and comparative analysis of the variety of such marginal systems than does focus on the code alone. Also, more generally, it leads into description and comparison of whatever may characterize such an event or relationship, e.g., talk to babies, whether or not special features characterize it from the standpoint of the code as such. It is equally important to know the characteristics to talk to babies in societies where "baby talk" is eschewed. With regard to message-form, there is much to be discovered and described in the sequential patterning of speech as routines, specialized to certain relationships.)

Ervin-Tripp suggests that the structures of relations with respect to language will prove to be specific in some ways, to be more than illustration of more general sociological or psychological or cultural notions. The same is likely to prove true for each of the kinds of codes employed in a community. The heuristic assumption is that their separate maintenance implies some specific role for each which is not wholly duplicated by any other (including language). On the other hand, studies focused on the relations among components of communicative events are likely to discern patterns general to them, but partly independent of, and cutting across, the other departments of study into which the events might be cast ethnographically. Once looked for, areal styles, in the use of specific codes, and areal communicative styles generally, are likely to be found. Lomax (1959) has suggested such for musical performance, and Melville Jacobs has suggested such may be the case for the dramatic performances that enact myths.

It is especially important to notice that delineations of communities in these respects are crucial to understanding of the place of language in culture, and to understanding of the particular place of language in culture signalled by what is commonly called the Sapir-Whorf hypothesis. To assume that differences in language shape or interact with differences in world view is to assume that the functional role of language in relation to world view is everywhere the same. Indeed, anthropological thought quite generally has tended to assume identity or equivalence of function for language throughout the world (see discussion in Hymes 1961; 1962; ms. a).

When a particular code is considered but one component of communicative events, the studies of the structure of communicative events in a society will provide detailed evidence on the differential ways in which the code enters into communicative purposes and cultural life. The different ways and stages in which a language enters into enculturation, transmission of adult roles and skills, interaction with the supernatural, personal satisfactions, and the like will appear. Languages, like other cultural traits, will be found to vary in the degree and nature of their integration into the societies and cultures in which they occur. It will be possible to focus on the consequences of such differences for acculturation and adaptation of both languages and peoples. Such information has been brought to attention in studies of acculturation, bilingualism, and standard languages. What is necessary is to realize that the functional relativity of languages is general, applying to monolingual situations too.

With particular regard to the Sapir-Whorf hypothesis, it is essential to notice that Whorf's sort of linguistic relativity is secondary, and dependent upon a primary sociolinguistic relativity, that of differential engagement of languages in social life. For example, description of a language may show that it expresses a certain cognitive style, perhaps implicit metaphysical assumptions, but what chance the language has to make an impress upon individuals and behavior will depend upon the degree and pattern of its admission into communicative events. The case is clear in bilingualism; we do not expect a Bengali using English as a fourth language for certain purposes of commerce to be influenced deeply in world view by its syntax. What is necessary is to realize that the monolingual situation is problematic as well. Peoples do not all everywhere use language to the same degree, in the same situations, or for the same things; some peoples focus upon language more than others. Such differences in the place of a language in the communicative system of a people cannot be assumed to be without influence on the depth of a language's influence on such things as world view.

More particularly, if a language is taken as a device for categorizing experience, it is not such a device in the abstract. There remains the question of what may be the set of events in which categorizing dependent upon the language occurs. (The set includes events in which a single person is using a language excogitatively.) Although anthropologists have sometimes talked of the use of language "merely" as a tool of communication, and of the categorizing of experience as if it were a superior category, the role of a language as a device for categorizing experience and its role as an instrument of communication cannot be so separated, and indeed, the latter includes the former. This is the more true when a language, as is often the case, affords alternative ways of categorizing the same experience, so that the patterns of selection among such alternatives must be determined in actual contexts of use—as must also, indeed, the degree to which a language is being used as a full-fledged semantic instrument (as distinct from its use as an expressive, directive, etc., instrument) at all in a given case.

Such considerations broach the third aspect of our frame of reference.

CAPACITY AND STATE OF COMPONENTS

So far we have considered the identification of events and components, and the structures of relations among them. Now we must consider their capacities, or capabilities, and states. It is here that "communication theory," in the sense in which the term is equivalent to "information theory," enters, with its concern for the measurement of capacity. Although associated primarily with the capacity of channels and codes, the underlying notion extends equally to all components of a communicative event, and to the events of a system.

Questions of capability can be broached in terms of focus upon some one of the components of an event (or the event itself) in relation to all other components in turn. Some topics of long-standing anthropological interest find a place here. The relation of language to environment, both natural and social, in the sense of elaboration of a code's capacity, especially via vocabulary, to deal with snow, cattle, status, etc., as topics, is one. Another is the relationship between the capability of a code, and the capabilities of its users, in the sense of the Whorfian concern with habitual behavior and fashions of speaking. In both cases there must be reference from the start to the distribution in use of the portion of the code in question, both among communicative events and in relation to their other components. (The necessity of this has been argued for the Whorfian problem above; on cultural focus, elaboration of vocabulary, and folk-taxonomy of semantic domains, cf. the views on dependence on context of situation of Brown [1958:255–258], Frake [1961:121–122], Gluckman [1959], Meillet [1906], and Service [1960].)

With regard to participants, differential competence and performance are salient concerns of Bernstein's analysis of elaborated and restricted codes. Gumperz' concept of verbal repertoire also singles out a participant's capabilities in relation to the code component. Albert and Frake touch upon the subject with regard to special forms of usage. Code-switching, ability to translate, range of dialects or levels or socially advantageous routines at command, are familiar examples. John Roberts (ms.) has undertaken ingenious studies of capacity with respect to communicative tasks. Often this level and the preceding one are but faces of the same coin, the formal structure of relations being grounded culturally in judgments (and facts) as to capability, and circumstances as to capability being dependent upon the structures of relations.

The ethnography of communication deals in an empirical and comparative way with many notions that underlie linguistic theory proper. This is particularly so when linguistic theory depends upon notions such as those of "speech community," "speech act," and "fluent speaker." How varied the capabilities of speakers can be in even a small and presumably homogeneous tribe is sketched incisively by Bloomfield (1927) in a paper that deserves to be classic for its showing that such variation, including possibilities of grammatical mistake, is universal. The range and kind of abilities speakers and hearers show is an area largely unexplored by ethnographers and linguists, but one of great import both to cultural and linguistic theory. (I have tried to draw some implications of a focus on the concept of speakers' abilities in another paper [Hymes 1964b].)[7]

Capacity varies with event, and with the states in which participants, channels, etc., may be in the event, including the values and beliefs of participants, as properties of their states that help constitute events as communicative, and that determine other properties. Here Albert's paper illustrates possibilities of approach. In part the question is one not of what a language does for and to participants, their personalities, culture, and the like, but of what participants, their personalities, and the like, do for and to a language.

Only by reference to the state of participants, moreover, does it seem possible to introduce in a natural way the various types of functions which communicative events may serve for them.

There has been a bias in American linguistics, and in American extensions of linguistic methodology, favoring a "surface-level" approach that stresses identification and segmentation of overt material, and hesitates to venture far into inner structural relations and ascription of purpose. (The bias perhaps reflects the favoring of visual over acoustic space, the trust of the eye, not the ear, that Carpenter and McLuhan [1960:65–70] find characteristic of our society.) In Kenneth Burke's terms, there has been a tendency to treat language and its use as matters of "motion" (as if of the purely physical world), rather than as matters of "action" (as matters of the human, dramatistic world of symbolic agency and purpose). With all the difficulties that notions of purpose and function entail, there seems no way for the structural study of language and communication to engage its subject in social life in any adequate, useful way, except by taking this particular bull by the horns (cf. the introductory discussion in Hall's paper). The purposes, conscious and unconscious, the functions, intended and unintended, perceived and unperceived, of communicative events for their participants are here treated as questions of the states in which they engage in them, and of the norms by which they judge them. (Those aspects of purpose and function that have to do with feedback, exchange, response to violations of norms, and the like, are considered with the fourth aspect of the present frame of reference, that of the activity of the system.)

For ethnographic purposes, an initial "etic grid" for delineating and "notating" possible types of functions is needed, and it does seem possible to provide one, by considering the possibilities of focus upon each component in turn in relation to each of the others. The grid so derived has proven adequate to accommodate the various schemes of functions, and of functional types of messages, which have come to my attention. Ethnographic work will of course test and probably enlarge and revise it, just as experience of additional languages has enlarged and revised phonetic charts. Literary, philosophical, and other schemes of functions, and of functional types of messages, are also useful as sources of insight and details. (It may prove desirable to undertake a comparative and historical analysis of such schemes, as "home-made models" from our own culture. Among reviews, note Schaff 1962, Part 2, and Stern 1931, Ch. II.)

It must be kept in mind that functions may prove specific to individuals and cultures, and that they require specific identification and labeling in any case, even when subsumable under broad types. The "etic grid" serves only to help perceive kinds of functions that may be present, and possibly to facilitate comparison.

Focus on the addressor or sender in relation to other components entails such types of function as identification of the source, expression of attitude toward one or another component or toward the event as a whole, excogitation (thinking aloud), etc. Such functions may be of course intended, attributed, conscious, unconscious. *Focus on the addressee* or other receiver entails such types of function as identification of the destination, and the ways in which the message and event may be governed by anticipation of the attitude of the destination. Persuasion, appeal, rhetoric, and direction enter here, including as well the sense in which the characteristics of the addressee govern the other aspects of the event as a matter of protocol. Effects on receivers may be of course intended, attributed, conscious, unconscious, achieved, frustrated. *Focus on channels* in relation to other components entails such functions as have to do with maintenance of contact and control of noise, both physical and psychological in both cases. *Focus on codes* in relation to other components entails such functions as are involved in learning, analysis, devising of writing systems, checking on the identity of an element of the code use in conversation, and the like. *Focus on settings* in relation to other components entails all that is considered contextual, apart from the event itself, in that any and all components may be taken as defining the setting of the event, not just its location in time and space. Such context has two aspects, verbal and nonverbal from the standpoint of speech, kinesic and nonkinesic from the standpoint of body motion, and, generally, for any one code or modality, context constituted for a message by other messages within the same code or modality, as distinct from context constituted by all other facets of the event. *Focus on message-form* in relation to other components entails such functions as proofreading, mimicry, aspects of emendation and editing, and poetic and stylistic concerns. *Focus on topic* in relation to other components entails functions having to do with reference (in the sense both of linguistic meaning proper and denotation) and content. *Focus on the event* itself entails whatever is comprised under metacommunicative types of function. If the message is taken as subsuming all, or all the immediately relevant, other components, then focus on the message as surrogate of the whole event may be taken as entailing metacommunicative functions ("the message 'this is play'"; Russell's types, etc.; see Bateson 1963 on the importance of this function).

Common broad types of functions associated with each type of focus can be variously labelled: expressive, directive, contact (phatic), metalinguistic, contextual, poetic (stylistic), referential, and metacommunicative are useful. The etic framework implied here can be handled with pencil and paper for visual purposes (and expanded also) by two devices, one of horizontal placement, one of vertical placement, of components relative to each other. In handling the five broad types of components of action used in his analysis (Scene, Act, Agent, Agency, Purpose), Burke devises various "ratios"; thus, the relation of Scene to Act is the Scene-Act ratio, and can be represented as if a numerator over a denominator: Scene/Act (Burke 1945). In explicating grammatical categories in terms of the components of speech events, Jakobson (1957) discriminates speech events (E^s) and narrated events (E^n), and participants in each (P^s, P^n), expressing relations with a diagonal; thus, the relation of the narrated event to the speech event (involved in verbal categories) is expressed E^n/E^s. Either device could be used to express all the possible combinations and permutations of focus upon the relation of one component of a communicative event to each of the others. Either device is useful in explicating other logical and empirical schemes of functions and functional types of messages in terms of a common denominator, a problem which is a converse in effect of the usual problem of componential analysis. (There one proceeds from etic grid to discover an emic system, here one is concerned to proceed from a possibly emic system to discover an etic grid.)

Most of the functions and components noted above have been discussed with examples of Jakobson (1960) and Hymes (1962).

ACTIVITY OF THE SYSTEM

In formation theory is one topic notably associated with communication; cybernetics is the other. Having taken information theory in its quantitative sense as pertaining to the third aspect of the present frame of reference, we take cybernetics as pertaining to the fourth. Studies concerned with the information theory aspect of ethnographic systems of communication are almost nonexistent, and the case is the same for studies concerned with the cybernetic aspect. One can think in both respects of work by John Roberts that should become far better known than it is (note his forthcoming book, *Four Southwestern Men*), and of a few celebrated and isolated examples in the work of Levi-Strauss (1953) and Bateson (1949; 1958) where cybernetic notions are applied.[8]

Apart from its discussion by Hall, cybernetics does not enter overtly into the papers presented [in the original collection], which are largely concerned with the need to develop more limited empirical and analytical contributions. Nevertheless, the activity of systems of communication and of communicative events is involved in much of the work they represent. Most salient, perhaps, is the concern with the conduct of selves and of gatherings in the work from which Goffman's paper stems. Notice also Bernstein's attention to the workings of different types of codes, and Gumperz' delineation of personal and transactional modes of switching, with regard to the linguistic dimension of interaction, as well as the dynamic aspect of the shifts of language with topic that Ervin-Tripp treats. Frake sketches dynamics of Subanun drinking activity, and Albert gives notable Burundi examples of speech behavior as a system of action. Labov touches upon the specific courses of linguistic evolution, which of course involve the activity of systems of communication; and Malkiel models a case of such involvement as an illustration of glottodynamics.

The activity of the system is the most general aspect of the four, and ultimately the one in terms of which it is necessary to view the rest. For particular purposes, of course, any one aspect, or part of one, can be segregated for analysis, and there is much to be done in the ethnographic and comparative study of every aspect and component. To take the channel component as an illustration, there are few if any ethnographic studies to compare with Herzog's multi-faceted account of the system of channels elaborated among the Jabo of Liberia, considering, as it does, the structure of the code in each, the relation of code and messages in each to base messages in speech, native categories and conceptions, social correlates, and circumstances of use (Herzog 1945). There is a fair variety of reports of specialized uses of the vocal channel, but the account of Mazateco whistle talk by Cowan (1948) again is almost unique in providing a technical linguistic base and ethnographic context that could support controlled comparison. We have noted that paralinguistic and kinesic investigations have but begun to be extended cross-culturally, and attention to the sociopsychological context of attitude toward use of a channel, or modality, such as voice and gesture, such as Devereux (1949, 1951) has shown in work with the Mohave, is far to seek. The two recent general comparative studies (May 1956, Stern 1957) look toward historical interpretation in terms of distribution and origins, but not toward controlled comparison of structures and functions, perhaps because the available data offer little encouragement. Stern's classification of speech surrogates, derived from notions of communication theory, needs clarification and extension to include writing systems, which are logically comprised by the categories. As for the structural and functional aspects of writing and literacy, empirical studies of the diversity of the patterns that occur are few, and as for contrastive studies of their absence, that of Bloomfield (1927) is the only one known to me. Interpretations of the determinism of particular channels, such as those of McLuhan (1962) and of Goody and Watt (1963), and interpretations of the determinism of media (channels) generally, such as are expressed in the orientation of Carpenter and McLuhan (1960) and McLuhan (1964), interesting as they are, seem oversimplified, where not simply wrong, in the light of what little ethnographic base we have. There is a tendency to take the value of a channel as given across cultures, but here, as with every aspect and component of communication, the value is problematic and requires investigation. (Consider for example the specialization of writing to courtship among young people by the Hanunóo, and to a borrowed religion among the Aleut; and the complex and diverse profiles with regard to the role of writing in society, and in individual communicative events, for traditional Chinese, Korean, and Japanese cultures, with regard both to the Chinese texts shared by all and to the materials specific to each.) To provide a better ethnographic basis for the understanding of the place of alternative channels and modalities in communication is indeed one of the greatest challenges to studies of the sort we seek to encourage. At the same time, such work, whether on channels or some other aspect and component, profits from taking into account the complete context of the activity of the system of communication of the community as a whole.

It is with this aspect that the ethnographic study of communication makes closest contact with the social, political, and moral concerns with communication, conceived as value and a determinant in society and in personal lives.

The frame of reference just sketched can be summed up as asking a series of questions: What are the communicative events, and their components, in a community? What are the relationships among them? What capabilities and states do they have, in general, and in particular cases? How do they work? . . .

Among general methodological trends, one each in ethnography and linguistics should be singled out. In addition to the ethnographic work already mentioned, that of Metzger and Williams is a prime example of work, not concerned primarily with communication, that makes a contribution to its understanding through precision of focus and detail. From one of their accounts (1963:218–219, 227–228), for example, one could determine the place of speech in the hierarchy of ritual means of the community in question for controlled comparison with other cases. Their ethnographic method results in detail specified at the levels of the components of communicative events and of the interrelations. In complementary fashion, linguistitc work concerned with the abilities and judgments of appropriateness on the part of native speakers that generative grammar brings into focus can contribute to the third and fourth aspects of the communicative ethnography. Such notions, pursued fully, lead into full scale studies focused on the full range of factors conditioning the exercise of judgment and ability.

There is perhaps a convergence between the professional field of speech and linguistics in the increased interest of the former in behavioral approaches, and of the latter in poetics and logic. It ought to be the part of anthropology to contribute to a truly comparative poetics, logic, and rhetoric, and what perhaps distinguishes the ethnography of communication as a perspective from sociolinguistics and psycholinguistics, as commonly conceived, is its inclusion of such humanistic subjects. If it can encourage the trend in folklore to the joint study of the structures of codes, messages, and performances, there will be mutual benefit.

There are a number of other particular lines of study where mutual benefit can result. The study of folk taxonomies, and of ethnographic semantics generally, needs specification of communicative contexts if it is to achieve the implicit goal of discovering the structure of vocabularies as wholes. (See argument in Hymes 1964a.) The methods of ethnographic semantics, in turn, are needed in discovering the components of communicative events. A like relationship holds with the work of observation and participation characteristic of paralinguistics, kinesics, and other aspects of the discovery of codes additional to language in the presentation of self in everyday life. (Note most recently Hockett 1960; Pittenger, Hockett, Danehy 1960; and Sebeok 1964.) Ethnographic and comparative studies in the context of communication are needed to extend the etic frameworks, and to ascertain emic relevance amidst the wealth of data even a few minutes can supply. In turn, these investigations are needed to delimit the place and interrelations of individual modalities, such as spoken language, in the communicative hierarchy of a community, and as a basis for understanding the evolution of communication (Birdwhistell 1960).

The potential richness of studies of socialization, enculturation, child development, etc., is manifest. There is here a situation analogous to that with regard to the description of adult verbal behavior. Studies focused on the linguistic code as such need extension to concern with the whole of the child's induction in the communicative economy of its community. (Some notes and queries as to the child's induction are indicated in Hymes 1962; 1964c.) Such studies are beginning to appear (e.g., John 1963; 1964). The importance of concern with the child is partly that it is a favorable vantage point for discovering the adult system, and that it poses neatly one way in which the ethnography of communication is a distinctive enterprise—i.e., an enterprise concerned with what abilities the child must acquire beyond those of producing and interpreting all grammatical sentences in order to be a competent member of its community, knowing not only what may be said, but also what should and should not be said, and when and where.

There is a growing extension of interest among philosophical analysts from meanings of words and sentences to speech acts and empirical modes of language use. Studies of the ethnography of communication offer empirical testing grounds for the adequacy of logical analyses of rational communication (Harrah 1963), types of acts such as promises (Searle 1962), and of modes of use such as metaphor. In turn, ethnography cannot but benefit from additional precision of concepts for etic and typological purposes.

Work in fundamental education and literacy raises problems of particular interest, and can be both a source of empirical data and insight, and a practical area to which ethnographic studies of communication can contribute. Just as there may be interference in the speech of bilinguals, or in the perception of those mastering another code, due to carryover of linguistic patterns already acquired, so there may be interference in the communicative conduct of bilinguals and newcomers to a community, due to carryover of sociolinguistic or communicative patterns already acquired. (Hall [1959] provides a good account of some factors, and his paper in this volume [i.e., the original volume] is similarly concerned; on a cognitive aspect, see the forthcoming study by Roberts [ms.].) The various purposes of educators, workers in literacy, translators, missionaries, and applied anthropologists may be facilitated on occasion by prior ethnographic study of the local communicative economy, as may the purposes of teachers in our own society (here should be cited current work in Great Britain of Michael Halliday, Angus McIntosh, J. Catford, and others).

To the study of mental health in its communicative aspect, an ethnographic approach may contribute the expected anthropological perspective on comparative range, and on what is social in the given case, against which personal departure can be assessed (cf. Sapir 1927; Ruesch 1961).

The problems of the study of primate communication are in principle the same as those of the ethnographic study of communication in human communities. The importance of studies of primate and animal communication to help determine, by comparison and contrast, the distinctive properties of human language, and to help picture its evolutionary emergence, has gained new recognition in recent years (e.g., Sebeok 1962 and the various presentations by Hockett, cited and summarized in Hockett and Ascher 1964). Ethnographies of communication here play a complementary role, which has yet to gain recognition, since it tends to be assumed that the functions and uses of human language are constant and already adequately known. Empirical questions as to such things as the minimum role that a language can play in the communicative system of a small hunting and gathering society, and of the adequacy of minimal codes in close-knit communities, are not taken into account. Extrapolations as to the relations between code and communicative context at stages of human evolution, however, of the sort attempted by Hockett and Ascher (1964), need a basis in comparative ethnography (cf. Bartholomew and Birdsell

1953) as well as in the comparison of codes. (See discussion in Hymes 1964a: 105–106.) Not codes alone, but whole systems of communication, involving alternative modalities and specific needs, must be considered and compared. The reciprocal gain to ethnography from studies of ethnology and animal communication is indicated here by Hall's paper.

To the evolutionary approach to culture, ethnographic studies of communication can contribute a framework within which languages can be treated adaptively in ways which articulate with the study of cultural evolution as a whole, and with microevolutionary studies of individual cases (cf. Hymes 1961, 1964a).

Most of what can now be sketched is but an outline of a future in which, one can hope, ethnographic studies of communication will be commonplace, and an ethnographic perspective on the engagement of language in human life will be the standard from which more specialized studies depart.

NOTES

[1] To Susan Ervin-Tripp, John Gumperz, Michael Halliday, Sydney Lamb, Sheldon Sacks, and Dan Slobin, I am indebted for warm discussions of language and its social study; to Bob Scholte and Erving Goffman, for pointed argument as to the notion of communication; to Harold Conklin, Charles Frake, Ward Goodenough, Floyd Lounsbury, and William C. Sturtevant, for discussion through several years of the nature of ethnography. To all much thanks and no blame.

[2] I have elaborated some of the notions in this section and the next in other papers (Hymes 1961, 1962, 1964a, 1964b). Where this paper differs from the others in conception, it takes precedence. [Editor's note: Part of the initial section is omitted.]

[3] Spier and Sapir (1930:217, n. 97). The point and the language indicate that the comment is due particularly to Sapir. The Wishram avoidance is due to the severe punishment, even death, visited for constructive adultery, which offense may be attributed in some circumstances even for private conversation or physical contact.

[4] With regard to the first and second communities, babyhood lasted "until they could talk clearly" (Spier and Sapir 1930:218)—in Wishram, of course. With regard to the second, "Such guardian spirits could understand the language of babies. They maintain that a dog, a coyote, and an infant can understand each other, but the baby loses his language when he grows old enough to speak and understand the tongue of his parents" (ibid.: 255). With regard to the third, the group may have been individuated into various dyadic relationships between particular persons and spirits, for the example is given as "For instance, one who had gained the protection of Coyote could tell, on hearing a coyote's howl, what person was going to die" (ibid.: 239). The matter would depend on information, probably now unobtainable, as to whether the language of the spirits was common to all of them.

[5] The classical writer Ssukung Tu discriminated 24 modes, translated as Grand Mode, Unemphatic, Ornate, Grave, Lofty, Polished, Refined, Vigorous, Exquisite, Spontaneous, Pregnant, Untrammeled, Evocative, Well-knit, Artless, Distinctive, Devious, Natural, Poignant, Vivid, Transcendent, Ethereal, Light-hearted, Flowing (Ssukung Tu, as translated [1963] with accompanying discussion by Wu Tiao-kung, "Ssukung Tu's poetic criticism," 78–83).

[6] Notice Conklin (1962:199): "An adequate ethnographic description of the culture (Goodenough 1957a) of a particular society presupposes a detailed analysis of the communications system and of the culturally defined situations in which all relevant distinctions in that system occur."

[7] The term "capability" is used with conscious reference to Tylor's definition of culture (or civilization) as all those capabilities acquired by man in society (1873:1). I

subscribe to the view that what is distinctively cultural as an aspect of behavior or things is a question of capabilities acquired, or elicited, in social life, not a question of the extent to which the behavior or things themselves are socially shared. The point is like that made by Sapir (1916:425) with regard to similarity due to diffusion, namely, that its difference from similarity due to independent retention of a common heritage is one of degree rather than of kind, since the currency of a culture element in a single community is already an instance of diffusion that has radiated out, at last analysis, from a single individual. Sapir's point converges with the focus of generative grammatical theory on the individual's ability to produce and interpret novel, yet acceptable, sentences. The frequency and spread of a trait is important, but secondary, so far as the criteria for its being a product of cultural behavior, as having a cultural aspect, are concerned. A sonnet, for example, is such a product, whether or not it survives the moment of completion. In the course of the conduct of much cultural behavior, including verbal behavior, it will not be known, or will be problematic to the participants, whether or not some of what occurs and is accepted as cultural, has in fact ever previously occurred. For many typical anthropological problems, it is essential to single out for study cultural behavior that is shared to the limits of a community, or as nearly so as possible. For other problems, a group, family, person, or the ad hoc productivity of adaptation to an event, will be the desired focus. To restrict the concept of the cultural to something shared to the limits of a community is an arbitrary limitation on understanding, both of human beings and of the cultural. The viewpoint sketched here has the same fulcrum as that of Sapir's "Why Cultural Anthropology Needs the Psychiatrist" (1938), but Sapir's insights need not imply his virtual reduction of cultural behavior to psychiatric subject matter.

[8] Goodenough (1957b) introduces communication theory in the Shannon sense into his critical review of an anthropological book on communication (Keesing and Keesing 1956) that does not itself make use of such theory.

REFERENCES CITED

BARTHOLOMEW, GEORGE A., JR. and
JOSEPH B. BIRDSELL
    1953 Ecology and the protohominids. American Anthropologist 55:481–498.
BATESON, GREGORY
    1949 Bali: the value system of a steady state. In Social structure: Studies presented
           to A. R. Radcliffe-Brown, Meyer Fortes, ed. New York.
    1958 Naven. 2nd ed. Stanford.
    1960 Minimal requirements for a theory of schizophrenia. A.M.A. Archives of General Psychiatry 2:477–491.
    1963 Exchange of information about patterns of human behavior. In Information
           storage and neural control, William Fields and Walter Abbott, eds. Springfield, pp. 1–12.
BIRDWHISTELL, RAY L.
    1960 A look at evolutionary theory in the light of developments in communication
           theory. In Report of the ninth annual round table meeting on linguistics and language study; anthropology and African studies, William M. Austin, ed. Washington, D.C., 175–193.
BLOOMFIELD, LEONARD
    1927 Literate and illiterate speech. American Speech 2:432–439.
BOAS, FRANZ
    1911 Introduction. In Handbook of American Indian languages, Franz Boas, ed. Washington, D.C., 1–83.
BROWN, ROGER
    1958 Words and things. Glencoe.
BURKE, KENNETH
    1945 A grammar of motives. Englewood Cliffs, N.J.

CARNEIRO, ROBERT L.
    1964   The Amahuaca and the spirit world. Ethnology 3:6–12.
CARPENTER, EDMUND and
MARSHALL McLUHAN, eds.
    1960   Explorations in communication. An anthology. Boston.
CHERRY, E. COLIN
    1961   On human communication. A review, a survey, and a criticism. New York,
            Science Editions. First published, Cambridge, Mass., and New York, 1957.
CONKLIN, HAROLD C.
    1955   Hanunóo color categories. Southwestern Journal of Anthropology 11:339–344.
            Reprinted in Hymes 1964d.
    1962   Lexicographical treatment of folk taxonomies. In Problems of lexicography,
            Fred W. Householder and Sol Saporta, eds. Supplement to International Jour-
            nal of American Linguistics 28 (2), Part II; Publication 21 of the Indiana
            University Research Center in Anthropology, Folklore, and Linguistics, 119–
            141.
    1964   Ethnogeneaological method. In Explorations in cultural anthropology, Ward
            H. Goodenough, ed. New York, pp. 25–55.
COWAN, GEORGE
    1948   Mazateco whistle speech. Language 24:280–286. Reprinted in Hymes (1964d).
DEVEREUX, GEORGE
    1949   Mohave voice and speech mannerisms. Word 5:268–272. Reprinted in Hymes
            1964d.
    1951   Mohave Indian verbal and motor profanity. In Psychoanalysis and the social
            sciences, vol. 3, Geza Róheim, ed. New York, pp. 99–127.
FRAKE, CHARLES O.
    1961   The diagnosis of disease among the Subanun of Mindanao. American Anthro-
            pologist 63:113–132. Reprinted in Hymes 1964d.
    1962a   Cultural ecology and ethnography. American Anthropologist 64:53–59.
    1962b   The ethnographic study of cognitive systems. In Anthropology and human
            behavior, Thomas Gladwin and William C. Sturtevant, eds. Washington, D.C.,
            pp. 72–85.
    1964   A structural description of Subanun "religious behavior." In Explorations in
            cultural anthropology, Ward H. Goodenough, ed. New York.
GLUCKMAN, MAX
    1959   The technical vocabulary of Barotse jurisprudence. American Anthropologist
            61:743–759.
GOODENOUGH, WARD H.
    1956   Residence rules. Southwestern Journal of Anthropology 12:22–37.
    1957a   Cultural anthropology and linguistics. In Report of the seventh annual round
            table meeting on linguistics and language study, Paul L. Garvin, ed. Washing-
            ton, D.C., pp. 167–173. Reprinted in Hymes 1964d.
    1957b   Review of Keesing and Keesing 1956. Language 33:424–429.
    Ms.   Formal properties of status relationships. Paper read at the annual meeting of
            the American Anthropological Association, November 16, 1961, Philadelphia.
GOODY, JACK and
IAN WATT
    1963   The consequences of literacy. Comparative Studies in Society and History
            5:304–345.
GREENBERG, JOSEPH H.
    1948   Linguistics and ethnology. Southwestern Journal of Anthropology 4:140–148.
            Reprinted in Hymes 1964d.
HALL, EDWARD
    1959   The silent language. New York.
HALLOWELL, A. IRVING
    1964   Ojibwa ontology, behavior, and world view. In Primitive views of the world.

Stanley Diamond, ed. New York, 49–82. (Selections from Culture in history, Stanley Diamond, ed. New York, 1960.)

HARRAH, DAVID
1963 Communication: a logical model. Cambridge.

HERZOG, GEORGE
1945 Drum-signaling in a West African tribe. Word 1:217–238. Reprinted in Hymes 1964d.

HOCKETT, CHARLES F.
1948 Biophysics, linguistics, and the unity of science. American Scientist 36:558–572.
1955 A manual of phonology. Memoir 11 of the International Journal of American Linguistics; Indiana University Publications in Anthropology and Linguistics.
1958 A course in modern linguistics. New York.
1960 Ethno-linguistic implications of studies in linguistics and psychiatry. In Report of the ninth annual round table meeting on linguistics and language study; anthropology and African studies. William M. Austin, ed. Washington, D.C., pp. 175–193.

HOCKETT, CHARLES F. and
ROBERT ASCHER
1964 The human revolution. Current Anthropology 5(3):135–168.

HYMES, DELL
1961 Functions of speech: an evolutionary approach. In Anthropology and education, Fred C. Gruber, ed. Philadelphia, University of Pennsylvania Press, pp. 55–83.
1962 The ethnography of speaking. In Anthropology and human behavior, Thomas Gladwin and William C. Sturtevant, eds. Washington, D.C., Anthropological Society of Washington, pp. 15–53.
1964a A perspective for linguistic anthropology. In Horizons of anthropology, Sol Tax, ed. Chicago, pp. 92–107.
1964b Directions in (ethno-) linguistic theory. American Anthropologist 66, No. 3, Part 2:6–56.
1964c Formal comment. In The acquisition of language, Ursula Bellugi and Roger Brown, eds. Lafayette, pp. 107–112.
1964d [Editor.] Language in culture and society; a reader in linguistics and anthropology. New York.
Ms. a Two types of linguistic relativity. Paper presented to conference on sociolinguistics, UCLA, May 17, 1964.
Ms. b The anthropology of communication. In human communication theory: original essays, Frank X. Dance, ed. New York.

JAKOBSON, ROMAN
1953 Chapter two. In Results of the conference of anthropologists and linguists, by Claude Levi-Strauss, Roman Jakobson, C. F. Voegelin, and Thomas A. Sebeok. Memoir 8 of The International Journal of American Linguistics; Indiana University Publications in Anthropology and Linguistics, pp. 11–21.
1957 Shifters, verbal categories, and the Russian verb. Cambridge, Mass, Harvard University, Russian language project.
1960 Concluding statement: linguistics and poetics. In Style in language, T. A. Sebeok, ed. Cambridge, Mass., and New York, pp. 350–373.
1963 Efforts towards a means-ends model of language in inter-war continental linguistics. In Trends in modern linguistics, Christine Mohrmann, F. Norman, and Alf Sommerfelt, eds. Utrecht and Antwerp, pp. 104–108.

JOHN, VERA P.
1963 The intellectual development of slum children: some preliminary findings. American Journal of Orthopsychiatry 33:813–822.
1964 The social context of language acquisition. Merrill-Palmer Quarterly (spring).

KEESING, FELIX and
MARIE M. KEESING
1956 Elite communication in Samoa. Stanford.

KLUCKHOHN, CLYDE
  1961   Notes on some anthropological aspects of communication. American Anthropologist 63:895–910.
LAMB, SYDNEY M.
  1964   The semetic approach to structural semantics. American Anthropologist 66, No. 3, Part 2:57–78.
LEVI-STRAUSS, CLAUDE
  1945   L'analyse structurale en linguistique et anthropologie. Word 1:33–53. Reprinted in translation in Hymes 1964d.
  1953   Social structure. In Anthropology today, A. L. Kroeber and others, eds. Chicago.
  1960   L'anthropologie sociale devant l'historie. Annales 15(4):625–637.
LISKER, LEIGH, FRANKLIN S. COOPER, and
ALVIN M. LIBERMAN
  1962   The uses of experiment in language description. Word 18:82–106.
LOMAX, ALAN
  1959   Folk song style. American Anthropologist 61:927–954.
LOUNSBURY, FLOYD G.
  1955   The varieties of meaning. In Report of the sixth annual round table meeting on linguistics and language teaching, Ruth Hirsch Weinstein, ed. Washington, D.C., pp. 158–164.
  1956   A semantic analysis of the Pawnee kinship usage. Language 32:158–194.
MAY, L. CARLYLE
  1956   A survey of glossolalia and related phenomena in non-Christian religions. American Anthropologist 58:75–96.
McLUHAN, MARSHALL
  1962   The Gutenberg galaxy. The making of typographic man. Toronto.
  1964   Understanding media. The extensions of man. New York.
MEILLET, ANTOINE
  1906   Comment les mots changent de sens. L'Année Sociologique. Reprinted in Linguistique historique et linguistique générale, vol. 1, 230–271.
MERRIAM, ALAN
  1964   The arts and anthropology. In Horizons of anthropology, Sol Tax, ed. Chicago, pp. 224–236.
METZGER, DUANE and
GERALD WILLIAMS
  1963   Tenejapa medicine I: the cure. Southwestern Journal of Anthropology 19:216–234.
MORRIS, CHARLES W.
  1946   Signs, language, and behavior. Englewood Cliffs, N.J.
PIKE, KENNETH L.
  1954   Language in relation to a unified theory of the structure of human behavior, Part I. Preliminary ed. Glendale, Summer Institute of Linguistics.
PITTENGER, ROBERT, CHARLES F. HOCKETT, and
J. S. DANEHY
  1960   The first five minutes. Ithaca.
ROBERTS, JOHN M.
  Ms.   Four Southwestern men.
RUESCH, JURGEN
  1961   Therapeutic communication. New York.
RUESCH, JURGEN and
WELDON KEES
  1956   Nonverbal communication. Notes on the visual perception of human relations. Berkeley and Los Angeles.
SAPIR, EDWARD
  1916   Time perspective in aboriginal American culture: a study in method. Canada, Department of Mines, Geological Survey, Memoir 90; Anthropological Series,

No. 13. Ottawa, Government Printing Bureau. *Reprinted in* Selected writings of Edward Sapir, David G. Mandelbaum, ed. Berkeley and Los Angeles, 1949.
1921   Language. New York.
1925   Sound patterns in language. Language 1:37—51. *Reprinted in* Selected writings of Edward Sapir, David G. Mandelbaum, ed. Berkeley and Los Angeles, 1949.
1927   Speech as a personality trait. American Journal of Sociology 32:892–905. *Reprinted in* Selected writings of Edward Sapir, David G. Mandelbaum, ed. Berkeley and Los Angeles, 1949.
1929   The status of linguistics as a science. Language 5:207–214. *Reprinted in* Selected writings of Edward Sapir, David G. Mandelbaum, ed. Berkeley and Los Angeles, 1949.
1938   Why cultural anthropology needs the psychiatrist. Psychiatry 1:7–12. *Reprinted in* Selected writings of Edward Sapir, David G. Mandelbaum, ed. Berkeley and Los Angeles, 1949.
(Pages for Sapir 1916, 1925, 1929, 1938 cited in text as of Mandelbaum 1949.)
SCHAFF, ADAM
1962   Introduction to semantics. London, Warsaw.
SEARLE, JOHN
1962   Meaning and speech acts. The Philosophical Review 71:423–432.
Ms.   How to promise.
SEBEOK, THOMAS A.
1962   Coding in the evolution of signalling behavior. Behavorial Science 7:430–442.
1964   Approaches to semiotics: cultural anthropology, education, linguistics, psychiatry, psychology. 'S-Gravenhage, Mouton.
SERVICE, ELMAN R.
1960   Kinship terminology and evolution. American Anthropologist 62:747–763.
SMITH, M. G.
1957   The social functions and meaning of Hausa praise singing. Africa 27:26–44.
SPIER, LESLIE and
EDWARD SAPIR
1930   Wishram ethnography. University of Washington Publications in Anthropology 3(3):151–300. Seattle.
SSUKUNG TU
1963   The twenty-four modes of poetry. Chinese Literature 7. Peking.
STERN, GUSTAV
1931   Meaning and change of meaning. Göteborg.
STERN, THEODORE
1957   Drum and whistle languages: an analysis of speech surrogates. American Anthropologist 59:487–506.
TRAGER, GEORGE L.
1949   The field of linguistics. Studies in Linguistics, Occasional Papers, 1. Norman, Oklahoma.
TYLOR, EDWARD B.
1873   Primitive culture. 2nd ed. London, John Murray. 1st ed., 1871. *Chs. I–X re-printed as* The origins of culture, with an introduction by Paul Radin, New York, 1958.
ULDALL, HANS
1957   Outline of glossematics, Part I. (Travaux du Cercle Linguistique de Copenhague, vol. 11.) Copenhagen.
WHORF, BENJAMIN LEE
1940   Linguistics as an exact science. Technological Review 43:61–63, 80–83. *Also in* Language, thought and reality: selected writings of Benjamin Lee Whorf, John B. Carroll, ed. New York and Cambridge, 1956, pp. 220–232.
WILLIAMS, RAYMOND
1960   Culture and society 1780–1950. Garden City.

LANGUAGE, MEANING, AND SYMBOLIC PRESENCE

Garth Gillan

GARTH GILLAN was born in 1939. He was educated at St. John's University in Collegeville, Minnesota, and Duquesne University in Pittsburgh, where he received his Ph.D. in 1966. He is presently an assistant professor in the Department of Philosophy at Southern Illinois University at Carbondale. His research deals mainly in continental European philosophy, phenomenology, existentialism, and structuralism. Professor Gillan has written numerous articles on the phenomenology of language and is currently editing a series of essays on Merlean-Ponty.

Compared with the definition of the linguistic sign within the phenomenological tradition, the structuralist tradition stemming from the *Course in General Linguistics* of Ferdinand de Saussure poses new questions and strange directions for the philosophy of language in defining the linguistic sign as an internal rapport between signifying and signified. The *Logical Investigations* view the linguistic sign as inherently expressive of the meaning (*Bedeutung*) immanent within the subjective act of expression. The linguistic sign is for Husserl a conscious act which through its meaning, ideal and objective in character, is directed to objects within the world or directed toward ideal objects within the universe of thought. The *Course in General Linguistics* opposes to that interpretation of the linguistic sign as meaningful act a definition of the sign that calls into question the nature of the signifying element within language. For de Saussure the linguistic sign signifies not as act or as speech, but as a value within language as a system of signs. The linguistic sign signifies, therefore, in and through its differences from other signs; the sign signifies in terms of its diacritical nature.

Rather than being an opposition rooted in the arbitrary choices of different theories and different methods, that opposition between the phenomenology of expressive language and the linguistics of structural meaning is a tension between the contrasting demands that the experience of language creates for philosophic thought. If the phenomenology of Husserl formulated its problematic in terms of formal logic, structural linguistics requires that a phenomenology be created to meet the demands of the social logic of language. For in addition to calling into question the interpretation of the linguistic sign, structural linguistics poses the question of linguistic meaning as social, since language as a system of signs is the principle of communication. Language for structural linguistics is an intersubjective object and not principally the experience of a transcendental and monadic subjectivity. The task of a phenomenology of language consequently is redirected by structural linguistics toward the description of the experience of expression, on the one hand, and, on the

Reprinted with permission of *International Philosophical Quarterly*, 9 (Summer 1969), 431–438.

other, toward the description of the inherence of intersubjective meaning within the consciousness and act of expression. The burden of the following pages is to move in that direction and to draw from the descriptive efforts of linguistics those consequences which create, for the philosophy of language, fundamental dimensions and perpetual questions.

I. SOUND AND MEANING

In the *Course in General Linguistics*,[1] Ferdinand de Saussure inaugurated a new era in the development of the science of linguistics. If structural linguistics has inherited the prinicple of structuralism from him, it has also inherited the crucial question of the relationship of sound and meaning. De Saussure formulated the framework in which the question is again asked today. Consequently the question of sound and meaning must begin with him.

For de Saussure, linguistics was to concern itself with language as a totality, as a *system* of signs, independent of the speech of the individual, *la parole*. Thus was announced the principle of *structuralism* which has borne so much fruit in the study of language. But for de Saussure in viewing language as a *system*, the question of meaning played a crucial role in determining the nature of the linguistic sign within the context of language, *la langue*, as a social institution.

De Saussure defined the linguistic sign by a double rapport. What made a certain sound combination a linguistic element for him was not only its phonemic structure, but its signification. For de Saussure the linguistic sign was a unity composed of two elements, the acoustic image and the concept, the *signifié* and the *signifiant*.[2] And the term, sign, designated the totality formed by this rapport. But for de Saussure the connection between *signified* and *signifying* was not a *natural* relation. For him the linguistic sign was not, strictly speaking, a product of nature, since the union of a particular sound with a specific meaning is arbitrary and each sign is part of a total system of signs, *la langue*.

But while each sign is a positive rapport between what is signified and the signifying, the values that each sign has, what stands for the signified or the signifying, are determined by the relation of sign to sign. Consequently for de Saussure the linguistic sign is *diacritical*. It is not something absolute, but determined precisely by its place within the system of signs which is language, *la langue*. In language, therefore, there are, strictly speaking, only differences, such that a change in one sign will bring about a shift in the meanings of other signs and in the signifying sounds.[3]

As a consequence of the diacritical nature of the linguistic sign, for de Saussure *la langue* is a matter of formal relations and not of the sound substances; it is formal and not substantial.[4] And the linguistic sign as the combination of values given to the signifying and signified is "a form and not a substance." Language, then, for de Saussure consists essentially in the formal elements that compose it. Language is not an assemblage of definite sounds and meanings, but rather is the totality of the functional relations that signs possess. *La langue* is a system of signs, while, on the other hand, the sound substances only belong to the spoken language, *la parole*.

But it is this break within the core of language that leads us to ask, is the distinction between form and substance lived within the experience of language? And further, can one make the distinction between language as a formal system and the spoken language? Certainly for de Saussure the linguistic sign as *form* is the concrete element of language and not an abstraction.[5] But then are the sound substances immaterial to the inner movement of language toward meaning, toward the creation of the linguistic sign? Is sound an accident or does meaning inhabit sound in an essential manner?

Taking into consideration the distinction between morphological elements as the ultimate carriers of semantic meaning within language and phonemes as the ultimate significant sound elements, for Jakobson and Halle, the features that set off morphological units from each other are oppositions and distinctions heard within the flow of sound. Each phoneme is a bundle of these distinctive features.[6] The semantic signs or morphological units, such as words or terminal endings, are heard as distinct from one another through the differentiations brought to the fore by heard significances, the distinctive features.

The distinctive features and the phonemes which are combinations of them are significant within any given language only inasmuch as they are differentiated from one another. They are significant inasmuch as they set each off from the other by way of oppositions and contrasts: "Any such feature denotes that the morpheme to which it pertains is not the same as a morpheme having another feature in the corresponding place. . . . All phonemes denote nothing but otherness."[7]

Not all features, however, are distinctive in every language. From among the features that set off phonemes such as the sonority features: vocalic/nonvocalic, consonantal/non-consonantal, compact/diffuse, tense/lax, voiced/voiceless, nasal/oral, discontinuous/continuant, strident/mellow, checked/unchecked, and the tonality features: grave/acute, flat/plain and sharp/plain, each language selects those that will be significant for it in the demarcation of semantic units.[8] Besides the distinctive features, other sound features operate to differentiate and organize the utterances into sentences or words.[9] Such are sentence and word stress in American English. In addition there are expressive features which place differing degrees of emphasis on parts of the utterance and convey the affective tone of the utterance.

As Jakobson and Halle have shown, in hearing a spoken utterance, two factors must be taken into consideration. The significant sounds of language are heard in terms of opposition of features, or aspects which the different phonemes possess and in terms of contrasts, as they are set off from other sounds within the context of the utterance. Each sound element has its significance in terms of the sounds to which it is opposed and within the context in which it appears or is able to appear. Phonemes as distinctive elements in language, consequently, presuppose the context of words; words, that of the total utterance. The configurative features or sound aspects that serve to set off syllables, words, and sentences are configurations that occur in a total utterance and are continuous over the whole spoken utterance. As they play over the whole utterance, they act upon the individual phonemes as in English: án áim, but, a náme.

The Gestalt character of the perception of the phoneme as a combination of heard differentiations is brought out in the above descriptions and more poignantly by the case of the Danish [a]. Jakobson analyzes the situation as follows:

> A pair of palatal vowel phonemes genetically opposed to each other through relative wideness and narrowness and, acoustically, through a higher and lower concentration of energy (compact/diffuse), may in some language be implemented in one position as (ae)—(e) and in another position (e)—(i), so that the sound (e) in one position implements the diffuse, and in another, the compact term of the same opposition. The relation in both positions remains identical. Two degrees of aperture and, correspondingly, of concentration of energy—the maximal and minimal—oppose each other in both positions.[10]

In the case of the Danish [a] the same phonetic sound may function as an allophone or variant of one phoneme in one context and in another context as that of another. While it is articulated in the same way in each case, it is heard as a different phoneme, since the features in question are relative to the context. This lack of absolute identity of the sound in every situation indicates that the sound is perceived by the ear within a figure/ground configuration. The ground is the same, the phonetic sound [e], but the different features form significantly different configurations depending on the context.

There is a correlation, however, between articulation and hearing as the basis for the identity of phonemes, but as the Danish [a] clearly shows, the heard configuration is the final basis for the determination of the phonemic character of an articulated sound. The same situation prevails in esophageal speech where there is a transfer of function in articulation. In abnormal cases where the larynx is removed, the voiced feature is sounded or has its source often in the vibration of the mucous tissue in the pharynx. The heard feature does not disappear, as one might be led to believe if the point of articulation alone served to differentiate phonemes. In those cases, another way of articulating the heard significance is found.[11]

The articulation of sound, therefore, is a gesture which realizes through the movements of the lungs, tongue, and lips the heard significances operative in language, and as a heard significance the phoneme is at once an acoustic-articulatory phenomenon. But, as we have seen in esophageal speech and from the Danish [a], from the side of the articulatory gesture, each sound flows into the other; on the side of the heard significances, each heard feature and phoneme are the result not of the union of form and content, but of the perception of a sound-Gestalt, a meaning formed through the configuration of oppositions and contrasts into distinctive features. And while for the ear each phoneme is distinct and the progression from one to the other in the flow of sound is not that of a gradual change, but one of definite transitions, the articulatory gesture forms a total movement whose first movements are an anticipation of the whole and whose final effort is the completion and fulfillment of a total project.

Consequently to say that the flow of sound belongs to the sound substance and the distinctness of phonemes to the form of language is to obscure the fact that the heard significances of language are at the same time articulated and spoken sounds. And it is, at the same time, to ignore the fact that no phoneme is spoken for its own sake alone but within the realization of a total gesture and within a more comprehensive totality, the utterance.

If one makes the distinction as is often done by linguists between phonetics and phonology, between the study of the different sounds that are found in a language and the study of the *significant* sounds, the distinctive features and phonemes, then not every phonetic difference is a phonemic or phonological difference. The articulated sound is spoken within the utterance not as a phonetic sound, but as phonemic, a configuration of features that form themselves through opposition and contrast within the language as a whole and within the utterance.

The principle of relativity such as it exists on the phonological level and is so recognized by all linguists, rules out the existence, or supposed existence, of absolute stimuli within the perception of significant sound. No sound within the spoken utterance is self-contained, but only has significance in its relation to the other configurations of sound and within the pattern of distinctive features that each language realizes on the phonological level. To speak, then, of purely physical sound and the addition of linguistic form is phenomenologically and theoretically to retreat into an abstraction.

But although we can say that the gesture of speaking is the realization of heard meaning, the experience of heard significances is dependent at the same time on the act of speaking, for it is in the speaking act that they come into existsence and unfold themselves as heard meaning. The phonemic entity or unity is not realized prior to the spoken utterance within its distinctive, configurative, expressive, and redundant features. The speaking act has a priority, then, as the original expressing of sound, but its goal is not just any type of sound, but phonologically significant sound. And since the speaking act is the articulation of sounds whose significance is a heard significance, here is revealed a teleology within the speaking act: speaking is *speaking to be heard*.

It is on the level of hearing and speaking as selective activities or *Sinngebungen*, therefore, that we must find the lived experience of language sounds as significant and meaningful. Sound distinctions vary from language to language and although the sounds may be phonetically the same, from English to French and from German to Russian, from the different systems of phonemic distinctions utilized by a tonal language such as the Chinese to the Western languages, the phonemic oppositions and contrasts are perceived within the flow of speech and realized within the articulatory gesture. There is a French ear and an English ear, not in terms of physiology, but in terms of perceiving within the flow of sound different phonemic differences. The articulatory gesture that realizes such heard significances is, consequently, a realization of meaning.

In the meaningful organization of linguistic sound, then, the selectivity present in the distinguishing of features takes place. But features only have significance in relation to the other parts of the sound sequence; they do not have an absolute character, but their soundful meaning lies, as Jakobson has said, in their complete otherness. Thus the perception of meaningful sound, the phoneme, is the perception of a *sound-Gestalt*, for it is heard as a combination of oppositions and contrasts within the flow of the utterance actually heard and in terms of the total system of oppositions which comprise the phonological pattern of a language.

Thus at no level and at no stage of speaking are sounds uttered in isolation. As we have seen from the phonological structure of language, each phoneme anticipates the next and the immediate horizon of each is the possibility of the next. And as joined together in the word, phonemes have features that they do not have separately, for the configurative features go beyond each phoneme as a bundle of inherent features and place its configuration within the utterance as a whole. Each morpheme, too, does not take up its meaning in isolation, but within its reference to other forms. Thus arises the syntax of the utterance which in turn embodies the interrelationships of morphemes and sound configurations within the realization of the soundfully unified utterance. Consequently, it is to the soundfully complete utterance, the unification of sound, form, and syntax, that we must turn to find the essential structure of hearing and speaking the spoken word. The primary spoken word is not the individual word, but the word is soundfully complete meaning, not the proposition, but the unity of sound and meaning achieved through an original project of expression.

Linguistics can, of course, analyze the different levels of utterance after it has been spoken. Yet as we saw in discussing the articulatory gesture, the elements of language originate within the awareness of the act of speaking. Its temporal flow and realization are also the flow of sounds and forms which originally come to be within the utterance as the speaking of soundfully complete meaning. Here we come head-on to our fundamental question: what is this awareness which characterizes the speaking act as the realization of soundful meaning? How do combinations of significant sounds come to have semantic significance?

Not only is it possible, as we have seen, to differentiate in a valid manner the different levels of language by concentrating on one level to the exclusion of others, but such a differentiation also takes place in pathological situations. In those cases meaning is separated, so to speak, from sound and sound from meaning. In his studies on aphasia, Kurt Goldstein[12] has shown that to perceive words, for example, as meaningful, a definite voluntary attitude is necessary. In cases where this is impossible, the simple repetition of sounds and their imitation become difficult. In disturbances of heard language, the perception of phonemes may be impaired, while the words remain meaningful. In such cases, the words cannot be repeated in their sound structure, but their meaning is present to the speaker.

Imitation of a heard sound, on the other hand, combines a different number of factors. It appears that a certain degree of abstraction is demanded in order to reproduce or imitate a heard sound exactly as it is heard. If the subject is not capable of ignoring the meaning of the word for a while, the sound produced will be that of his normal pronunciation. The general attitude of the subject in such cases is to consider language first of all in the meanings of words, consequently, it requires a real effort for him to abstract from this attitude and concentrate on the motor activities and the perception of sound for its own sake, both of which are needed to imitate successfully.

In other cases, however, meaning makes the repetition of sound complexes easier. That was observed in patients whose perception of words as sound complexes was disturbed and an attempt at repetition was made on the basis of the presumed meaning of the word. Sounds for them did not evoke definite meanings, but the word finally pronounced was within the range of meaning of the word called for. The patient would repeat, not the word spoken to him, but one that had a similar meaning.

What meaning do these pathological situations have for our present question? Only within pathological language are meaning and sound experienced as different levels as in disturbances of heard language. But on the other hand, exact imitation of sound complexes is difficult for some subjects since the word is experienced as a unity: sound and meaning co-signify each other, so to speak. And when imitation was successful, it was not because language itself was disturbed, but because the sound complexes were concentrated on to the exclusion of meaning. And in the last example, where the perception of sound was impaired, the spoken sound was not without semantic meaning, but evoked from the patient a response close to the meaning of the original word.

What do these situations mean, if not that for impaired language and for the normal subject sound and meaning "co-signify" each other within the unity of the word? Even when the perception of sound was disturbed, its inner relationship with semantic meaning was preserved, although in rudimentary form. Within the flow of significant sound, we had to reject the dichotomy between the physical sounds and the form of significance. More fully, then, how does semantic meaning inhabit language?

II. MEANING AND SYMBOL

On the surface, it would seem possible to separate the meaning of the word and the sound combinations which signify that meaning. That is precisely the position that de Saussure took in the *Course in General Linguistics* when he defined the linguistic sign as the rapport of concept and sound, the signified and the signifying. There was no doubt in de Saussure's mind, as there is none for us, that phonemic combinations carry and signify semantic significance, but the problem is, in what way do they do so? Is the meaningfulness of the spoken word its association with a "concept"? Or does not the intentionality of language bespeak a deeper dimension in which the becoming of sound is the unfolding of meaning?

In one of his later works, Noam Chomsky has pointed out that the differentiation of phonemes and the discernment of the morphemic elements within an utterance can be done without recourse to semantic meaning. In the commutation test, for example, where different sound elements are substituted for each other to determine whether they are significant for the native speaker, all that is required is the response of the speaker and not a knowledge of the semantic significance of the individual words.[13]

According to Chomsky, the same situation arises in setting up a structurally adequate grammar for a language. Semantic significance does not seem to be crucial in this area either, for the grammar can be *formally* set up without recourse to the semantic usage of the words within the syntax. Take the two sentences: "colorless green ideas sleep furiously" and "furiously sleep ideas green colorless." Both sentences, taken as they are, are nonsensical, but only the former is seen as grammatical.[14] It would seem, then, that a sentence cannot have semantic significance without being grammatical, but that it can be grammatical without having semantic meaning. Thus in Chomsky's transformational grammar, the grammatical structure consists in the kernel sentences of the language and the different transformations that can be worked on those sentences in order to derive more complex sentences. The grammatical structure is not determined by the meaning of the sentences, but by formal operations.

The possibility of such formal analysis does not rule out, however, the semantic role of linguistic elements, but does point to the fact that semantic significance is not discernible in formal structures *per se*. The question of semantic meaning remains and lies beyond them. But is it as clear as all that? Benjamin Lee Whorf has described grammatical categories that have no overt appearance within a sentence or utterance, but are covert categories, such as the distinction between round and long objects in Navaho and gender in English. In Navaho, certain verb stems go with one class and others with another, while some verb stems do not react to the difference.[15] "Sorrow" in this situation is a round noun. Yet it cannot be denied that the difference between the two classes of nouns can be discerned from an examination of the syntax of the sentences in which they are found and hence can be formulated without reference to their meaning. Yet Whorf maintains that such categories which do not have a specific form to denote them, but only a reactance within the sentence, only reveal themselves completely, beyond mere suspicion of their existence, to one who lives within the language and ceases to observe it from without. Consequently we must question the tenet of formalism in excluding semantic significance. Here it is important to realize that the meaning of a word or form, as semantic meaning, includes grammatical usage, just as it includes when it is spoken, sound combinations. But only the spoken awareness of the word within the utterance engages us within the unfolding where sound, grammatical usage, and semantic significance take their being, not as a dispersion, but as a field of variations and dimensions.

It is well known in structural linguistics that the semantic horizons of each word or utterance are determined within the language itself and by the language community. That is what de Saussure referred to in speaking of the arbitrary nature of the linguistic sign. The French word, *pomme*, for example, covers an area of meaning that is not covered by the literal translation of the English word, apple. In the phrase, *pomme de terre*, what is meant is the potato in English or in the current French saying, *pommes frites*, in English, fried potatoes are meant. As we see from the translations of the same word as knob, ball, or cone, no English word covers the same *area* or *field* of meaning that *pomme* covers, since it takes in an aspect of *roundness* in all its references.

Because of that arbitrary character, the word, consequently, does not refer to the perceived object in its *complete* configuration: the word does not *mean* the perceived object as such. Rather the word refers to those features within the perceived world which a specific language determines as its meaning. As Bloomfield says, the meaning of a word consists in the semantic features or the distinctive features of meaning.[16] Von Humboldt noted very early that the Greek word for the moon, *men*, and the Latin word, *luna*, do not denote the same aspects of the moon. The Greek refers to the importance of the moon as the cyclic measure of time, while the Latin word denotes the brightness of the moon. In each case it is the same object that is referred to, but not the same *meaning* or *meant object*.

Yet to speak of the meaning or meant object of the word, if carried out rigorously, creates a fission within the spoken awareness of the word, for the spoken word is, at once, its *meaning* and the *meant object*. For the speaker as he speaks or for the hearer as he hears the words spoken within the utterance, the understanding of the meaning of the word is one with the hearing of the sounds which compose it and its usage, be that as noun, verb, or article. In the temporal unfolding of the utterance within the flow of sound and the progressive constructtion of the syntax, which anticipates what is to come and takes up what has become, the awareness of meaning unfolds itself within the unfolding of sound. Meaning is not added to sound or inferred from its configurations, but becomes an aware presence within the unfolding of sound combinations. As it is heard and spoken, the utterance and word are an awareness which dwells within sound and syntax, which pulsates within the reverberations of sound and meaning.

On the other hand, the meaning which is disclosed in the hearing of sound is not a meaning that the individual speaker has decided will be its meaning. Rather it is an arbitrary meaning that is such because it has come to be so determined within the history of a specific language and within the language community. It is not solely the possession of the individual, but of all who speak the language. Consequently, the word in its spokenness is an individual possession and at the same time partakes of a cultural being. One could decide to redefine all the words in a language and give them new meanings, but his words would not be understood by others until he had taught his redefinitions to them. And that would be, in effect, to teach them a new language. However, language does not evolve in that way; the changes that take place in language occur over long periods of time and without the explicit notice of anyone, yet language remains full of meaning.

Consequently, since it is arbitrary, the word possesses its intentionality, not in the intending of a univocal definition, nor in the presentation of an object, but in the disclosure of itself as a field of meaning. Certainly, the semantic field of the word lies within the perceived world; *men* and *luna* both refer to the perceived moon. But the meaning of the word is not, as we have already seen, the intention of the perceived object, but the configuration of semantic features. That *field* of meaning is the word, an awareness unfolding itself temporally within the flow of sound, within the becoming of gesture. As they are temporally unfolded, the word and the utterance as a whole are an awareness of the meaning which is there unfolded. If the spoken meaning is viewed outside of the horizons of hearing and speaking, then it certainly seems that it directly intends things in the world and states of affairs. But meaning within the speaking gesture does not intend configurations of the perceived world directly, but intends them for the Other who can hear, whether that be the speaker himself or the one to whom he speaks.

If the meaning of a word was its reference to an object within the perceived world in its strictly perceived configurations, its meaning could not be grasped until the object could be viewed. Yet the word and utterance are meaningful even in the absence of which they speak. What is always present is the awareness which is unfolded in hearing and speaking. The word, hence, incorporates its reference, so to speak, within itself. For it is at once, sound, meaning, and syntax. It leads beyond itself into the perceived world, but only through its soundfully immanent meaning. As for itself, when it is heard or spoken, it is an awareness that is complete in itself.

Here we come face to face with a unique type of intentionality which testifies to the mutual inherence of *noesis* and *noema*, for the utterance is both the *intending* and the *intended*. The utterance is not only meaning heard, but also meaning spoken, meaning realized through an *intending* gesture. As an expression of selected configurations within the perceived world, the word is the soundful awareness which creates itself through gesture. The soundfully complete utterance, too, in taking up a *situation* or *state of affairs*, is the realization of itself, for as utterance, it is the speaking and the heard, the *meaning made present* and the *making present*, the *cogito* and the *cogitatum*.

The meaning that each has, therefore, the word and the utterance, is present to the speaker as the goal of his own gesture toward which the articulated sounds flow and which comes into being in their temporal unfolding. For the speaker, each demarcation of sound combinations constitutes a new meaning which incorporates itself into the whole of what is being said. The utterance is complete when the falling or rising of the voice marks it as complete and when the sounds form a complete structure according to the pattern of sound and syntax incorporated into the language. Thus meaning is not present within meaning spoken or heard as a pure awareness, present to itself all at once and with full clarity, but an awareness which fades off into a past which it retains within its movement toward completion and which anticipates itself in setting up the goal of its own sonority.

The meaning that lies thus within the utterance is not an explicitly held meaning, a meaning open to the full light of day and to the constituting rays of a subjectivity in full possession of itself and without the slightest shading or presence of shadows, but an embodiment in sound, a field of shadowy horizons which rather than being objects known, are hidden movements of meaning in which one dwells. But is that not a contradiction or, at the very least, a paradox? If I, the solitary individual, had created the language I speak, certainly it would be completely open to my gaze. But is it not the case that the meanings which I, the individual, speak are not mine, but rather "ours"? Those horizons which exist in their absence and ambiguity are the past of the language which has been given to the individual but which is also a history far beyond his remembrance, yet present to him as he dwells within the speaking act. The awareness which unfolds for the individual in the speaking of sound and in hearing the spoken word of Others has a past that is not only his past, but the past found in the slow evolution of idioms, formations, and etymologies. But they can be known by him, if he examines the contexts within which he speaks this or that word. Yet there is first the act of speaking and the contexts arise from the awareness within which the individual speaks, but which, at the same time, escapes into shadowy horizons of meaning, present in their absence and absent in their presence, rather than being open to a full and explicit gaze. Here within the deepest dimensions of soundful meaning are echoes which are, so to speak, not heard, but silent, but which, for all that, are what is said and are what is heard. Here we are in the realm, not of the signified and of the signifying, but of the *symbolic*.

The spoken word is a *symbolic* awareness, not as *symbol of something*, not as *symbolic of something other than itself*, but as the dwelling of *presence* within absent horizons which define its mode of *presence*. The word is *symbolic* since it embodies within itself a semantic field as an ever present field of present-absent horizons and because it dwells within that field as its own realization within the sound and gesture which it also is. And, again, the word does not possess itself in isolation, but as it is spoken within soundfully complete utterances. It is within its *spoken-ness*, taking place within the horizon of other events of sound and gesture, other contexts, that it takes to itself meaning within the unfolding of sound. As a consequence, rather than circumscribing one meaning or being univocal, the spoken word is a *symbolization* in which sound, syntax, and meaning form a living *presence* which holds within itself a past which escapes its grasp and a future which remains unknown. Or said more simply, that past and that future are the past and future of the language community of which the individual is a member.

That language community is present at the very beginning of language. The learning of a language by the child is a response to being spoken to by Others and to living within a world of spoken meanings. This acquisition of language is a matter of capturing the *style* embodied in the movements of sound and syntax. Roman Jakobson has shown that the sounds that a child has uttered in the babbling period have to be relearned with great effort when the child begins to pick up the style of the language he will speak. In the babbling period, the child is just articulating sounds, but he does not begin to speak, even in monosyllables, until he utters sounds in terms of the oppositions and contrasts which he hears in the language of Others. But at its inception such a structure of sound and syntax, the *style* of a language, presents the Others or Other as an horizon of Otherness within the speaking act itself, for the speaking act will be a speaking to be heard in the *style* presented by Others. The sounds of language in their *style* and the meanings of language in their *fields* of present-absent horizons are, then, not only mine but Ours, and the Other is there in the modulations of the *symbolic*, as the horizon which disincarnates language.

If the word were a pure awareness to itself and not *symbolic*, it would be constituted in the fullness of its genesis and the history which defines it. But the spoken word is not just the embodiment of the experience and awareness of a people. The history of its meaning and its etymology are linked together in the untold utterances of men long dead and forgotten. That presence of the Other as a horizontal dimension within the intentionality of language is also found on the level of sound and gesture. The patterning of sound and form which unfolds itself within the gesture of speaking is not only a temporality, a flow of sound, of the spoken meanings heard by the individual from his own lips, but also the flowing modulation of the words spoken to him by Others. The temporality of the spoken meaning is "his" time and "my" time. Certainly, hearing his words unfolds itself within the flow of my perceptive acts, yet the meaning and emotion manifested in his speech are the realization of his gestures, not mine. And within the flow of my perceptive acts I not only live the surging of my awareness, but I live the *tempo* of his life and consciousness as it is manifested in sound and gesture. Here is clearly an intersubjective temporality which is a temporality articulating itself within the structure of Otherness. Hence even in the word spoken in solitude, the Other is there as the horizon attendant to the flow of sound and within the structure: speaking to be heard and hearing gestural sound.

How are we to understand this temporality, the intervweaving of sound and gesture into the symbolization of spoken meaning? Are we in the presence of an act of *incarnation* of meaning in sound? It would seem that that word, incarnation, expresses the dwelling of meaning within the interweaving of sound and gesture and at the same time breaks down the distinctions that formalism carves out within the interior of language. But we must understand its meaning as the act of embodying and incarnating, an act which is one with what is realized and unfolds itself within the horizons of past, present, and future. But yet those horizons of the symbolic are just as much *disincarnate*, horizons that form the symbolic intention through their testimony to the presence of Others and hence inhabit that presence as the hollowing out of presence, the very escape of presence into the negation of its own incarnation. And, at the same time, that incarnation into sound is the act of a gesture which vanishes as soon as it comes into being, for the gesture of sound incarnates the presence of meaning only to disperse, scatter, and fade into the past.

The theme of incarnation cannot encompass the full movement of the presence of meaning in sound and gesture because language is not only the tradition of Others and bears their stamp, but because that tradition becomes an experience before the presence of the Other. Meaning abides within the word because it has been confirmed by the presence of the Other and by his word. The silence of the perceiving self is only broken at the moment when meaning reaches out for confirmation and the dialogue of discourse is initiated. The autonomy of the intentionality of language is not so much an illusion as one-dimensional. The act of speaking not only brings forth the presence of meaning, but that presence is only the reality of the word when the presence of the Other turns it into a meaning that is shared, a meaning which is only fulfilled and actualized through the witness of the word of the Other.

It is not only temporality and tradition, therefore, which explain the elusive, symbolic nature of language. The full significance of discourse and its symbolic essence lies in the dimension which the Other creates. For the Other in his confirming act finally constitutes meaning within language. His presence is more than a mere pole of orientation. Words do not signify in the fullest sense as communication, as meaning given without the possibility of their eliciting the response of another. They would be merely the solitary discourse of dreams. In speaking, the self alienates itself, in order to be expressive and do more than contemplate the world from behind an implacable mask. Rather, to speak is to appropriate the unknown dimension of exteriority so that the act of speaking can signify an actual presence of meaning. The word in its temporal horizons eludes itself, because it is constituted in more than the relation of act to meaning within one subjectivity. The word as symbolic is constituted in the relation of act to meaning within intersubjectivity. And the symbolic thus acquires the significance of a meaning suspended between the self and the Other.

The body adds another dimension to that plunge of language into elusive ambiguity. As Merleau-Ponty saw, language is not independent of the body, but in a way is the completion of the intentional life that the body leads within the perceived world. The presence of the symbolic in language as soundful expression is possible because the body itself is expression and is the foundation of the permanence of the symbol as incarnate presence. For meaning to exist in language, there must be the promise of bringing it to the fore of awareness time and time again. That promise is the temporality of the symbol as the permanent presence of sound and gesture within the horizon of the Other. It is the continuity of my bodily gestures of articulation that sustains the becoming of meaning and it is the presence of the body that makes possible its realization, for the complete realization of meaning is the completion of a movement of sound. Such a symbolic intentionality is an awareness that becomes and establishes itself as an achieved meaning in sound, and hence its permanence is the possibility of a response articulating that sound again and again. But as an act of soundful symbolization, the articulatory gesture is an expression, itself; it is the becoming of a symbol.

In the *Phenomenology of Perception*, Merleau-Ponty tied up that expressiveness of the body with the theme of temporality. There temporality is the temporality of the body. The living present in its most concrete form is the incarnate presence of the body to itself in the pre-reflective life of perception and of the perceived world. Because I have a body which is the field of temporal presence, I am in time and am temporality myself, but without being submerged in its passing and disruption. I am present at the self-generation of time in the present, in the renewal of the "now." As such, time is not just being in the sense of immediacy, but a manifestation to itself: it constitutes itself for itself. It is in time that consciousness is given to itself and comes into being. Yet consciousness does not do so outside of time, but, as Merleau-Ponty says in what is just a passing phrase, by raising up symbols for itself in succession and multiplicity "which are it, since without them it would, like an inarticulate cry, fail to achieve self-consciousness."[17]

The speaking gesture which realizes, and is one with, this temporal movement of symbolization unites the movements of the tongue, lips, and chest into the expression of meaning. And in doing so, it takes for its own in the creation of symbols the experience of breathing. The sounds that are spoken are not separated from my intentions, rather they are my intentions become symbols. They are part of myself as my breath, and spoken meaning is realized through the very movement by which I breathe.

In breathing there is no surface to separate me from the depth of the world. In breathing the fresh breeze which moves through the heavily scented pines, I do more than carry out respiration. I take the scene into myself and witness to my incorporation into the density of the trees and the green growth of the underbrush. And in exhalation I do more than empty my lungs, but I breathe out my own substance into the surrounding world. To refuse to release that substance into the intermingling of myself and the world, to retain it and capture it, is to choose death and not life. That life is, here, not the possession of itself, but in breath the communion with a world. The experience of spoken meaning dwells within that communion, for it is my breath realizing itself in a new dimension, that of the symbolic.

But that is not an isolated experience. As Schilder has shown, the openings of the body are not only the schema into which the body image forms itself, but also the primordial points of contact for the body and the world. The excretions of the openings of the body, such as those of the anus in bowel movements, are not experienced by the child as separate from the body; they are in some way still part of the body. And after the mouth has taken in food, the food does not have to wait for digestion to be experienced as part of the body.[18] And so the breath that becomes the sound of language is not other than the body, but the pouring forth of breath into a world with which it is one, is, in a sense, the hovering of the world over chaos and darkness.

Thus from the very beginning of the speaking act as the realization of the incarnate presence of meaning, we are dwelling within a world. And the symbols that it realizes are one with that movement, for they are the achievements of that primordial experience symbolizing in a new and unique way. It is not a question of separating breath and linguistic sounds, for the sounds of language are breath, and the realm of the symbolic arises with the birth of new meaning in the soundfully complete utterance. Here we have in the realization of incarnate meaning which escapes into the shadows of its own presence, a symbolic intentionality as the way subjectivity dwells within the world on the level of spoken meaning. Subjectivity does so by taking all those aspects of the world which it has through the body and by unifying them into a new totality of symbols, *logos*.

NOTES

[1] Ferdinand de Saussure, *Cours de linguistique générale* (Paris: 1955); *Course in General Linguistics*, trans. Wade Baskin (New York: 1959).

2 *Ibid.*, p. 99. Reference is to the French text.

3 *Ibid.*, pp. 155–69.

4 *Ibid.*, p. 169.

5 *Ibid.*, p. 157.

6 Roman Jakobson and Morris Halle, *Fundamentals of Language* ('S-Gravenhage, 1956). Janua Linguarum NR 1., pp. 4 and 6.

7 *Ibid.*, p. 110.

8 *Ibid.*, pp. 29–31.

9 *Ibid.*, p. 9.

10 *Ibid.*, p. 15.

11 B. Malmberg, *Structural Linguistics and Human Communication* (New York: 1963), p. 37.

12 Kurt Goldstein, *Language and Language Disturbances* (New York: 1948), p. 73.

13 Noam Chomsky, *Syntactic Structures* ('S-Gravenhage: 1957). Janua Linguarum NR 4., p. 96; 9.2.4.

14 *Ibid.*, 2.3.

15 Benjamin Lee Whorf, "Grammatical Categories," *Language, Thought and Reality*, ed. John B. Carroll (Cambridge: 1964), p. 91.

16 Leonard Bloomfield, *Language* (New York: 1964), p. 141.

17 Maurice Merleau-Ponty, *The Phenomenology of Perception*, trans. Colin Smith (New York: 1962), p. 427.

18 Paul Schilder, *The Image and Appearance of the Human Body* (New York: 1964), p. 188.

ADUMBRATION AS A FEATURE
OF INTERCULTURAL COMMUNICATION
Edward T. Hall

EDWARD T. HALL is professor of anthropology in the College of Arts and Sciences at Northwestern University. For the past ten years he has been conducting research and writing about man's perception of space both in the United States and abroad. His most recent book, The Hidden Dimension, deals with proxemics, man's use of space.

Dr. Hall received his Ph.D. from Columbia University. After army service during World War II, he conducted field work in Micronesia. For five years he was director of the State Department's Point IV Training Program preparing Americans for service overseas. He has taught at the University of Denver, Bennington College, the Harvard Business School, and the Illinois Institute of Technology.

A consultant to government, private foundations, and business, Dr. Hall is a Fellow of the American Anthropological Association, lecturer, and author of The Silent Language, The Hidden Dimension, and numerous articles in professional journals. He is a director of the Ansul Company and the Brookfield Zoo and is a member of the Advisory Committee of the Northeastern Illinois Planning Commission.

More than two decades of observing Americans working with other cultures lead me to believe that the majority fall into two groups. One group—mostly professional linguists and anthropologists—is convinced that it is a waste of time to send a man abroad until he is thoroughly conversant with the language and culture on all levels. The other group, appalled by the cost of implementing such a policy and drawing from naive experience, sees language and culture only as screens that have to be penetrated in order to find the real man or people underneath. This second group believes that there is a dichotomy between man and his language-culture and also that good will is the primary material needed to pave the road to understanding.

Intuitively, the specialist in intercultural communications has known for a long time that neither of these positions is appropriate as a matter of policy. There are many times when all the good will in the world would not reach the mind of, say, a Japanese. On the other hand, knowledge of the language and culture will not enable one to "get through" to the other fellow in every instance, even if he is member of one's own culture.

Anyone who has lived and worked abroad knows that the overseas world is full of surprises, not all of them pleasant, which are due to accumulated slippage in reading subtle signs of which we are often unaware. The surprises that characterize life abroad, as well as at home, are due not so much to ignorance of overt culture as to changes or shifts in the signs that we read to penetrate people's façades, signs that tell us what's going on underneath. Goffman (1957, 1959) refers to this process as "going backstage." Ability to read these signs enables us to be "sensitive," to know how the other person is reacting to what we are saying and doing.

Reproduced by permission of the American Anthropological Association from American Anthropologist, vol. 66, No. 1, 1964.

To do this, one must be able to read and interpret correctly what I have termed "adumbrations": those indications preceding or surrounding formal communications which enable organisms to engage in the mutual exchange and evaluation of covert information on what each can expect from the other. Adumbrations are the feedback mechanisms that enable us to steer a smooth course through life or to prepare for attack when combat cannot be avoided. They foreshadow what organisms will do, perform corrective functions, and help set the directions a given communication will take, as well as the actions resulting from it. As we shall see, absence of the adumbrative feature can have catastrophic consequences. In addition, adumbrations are often closely linked with territory, or personal space, occur on different levels, and have proxemic implications (Hall, 1955, 1959, 1963a, 1963b).

Most, if not all, of the conceptual models I have examined have implicit in them the concept that the events referred to occur at different levels in depth. Thinking in the fields of depth psychology, ethnography, and descriptive linguistics has from the very beginning been intermingled on the matter of levels. Freud made the original contribution. Since then, recognition of the need to distinguish between different analytic levels has become fairly widespread, owing to work of Boas (1911), Linton (1936), Kluckhohn (1943), Sapir (1921, 1925, 1927), Sullivan (1947), and others.

Recently, there has been a shift to another dimension. Goffman's frontstage-backstage model implies a horizontal rather than a vertical dimension. Recent studies in ethology suggest that a temporal dimension should be added to our ever-growing inventory.

A LINGUISTIC MODEL FOR ANALYSIS OF CULTURE

In 1953, Trager and I introduced the notion that cultural events occur not on two but on three levels: the formal, the informal, and the technical. We described how these different levels function and can be identified. My own description (Hall 1959) does not deviate in any significant degree from the joint version. However, I have come to feel that it was somewhat oversimplified and this I shall attempt to correct.

Originally, Trager and I had collected microtexts of references to time as they occurred in the context of conversations in natural settings. After a while (an informal reference) we noted that the items we were collecting were not at all of the same degree of specificity but were in fact quite different. This observation suggested a three-part classification that we later called formal, informal, and technical. Brief examples will suffice here: *Technical:* "Resolving time is 1 μsec"; *Formal:* "We always start services promptly at 11"; *Informal:* "I'll see you later." In English we have not only a word for time but an extensive formal vocabulary devoted to it. Whorf's description of linguistic events (see papers in Carroll 1956) is based on *formal* differences between languages, and this is one reason why they are so difficult to grasp, a generalization which still holds. (On technical, formal, and informal, see Hall 1959, Ch. IV for extended discussion.)

To use a spatial metaphor, the formal-informal-technical concept is like a river: the readily perceived main current is the technical, surrounded by the informal back eddies and quiet pools, all of which are contained in a formal channel. Like all analogies, this one has limitations, yet it did help in the organization of our data and in talking to outsiders about what we were doing. When we were developing it, we suggested (Hall and Trager 1953; Hall 1959) that a linguistic model was an excellent one for the analysis of culture; that, in fact, all culture could be viewed as communication and all cultural events could be analyzed with the methods of linguistics.

The linguistic model has served us well and will continue to do so, but it requires some broadening, as noted by several linguists (Hockett 1958; Sebeok 1962). The great strengths of linguistics are that it has distinguished between *etic* and *emic* events (Hymes 1962; Greenberg 1959a, 1959b) and has been able to handle greater and greater complexity. Descriptive linguistic models break down, however, when it is necessary to deal with feedback or teleology. The ability to handle the complexity necessary for discourse analysis has not proceeded with any degree of sophistication, with one exception (Joos 1962).

Recent advances in isolating the relationship of biochemistry to the environment (Christian 1961; Deevey 1960), however, explain population control as the result of a series of interlocking and interdependent servomechanisms that conform to information theory principles as laid down by Wiener (1948), Shannon (1949), Pierce (1956), and their followers. Gilliard (1962) has shown how display behavior also fits this pattern and is also an important process in evolution. Hockett (1958) defined communication so generally as to comprise any event that triggers a response in another organism.

It would seem then that the time is ripe to take the first (even though faltering) steps towards the integration of linguistic models with the communication models of wider scope recently developed in the fields referred to above.

It is suggested that interpersonal communication occurs as a hierarchy of formally determined cybernetic responses. Two processes to which adumbrative behavior is particularly important are those beginning with the informal and becoming increasingly technical, in stages, whenever an inappropriate response is met on either side, and, conversely, those beginning with the technical, and becoming increasingly informal, as appropriate responses are met. Courtship and business negotiation offer many examples of such processes. When the parties know each other well and have enough in common, there is very little need for technical statements. The greater the distance (and the greater the investment), the more necessary it becomes to spell things out, even to the point of specifying which language version, say English or Spanish, of a contract will hold in case of litigation. In other words, the degree of explicit information content of a communication is a function of the degree to which the other party is already appropriately programmed. Less explicit means serve the ends of economy, and often avoid the commitment of organisms beyond a point of no return if things don't seem to be going well. On the other hand, some things can be accomplished only if the less explicit means can be successfully employed. Much interaction is under constraints like those set by the girl who wants to be kissed but not to be asked.

These same processes hold true to a lesser degree within a primarily technical sphere, such as conversations between scientists on scientific topics, in the laboratory, as contrasted to publication in a scientific journal.

All this represents a redefinition of the formal, the informal, and the technical levels and is a first attempt to bring these concepts into line with the general principles (but not the details) of information theory.[1] This change in definition is made possible by recognition of constant feedback in man and in animals on every level, from the biochemical to the international (Hall 1959).

IMPORTANCE OF ADUMBRATION IN COMMUNICATION

This paper focuses on the informal adumbrative process. It advances the hypothesis that the formal or technical message is more often understood than the informal, but, since the latter influences the meaning of the former, there is always a parataxic element (noise) present in any conversation and this element becomes greater as cultural distance increases.

In essence, every communication appears to comprise three interrelated parts or phases: A beginning phase, a peak phase, and a terminating phase, analogous to a sine wave on an oscilloscope. Musicians refer to the first and last as the attack and decay phase of a musical note.

What happens in one phase apparently influences the other two very considerably. That is, communications have an adumbrative phase (the part that indicates what is coming), the message itself, and a terminal or transition phase that signals how things went or the nature of reply expected. It is my hypothesis that the greatest confusion in intercultural communication can often be traced to failures in catching the true significance of the adumbrative and/or the terminal-transition phase, while, as a general rule, the message itself is often understood. Since the communication is taken as a whole in which the parts are interrelated, however, distortion of or failure to grasp the beginning or end can result in *total* distortion, or what Sullivan (1940) called parataxic communication. (For intracultural consequences as within a family, of contradiction between the message and its context, including the temporal phases dealt with here, see Bateson [1960, 1963] and cf. Ruesch [1961: passim].)

I am going to dwell chiefly on nonverbal communication of which there are many varieties (Hall 1959; Hymes 1962), drawing chiefly on my work in time and space as communication. One can begin with the setting which is a form of communication; changes in the setting foreshadow other changes. One might assume that we are talking about the cues, but this is not so. The cue is a short message of minimal redundancy in full awareness from A to B that indicates what A wants B to do. The adumbration, on the other hand, is a perceivable manifestation of A's feelings of which he may not even be aware: his tone of voice (paralinguistic behavior), facial expression, even his dress, posture, and handling of appointments "in time." While most of us are familiar with cues as a special type of communication, adumbrations are less well understood. They were first described under a different name by ecologists studying the behavior of other life forms (ranging from lizards to birds), courting, fighting, socializing, and caring for their young.

PRE-HUMAN ADUMBRATIVE BEHAVIOR

Adumbration can be observed in all vertebrates, although it is easier for man to recognize it in some forms than in others. Display is the principal vehicle of adumbration among animals. Gilliard (1962) lists four types of display: vocal, mechanical, mobile, and static-terrestrial. Most, if not all, bird calls can be classified as vocal display. Various mechanical means are also used to produce display by sound. The peacock's tail feathers rustle as he spreads them in display. The bowerbird snaps his bill, the gorilla thumps his chest (Schaller 1963), and the rattlesnake vibrates his tail to produce a threatening buzz. Movement displays are varied; their most familiar form is the strutting of male pigeons, the neck-stretching and head-bobbing of the gulls. Almost anyone familiar with chickens will recognize the static-terrestrial posturing of the barnyard cock as a display.

Recently display has received more and more attention from the ethologist and the animal psychologist and is seen as an active agent in evolution. It also performs a number of extraordinarily important and vital functions, many of them associated with language in man. Correct interpretation of the significance of given displays is normally limited to within the species, sometimes to within genera.

Display behavior is not limited to a single act but is a sequence of events that combine in different ways with different results. Anyone who has observed gulls will have noted a good deal of posturing and head-bobbing. Timbergen (1954) gives an excellent description of the significance of this behavior, which appears so bizarre at first glance.

During the mating season, a male blackheaded gull lays claim to a territory, a small plot of land that he defends against his own kind, particularly other males. Whenever another gull lands on his turf, the gull responds with a "long call" (vocal display) and postures his body obliquely (static-terrestrial display). This is the first in a series of "threat displays." During the second step, the two gulls draw closer together, lean forward, and often perform movements of the head and neck (movement displays) that look as if they were choking each other. Then they assume "upright posture" (static-terrestrial display). The third step in the sequence is "head flogging." Performed by only one of two males, it signals submission and serves to suppress further aggression. During courtship, head flogging is performed by both the male and the female to signal appeasement. This three-step scene (approach, threat, appeasement) is played over and over again until the two gulls apparently get to know each other (are mutually programmed) and learn that in this instance both can be counted on to end the aggressive exchange sequence by giving the appeasement display. Repetition and the ability to recognize individuals are important elements in communication sequences such as these.

In still another context, male sea lizards on the Galapagos Islands, defending their territories during mating, engage in mutual display and nobody gets hurt. The ethologist Eibl-Eibesfeldt (1961), recognizing and wishing to test the function of display in suppressing aggression, put male sea lizards in other lizards' territories, thereby short-circuiting the normal display sequence. As soon as this happened, terrible fighting broke out.[2]

Those who have studied display are generally agreed that it performs several important communicative functions both within a species and between species. It reduces the amount of actual combat and limits serious fighting to interspecies. During courtship it synchronizes the behavior of the sexes, gets attention, suppresses nonsexual responses, and releases the submissive posture in the female. On the other hand, lack of participation in a given display pattern isolates even closely related species from each other, thus acting as an evolutionary force in the maintenance of reproductive isolation.

In encounters between species, ability to interpret correctly at least part of the display sequence is of critical importance. Hediger (1955), the animal psychologist, has stressed the necessity for men to be able to identify the adumbration behavior of other species. Pandas, bears, and snakes are dangerous to man because it is difficult to know how they are feeling from moment to moment.[3]

The hypothesis can be advanced that: *Unless the adumbrative sequence is known, two species or societies or two individuals cannot interact in any way towards each other except in a parataxic manner and with ultimate aggression.* Within species, short-circuiting the adumbrative sequence leads to serious fighting.[4]

THE ADUMBRATIVE FUNCTION IN MAN

As we have seen, some of the functions of adumbration are: To protect organisms (including man) from becoming over-committed, to give them some control over their encounters with others, to protect egos, and to provide an automatic buffer or means of transition from one segment of a communication sequence to another; adumbration may also serve to establish intimacy. In many cultures, there are intermediaries who act in an adumbrative role, relative to the focal messages of a relationship. They may serve as buffers to save face and prevent over-commitment, on the one hand, to establish the necessary or desired closeness on the other. In our own culture, time, space, and materials communicate on many levels including the adumbrative level.

The examples I shall use are drawn from my studies of proxemics, the human use of microspace (Hall 1963a, 1963b). There are three different types of microspace (Hall 1963a, 1963b): Fixed-feature space (including the setting); semifixed-feature space (components that are part of the setting and can be moved); and dynamic space (man's informal repertoire for handling space). The desirability of choosing a proper setting for a communication is so well known that there would be no need to mention it, if it were not for the fact the choice of setting differs from culture to culture, often for the same act.

This is one reason why Americans in foreign lands who become ill often suffer from anxiety as soon as they go to the doctor. Sivadon (ms.) has stressed the importance, even for the indigenous population, of recognizing the adumbrative side of the setting. He states that hospital waiting rooms and doctors' offices should emphasize the familiar and be as free as possible of the un-known, such as glass cases full of chromium instruments which are familiar to the physician but not to the patient.

In the international political arena, adumbrative space has proved to be sig-nificant indeed. All other things being equal, and given a willingness to negoti-ate in the first place, there is little adumbrative significance for Americans re-garding the choice of the place of a negotiation. Our approach is to get on with negotiations and "not hold up the show." Allowing the other party to choose or move a negotiation site, once it has been established, signifies only that we intend to be "reasonable." However, when the American negotiators readily agreed to move the setting of the Korean truce negations from the Swedish peace ship in Seoul harbor to Panmunjom, the Chinese Communists apparently assumed that this represented an "appeasement" display. As most Americans will remember, it took a while to disabuse them of this misconception.

In the international business context, there are numerous examples of how familiarity with the differences in the adumbrative significance of the setting helped negotiations, while ignorance hindered them. Some of our more adept American firms have learned that they do better if they create settings with de-sign features which enable their Latin American counterparts to progress, like Tinbergen's gulls, through known stages in the business courtship. One very successful Wall Street executive specializing in Latin America chooses a club that features dark, oak-panelled walls, heavy, leather-covered chairs, high ceil-ings, and stained-glass windows, a setting that is impressive and at the same time "simpatico" to his clients. A little settee with a low table in front permits the necessary closeness to begin a relationship. As many American business men have discovered, the home is *not* the setting that a Latin American chooses to consummate a business deal. The home is for the family and not for business.

In Japan, business men often take the preliminary steps in a negotiation on the golf course. As one oil executive put it, "We soon learned, from the num-ber of golf games involved, how to compute the size of the contract we were going to negotiate."

Even on familiar home ground in the United States, there are instances when inferences drawn from spatial behavior have proved to be in error. This type of mistake can be due either to socio-economic or regional differences in the background of the two individuals. Courting provides us with some excel-lent examples of breakdown in the adumbrative phase that is often serious enough to kill a budding romance. Difficulties of this type have been fully de-scribed in our printed folk literature. I would like, however, to use one of my own examples because it seems quite appropriate.

In the early thirties, when automobiles were just beginning to be commonly used for courting, where the girl sat when she entered the car foreshadowed what kind of evening the couple was going to have. This was particularly true of the first date. The convention in my part of the country was for a "nice" girl to sit as far away from the driver as she could get (which wasn't very far). There was, however, a category of female, a member of a particular subculture, for whom it was not only permissible but customary to "snuggle up" to her date, even on a first night out, without the slightest intention of putting ideas into his head about what kind of a girl she was. Undoubtedly there were boys who were sufficiently motivated to surmount this particular source of adumbrative interference in communication when they faced it for the first time, and who eventually pieced together successfully the foreshadowing features of each successive stage in the courtship. In most instances, however, reproductive isolation was successfully maintained. Those I have talked to who ran afoul of this difference in pattern were so frustrated by it that they gathered up what was left of their wounded egos, said good night, and quickly shifted their attention to women in whom there was a more predictable connection between what one observed and what was going on inside.

Some of the most familiar instances of adumbrations in which the feelings are at variance with the overt behavior pattern are those having to do with where people stand and sit in relation to each other and whether they touch each other. There is, first of all, a large group in which touching is important, even with strangers. An equally numerous group of people avoids touching. Those who are not used to being approached closely are made uncomfortable by the laying-on of hands and take it as preliminary to either a fight or a sexual "pass."

Stated this way, there seems to be nothing mysterious about adumbrative communication and, *in fact, the idea is deceptively simple*. My hypothesis is that the specific technical communication on the overt level is seldom seriously misinterpreted, even in cross-cultural contexts, if the adumbrative part is read correctly. What is most often misinterpreted is the adumbration. In some instances, this can be serious enough to prevent the real communication from ever emerging or even to result in a fight.

In the course of this discussion, nothing has been said about transitions or juncture phenomena in transcultural encounters, mostly because virtually nothing is known about it. Our own version of Western culture seems to emphasize the build-up or attack phase and to pay little attention to the equivalent of terminal junctures and transitions. Yet I recall numerous instances when I was forced to look back on a sequence of events that seemed to be going well at the time and reappraise what I thought was going on because of an ending that appeared abrupt. In most instances it was impossible to judge whether things went well or badly until someone familiar with the local dialect of behavior could be consulted.

SUMMARY

In this article there has been no attempt to be definitive, and only broad outlines have been sketched. In summary, the view seems to be gaining currency that communication occurs simultaneously on several levels in depth, as well as proceeding sequentially according to quite rigid but unstated rules. How a given communication sequence develops can be seen as a function of the strength of motivations of the two parties, their knowledge of the system, and how they respond to each others' adumbrations. All communication in this sense can be viewed as a discourse, even though different styles (Joos 1962) are used, while ability to participate in the discourse is a function of programming.

In the display sequences of animals, we find simple models of behavior that may have relevance to man within cultures and across cultures. The study of animal behavior is relevant because man does not experience as much difficulty with speech (even if the language is different) as he does with these older, more primitive, and possibly more basic communications which are currently in the early stages of examination. In the larger sense, display is seen to perform important functions in evolution and in population control which may also be of some relevance to man.

NOTES

[1] See also Sebeok (1962) for integration of ethological data with information theory; Reusch and Kees (1956) use an information theory model but not a linguistic one as a point of departure.

[2] For a more detailed treatment of display, the reader is referred to Hinde and Tinbergen (1958).

[3] It is also distortion, or absence, of normal adumbrative functions that makes the assaultive psychotic so dangerous. Personnel treating such patients are in constant danger until they learn to pick up the subtle signs that foretell impending aggression.

[4] One of the consequences of overcrowding may be that there is not enough room for proper display.

REFERENCES CITED

BOAS, FRANZ
  1911   Introduction. In Handbook of American Indian languages, F. Boas, ed. Bulletin of the Bureau of American Ethnology, vol. 40, part I. Washington, D.C.
BATESON, G.
  1960   Minimal requirements for a theory of schizophrenia. A.M.A. Archives of General Psychiatry 2:477–491.
  1963   Exchange of information about patterns of human behavior. In Information storage and neural control, W. Fields and W. Abbott, eds. Springfield, Ill., 1–12.
CARROLL, JOHN B.
  1956   Language, thought and reality. Selected writings of Benjamin Lee Whorf. New York.
CHRISTIAN, JOHN J.
  1961   Phenomena associated with population density. Proceedings National Academy of Sciences 47 (April):428–449.
DEEVEY, E. S.
  1960   The hare and the haruspex: a cautionary tale. American Scientist 48(3):415.
EIBL-EIBESFELDT, I.
  1961   The fighting behavior of animals. Scientific American 207 (December):112–122.
GILLIARD, E.
  1962   On the breeding behavior of the cock-of-the-rock (aves, rupicola rupicola). Bulletin of the American Museum of Natural History, vol. 124, article 2. New York.
  1963   The evolution of bowerbirds. Scientific American 209(2):38–46.
GOFFMAN, E.
  1957   Alienation from interaction. Human Relations 10 (1): 46–60.
  1959   The presentation of self in everyday life. New York.

GREENBERG, J.
1959a Language and evolution. *In* Evolution and anthropology, Betty Meggers, ed. Washington, D.C.
1959b Current trends in linguistics. Science 130(No.3383):1165–1170.
HALL, E. T.
1955 The anthropology of manners. Scientific American 192:85–89.
1959 The silent language. New York.
1963a Proxemics—the study of man's spatial relations. *In* Man's image in medicine and anthropology, Iago Gladston, ed. New York.
1963b A system for the notation of proxemic behavior. American Anthropologist 65:1003–1026.
HALL, E. T. and
G. L. TRAGER
1953 The analysis of culture. Washington, D.C., American Council of Learned Societies.
HEDIGER, H.
1955 Studies of the psychology and behaviour of captive animals in zoos and circuses. London.
HINDE, R. and
N. TINBERGEN
1958 The comparative study of species' specific behavior. *In* Behavior and evolution, Anne Roe and G. G. Simpson, eds. New Haven.
HOCKETT, C. F.
1958 A course in modern linguistics. New York.
HYMES, D.
1962 The ethnography of speaking. *In* Anthropology and human behavior, T. G. Gladwin and W. C. Sturtevant, eds. Washington, D.C., pp. 15–53.
JOOS, M.
1962 The five clocks. Supplement to International Journal of American Linguistics 28, part V. Bloomington.
KLUCKHOHN, C.
1943 Covert culture and administrative problems. American Anthropologist 45:213–227.
LINTON, R.
1936 The study of man. New York.
PIERCE, T.
1956 Electrons, waves and messages. New York.
RUESCH, J.
1961 Therapeutic communication. New York.
RUESCH, J. and
W. KEES
1956 Nonverbal communication. Berkeley and Los Angeles.
SAPIR, EDWARD
1921 Language. New York.
1925 Sound patterns in language. Language 1:37–51.
1927 The unconscious patterning of behaviour in society. *In* The unconscious: a symposium, E. S. Dummer, ed. New York.
SCHALLER, G. B.
1963 The mountain gorilla. Chicago.
SEBEOK, T. A.
1962 Coding in the evolution of signalling behavior. Behavioral Science 7:430–442.
SHANNON, C. A. and
W. WEAVER
1949 The mathematical theory of communication. Urbana, Ill.
SIVADON, P.
Ms. Techniques of sociotherapy.

SULLIVAN, H. S.
  1947 Conceptions of modern psychiatry. Washington, D.C.
TINBERGEN, N.
  1954 The origins and evolution of courtship and threat display. *In* Evolution as a
        process, A. C. Hardy, T. S. Huxley and E. B. Ford, eds. London.
WIENER, N.
  1948 Cybernetics. New York.

ATTITUDE FORMATION
AND OPINION DEVELOPMENT

The announcement on August 30, 1961, that the Soviet Union planned to resume atmospheric tests of nuclear and thermonuclear bombs caused considerable public outrage throughout the world. In October, eighty-seven national delegations at the United Nations sponsored a joint resolution appealing to the Soviet Union to refrain from exploding its preannounced fifty-megaton bomb. On October 30, when Soviet Ambassador Valerian Zorin verified that the Soviet Union had set off a bomb even larger than fifty megatons, American Ambassador Adlai Stevenson stated tersely: "They have contemptuously spurned the appeal of the United Nations and of all peace-loving peoples." Ambassador Stevenson emphasized on November 15 that the Soviet Union "becomes doubly answerable to world opinion. The world will look to them in this debate to answer not one but two burning questions: do you or don't you want disarmament? and—once again—do you or don't you want an end to nuclear weapons, in fact or just in rhetoric?" Immediately following Stevenson's address, Zorin sharply chided him for "upbraiding" the Soviet Union:

> Excuse me, Mr. Representative of the United States, you came out against our position not from the point of view of the general demand of mankind, but from the point of view of your own military interests. . . . There is not a shred of humanism, not an iota of humanitarian consideration that you need now; what you need, what you preserve, is the military interest of the United States. There is your humanism; there is your morality, Mr. Representative of the United States. Therefore, it is not suitable for you to preach to us [Prosser 1969: 313–315].

In the 1967 Middle East Crisis, Yumjaagiin Tsedenbal, Chairman of the Council of Ministers of the Mongolian People's Republic, condemned Israel in the Fifth Special Emergency Session of the United Nations because "World public opinion is deeply indignant at the bestial violence and arbitrary atrocities inflicted by the Israeli invaders on their victims. . . . We are here witnesses of a crime against humanity, a crime forbidden by international law. This is an open and blatant case of aggression which should be condemned as an act of international brigandage. This is required by the conscience of mankind itself" (Tsedenbal 1970: 1200). Prime Minister Mohammad Hashim Maiwandwal of Afghanistan argued that the Israeli aggression had placed the world organization "on trial before humanity": "If, in this crucial moment, the United Nations yields to the aggressor and fails to eliminate the consequences of the aggression, the world's faith in the Organization will be shaken, while the Israeli extremists will consider such a failure of the world body as a monumental reward for their acts of aggression" (Maiwandal 1970: 1211–1219).

It is obvious that sentiments directed toward an "indignant world opinion," "the appeals of all peace-loving states," "the conscience of mankind," and "the world's faith in the United Nations" can be offered with equal fervor by American, socialist, and neutral diplomats. At the same time, public opinion polls of segments of populations are taken to demonstrate the formation of attitudes and opinions that are widely considered representative. For example, in Israel, after the Six-Day War, the Research Institute Dahaf polled almost five hundred Arab men in forty Arab localities in Israel, and the pro-Arab newspaper Davar published the results showing that these Arabs living in Israel believed that a new war with the Arab states would come in two years, that had the Arabs won, "our position would have been worse," that the Arab leaders had "betrayed their people," and that, with some reservations, closer ties should be made with the Jews. In fact, although as many as 22 percent refused to answer some questions relating to the war, 79 percent of the Arabs responded that they were willing to live in the same town with Jews; 74 percent would live in the same neighborhood; 55 percent would live in the same house; and 59 percent would want their children and Jewish children to attend the same schools. Of the respondents, 76 percent considered themselves as Israeli Arabs in contrast to Palestinians, Arabs, or Israelis. Davar offered its own bias to the results of the poll:

The following public opinion poll on what the Arabs of Israel believe following the Six Day War is significant, not only for the insight into what this important minority thinks but as a clue to Israel as to her relations with the now-hostile Arab world. It has been said often, and truthfully, that Israel's Arab citizens could be the bridge to peace with Israel's neighbors. The poll should be a considerable help in crystallizing the thinking of the Israel regime [Davar 1967].

In a public opinion poll, sponsored by Radio Free Europe, of 10,500 West Europeans and 5,654 East Europeans visiting in eight European countries within the first year after the Six-Day War, the researchers concluded that East European and West European public opinion coincided on the Arab-Israeli issue, indicating a common European public opinion. Pro-Israeli sentiment in both sections of Europe tended to subside from the high emotional peak during and immediately after the June 1967 war, though pro-Israeli attitudes still exceeded pro-Arab sympathies by a wide margin (47 percent to 11 percent in Eastern Europe and 39 percent to 5 percent in Western Europe). In Eastern Europe, age, educational background, and the political allegiance of the respondents played an important part in determining their sympathies with strong pro-Israeli sentiment among better educated and anti-communist population groups, whereas pro-Arab support came almost exclusively from regime supporters. The majority of East Europeans who sided with either the Israelis or the Arabs also wanted their countries to give active support to the side they favored. Finally, opinion among East Europeans was in sharp conflict with the Soviet pro-Arab policy and as reflected officially by the East

European governments, except in Romania, where both citizens polled and the government were highly pro-Israeli [Radio Free Europe 1968].

The concept both of a world public opinion and of selective polls present problems in understanding the role of attitude formation and opinion development, despite the success of the latter in preelection polls. Leo Bogart, currently vice-president and general manager of the Bureau of Advertising for the ANPA questions in this section's first essay, "Is There a World Public Opinion?" whether or not the concept of world opinion is a reality to study and contend with or a rhetorical artifact. Although he agrees that public opinion polling has taken on world-wide proportions, the term as related to polling takes on a considerably different meaning than the collective representation of mankind concept. He argues that there is no responsible political mechanism involved in world public opinion analogous to that in a national state. And even on a comparative basis between states, it is difficult to equate the public opinion of a highly literate society vs. a preliterate state. That public opinion causes either "the revolution of rising expectations" as Dr. Kenneth D. Kaunda, President of the Republic of Zambia (1970: 1103–1116), suggested or the "revolution of rising frustrations" afflicting the developing countries is questionable. Bogart and Lasswell (1953) agree that when opinion can be moulded into action, violence and revolution do occur either nationally or cross-nationally. Still, the actual revolution is often sparked by a single accident of history. Bogart insists that "the opinions of mankind" on major issues are simply platitudes about peace, economic growth, scientific progress, and their opposites. Such broad consensus through the ranks of humanity may exist. Bogart suggests, "perhaps on the rules of interpersonal conduct: hospitality to guests, deference to the aged, courtesy to strangers."

Among the problems of opinion polls, Arthur Kornhauser (1950) lists as the core issue the question: "Do the inclinations or prepossessions of those responsible for an opinion survey lead to results and conclusions that are one-sided, untrue, or misleading in reference to what they purport to describe?" He suggests two elements in judging bias, the detection of flaws, which means that opinions under study are misrepresented, and the interpretation, which ascribes these errors to predispositions or desires of the researcher. A suggestion of the suspicion that rural Japanese might hold for such a respected American political opinion analyst as Douglas Mendel, Jr. (1969), is seen in questions that would be typical for Americans or Western-oriented Japanese in which they respond "yes," "no" or "I don't know." Some rural Japanese would respond "I don't know" meaning "You are an American, and how could you therefore ask me such questions?" or "Of course I have an opinion, but it is my duty to take in information, and not to give it out." Herbert Blumer (1948) notes the inability of public-opinion polling to isolate public opinion as an abstract or generic concept that could thereby become the focal point for the formation of a system of propositions. He believes that opinion analysts are afflicted naturally by bias because they are so wedded to their technique and so preoccupied by its improvement that they shunt aside the vital question of whether the technique is suited to the study of what they are ostensibly seeking to study. Blumer recommends these criteria for judging public opinion studies: (1) Public opinion must obviously be recognized as having its setting in a particular society and as being a function of that society in operation. (2) The society has its own organization and is not an aggregation of disparate individuals. (3) Since the society is made up of varying functional groups, they must act through the channels available to them in their society. (4) The decision makers are almost inevitably confronted with the necessity of assessing the various influences, claims, demands, urgings, and pressures that are brought to bear on them. (5) Public opinion is formed and expressed in large measure through the functional composition and organization of the society, often forming attitudes and moulding opinions through the unequal interaction and participation of disparate individuals wielding entirely different kinds of influences. (6) Public opinion consists realistically in the patterns of diverse views and positions on the issue that come to the individuals who have to act in response to public opinion (Blumer 1948).

The second essay in this section, by Council of Europe official Gerard Herberichs, "On Theories of Public Opinion and International Organization," is in agreement with Bogart that public opinion as a dynamic and constructive force shaping international or national policy does not exist. At best, public opinion is almost exclusively a power to say no, and at worst, the final power to revolt. Nevertheless, international organization theorists attach very special importance to public opinion, considering it their most promising ally, for they believe that the voice of public opinion is the voice of reason, justice, and the universal conscience of mankind. The Hague Convention of 1907, the League of Nations, and the Universal Declaration of Human Rights all undertake to establish international law defining public opinion. Herberichs treats the role of public opinion as a presumed factor in relation to international organizations and moves toward what he believes is a realistic theory based on the constructs of Maurice Hauriou, who attempted to demonstrate that institutions, once they are created without the public's intervention, subsequently do need the active support of the public, which has the final power either to accept or reject them.

Although diplomats at the United Nations obstensibly speak to the peoples of the world in behalf of their own national public, their primary audience actually consists of their fellow diplomats. No matter how influential they are with their home governments, most of them are governmental spokesmen rather than policy makers (Prosser 1963, 1965, 1969). Jack E. Vincent, in "The Convergence of Voting and Attitude Patterns at the United Nations" (1969), assumes that the delegates possess influence potential, which sometimes allows them to make decisions without directions from their home governments and frequently allows them to inform their governments, inserting their personal evaluations, about how attitudes ought to change in relation to particular issues facing their delegation. Several studies (for example, Hovet 1960) have attempted to assess state attitudes, but few have evaluated the individuals' attitudes, which considerably affect the development of the opinion of the home governmental decision makers. Despite the exploratory nature of the study, Vincent feels justified in questioning whether or not attitudes and voting patterns at the United Nations would persist as new developments occur, for example, in relation to the dimension of the Western Community as a predictor of United Nations voting.

The original hypothesis, "Ideas often flow from radio and print to the opinion leaders and from them to the less active sections of the population" (Lazarsfeld, Berelson, and Gaudet 1948), has been revised and retested continuously since it was first proposed. The importance of the two-step flow theory has been considerable in the development of public-opinion studies, both in the United States and abroad. Among the frequently cited studies have been the Katz revision (1957), in which he stresses the functioning of interpersonal relations as communication networks and as sources of social pressure or support, and van den Ban's revision (1964), in which he argues that people generally develop their opinions from personal friends or acquaintances and only secondarily by the mass media. He concluded that when people urgently need information, the two-step process is more frequent, but they usually go directly to high social status people, and the relation between pioneering and opinion leadership is closer in progressive than in traditional groups. In his essay printed here, "The Two-Step Flow Theory: Cross-Cultural Implications," Lloyd R. Bostian reviews the varied revisions, including the Katz and van den Ban studies. Bostian's own conclusions are that the two-step flow hypothesis explains very few communication situations and is too simple a concept for great utility in explaining the process of communication. He recommends further research on the hypothesis, and indeed, the essays by van den Ban and Dasgupta in the section on communication as agent and index of social change do test the hypothesis further. Bostian suggests, first, that research is needed which separates the relay function from the influence function. Second, we need to reevaluate our ideas about the flow of information, especially the concept that an opinion leader is a voluntary transmitter of information. Third, we must specify the type of information being transmitted and consider its utility to the receiver.

In his essay, "Misconstruction and Problems in Communication," anthropologist Brian M. DuToit relates an incident that affected the attitudes of east central highlanders of Australian New Guinea while he was conducting a year of anthropological fieldwork there among the Gadsup linguistic group. The events that preceded and accompanied the solar eclipse of 1962 in New Guinea produced what DuToit calls the preconditions for a movement of cultural revitalization among the natives with whom he was working. Offered as a case study, it shows the kind of misinterpretation and misrepresentation that frequently occurs where linguistic and cultural barriers compound administrative problems. This study suggests a field for research—for example, to uncover millenarian patterns in mythical traditions—in which anthropologists and folklorists can successfully participate.

In his essay "Consensus and Dissent in Ghana," Jack Goody relates his experience in Ghana before and after the coup against Nkrumah in which a sudden and complete reversal in belief, commitment, ideology, consensus, attitudes, and opinion occurred. Before the coup, there was no community of dissent, but Nkrumah's successor, Colonel Kotaka, told Goody that he had predicted that 95 percent of the people would be in favor of the coup, eliminating any need for bloodshed. Consensus about the immediate past was overwhelming and became largely negative by emphasizing the mistakes of the Nkrumah regime. Although university students rejected the one-party government, no coherent opinion could be found about what future directions Ghana should consider, ranging from an elimination of party politics altogether to a desire for a prolonged army rule. Goody believes that a major problem facing the development of political attitudes in countries such as Ghana lies in the inherent economic and social situation of the third world, in which citizens are almost entirely dependent upon the government for employment and social development. Goody warns that Western academic observers must avoid stressing Western models related to political attitude change in third-world countries in which a strange mixture of Western and tribal mythology and beliefs coincide in the development of a sense of nationhood.

The final essay is methodological. In "Interviewing Cross-Culturally," Hal Fisher assesses the core of the problem of perfecting the techniques of analyzing attitudes and taking opinion polls as conducting successful interviews. He considers the relationship between the interviewer and interviewee across cultural boundaries, the informant's own setting, problems caused by holding interviews in either the interviewer's or the interviewee's second language or through translation, and the equivalencies of meaning between interviewer and informant. As a methodological essay, it accepts the objective of Hunt, Crane, and Walke that interviews are most useful as tools for genuine comparative behavioral research. Fisher adds that by constructing scientifically rigorous interviews, the researcher will gain an understanding of attitudes, opinions, and cultural values that serve as a link for communication among peoples.

REFERENCES CITED

BLUMER, HERBERT
   1948   Public opinion and public opinion polling. American Sociological Review 13:542–547.
HOVET, THOMAS, JR.
   1960   Bloc politics in the United Nations. Cambridge, Mass.
KATZ, ELIHU
   1957   The two-step flow of communication: an up-to-date report on an hypothesis. Public Opinion Quarterly 21:61–78.
KAUNDA, KENNETH D.
   1970   The revolution of rising expectations. In Sow the wind, reap the whirlwind: heads of state address the United Nations. Michael H. Prosser, ed. New York.
KORNHAUSER, ARTHUR
   1950   The problem of bias in opinion research. In Reader in public opinion and communication. Bernard Berelson and Morris Janowitz, eds. New York.
LASSWELL, HAROLD D.
   1950   Democracy through public opinion. In Reader in public opinion and communication. Bernard Berelson and Morris Janowitz, eds. New York.
LAZERFELD, PAUL F., BERNARD BERELSON, and
HAZEL GAUDET
   1948   Time of final decision. The people's choice: how the voter makes up his mind in a Presidential campaign. New York.

MAIWANDAL, MOHAMMED HASHIM
   1970   Can a country invade another country and dictate its own terms? *In* Sow the wind, reap the whirlwind: heads of state address the United Nations. Michael H. Prosser, ed. New York.
MENDEL, DOUGLAS H., JR.
   1969   Japanese opinion on key foreign policy issues. Asian Survey August: 625–639.
PROSSER, MICHAEL H.
   1963   Communication problems in the United Nations. Southern Speech Journal Winter: 125–132.
   1965   Adlai E. Stevenson's audience in the United Nations. Central States Speech Journal November.
   1969   An ethic for survival: Adlai Stevenson speaks on international affairs, 1936–1965. New York.
RADIO FREE EUROPE
   1968   The Arab-Israeli conflict and public opinion in Eastern Europe (including a comparison with West European opinion). Radio Free Europe December: 35 pp. and appendix.
TSEDENBAL, YUMJAAGIIN
   1970   We are witnesses of a crime against humanity. *In* Sow the wind, reap the whirlwind: heads of state address the United Nations. Michael H. Prosser, ed. New York.
VAN DEN BAN, A. W.
   1964   A revision of the two-step flow of communication hypothesis. Gazette 10:237–250.

IS THERE
A WORLD PUBLIC OPINION?*
Leo Bogart

LEO BOGART *is executive vice-president and general manager of the Bureau of Advertising, American Newspaper Publishers Association. He is a fellow of the American Sociological Association and of the American Psychological Association. He is a past president of the American Association for Public Opinion Research and of the World Association for Public Opinion Research. He is author of* Strategy in Advertising, The Age of Television, Social Research and the Desegregation of the U.S. Army, *and editor of* Current Controversies in Marketing Research. *This paper, delivered as an address before a WAPOR regional congress in Yugoslavia in 1965, appears in a modified form in Bogart's book* Feedback, *to be published by Wiley in 1972.*

The phrase "world public opinion" acquires ever more widespread currency as international organizations apply collective pressure in an effort to keep the peace. In 1965, world opinion was cited by statesmen in various countries to support their positions on such matters as the Greek Constitutional crisis, the American use of teargas in Viet Nam, the Pakistani-Indian war, and the unsuccessful coup in Indonesia. In the United States, mounting doubts have been raised about the significance of world opinion as a reference point for foreign policy. Can a great power expect universal love and approval to pursue its national goals? The assumption behind such a question is that world opinion may be weak or ill-informed, *not* that it does not exist.

Is "world opinion" a reality to study and contend with? Or is it no more than a rhetorical artifact, a latterday version of the particularistic and protective Deity who served every national cause in the wars of the past?

INTERNATIONAL OPINION OR INTERNATIONAL RESEARCH?

It is impossible to speak of public opinion today except in relation to the measurements made in surveys. By this criterion, the emergence of polling on an international scale suggests that public opinion is itself now a world-wide phenomenon. But does multi-national polling prove any more than that parallel research exercises may be carried out in many places at once, like the spring maneuvers of armies not allied?

The term "public opinion" as used in polling is quite distinct from the concept of public opinion as a "collective representation" or state of mind, diffuse,

Reprinted with permission of Steinmetz Institute, publishers of *Polls* and the author, *Polls* (Spring 1966), pp. 1–9.

* This article is an adaptation of a paper originally presented before the Eastern European Regional Conference of the World Association for Public Opinion Research, Dubrovnik, Yugoslavia, May 1965.

shapeless and shifting as a cloud. It is also distinct from the concept of public opinion as a force interacting with other sources of political power.

Opinion research has introduced a new element of self-consciousness into the relationship between leaders and peoples. During the period 1939–1941, President Franklin D. Roosevelt took a number of actions aimed to help the Western Allies without bringing America into the war. These measures were taken with cautious awareness of what public opinion polls showed about the complex feelings of the American people toward the European conflict. Naturally, Roosevelt's actions, like any strong executive behavior, had important consequences in the evolution of public sentiment. It is of interest to compare this feedback process with the decisions taken by President Lincoln at the outset of the Civil War, when the real condition of public opinion in the Northern States could be evaluated only by judgment and not by poll statistics. How different would Roosevelt's actions have been if he had not had opinion survey data, or Lincoln's if he had?

To measure opinion demands that there be a definable universe, a particular public, whose true dimensions can be sampled. The base may be described in terms of political geography, or it can be further limited in demographic terms, still within the boundaries of some political entity.

Public opinion polling implies that there are common yardsticks, meanings and terms of reference among the people questioned. This implies further the existence of a social-political system whose unifying character is recognized by the public itself.

Does such a social system exist today on a world-wide scale? There are indeed certain signs to encourage cautious hopes that a world society is emerging: the trend toward universal cultural symbols, the diminution of distances and the growing interdependence of national economies. The dislocations of war, the expansion of trade in peacetime, and the incredible growth of air transportation have all made for an enormous increase in personal mobility across national boundaries. But the political ideal of a world order remains remote.[1]

Within a national state, "public opinion" implies the existence of an authority in some way responsible to the public, either directly, as in the ideology of avowed democracies, or in the traditional sense, in which the king or dictator rules "on behalf of" the people or of some divine national mission. Such a recognition is implicit even where a political ideology regards the mind of the masses as something to be played upon and controlled.[2] There is no "responsible" political mechanism involved in world public opinion analogous to that in the national state. International organizations like the United Nations have as their constituents individual national states rather than the world community at large.

The mechanics of survey research may help to create the illusion that opinions are international, because they can be traced from one country to the next. Polling results are commonly reported as percentages without regard to the intensity or certainty with which opinions are held. Thus, when the findings of cross-country surveys are published, the implication is that similar answers to the same questions reflect similar salience or significance for these questions in different countries. Yet, identical responses may emerge by coincidence from entirely different causes, or in entirely separate historical or cultural contexts. Similar percentages responding "yes" in Italy and England, say, may actually reflect deep-seated convictions in one case and in the other no more than a conventional playback of the prevailing views expressed by the institutions of mass persuasion.

For understandable pragmatic reasons, reports of multi-national surveys customarily ignore this type of qualitative distinction. What is the meaning of "public opinion" in societies where literacy is universal and where the media are highly developed, compared to its meaning in those societies whose mass media are within access of only a small literate elite? Can the same phrase, "public opinion," be applied in countries which enjoy a high degree of political freedom and those in which deviant utterance is repressed or discouraged? Can one regard "public opinion" as comparable in countries where polls are a familiar part of the life of politics and marketing and countries in which the state of public opinion is itself a matter of diverse opinion among experts? Such questions raise their own doubts about the meaningfulness of a world opinion which takes so many different shapes.

OPINION, SOCIAL ACTION AND SOCIAL REVOLUTION

Public opinion is a twilight realm between the learning of information and overt behavior. Many recent research findings lead us to the conclusion that these domains are not wholly interdependent. A change in information does not necessarily lead to change in opinions. Behavior appears to be particularly resistant to change even when the verbal expression of opinion *does* shift.

There are remarkably few authenticated instances of behavioral change directly attributable to changes of opinion induced by exposure to persuasive argument.[3] Laboratory experiments have shown under controlled conditions what recent history illustrates in gruesome detail—that people can be readily induced to behave in contradiction to their deeply felt opinions and moral standards, provided that they have some kind of socially acceptable rationale (such as "obedience to authority") to sustain them.

Leon Festinger's theory of cognitive dissonance has described the mechanisms by which human beings rationalize their beliefs and unconsciously resolve or reduce the apparent discrepancies among their opinions. One signal contribution of this theory is that it forces all those who study public opinion to acknowledge that the data we work with—what people tell us in interviews— are inseparable from personal value-systems *in toto* and cannot be dealt with as isolated facts, or as facts with an independent reality.

Just as the individual minimizes tension by "bridging" the inconsistencies of his beliefs, so does he minimize any threat to his complacency by the mechanisms of selective self-exposure to information and opinion-forming media, and by selective perception of messages within media. Consciously and unconsciously we seek and see what we want to see—we confirm what we already believe.

Theories of public opinion and theories of social revolution have developed in the same epoch with remarkably little cross-reference. Social revolution may emerge from the force of a public opinion whose expression finds no legitimate channels. But it may also result from the effectively organized actions of a minority which seizes control of state institutions and thereby acquires legitimacy, authority and leadership over public opinion itself. For reasons which are only now being clarified by experimental studies of attitude change, when people are forced to accommodate to a changed social order, the need for consistency impels them to adopt many of the explanations by which the new order justifies itself.[4] Direct social pressure and restricted access to alternative viewpoints may be less important in bringing about this change than the inner need to feel comfortable with what one outwardly accepts.

Yet, even when public opinion is considered from this perspective, it is apparent that social revolution, with rare exceptions, has taken place within the framework of national states. Even when revolution has been international, it has not been world-wide.

OPINION AND CONSENSUS

To speak of "the opinions of mankind" (as the American Declaration of Independence did in 1776) implies that there are subjects of broad consensus throughout the ranks of humanity. Are there indeed such subjects? Perhaps on the rules of interpersonal conduct: hospitality to guests, deference to the aged, courtesy to strangers.

Public opinion arises not from agreement but from conflicts in values. Opinion implies the articulation of a point of view which can be recorded and measured. Consensus is simply not measurable in the same terms as opinion. Only those subjects on which there is no consensus are controversial and provocative of opinion, of divergent answers to the same questions.[5] When we move from comparative anthropology to the most sophisticated spheres of political or economic thought, the collective opinions of mankind on major issues (peace, economic growth, scientific progress) resolve into a series of platitudes. Lack of agreement about means rather than ends represents the chief obstacle to a world-wide public opinion.

In the famous Eleventh Edition of the *Encyclopaedia Britannica*, an article on Balkan history refers to the shocked reaction of "world public opinion" to atrocities committed in the course of the Greek war for independence. If one can speak of an articular international public opinion in the 1820's, can one speak of an incensed public opinion at the time of the Crusades, of the Hun invasions, or of the Goths and Vandals centuries earlier?

It is interesting that this kind of early reference to public opinion finds its clearest expression as a sense of outrage. At this point it is no longer opinion at all in an intellectual sense, but rather a state of emotional shock, a visceral response of readiness for action. Such a reaction is what people normally feel when they learn of a particularly vicious crime. To the extent that the crime itself is important or interesting enough to come to the attention of the entire community, there is a common instinctive feeling that something must be done. This kind of clear-cut emotional response cries for expression and action.

When opinion is divorced from it, its nuances are infinitely more difficult to trace and test; it is harder to find a consistent point of view. A vague or confused state of public opinion crystallizes into sharp divisions when specific alternative choices are in the balance. It is only through action that opinion influences history. On the great issues of the time opinion may move in fits and starts, by jumps and leaps, rather than by a slow process of change or attrition.

PUBLIC OPINION AND THE MASS MEDIA

The identification of public opinion with survey findings means that it is often talked about as though it were an unconnected series of attitudes on discrete subjects ranging from the flavor of toothpaste to the exploration of the moon. In fact it represents a unified though inconsistent perception of the world, shaped in large measure by selective experience of it through the mass media. This is not to say that media opinion is public opinion, which is rarely the case in any society. But it is inconceivable for a "public opinion" to exist in a society into which there is no means of injecting ideas and information on a massive scale.

There may be a form of public opinion in a pre-literate society without any media, but this kind of "opinion" is almost indistinguishable from the social mores as such. In impoverished pre-industrial countries the messages of the mass media are carried by word-of-mouth far beyond the primary audience to reach many people who themselves have no direct contact with radio, television or the press.

For the past hundred years, sociologists have been intrigued by the contrast between folk and industrial society. Industrial society is by definition a complex order full of internal contradictions and conflicts among antagonistic groups and social classes. Its values and beliefs are not universally shared. The classic view of a folk society is one of simple structure and commonly held beliefs. But today every folk society must contend with an increased flow of new information and with the repercussions of events in the world at large. The common symbol of this is the Bedouin on his camel looking up at the jet airplane in the sky. Even in the most primitive areas of the world today there is at least a dim awareness that the price of salt or kerosene is in some way influenced by the decisions of powerful men a long way off. The names of these men and the slogans that identify them are known even in the depths of the bush.

Broadcasting changes the requirement that public opinion be dependent on mass literacy. Broadcasting makes significant personalities and events familiar to more people; perhaps even more important, it creates an illusion of such familiarity where this may not be justified. Power over broadcasting is generally more concentrated than control of the press; moreover, nation-wide broadcasting systems tend to create a centralized common experience, while the reading of a newspaper or magazine is selective both in the reader's choice among periodicals and in his choice of items to read.

BARRIERS TO INTERNATIONAL MASS COMMUNICATION

In recent years there has been a rapid acceleration of the forces making for global unity of information and culture. But this tendency has taken place largely within the framework of national mass media systems rather than through international mass media, communicating directly with a world-wide audience. While specialized or technical publications have international audiences, and while the same is true for the living arts—literature, painting, music and theater—this kind of international public does not really exist for the mass media as we usually define them. Here tremendous barriers still exist.

1. First and foremost is the barrier of language. Most people in most countries are unable to communicate except in their native tongue. And even among those who know other languages, few indeed have either the intellectual stamina or the incentive to eavesdrop, as it were, on broadcasts or publications addressed to the audience of another nationality.
2. Another barrier arises from differences in the mores of different societies. Even when they are clearly communicated, symbols do not necessarily signify the same meanings, nor do they have the same importance to people of different cultures. This is all the more serious because people tend to insulate themselves from experience or information which is in any way not in conformity with what is customary and comfortable. In an institutionalized form, this kind of barrier is defined as political or ideological in nature. Countries in many parts of the world and of varying political persuasions censor or restrict access to incoming foreign mass media in order to protect their citizens from communications which are deemed to be hostile, tendentious or false. Sometimes what appears to be a political barrier may actually have a very simple economic basis, as when countries limit the importance of films because they lack foreign exchange.
3. Media distribution across national boundaries is inhibited by a variety of nonpolitical factors: the expense or physical difficulty of transporting publications, records or films, the absence of needed equipment or trained technicians, the slowness of transport.
4. Finally, there are differences in the popular taste and interests of different cultures, as in the case of national games, dances and musical forms. This is often carried over into areas of intellectual content. In any case, the effect is to discourage voluntary exposure to media of non-local origins.

All these factors together have inhibited the emergence of international mass media, with only a few exceptions, of which the *Reader's Digest* is perhaps the most remarkable, since its editorial origins are predominantly American.

PICTURES OVER WORDS

Since the earliest years of this century, the motion picture has been a tremendous force for the creation of universal symbols and values and for the sharing of common human experiences. Seen in the dark, under conditions which arouse the most intense dramatic identification on the part of the audience, motion pictures can create empathy with protagonists who stem from a different culture, speak a strange language, and live in an unfamiliar geographic environment.

When this quality of audio-visual communication is translated through documentary television into the world-wide reporting of great events at the moment they happen, new possibilities are opened to the sharing of collective experience. So far, international television has been largely a matter of sports, entertainment and ceremony, like the funeral of Churchill. But the intensity with which strong mass sentiments can be mobilized, as at the time of the Kennedy assassination, suggests the beginnings of a new dimension in the creation of history.

James Reston, the noted columnist of the *New York Times*, has observed that "it is the almost instantaneous television reporting of the struggle in the streets of Selma, Alabama, that has transformed what would have been mainly a local event a generation ago into a national issue overnight. Even the segregationists who have been attacking the photographers and spraying black paint on their TV lenses understand the point." Consider the repercussions of this observation on a global scale.

The launching of communication satellites by both the United States and the Soviet Union represents a major event in international communication, with great implications for the creation of a world-wide public opinion. Within a few years it will become technically possible, with only minor adaptations, for both radio and television signals to be sent (or jammed) from any transmitter to any receiver in the world. But until this is a reality, the world-wide flow of ideas and information must depend on the national mass media systems which mediate, edit and interpret for their different audiences.

LIMITATION OF NATIONAL MASS MEDIA SYSTEMS

In all countries, socialist and capitalist alike, mass media tend to be devoted to recreation more than to information. They tend to be parochial in orientation and conservative in relation to the national power structure.

Each of these points deserves some expansion:

1. Media content is primarily entertaining rather than informative or political, when we consider the full spectrum of media exposure to most people in most countries. Typically, mass media are experienced as a pastime, as a form of relaxation rather than as instruction or enlightenment. Mass media content lends itself less to the creation of public opinion than to the establishment of commonly understood reference points. These may have technological or even political connotations, like Sputnik or Gemini, but more often they are in the domain of popular culture: The Beatles, Brigitte Bardot, Mickey Mouse. One of the curious byproducts of the newer mass media is that they have placed political figures, imaginary cartoon characters and movie actresses in the same fantasy world of stardom.

2. The mass media are essentially parochial in character. In every country they look at the world from a national perspective. They focus strongly on local interests and personalities. Not only in the press but in audio-visual media, the "news" tends to be what is happening close to home. Things happening nearby are perceived as familiar and amenable to control. Disproportionately little attention is typically paid to distant events of far greater ultimate consequence.

In my personal observation this parochialism exists in both socialist and capitalist countries, in industrialized and underdeveloped ones. It is true in spite of the existence of world-wide news services, in spite of shortwave broadcasting which reaches listeners across vast distances, in spite of the wide-spread dissemination of films, recordings and television programs. Those common threads of information which filter through all the many different selective nets of national media systems become world-wide knowledge in spite of those national systems and not because of them.

3. The mass media reflect the power structures of national states. This is clearly and unmistakably a matter of intention in those countries—including the socialist countries—where the media express the official position of the government or the Party and where they are assigned a definite mission in mobilizing public support for national policies. It is no less true in Western countries in which operational control of the mass media is in private hands, but where their financial foundation is inseparable from the prevailing economic institutions. (To be sure, mass media may be voices of dissent, outspoken or guarded, but rarely loud or powerful. Interestingly enough, the ideology of dissent is more often universal than nationalistic.) Whether under private or official control, mass media tend to be voices of conformity. This inherent conservatism reinforces their tendency to be parochial in outlook.

The psychoanalyst Harry Stack Sullivan refers to what he calls the "parataxic distortions" which arise in interpersonal conduct.[6] These distortions represent one individual's self-centered and particularistic views of events which involve other people. Sullivan is not concerned with paranoid delusions, but with the common misperceptions that arise in the stress and strain of ordinary interpersonal conduct. Private motivations and needs shape perception so that the same objective reality takes on completely different meaning in the eyes of two participants.

There is an obvious parallel between this type of neurotic behavior at the level of lovers, parents and child, husband and wife, superior and subordinate, rivals or competitors, and the behavior of nations engaged in a conflict of vital interest.

In the classical Chinese opera, the faces of the actors are painted in a mask-like manner to designate symbolically the character of the personages they portray: virtue, duplicity, vengefulness, etc. What the characters actually say and do is almost irrelevant because their true nature has already been revealed by the color of their face paint.

In today's mass media, particularly in wartime, not only cartoons and caricatures but verbal clichés and stereotypes are used to represent the character of the national adversary. What the adversary says or does may be irrelevant if his inherently evil nature is already known to us by the color of his mask. His motives are predictable, his actions can no longer be explained by the ordinary human standards. This kind of distortion is more or less generally true of the way in which media in most countries depict the outer world, and particularly those sectors they define as hostile.

Until national mass media systems overcome these limitations, it is hard to see how a world opinion can emerge.

WORLD OPINION AND PROFESSIONAL RESPONSIBILITY

The pollster who is engaged in multi-national research is apt to be especially sensitive to the subtle necessities of transcending his own national perspective. But every research practitioner must acquire such sensitivity if the growth of opinion surveys is itself to be an influence on the development of a world opinion.

There is a division between those who are concerned with analysis of the complexities of human nature and those who prefer to describe it in simple terms. Consider the "yes" or "no," the "either-or" of the classic opinion poll, whether it deals with political candidates or with commodity preferences. Is this not akin to the ideological "either-or" of the world view that divides humanity into two opposing camps? Political choices may perforce be clear-cut. Analytical judgments can seldom be so. Regardless of his personal commitments, his ideological loyalties, his social position, his economic or political self-interest, the pollster can only perform his job with competence if he performs it objectively.

There is a great temptation for public opinion research to follow the lead of the media, to deal in clichés and stereotypes, to simplify issues which are really extremely complex and subtle, to ask questions which assume that opinions can be polarized along ideological lines.

In constructing questionnaires, the professional researcher is trained to avoid terms which may be part of the working vocabulary of his own political environment: "the Free World," "the building of socialism," and the sinister epithets applied to the adversary. Yet, the political naiveté implicit in such terms may well intrude into the over-all concepts which shape the design and analysis of research.

Experiments have shown that it is possible to elicit opinions from some people on nonexistent subjects. It is all the easier to get opinions on matters which seem plausible because they are familiar but which really exist only in the mind of the questioner. When political clichés and nonsense terms enter the language of opinion research, they achieve an undeserved dignity and veil the truth both from the researcher and from those who take his findings seriously.[7]

The answers to questions in surveys should never be confused with the fluid changing reality of public opinion. When we consider the vague and ephemeral nature of many verbal expressions of attitude, their sensitivity to changes in question wordings, question sequence, and the authority of the questioner, we are made more aware of the vast difference between the reality of public opinion and our polling measurement of the Platonic shadow cast upon the wall of the cave.

Human nature is something more subtle, fragile and complex than what can be measured by a question which asks, "Do you agree or disagree?" Opinions are contradictory and illogical, subject to constant shifting and change. They are amenable to influence and evolution; they are swayed by crass material interest, but also by poetry. To the extent that this viewpoint governs the professional attitude of the opinion research practitioner, he may help foster that tolerance of diversity which is essential to the future history of this century if there is to be any future history at all.

Opinion surveys are being conducted throughout the world at an ever-accelerating pace. A common experience is shared by the Senegalese tribesman who is queried about the rising cost of living, the Siberian schoolgirl who reports on her favorite motion picture themes, and the Argentine housewife who reveals her motivations in serving maté. Once the survey mechanism is set in motion within a country, it cannot be confined to the trivia of consumer preference, because these can only be understood in the light of a deeper understanding of the values that men cherish. If a world public opinion can emerge from a world-wide consciousness of opinion, the research profession must be a major agency of change.

NOTES

[1] For an optimistic (and outdated) view, cf. Th. Ruyssen, "Existe-t-il une Opinion Internationale?" *L'Esprit International*, No. 45 (January, 1938), pp. 71–89.

[2] E.g., "The role that public opinion plays in America and Germany is very different. In the great 'democracy' on the other side of the ocean it has the function of a corporation whose millions of stockholders dictate the policy of the enterprise. In National Socialist Germany, it seems to us rather as the body of the people (*Volkskörper*) which receives its orders from the head and guarantees their accomplishment, so that through the working together of head and limbs transcendent political and cultural values can be achieved. In one case public opinion rules; in the other it is led." Elisabeth Noelle, *Meinung und Massenforschung in U.S.A.*, Frankfurt/Main, 1940, p. 1. The same author also quotes approvingly from Reichsminister Goebbels: "The people shall begin to think as a unit, to react as a unit and to place itself at the disposal of the government with complete sympathy" (*Ibid.*, p. 134).

[3] For a review of the evidence, cf. Leon Festinger, "Behavioral Support for Opinion Change," *Public Opinion Quarterly*, Vol. XXVIII, No. 3 (Fall, 1964), pp. 404–417.

[4] For a summary of the literature and theory on this subject, see the chapter on "The Effects of Enforced Discrepant Behavior" in Arthur R. Cohen, *Attitude Change and Social Influence*, New York, 1964.

[5] A Gallup poll a few years ago found that 96 percent of the American people believe in God and 61 percent in the Devil. God's existence is a matter of consensus; that of the Devil evidently a matter of opinion.

[6] Harry Stack Sullivan, *The Interpersonal Theory of Psychiatry*, New York, 1953.

[7] An illustration of this is to be found in Jean-Paul Sartre's cancellation of a 1965 lecture tour in the United States, not on the grounds that he disagreed with American policy on Viet Nam but because a survey showed this policy was approved by a majority of the American public.

ON THEORIES OF PUBLIC OPINION
AND INTERNATIONAL ORGANIZATION

Gerard Herberichs*

GERARD HERBERICHS, a Dutch national, was born in 1928. He studied law and
political science at the Universities of Leyde, Nijmogen (Netherlands) and Poitiers
(France). Dr. Herberichs was the foreign editor of a Dutch daily newspaper before
joining the Council of Europe where he was information officer and is now cultural
development officer. He has published a book on the councils of peace and international organization that have been held by modern popes, Theorie de la Paix
selon Pie XII (Paris, 1964), and many articles dealing with various aspects of
political science.

One of the most significant features of our time is the rapid progress
of international organization. The United Nations and the specialized agencies, despite the continuing absence of a country of 700 million
people, are rapidly developing into truly universal institutions.[1] At the same
time, regional intergovernmental organizations are springing up all over the
world. Their number is steadily expanding. The Yearbook of International
Organisations 1964–1965 lists 150 of them, the United Nations, the specialized agencies, and the three European Communities not included.[2] Not less
than 112 of them have been established since 1945.

The increasing popularity of institutionalized cooperation among governments cannot simply be explained as a temporary phenomenon, a matter of
fashion. International organization rather responds to a need which has always
existed but which has been intensified and made obvious by the prodigious
development of communications. As this development is likely to continue,
and even to accelerate its pace, the need for international organization, regionally as well as globally, will probably make itself felt with more and more
urgency. This of course amounts to saying that governments, in order to promote their national interests, are finding themselves more and more obliged
to have recourse to at least some forms of institutionalized cooperation. A kind
of irreversible process has thus been set in motion. Major conquests of civilization can never be done away with; we can only go forward on the road they
set. Proudhon might say that the necessity of international organization has
been "revealed" to modern society "by history"—or, more precisely, by the
development of communications.

To what extent is this process in step with, and representative of, the aspirations of men and women in the various countries of the world? Does public

Reprinted with permission of Public Opinion Quarterly, 30 (Winter 1966–1967),
624–636, and the author.

* The author is very grateful to his colleague, Dr. William Worsdale, who kindly
offered to translate all French quotations. Footnotes refer to the original sources from
which he translated.

111

opinion play any role in it? Can it play a role? Should it play a role? Such are the main themes to be touched upon in this article.

PUBLIC OPINION AS A NONEXISTING FORCE: ITS FUNCTION

Public opinion is usually defined as a social or political force. The function attributed to it is to exercise pressure or influence on leaders. Political theorists since Plato have given close attention to this phenomenon. David Hume, in his essay *Of the First Principles of Government*,[3] comes to the conclusion that all governments in the world, however despotic, are based upon opinion, and this view is shared by most modern writers.

This assertion seems to imply that public opinion is a dynamic and constructive force shaping policy or, at least, the broad lines of a policy. Experience shows, however, that this assumption is seldom confirmed, more particularly as far as foreign policy and international cooperation are concerned. By lack of interest, lack of knowledge, and lack of tools, the general public is prevented from playing any active and positive role. Its almost exclusive tool is of a negative nature: the power to say "No," that is, in the last analysis, to revolt. But in saying "Yes," the public does not really shape the course of events; it just allows things to run on, at least for a time, and it may very well be, especially with regard to foreign affairs, that such an attitude is the logical consequence of an almost complete absence of opinion.

What really matters, then, is the fact that the public at any time may react, notably by suddenly manifesting its anger. Precisely because public opinion is so uncertain and unpredictable, all those who are in power fear it. This, of course, is the factor that, apart from all considerations of institutional democracy, obliges decision makers to respect at least some limits and incites them to at least some moderation. This moderating influence is an essential function of public opinion. But what is stressed here is that public opinion, in order to make its impact felt, need not really exist. It is to be defined not so much as an actual but as a virtual force.

No power can ever be maintained by mere force; it always needs a minimum of, at least passive, popular consent. But, even in the long run, it can very well do without any active support of the public. It cannot be said, therefore, that government is really based upon opinion. For how could it be based on something which, in too many cases, does not exist?

OPTIMISTIC AND PESSIMISTIC IDEOLOGIES

Theorists of international organization attach very special importance to public opinion. They generally consider it to be their most promising ally, at least in the long run. Such an attitude is typical of propagators of new ideas. The future is their historical dimension: a golden age to come, a great task to be accomplished, a better world to be built for our children, etc. On the other hand, those who distrust public opinion seem rather to be oriented toward the past, in the sense of a more or less static established order. Here we find an additional explanation of the fact that all rulers, whatever be their régime, fear public opinion. Power is naturally conservative. The battle cries and revolutionary slogans best serve the opposition, i.e. the group that wields no power.

In the evaluation of public opinion we also find a characteristic difference between the more conservative and the more progressive temperament. On the one hand, those one might call the pessimists would not say, with Pascal, that "opinion rules the world like a queen," but rather that opinion is the world's tyrant. The pessimists will assert that it may be necessary to attach importance to public opinion, and even to give it an institutional place in the political system, but, they ask, what can be the value of this collective phenomenon? We know Plato's reply: "The public itself," he says, "is the great sophist."[4]

On the other hand, a second category of people, who might be called the optimists, show a tendency to place confidence in public opinion. Deep in their hearts, they believe that public opinion is equivalent to common sense; they believe that "the voice of public opinion" (provided, presumably, that it makes itself heard), is the voice of Reason, of Justice, of the Universal Conscience of Mankind. Here one has no trouble in recognizing a whole series of concepts dear to "democratic" ideology, and more specially left-wing democratic ideology. One will seldom find a true reactionary believing in public opinion.

Faith in public opinion is, however, not entirely a modern attitude. It is an irrational conviction that seems to have very deep and ancient roots, worthy of thorough psychoanalytical investigation. "Public opinion," says Aristotle (and here he tackles one of the points on which he completely disagrees with his master, Plato), "must be admitted to be not only an unavaoidable force but also, up to a point, a justifiable standard in politics. It is possible to argue . . . that in the making of law the collective wisdom of a people is superior to that of even the wisest lawgiver."[5] From the Middle Ages comes the well-known proverb, alleged to be Alcuin's reply to Charlemagne: Vox populi, vox Dei. And Mme. de Sévigné, contemporary of Blaise Pascal and Louis XIV, one century before the Revolution, wrote this remarkable sentence: "It has long been my view, for which I shall one day be taken to task, that the public is neither mad nor unjust."[6]

INTERNATIONALIST DOCTRINE: THE WORSHIP OF PUBLIC OPINION

Modern theorists of international organization invariably adopt the optimistic point of view. Still more significantly, from its very beginnings the modern idea of international organization was closely associated, explicitly, with the concept of public opinion and, implicitly, with the concept of democracy. We refer in particular to the late days of the Age of Reason, which was also the great era of Cosmopolitanism, ending with the American and French Revolutions. It is the period of Immanuel Kant's essay Zum ewigen Frieden (1795) and Jeremy Bentham's Plan for an Universal and Perpetual Peace (1789). Two new ideas, different but complementary, begin to make their way in the optimistic climate of the dying century. The first is that war is an evil that should be abolished; the second, that peace should be organized. Each of these ideas has a counterpart in a specific conception of public opinion. The first idea corresponds to the belief that public opinion is peace-loving; the second idea, to the belief that public opinion is a useful instrument, the main driving force to achieve international organization.

Condorcet, writing in 1786, refers to American public opinion as a stronghold against war: "A number of eloquent philosophers of the Old World, especially Voltaire, protested against the injustice and the absurdity of war; but they were scarcely able to do more than curb martial fury in a few respects. . . . In America, however, these peaceful opinions are those of a great people. . . . Any idea of a war prompted by ambition or desire for conquest withers there before the tranquil judgment of a humane and peaceful nation. There the language of humanity and justice cannot be held up to ridicule either by the warring courtesans of a king or by the ambitious leaders of a republic."[7] Elsewhere, he writes: "Institutions, better planned than these ideas of everlasting peace that have occupied the time of some philosophers and brought consolation to their souls, will speed up the progress of this brotherhood of nations."[8]

James Mill, disciple of Jeremy Bentham, writing in the years 1816 to 1823, recommends that "a code of international law" be drafted and published in the principal languages. Such publication would have two great advantages:

> The first would be that the intelligence of the whole world being brought to operate upon it, and suggestions obtained from every quarter, it might be made as perfect as possible. The second would be, that the eyes of all the world being fixed upon the decision of every nation with respect to the code, every nation might be deterred by shame from objecting to any important article in it. . . . A moral sentiment would grow up, which would, in time, act as a powerful restraining force upon the injustice of nations, and give a wonderful efficacy to the international jurisdiction.[9]

It is interesting to note that James Mill, in his first point, attributes an active and constructive role to public opinion—an idea which, we fear, has not often been confirmed. His belief in the virtue of publication is paralleled by Kant, who writes at the end of his essay that all maxims that need publicity in order to attain their aims are in accordance with both justice and politics.[10]

In 1828 William Ladd founded the American Peace Society. A circular letter, published on that occasion, described the movement's aim as the establishment of a "Congress of Christian nations." Public opinion was to play an essential role:

> We hope to increase and promote the practice already begun, of submitting national differences to amicable discussions and arbitration; and, finally, of settling all national controversies by an appeal to reason, as becomes rational creatures, and not by physical force, as is worthy only of brute beasts; and that this shall be done by a congress of Christian nations, whose decrees shall be enforced by public opinion that rules the world;—not by public opinion as it now is, but by public opinion when it shall be enlightened by the rays of the gospel of peace. . . .[11]

As early as 1829, the Society organized a competition of prize essays on the idea of a congress of nations. All successful authors dealt at some length with public opinion. One of them, writing under the name of Hamilton, asserted that the congress of nations "must be upheld by public opinion, or it cannot be efficient. This is indispensable to its success. What public opinion is and has been, in reference to this great plan of national reform, is but another form of enquiring what the condition of men is and has been in reference to it; and here we may confidently rest as on the strongest ground for belief in the ample success of the Congress."[12]

Another prize winner, who signed himself a Friend of Peace, said:

> . . . the law of nations is placed, in the first place, under the protection of public opinion. It is enforced by the censures of the press, and by the moral influence of those great masters of public law who are consulted by all nations as oracles of wisdom, and who have attained, by the mere force of written reason, the majestic character, and almost the authority, of universal lawgivers, controlling by their writings the conduct of rulers, and laying down precepts for the government of mankind. . . . It is public opinion that regulates all the concerns of this great world of ours. This is it that forms men into communities, and institutes the necessary regulations for the public weal; that decides what shall be the form of government, making one country a republic, and another a monarchy; and that regulates manners and customs, perpetuating or changing them to suit itself. How pervading its influence! How tremendous its power![13]

In the concert of optimism, only one dissenting voice made itself heard—that of Alexis de Tocqueville. This brilliant political author saw much farther than his contemporaries. He was not a theorist of international organization. He believed passionately in freedom of the press, in public opinion also, but this belief was not unconditional; it was tempered by his remarkable lucidity. In 1840 he wrote:

> People living in an aristocratic age are unwilling to acknowledge the infallibility of the mass. In times of equality the reverse is true. I have shown how equal conditions give men . . . a lofty and frequently exaggerated idea of human reason. . . . Willingness to believe the mass grows, and it is public opinion that increasingly leads the world. . . . In the United States, the majority takes it upon itself to provide individuals with a host of ready-made ideas, which relieves them of the responsibility of forming their own. . . . Whatever political laws may govern men in ages of equality, we can foresee that faith in common opinion will become a sort of religion with the majority as its prophet.
> Intellectual authority will thus be different but in no way diminished; rather than that it should disappear, I foresee that it might easily become too great and that it might eventually enclose the action of individual reason within stricter limits than are compatible with the greatness and happiness of mankind. In equality I clearly discern two trends: one which leads each man's mind to new thoughts, and the other which might easily lead him to think no longer. Again, I can see how, under the influence of certain laws, democracy could extinguish that intellectual freedom which the democratic social state promotes, so that having removed all the fetters that were for-

merly imposed on it by classes or individuals, the human mind could be closely chained to the general will of the greater number. . . .

This, which cannot be repeated too often, should give much food for thought to those who see freedom of the intelligence as something sacred and who hate not only the despot but also despotism. When I feel the hand of power heavy upon my brow, little do I care who my oppressor is, and I am no more ready to put my head into the yoke because it is held by a million hands. . . .[14]

THE ERA OF PEACE CONGRESSES

Tocqueville's almost prophetic warnings do not seem to have found many echoes in his time. The dominant optimistic ideology of public opinion was carried further on the wings of pacifism and internationalism.[15] After 1843, the followers of the various peace movements organized peace congresses at regular intervals: London (1843), Brussels (1848), Paris (1849), Frankfurt (1850), London (1851), etc. These congresses were of private (nongovernmental) origin and their aim was, precisely, to rouse up public opinion. The pacifists certainly did not succeed in mobilizing the masses; their great merit was that, through many decades, they kept alive the idea of international organization in the minds of an élite who sometimes lacked realism but never courage or broadmindedness. The (governmental) Hague Peace Conferences of 1899 and 1907 and, in a later stage, the League of Nations, were, to a large extent, the fruit of their activities.

In the middle of the last century, the idea of international organization was conceived of not so much on a world level as on a European (or, at the maximum, a Euro-American) level. Victor Hugo was one of the prominent pacifists of that era. In his powerful rhetoric, he often referred to European unity, as in 1867, when he wrote:

> In the twentieth century there will be an extraordinary nation. . . . This nation will have Paris as its capital and will not be called France; it will be called Europe. It will be called Europe in the twentieth century, and in the following centuries, after still further transfiguration, it will be called Humanity. Humanity, as the definitive nation, is already foreseen by thinkers in their contemplation of the shadows; however, the nineteenth century is witnessing the formation of Europe.[16]

Earlier, in 1849, Hugo had been elected chairman of the Paris Peace Congress. At the opening session, he gave a speech that made a deep impression on the audience:

> There will come a day when you, France, you, Russia, you, Italy, you, England, you, Germany, you, all nations of the continent, without losing your distinctive qualities and your glorious individuality, will join closely together in a higher unity and constitute a European fraternity. . . . There will come a day when bullets and bombs will be replaced by votes, by universal suffrage of the peoples. . . . There will come a day when we shall see those two immense groups, the United States of America, the United States of Europe [applause] facing each other, extending their hands across

the ocean. . . . It will not take four hundred years for such a day to come, because we are living in an age of speed and are being borne along by the most impetuous current of events ever experienced by mankind, so that a year of our time sometimes does the work of a century. . . . [Hear, hear!][17]

One may have noticed the definitely "democratic" ideas of the poet: he places his hopes in universal suffrage. The man in the street, so is the assumption, will certainly oblige rulers to do away with wars and to create European unity. Similar ideas are expressed in, for instance, the writings of Frédéric Passy and of the Freemason Félix Santallier, who in 1867 created at Le Havre the "Union de la Paix." A year later, not less than seventy-two lodges had declared themselves in favor of this initiative. Santallier, too, expected all salvation to come from public opinion. He stressed the need for propaganda campaigns in the various countries in order to organize "a popular experience" for peace: "Since Peace has never managed to descend the steps of thrones, let us try to make it rise up from within the hearts of peoples!" Elsewhere he wrote: "It is therefore from public opinion, in its universal expression, that we should ask for the sovereign sanction of the powers of a tribunal able to judge nations."[18]

There is not much point in quoting further texts here. The irrational belief in the value and efficiency of public opinion is today, as Tocqueville foresaw, no less topical than one or two centuries ago. In a concluding editorial in the *Yearbook of International Organisations 1964–1965*, Mr. G. P. Speeckaert writes:

> Let us hope that the next step . . . will see the blossoming of a genuine spirit of co-operation between states. That is what all peoples want, the world over, and the contribution of international non-governmental organisations in the work of the intergovernmental bodies . . . is inspired and sustained by belief in the greatness of the task of the United Nations and its Specialised Agencies.[19]

But this statement, of course, takes for granted what needs to be proved.

INTERNATIONAL LAW DEFINING PUBLIC OPINION

Contemporary theorists and writers of many kinds are not alone in adopting the ideology described here. International treaties, signed and ratified by governments, also pay lip service to the somewhat simplistic doctrine that public opinion wants peace and international organization. Here, again, the examples are abundant.

The preamble of the fourth Hague Convention (1907), for instance, recognizes the "principles of the law of nations, as they result from the usages established among civilized peoples, from the laws of humanity, and the dictates of public conscience." Article 12 of the Covenant of the League of Nations, in instituting the *moratoire de guerre*, presupposes the influence of an active and peace-loving public opinion. In its preamble, the Universal Declaration of Human Rights refers to the outraged "conscience of mankind"; "the advent of a world in which human beings shall enjoy freedom of speech and belief" is proclaimed as "the highest aspiration of the common people." Article 1 of the Declaration states that "all human beings are . . . endowed with reason and conscience." And the UNESCO Constitution's preamble says that, "since wars begin in the minds of men, it is in the minds of men that the defences of peace must be constructed." It also refers to "a peace which could secure the unanimous, lasting and sincere support of the peoples of the world," etc.

Some of the treaties establishing international organizations are very explicit. The preamble of the Arab League's Pact, for instance, speaks of the "aspirations and hopes" of "all the Arab countries" and of "the wishes of public opinion in all Arab countries." The Council of Europe's Statute says that the organization is created in order to respond "to the expressed aspirations" of the European peoples.

THE COUNCIL OF EUROPE'S CASE

Among the texts that have been mentioned here (and many more could be quoted), the Statute of the Council of Europe holds a special place. It is the only treaty in which the reference to public opinion corresponds to hard and precise facts. But, at the same time, the Council of Europe may go down in history as the unique example of an international institution owing its existence to the pressure of "public opinion." In other words, the Strasbourg institution appears to confirm that it can happen, in exceptional circumstances, that public opinion plays an active and constructive role in the process of international organization.

It is generally agreed that the preamble of the Council's Statute refers to the Federalists' Congress, which took place at The Hague in May 1948—one hundred years after Victor Hugo's appeal in Paris. This Congress, too, aimed at rousing public opinion, and it was also of private (nongovernmental) origin. Representatives from almost all Western European countries took part, urging the governments to set up the Council. Many of us will remember the wave of enthusiasm all over Europe in those days. In the streets people talked about European unity as the dawn of a new era and many believed that the United States of Europe were to be created in Strasbourg almost at once. Less than twelve months after the Hague Congress, that is to say, within an extremely short period, the governments had elaborated and signed the statute of the first political European institution.

According to certain witnesses, a similar, though undoubtedly much more ephemeral, phenomenon had taken place in 1919 when Woodrow Wilson came to Europe as the founding father of the League of Nations. If this were to be confirmed—and the question deserves some serious research—the League might be considered as a second exception. Be this as it may, the wave of popular enthusiasm of the year 1948–1949 was unprecedented and will not often be repeated. Only under very exceptional psychological conditions does the public seem capable of acting as a constructive driving force. A general awareness of living through a historic moment might well be the decisive factor that makes the masses measure up to their responsibilities.

Sudden passions are not necessarily lasting, and the popular origin of an international institution, however exceptional the case may be, is not warranty that the public will show a continuing interest in its own creation. In the factor of *duration* we come to the heart of the problem.

TOWARD A REALISTIC THEORY: MAURICE HAURIOU

Maurice Hauriou, one of France's most brilliant political theorists, who died almost thirty-five years ago, succeeded, I think, in giving a satisfactory and rational explanation of the assertion that public opinion should play a vital role in political institutions. In the work of most authors, this assertion, as we have seen, is not much more than a gratuitous inference—a hypothesis of a rather ideological nature. But Maurice Hauriou methodically excluded all preconceived doctrine and in this way showed why institutions, once they exist, having been created without the public's intervention, subsequently badly need the active support of public opinion.

Hauriou did not deal specifically with public opinion, but his works, in particular the *Théorie de l'Institution*, have far-reaching implications, in my opinion at least, for contemporary study of the problem, especially in regard to international organization. What is an institution? According to Hauriou, it is essentially an *idea*. It is an idea that has been "found," as he puts it, by an intellectual "elite" and which, by the intervention of a second "elite"— those who are in power ("les élites du pouvoir")—has been embodied in a certain organization. Only from that stage onward, once the "elite" of decision makers have actually created the institution, is the public called upon to play a role, by accepting, at least passively, the new body. It is the public, in this theory, that makes institutions last, because it has the power either to accept or to reject them.

"A social institution," he writes, "is essentially made up of an objective idea transformed into a social fact by a founder; the idea then attracts an unspecified number of supporters from the social group and thus subordinates to its service indefinitely renewed subjective wills."[20] Elsewhere, he stresses that the attachment of the public is the element that determines the duration of an institution:

> A social organization becomes durable, i.e., preserves its specific form, despite the continuous renewal of its human content, when . . . the guiding idea . . . has managed to subordinate to itself power of government, . . . and when . . . this system of ideas and balance of power has been confirmed . . . by the consent of the members of the institution and of the social group. In sum, the form of the institution, which is its durable element, consists of a system of balance of power and consent built around an idea.[21]

It is obvious that the phenomenon of the basic concept of the institution, recruiting "an unspecified number of supporters from the social group," is actually a process of public opinion. It is the agreement of the people, be it only the tacit agreement—people abstaining from revolt, which makes institutions last. Hauriou, in saying this, acknowledged a *fact*, whereas too many others saw and see here a point of doctrine, of "democracy," for instance. If such are the facts, the unavoidable conclusion is that institutions can but vegetate, that is, just perpetuate themselves, as long as they command only passive support. In order to develop and to prosper, they need the active support of a conscious and interested public. They must be more than purely technical or administrative machinery: the idea that caused their formation should be anchored in the minds of citizens.

Hauriou's theory states the case for information on international institutions, which today arouse no real interest, as opinion surveys show. International institutions are entities too remote, too far off from everyday life. We shall never be able to build a true international society unless we find ways to prove to the public that its own vital interests are really at stake. With international institutions, the public does not even dispose of that elemenary means to express itself which, in a national democracy, is the right to vote. There are no general elections to appoint the members of the Consultative Assembly of the Council of Europe or of the European Parliament, let alone the governmental delegations to the United Nations. This shows that democracy on the international level still has a long way to go; even its purely formal institutionalization has not yet been achieved.

CONCLUSIONS

Neither the reason nor the virtue of the nations has brought about the present (and certainly encouraging) degree of international organization, but rather the progress of communication, rightly understood by governments.

As regards international institutions, perhaps public opinion, in the true sense of the word, does not really exist; at least it has not often manifested its presence. With Claude[22] and many others, one can wonder whether the so-called "opinion of the public" must not rather be described as the "opinion of the few," the small group who have a deep knowledge of the problems at stake —a handful of politicians, high officials, journalists, and diplomats. These are the people who really influence the course of events, who actually participate in decision making and who, in this way, give major impulses to the shaping of the public's opinion. This view also corresponds to Maurice Hauriou's theory on the origin of institutions.

The question remains whether public opinion is capable of playing the vital role in international affairs attributed to it by optimistic ideology. I do not think that this ideology is a myth, as some very respectable authors say; I am rather inclined to consider the concept of public opinion playing a vital role in international organization as an ideal. It is an ideal, like peace or democracy, toward which we must by all means work, using education and information as instruments, an ideal that will never be entirely realized.

The belief in education presupposes that men, even collectively, are capable of at least some reason and that human nature is endowed with at least some goodness. Such a hypothesis, of course, is again largely a question of doctrine, of ideology, or, more precisely, of attitude. And not attitude as such, but only a clear perception of facts, can help us advance along the road to truth.

NOTES

[1] According to the *Yearbook of International Organisations 1964–1965*, membership in the UN almost doubled from January 1, 1952 (60 members), to December 31, 1963 (112 members). Of the 52 new members, 30 were African, 15 European, 4 Asian, and 3 American states.

[2] Geographically, the 150 intergovernmental organizations are divided as follows: 34 European (Eastern and Western), 28 American, 14 African, 3 Asian, and 71 "intercontinental" organizations.

[3] *Essays and Treatises on Various Subjects*, London, 1957, p. 31.

[4] George H. Sabine, *A History of Political Theory*, New York, 1951, p. 43.

[5] *Ibid.*, p. 96.

[6] *Lettre au Comte de Grignan*, 6 août 1670, in *Lettres*, Paris, 1953, Vol. I, p. 172.

[7] Quoted in Jacob Ter Meulen, *Der Gedanke der Internationalen Organisation in seiner Entwicklung*, Vol. II, The Hague, M. Nijhoff, 1929, p. 16.

[8] *Ibid.*, p. 20. Another aspect of Condorcet's theory is that he stresses, like Jeremy Bentham, that it is in the *national interest* of states to promote international organization. This point would deserve a special study.

[9] *Ibid.*, pp. 268–273.

[10] *Zum ewigen Frieden*, Leipzig, 1947, p. 64.

[11] Ter Meulen, *op. cit.*, p. 274.

[12] *Ibid.*, p. 286.

[13] *Ibid.*, pp. 293–294.

[14] *De la Démocratie en Amérique*, Paris, 1963, pp. 225–227.

[15] For the significance of these equivocal terms, see Gérard Herberichs, *Théorie de la Paix selon Pie XII*, with a preface by Charles de Visscher, Paris, 1964, pp. 141–154.

[16] Ter Meulen, *op. cit.*, Vol. III, p. 24.

[17] *Ibid.*, Vol. II, pp. 318–319.

[18] *Ibid.*, Vol. III. pp. 25–27.

[19] P. 1539. Other examples of contemporary authors writing in the same sense are given in my book, cited above, pp. 192–209.

[20] *Précis de Droit Constitutionnel*, Paris, 1923, p. 76.

[21] *Ibid.*, 1929, p. 73.

[22] Inis L. Claude, Jr., "Open Diplomacy Revisited" in *International Spectator*, The Hague, Jan. 8, 1965, pp. 24–27.

THE TWO-STEP FLOW THEORY: CROSS-CULTURAL IMPLICATIONS

Lloyd R. Bostian

LLOYD R. BOSTIAN received his B.S. in agricultural economics at North Carolina State University in 1954, and his M.S. in agricultural journalism in 1955, and his Ph.D. in mass communication in 1959 at the University of Wisconsin. He has taught at the University of Wisconsin since 1954 and is currently chairman of the Department of Agricultural Journalism. His teaching specialty is the role of communication systems in rural development. He has published papers on the communication behaviors of farmers in Southern Brazil in Brazilian journals and has contributed essays to such journals as the Journal of Broadcasting and the Journalism Quarterly. He is a charter member and founder of the Associacao Brasileira de Informacao Rural.

Few recent studies testing the two-step theory of communication with respect to diffusion of general media content in this country have shown significant results in its favor, and reconceptualizations have not proved fruitful. However, before the theory is given up for dead, it may be productive to examine it in the context of less developed societies where media are scarce, and in special situations involving purposive, persuasive communication.

This paper reviews some of the major components of the original theory, discusses theoretical additions and modifications provided by later researchers, and calls attention to the possible utility of the theory in development oriented communication studies.

The two-step flow hypothesis emanating from the study of voter decision-making in the 1940 presidential campaign by Lazarsfeld, Berelson and Gaudet was originally stated clearly and simply: "Ideas often flow from radio and print to the opinion leaders and from them to the less active sections of the population."[1]

This hypothesis became a major stimulus for research concerning the diffusion of information. In fact, Elihu Katz, who took an early interest in the development of the theory at the Bureau of Applied Social Research at Columbia University, calls the original study "a major turning point in the conceptualization of the process of mass communication."[2]

In the original study of voter decision-making, mass media had less effect on voters than had been hypothesized. The major source of influence seemed to be other people. These influentials or "opinion leaders" were identified as those who tried to convince others of their own opinions or those who were sought out by others for their opinions. Opinion leaders were thus defined as those who exercised personal influence.[3]

These opinion leaders were found to be quite similar to the people they influenced. The major difference was in exposure to mass media information

Reprinted with permission of Journalism Quarterly (1970), 109–117.

and in exposure to content related to leadership. Here the opinion leaders excelled. Thus the authors surmised that the opinion leaders were transmitting information they received from the media and formulated their two-step flow hypothesis.

It is important to note that this early research *did not actually measure a two-step flow*. It simply showed the *absence of a one-step flow;* that is, most people were not *directly* influenced by mass media in deciding how to vote. The two-step idea was an inference, or hypothesis, drawn from the combination of facts that opinion leaders did persuade non-influentials, and did have higher exposure to mass media information regarding the election. The research measured general media exposure, not transmission of particular pieces of information from media to opinion leader to follower.

The original hypothesis contained several ideas or variables which stimulated additional research. A major variable and a topic of later studies was the opinion leader and the role of interpersonal relationships in communication situations. In his 1957 updating of the two-step theory, Katz stressed the functioning of interpersonal relations as communication *networks* and as sources of *social pressure or support.*[4]

In fact, Katz and Lazarsfeld indicated that the original and succeeding pieces of research by the Columbia Bureau emphasized the role of the interpersonal network. They also pointed out the similarity between their term *opinion leader* and Kurt Lewin's term *gatekeeper*. (Lewin had conceptualized the gatekeeper as one who controls a strategic portion of a channel.) They reported that the gatekeeper may or may not transmit information within the group and may or may not be influential: he only introdurces the idea to the group. Referring to studies in Greece and Lebanon, they reported an additional idea: the possibility that the availability of new information may give rise to new gatekeepers, who soon become influentials as a result of their transmission of information. Unfortunately, this latter conceptualization as to differences between gatekeepers and opinion leaders seems to have been largely ignored since this report.[5]

Later studies told the Columbia researchers even more about interpersonal communication networks. The two-step flow became a multi-step flow—with information flowing from mass media through several relays of opinion leaders who communicate with one another and with followers. It became clear that influence or innovation spreads gradually through a society via various combinations of mass media and interpersonal networks. This led to Coleman, Katz and Menzel's study of "The Diffusion of an Innovation among Physicians."[6] These researchers introduced the variable of *time*. Earlier studies had shown that the opinion leaders were more exposed to mass media information. The Coleman *et al.* study further showed that the opinion leaders were also more likely to be innovators, indicating with greater certainty that they were innovating as a result of the *first-step* of getting information from mass media, before taking the *second-step* of influencing others to adopt new drugs. Many diffusion studies have produced the same finding.[7]

Recently, Bemis reached the same conclusion, that the early adopters who are also opinion leaders have earlier first knowledge. This is reported in his

1968 Ph.D. dissertation concerning the diffusion-adoption process among two groups of Wisconsin pesticide users with special emphasis on opinion leadership and other communication factors.[8]

Another variable contained in the original hypothesis is that of *influence*. The original study made no attempt to separate *information* from *influence*, being concerned only with persuasion. Obviously, however, the function of a message may be either to *inform* or to *persuade*. Only later did the conceptualization that the gatekeeper relays information and the influential endorses it become established. Neither was it clear originally as to exactly what functions gatekeepers play versus opinion leaders. Nor was it shown to what extent one individual performs both functions.

LATER STUDIES

Later studies have been primarily of two types—those studying news flow, especially the diffusion of information from major news events, and studies specifically designed to retest the original two-step flow theory. A few articles of both types are reviewed here.

In 1960, Deutschmann and Danielson reported a summary of results from several studies of the diffusion of knowledge of major news stories.[9] They listed two functions involved in opinion leadership—the relay function and the reinforcement function. Their resume listed several key findings:

1. Initial mass media information on important events goes directly to people on the whole and is not relayed to any great extent.
2. People talk about important news they have learned from the media.
3. Opinion leaders, who have more information, may do supplementary relaying (concurrent with the reinforcement function) when the topic arises.

The authors found little confirmation for a two-step flow of communication in these research results regarding major news events. And they urged caution and qualification in applying the two-step flow hypothesis. Interpersonal communication regarding the news was present, but unimportant as far as diffusion was concerned.

In evaluating the Deutschmann-Danielson findings, two items stand out. First, they were dealing not with persuasion or influence, as were the originators of the theory, but with transmission of news. Second, they were dealing with information concerning important events—characterized by high interest and rapid diffusion. And the findings, though extremely valuable and clear cut, could not likely be expected to apply to diffusion of low-interest, non-crisis information. They did hypothesize, however, that word-of-mouth transmission would be smaller when the story has less news value.

In late 1963, Greenberg[10] commented on the Deutschmann-Danielson findings, suggesting that with regard to recurring issues in public affairs, interpersonal channels are used primarily for reinforcing existing opinions, rather than for creation or conversion of attitudes. His school communication study indicated that in measuring conversations about school activities, more horizontal than vertical conversation occurred—citizens and school personnel talked primarily with their peers (79% and 67% respectively). Thus Greenberg found a striking absence of the *relay* function. Further, communication was initiated more often by the less-informed than by the more-informed—an indication of information seeking. Finally, most successful influence attempts consisted of *reinforcements*, not conversion or new opinion.

Hill and Bonjean, in their 1964 article, came to a conclusion opposite to that of Deutschmann-Danielson, that "the greater the news value of an event, the more important will be the interpersonal communication in the diffusion process.[11] They based their conclusion on the fact that interpersonal communication accounted for 57% of first learning of John F. Kennedy's assassination. This is one of the few U.S. news diffusion studies reported in the past 20 years finding that interpersonal communication accounted for a greater percentage of first knowledge than did mass media. Hill and Bonjean also indicate that interpersonal learning was almost as rapid as learning from mass media.

In his article in fall of 1964, Greenberg verified the Deutschmann-Danielson finding that major news through mass media goes directly to a majority of the receivers.[12] However, he hypothesized that person-to-person communication as the first source of news has its primary role in the diffusion of events which receive *maximum* and *minimum* attention from the populace. In other words, where personal channels are most often cited as the first source of information, the events are likely to be those which come to the attention of nearly everyone or practically no one. Greenberg hypothesized in this manner because he conceptually differentiated between the "importance" of a news event (interest in it) and the "attention" given to it (number of people aware of it). He was concerned with the type of information involved, believing that interpersonal communication will play different roles given differences in the above factors. He further pointed out that his results were based on "special events" with virtually no competing messages in the system. (This is also a characteristic of the communication situation of many news diffusion studies reported.)

In a recent news diffusion study concerning President Johnson's March 31, 1968, decision not to run again for the presidency, Allen and Colfax[13] found only slight two-step passage of this important news—only 5% of those interviewed heard the news by word-of-mouth. They hypothesized that the major factors determining this percentage would be the level of attendance to media when the news breaks, plus the time-space opportunity to receive word-of-mouth information before casual or customary exposure to the ubiquitous mass media.

Adams and Mullen added a new dimension in their report of a study measuring diffusion of the announcement of Pope Paul regarding the Catholic Church's position on birth control.[14]

Several hypotheses were advanced concerning the type of information involved: information of personal relevance and considerable emotional impact (for the Catholic audience). Of those who had heard of Pope Paul's announcement, virtually all (97.8%) heard from mass media or noninterpersonal channels. In finding acceptance for all major hypotheses, Adams and Mullen found that a large proportion of Catholics in comparison to non-Catholics had heard the news, had attempted to verify it, had told others of the news and had received information from others regarding the announcement.

Of the second type of studies, those concerning direct re-testing of the two-step flow, much of the reported work is by Troldahl. In 1965, Troldahl and Van Dam reported a study of face-to-face communication about major topics in the news.[15] They measured opinion leaders by asking both whether anyone had asked the person for his opinions on the topic and whether the person had asked anyone about the topic. Thus they identified Opinion Givers and Opinion Askers. An important finding, regarding the two-step flow, was that three-fourths of the conversations involved both giving and asking, in other words there was substantial *opinion sharing*.

The authors further reported that givers and askers did not differ significantly on mass media use, nor on gregariousness, nor on perceived (self) opinion leadership. This led them to conclude that earlier studies had erred in not separating out the *inactives* from the follower or non-leader category. They defined inactives as non-sharers of information—people who had not talked to anyone about the topic (79% of non-givers were inactives). When Troldahl and Van Dam eliminated inactives from their analysis, they found clear cut differences between Givers, Askers and Inactives. Givers conversed with askers but not with (by definition) inactives. They concluded that there may not be a second-step flow from givers to askers, but rather a shared conversation among people much alike.

Troldahl and Costello examined the mass media exposure patterns and interpersonal communication behavior of teen-agers.[16] Through factor analysis they identified various two-step flow patterns. Regardless of the medium used *heavily*, the teenager talked to friends about what he had been exposed to in that medium. In other words, heavy mass media exposure led to second-step conversations.

Troldahl developed a modified model in 1961.[17] He pointed out that most news flow research had involved *information*, while the original studies concerned *attitudes and behavior*. Since the theory had proved of little value to explain news flow, Troldahl concluded that the two-step theory seemed more applicable to attitudinal studies. He was also concerned with the fact that previous theories stressed the *notion* that opinion leaders initiate the second-step flow, but research had not shown this. He hypothesized that the two-step flow is expected to operate only when a person is exposed to mass media content that is inconsistent with his present predispositions—in such cases, that person seeks his opinion leader. Troldahl derived this idea from "balance" theory.

To test this idea, he injected experimental messages into a natural social system, with before and after measurements, experimental and control groups. He hypothesized a *"two-cycle flow of communication"* as a prerequisite to changes in beliefs or behavior. He expected that an opinion leader would not function as an influential until he had completed his own influence cycle—that is, before he would exercise influence on a particular issue, the opinion leader would have already been exposed to the information in question, sought advice from his own opinion leader, and would have changed or re-affirmed his own belief. Thus the "two-cycle" idea.

Troldahl's findings did not conform generally to his own predictions arising from his two-cycle hypothesis, and little confirmation for a two-step flow was obtained.

Arndt provided one of the most recent tests of the two-step flow in his study of the diffusion of a new product.[19] He pointed out that one contribution in the original research, in addition to those heretofore mentioned, was that the conceptualization contributed to the "rediscovery of people" in social research. Further, the theoretical framework appeared to have guided most of the later research on the flow of mass communications and the diffusion of innovations. Therefore, he found it surprising that the hypothesis as a whole had never really been subjected to the test of empirical verification.

In Arndt's review of previous research, he stressed the lack of study of the flow of specific content from media to opinion leader to nonleader.

In order for a researcher to make a rigorous test of the original hypothesis, Arndt listed four requirements:

1. It should be possible to measure the differential impact of the messages from impersonal sources on opinion leaders and nonleaders.
2. It should be possible to trace the flow of personal influence among leaders and nonleaders.
3. It should be possible to compare the content of the messages from the impersonal sources with the content of the word-of-mouth communication at the second step.
4. It should be possible to isolate the effect of word-of-mouth messages on the receivers of those messages.

Arndt found some confirmation for the original theory, though not all of his results were statistically significant. He concluded that opinion leaders seemed to be more influenced by the impersonal source (direct mail letter) than were the nonleaders, hence support for the first-step flow of influence. In regard to the second step, leaders were more active communicators, both as transmitters and receivers of word-of-mouth communications. An unexpected finding, which agreed with that reported in the Troldahl-Van Dam study, was the amount of *opinion sharing*, via the relatively large amount of word-of-mouth communication flowing from nonleaders to leaders.

Deutschmann[19] was interested in applying the two-step theory to information diffusion in small communities—for cross-cultural application. He used a machine simulation with the following five operating conditions for his model:

1. Any message will inform the receiver, if it is delivered.
2. Reception of messages is selective, in relationship to channel orientations.
3. Any external message will touch off face-to-face messages.
4. Face-to-face local messages flow more frequently within groups than between groups.

5. There is a small group of individuals (tellers or communicators) who encode messages they receive.

In the machine test of this model, Deutschmann found that most individuals were informed by face-to-face means, and most face-to-face telling was within groups rather than between.

In his summary of two-step flow studies, van den Ban[20] concludes that these studies give one the impression that people usually get their news first from the mass media, except in cases of very important and unexpected events which cause a lot of excitement and comment. If they are interested in the event, they may consult mass media for additional factual information, but they are perhaps more inclined to listen to personal sources for interpretation and evaluation of these events.

Van den Ban's own study showed that opinion leaders as well as followers are influenced both by mass media and by other people, but during different stages of the adoption process.

Of substantial interest regarding application to developing societies are these two conclusions:

1. When people urgently need information, a two-step process is more frequent, but people will go to the best informed, people of high social status, not friends and neighbors.
2. The relation between pioneering (innovation) and opinion leadership is closer in progressive than in traditional groups.

APPLICATION TO DEVELOPING COUNTRIES

A brief presentation of some generalizations concerning mass media and interpersonal communications in developing countries will give a basis for generating hypotheses regarding the applicability of two-step flow theory to communication situations in those countries. Obviously, no two countries are alike. However, we must generalize regarding characteristics of these countries if we are to have a base for applying the two-step theory.

Developing countries have a scarcity of mass media, transmission facilities and receiving capabilities. Low personal incomes are a disstimulus to support of both commercial and governmental media. Such media as are available are usually located in the largest population centers and are urban oriented. Mass media are directly available in few homes, substantially fewer in rural areas.

Interpersonal communication occurs within small social groups and work groups. Such communication is more personalized and thus often assumed to be more persuasive than in developed countries (industrialized, urban societies).

Opinion leaders in developing countries are more local (serve fewer people) and use more personal channels of communication. There is a high correlation between opinion leader and gatekeeper functions, i.e. the opinion leader is also likely to be a gatekeeper, and this function is a general one, i.e. the leader or gatekeeper transmits a wide array of information across subject matter lines.

With these basic assumptions, and backed by communication research results from developing countries,* we can make the following generalizations regarding the performance of the two-step flow in developing countries (non-industrialized, mostly rural societies).

1. *Mass media messages are normally non-influential.* Even for the opinion leader, mass media carry a low ratio of instrumental information, or information which would contribute to decision-making or to changing attitudes, as compared to non-utilitarian messages. People do not normally expect to receive instrumental information via mass media, nor do they readily perceive its utility when it is present.

2. *The two-step flow is rarely operative.* There is little influential information available and little reason for opinion leaders to function using information transmitted by mass media as their source.

3. *When locally relevant, instrumental, persuasive information is available via mass media, the two-step flow operates at a higher level than in developed countries.* Normal communication is personal and local; leaders are on the lookout for instrumental information; a local demand exists for such information, thus increasing the two-step flow.

4. *Interpersonal channels and thus the two-step flow are more important for news of maximum interest than in developed countries, but less important for news of minimum interest than in developed countries.* Since media are not ubiquitous, "important" news has a high two-step flow rate. Minimum interest news has a low interpersonal flow because news important to special interest groups is rarely available via mass media.

5. *Influence is an important motive for relay of information.* That is, most information is relayed because of a persusasive element. There is a low degree of information-seeking and a high degree of information-sharing. This increases passage of influence and influential information versus a relay of news per se.

6. *Opinion leaders and followers share fewer characteristics than do their counterparts in developed countries.* A greater proportion of opinion leaders are formal leaders rather than simply members of the community, neighbors or friends. But since communication is more personal and local, this does not diminish the information flow nor the flow of persuasive influence.

7. *When opinion leaders are neighbors and friends (share characteristics of their followers) they normally innovate or adopt the behavior or attitude in question, before informing others. . . .*

8. *Initiation of the information flow between leader and follower is normally made by the follower.* Leaders do not normally transmit to followers except after information-seeking or request of the follower.

* The author is not aware of studies conducted in developing countries which have specifically tested the two-step flow theory, and he is reluctant to cite the multitude of peripherally related studies, a majority of which fall into the diffusion research category.

9. *Information availability via mass media creates new gatekeepers, and these gatekeepers eventually become opinion leaders.*

Since none of these generalizations is backed by sufficient data, all should become hypotheses for future two-step flow research.

SUMMARY AND CONCLUSIONS

The two-step flow hypothesis appears to explain very few communication situations and is likely too simplified a concept for great utility in explaining the process of communication.

Research shows that the two-step hypothesis can perhaps best explain some communication situations involving influence—where opinion leaders influence followers, they often use information gained via the mass media.

Research does not tell us the optimum level of operation of this concept. That is, with everyone receiving messages directly by mass media, we have a very efficient system in terms of time involved but not in terms of equipment needed, yet one in which two-step flow is zero. Contrarily, it would be possible to achieve a perfect two-step flow by only one person in the community receiving information via mass media and ultimately informing all others in the community, an inefficient diffusion system in terms of time but efficient in the sense of raising the number of people reached per unit of equipment.

From a purposive communications point of view, which one of these extremes is better (if not something in between) depends not only on the type of efficiency desired, but also on the effectiveness of the communication, a factor influenced by the type of information transmitted, the objectives of the communicator and by the needs and interests of the ultimate receivers or the community as a whole. This indicates the futility of specifying an optimum level of two-step flow, unless with specification and definition of the conditions surrounding the communication situation.

The following areas appear especially appropriate for further research both in the United States and elsewhere:

First, we need research which separates the relay function from the influence function. We must know the role of information and the role of personal influence as they both relate to the communication of information through interpersonal channels. Put another way, we must separate the opinion leader function from that of the gatekeeper. We further need to see to what extent we can create gatekeepers by providing people with new information, and to what extent such new gatekeepers subsequently become opinion leaders.

Second, we need to reevaluate our ideas about the flow of information, especially our concept of an opinion leader as a voluntary transmitter of information. Evidence indicates that the initiation of the flow of information is often the reverse—the follower initiates the conversation, and often the flow is in both directions, with information shared. Because the leader is a source of information does not mean that he voluntarily transmits it. The concept of information-seeking is more relevant than ever, and certainly it deserves a greater place in research than its recently emphasized converse of information-avoidance.

Third, we must specify the type of information being transmitted and consider its utility to the receiver. Research has given us some clues as to influential versus non-persuasive information, important versus unimportant news, high interest versus low interest, but other characteristics of information can relate both to the flow of information and to its influence on the receiver, and these demand study.

NOTES

[1] Paul F. Lazarsfeld, Bernard Berelson and Hazel Gaudet. *The People's Choice*, 2nd ed. (New York, 1948).

[2] Elihu Katz, "The Diffusion of New Ideas and Practices," Voice of American Forum Lectures: Mass Communication Series, No. 7.

[3] Paul F. Lazarsfeld, "Mass Media and Personal Influence," Voice of America Forum Lectures: Mass Communication Series, No. 8.

[4] Elihu Katz, "The Two-Step Flow of Communication: An Up-to-date Report on an Hypothesis," *Public Opinion Quarterly* 21:61–78, 1957.

[5] Elihu Katz and Paul F. Lazarsfeld. *Personal* Influence (Glencoe, Ill., 1955).

[6] James Coleman, Elihu Katz and Herbert Menzel. "The Diffusion of an Innovation Among Physicians," *Sociometry* 20:253–70, 1957.

[7] Gwyn E. Jones, "The Adoption and Diffusion of Agricultural Practices," *World Agricultural Economics and Rural Sociology Abstracts*, Vol. 9, No. 3 (Sept. 1967). (This paper includes several hundred bibliographic listings. Professor Jones is at the Agricultural Extension Center, University of Reading.)

[8] James H. Bemis, Jr., "A Study of the Adoption-Diffusion Process among Two Groups of Wisconsin Pesticide Users with Special Emphasis on Opinion Leadership and Other Communication Factors." Ph.D. Dissertation, University of Wisconsin, 1968.

[9] Paul Deutschmann and Wayne Danielson. "Diffusion of Knowledge of the Major News Story." *Journalism Quarterly*, 37:345–55 (Summer 1960).

[10] Bradley S. Greenberg, "Dimensions of Informal Communication" in *Paul J. Deutschmann Memorial Papers in Mass Communication Research*. Scripps-Howard Research, December 1963.

[11] Richard J. Hill and Charles M. Bonjean. "News Diffusion: A Test of the Regularity Hypothesis," *Journalism Quarterly*, 41:336–42 (Summer 1964).

[12] Bradley S. Greenberg, "Person-to-Person Communication in the Diffusion of News Events," *Journalism Quarterly*, 41:489–94 (Autumn 1964).

[13] Irving L. Allen and J. David Colfax, "The Diffusion of News of LBJ's March 31 Decision," *Journalism Quarterly*, 45:321–4 (Summer 1968).

[14] John B. Adams and James J. Mullen, "Diffusion of the News of a Foreign Event: A Nationwide Study," *Journalism Quarterly*, 46:545–57 (Autumn 1969).

[15] Verling C. Troldahl and Robert Van Dam. "Face-to-Face Communication about Major Topics in the News," *Public Opinion Quarterly* 29:626–34 (Winter 1965).

[16] Verling C. Troldahl and Daniel E. Costello. "Mass Media Exposure Patterns and Interpersonal Communication Behavior of Teenagers." Paper presented to the Theory and Methodology Division of the Association for Education in Journalism, Iowa City, Iowa, 1966.

[17] Verling C. Troldahl, "A Field Test of a Modified 'Two-Step Flow of Communication' Model," *Public Opinion Quarterly* 30:609–23 (Winter 1966).

[18] Johan Arndt, "A Test of the Two-Step Flow in Diffusion of a New Product," *Journalism Quarterly*, 45:457–65 (Autumn 1968).

[19] Paul J. Deutschmann, "A Machine Simulation of Information Diffusion in a Small Community," mimeo of Programa Interamericano de Informacion Popular, September, 1962.

[20] A. W. van den Ban, "A Revision of the Two-Step Flow of Communication Hypothesis," *Gazette*, 10:237–50 (No. 3, 1964).

MISCONSTRUCTION AND PROBLEMS IN COMMUNICATION

Brian M. Du Toit

BRIAN M. DU TOIT received his B.A. and M.A. from the University of Pretoria, South Africa, and his Ph.D. in 1963 at the University of Florida. His dissertation is based on a year's research in the east central highlands of New Guinea. He has taught at the University of Stellenbosch and the University of Cape Town. Currently he is associate professor of anthropology at the University of Florida, where he also teaches in the African Studies Center. He has served as associate editor of the Journal of Asian African Studies, is a fellow of the American Anthropological Association, an associate of Current Anthropology, and a member of Sigma Xi. Du Toit is the author of Beperkte Lidmaatskap (Cape Town, 1965) and the editor of Culture Change in Contemporary Africa (Communication of the African Studies Center, vol. I, no. 1, 1970). He has published articles in American Anthropologist, Anthropological Quarterly, Human Organization, Journal of American Folklore, South African Journal of Science, International Journal of Comparative Sociology, Journal of Asian and African Studies, Oceania, Tydskrif vir Volkskunde en Volkstaal, Tydskrif vir Geesteswetenskappe, Psychologia Africana and contributed chapters to E. Eddy's Urban Anthropology: Research Perspectives and Strategies (University of Georgia Press, 1968) and E. de Jager's Man: Essays Presented to O. F. Raum (in press).

My aim in this paper is to show how a condition of uncertainty and nervous stress that has been complicated by problems in communication may set the field for a cargo-type reaction.[1] Anthropological literature records an ever-growing number of cases in which situations of culture change and contact lead to reactions among a society's members. Such reactions are variously described as nativistic, revitalistic, vitalistic, millenarian, messianic, or cargo movements. Each type requires a necessary set of conditions, a leader, and an aim or program of action that in the last analysis allows typification. On the whole, these movements are studied in retrospect and usually at a distance. Cases in which an observer was on hand to record the field conditions and early phases of the movement are limited, for many situations that contain the necessary and sufficient causes for such a movement never develop because of sudden changes in the forces that precipitated the conditions.[2]

The situation to be discussed here contained the conditions that could have given rise to such a movement. Certain individuals did in fact capitalize on the mental state of the people, but the situation was soon over, and the stress that could have been manipulated was removed.

The data presented here will sound like an unlikely, disconnected series of events. They in fact occurred during 1961/62 in the eastern central highlands of New Guinea. These events are discussed as they occurred, and also as they

Reproduced by permission of the American Anthropological Association from American Anthropologist, Vol. 71, No. 1, 1969.

were observed and experienced by the anthropologist who unwittingly contributed to the misconstruction that produced the situation.

I

The first event occurred during September 1961. We had just attended some festivities in the eastern extreme of the Arona Valley and were crossing the valley, a distance of approximately fifteen miles, to return to our home village. The sun was hot and my interpreter inquisitive. He was a young fellow, perhaps eighteen years of age, who had been as far west as Chimbu to attend a Lutheran Mission school. He had been introduced to the world beyond the valley and was continually asking questions or requesting explanations of things he had heard.

We had crossed more than half the valley floor, discussing the events of the previous days, when we sat down under the shade of a tree to rest a while. He took this as the cue that he could initiate the next topic and inquired, "Master, what is this I heard about people who are flying very, very high—not aeroplanes, but things that can go much higher?" For the next couple of miles, as we slowly walked the track, I explained as well as Neo-Melanesian would allow what the space project envisages—that we wanted to reach the moon first with unmanned spacecraft, later to construct a "half-way house" in space, and finally to land a man on the moon. Waʔiyo, my companion, listened intently and asked a number of questions of a practical nature regarding this venture. As shadows were lengthening, we reached Akuna and set about preparing our evening meal, completely forgetting our discussion. It was not raised again.

II

On the afternoon of January 20, 1962, a number of the old men in the village, led by the *luluai*[3] of Akuna came to my house. They were clearly upset. After the usual formalities the luluai turned to me and with a grave expression informed me that they had just returned from Kainantu. The *kiap*[4] had called all the village headmen from the sub-district to the administrative headquarters and had warned them of two things. The first and foremost was that there was to be a solar eclipse on the fourth of February and that they should not be affected by any teachings people might express. "In two weeks, the fourth of February, the sun will disappear for five minutes," the kiap said. The luluai returned to Akuna and told his people and me, "The kiap says that on the fourth day of February the sun will disappear for two weeks." The second warning was that when the sun disappeared, the people should not look into the sky unless they had sunglasses to protect their eyes.

That evening I accepted an invitation to attend a meeting of the old men in the village. Answering questions, I told them that the sun would be obscured for a few minutes but after that the day and the following days would be normal. During the following two weeks representatives from neighboring villages, even from a neighboring linguistic group, the Tairora, came to my house to hear it explained. They would say, "Tell us what you told the men from

Tompena who came to you." Repeatedly I explained that nothing out of the ordinary was going to happen, that if it were I would certainly prepare for it; but look, "I am remaining right here with you people," I would conclude.

During the following and final week repeated reports were received about preparations for the tudark, as it had been dubbed in Neo-Melanesian. The radio reported shortages of kerosene and sunglasses throughout New Guinea because the natives were preparing for the darkness by seeking the magical powers the sunglasses would give them. A missionary allegedly was telling his converts that the whites were not afraid of the impending darkness because they wore neckties. From a friendly old lady in Boston he had received a large number of old wide ties, which he sold to his "congregation." On a trip beyond the Arona valley I encountered a person who was "safe"; he wore a traditional grass skirt, a zoot American tie, and sunglasses. The administrative officer at Kainantu explained later that certain persons, especially among the Auyana[5]—long a hotbed for cargo movements—were in fact capitalizing on the state of mind of the people,[6] manipulating their fears and their uncertainty to their own advantage.

During the week immediately preceding the tudark people in Akuna repeatedly asked me about the coming events. They wanted to safeguard themselves by being repeatedly assured. During those last days there was much talk about preparing a large men's house in which all the people could assemble. That was being done by other villages, but Akuna did not go that far, possibly due to my presence. A few days before the event was to occur, we visited Wayopa, a daughter village of Akuna that had split off and contained many kinsmen of the mother village. As we entered the village, I noticed a large house under construction. It was built in the traditional round form rather than in the square, which the people now build because of administrative pressures.

When the village headman, Opura, told us that it was associated with the problems created by the tudark, I questioned him about his fears. "How do you think it is possible for the sun to disappear for two weeks, and even if it did, what would that do to you?" He sat down and told me about the ancestors and what had happened when his father was young. Once during those years it had grown dark, he explained, and the earth was covered with white powder (sometime in the past there was a volcanic eruption in that area of the highlands).[7] The pigs had become vicious, and large wild pigs had come out of the forests. When he was asked what that had to do with the house they were building, he explained that they would all gather in there—the entire village—and that the people were already gathering large supplies of firewood, food, and water in bamboo containers. They feared, he said, that the long period of darkness would result in a repetition of the earlier situation and that the large wild pigs would come down from the forest and attack people. They also expected the ancestors to return, and they were all going to be waiting for them in a central ceremonial structure. We departed in late afternoon for Akuna and did not see Opura or anybody from his village until the following week, in spite of the fact that they normally visited Akuna frequently and regularly.

III

When an anthropologist is in the field, he cannot always easily get the supplies he needs. We had an arrangement with members of the Summer Institute of Linguistics, who have a headquarters about ten miles from Akuna, across the mountain. Whenever necessary I would walk in and borrow their Land Rover to go shopping; somebody from their group would accompany us to Akuna and then drive the Land Rover back. This meant, however, that when we made our shopping trip once every two months, we returned to the village with an impressive load of canned foods, tins of kerosene, etc. A shopping trip was scheduled for February third, but only after we returned to Akuna did this strike me. As we were unloading the Land Rover, I noticed the luluai and a number of the old men looking at us. They did not say a word, but just looked, their faces drawn with indecision. Still the reason for this cool reception did not dawn on me. But as soon as we had unpacked the supplies and sat down to a hurriedly prepared meal, Wa?iyo came in and told me that the old men wanted to speak with me in the luluai's house. By then it was dark, and, flashlight in hand, I walked with Wa?iyo to the luluai's house. Squatting around the hearth in the center of the hut were most of the older men of Akuna. I sat down and accepted the food that was offered me in typical Gadsup hospitality. In the glowing embers there were a number of sweet potatoes for anyone who wanted more food.

The luluai turned to me and said, "Mata?o,[8] you have been telling us that we need not fear the tudark." I affirmed that. "Mata?o, you said we need not be afraid because you were not afraid and would be here in Akuna." Again I affirmed his statement. "Mata?o, then why did you today go and get enough food and kerosene for two weeks?" Suddenly I realized why I had received such a cool reception that afternoon and why I had been summoned to this meeting as soon as they had discussed the situation. All I could do was laugh and attempt to explain. I explained that they well realized that I did not go into the trade store very frequently, and that when I did it was to buy supplies for a long time. Again the luluai asked, "Mata?o, if you people are not scared of the tudark, why is it that all the Americans are escaping to the moon?" That question completely floored me; when I asked him to explain, he said, "Didn't you tell Wa?iyo that the Americans were going to the moon in large flying houses?" I remembered our conversation of some months ago on the way back from eastern Gadsup, and again a long and technical explanation was called for.

Since it was the eve of the solar eclipse that had caused much concern and nervous tension, I decided to explain in detail what caused the eclipse. We were still squatting around the hearth, with the only light coming from glowing coals. On the floor in front of me lay my second roasted sweet potato and some little distance away another. Suddenly an idea struck me, and I said to the men, "Look here, do you see this sweet potato on the floor? This is New Guinea, and this little stick I am putting on it is our village. Look, luluai, here you are!" (I must admit that my introductory astronomy was completely forgotten; in fact, I could not even remember what turned around what, but

I had to speak fast.) Next I held up the flashlight in my right hand to about twenty-four inches above our earth-sweet potato, explaining that it was the sun. Then with the second sweet potato in my left hand I explained how the moon turned around the earth. Day and night were caused by the earth turning around its own axis allowing sunshine to fall on various parts alternately. At that stage the sweet potato in my left hand passed between the flashlight and the earth-sweet potato, casting a dark shadow on the earth and hanging over our village for a brief spell before moving on. Around the fire twenty pairs of eyes looked on in deep concentration, waiting for the next development. "That's the way it is going to be tomorrow morning. We will feel and see the shadow of the moon on our village and then it will move over like this . . . and then it is all over. That is all that is going to happen." Again the eclipse had to be acted out, and long discussions ensued about how the sun could be so hot and similar topics. The luluai and his friends assured me that they understood and believed the explanation. I again assured them that at nine the next morning I would stand in the village square with my wife and two-year-old daughter and they should join me there. This was agreed upon, and Waʔiyo and I climbed down from the house and walked across the quiet and deserted village square.

IV

Sunday, February 4, was a typical morning in the highlands. The air was crisp but not cold, and toward the east light, filmy clouds covered the sky. By eight that morning the sun was baking down on Akuna, and I walked out into the village square. It was quiet and deserted. The usual hustle and bustle of women sweeping the area in front of their houses, while children played around or nestled against the wall to escape the cool morning breeze was absent. The men who usually emerged yawning and stretching to discuss the day's activities with kinsmen or neighbors were not there.

Shortly after my arrival Waʔiyo emerged from his house, where he lived with his widowed mother. He came over to the center of the village square, where we stood talking. It did not seem advisable for me to approach any of the other houses or any of the people. This was a decision they had to make for themselves. After about thirty minutes Waʔiyo's cousin, Iripe, and another young fellow emerged from their houses but did not approach us. They squatted in the sun, watching us yet remaining very close to the doors to their houses. In the distance, west of us, I could see the Kate evangelist of the Lutheran mission leaning against the fence and watching us very closely. He did not greet us, as was his custom, nor did he come closer. At a quarter to nine my wife and baby daughter joined us in the village square. Nobody had emerged and nobody spoke. We knew there were people watching us in the dark entrances to the houses that surround the village square.

At last, after what seemed like a whole day of waiting, it was close to nine o'clock. It felt as if somebody had turned an air conditioner against my back as a shadow gradually engulfed the square and the whole village. The shadow increased to dusk. Then after a few long minutes the warmth gradually crept up my spine again, and the sun was once again shining brightly. Waʔiyo, who had stood between my wife and me was quiet, but I could hear his breathing return to normal.[9] His friends were still crouched at the entrances to their houses. The evangelist was still leaning against the fence watching us.

Since we knew that we had been watched throughout this event, my family stood around for a few minutes and then returned to our house. "It's all over now," I told Waʔiyo; he gave a nervous little laugh and called out to his friends to join us. As they were approaching, the evangelist climbed the fence and slowly came up to me, asking, "Is it over?" I assured him that the eclipse had passed. "Tomorrow ollesem?"[10] he asked, and I told him that this was all—the eclipse would not be repeated tomorrow or again soon. He was clearly disappointed at this news and slowly walked up to his house just west of the village fence.[11]

Except for the young people who were standing near us in the village square nobody had emerged, and I remained to see when life would return to normal. It was close to 11:30 A.M. before the older men emerged from their dark houses, and I assured them that it was all over and that life could now return to normal. The usual morning activities had been abandoned, and by noon a number of the men had joined us to make sure that it was safe and then returned to inform their wives that they could leave the safety of their houses. Little work was done that day because the people remained in or near the village discussing the great thing that had happened—and yet not happened.

V

Whether a revitalization movement would have developed if the administration had not called the luluais for a briefing is unknown. It is felt, however, that occurrences among neighboring groups, the general atmosphere at the time, and the train of events known to mission and other agents allowed for this possibility. The kiap in fact justified his action on that basis. Among the Gadsup speakers in and around Akuna the preconditions for such a movement were present. Had someone appeared to call on them to identify and associate with him because that great thing was going to happen and the ancestors were going to return, he would have been accepted. They did in fact go so far as to build ceremonial houses and congregate in them.

There are, of course, a number of points that can be made regarding this series of events. It is obvious that we have here the old problem of conceptualization. Cargo cults and variations on them in the form of other revitalization movements have repeatedly shown that they are likely to appear where there is cultural distance—differences in complexity, education, and similar aspects. In this case, people who had very little knowledge of physics were confronted with news of revolutionary changes in the system they were accustomed to and had accepted as set. But added to this is the fact, as Raymond Firth pointed out, that "cargo cults feed on rumour" (1955:131). Once the idea was distorted—for whatever reason—the rumor spread throughout this part of the highlands, and new elements were added. One of the major reasons for the distortion seems to have been the inability of most of the villagers to understand and internalize the phenomena that were reported to them.

A second point, related no doubt to the first, is the problem in communication and the linguistic barriers that had to be crossed. Catherine Berndt (1954) has pointed out the problems that exist even in translating material from one language in this region into another. The speaker of one language is faced with vocabulary, phonetic, and grammatical differences when he uses another language. That then complicates communication between different cultural and linguistic groups. When the speaker formulates his ideas in English, speaks in what Reinecke calls a *marginal language* (1964:535), such as the Neo-Melanesian used in this case, and then has his statement translated into native languages and dialects, these problems are compounded. The luluais who attended the meeting in Kainantu are in most cases unilingual. They returned to their villages and reported a situation that they could not understand, that was most likely distorted in transmission, and that they would tend to attach to the known to give it meaning. For that reason the rumor became linked to apocalyptic events that were said to be approaching. Even in cases where the luluai was a speaker of Neo-Melanesian or where he was accompanied by his *tultul* (who is always bilingual), we are still faced with the cultural differences. Haugen (1961) has discussed the problems of bilingualism, and he points out that languages must be seen and learned as *systems*. The units and individual items of a language might be learned and the speaker may be able to organize them into meaningful sentences, but he still does not know the language. He still is not familiar with cultural referents, with idioms and nuances, with speech habits and related aspects of communication. The cultural and linguistic distance between these two peoples, the initiators of the explanatory statement and the receivers of the distorted rumor, are the basic cause of this misconstruction.

But there is a further element in this series of events, namely the form and direction the reaction took. Discussing his Tikopian experience Firth states that "another later rumour was of the apocalyptic type which often is an accompaniment of, or alternative to, a 'cargo' movement" (1955:131). Melanesia, and especially New Guinea, has produced a large number of revitalization movements, all of which have certain elements in common; two elements that appear very frequently in these cultural reactions are the elements of the apocalypse—a slot that can be filled by any believer with initiative—and the millenarian trend. The latter in fact seems to have been present before Western cultural contact (du Toit 1965:117), and in the case of the Koreri especially we are dealing with very old cultural traditions (Kamma 1954). This may be true as well in the case of the Tangu, discussed by Burridge (1960). Professor Lanternari, in a private communication, suggests that we might have a mythological undertone that inspires exactly that kind of reaction in revitalization movements. He states, "I mean, that an exceptionally strongly impressive event like the solar eclipse, but also the arrival of an aeroplane, or of the whites for the first time,[12] may be the catalyzing factor for the *resurgence* of such millenarian expectations and ritualistic activities as you have shown . . . I say 'resurgence' rather than 'rising' because I am convinced that a millenarian pattern is underlying in many mythical traditional themes and attitudes." The study of this is an area in which anthropologists and folklorists can cooperate.

I hope that this account of events in the highlands of New Guinea will prompt others to report similar experiences. Only then will a clearer understanding of the preconditions of such cultural reactionary movements be reached.

NOTES

1 The events discussed in this paper occurred while I was carrying out a year's anthropological fieldwork among the Gadsup linguistic group in the eastern central highlands of Australian New Guinea as a member of an interdisciplinary research team of the Micro-Evolution Studies Project. This phase of the project was sponsored by a grant (G. 17283) from the National Science Foundation and functioned under the auspices of the University of Washington.

I decided to present these data in this form so that the reader can closely follow the series of events that occurred without being bogged down by theoretical or referential material and discussions. Comments on an earlier draft by Peter Worsley at the University of Manchester and Vittorio Lanternari in Rome are greatly appreciated and have been incorporated in this final draft.

A copy of this paper was read at the annual meeting of the American Folklore Society in Toronto, Canada, on November 18, 1967.

2 The primary reason for offering this material here, even though we have no proof or assurance that a movement of cultural revitalization would have followed, is the need for information at this level. Kopytoff states, "We need studies of cases where the preconditions (including the ideological) for a movement exist and yet no movement develops" (1964:85). Anthony Wallace has postulated five temporally overlapping but functionally distinct stages in such a movement (1962:146–152). We may in fact suggest that this community progressed to the second stage without developing any further. Referring to such a movement in Tikopia, Raymond Firth explains that "there can be a 'cargo-cult type of behavior,' without it attaining the organized coherence of a movement or a cult development" (1955:131).

3 Luluai is a Neo-Melanesian term that refers to a government-appointed village chief in New Guinea.

4 As in the previous case, kiap is Neo-Melanesian and refers to any government official, especially those associated with administration and taxation.

5 Among the Auyana speakers, a group living southwest of the Gadsup and separated from the latter by the Tairora, there were in fact strong cargo-type beliefs at this time. The natives believed that all the whites in the area would leave and their property and wealth would be left for the Auyana. Again there was a coincidence in that all the missionaries were leaving the area at that time to attend a Lutheran Missionary Conference in Madang on the north coast. As they left one after another, the belief that these things were in fact coming to pass was confirmed.

6 Melanesia, and New Guinea in particular, has produced a great number of revitalization movements primarily of the cargo type. Also in this part of the eastern highlands (Berndt 1952–53; 1954) such reactions have occurred. A similar movement in the Kainantu area in 1947 spread west to the Goroka district (Salisbury 1958:71–72). Although the Gadsup have less contact with people in the Markham valley, they traditionally traded with them, and there too such a movement had occurred (Read 1958). One of the most complete chronological and analytical studies to appear on this subject is that of Peter Lawrence (1964). He shows how in the Madang district on the north coast the cultural revitalization movement was grafted onto preexisting cultural prototypes. The Road Belong Cargo then was simultaneously leading from the accepted mythological and religious traditions and to a new way for which God would provide

the cargo. This may in fact be the type of situation Lanternari speaks of (1967) as a mythological pattern for millenarianism. When the administrative officer in Kainantu learned that similar tendencies were developing among the Auyana, he was justified in calling all the village chiefs in his district for a briefing session. The impending visit of scientists from various countries had in fact been reported in a Neo-Melanesian paper published in Lae, and since only the evangelists and a number of acculturated persons were able to read this, the man in the village could well have been exploited. The mistranslation, misinterpretation, and misconstruction of his words of caution could not be foreseen by the official.

[7] Bulmer and Bulmer (1964:56–57) in their survey study of the prehistory of the New Guinea Highlands refer to "volcanic ash falls, which are described in folk histories from several parts of the Highlands" as a possible reason for the covering over of archaeological finds. Also, the geographer Brookfield (1961:440), in discussing volcanism, mentions these traditional stories among the peoples of the western highlands. Referring to similar folkloristic data that he attempted to date. Watson (1963) has suggested that this eruption and the subsequent ash fall might not have occurred on the main island of New Guinea. He says that it might represent the eruption of Krakatoa in 1883. More empirically, Lloyd Rhys (1942:203–205) refers to tremors and earthquakes that have affected the northern area especially. One such case occurred on September 20 and 21, 1935, in the Torricelli mountains. McCarthy (1963:158) says that the loss in human lives was under 150 people but that the damage was severe and widespread. Volcanic eruptions such as Mount Lamington (Keesing 1952) occurred more recently.

[8] This is a local phonetic corruption of the general form of address, "Master."

[9] The impressiveness of this event cannot be overstated. Here are a group of people who have been accustomed to the regularity of natural events and the certainty of sunrise and sunset separated by a day of light, a day during which the sun will shine and even when visibly obstructed by a cloud can still be seen and the effects perceived and explained. These people do not understand the conditions that cause the disappearance of the sun. In private communication Professor Lanternari states, "I saw that eclipse in February 1962. There was a strong impulse to apocalyptic visions or imaginations, even in an urban milieu such as Rome!"

[10] Neo-Melanesian: "Tomorrow all the same?"

[11] Although this cannot be stated categorically, I had the feeling during the days preceding the eclipse that the evangelist was somehow enjoying the fear of the local people and possibly even baiting it. If this was the case, I never learned of any attempt to use it to his personal advantage. A number of writers have remarked on this subject, but Lawrence (1964:82–83) discusses the whole problem created by evangelists who have settled in native villages and misrepresent the missionary teachings. For this reason too the Lutheran church that stands in Akuna and is served by an evangelist is already syncretistic to a great extent.

[12] Both of these historic events, namely the first view of an aeroplane and the first contact with a white missionary in his valley, produced very similar reactions. The first thought, as informants report it, was that the ancestors had returned. A full account of these changes will appear in du Toit (in press).

REFERENCES CITED

BERDNT, CATHERINE H.
    1954   Translation problems in three New Guinea highland languages. Oceania 24:289–317.
BERDNT, RONALD M.
    1952–53   A cargo movement in the eastern central highlands of New Guinea. Oceania 23:202–234.
    1954   Reaction to contact in the eastern highlands of New Guinea. Oceania 24:256–274.

BROOKFIELD, H. C.
1961   The highland peoples of New Guinea, a study of distribution and localization. Geographical Journal 127:436–448.
BULMER, S., and
R. BULMER
1964   The prehistory of the Australian New Guinea highlands. American Anthropologist 66 (4, pt. 2):39–76.
BURRIDGE, K. O. L.
1960   Mambu, a Melanesian millennium. London.
DU TOIT, BRIAN M.
1965   Beperkte Lidmaatskap. Cape Town.
In press Akuna: A New Guinea Village Community.
FIRTH, RAYMOND
1955   The theory of "cargo" cults: a note on Tikopia. Man 55:130–132.
HAUGEN, EINAR
1961   The bilingual individual. In Psycholinguistics. Sol Saporta, ed. New York.
KAMMA, F. C.
1954   De Messiaanse Koreri-Bewegingen in het Biaks-Noemfoorse Cultuurgebied. The Hague.
KEESING, F. M.
1952   The Papuan Orokaiva vs. Mt. Lamington: cultural shock and its aftermath. Human Organization 11(1):16–22.
KOPYTOFF, IGOR
1964   Classification of religious movements: analytical and synthetic. In Symposium on new approaches to the study of religion. June Helm, ed. Seattle (for American Ethnological Society).
LANTERNARI, VITTORIO
1967   Personal communication.
LAWRENCE, PETER
1964   Road belong cargo. Manchester.
McCARTHY, J. D.
1963   Patrol into yesterday. Melbourne.
READ, K. E.
1958   A cargo situation in the Markham Valley, New Guinea. Southwestern Journal of Anthropology 14:273–294.
REINECKE, JOHN E.
1964   Trade jargons and creole dialects as marginal languages. In Language in culture and society. Dell Hymes, ed. New York.
RHYS, LLOYD
1942   Highlights and flights in New Guinea. London.
SALISBURY, RICHARD F.
1958   An "indigenous" New Guinea cult. Kroeber Anthropological Papers 18:67–78.
WALLACE, ANTHONY F. C.
1962   Culture and personality. New York.
WATSON, JAMES B.
1963   Krakatoa's Echo. Journal of the Polynesian Society 72:152–155.

CONSENSUS AND DISSENT IN GHANA

Jack Goody

JACK GOODY, a fellow of St. John's College, Cambridge University, and director of its African Studies Centre, has undertaken field research in Ghana from 1950 to 1952, from 1956 to 1957, from 1964 to 1966, and from 1969 to 1970. He was also a fellow of the Centre for Advanced Study in the Behavioural Sciences. He is the author of The Social Organization of the Lowiili (1956), Death, Property and the Ancestors (1962), Comparative Studies in Kinship (1969), and Technology, Tradition and the State in Africa (1971) and is editor of The Developmental Cycle in Domestic Groups, Succession to High Office (1966) and Literacy in Traditional Societies (1969).

In the larger towns of Ghana, the Young Pioneers[1] used to parade through the streets singing party songs and carrying banners proclaiming that "Nkrumah never dies," "Nkrumah is the new Messiah." Meanwhile the press extolled the virtues of Nkrumahism and of African socialism, and the party controlled virtually all trade-union, cooperative, and similar activities. The local administration, too, had been "politicized" and both regional and district commissioners were party appointees.

Both administratively and ideologically the party was in charge. Of dissensus there was little evidence: the ballot boxes announced massive support; the mass media showed no dissent; Nkrumah (political scientists maintained) was a charismatic leader. Moreover, few if any of the many academic commentators who visited the country ventured to predict any radical change in the situation.

On February 24, 1966, Colonel Kotoka led a military coup against the existing regime. On this day, I spent some hours in the streets of the capital, Accra. The public reaction was immediate and visible, and the change-over was widely welcomed: almost at once posters appeared which caricatured the deposed leader and cast aspersions on the circumstances of his birth; the relics of his rule were torn down from public buildings; market women danced through the streets wearing the white headscarves of victory; some Young Pioneers (just before they were officially disbanded) marched through the streets of the capital bearing banners that proclaimed "Nkrumah is NOT our Messiah."

Some two weeks after the coup I traveled to several small administrative centers in Northern Ghana that I had known over a period of years. Only the district commissioners and members of Parliament were in prison. Nevertheless the whole of the party structure had totally vanished. The Young Pioneer organizers had literally disappeared "into the bush"; the ex-party chairman of the small modern town of Salaca was busy making public gestures of commitment to the new regime (donations to the army, presents to the populace).

Reprinted with permission from the Political Science Quarterly, 58 (September 1968), 337–352.

The large majority of party supporters had become forthright in their criticism of its rule.

There are many questions which this situation raises. The main one that comes to mind is, How was such a sudden and complete reversal possible? Subsidiary to this are the questions, Why was it not foreseen and how permanent is the new situation? In this paper I want to try to elucidate some aspects of the change in "support" and to discuss some implications of the process for the study of political institutions.

In speaking of a reversal I am not primarily concerned with the method of changing political power—that was accomplished by the army. I am concerned rather with the reversal of "belief," "commitment," "ideology," "consensus," "attitude," "opinion."

I

In the later years of Convention People's party rule, "support" was difficult to assess; the ballot box was no longer an adequate instrument for the measurement of opinion; at the time of the latest election (1965) many reliable reports spoke of the sealing of the "No" boxes, and the burning of negative papers. On the interpersonal level, it was generally thought injudicious to express critical opinions, and individuals one had known over many years avoided the subject of politics, except where their views coincided with those of the government; that is to say, the regime got considerable support from "intellectuals" over such issues as Rhodesia (the call for volunteers appeared on university notice boards and received a reasonable response) partly because of the reservations they had on other issues.

There had been, of course, a change in the nature of the "support" over time. Before independence, the Convention People's party received the majority of votes cast by the citizens of Ghana[2] at a period when it was possible to present alternative views to the voting public.[3] At this time there was no doubt at all about its popular appeal. With the proscription of other political groups and with the penetration of the party into virtually all fields of advancement, it became more difficult to gauge the level of "support"; the ballot box certainly provided no measure. Nor was there any satisfactory alternative. The failure to recruit many intellectuals (university students and lecturers, for example) to the party was some indication that things were not as they had been. But those who were committed to the *status quo* could easily dismiss such groups as unrepresentative or as holding views based upon particular (for example, bourgeois) interests. Moreover, the network of paid informers, the preventive arrests, above all the desire for a peaceful life, meant that open discussion of disapproval took place only between foreigners or between very close friends,[4] if at all. As a consequence, expatriate commentators were always inclined to equate official statements with popular attitudes, while even the dissenters themselves could never be sure of the extent to which their views were shared by others. There was no community of dissent.

Some two weeks after the events of February 24 (originally known as coup or revolution depending upon the political persuasion of the speaker), Colonel

Kotoka told me that he had estimated ninety-five per cent of the people would be behind the coup and had therefore anticipated little bloodshed. His forecast proved correct, but such prescience was rare. Few foreign commentators (and fewer political scientists) came out with such a view (in advance), and it is clear from the ex-President's post-coup exhortations from Guinea that he was equally misinformed about the temper of the populace; otherwise he would have realized the futility of trying to galvanize the Young Pioneers and the Workers Brigade into action against the new authorities.

And so, both among the politicians, hearing what they wanted to hear, and among the political scientists, located in some newly created *zongo*, whether university compound, international hotel, or "residential" area, there was a tendency to gauge present support in terms of past evidence. But such an approach failed to take account of trends in ruler-subject relationships. In no political system, business organization, or university department can the leadership fill all the expectations of the personnel. The less "realistic" the demands, the greater the gap between wish and fulfillment. When Ghana achieved independence, certain of the expectations of the people were economically "irrational" under the conditions that obtained. In 1957, my assistant (later a Young Pioneer Organizer) thought of increased American imports, especially of "cowboy" hats, as the most desirable of the future benefits. Others, with the general interest more at heart, pinned their faith on mechanized agriculture, still not successfully tested in West Africa. Hopes of this kind (found in all modern political systems) are bound to remain at least partly unfulfilled; from the standpoint of the supporters, all political programs have an aspect of the cargo cult about them.[5] While the failure, or postponement, of expected benefits may lead to a temporary reinforcement of beliefs, in the end a measure of disillusionment is bound to set in.[6] In multi-party regimes, the movement in and out of power provides a mechanism whereby such beliefs can continue to be sustained without rejecting the system itself; the possibility of a new president, or the next prime minister, represents the prospect of a new dawn, at least for a substantial part of the electorate; even the cabinet reshuffle has its cathartic effects. In monarchical regimes a similar function is served by the natural turnover of royalty; a new ruler brings into being new hopes, "a new Elizabethan age." Indeed, in some societies a new era began with every reign; the calendar was a calendar of kings. In others, the desire to install a new ruler may have led to the extinction of the old.[7] But in one-party states, succession to high office can rarely be routinized; even open discussion of the problem is likely to be identified as potential rebellion. Consequently there is no such outlet, no safety valve, for the frustration that inevitably arises not only out of the power situation, but also from the inevitable discrepancy between expected and actual returns.[8] In the absence of either institutionalized "rituals of rebellion"[9] or anticipated changes of personnel, commitment (if not "consensus") is bound to diminish with the passage of time; the revolutionary momentum cannot be indefinitely sustained; slogans such as "Nkrumah will never die" are no balm for incipient discontent.

The rise and fall of such a ruler's "popularity rating" (or that of his government), the developmental cycle of support for change-oriented leadership, is concealed by the manipulation of ballots, by organized demonstrations, and by people's inhibitions about openly expressing their views.

In many respects this progress of events, the disenchantment of the populace, exemplifies Frantz Fanon's model for the aftermath of independence.

> The bourgeoisie who are in power vainly increase the number of processions; the masses have no illusions. They are hungry; and the police officers, though they are now Africans, do not serve to reassure them particularly. The masses begin to sulk; they turn away from this nation in which they have been given no place. . . . Since [independence the] party has sadly disintegrated; nothing is left but the shell of a party, the name, the emblem, the motto. . . . Today the party's mission is to deliver to the people the instructions which issue from the summit. . . . After independence, the party sinks into an extraordinary lethargy. The militants are only called upon when so-called popular manifestations are afoot, or international conferences, or independence celebrations. The local party leaders are given administrative posts, the party becomes an administration. . . . The party is becoming a means of private advancement.[10]

Fanon regarded this progression as characteristic of "bourgeois" parties alone. The Convention People's party was not of this kind, though for some it became a means of attaining bourgeois status: indeed, the system of stratification in Africa south of the Sahara hardly allowed of the growth of parties which were differentiated along lines of economically based classes. Orthodox Marxist attempts to apply class analysis to Africa usually fail to recognize the quite different kind of production relationships that existed in the pre-industrial systems, and that still exist today.[11] Neither here, nor in other spheres of social life, does the mechanical importation of European schemes have much to contribute to Africa. As far as Fanon's analysis is concerned, his idealistic viewpoint prevents him from isolating the general factors in the growth cycle of popular support that are common to all regimes, whether the parties are "single" or "multiple," "bourgeois" or "mass," "progressive" or "reactionary," "Left" or "Right."

When the regime in Ghana ended, by sudden and unanticipated military moves, the reaction was powerful and immediate: consensus, at least about the immediate past, was overwhelming, and even ministers and confidants of the ex-President hastened to express their misgivings; at least in the towns, the masses enthusiastically celebrated their relief; the university became, overnight, a center of vigorous discussion about the affairs of state, and has continued as such to this day.

The reaction to the coup was primarily negative in the sense that it was directed first and foremost toward eliminating the faults of the past. "What went wrong in Ghana?" was the title of a popular series of lectures, launched in March 1966 by the extramural department of the university. On the day of the coup itself, an element of spontaneous regression was very noticeable. I overheard a couple refer jokingly to their country as Gold Coast rather than Ghana, and there were shouts for the former opposition party (National Liberation Movement) until it was rumored that army policy was against all parties, not only the one which had recently monopolized political office.

This situation did not, of course, persist. Agreement about the past was accompanied by an increasing diversity of views about future action. Many constitutional flowers are now in bud. Some would reject political parties, single or multiple; others would retain military rule, and others stress the role of traditional rulers.[12] No doubt this plurality of belief, this condition of loose ideological structure, will persist until the situation is crystallized, until opinion is mobilized, for example, by the formation of political parties that serve to polarize in simple binary form the current diversity of views.

If any new consensus were to develop this might be expected among the fairly homogeneous body of students at the University of Ghana, Legon. However, a recent survey[13] shows a considerable range of views even about something as basic as the return to civilian rule. "About one third think civilian rule should come within eighteen months, but 43% think it will take at least five years or that no limits can be set" (p. 7). While students were in complete agreement about rejecting one-party rule, a tenth of the students rejected political parties altogether. As with the chiefs, parties were seen as instruments of conflict rather than as bases of consensus.

The issues on which the students did show large measures of agreement, namely, the desirability of a unitary constitution (seventy-six per cent) and a unicameral legislature (seventy-two per cent), were rather less significant than those on which they showed a great spread of opinion, or even a retreat from decision-making. The desire for a prolongation of army rule was expressed before Dr. Busia's reminder of the dangers facing military governments, a timely reminder that was quickly followed by an attempted coup on April 17, 1967.[14] But the basis of this desire appears to be not so much a positive inclination to military government as fear of the alternative possibilities. Indeed, the same might be said for no-party proposals supported by the chiefs, for as yet no one knows what a no-party electoral system would look like. In putting this view before the Constitutional Committee, one of the supporting speakers said "the chiefs did not have in mind that the country should stick forever to no-party governments; they intended the system to be only a stop-gap, while the country was getting 'ripe' for party politics."[15] This lack of certainty is also apparent from the fact that twenty-five per cent of students gave no answer when asked "What measures would you suggest for encouraging a stable and continuous democratic system in Ghana?"

The effect of relaxing the general pressure toward "enforced consensus," of lifting the lid, can be seen not only in ideological uncertainty but also in restlessness to discipline of any kind; the more permissive atmosphere is more tolerant of protest and of dissent. The results of political decompression are most visible in the student population where "revolts" have occurred both at the universities and in the schools. The former were discussed by Professor A. Kwapong, vice-chancellor of the University of Ghana, in his address to the Congregation on March 26, 1966.

> Since the return of freedom to this country, we have witnessed a wave of restlessness and a sense of malaise among the young in our schools and Universities. In a way, this questioning of authority and restlessness have always been the natural condition of the young throughout history, and we

have all of us been young before. . . . For the past six years, until the 24th of February, 1966, freedom of expression and conscience, and with this, freedom of the young to rebel had been effectively silenced. Now, with the removal of our frustrations and the return of liberty, there is the danger that the sudden access of this almost unfamiliar blessing may be taken by some for licence. . . .[16]

These reactions against authority occurred at the Universities of Legon and Kumasi (where they led to the resignation of the principal) and in a number of secondary schools. It has been suggested that these activities were connected with the tightening up of entrance standards to the university. While educational advancement is certainly a matter of considerable concern (since the ban on party politics, the university has become second only to the army as the main avenue of social advance), the revolts started long before there were any announced or even anticipated changes.[17] And in the university at least, the aims of the students were domestic rather than educational or "political."[18]

In Ghana today there is continual exploration of alternative possibilities for good government. Many are in favor of a multi-party system, and they are backed by a good deal of legal thinking which, having been in the forefront of the early phases of nationalist endeavor, is now oriented toward those "Western" forms in which they see "the law" and themselves as most easily operating. All, however, are aware that a multi-party system can simply be a prelude to the establishment of a one-party regime by the victors. Nowhere in independent Africa has a regime allowed itself to be changed by means of the ballot box.[19] This situation does not arise from "political immaturity" but from the rejection (primarily by political leaders) of specific ways of transmitting office implicit in the electoral system. Unless these rules of the game are accepted by the participants, the result must be a one-party regime, either nominally (as in the regions of Nigeria) or legally (as in Ghana). When this happens, the only instrument of change is the armed forces.

It is the fear that the multi-party system will be manipulated by those who do not accept its basic rules which makes many Ghanaians wary of recourse to a political system where the party is the all-dominating institution it has so often become in Africa and elsewhere. But such hesitation is also motivated by the fear of a return to the violence of extra-electoral conflict that occurred between the CPP and the NLM during the years 1954 to 1956.[20]

The discussion concerning the no-party state is a widespread reaction to one-party rule and the violence that marked the final years of the two-party system. A recent example of this discussion is found in K. O. Adjei, "No Party System—A Revolution in Political Thinking," The Ashanti Pioneer, June 17, 1967. In "Proper Approach to Party Politics is Needed," The Ghanian Times, June 17, 1967, H. K. Bidi Setsoafia advocates a return to party politics, but he does so very guardedly, giving sympathetic treatment to both the chiefs' case and to the suggestion put forward by Mr. Yaw Twumasi, university lecturer in political science and editor of the influential Legon Observer, that "perhaps the safest way to take in planning the future constitution of this country was to build on our chieftaincy, our institution which has for many years been practised in this country, than perhaps adopting again party politics which is completely foreign to us in Ghana." In a situation of political reversal, where a new system of government and its operators have been found wanting on grounds both of morality[21] and social organization, it is not surprising that there should have been a renewal of interest in the chiefship and in churches.

It is considerations of this kind, combined with a general distrust of "politicians" (which has increased since a plethora of commissions publicly revealed their private activities) that makes many people advocate a prolongation of military rule or express an aversion to party government. Such an attitude immediately raises grave problems. If parties are out, the main problem for an electoral system becomes the selection of candidates and the formulation and communication of alternative policies. The suggested solutions to the initial choice of candidates (the selection of the "eligibles") vary between central nomination by Parliament or by temporary parties ("to be dissolved after the election") and local nomination by bodies of rate-payers, chiefs, trades unions, etc.

Such ideas, as yet adumbrated only in memos to commissions, letters to the newspapers, and in personal discussions, are countered by the constitutional traditionalists. These others believe that it was the party and the politicians who have failed, not the system itself.[22] As one journalist recently asked, "If party politics has succeeded in many other parts of the world, why should it not succeed in Africa?"[23]

II

An attempt to answer this fundamental question is an essential preliminary to the planning of any new governmental system. It is not sufficient to pronounce upon the necessity for, or the futility of, the "Westminster model" without trying to analyze the particular difficulties involved. We should begin by recognizing the costs (as well as the gains) of the multi-party system. Such a system means nothing unless there is some oscillation between the parties; in a situation of "pure" competition, the developmental trends we have already noted will ensure that such changes occur. If the opposing parties do not simply offer the electorate a change of personnel, but a change of policy as well, then it is clear that an element of discontinuity will be introduced into key areas of planning. The problem is a basic one for all Socialist parties in an electoral regime, whether in Europe, Asia, or Africa, and in just the same way the system often acts as a brake on unrestricted "capitalism." But continuity of planning and the mobilization of national effort may be seen as having greater importance in those new nations where rapid development is the major aim of the ruling elites; and these ends the single party can more easily promote.

However, the principal threat to multi-party rule is not, I think, the planned economy. Nor (as I have remarked) is it a question of "political immaturity"; there is nothing immature about wanting to consolidate one's power. Neither is it only a matter (as some of the present defenders of the multi-party system suggest)[24] of the venality of particular politicians. While the "intellectual" politicians of present-day Ghana are certainly not "rogues," the demagogic atmosphere of competitive politics will bring to the fore less conscientious contestants and less scrupulous tactics.

If the problem existed only on the "political" level, it would be easier to deal with. But in a situation where superiors are traditionally offered gifts of solicitation and thanksgiving, where politicians (like chiefs in earlier times) can easily influence appointments to jobs, where these jobs are becoming increasingly scarce as the growth of education outstrips the capacity to absorb the educated in non-traditional occupations—under these conditions, support is easily bought by those who succeeded in reaching positions of power. Moreover, those holding such positions, lucrative in terms of both salary and power, have little to fall back on when they relinquish their grip on office. In Britain, the defeated M.P. can retire to a company directorship or a trade-union post; in West Africa, a change to the position of village schoolmaster or council clerk represents a great drop both in salary and status, and even these jobs may fall within the patronage of one's political opponents.

This general problem of developing countries crops up in a particular form in present-day Ghana. While the party machinery virtually disappeared overnight, the absorption into other jobs of former members of Parliament, district commissioners, and party officials was a major social problem. In those areas in Northern Ghana with which I am personally acquainted, the majority of such individuals have returned to their former occupations, usually school teaching. But some had no substantial qualifications for "white-collar" jobs, and others have been unwilling to make the adjustment; these are either "roaming" or "farming," that is, sitting around the house. Clearly this category of ex-functionary represents a potential focus for dissatisfaction; even those among them who now express doubts about the previous regime cannot help regretting the glory it imparted to their lives. It was not surprising, therefore, that when the coup of Lieutenant Arthur on April 17 looked as though it would be successful (he had captured the radio and proclaimed his victory), some of these former officials openly celebrated the demise of the National Liberation Council, even though there was no suggestion that the new junta was more inclined to support Nkrumah than the first. Many of the individuals who engaged in this premature rejoicing were promptly placed under protective custody. Nevertheless, there is little evidence to show that the majority was primarily interested in the re-establishment of the previous regime. It was rather the reoccupation of their former positions; and they will be equally anxious to "get their own back" when an electoral system offers them the opportunity.

The problems of party government in developing countries like Ghana, then, lie not so much in a lack of political education, nor in the failure to achieve consensus, as in the economic and social situation of the third world. With the virtual absence of private employers, those who want jobs have to get them from government agencies; the educated exceed the employed. The temptations to manipulate are enormous and there is little institutional plurality to compensate, and few checks and balances to the exercise of politicians' power. Under such conditions we cannot visualize effective multi-party government of a

Western kind, while to many, the costs of one-party rule make this a yet less attractive proposition. The military provide the only ultimate sanction against the monopolization of power, and, while they claim to regard their rule as only temporary (and indeed appear to act on this assumption), their first intervention is hardly likely to be their last.

The alternation of civilian and military rule will, I think, dominate the pattern of West African government over many years to come, and such a pattern will to some degree reflect popular demands, or at least receive the approbation of the masses. But the swing of the pendulum could be controlled, by trying to limit the role of political parties and of the military forces.

In suggesting that an attempt could be made to restrict the power and function of parties, we need to remind ourselves that there is, after all, no divine law that allows them to operate, everywhere, in a situation of uninhibited competition; one could even legislate for a regular rotation between alternative lists (as in nineteenth-century Portugal), a system which provides a considerable check upon the action of the political haves against the temporary have-nots. What would be the sanctions against a breach of the rules? Here one has to recognize the *de facto* role of the army in political systems of all kinds, but especially in the new nations. It would seem possible to allocate to the army (or perhaps a supreme court, backed by the army) the function of preserving the agreed constitution. To specify the conditions under which the army should intervene might at least limit its arbitrary role in government and make its interference less unpredictable than it is now in so many West African countries. To make this attempt is to recognize that, for any political system, consensus is desirable, but force is essential.

III

There are many reasons why academic observers of the Ghanaian scene, political scientists, historians, sociologists, failed to assess reaction to a coup, in particular the virtually complete disintegration of the party and its auxiliaries. To discuss all these reasons here would be unnecessary, but there is one point of general interest which is not easily sidestepped.

Academic observers from Western Europe and America have inevitably tended to extrapolate from their own cultural experience in analyzing contemporary Africa. They have placed great stress on research into the growth of political parties, on electoral processes, on the development of consensus, and on other elements in the political system that strike a chord in their own tradition. They tend to make a rigid distinction between consensus as the instrument of politicians and force as the instrument of the military. A clearer appreciation of their own past and indeed present might have modified this view; so, too, would a recognition that a state organization involves the control of armed force.

The idealist position over-emphasizes the role of ideological consensus, and such a view is reinforced by the anthropological approach, recently imported into "modern" political studies, that calls for an analysis of the "political culture." As in many "anthropological" studies, culture gets reified, norms rigidified, social action homogenized, and "models" acquire a specious generality and an unsanctioned authority.

The situation in contemporary Ghana illustrates the ease with which apparent support can evaporate, especially following a change from a condition of "enforced consensus." One aspect of the reaction to political decompression is a state of ideological restlessness, and a proliferation of solutions to the problems of social organization. In Ghana, these preferred solutions do not derive primarily from any systematic ideology, but consist of attempts to arrive at "more adequate" social arrangements by building upon certain pre-existing elements of organization and belief, and trying to arrive at new combinations.

Just as Western social science has tended to place too much stress upon consensus, as against coercion, so, too, it has given too much attention to ideology and belief as "systems" on the group and individual level.

In the recent volume *Ideology and Discontent*,[25] we are offered little by way of a definition of ideology, apart from the editorially approved statement of Erikson that it is "an unconscious tendency underlying religious and scientific thought as well as political thought."[26] Given the somewhat limited techniques that social scientists have produced to deal with conscious elements in verbal (and quasi-verbal) behavior, it is difficult to see them making much headway with the unconscious. Indeed, another contributor finds the term ideology "so muddied by diverse uses" that he substitutes "belief system," defined as "a configuration of ideas and attitudes in which the elements are bound together by some form of constraint or functional interdependence."[27]

In the last analysis, all behavior of man and nature is "functionally interdependent." The question here is one of relevance. Too great a stress on the systematic aspects of beliefs, ideologies, societies, and cultures renders incomprehensible the inconsistencies in behavior (on "normative" and "actual" levels), the contradictions between attitudinal elements ("personal" and "group"), and the developmental aspects of belief. The logic behind the internal dynamics of the changing situations that characterize Africa today lies not so much in functional interdependence of belief, nor in the coherence of culture, but in the conflicts within social structure and in the fact that on the folk level, beliefs are rarely as systematic, as consensual, as univalent, as they are presented analytically. Comprehensive ideologies, systematic structures of belief, these are social artifacts of strictly limited distribution, both within and across societies.

NOTES

[1] The Young Pioneers was the youth wing of the one party, the Convention People's party (CPP).

[2] Even here, the dropping of a paper into a box with a similar mark cannot, as many numerical studies tend to assume, be taken as an equivalent act in different communities at different times. Voting is a social action whose meaning depends upon the particular situation; this fact presents a source of complication for cross-cultural psephology.

[3] The "balance of presentation" clearly differed from place to place, depending upon the local political situation, control of mass media, and the like.

[4] In this kind of situation the reactions of foreign residents need to be treated with

particular care; since their major ties (of kinship and citizenship, for example) lie elsewhere and since they are occupationally more mobile, they are freer to take risks in their comments; in any case, these would not have earned them detention, but at worst expulsion. Unlike a country's citizens, they always carry a return ticket in their pocket, a fact that conditions their assessment of the political situation.

[5] See P. Worsley, *The Trumpet Shall Sound* (London, 1957).

[6] See L. Festinger's work on cognitive dissonance, and, in particular, L. Festinger, H. W. Riecken, and S. Schachter, *When Prophecy Fails* (Minneapolis, 1956).

[7] This is, of course, a central theme of Sir James Frazer's work *The Golden Bough.*

[8] See my discussion in Jack Goody (ed.), *Succession to High Office*, Cambridge Papers in Social Anthropology, Vol. 4 (Cambridge, 1966).

[9] M. Gluckman, *Rituals of Rebellion* (Manchester, Eng., 1954).

[10] Frantz Fanon, *The Wretched of the Earth* (London, 1965), 137–38.

[11] This point is appreciated by Max Gluckman and W. Arthur Lewis. The latter comments: "West African politics is not a Marxist-type struggle between haves and have-nots. Neither is it a struggle between a new modernising middle-class elite and a backward aristocracy. . . . West African society does not fit into the Marxist categories. The area is under-populated, so land is abundant, and in most tribes a man has a right to as much land as he can cultivate. Hence landlords, rents, oppressed peasants and landless labourers are rare. . . . Landlordism is not a political factor. Neither is capitalism." (*Politics in West Africa* [London, 1965], 18.) The basic reason behind this situation is technological; nowhere in Africa do you find any great development of intensive agriculture because nowhere do you find the plough. The implications of this fact are rarely understood by those historians who talk of African "feudalism," nor yet by those agriculturalists who want to jump straight from hoe to tractor.

[12] The Joint Standing Committee of the House of Chiefs submitted a memorandum to the Constitutional Committee who were hearing views on future political organization. In presenting this statement the Adansihene advocated no-party government because of the "inherent evils" of the party system. "Western democracy was imposed on this country by a few educated people . . . our proposals can create for this country a government by consent without incurring the unsavoury features of party politics. . . . He said although they recommended the banning of political parties, they were not against people with common political ideology coming together. The Chairman of the Constitutional Committee, the Chief Justice of Ghana, then asked them to reconsider this view." (*Daily Graphic*, June 23, 1967.)

[12] M. Peil and E. O. Odotei, "Return to Civilian Rule (Report on a survey of university students)," *The Legon Observer*, June 9–22, 1967; a randomly selected ten per cent sample of 198 students were interviewed in February 1967.

[14] See K. A. Busia, "One Year after the Coup," lecture delivered on March 30, 1967, *The Legon Observer*, April 14–27, 1967: "Military regimes are notoriously unstable. Africa has so far not shown any signs that her military regimes will be an exception to the historical pattern." Dr. Busia was commenting on a speech of Brigadier Afrifa and was in turn criticized by Professor Adu Boahen for wanting so swift a return to civilian rule.

[15] *Daily Graphic*, June 26, 1967.

[16] Reprinted in *Minerva*, IV (1966), 542–54.

[17] For example, the Asanteman Secondary School, Kumasi, was temporarily closed for a month (May to June 1967) following student violence. Students claimed that the headmaster registered five students as private candidates for the G.C.E. examination, an allegation later denied by the African Examinations Council (*Evening News*, June 19, 1967). The extent of the problem can be seen from the fact that two days earlier the *Ghanaian Times* reported the warning of Lt. Col. E. A. Yeboah, member of the Eastern Region Committee of Administration, against students' strikes and demonstrations. Conflict at Asanteman had developed over the year and was partly due to the measures introduced by a new headmaster trying to rectify a situation that had arisen under the previous non-graduate head. But, as at Nungua and elsewhere, an element of "student power"

was present; the freer atmosphere encouraged protest. Moreover, Nkrumah himself had been overthrown by force; and the process of "destooling" a leader by pressure from below was and still is a widespread feature of the traditional sector of Akan life.

[18] For example, in July 1966 the students at Akuafo Hall, Legon, wanted to use a room reserved for senior staff as a television room and turned to activist methods when they were refused.

[19] In 1967 Sierra Leone almost effected such a change, but a close finish in the electoral competition and a subsequent recourse to the army led to the collapse of the parliamentary system and its replacement by a military regime.

[20] For a detailed account of these struggles, see Dennis Austin, *Politics in Ghana, 1946–60* (London, 1964).

[21] There are those who are still interested in a secular Socialist morality, but disillusion with the political representatives of such a view has gone far. A widespread attitude is that illustrated by the comment an electrician made to me on the day of the coup (February 24) as he poured a libation from the E of the neon sign KWAME NKRUMAH, just ripped from the decorations of what is now known as National Liberation Circle: "In this country it was socialism for the poor and capitalism for the rich."

[22] See, for example, the argument of J. K. Tawiah, a lawyer (*Daily Graphic*, June 26, 1967) and the Chief Justice's criticisms of the proposals put forward by the chiefs for a period of no-party rule.

[23] H. K. Bidi Setsoafia in the *Daily Graphic*, June 19, 1967.

[24] See, also, Lewis: "It may even be true that half the ministers in West Africa are rogues" (p. 34).

[25] David E. Apter (ed.) (Glencoe, 1964).

[26] P. 21. Quoted from E. H. Erikson, *Young Man Luther: A Study in Psychoanalysis and History* (London, 1958).

[27] P. E. Converse, "The Nature of Belief Systems of Mass Publics," *Ideology and Discontent*, 207.

INTERVIEWING CROSS-CULTURALLY

Hal Fisher

HAL FISHER *has lived and worked in three foreign cultures over the past sixteen years. He was lecturer in broadcasting and audio-visual communication at the Beirut College for Women, Lebanon, for ten years. This was followed by a three-year period of service as program director of a large short-wave broadcasting station in Ethiopia. Most recently, he has been a broadcasting and audio-visual communications consultant and training officer in Kenya. He received his B.A. degree from Dubuque University and his M.A. from Indiana University. He is currently a candidate in the mass communications doctoral program at Indiana University and is specializing in cross-cultural applications of the communications media.*

The interview, "one of the earliest methods to develop for investigating intergroup attitudes" (Remmers 1954, 365), constitutes a vital ingredient in today's growing body of cross-cultural research.[1]

Studies indicate that numerous aspects of cross-national and single societal interviewing are similar.[2] However, cross-cultural situations present some serious impediments to the interview's effective service as a research tool. The burden of this paper is to isolate these problems and, where possible, to propose means for overcoming such limitations.

THE INTERVIEWER IN ANOTHER CULTURE

Upon entry into another culture, the interviewer faces his initial critical problem—"how to present himself to that society" (Maccoby and Maccoby 1959: 473). In some societies, the research interviewer is as yet unknown. To preliterates, his role may be unintelligible. In many cultures, he is regarded as an intruder. Yet, essentially, the field worker must be accepted before his interviewing can commence. Gaining acceptance is frequently a slow, arduous task. One researcher in an Afghanistan village first had to establish himself by wrestling the local champion and by taking high hurdles on horseback before he was allowed to interview (Maccoby and Maccoby 1959). After interviewing French and Austrian parliamentarians, one team of researchers concluded that "local habits and mores either incline people to resist interviewing or to structure their thoughts . . . as to preclude getting reliable data from them, or both" (Hunt, Crane and Wahlke 1964: 59).

Acceptance of the interviewer is highly dependent upon the degree to which he knows the respondent's culture and can identify with it. This suggests that he acquaint himself fully with the interviewee's culture prior to entering it. Then, upon entry, the interviewer will further benefit by talking to people informally, observing activities, and listening to conversations (Bennett 1948). DuToit's experiences in New Guinea suggest that this period of observation

Printed with permission of the author. This essay was written for this volume.

should be sufficiently long to minimize misinterpretation (DuToit 1969). As the interviewer establishes rapport and gains understanding of the host culture, his precision in ability to ask appropriate questions should increase.

A key problem for the cross-cultural interviewer is that his role is determined partly by his approach and partly by the situation. Therein, according to Paul, lies the dilemma, for the researcher "assumes a role in order to study the culture; yet he must often know the culture before he can assume a satisfactory role" (1965: 431). His success is at least partially dependent upon his ability to play his role satisfactorily: "The more successful the field worker is in playing his role, the more he will 'enter' the informant's role" (Gold 1957–1958: 218). In so doing, the interviewer must know how to subordinate himself, blend self-expression and integrity, minimize cultural and social differences, and sense when to change his role tactics.

Gold (1957–1958) postulates an interviewer role spectrum ranging from "complete participant" (identity and purpose hidden) through "participant-as-observer" and "observer-as-participant" to complete observer (systematic, detached eavesdropping). This continuum may be extended to include the questioner-respondent relationship typically implied in the survey questionnaire.

Because cultures differ, the interviewer functioning in another society may not be fully aware of important situational variables. Thus, as Richardson, Dohrenwend and Klein note, "the observer will often not know which of its aspects to look for, or . . . will not understand the significance of what he observes" (1965: 14).

Moreover, the cross-cultural interviewer's effectiveness is frequently tempered by political considerations. His very presence may render his motivations politically suspect. Consequently, his unique burden of proof becomes the presentation of an image of himself that is neutral, credible, trustworthy, and acceptable to the host culture. One veteran of extensive interviewing in tropical Africa proposes that the investigator's image must be such that the satisfactions of both officials and informants are maximized (Hanna 1964–1965). His purpose must be legitimate and must pose minimal threat. At the same time, establishing proper contacts, observing formalities, and gaining official clearances become vitally important.

The exact impact a foreign interviewer has on his respondent's replies is unknown. On the one hand, the interviewer may "actuate perceptions that he is impartial. . . . On the other hand, respondents may slur over esoteric details because they believe the foreigner will not understand them" (Hunt, Crane, and Wahlke 1964: 62). In studies of subcultures in the United States, Negroes tended to respond differently when interviewed by whites than by other Negroes. Also, working-class respondents were less inclined to talk freely to middle class interviewers than to peers (Jahoda, Deutsch, and Cook 1959). Similarly, Hunt, Crane, and Wahlke concluded that, in Europe at least, "interviewing difficulties vary . . . with status relationships" (1964: 62).

It appears, therefore, that perception of and response to the interviewer is highly dependent on how he handles his role and projects his image. Among Africans, Hanna (1964–1965) posed variously as respected professor, peer, friendly participant, stranger, neutral, and an American, depending on which appeared to establish the greatest trust relationship in each particular situation. Powdermaker (1966) became "Visiting Teacher" in the south and "Professor" on the Zambian Copperbelt. Paul (1965) assumed the role of trader among Guatemalian Indians.

The thought patterns and pace of thought characteristic of the interviewer and his society further complicate cross-cultural interviewing. Does, for example, Western haste in pressing for replies confuse other peoples? Do variant cultures approach a reply in different ways—one perhaps by analogy or story, another by a quantitative response, and a third by a philosophical reply? In the midst of such potential discrepancies, the interviewer is urged to "guard against imposing his own frame of reference and thought patterns, because they may well be meaningless and irrelevant to the respondent" (Richardson, Dohrenwend, and Klein 1965: 219).

It seems clear, then, that the cross-cultural interviewer must never forget that "the social characteristics, the style of presentation of the self, his interview style and other qualities . . . have important effects on the person he interviews" (Pelto 1970: 96).

THE RESPONDENT AND HIS SETTING

Cross-cultural interviewing is further confounded by variables related to the interviewee and his cultural context.

First, the informant's responses will reflect his own culture. European interviewees reacted negatively to precoded questions, considering them "too brutal" because they provided no opportunity to register nuances and personal positions. Multiple choice questions were rejected because examinations of this type are not normally given in European schools (Hunt, Crane, and Wahlke 1964). In like vein, Lerner (1956) observed that the highly defensive style of French interviewees provided them with an elegant means of maintaining proper social distance and enabled them to gradually reshape the interview format.

Informant reliability may also vary from culture to culture. Frank and Ruth Young's informants differed widely on trustworthiness of information, especially in replies to evaluative questions, leading the researchers to conclude that "There is seldom precise agreement on any question or for all communities" (1962: 148).

Informant accuracy can be verified by observation, by cross-checking with other informants, by examination of the internal self-consistency of the replies, or by asking the informant to give a retrospective account. Sometimes, if given an opportunity, an informant will correct misinformation. By being tactful, Evans-Pritchard encouraged Nuer informants to confess good-naturedly, "What we told you yesterday was all nonsense! Now we will tell you correctly!" (quoted in Paul 1965: 446).

Frey considers that there are three types of snares set by respondents for the cross-cultural researcher:

1. A respondent's tendency to react to questions "en bloc" and in terms of some irrelevant fixed orientation.
2. The acquiescence to "set" or "courtesy bias" in which the respondent says what he thinks the interviewer wants.
3. Respondent reaction to please some reference group.

Such "sets" may both produce a false appearance of validity and preclude accurate measurement (Frey 1970).

Statements by the informant unaffected by any response "set" will, nonetheless, differ with the social context of the interview. Alone, the interviewee may respond in one way; with others, differently. In Kenya, a young person would become guarded if an elder entered the room. Among the Navaho, the group would never interrupt the spokesman; in Tanzania, the opposite would be true. In Nigeria, Nadel got his best information from group arguments (cited in Paul 1965).

Also, the interview is a form of social interaction and, consequently, the personality of the interviewee bears on the process (Bennett 1948). Such interaction of interviewer and interviewee personalities across cultures is "a complex social process" (Pelto 1970: 97). Ego defense mechanisms and other psychological factors, variable across cultures, compound this interaction still further (Williams 1967).

Obviously, then, individual and contextual variables operate to provide "cultural differences in both those things respondents are able to talk about and those things they are willing to talk about" (Deutscher 1968: 334).

PROBLEMS RELATED TO TRANSLATION

Translation often constitutes a formidable problem for the researcher interviewing in another culture. Whenever interviewer and respondent languages differ—a situation which normally prevails—translation problems arise.

Some believe translation difficulties exist even within a single society at any time the same question is asked of people from differing backgrounds (Anderson 1967). Deutscher subscribes to the same view: "Many . . . errors in translation and interpretation—the semantic slipups—also occur between interviewer and interviewee within our own society" (1969–1970: 21).

Because in the cross-cultural interview situation each language typically represents a different culture, Phillips believes the interviewer's fundamental problem is that "he must not only translate language, but inevitably must translate culture" (1970: 389). Casagrande elaborates reasons for this phenomenon: "The attitudes and values, the experiences and tradition of a people, inevitably become involved in the freight of meaning carried by a language" (1954: 336). Moreover, translation "involves the explication of material and experiences which are not culturally or socially shared" (Phillips 1968: 390). To Blanc (1956), such lack of shared experience means there can be no meaningful equivalents. Because divergent cultural experiences fortify translation barriers, "the researcher is seldom capable of viewing native culture as an 'insider'" (Cicourel 1969–1970: 50).

Linguistic distinctions in meanings of words, in syntactical contexts, and in the requirements of languages add to translation distortion (Ervin and Bower 1952–1953). Deutscher gives yet another reason for distortion: "Different languages sometimes provide lingual markers at different points on a continuum" (1968: 32 f.). For example, "friend" implies a range of acquaintances to the American, an inner few to the German, a form of address to the Spaniard, and empathetic identity to the Arab. This problem of categories exists both for attitudinal responses and even for dichotomous distinctions such as "yes" and "no."

Because of differences in culture, language, word meanings, and grammatical syntax, the expectations of the interviewer and the informant differ. Grimshaw (1969–1970) observes that this divergent evaluation in turn activates cultural norms of privacy and its violation and of propriety in getting and in giving of information. This process further blocks vital information just when channels should convey maximal data.

A cluster of corollary problems further impede effective cross-cultural interviewing. Variations in phonology, pronunciation, semiotics, kinesics, and proxemics complicate translation and interpretation. The experiences of den Hollander (1967) confirm that the conventional extralingual means of expression of the host culture may convey nothing to the interviewer. Mahl (1968) found that gestures and movements may fortify concurrent verbal statements, deny them, anticipate later statements, or be a direct function of interaction with the interviewer. Cicourel (1969–1970) sees the continuing alteration and transformation of social meanings in both societies as yet another basic reason for loss of information through translation. Finally, the researcher's budget and time in the field are variables that impinge on translation accuracy (Phillips 1970).

The basic overarching problem under which all translation difficulties may be subsumed is how to determine with confidence that interviewer and interviewee are mutually communicating about the exact item being considered with maximal transfer of information.

ATTEMPTS TO ACHIEVE MEANING EQUIVALENCE

Cross-cultural interviews have employed several devices with varying success in their attempts to override translation difficulties and to achieve a greater degree of meaning equivalence in interviewing.

Some have used a contact language, which is defined as "a second language spoken by both field worker and informant" (Maccoby and Maccoby 1959: 473). My own experiences in the Near East and Africa confirm that, unfortunately, often only the educated speak a second language and that there is usually a mismatch between interviewer and respondent ability to speak and understand it. Cicourel (1969–1970) points out that those using a contact language often find it difficult to fill in appropriate meanings, especially when educational and social differences exist.

When a dialect such as pidgin English is used, barriers to communication increase. In the use of dialect, cultural conditioning elicits particular patterns of interaction and prevents others from occurring, so that the language shifts with the interaction (Chapple 1970). Therefore, the use of a dialect or a contact language does little to assure equivalence of meaning across cultural barriers.

Another device for surmounting translation problems is the employment of interpreters. Although his help is valuable, the interpreter is rarely the passive agent for transferring messages that he should be. His language competence and time pressures on his intermediary role introduce errors of translation (Phillips 1970). Three additional serious interpreter effects are: (1) his deliberate or unconscious biases, (2) his social status, and (3) the consequences of the diminished privacy inherent in the three-way relationship (Paul 1965). Kluckhohn comments that, with the introduction of the interpreter, "At best, an awkward third set of variables have been introduced into an already complex problem" (1945: 97). Thus, it appears highly dubious that the interpreter can provide translation with meaning equivalence in which the researcher can place unreserved confidence.

Another method, back or reverse translation, promises help in gaining lexical equivalence. But the process is involved:

> First, the original question is translated into the local language, and then another translator later independently translates this translated version back into the original. The original re-translated versions are compared and the discrepancies are clarified [Deutscher 1968: 320].

Frey (1970) declares the translation becomes acceptable if the original suffers minimal distortion in the double translation process. Serial translation and parallel translation comprise other more elaborate variants of the back translation technique.

Obviously, back translation is time consuming and costly. Moreover, when using this method in Thailand, Phillips (1970) discovered he could spot error only after lengthy experience. Schuman encountered trouble with back translation in Pakistan because translators represented social and educational levels different from those of the respondents (reported in Deutscher 1968). In addition, there is the danger of spurious lexical equivalence. Such shortcomings render back translation somewhat less than the ideal tool for achieving meaning equivalence in cross-cultural interview situations.

Other sophisticated devices for inspecting translation equivalence exist. Frey (1970) suggests statistical checks on the level of redundancy in each version of the back translation instrument, syntactical investigations, use of the semantic differential to indicate connotative similarity, and adjective-verb-noun ratios. Almond and Verba (1970) propose, additionally, the use of dichotomized intensity questions and adoption of ways of analyzing data that reduce researcher dependence on complete equivalence.

In the final analysis, however, it is conceptual equivalence that is of ultimate importance. Deutscher makes it an axiom that "the greater efforts should be directed toward obtaining conceptual equivalence without concern for lexical comparativity" (1968: 337). Przeworski and Teune clarify that no problem of conceptual equivalence exists where the same phenomenon has identical observable manifestations in both social systems being compared or represented by the interviewer and interviewee. For example, if a "president" is chief executive of the same type of government in two different state systems, no problem of measurement usually exists. However, "the question of equivalence arises . . . if system interference is present and measurement involves interference" (Przeworski and Teune 1970: 106 f.). When this condition prevails (and it would seem to the predominant number of times), the only way to attain conceptual equivalence is to establish the validity of a value or inference as it exists in each system and then and only then can reliable inferences be made across systems.

This implies the interviewer may be required to frame an entirely different question than would normally be asked in his own culture to get at the parallel value or information in the respondent's culture. Thus, each question would require thorough conceptualization before it is framed to ascertain whether or not it reliably probes for the exact information sought. Such a process makes it imperative that the interviewer transcend the bounds of his own culture in order to stand objectively and culture-free above both his own culture and that of his informant.

Some interviewers may never master this procedure. All will find it painstakingly slow and costly. However, it may well be the only conceivable means of establishing valid and reliable conceptual equivalences across cultures where direct measurement is impossible. Discovery of a small amount of reliably equivalent concepts will, in the long run, be preferable to the cross-cultural interviewer's eternal wandering in the maze of indeterminate relationships.

SUMMARY AND CONCLUSION

Interviewing in another culture is confounded by important interviewer, respondent, and cultural variables. Language translation problems are among the researcher's most formidable hurdles, and devices to overcome them fall short of being ideal. Contact languages and interpreters have their shortcomings. Back translation offers hope limited to the achievement of lexical equivalence. And the way to conceptual equivalence, the ultimate "must" if cross-cultural interviewing is to bear useful scientific fruit, is painstakingly slow, arduous, and expensive.

Despite such imposing obstacles, the interviewer must not surrender in despair. He should remember, instead, Hunt, Crane, and Walhke's confidence that "interviews are a most useful tool for genuinely comparative behavioral research" (1964: 68). He can take confidence in the facts that there are already a number of instruments, limited though they may be, in use to improve interviewing and that scientific methodologists are continually improving the available tools and developing others. However, he will be wise if he selects those interview techniques that will provide maximal scientific rigor within the limits of his time, budget, and research design. This implies that he may have to remain content with findings less global and generalizable than he desires.

Nonetheless, if through his interviews he can make some small contribution to the building of social science theory and man's understanding of other humans, what he accomplishes may be of crucial significance. In so doing, he will have employed one means of human communication—the interview—to gain appreciation, understanding, and some useful scientific knowledge of the vast reservoir of information and values cultures have to contribute and communicate to one another.

NOTES

[1] Lapiere used the interview for comparing racial prejudices in 1927. In the early 1930s, Zawadzki and Lazarsfeld compared depressed Poles and Americans by the interview technique. Anthropologists have long depended heavily on the interview.

[2] Eleanor Maccoby and Nathan Maccoby, "The Interview: A Tool of Social Science," in Gardner Lindzey (ed.), Handbook of Social Psychology, vol. I (Cambridge, Mass., 1959), pp. 449–487; S. Richardson, B. Dohrenwend and D. Klein, Interviewing: Its Forms and Functions (New York, 1965); and Mark Benney and E. Hughes (eds.), "Of Sociology and the Interview," The American Journal of Sociology, 62 (2) (September 1956, entire issue), comprise a few of numerous resources on use of the interview in research.

REFERENCES CITED

ALMOND, GABRIEL, and
SIDNEY VERBA
    1970   Some methodological problems in cross-national research. In Comparative Perspectives: Theories and Methods. Amitai Etzioni and Fredric Dubow, eds. Boston, 349–364.
ANDERSON, R. B. W.
    1967   On the comparability of meaningful stimuli in cross-cultural research. Sociometry 30:124–136.
BENNETT, JOHN W.
    1948   The study of cultures: a survey of technique and methodology in field work. American Sociological Review 13:6, 672–689.
BENNEY, MARK, and
EVERETT HUGHES
    1956   Of sociology and the interview. The American Journal of Sociology 62:2, 137–142.
BLANC, HAIM
    1956   Multilingual interviewing in Israel. The American Journal of Sociology 62:2, 205–209.
CASAGRANDE, JOSEPH B.
    1954   The ends of translation. International Journal of American Linguistic Society 20:4, 335–340.
CHAPPLE, ELIOT D.
    1970   Culture and biological man: explorations in behavioral anthropology. New York.
CICOUREL, AARON V.
    1969–1970   Language as a variable in social research. Sociological Focus 3:2, 43–52.
DEN HOLLANDER, A.
    1967   Social description: the problem of reliability and validity. In Anthropologists in the Field. D. G. Jongmans and P. C. W. Gutkind, eds. Assen, pp. 1–34.
DEUTSCHER, IRWIN
    1968   Asking questions cross-culturally: some problems of linguistic comparability, In Institutions and the person. Howard Becker et al., eds. Chicago, pp. 318–341.

1969– Asking questions and listening to answers: a review of some sociological
1970   precedents and problems. Sociological Focus 3:2, 13–32.
Du Toit, Brian M.
  1969   Misconstruction and problems in communication. American Anthropologist
         71:46–53.
Ervin, S., and
H. Bower
  1952–1953   Translation problems in international surveys. Public Opinion Quarterly
             16:4, 596ff.
Frey, Frederick
  1970   Cross-cultural survey research in political science. In The methodology of
         comparative research. Robert Holt and John Turner, eds. New York, pp.
         173–294.
Gold, R. L.
  1957–1958   Roles in sociological field observations. Social Forces 36:217–223.
Grimshaw, Allen D.
  1969–1970   Some problematic aspects of communication in cross-racial research in
             the United States. Sociological Focus 3:2, 67–85.
Hanna, William J.
  1964–1965   Image-making in field research: some tactical and ethical problems
             arising from research in tropical Africa. American Behavioral Scientist 8:15–20.
Hunt, W., W. Crane, and
J. Wahlke
  1964   Interviewing political elites in cross-cultural comparative research. American
         Journal of Sociology. 70:1, 59–68.
Kluckhohn, Clyde
  1945   The personal document in anthropological science. Social Science Bulletin
         53:97ff.
Lerner, Daniel
  1956   Interviewing Frenchmen. American Journal of Sociology 62:2, 187–194.
Maccoby, Eleanor, and
Nathan Maccoby
  1959   The interview: A tool of social science. In Handbook of social psychology,
         Gardner Lindzey, ed. Vol. 1. Cambridge, pp. 449–487.
Mahl, George
  1968   Gestures and body movements in interviews. Research in Psychotherapy 3:295–
         346.
Paul, Benjamin D.
  1965   Interview techniques and field relationships. In Anthropology today. A. L.
         Kroeber et al., eds. Chicago, pp. 430–451.
Pelto, Pertti
  1970   Anthropological research: the structure of enquiry. New York.
Phillips, Herbert P.
  1970   Problems of translation and meaning in field work. In Comparative perspec-
         tives: theories and methods. Amitai Etzioni and Fredric Dubow, eds. Boston,
         pp. 385–404.
Przeworski, Adam, and
Henry Teune
  1970   The logic of comparative social inquiry. New York.
Remmers, H. H.
  1954   Introduction to opinion and attitude measurement. New York.
Richardson, Stephen, Barbara Dohrenwend, and
David Klein
  1965   Interviewing: its forms and functions. New York.
Sellitz, Claire, et al.
  1959   Research Methods in Social Relations. Vol. I. New York.

WILLIAMS, THOMAS R.
  1967   Field methods in the study of culture. New York.
YOUNG, FRANK, and
RUTH YOUNG
  1962   Key informant reliability in rural Mexican villages. Human Organization 20:3, 138–155.

THE COMMUNICATION
OF LEADERSHIP

Leadership has been studied variously by such disciplines as social science, history, and psychology. Modern sociology itself developed in part as an intellectual debate over definitions and treatment of leadership. The philosopher-king concept of Plato, the citizen-ruler-orator idea of Isocrates, and the philosopher-orator-statesman of Cicero were prevalent theories until Thomas Hobbes and John Locke began emphasizing the rights of individuals more than the duties of rulers. Karl Marx, sometimes called the father of international communication, changed the role of leader by the grace of God (Gottesgnadentum) to the leadership of the anonymous masses or the dictatorship of the proletariat. Marx discovered the mainspring of history in the recurrent tensions between the forces and the relations of economic production and the human past as the manifestations of timeless national genius— not the leadership of a single isolated ruler, but that demonstrated by the will of the people (Rustow 685). The progression of the Marxist position is seen clearly in Premier Nikita Khrushchev's October 3, 1960, statement justifying his appearance at the United Nations assembly: "We, by the will of our people, have come here and are tirelessly sowing the seeds of peace" (Khrushchev 1970a:548). During the same session, President Achmed Sukarno echoed similar sentiments when he reminded the delegates:

> Today, it is President Sukarno who addresses you. But more than that, though, it is a man, Sukarno, an Indonesian, a husband, a father, a member of the human family. I speak to you on behalf of my people, those ninety-two million people of a distant and wide archipelago, those ninety-two million who have lived a life of struggle and sacrifice, those ninety-two million people who have built a State upon the ruins of an empire [Sukarno 1970:507].

To be sure, whether the leader leads by divine appointment or by the will of the people as do elected or even certain dictatorial leaders, his leadership cannot occur in isolation. Dankwart Rustow suggests:

> It is never enough to ask: Who is this leader? A more meaningful question is fourfold: Who is leading whom from where to where? The leader's character, the expectations of his contemporaries, the play of historic circumstance, and the success or failure of a movement in reaching its goals are equally important parts of the over-all process [Rustow 684].

In The Nerves of Government, Karl Deutsch stresses that one of the best ways to perceive leadership is to see it as a process of communication, or connection, between leader and followers (Deutsch 1966:157–160, 172–176). Rustow's "who" or Lasswell's "who" in his model "Who says what to whom in what channel with what effect," becomes the leader seeking to communicate his goals and accomplishments to his followers. As a process their perception of him as decision maker, originator of ideas, recipient of voter or follower feedback, and fulfiller of hopes changes as he perceives his own function changing.

Jean Lacouture theorizes that the heroic leader creates the inevitability of his own downfall. He begins to believe in his own miracles, he is oppressed by false proofs of his infallibility, and he is in constant danger of being unhinged by the absurdity of his own propaganda (Lacouture 1970). Among the four charismatic leaders whom Lacouture treats, Bourguiba, Nasser, Nkrumah, and Sihanouk, all were masters of propaganda and public relations. Still only Bourguiba remained in power in mid-1972. Sihanouk's "government by laughter" fell because he was so insensitive to his inability to communicate effectively with his followers that he, like Nkrumah, dared to leave his country, opening himself to a bloodless coup. Mazrui, reflecting in this volume on assassinations and deposings that have occurred frequently in Africa during the months of January and February, suggests that there may be a symbolic correlation—a new year, a new nation, a new manifestation of instability. The decline and fall of such leaders as Khrushchev, Nkrumah, DeGaulle, Johnson, Sukarno, Sylvanus Olympio, and Sihanouk may be attributed in part to their failure to communicate properly their own concern for their people. The loss of credibility on major issues may so undermine their base of support that their usefulness is destroyed. Rustow argues that the leader whose career ends in disaster differs from the leader "who lives long and rules well" in that the former becomes set early in his responses to situational events for which his followers demand innovative and credible answers, whereas the latter can summon new resources and adapt to new situations until a far more advanced age (Rustow 1968:690).

We might postulate, as Rustow has suggested, that leadership is a process of communication between the leader and his followers, an experimental learning event for both the leader and his followers, and a perception of a sense of timing not only for the leader but also for his followers. The leader's longevity depends upon all three aspects of the process, which is itself dynamic and changing. When the leader fails to communicate effectively with his constituents or misperceives their response to his leadership, or when he cannot generate enthusiasm or credibility for his goals and programs, or when he becomes so routinized as a bureaucratic functionary that he can no longer maintain the momentum of dramatic leaders such as DeGaulle, Atatürk, Mao, or Castro, who give the appearance of an intensely intimate feeling of communication with their followers, he may continue to rule for a time in a titular sense, but he no longer fulfills the basic functions of a leader, leading his followers creatively and innovatively to new aspirations and goals.

The essays in this section treat the final plateau of violence, which occurs against leaders through assassination or deposition, the cross-cultural communication of the heads of superpowers, and the concept of charismatic leadership of the individual, the institution, and the party. In an international organization, the individual leader may be overshadowed by the fact that he is a government spokesman and not a creative leader as an individual. The American ambassador to the United Nations is placed in the curious position of holding cabinet rank nearly equal to that of secretary of state and at the same time of having to answer to the Bureau of International Organization Affairs, which is headed by an assistant secretary of state. This was particularly galling to Ambassador Adlai Stevenson, who had been a recognized national leader before he became a diplomat at the United Nations. Reputed to have been called "my official liar" by President Kennedy after the Bay of Pigs crisis, Stevenson believed his own credibility as a leader so jeopardized that he felt that he ought to resign, except that the Kennedy government was so new that even more serious harm might have been done to the entire United States image by his resignation in protest (Prosser 1969). In the 1961 Indian invasion of Goa, Diu, and Damão, Ambassador Stevenson demanded Security Council condemnation of India, saying: "This is an urgent and pressing matter. This is war. People are being killed." His colleague on the council, Ambassador Barnes of Liberia, was similarly affected, as Stevenson had been earlier, by the inability to take individual action. Barnes requested that the council postpone a vote until morning so that he could telephone his government for voting instructions, by which time the invasion was completed.

The executive director of an international organization has not only the difficulty of sometimes being a national of a government involved in critical disputes, or of seeming to favor one group of states over another, but also the problem that if he is innovative in a dispute, he loses the goodwill of one group of states, and if he is inactive, the effects of the dispute might worsen or the organization become simply a technical information exchange organization (Cox 1969). A primary example of this dissatisfaction was apparent in the socialist governments' response to Dag Hammarskjöld's handling of the Congo situation. In his first address to the world summit meeting at the United Nations, September 23, 1960, Premier Khrushchev reacted as follows:

> Mr. Hammarskjold, the Secretary-General, has taken a position of purely formal condemnation of the colonialists. In actual practice, however, he is following the colonialists' line, opposing the lawful Government of the Congo and the Congolese people and supporting the renegades. . . . Conditions have clearly matured to the point where the post of Secretary-General, who alone directs the staff and alone interprets and executes the decisions of the Security Council and the sessions of the General Assembly, should be abolished [Khrushchev 1970b].

In his next address, on October 3, 1960, Khrushchev stated the socialist position more starkly:

> In order to prevent any misinterpretation, I should like to repeat: we do not, and cannot, place confidence in Mr. Hammarskjold. If he himself cannot muster the courage to resign in, let us say, a chivalrous way, we shall draw the inevitable conclusions from the situation. There is no room for a man who has violated the elementary principles of justice in such an important post as that of Secretary-General [Khrushchev 1970a:542].

During the session, Premier Khrushchev and other socialist leaders urged the creation of the troika in the secretariat, by which a man from each of the three world blocs, representing the Western, socialist, and neutral countries, would collectively manage the position of secretary-general. Because of widespread support for Hammarskjöld and against the troika proposal by members of the neutralist states, the socialist proposals were eventually dropped.

To prevent precisely such a loss of support as Hammarskjöld suffered, Robert Cox offers four important propositions for the relations between the executive head and the member states of the international organization which he serves: (1) Issues often do not have the same rank of importance for the executive head and the member states, (2) strong local pressures affect national delegations more than the personality of the head of the international organization, (3) the interests of the international organization must be advanced within the domestic context of its major member states, (4) the executive head must fortify his position by alliance with domestic pressure groups. In effect, then, the executive head must have the ability to communicate the goals of the international organization to the nation states so effectively that dominant local conflicts will not prevent concerted action by the international organization as representative of all the member states (Cox 1969:250).

In the first essay in this section, Ali Mazrui, an East African, reflects upon the situations that give rise to violence against the national leader. The plateau of violence represented by assassinations and depositions suggests the ultimate form of communication breakdown. On the international level, Mazrui finds no treaty that betrays a greater sensitivity to the risk of assassination than the Charter of the Organization of African Unity, which expresses its "unreserved condemnation, in all its forms, of political assassination, as well as of subversive activities on the part of neighboring States or any other State." Mazrui defines assassination more from the political importance of the victim than from the motives of the killer, that is, the status of the victim is in itself highly communicative in terms of the stability of leadership. Some assassinations utterly destroy the government in power, whereas others have the effect of creating hero worship and thus becoming a great symbol of national unity. Mazrui concludes that African consensus may occur in spite of the increasing assassinations and depositions, or the fostered hero worship may actually be the cause itself of the consensus.

Of concern to all the writers in this section is the difference between the bureaucratic and the charismatic leader. In the second essay included here, Thomas E. Dow explicates and expands the Weberian theory of charisma and offers an excellent formulation of the theory. Charisma of leadership is a universal and can, according to Dow and other contemporary theorists such as Bendix (1967) and Tucker (1968), be found in any time or age and in any geographical situation. Conditions most generally leading to the rise of charismatic authority, except where charisma resides between community and a certain office, for example, the residual partial charisma in the American Presidency, the British Crown, or the papacy, are chiefly those of extreme stress in which the leader perceives himself and is perceived by his followers as being able to revolutionize events in such a way as to overcome extraordinary obstacles by his own gift of grace. If, as Karl Lowenstein suggests, the concepts of charisma and the charismatic leader have had a greater impact upon the thinking of our time concerning leadership than nearly any other (Lowenstein 1966), it is well that we ponder the constituents of charisma and the intense role of communication that exists between the charismatic leader and his followers and whether the charismatic leader becomes routinized, or deposed, or assassinated because he no longer can communicate effectively his Messianic mission. Or it may be that the very nature of charisma is inherently so unstable that no matter how effectively the leader communicates, he must ultimately fail.

An excellent example of summit-level, cross-cultural communication between world leaders and between a foreign government and the citizens of another government (for a model see Wedge 1969) were the visits of Soviet Foreign Minister Anastas Mikoyan to the United States in January 1959; the visit of Vice-President Richard M. Nixon to the Soviet Union from July 24 to August 2, 1959, and the visit of Premier Nikita Khrushchev to the United States in September 1959. My wife and I were among the first fifteen thousand Americans to receive visas to visit the Soviet Union under the cultural exchange program that the Soviets and Americans had signed. We were there between the visits of Nixon and Khrushchev. Before leaving the United States we saw the Soviet exhibit in New York; and while in Moscow, we attended the American exhibit where Nixon and Khrushchev had held their famous "Kitchen Debate," described in Nixon's Six Crises (1962; see also Young 1962). We saw many Russians turned away from the American exhibit. The many Russians who were inside had considerable difficulty believing in the "typicality of the American worker's home" though to us it seemed fairly typical of the tract homes found in American suburbs. Curiously, although most of the exhibit was well guarded to protect against loss of products, art, and crafts, there were no guards in the section where books by American authors were on display. When this exhibit opened in late July, fifteen thousand books were displayed. By late August, when we were there, more than half had disappeared. By what we learned was a calculated design, the Americans were assured that several thousand American-authored books would find their way into Moscovite homes.

In his essay "The Rhetoric of Peaceful Coexistence: Khrushchev in America, 1959," Theodore Otto Windt, Jr., discusses the Soviet premier's attempts at artful diplomacy in which he tried to carry specifically different messages to the general American populace and the American leaders, while at the same time demonstrating at home that he was skillful in negotiating with the capitalists without losing crucial Soviet objectives. At least five editions of his speeches have been published (1960a, 1960b, 1961a, 1961b, and 1963) and several critical theses about his speeches have been prepared (see, for example, Sharp 1962, Pruett 1962, and Windt 1965). Windt suggests that American audiences became less convinced of Khrushchev's satanic powers and began to see Khrushchev as more human; but they still disregarded his proposals as Soviet propaganda. The irony of this fear can be seen in considering his 1959 address to the United Nations, when he made some of the most sweeping disarmament proposals ever made by an American or Soviet head of government (Khrushchev 1970c). Windt accepts the idea that whereas Khrushchev forced a somewhat softened idea on Americans toward Soviet leadership, at home his 1959 American visit represented the zenith of his career as premier, for he had proved that he could talk to American leaders without sacrificing Soviet interests, and he had made friendly contacts with the American people for the Soviet people. Unfortunately for Sino-Soviet relations, his personal diplomacy marked the beginning of deep ideological divisions between the two governments, leading to the eventual Chinese denunciation of Khrushchev as a revisionist. If, as Windt believes, the 1959 visit of Khrushchev marked a major change in the hostile attitudes between the Soviet and American governments and peoples, this display of his rhetorical leadership deserves considerable praise and respect when we consider the difficulties the leader must face when he wishes to speak successfully for his people across national boundaries to a people whose ideological perspectives are diametrically different.

In the last two essays in this section, case studies are offered to demonstrate the role of the charismatic leader and the charismatic party in third-world nations. The summer 1968 issue of Daedalus devoted itself to an idea called "Philosophers and Kings," in which such charismatic leaders as Gandhi, Nkrumah, De Gaulle, and Atatürk are considered. Similarly, the June 1967 issue of Asian Survey presents individual case studies of charismatic leaders Sihanouk, Nehru, Kim Il-Song of North Korea, and Mao Tse-tung. Lacouture's The Demigods: Charismatic Leadership in the Third World (1970) deserves careful reading. Since the longevity of the individual charismatic leader is questionable, such case studies can be viewed only as tentative and illustrative. Though somewhat dated, the essay, "Charismatic Authority and the Leadership of Fidel Castro," by Richard R. Fagen, the author of Politics and Communication (1966), develops the charismatic leadership of Fidel Castro in a very useful fashion. Fagen applies the five elements of the Weberian formulation of charismatic authority to Castro's exercise of power during his first years as the Cuban premier. That Castro's authority remains strong at the time of this writing suggests that he has retained an ability to convince his people that he is still the Messianic revolutionary leader in which they first placed their trust and is so despite all the odds placed against his continued leadership.

In the final essay, "Party Charisma: Political Practices and Principles," Irving L. Horowitz develops the thesis that the one-party system itself possesses charisma in third-world nations. Weber would not have accepted the concept of party charisma since he saw a distinction between "the sovereignty of the charismatic man" and the "superordination of the institutions." However, leadership, by the will of the people or in the name of the anonymous masses, places its ideological rationalization in the cult of the greatness of the people. Thus, the state itself becomes God-like—the supreme authority, arbiter of law, and great unifier. It is clear that the most effective charismatic leaders increase their own intense communication with their followers by bestowing on the people the same charismatic qualities which they themselves, by the grace of God or by the will of the people, possess. When the charismatic leader falls, party charisma may serve to sustain belief or to deny it for the leader. Or the

*party's charisma itself may be destroyed, at which point the party reaches
what I have called the final plateau of conflict in communication.*

REFERENCES CITED

BENDIX, REINHARD
    1967   Reflections on charismatic leadership. Asian Survey 7:341–352.
COX, ROBERT W.
    1969   The executive head: an essay on leadership in international organization. In-
            ternational Organization 23:205–230.
DEUTSCH, KARL W.
    1966   The nerves of government: models of political communication. New York.
FAGEN, RICHARD R.
    1966   Politics and Communication. Boston.
KHRUSHCHEV, NIKITA
    1960a   For victory in peaceful competition with capitalism. With a special introduc-
            tion for the American edition. New York.
    1960b   Khrushchev in America: full texts of the speeches made . . . on his tour of the
            United States, September 15–27, 1959, New York.
    1961a   Conquest without war: an analytical anthology of the speeches, interviews,
            and remarks of Nikita Sergeyevich Khrushchev with commentary by Lenin,
            Stalin, et al. N. H. Mager and Jacques Katel, eds. and comps. New York.
    1961b   A peace treaty with Germany: three speeches. New York.
    1963   Khrushchev speaks. Thomas P. Whitney, ed. Ann Arbor.
    1970a   The seeds of truth. In Sow the wind, reap the whirlwind: heads of state
            address the United Nations. Michael H. Prosser, ed. New York.
    1970b   Misleading the people is like trying to wrap up fire in a piece of paper. In
            Sow the wind, reap the whirlwind: heads of state address the United Nations.
            Michael H. Prosser, ed. New York.
    1970c   Let us disarm completely. In Sow the wind, reap the whirlwind: heads of state
            address the United Nations. Michael H. Prosser, ed. New York.
LACOUTURE, JEAN
    1970   The demigods: charismatic leadership in the third world. Patricia Wolf, trans.
            New York.
LOWENSTEIN, KARL
    1966   Max Weber's political ideas in the perspective of our time. Amherst.
NIXON, RICHARD M.
    1962   Six crises. New York.
PROSSER, MICHAEL H., ed.
    1969   An ethic for survival: Adlai Stevenson speaks on international affairs, 1936–
            1965. New York.
PRUETT, ROBERT E.
    1962   A comparative analysis of Lenin's speeches on the communist *International*
            with Khrushchev's "Central Committee Reports." Unpublished Master's
            thesis, Northern Illinois University.
RUSTOW, DANKWART A.
    1968   Introduction to the issue "Philosophers and kings: studies in leadership."
            Daedalus 97:683–694.
SHARP, DAWN
    1962   A study of the persuasive techniques employed in the public speaking of
            Nikita Sergeyevich Khrushchev during his tour of the United States. Un-
            published Master's thesis, Florida State University.
SUKARNO, ACHMED
    1970   Riding the whirlwind. In Sow the wind, reap the whirlwind: heads of state
            address the United Nations. Michael H. Prosser, ed. New York.

TUCKER, ROBERT C.
1968   The theory of charismatic leadership. Daedalus 97:731–756.
WEDGE, BRYANT
1968   Communication analysis and comprehensive diplomacy. In International communication and the new diplomacy. Arthur S. Hoffman, ed. Bloomington.
WINDT, THEODORE OTTO
1965   The rhetoric of peaceful coexistence: a criticism of selected American speeches by Nikita Khrushchev. Unpublished Ph.D. dissertation, Ohio State University.
YOUNG, RONGAL RAYMOND
1962   Richard Nixon speaking in Russia: July 24–August 2, 1959, a study in audience adaptation. Unpublished Master's thesis, University of Washington.

THOUGHTS ON ASSASSINATION
IN AFRICA*

Ali A. Mazrui

ALI A. MAZRUI was born in 1933 at Mombasa, Kenya. Currently, he is professor and head of the Department of Political Science at Makerere University, Kampala, Kenya. He is vice-president of the International Political Science Association and vice-president of the International Congress of Africanists. He has been a visiting professor at the University of Chicago, a research associate at the Center for International Affairs of Harvard University, and a visiting professor on a joint appointment at the Universities of London and Manchester during 1970 and 1971. His published books include: Towards a Pax-Africana: A Study of Ideology and Ambition (London, 1967), On Heroes and Uhuru Worship (London, 1967), The Anglo-African Commonwealth (Oxford, 1967), Violence and Thought (London, 1969), Protest and Power in Black Africa (New York, 1970), which he edited jointly with Robert I. Rotberg, and The Trial of Christopher Okigbo: A Novel of of Ideas (London, 1971).

Perhaps no international treaty betrays a greater sensitivity to the risk of assassination than does the Charter of the Organization of African Unity. The Charter consecrates its disapproval of this phenomenon in Article III, in which it expresses its "unreserved condemnation, in all its forms, of political assassination, as well as of subversive activities on the part of neighboring States or any other State."[1]

Independence is a beginning. So is the month of January every year, sometimes spilling over into February. For some reason a disproportionate number of the historic acts of violence in Africa since independence have tended to happen in the months of January and February. It was in January 1961 that Patrice Lumumba was handed over to Moise Tshombe, his enemy in Katanga. That was the prelude to one of the most significant assassinations in Africa's history. The following month the death of Lumumba was announced.

In January 1963 President Sylvanus Olympio of Togo was assassinated. And it was with Olympio's fate in the background that the Charter of the Organization of African Unity was signed a few months later.

In January 1964 the Zanzibar revolution exploded in East Africa, with vital consequences for the region as a whole. Among the immediate effects were the army mutinies of Tanganyika, Uganda, and Kenya which happened later the same month.

In January 1965 the prime minister of Burundi was assassinated. The heads

* This paper was written for the panel on "Consensus and Dissent, with Special Reference to the Developing Countries" at the Seventh World Congress of the International Political Science Association in Brussels in September 1967.

Reprinted with permission from the Political Science Quarterly, 58 (March 1968), 40–58.

of neighboring Kenya, Uganda, and Tanzania discussed the event and jointly expressed their sense of shock.[2]

Within the same period Kenya had its first assassination since independence —the killing of Mr. Pinto, a prominent member of Parliament.

In January 1966 came the Nigerian coup, which cost the lives of Federal Prime Minister Balewa and the premiers of the northern and western regions. The following month Nkrumah fell. His regime was overthrown while he was on his way to Peking. From the point of view of the theme of assassination the Ghanaian coup had a different kind of significance; it seems to have been a studied policy of the soldiers to avoid the risk of assassinating Nkrumah. That seems to have been one reason why the coup was timed to take place after his departure for Peking.

Is there any special reason why the opening months of January and February from year to year should have had such a disproportionate share of Africa's great acts of turbulence? Other months have had their events, too. But the deaths of Lumumba, Olympio, Balewa, and the Sardauna of Sokoto; the regionally transformative Zanzibar revolution; the East African mutinies; and the fall of Nkrumah are almost in a class by themselves as events which shook Africa. Yet, while sharing January and February for their anniversaries, the events provide little evidence for a Montesquieu-like hypothesis about the effect of climatic changes on major political events. Our collection of events is too widely distributed to be correlated with weather conditions in January and February. The most that one can hope for is a symbolic correlation—a new year; a new nation; a new manifestation of instability.

What is of greater interest than the month in which it occurs is, of course, the phenomenon of assassination itself. Everything considered, there might easily have been many more assassinations in Africa than we have had so far. The potentialities of this and other forms of political violence have been there from the start. What this paper hopes to analyze are, in part, precisely those potentialities. But it will be a postulate of mine that the risk of assassination was not only objectively there, but was keenly felt to be there by many of the leading participants in African politics. African leadership soon developed a conscious or subconscious fear of the assassin. This fear exerted an important influence not only on their personal behavior from day to day, but also on their policies and ideologies.

In our analysis we shall first place the issue of assassination within the context of the problem of legitimacy in a newly invented state. We shall then link this up with different levels of consensus, and examine these in relation to personal leadership as a functional alternative to weak legitimacy. Where authority is too personified, challenge to authority also tends to take the form of personal violence. The possibilities of assassination are maximized. Ideology, however, tries to mitigate these possibilities. And in any case there are assassinations which, in their impact, produce the kind of retrospective hero-worship which is itself a contribution to national identity. We shall conclude with an examination of the influence of assassination on certain aspects of Pan-African behavior and diplomatic thought.

But, first, a definitional problem has to be tackled.

WHAT IS "ASSASSINATION"?

An alternative rendering to the term "assassination" is sometimes supposed to be "political murder." But this rendering only shifts the definitional problem. When is a murder "political"? If the answer is "When it is committed for political reasons," then not every political murder is an assassination. In the course of the Zanzibar revolution thousands of people were killed, and many of these were killed for reasons which, in their racial implications, could only be described as "political." Yet the killing was at the grass-roots level—a petty Arab shopkeeper killed by his African neighbor; a petty landlord killed by a tenant. One of the curious things about the Zanzibar revolution—in contrast to, say, the Cuban, with which it has often been compared—was the relative toleration shown toward leading members of the previous regime under the Sultan. The Zanzibar revolutionaries showed little immediate desire to "make a public example" of their predecessors in power. Not only were there no executions, but a special effort was apparently made by the revolutionaries to spare Sheikh Ali Muhsin, the leader of the overthrown Nationalist party, any public indignity. Even John Okello, the temperamental Ugandan who appeared to have spearheaded the coup, made threats on Zanzibar radio against anyone who had "violent designs" against Ali Muhsin. A long detention awaited him and his kind, but there was a marked reluctance to sentence them to a physical penalty.

Yet this tolerance of the revolutionary leaders toward their predecessors was in marked contrast with the outbreak of racial vendetta at the grass-roots level— neighbor against neighbor, farmer against farmer. Many of these were politically-inspired killings. But were they "assassinations"? It is possible to argue that the Zanzibar revolution unleashed a large number of "political murders"— but not a single "assassination." For the term "assassination" does not merely mean "killing for political reasons." In fact, the reasons can be quite irrelevant. For example, in November 1963 headlines in different parts of the world proclaimed "Kennedy Assassinated"—before we knew who had killed him, let alone for what reasons. Perhaps we still do not know for what reasons. Yet the death of John F. Kennedy remains a case of assassination.

What seems more plausible is that the term "assassination" derives its meaning less from the motives of the killing than from the political importance of the victim. The victim need not be a professional politician, nor hold a formal office of state. Neither Mahatma Gandhi in 1947 nor Malcolm X in 1964 was a politician or state official in this professional sense. Yet we think of their deaths as instances of "assassination."

Victor T. LeVine prefers to base the definition of "assassination" on the role of the killer rather than the status of the victim. LeVine would also add the element of surprise to his definition. As he himself put it, "the difference between assassination and political murder is admittedly a tenuous one; I would contend that it lies in two areas, the role of the killer, and the element of surprise. Assassins are usually hired or delegated, and they generally strike without warning to the victims."[3]

That assassins usually carry out their purpose "without warning their victims" can surely be taken for granted. Assassins do not normally warn the police, either. As for the claim that "assassins are usually hired or delegated," surely this—even if it were statistically true—could have no bearing on the definition of assassination. A king can be assassinated by his own prospective successor.

As for the element of surprise, again this is at best an accompanying characteristic of assassination rather than a defining one. What if the killer is "theatrical" enough to telephone his victim anonymously and tell him that he has only until Thursday the following week to live? And what if on that Thursday the man is indeed killed? Was the theatrical forewarning enough to deprive the killing of the status of an assassination?

What about Lumumba when he was handed over to his enemies in Katanga? The news of his death was announced a month later. Many people were "shocked" without really being "surprised." The phenomenon of "surprise" implies a high degree of unexpectedness. And yet Lumumba already bore the marks of a violent beating even before he was handed over to his worst enemies. He was being publicly manhandled as he was being transported to Katanga, and the press informed the world with photographs of an abused Lumumba being dragged about by soldiers. There followed the weeks of mystery and speculation. Was Lumumba still alive? When the answer came in February 1961 many people, especially in the Third World, were indeed shocked that the worst had come to the worst. And yet somehow it was the shock of anger, and perhaps of political anguish, rather than the shock of surprise.

From this it can be concluded that neither the speed of killing nor the role of the killer is crucial in defining assassination. What is crucial is the status of the victim. The core or minimal definition is that an assassination is the killing of someone politically important by an agent other than himself or the government—for reasons which are either political or unknown.

LEGITIMACY VERSUS INTEGRATION

Perhaps the most fundamental problems confronting African countries are reducible to two crises—the crisis of national integration and the crisis of political legitimacy. For our purposes, the crisis of integration may be seen as a problem of horizontal relationships. It arises because different clusters of citizens do not as yet accept each other as compatriots. The sense of a shared nationality has yet to be forged.

The crisis of legitimacy, on the other hand, is a problem of vertical relationships. It arises not because one citizen does not recognize another as a compatriot, but because significant numbers of citizens are not convinced that their government has a right to rule them. Integration is a problem of neighbor against neighbor, legitimacy a problem of the ruled against their rulers.

Assassinations arise both in situations of inadequate national integration and in situations of weak legitimacy or accepted authority. But it would be a mistake to assume that the crisis of integration and the crisis of legitimacy need necessarily go together. It is possible for a country to have attained a high degree of integration or sense of nationhood while its capacity for accepting shared authority remains underdeveloped. The reverse phenomenon is also quite possible, and has perhaps even more examples in history.

Assassinations are often symptomatic of both crises. But here again it is not necessary that both crises be present. Recurrent assassinations have been known to happen in countries with a highly developed sense of shared nationality. Japan provides one dramatic example. Robert E. Ward has argued that Japan's history as a whole is a strange mixture of docility and violence:

> Violence and the use of armed force to accomplish political ends have a long and honourable tradition, which is by no means limited to pre-Restoration times. The phrase "government by assassination" gained broad currency in Japan as late as the 1930's and with considerable justification.[4]

Ward points out that the fourteen-year period of 1932–45 marked a reversion to this form of political behavior. The period began with the assassination of Prime Minister Inukai Tsuyoshi on May 15, 1932: "This was merely the most conspicuous of a number of such incidents that represented protests against widespread economic—especially agrarian—distress . . . and a foreign policy held to be insufficiently nationalistic and aggressive."[5]

Here were a people with a marked degree of national consciousness. Indeed, many of the killings were widely regarded as "*patriotic* assassinations," carried out for the sake of national honor. And yet the widespread approbation of many such acts in the country was an indication that the successful creation of national identity in Japan had not been accompanied by a successful tradition of governmental legitimacy. It is true that the emperor himself had more than political acceptance. He commanded mystical reverence as well. But in the final analysis the emperor was perhaps more a symbol of nationhood than of secure governmental authority.

In Africa the crises of both integration and legitimacy are still acute. And political violence is often symptomatic of both. Assassination itself as a political solution was rare during the colonial period. One can almost say that—in the light of our definition of it as "the killing of someone politically important, by an agent other than himself or the government, for reasons which are either political or unknown"—assassination comes near to being a post-independence phenomenon in Africa. Rival political groups in colonial Africa might have killed each other before. But the kind of political importance which a victim had to have if the killing was to be defined as an "assassination" was, to some extent, camouflaged by the colonial situation. Thus, if Patrice Lumumba had been killed mysteriously before the Congo became independent and afforded him a chance to be prime minister, the killing would have appeared less obviously as an assassination than it did when it took place some months after the country's independence.

But reasons of definition are not the only ones which make the killing of politically important African figures a post-independence phenomenon in the main. More weighty reasons are tied up with problems of the crises we have mentioned.

British colonial governors were hardly ever killed in office whereas within a few years of independence African heads of governments found themselves victims or near-victims of assassins. Why the difference? One possible answer is that the British colonial governor was well guarded. Another answer is that he mixed less with the general populace, and therefore exposed himself less to possible assassination. Both these statements might be true, and yet as reasons they might be of only marginal relevance.

We might get nearer the real reasons if, first, we reflected on this hypothesis: That there had been few attempts on the lives of colonial governors in Africa for the same reason for which there had been few mutinies by African soldiers under the colonial regime—the range of possible retaliatory signals was wider in the British power-spectrum than in that of the new regimes.

And yet the range of possible changes in the situation which could result from an assassination was seemingly narrower in a colonial situation than in a post-independence one. An assassin asks himself in a colonial situation what will happen if he kills the British governor. On the one hand, British power seemed great enough to be able to inflict a whole range of possible acts of revenge on the assassin alone, or on the assassin and others as collective punishment.

On the other hand, British power also seemed great enough to prevent any fundamental change in the political situation being brought about by the mere assassination of a governor. A replacement could be sent, and the colony would remain a colony under basically the same policy. British capacity for varied forms of revenge could put off an assassin through fear of credible consequences. British capacity for maintaining the political *status quo* despite the loss of a governor could put off an assassin through fear of futility.

But in a post-independence situation, getting rid of a prime minister could cause a more significant change in a country's orientation—just as an army mutiny after independence can effect an important change, unless it is thwarted by appeal to the former colonial power.

And even when thwarted it could—on issues like the Africanization of the officer corps in the army—prove to be a victory of the vanquished. The fluidity of the basis of legitimacy in a post-independence situation maximizes the temptation to revolt—and both military insubordination and attempted assassinations become a more common phenomenon than in pre-colonial days.

That is one reason why African independence and increased African violence are often companions—at least for a time.

CONSENSUS, PRIMARY AND SECONDARY

Linking this up with more traditional categories of political analysis, we may say that the problem of legitimacy is the old problem of "political obligation" in political philosophy. It is the problem of why and when one obeys or ought to obey the government. Where legitimacy is fully secure, the citizens do not question the government's right to govern, though they may question the wisdom of this or that governmental action. When it is not secure, challenges to authority may allow little differentiation between dissent, insubordination, rebellion, and outright treason.

In traditional political theory, the problem of political obligation involves a shifting balance between the area of consent in government and the area of compulsion. And the area of consent itself has different levels. To take Uganda as an example, one might note that there is a difference between consenting to being ruled by President Obote's government and consenting to this or that *policy* of his government. It is possible for an opponent of Dr. Obote's regime to be in favor of this or that policy pursued by the regime. Thus there were many Ugandans outside Obote's party who supported his toughness against the kingdom of Buganda although they would not vote for Obote in a general election. In this case they accept the policy though, given a choice, they would not accept the government.

But even the idea of accepting Obote's government, or consenting to be ruled by it, has two levels. The more obvious level is in the sense of having voted for Dr. Obote's party at the last election. Yet there is a sense, of course, in which even the Democratic party, although in *opposition*, consented to be ruled by Obote's Uganda People's Congress. The very idea of a loyal opposition implies consenting to be ruled by the constitutional government in power, although reserving the right to disagree with almost every one of its policies.

The problem in Africa in the first few years of independence was of trying to ensure that every Opposition remained a loyal opposition. It was a quest for a situation in which one could challenge decisions of the government and not the government's right to execute them.

In the final analysis, this was the ultimate problem of *consensus*—not a consensus on policies (that is, secondary consensus), but a consensus on legitimate methods of policy-making and legitimate methods of implementation (primary consensus). Thus even those who did not vote for the majority party in Uganda but took advantage of the elective principle concede the right of governance to their rival party.

In this primary sense, consensus is that which makes it possible to have *compulsion by consent*. It is what makes citizens accept a certain degree of force from the government, or even complain about that force, without feeling that the government lacks the right to govern them at all.

But the degree of compulsion needed is sometimes in inverse proportion to the degree of secondary consensus already achieved. This secondary consensus, or agreement behind certain policies, is sometimes known as "national unity" at a particular moment in time. There are occasions when we have to think of compulsion as that which we have to put into a governmental system in order to make up for deficiencies in unity. The Congo is less united than Uganda; therefore the Congo needs more coercion or compulsion in its system than does Uganda. Mainland Tanzania is more united than Uganda. Therefore mainland Tanzania or Tanganyika needs less coercion for minimal system-maintenance than does Uganda. Coercion and consensus are sometimes functional alternatives for system-maintenance.

But secondary consensus is not necessarily agreement behind policies; it can sometimes be agreement behind a leader, almost regardless of the policies he pursues.

African countries, faced with inadequate primary consensus, have sometimes invoked diverse devices in order to consolidate at least secondary consensus behind the leader. There is a tragic paradox involved in the process. On the one hand, the absence of primary consensus creates the danger of assassination because of the very inadequacy of legitimacy. On the other hand, the attempt to create secondary consensus leads to the personification of government. "Nkrumah is the CPP; the CPP is Ghana; Nkrumah is therefore Ghana." This is the syllogism which, in its conclusion, legitimates African equivalents of Louis XIV. But the doctrine of "I am the State," by personifying government, can be an invitation to regicide in conditions of primary dissensus. To challenge the leader is to challenge the state. The transformation of the state therefore "requires" the elimination of its present embodiment.

African attempts to promote "leader-worship" are, therefore, caught up in this contradiction. The whole idea of promoting it is partly inspired by a desire to mitigate the potential for regicide inherent in primary dissensus. And so leader-worship sometimes verges on being almost literal. Nkrumah was the clearest example in recent African history, though by no means atypical. He permitted himself to be portrayed as a messiah. But he needed to be a political Christ without a political crucifixion. Indeed, the reason for portraying him as a messiah was to avert the danger of crucifixion. But the sacralization of authority has entailed a personification of authority as well. And it is this which leads to the personification of opposition as well.[6]

DEATH AND HERO-WORSHIP

Then there are occasions when it is, in fact, the "crucifixion" which achieves the leader-worship so vainly sought by propaganda. The clearest example is probably the place of Lumumba in the Congo. Before his death Lumumba was perhaps more a hero of Pan-Africanists outside the Congo than of the Congolese themselves. It is true that he was "the nearest thing" to a national leader that the Congo had; but that was not all that "near." Lumumba stood for Congolese unity, but he was not himself popular enough or strong enough to ensure that unity without external help. Perhaps the forces against unity were in any case greater than any single leader could cope with. Lumumba might well have been a casualty of circumstances. Yet one thing was clear: while he lived he was essentially a factional hero rather than a national one.

But after his death the myth of Lumumba was rapidly nationalized. His death was announced in February 1961. By the summer of the same year a coalition government was formed under the premiership of Cyrille Adoula, with Kasavubu still president. When the new Prime Minister Adoula ventured into Stanleyville, he made a point of placing flowers at a temporary monument of Lumumba and he exclaimed: "We have achieved what Lumumba wanted: one Congo, one Congo, one Congo."

Commenting on this situation, Henry Tanner said:

The gesture . . . showed that Lumumba's place in Congolese politics has undergone a subtle but far-reaching change. Before the formation of the coalition government, the Lumumba legend had been the exclusive tool of one political faction. Now it is being invoked, with different shades of meaning and enthusiasm, by both parties in the coalition . . . even a politician who owes his power to Kasavubu, Lumumba's earliest rival, may find it wise to worship at the shrine.[7]

In July 1964, to the astonishment of the world, Moise Tschombe, the former secessionist of Katanga, was invited by President Kasavubu to succeed Adoula as prime minister of the Congo. Tschombe was widely regarded as the man behind the murder of Lumumba. Yet he had now come back from his exile in Europe to take over the reins of national power. On July 19, 1964, he addressed an enthusiastic crowd of 25,000 at the Baudoin Stadium in Leopoldville and proclaimed: "Give me three months and I will give you a new Congo."

On July 26 he was in Stanleyville, the Lumumbist stronghold. He repeated his theme of "give me three months" to a major rally. And as one more step toward that goal of a "new Congo," Moise Tschombe laid a wreath at the monument of Patrice Lumumba.[8]

Yet instability continued in the Congo. Tschombe scored a victory over the rebels, but the entire political regime ended with General Mobutu's coup in December 1965. On the first Independence Day anniversary following the coup a great crowd assembled in the capital to celebrate the occasion. The day was June 30, 1966, and President Mobutu was delivering a speech. Suddenly he made an unexpected statement:

> Glory and honour to an illustrious citizen of the Congo, to a great African, and to the first martyr of our independence. Patrice Émery Lumumba, who was the victim of the colonialist plot. In the name of the Government, we proclaim his name on this national heroes' day. . . .

Mobutu also declared a new policy toward the Belgian mining interests in the Congo, implying a greater assertion of Congolese control over the country's economy. Opposition to the autonomy of mining interests in the Congo was certainly in the tradition of Lumumbist thought in the Congo.[9]

Not long after, George Penchenier devoted one of four articles on the Congo in Le Monde to Mobutu's move in proclaiming Lumumba a hero. Penchenier pointed out that it was not merely in the rebel-held areas that Lumumba was regarded in such terms. "The three short months in which he held power were enough to make him a legend, and the circumstances of his death made him a martyr." Penchenier went on:

> Six years have passed. . . . The old street named Leopold III will be known in future as Patrice Émery Lumumba and a monument will be erected to his memory. The Congolese welcome these acts without stopping to think about the strange fate of a man who was followed, then betrayed, and now rehabilitated. General Mobutu has taken a political step. After having defeated the Lumumbist rebellion, he is trying to create a united Congo. Who better to help him than Patrice Lumumba?[10]

It looks as if the memory of Lumumba may contribute more to the "oneness" of the Congolese than anything Lumumba himself actually did while he was still alive. It all depends upon whether shared heroes constitute one of the factors which help to create national consciousness.

But why should Lumumba be a hero for reasons other than what he actually accomplished for his country while he lived? This takes us back to the place of violence in political mythology at large. Criteria for heroism in relation to violence can take one of three main forms. First, a person can be a hero because of some accomplishment in a violent activity like war. These are, of course, the war heroes. Secondly, a person can be a hero because of his capacity for non-violence in the face of provocation. Mahatma Gandhi and Jesus Christ fall within this second category. And, thirdly, a person can be a hero simply by being a victim of someone else's violence in a particular set of circumstances. It is within this third category that Patrice Lumumba falls.

Young nations often feel a need to have an antiquity. The desire to be old becomes part of the quest for identity. And dead heroes even of the immediate past are history personified. In that lies their relevance for the development of national consciousness. Hero-worship when the heroes are alive is at best a case of secondary consensus; hero-worship when the heroes are dead might well be a contribution to primary consensus.

But the secret both of national pride and national cohesion is to know what to forget. The desire to be old and wrinkled as a nation must be accomplished by a determination to have a failing memory. In Kenya, for example, this phenomenon is tested against what happened during the Mau Mau insurrection. On the one hand, there is a desire that yesterday's villains—the Mau Mau fighters—should become today's heroes. On the other hand, there is a determination that yesterday's heroes—the "loyalists" who fought against the Mau Mau—should not become today's villains. A similar selectivity will be demanded of the memory of the Congolese. In the case of the legend of Lumumba, it is a selectivity which has already taken place.

As we have argued before, the very idea of a nation can sometimes be a little too abstract, and hence a little too cold, to command ready human allegiance. To give the idea of a nation warmth, it is often necessary either to personify it metaphorically, or, more effectively, to give it specific human form in national heroes. This is why ancestor-worship is important not only among tribes but also within nations. And this is indeed why the assassination of Patrice Lumumba remains one of the most important single contributions to the development of primary consensus in the Congo.

PAN-AFRICANISM AND THE ASSASSIN

The distinction between national consensus and regional consensus in Africa is not always easy to draw. The same factors which make nationalism and Pan-Africanism in the continent so intimately connected have also produced an overlap between problems of domestic territorial identity and problems of continental racial identity. The very fact that Lumumba was a Pan-African hero before he became a Congolese national hero emphasizes this overlap.

Problems of separatism in Africa often get into a paradoxical relationship with problems of Pan-regionalism. The old issue of Katanga's secession, the continuing difficulty of secessionist Somalis in Kenya and Ethiopia, and even the isolation of Biafra, have in their different ways exemplified the tense connection between the politics of African separatism and problems of Pan-Africanism at large.

In what way is secessionism on the one hand and pan-regionalism on the other related to the phenomenon of assassination in Africa? A step toward an answer can be taken by asking yet another question: What sort of issues in such areas of political experience arouse the kind of passions which produce assassins?

One major category is of issues which imply a great sense of finality once a decision is taken. And these are issues which command such a degree of emotional involvement among those affected that the apparent finality of the decision, once it is taken, seems almost unbearable to the loser. This category of issues can produce assassins even though the immediate reason for killing a public figure might be a mere side-effect of the central factor which set the passions free.

Pre-eminent among the breeding grounds of assassins is a situation involving territorial partition—prospective, accomplished, or thwarted partition. Partition can take different forms. The term is normally used to apply to a case like that of Ireland or India where a foreign power was involved in the partitioning. But internally-generated secessionism is also a quest for partitioning a country.

Mahatma Gandhi lost his life in a situation involving separatist passions. Abraham Lincoln lost his life after frustrating a bid to partition the United States. More recently the issue of the separation of Algeria from France let loose emotions which resulted in a number of political murders, including several attempts on the life of de Gaulle.

The situation in the Algerian case was indeed complex. But to people like Jacques Soustelle, Algerian independence was at the time synonymous with the partition of France. The assassinative emotions generated were in part derived from the dread of partition, while the FLN was regarded as a secessionist movement.

When one considers this relationship between separatism and assassination, the prospect in Africa can be very disquieting. It was, after all, in Africa that Europe practiced the art of partition at its most elaborate. Where Europe attempted to unify those who were distinct, it left the seeds of future separatism—and Patric Lumumba was assassinated in a secessionist province. Where Europe divided, it sometimes left behind latent passions for reunification—and political killings at the grass-roots level have resulted from such division. In short, balkanization is a breeding ground of political violence, including the phenomenon of assassination. And balkanization is what Africa is burdened with for the time being.

Pan-Africanism is often an attempt to grapple with the consequences of balkanization. One early assassination which had Pan-African significance, as well as being somewhat connected with Africa's fragmentation, was the assassination of Sylvanus Olympio, first president of independent Togo. In this regard, we might begin by noting that, from the point of view of Pan-Africanism, there are three types of assassinations. There is the kind of assassination which might harm the cause of Pan-Africanism; secondly, the kind which might conceivably help the cause of Pan-Africanism; and thirdly, of course, the kind which has had little relevance for Pan-Africanism.

The assassination of Sylvanus Olympio remains perhaps the most dramatic case of a continentally divisive assassination which Africa has had so far. Olympio happened to be a pre-eminently "bicultural" or "tricultural" African leader in his upbringing. He was at home both among French- and English-speaking colleagues. And his country, Togo, under his leadership, was expected to be an important inter-lingual link between the two sectors of Westernized Africa.

However, a border dispute between Togo and Ghana marred this picture of potential amity. Nkrumah had become a champion of the reunification of the Ewe on the two sides of the border, hoping thereby to enlarge the boundaries of Ghana. Because of this border dispute and of personality factors in the relations between Olympio and Nkrumah, Ghana became a little too hospitable in the refuge it gave to discontented Togolese "at war" with the regime of their own country.[11]

When, therefore, Olympio was assassinated in January 1963, there was immediate suspicion in some circles that Ghana under Nkrumah was, either directly or indirectly, implicated. Nigeria's Foreign Minister at the time, Jaja Wachuku, articulated his suspicions perhaps a little too quickly. He regarded Olympio's assassination as "engineered, organized, and financed by somebody." He warned that Nigeria would intervene militarily if "the contingent of armoured Ghanaian troops lined up on the Ghana-Togo border" attempted to cross the border.[12]

Observers outside shared similar suspicions. Even the pro-Ghana American periodical at the time, *Africa Today*, saw a connection between a frontier dispute of that kind and the danger of assassination. In its own words:

> It is not the opposition which takes to the hand grenade but usually the neighbouring country whose leaders have taken up the cause of the opposition. . . . Africa balkanised will continue to be fertile ground for senseless political rivalries.[13]

But apart from the issue of frontiers, there was the issue of diplomatic recognition. With the murder of Olympio, African states were faced for the first time with the whole problem of "legitimate succession" following a case of regicide. West African governments were divided on the issue of whether or not to recognize the new Togolese government under Mr. Nicolas Grunitzky. From the east coast of Africa came the voice of Tanganyika, then almost alone as an independent state in its area. Tangayika cabled the secretary-general of the United Nations in the following terms:

> After the brutal murder of President Olympio, the problem of recognition of a successor government has arisen. We urge no recognition until satisfied first that the government did not take part in Olympio's murder or second that there is a popularly elected government.[14]

The first condition concerned the issue of whether assumption of power

was by legitimate means. The second concerned a possible subsequent legitimation of what was originally an illegitimate method of assuming power. Subsequent elections were, in other words, capable of giving a stamp of moral
dignity to a regime which originally acceded as a result of assassination or insurrection. It was like de Gaulle coming into power in 1958 as a result of
military insubordination—and then organizing a referendum throughout the
French community in order to validate his standing.

The year of Olympio's murder was also the year of the formation of the
Organization of African Unity. Only a few months separated the two events.
The ghost of Olympio virtually dictated that dramatic part of Article III of
the Charter of the new Organization: "unreserved condemnation, in all its
forms, of political assassination, as well as of subversive activities on the part
of neighbouring States or any other State."

Lumumba's martyrdom had perhaps, on the whole, been a positive contribution to Pan-Africanism. It gave Africa a shared hero as the memory of nationalism indulged in unifying selectivity. Olympio's murder, on the other hand,
at first deeply divided the continent, as suspicion and recrimination reigned
supreme. But history is beginning to reveal Olympio as essentially the first
major victim of a military coup in independent Africa. His death now appears
to have been an omen of things to come. Whether this prophetic symbolism
of his assassination would convert Olympio into a continental African hero
depends very much upon whether Africa will experience a fundamental disenchantment with military regimes—and turn back with nostalgia to the first
casualty of the wave of militarism.

If that were to happen, other heroes, too, of pre-military Africa—from Lumumba to Balewa—may contribute the vague mystique of their ancient names
to the slow growth of primary consensus in the consciousness of Africa.

NOTES

[1] The Charter is available in Boutros Boutros-Ghali, "The Addis Ababa Charter,"
International Conciliation, No. 546 (Jan. 1964), Appendix, 53–62.

[2] This was the second prime minister of Burundi to be assassinated. The first was
Prince Rwagasore, who was shot dead with a hunting-gun as he sat in a restaurant in
Usumbura, less than a month after his Lumumbist Uprona party had swept the polls in
September 1961. That, however, was before Burundi's independence. For an account of
the trial and retrial of those accused of complicity, see, for example, Clyde Sanger's
article in The Guardian (Manchester), Jan. 12, 1963.

[3] See Victor T. LeVine, "The Course of Political Violence," in William H. Lewis
(ed.), French-Speaking Africa, The Search for Identity (New York, 1965), 59–60;
68; 241, n. 15.

[4] "Japan," in Robert E. Ward and Roy C. Macridis (eds.), Modern Political Systems:
Asia (Englewood Cliffs, N.J., 1963), 60.

[5] Ibid., 30.

[6] See Ali Mazrui, "The Monarchical Tendency in African Political Culture," British
Journal of Sociology, XVIII (1967), 231–50. See, also, David E. Apter, "Political
Religion in the New Nations," in Clifford Geertz (ed.), Old Societies and New States
(New York, 1963), 82–84.

[7] Henry Tanner, "Over the Congo, Lumumba's Ghost," New York Times Magazine,
Oct. 29, 1961.

[8] *Africa Report*, IX (1964), 20.

[9] *Africa Digest*, XIV (1966), 22–23.

[10] *Le Monde*, Sept. 1, 5, 1966. The English rendering of the quotation is from *Africa Digest*, XIV (1966), 22–23.

[11] For a comprehensive recent treatment of the border problem and its ethnic implications, see Claude E. Welch Jr., *Dream of Unity* (Ithaca, 1966), especially Chaps. II, III.

[12] See Helen Kitchen, "Filling the Togo Vacuum," *Africa Report*, VIII 1963), 9.

[13] "Conspiracies and Balkanisation," *Africa Today*, X (1963), 3.

[14] *Tanganyika Standard* (Dar-es-Salaam), Jan. 26, 1963.

THE THEORY
OF CHARISMA

Thomas E. Dow, Jr.

THOMAS E. DOW, JR., *was born in 1936 and received his A.B. in history at Hunter College of the City University of New York, and his A.M. and Ph.D. in sociology at the University of Pennsylvania. He has taught at Russell Sage College, Mount Holyoke College, Fourah Bay College at the University of Sierra Leone in Freetown, and is currently associate professor of sociology at the State University of New York College at Purchase, New York. He served also as a staff associate in the Demographic Division of the Population Council during 1970 and 1971. He did research in Kenya during 1966 and in Sierra Leone from 1968 to 1970. He received two Ford Foundation grants administered by the Afro-Asian Studies Program of Amherst College, Mount Holyoke College, Smith College and the University of Massachusetts. He is a fellow of the African Studies Association and the American Sociological Association, and is a member of the Population Association of America and the International Union for the Scientific Study of Population. He has presented papers at the Fifth International Criminological Congress at Montreal in 1965, at the Population Association Annual Meeting in 1967, at the Nairobi Seminar on Population Growth and Socioeconomic Development in 1969, and at the African Studies Association's Annual Meeting in Boston in 1970. Professor Dow has contributed two sound seminars to the McGraw-Hill series on World Population Problems and has published essays in such journals as the American Sociological Review, Psychological Reports, The Journal of Criminal Law, Criminology and Police Science, Social Forces, Sociological Quarterly, Sierra Leone Geographical Journal, Journal of Modern African Studies, and Current History. Professor Dow is presently preparing a monograph on the population of Sierra Leone.*

Since its first systematic treatment by Max Weber in *Wirtschaft und Gesellschaft* in the early twenties, the concept of charisma** has been of only limited use to the social sciences. This is so because of fundamental disagreement concerning its meaning and application. In response to this, the present paper offers (1) a brief examination of Weber's contribution, (2) a critical analysis of this position based in part on the recent literature, and (3) a final formulation of the concept.

Reprinted with permission of *The Sociological Quarterly*, 10 (Summer 1969), 306–318.

* Research for this paper was supported by a Ford Foundation grant administered by the Asian and African Studies Program of Amherst College, Mount Holyoke College, Smith College and the University of Massachusetts. Supplementary funds were also received from the Mount Holyoke College faculty grants committee.

** Editor's note: Weber's writings on charisma have been translated, paraphrased, and interpreted by numerous modern writers. Henceforth the "Weber (1947)" reference will refer to the portions of *Wirtschaft und Gesellschaft* selected for translation by A. M. Henderson and Talcott Parsons. It should be remembered that Weber worked on *Wirtschaft und Gesellschaft* before and after World War I, and that the incompleted work was published after his death in June, 1920. For two other selective treatments by modern writers see Gerth and Mills (1946) and Bendix (1960).

For Weber, charismatic authority exists when an individual's claim to "supernatural, superhuman or . . . exceptional powers" (Weber, 1947:358) is acknowledged by others as a valid basis for their participation in a program of action which seeks to remedy "extraordinary . . . distress or [guarantee] the success of extraordinary ventures" (Gerth and Mills, 1946:251). Hence the leader's authority and program are specifically "outside the realm of everyday routine and . . . [therefore] sharply opposed both to rational . . . and to traditional authority. . . . Both . . . are . . . forms of everyday routine control . . . while charismatic authority repudiates the past, and is . . . a specifically revolutionary force" (Weber, 1947:361–362). In this sense "every [charismatic] leader . . . preaches, creates, or demands new obligations" while at the same time repudiating "any sort of [systematic] involvement in the everyday routine world" (Weber, 1947:361–362). This repudiation is of necessity ephemeral, and the "pure form [of] charismatic authority . . . [exists] only in the process of originating" (Weber, 1947:364). In time, primarily because of the inherent instability of charismatic authority (Gerth and Mills, 1946:248), the movement is brought back into the normal routine of the community (Weber, 1947:363–386) and "it is the fate of charisma, whenever it comes into the permanent institutions of a community, to give way to powers of tradition or of rational socialization" (Gerth and Mills, 1946:253).

Thus Weber speaks of charismatic leaders who reveal a transcendent mission or course of action which may be in itself appealing to the potential followers, but which is acted upon because the followers believe their leader is extraordinarily gifted. By accepting or believing in the leader's extraordinary qualities, the followers legitimize his claim to their obedience. This relationship prevails until the movement is destroyed by failure (Weber, 1947:360) or routinized by success. The evaluation which Weber placed on this latter process is a matter of controversy, and its discussion opens a Pandora's box of related issues in the social sciences. For the moment, it is enough to outline the shape of things to come.

On the one hand, Weber (Gerth and Mills, 1964:253) speaks of the "waning of charisma [as generally indicating] the diminishing importance of individual action." Gerth and Mills (1946:72–73) proceed from such statements to the following conclusion:

> Defensive pessimism . . . is a major theme of Weber's work, [and this theme] is reinforced by the fate he [Weber] sees for charisma in the modern world. . . . The concept [of charisma] serves him as a metaphysical vehicle of man's freedom in history. [This] freedom, as carried by charisma, is doomed. . . . For Weber, . . . freedom is identified with irrational sentiment and privacy . . . [and is] now on the defensive against both capitalism and bureaucracy.

Bendix (1960:328–329), on the other hand, suggests that Weber meant something very different:

> For Weber charisma and its routinization were omnipresent possibilities in all phases of history and had to be examined anew in each case. . . . He [Weber] did not identify all positive and dynamic historical forces with

"charisma" and all negative and retrogressive forces with routinization. . . . Accordingly, he did not subscribe to a theory of history that sees history's dynamic element in the charismatic "break-throughs" of great men and its stable element in the "decline of charisma" through routinization.

Obviously, these divergent interpretations do not resolve the question of charisma, but they do suggest that analysis of this concept involves facing some of the basic issues of social science: e.g., the role of the individual as a history maker, the independent role of ideas—vis-à-vis material, ideal and group interests, the explanation of social change, and the assessment of irrational forces in history. In the following sections, the concept of charisma is re-examined with these questions in mind.

CHARISMA AND TRANSCENDENCE

Throughout Weber's discussion, transcendence is attributed implicitly or explicitly to both the qualities of the leader and the content of his mission; the former being variously described as "supernatural, superhuman or exceptional," the latter as "new, outside the realm of everyday routine, extraordinary and revolutionary." Without this transcendent attribute one cannot speak meaningfully of charisma; with it, charisma can be distinguished both conceptually and objectively, from other forms of authority.

Marcus (1961:237), for example, argues that "the essence of the . . . charismatic hero lies in the belief he arouses that he can control the forces of history and achieve its transcendent objective." Following this pattern, Hitler, Churchill, and De Gaulle were able to inspire "in their followers [the conviction] that they were the masters of history and that in the long run history would be with them" (Marcus, 1961:238). This inspiration derives from the followers' faith in the charismatic figure, and not from the rational likelihood of success which, for each man in turn, could hardly have been less promising. It is this irrational bond, or identification between leader and led, that provides the follower with an opportunity for transcendence, and requires the leader, in turn, to maintain the revolutionary quality of the movement. Accordingly, distinctions between forms of leadership may then be made on the basis of whether or not the leader represents an "incarnation of some vision of a transcendent state" (Marcus, 1961:239).

But there remains the objection, expressed by Friedrich (1961:3–24), that Weber has grouped together two qualitatively different patterns of leadership only one of which is transcendent and hence truly charismatic. Friedrich (1961:15) contrasts "leadership based upon a transcendent call by a divine being, believed in by both the person called and those who follow," with secular forms of inspirational leadership which he characterizes as non-transcendent. Yet the appeal of a secular savior, whatever his personal integrity or intention, is fundamentally equivalent to that of a sacred prophet; in both cases one may observe a transcendent element, although it may not be theological in form. In this sense Weber's value-free extension of charisma, to include sacred and secular, "good" and "bad" movements, is quite consistent.

In all, this argument indicates the obvious significance of a transcendent element in any meaningful definition or analysis of charisma. It also provides a first impression of the important part played by (1) the gifted individual, (2) autonomous ideas, and (3) irrational forces in the charismatic process.

CHARISMA AND SOCIAL DETERMINISM: A THEORY OF SOCIAL CHANGE

Following Weber's suggestion (1947:370; Bendix, 1960:300) that charisma is manifested under certain circumstances more than others, some recent attempts (Friedland, 1964; Berger, 1963) have been made to locate the charismatic context. Friedland (1964:18), for example, suggests that "the concept [of charisma] can be useful . . . in the analysis of social change if [attention is focused] on the social context within which charisma develops rather than on charisma or charismatics." More specifically, he (Friedland, 1964:18) suggests what this context typically is: "Charisma appears in situations where (a) leaders formulate inchoate sentiments deeply held by masses; (b) the expression of such sentiments is seen as hazardous; (c) success . . . is registered." Unfortunately, this definition is seriously limited. There are always inchoate sentiments held by masses, expressing revolutionary ideas is always more or less dangerous, and success is always reinforcing. But having said this we are not really any closer to an understanding of the charismatic situation. We still do not know why leaders emerge in one case and not another, or why they succeed in one situation and not another.

Obviously people must recognize, accept, and follow the pretender before he can be spoken of as truly charismatic. The question is why do they do so? Do they do so because the times are particularly propitious for revolutionary change, or do they do so because of their belief that the charismatic figure, because of his extraordinary gifts, can achieve the transcendent image contained in his message? We would suggest that transcendent revolutionary change is never necessary, save as that necessity becomes part of retrospective analysis, and that such change is always—in rational terms—an improbable course of action, which is pursued because of the followers' faith in the "supernatural, superhuman or exceptional" qualities of the leader.

In short, we do not believe there is any usual or necessary context within which charisma naturally develops. The situation in which such a movement occurs may be relatively ordered, or it may involve military, political, or economic disorder. In either case, but particularly in the latter, such situations have not uniformly produced a revolutionary departure, a transcendent ideal, and have as often resulted in noncharismatic as in charismatic solutions. Thus, any analysis which concentrates exclusively on the social context in which charisma is supposed to develop, risks misunderstanding the fundamental nature of the charismatic movement, i.e., the relative independence of both the exceptional individual and his ideas. This is not meant to imply that either the man or his ideas are free agents in the process of historical transformation, but merely that they are perhaps more autonomous than Friedland imagined. Weber's analysis of ideas and interests, on the other hand, makes ample provision for this autonomy, and is therefore more relevant to an understanding of the charismatic element as an instrument of social change.

In this connection, it is clear that the charismatic figure and his ideas represent the cornerstone of Weber's attempt "to make intellectual allowance for the role of ideas and innovation in human affairs . . ." (Bendix, 1965:183). The relative autonomy of such ideas was affirmed by Weber's refusal "to conceive of [them] as being 'mere' reflections of psychic or social interest" (Gerth and Mills, 1946:62). Similarly, although the charismatic figure may be located in social space, "there is hardly ever a close connection between the interests or the social origin of the speaker . . . with the content of the idea during its inception" (Gerth and Mills, 1946:62–63). In the same way, "there is no pre-established correspondence between the content of an idea and the interests of those who follow from the first hour" (Gerth and Mills, 1946:63). Naturally, in time—"by a selective process"—ideas and interests "find their affinities" (Gerth and Mills, 1946:63). Finally, Weber (Gerth and Mills, 1946: 269–270) states:

> It is not our thesis that the specific nature of a religion [read charismatic idea] is a simple "function" of the social situation of the stratum which appears as its characteristic bearer, or that it represents the stratum's "ideology," or that it is a "reflection" of a stratum's material or ideal interest-situation. . . . However incisive the social influences, economically and politically determined, may have been upon a religious ethic [read charismatic idea] in a particular case, it receives its stamp primarily from religious [read individual or charismatic] sources, and, first of all, from the content of its annunciation and promise.

Personal charismatic leadership must be understood in those terms: as a movement in which neither the leader, nor the followers, nor the content of ideas can be explained as following directly from a specific context or constellation of interests. When the opposite argument is offered, as it was by Friedland, it is soon clear that it does not explain why charismatic leadership arises in one situation and not another, although both situations apparently contain the same necessary pre-conditions.

CHARISMA: A TIME BOUND CONCEPT

Weber (Gerth and Mills, 1946:245) suggests that "the further back we look in history, the more we find [charismatic leadership] to be the case." He also mentions Robespierre's apotheosis as "the last form which charisma has assumed in its long road of varied and rich destinies" (Gerth and Mills, 1958:72). From such statements, the question of charisma's relevance in the modern world arises.

Schlesinger (1960:6), for example, argues that Weber's use of charisma demonstrates "its irrelevance to the modern technical world." He stresses Weber's characterization of charismatic authority as being "specifically outside the realm of everyday routine" and "specifically irrational in the sense of being foreign to all rules." The nature of modern society and therefore modern leadership being, in Schlesinger's opinion (1960:7), just the opposite of this, one cannot use charisma to analyze leadership more complicated than that of "medicine men, warrior chieftains, and religious prophets." If the leadership is more complicated than this, it must be assumed that it has already been routinized and is therefore by definition no longer charismatic. But this over-simplification does justice neither to Weber's thesis nor the broader implications of charisma.

While it is true that Weber stressed the non-institutional character of charisma, his discussion of its routinization runs deeper than Schlesinger suggests. For Weber, charisma is routinized gradually as it is forced to administer day-to-day routine. Thus, it is implicit in the concept of routinization as a process that a charismatic figure may pursue, for a time, a transcendent purpose from within an institutional structure, as did Hitler, Churchill, De Gaulle and Napoleon. The argument here, is that their initial and continuing appeal was not to "intellectually analyzable rules" but to transcendent images, and that the basis of their relationship to their followers remained largely emotional and irrational. When these conditions exist one can speak of modern inspirational leadership, which is purely charismatic in its inception, largely charismatic during an indeterminate period of institutional control, and ultimately non-charismatic as transcendence recedes in the face of success or failure. Once again, the careers of Napoleon, Churchill, Hitler, and De Gaulle illustrate all phases of this process.

Furthermore, several recent contributions (Berger, 1963; Runciman, 1963) to the literature also suggest that charismatic leadership has existed and does exist within complex institutional structures. In particullar, Runciman (1963: 149) states that "under a [modern] bureaucratic or rational-legal system, the situations where charismatic leadership still finds expression are those where a leader can by his personal and exemplary qualities create a further legitimacy for actions going beyond his stipulated office. . . ."

From this, one may conclude that the charismatic phenomenon is not bound necessarily to any particular historical period. As we have argued, there is no likely time or place for the form of transcendent change contained in any charismatic movement. All times are against such change, and it is precisely the fact that charisma is not a necessary development from any set of present circumstances that makes it a truly revolutionary departure. That we, of necessity, lack a clear vision of the forms that such departures might take in the future, is not to be construed as a limiting factor on such possibilities. Thus while we accept Bendix's interpretation (1962:326–327), "that charisma has been a recurrent phenomenon because persons endowed with this gift of grace—for better or worse—have asserted their leadership under all historical conditions . . . in all phases of history," we do not accept a completely asocial or ahistorical perspective.

The occurrence of a specific charismatic episode is indeterminate—as to time and place—and yet the frequency of charismatic events may be greater under some circumstances than others. Similarly, the attempt "to clarify the social context that [favors]—in the sense of elective affinity—the emergence of innovating forces" (Berger, 1963:950) is certainly valuable. Yet, having said this, one must still conclude that charisma is in, but not of this world, and cannot be reduced to a simple pattern of historical determinism.

CHARISMA, ROUTINIZATION AND THE INDIVIDUAL

In Weber's thesis, pure charismatic authority is inherently unstable (Gerth and Mills, 1946:248), and must ultimately become "either traditionalized or rationalized, or . . . both" (Weber, 1947:364). In this "process of routinization the charismatic group tends to develop into one of the forms of everyday authority . . ." (Weber, 1947:369). Weber believed that in the course of this transformation charismatic elements might occasionally persist, but only in an impersonal rather than personal form. His resulting analysis of this process provides the basis for a continuing discussion of institutional charisma by contemporary sociologists.

Berger, for instance, notes "the non-institutional, even anti-institutional, character of charisma as understood by Weber" (Berger, 1963:949), but argues that recent findings concerning the Israeli prophecy require "a modification of the theory of charisma that would de-emphasize the latter's non-institutional character" (Berger, 1963:940). His thesis is that "the . . . prophets began their careers . . . located within the cultic institutions, but their message drove them beyond the cultic definition of their function. . . . The prophets do not [however] abandon their office, but radicalize it . . . [by] the astounding novum of their message" (Berger, 1963:948). Berger concludes that this finding does not contradict "Weber's insistence on the autonomy of . . . ideas," but merely indicates that "charismatic innovation need not necessarily originate in social marginality" (Berger, 1963:950). Charisma, representing "the sudden eruption into history of new forces . . . linked to . . . new ideas," may "be characteristic of socially marginal individuals . . . [but it] may also be a trait of individuals located at the center of the institutional fabric . . ." (Berger, 1963:950).

Obviously this argument, in combination with Runciman's thesis and our own analysis, is limited to the role of charismatic individuals under institutional circumstances; it indicates the potential for personal charismatic expression within rational-legal or traditional structures. In general, it suggests a greater role for the charismatic personality within an institutional setting than Weber was willing to acknowledge. But beyond this, being focused on the individual, it avoids the larger question of impersonal charisma; that is, the presence of a charismatic relationship in the absence of an extraordinary individual. This thesis of depersonalized charisma has been greatly extended in the work of Edward Shils.

Shils contends that Weber "did not consider the more widely dispersed . . . operation of the charismatic element in [a] . . . rational-legal [system] of society" (Shils, 1965:202), and suggests "that an attenuated, mediated, institutionalized charismatic propensity is present in the routine functioning of society" (Shils, 1965:200). This propensity is manifested in attributing "charismatic properties to ordinary secular roles, institutions . . . and strata

. . . of persons" (Shils, 1965:200). Shils explains this tendency as a reflection of man's need for order, which causes him to attribute charisma to those roles, institutions or strata which seem central in the creation or modification of order. These positions apparently inspire in man a sense of "awe-arousing centrality" because they are supposedly able to generate an order which provides "continuity, coherence and justice." The more powerful positions are most able to influence this order and hence have the most charisma attributed to them. It follows from this, that great power as such, and all effective possessors of it, will come to be endowed with charisma: "Corporate bodies—secular, economic, governmental, military, and political—come to possess charismatic qualities simply by virtue of the tremendous power concentrated in them" (Shils, 1965:207). And so "in the rational-legal system . . . charisma . . . is dispersed . . . throughout the hierarchy of roles and rules. . . . It is inherent in the massive organization of society" (Shils, 1965:205–206). The only qualification is that effective power "must also appear to be integrated with a transcendent moral order" (Shils, 1965:207).

The basic problem in this analysis is the degree of attenuation to which the charismatic element is subjected, as Shils moves from charismatic individuals, to specific charismatic offices, to the discovery of a charismatic propensity in the entire organization of society. In this extreme formulation, we are asked to imagine a charismatic relationship in the public's response to the routine offices of society, although such offices for the most part make no deliberate attempt—via specific ritual—to establish a charismatic basis for their authority. In Shils' thesis, however, they apparently achieve a certain charismatic legitimacy as a result of the concentration of power within them; the presence of such power apparently leads the community to attribute charismatic properties to these secular positions and their incumbents.

But in fact, power per se does not appear to have any necessary charismatic qualities. On the contrary, unless it actively and visibly pursues a transcendent end, while deliberately seeking to establish a charismatic basis for its authority, the public's relationship to corporate power as such will not be charismatic.

Shils (1965:207) of course is aware of this, and acknowledges that "power . . . does not automatically and completely legitimate itself simply by its effective existence." Such power "must also appear to be integrated with a transcendent moral order." At a superficial level, this argument suggests the tendency of all power to proclaim itself and its objective just. Whether they are so, and whether the power in question is charismatic merely because of this claim, is problematic.

More significantly, it is not entirely clear how effective rational-legal power —absorbed in the routine functioning of society—is to maintain a transcendent priority in its day-to-day administration of social and economic affairs. In short, if this "integration with a transcendent moral order" is evident only inferentially, in the behavior of the institution or in its formal rhetoric; and absent, in the sense of not being part of a radical movement toward a transcendent state of social, political, or economic affairs, then it is difficult to see in what way these mundane activities, this preoccupation with what Weber (Gerth and Mills, 1946:245) called the "calculable and recurrent needs . . . of a normal routine," can be considered or recognized by the public as a valid basis for entering into a charismatic relationship. Under these circumstances, the need for elaborate mechanisms of charismatic legitimation would be all the more evident. But it is precisely such rituals that are missing in the routine functioning of society.

Clearly such routine institutions, in their usual conduct of daily affairs and in their visibility to the public, would normally fall outside the realm of either personal or impersonal charisma; accordingly, the attempt to concentrate on residual or attenuated charismatic elements in such situations would seem to confuse rather than clarify their basic source of authority. In general, then, the extension of charismatic properties to the entire hierarchy of roles and rules in a rational-legal system, does not seem to represent a viable addition to the theory of institutional charisma.

A more balanced interpretation would be Weber's use of impersonal charisma to refer only to those offices that have made successful use of various practices and rituals to demonstrate or legitimize the charismatic qualities of the office. One would note especially the formulae and rituals to transfer the "supernatural, superhuman or exceptional powers" of the original charismatic predecessor to the office and present incumbent. This process of transmission, by which the "gift of grace" is presumedly kept alive, is crucial in establishing the presence of depersonalized charisma. In Weber's words (1947:364), "the way in which this problem is met—if it is met at all . . . —is of crucial importance for the character of the subsequent social relationships."

Obviously, therefore, if no popularly accepted process of charismatic discovery, designation, inheritance, or transmission exists, or is claimed, existing power will have to be justified in noncharismatic terms. This would seem to be the situation with regard to most of the routine functioning of modern society, in which a charismatic response is generally neither expected nor received in the relationship between corporate bodies and their clients.

CHARISMA: A FINAL FORMULATION[1]

There is no single charismatic temperament or personality type,[2] but there is a charismatic phenomenon which can be theoretically and empirically[3] isolated as an independent form of authority. Basically, it involves a distinct social relationship between leader and follower, in which the leader presents a revolutionary idea, a transcendent image or ideal which goes beyond the immediate, the proximate, or the reasonable; while the follower accepts this course of action not because of its rational likelihood of success—such a rational premise is in all instances missing—but because of an affective belief in the extraordinary qualities of the leader. Thus the leader appeals neither to intellectually calculable rules, nor to tradition, but to the revolutionary image and his own exemplary qualities with which the follower may identify. If such identification occurs, that is, if these reciprocal role expectations are met, the relationship is charismatic. This applies in small group dynamics as well as in large-scale social movements. It is, however, the larger stage of history that most concerns us here. Our analysis of charisma on this macro-level suggests the following points.

Initially, if no time is propitious for revolutionary change, except as the appearance of such necessity is read into retrospective analysis, then one cannot view history as a parade of equally qualified charismatic pretenders, one of whom is validated eventually because the time is "right." A better representation would be that of an individual who can inspire belief in his message not because of particularly facilitating conditions, but in spite of tremendous odds. Such a man is followed not because a revolutionary departure is imminent, likely, or normally to be anticipated, but because he can demand support for such change in spite of its improbable character. Thus Christ makes God believable; Mohammed, Allah; Churchill and De Gaulle make victory seem possible; while Kenyatta and Ghandi do the same for freedom and independence. It is not the inchoate feeling for freedom which makes such men believable, but the men who inspire belief that freedom can be obtained in spite of all odds—and the odds are always long!

From this, it is a short step to recognizing that the charismatic movement cannot be explained as a simple reflection or function of the social class, material interests or social situation of those originally involved. The religious message of Christ or Buddha, the revolutionary action of Ghandi or Nehru, the political military goals of Hitler, Napoleon and De Gaulle can hardly be viewed as a mere reflection of their social class or material interests. On the contrary, these men offered transcendent goals and revolutionary ideas which must be considered independent variables in the process of historical transformation. It follows from this, that the charismatic element, while obviously not the sole source of change (Bendix, 1962:325–328), must be considered a major factor in most revolutionary departures. Obviously, the consequences of such charismatically inspired departures need not be necessarily progressive.

Charisma, as Weber pointed out, is a value-free term and such charismatic leaders may—at the least—involve their followers in a cruel hoax or, as in Hitler's case, an epic tragedy. They provide in themselves and in their vision an opportunity for the follower to imagine himself and his society transformed into something entirely new. Unfortunately, it is a moot point whether this new order will represent an ethical improvement over the ancient régime, the outcome of such episodes being as unpredictable as their occurrence.

Charisma is neither old nor new, but an omnipresent possibility in all ages. This being so, we in the present are no more able to predict future charismatic departures than were those in the past able to anticipate the revolutions of today. Being "independent," charismatic possibilities are necessarily impossible to anticipate fully. One can safely assume, however, that such departures as do occur will not be monopolized by East or West, developed or developing societies. The civil rights revolution in the United States, for example, is an excellent illustration of a large-scale charismatic movement taking place within a highly developed society.[4] Other examples of charisma's diverse potential were suggested earlier in the work of Runciman and Berger. The former argued that in a developed society charismatic opportunities remain for the leader who can, by his "personal and exemplary qualities, create a further legitimacy for actions going beyond his stipulated office" (Runciman, 1963:149); while the latter contended that charismatic figures may arise at the center of the institutional fabric and radicalize it from within. The first point may perhaps be illustrated by Dag Hammerskjold's exercise of the office of Secretary General of the United Nations, Franklin Delano Roosevelt's exercise of the American Presidency and General De Gaulle's early exercise of the office of President of the Republic; while the second point is portrayed best by the actions of Pope John XXIII during his brief Pontificate. The argument that one can go further than this, and speak of depersonalized charisma residing solely in a secular office, role, strata, or concentration of power, was also considered.

In general, Weber's limited extension of charismatic properties to specific hereditary and institutional contexts, e.g., the Papacy and Kingship, seemed more defensible than Shils' attempt to attribute charismatic elements to a wide range of ordinary secular roles, institutions, and strata of persons. In the latter case, charisma ceases to have any independent descriptive or analytic value.

More specifically, Weber recognized the need for elaborate social rituals designed to make visible and explicit the manner in which the present incumbent receives the "gift of grace" which constitutes the basis of his claim on the loyalty of the community. Such legitimating procedures reach their most complete development in the "transmission of priestly charisma by anointing, consecrating, or the laying on of hands; and of royal authority, by anointing and coronation" (Weber, 1947:366).

Under these special circumstances, there may be—as Weber suggested—a certain charismatic relationship between the community and the office, irrespective of the person who fills it. And yet, having acknowledged the awe-arousing qualities of certain offices, it is necessary to add that this relationship is not static but dynamic; in that the behavior of the specific incumbent, in terms of his relatively ordinary or extraordinary gifts, will tend to influence the charismatic relationship with the community. In other words, the existential experience of charismatic obligation, by those involved with the institution, will vary in intensity with the content and style of contemporary leadership. Thus a particularly mediocre Pope or King may seriously weaken the powers of his office; while, conversely, under a truly "gifted" leader, the institution or office will realize the fullest measure of personal devotion on the part of the faithful.

Clearly, then, a certain charisma adheres to those offices which have carefully preserved and transmitted their extraordinary properties to all legitimate incumbents. But it is also clear that this relationship can be disturbed, if not destroyed, by the action of a particular office holder.[5]

So qualified, the concept of impersonal charisma—primarily, "hereditary charisma" (Erbscharisma) and "charisma of office" (Amtscharisma)—would seem to have a valid place in the general theory of charisma. In a sense, it represents a theoretical outpost beyond which the role of charisma is clearly marginal. Those going beyond such situations will probably find greater understanding in the use of rational-legal or traditional models of authority.

With this point we come full cycle from the purely personal context of charisma to the office itself. This closure represents the natural conclusion to the present analysis of charisma; an analysis which sought to establish the content, presence, and relative independence of charismatic authority in history.

NOTES

[1] This formulation has been used to analyze political leadership in tropical Africa (cf. Dow: 1968).

[2] Charisma has been correctly attributed to widely divergent personality types, e.g., Kenyatta and Kaunda, Nkrumah and Nyerere, Rousseau and Robespierre, Sukarno and Nehru, Calvin and Luther, suggesting that there is no specific temperament naturally associated with the possession of charisma.

[3] It should be possible to develop objective indices of charisma on two levels. First, the reasons men give for obedience to a leader, i.e., "why they feel compelled to obey," and the reasons advanced by the leader as to why he should be obeyed, may be categorized into distinct forms of authority. In any given situation, this would indicate whether power was primarily justified or legitimated on legal, traditional, or charismatic grounds. Second, the content of a leader's program, the proportion of all activities devoted to either the transcendent or the routine, may be empirically appraised, so that the relative position of these elements in any program of action would be apparent.

[4] That the action program of the civil rights movement represents a revolutionary departure from existing patterns of order is now largely accepted. We would go further and argue that from its inception to its present routinization, the movement corresponds to the formulation offered in this paper. Finally, one may consider Martin Luther King to have been the "ideal-typical" charismatic figure in this experience.

[5] History provides numerous examples of the loss of authority by those who had a legitimate claim to community loyalty on the basis of familial or institutional charisma. Moreover, in some cases the office itself was destroyed along with the incumbent.

REFERENCES CITED

BENDIX, REINHARD
    1965 "Max Weber and Jakob Burckhardt." American Sociological Review 30 (April): 176–184.
    1962 Max Weber: An Intellectual Portrait. New York: Doubleday.
BERGER, R. L.
    1963 "Charisma and religious innovation: the social location of Israelite prophecy." American Sociological Review 28 (December):940–950.
Dow, T. E., JR.
    1968 "The role of charisma in modern African development." Social Forces 46 (March):328–338.
FRIEDLAND, W. H.
    1964 "For a sociological concept of charisma." Social Forces 43 (October):18–26.
FRIEDRICH, C. J.
    1961 "Political leadership and the problems of charismatic power." The Journal of Politics 23 (February).
GERTH, HANS H. and
C. WRIGHT MILLS
    1946 From Max Weber: Essays in Sociology. New York.
MARCUS, J. T.
    1961 "Transcendence and charisma." The Western Political Quarterly 14 (March): 236–241.

RUNCIMAN, W. G.
  1963 "Charismatic legitimacy and one-party rule in Ghana." Archives Europeenes de Sociologie 4:148–165.
SCHLESINGER, A., JR.
  1960 "On heroic leadership." Encounter XV (December):3–11.
SHILS, E.
  1965 "Charisma, order, and status." American Sociological Review 30 (April):199–213.
WEBER, MAX
  1947 The Theory of Social and Economic Organization. Translated by A. M. Henderson and Talcott Parsons; edited with an Introduction by Talcott Parsons. New York.

THE RHETORIC OF
PEACEFUL COEXISTENCE:
KHRUSHCHEV IN AMERICA, 1959

Theodore Otto Windt, Jr.

THEODORE OTTO WINDT, JR., *is associate professor of speech and theatre arts at the University of Pittsburgh. He received his B.A. degree from Texas Lutheran College, his M.A. from Bowling Green State University, and his Ph.D. in 1965 from Ohio State University. He has spent much of his career in theatre as a director and an occasional writer of plays. Currently, he teaches courses in the rhetoric of the modern Presidency and argument in the Soviet Union.*

Premier Nikita Khrushchev's official visit to the United States in September 1959 culminated his drive for personal talks with President Eisenhower, a drive the former had initiated two years earlier. As a political event, it marked a major change in the cold-war atmosphere. Strident antagonism between the two countries faded briefly into cautiously guarded hopes for rapprochement on some outstanding issues.

The trip was not intended to serve as a setting for negotiations on major international issues.[1] Rather, it was conceived to establish a new atmosphere from which subsequent discussions could proceed. Each leader hoped to probe the other's intentions and policies. Publicly Khrushchev sought to identify areas of common interest. "It is important," he stated, "to find a common language and a common understanding on the questions we should settle."[2]

However, the carnival atmosphere that surrounded the trip obscured its significance. Some American leaders reacted to the exchange of visits with childish fears. Richard Cardinal Cushing compared Khrushchev's trip to "opening our frontiers to the enemy in a military war."[3] Vice President Nixon journeyed to Minneapolis to assure the American Legion that President Eisenhower would not be "taken in" or bluffed by the wily Russian into compromising American national security.[4] Furthermore, a "truth squad," dispatched by the State Department and led by Henry Cabot Lodge, accompanied Khrushchev, presumably to rescue soft-minded Americans who might be duped into embracing communism.[5] Seldom in the history of politics has the spoken word been endowed with such persuasive powers. President Eisenhower even added his bit to this miniature theatre-of-the-absurd by refusing to escort Khrushchev to his airplane when he departed for Moscow.

Khrushchev entered into the festivities with general good humor. He arrived on September 15 with an entourage fit for a czar. He blustered and laughed his way through tough question-and-answer sessions. In Hollywood he parodied the can-can and entered a lively debate with Spyros Skouras on the relative merits of communism and capitalism. Later, he bellowed when he learned he

Reprinted with permission of the *Quarterly Journal of Speech* (February 1961), pp. 11–22, and the author.

could not visit Disneyland. During his tour he ate hot dogs, exchanged trinkets, and campaigned as vigorously for the virtues of his government as an American politician campaigns for his party and himself.

These antics obscured the seriousness of the visit and the repercussions that issued from it. If this trip marked a definite change in Soviet-American relations, it also marked the beginning of the end of the uneasy Russian-Chinese alliance. To understand Khrushchev's rhetoric requires that we understand the political context in which he acted. The decisions Khrushchev made prior to his visit set the perimeters for the ideas he could advance while in America. To ignore this context is to ignore the essence of his rhetoric.

POLITICAL BACKGROUND

The Berlin crisis

Most commentators agree that the Berlin crisis of 1958–59 precipitated the invitation extended to Khrushchev to visit America.[6] On November 10, 1958 Khrushchev suddenly announced that the Soviet Union planned to sign a separate peace treaty with the German Democratic Republic.[7] During a press conference on November 27 he proposed that British and American occupation troops be withdrawn from Western Berlin, that West Berlin be unified with East Germany, and that the Soviet Union supply food and ensure industrial operations after these changes were made.[8] The Soviet note to the United States issued the same day proposed that the treaty be concluded *within six months.* This ultimatum has been interpreted in a variety of ways. Our best understanding can be gained if we attempt an understanding of Khrushchev's political position in 1958.

The political purposes of Khrushchev's visit

In June 1957 Khrushchev began his purge of the "anti-Party" group, led by Malenkov, Kaganovich, and Molotov.[9] Marshal Zhukov fell in October and Premier Bulganin in early 1958. By March 1958 Khrushchev was powerful enough to assume the position of Prime Minister as well as retain his power as Secretary of the Communist party. By March he had become sole ruler of the Soviet Union.[10] Now he would advance his own programs and bear responsibility for them.

As he proposed major changes in food production,[11] education,[12] agriculture,[13] and the military's relationship to the Party,[14] he met opposition. The *apparatchiki*, those Party bureaucrats who had vested interests in the old programs, were alarmed. Others who retained dreams of unseating Khrushchev saw his measures as offering future possibilities for ousting him from office. The major obstacle to his programs was the military-industrial complex, the "steel-eaters" as Khrushchev aptly named them, from whose budgets much of the money for new programs would have to come.

In 1958 Khrushchev found himself caught amid the mighty contradictions politics imposes on the exercise of power, contradictions that ideology either prohibits or ignores. To promise new domestic programs the Soviet economy could not support would raise expectations that could not be satisfied. To fail to act would leave him open to the charge that he could not govern. Khrushchev devised a strategy that would allow him to solve these problems at least temporarily without doing irreparable harm to his power base.

First, he sought rapprochement with the United States over several issues. If he could gain a limited *detente* with the United States, he could argue that the threat from capitalist nations was not as great as the military had led Russians to believe. Therefore, it did not deserve the vast expenditures lavished upon it. The *detente* policy marked Khrushchev's progressive thrust in foreign policy. Moreover, Khrushchev sincerely feared the possibility of nuclear war. This theme is sustained throughout his administration. Rapprochement with the United States could be a step toward realization of these goals.

On the other hand, Khrushchev could not afford charges of being "soft on capitalism" either from Stalinists or from Chinese. Therefore, he had to take a hard-line on a particular issue, which would subsequently protect him politically. Khrushchev probably instigated the Berlin crisis to shore up his defenses against conservative criticism. By stating his intention to sign a peace treaty with East Germany, he demonstrated his courage in facing the Western threat, an act he could readily point to if any severe criticism of his policy of *detente* arose.

The strategy was adroit. If the United States did not oppose the treaty, Khrushchev would have achieved a coup in international relations beyond his most imaginative expectations. He would hand over supervision of access to West Berlin to the East Germans. Then the Western powers would have to negotiate with East Germany, which would require recognition of that country, to secure new rights of access. Once the treaty was signed, Khrushchev could press for more concessions in Europe, especially for the incorporation of West Berlin into East Germany.

Conversely, if the United States did react, Khrushchev could use his ultimatum as a bargaining point for forcing a summit conference at which time he could pursue possibilities for rapprochement. If he achieved some limited agreements, he could return to Moscow to argue that the capitalist military threat had receded and thus could transfer monies from the military-heavy industry budgets to consumer goods and agricultural programs. Moreover, his acceptance by Western leaders would enhance his popularity with the Russian people, if the propaganda were well handled, by picturing him as one who could deal effectively with capitalist powers.[15] His opponents would think twice before attempting once again to depose a popular leader. In addition, Khrushchev would gain prestige. At the Moscow Conference in November 1957 Mao Tse-tung emerged as a formidable rival to Khrushchev's claim as international leader.[16] Recognition by Western leaders, especially by President Eisenhower, would enhance Khrushchev's diplomatic powers, even as it pointed to Mao's isolation.

These were the stakes in Khrushchev's gamble. They paid off. After he proposed the peace treaty, the United States responded by vigorously opposing any compromise of Western rights in Germany. As quickly as the lines of disagreement were drawn, maneuvers began toward easing tensions. In January 1959

Anastas Mikoyan toured the United States and smiled through the vilifications he was subjected to during several public appearances. On March 2 Moscow proposed a summit conference to negotiate the Berlin issue, an issue Americans did not consider negotiable. However, pressure from British diplomats caused Americans to take a less strident attitude. As a foreshadowing of the future, Vice President Nixon toured Poland and the Soviet Union in July and August. On August 3, 1959, a joint communique issued simultaneously in Washington and Moscow announced that Eisenhower and Khrushchev had agreed to exchange visits. Khrushchev would come to the United States in September.

The excitement of gaining this invitation must have been counterbalanced by the magnitude of rhetorical problems Khrushchev confronted in constructing a rhetoric appropriate to his political aims and to the diverse audiences who would scrutinize his every word and deed. This was a new situation in the cold war. Khrushchev could not come to America and argue seriously for *detente* and at the same time repeat standard communist condemnations of capitalist nations. He could not urge peaceful coexistence and the need for negotiated settlements of outstanding issues without appearing ready to negotiate. Such a strategy would only confirm suspicions held by American critics that his motives were pernicious as well as alienate his neutralist friends who looked to him for progressive leadership. On the other hand, he could not stray too far afield from standard ideology without making himself vulnerable to attacks of "revisionism," which the Moscow Conference had condemned. These were the political and ideological perimeters within which he would have to invent a rhetoric. During his trip he tip-toed the tightrope between the two major dangers he faced.

KHRUSHCHEV'S SPEECHES[17]

Leading ideas

Khrushchev sought to reduce world tensions, which had been intensified by threats of "rocket-rattling" and "massive retaliation," by placing disagreements in a more realistic context. In his farewell address to the American people Khrushchev turned to a folksy analogy to demonstrate the futility of continuing the strident rhetoric of the cold war:

> Imagine the following picture: two neighbors live side by side, each of them doesn't like the routine and way of life in the other's house. So they build up a fence and with their households abuse each other night and day. Is it a happy life such neighbors live? Anyone will say that it isn't. Sooner or later things may come to blows.
>
> However, bad neighbors still have a way out. One of them can sell his house and move elsewhere. But what can nations do? They can't move anywhere.[18]

As an alternative to mutual abuse, Khrushchev proposed peaceful coexistence. As he explained it in an article published in *Foreign Affairs*[19] to coincide with his visit, peaceful coexistence requires that nations desist from making belligerent speeches that only pollute the political atmosphere and make negotiations more difficult to conduct. Second, nations must renounce war as a method for solving political problems. Third, nations must cease interfering in internal affairs of other countries. Finally, nations must recognize certain mutual interests and problems that require settlement. Khrushchev contended the Soviet Union had always abided by these principles. However, he insisted that peaceful coexistence did not mean an end to ideological conflicts. Capitalism and communism remain antagonistic social and political systems.

As first steps toward peaceful coexistence, Khrushchev proposed three concrete measures: creating better trade relations, winding down the arms race, and signing the peace treaty with Germany. In his address at the United Nations he added several other topics appropriate to that international assembly. He called for admission of Peoples Republic of China to the U.N. in place of Nationalist China, a modified reorganization of voting procedures in the U.N., and complete and universal disarmament to be concluded within four years.[20]

Rhetorical Strategies

Khrushchev could scarcely have believed that the United States would agree to a peace treaty with East Germany. Such a treaty would have altered the balance of power in middle Europe and would have created untold crises over Berlin. Furthermore, Khrushchev readily dropped his ultimatum after only two days of talks with President Eisenhower at Camp David. In their official communique they stated they had reached an understanding that the Berlin question would be negotiated *"in accordance with the interests of all concerned."*[21] Previously, Khrushchev had maintained the Soviet Union would sign the treaty regardless of what other countries did.

Only naïveté would lead one to believe President Eisenhower's persuasive powers caused this change. A world leader does not shift his policy on a major issue without having prepared to do so well in advance. Khrushchev's insistence on the peace treaty was a "straw man" designed to arouse and heighten the suspense that surrounded the drama of his visit. Berlin was the major issue on which he appeared adamant. When he modified his position after the Camp David talks, he contributed to a modification of our perceptions of him. He conveyed the shadow, if not the substance, of a reasonable politician, a man prepared to negotiate. This strategy maintained concrete interest in his tour, even when it became repetitive, and gave Americans one piece of evidence that Khrushchev was not as unreasonable as he had been portrayed.

Khrushchev's second strategy was designed to place Americans on the defensive. He treated each issue he talked about as a prerequisite to peace, an alternative to war. At the United Nations he stated: "The tension in international relations cannot continue forever. Either it will reach the pitch at which there can be only one outcome—war—or else, by joint efforts, the states will succeed in abolishing this tension in good time."[22] Within this frame of reference with only "either-or" options, those who opposed his proposals seemed to advocate greater strains in Soviet-American relations and appeared to toy with the possibility of nuclear war. This strategy clearly gave Khrushchev an advantage in presenting his disarmament plan, especially since he seized the initiative with his dramatic plan for "general and complete disarmament" within a period of four years as a means for avoiding war.[23]

Khrushchev compounded his advantage by drawing proofs from American history and culture. When he argued that trade could contribute directly to world peace, he cited a motto on an American postage stamp, "World peace through world trade." In this same speech to the Economic Club of New York, he asserted that trade should always be conducted on the basis of equality and mutual advantage. In support Khrushchev quoted a Benjamin Franklin maxim, engraved above the entrance to the Commerce Building in Washington, "Commerce among nations should be fair and equitable."[24] At the United Nations, Khrushchev congratulated the newly emerging nations for rebelling against colonialism and compared the reverence future generations would have for these revolutionaries to the respect Americans have for George Washington and Thomas Jefferson. The Premier often used Eisenhower as an example of the new spirit in Soviet-American relations and praised him. One particular way in which he used Eisenhower's authority rested on beginning an argument with the gist of a statement by the President, agreeing with it, and subsequently developing his argument from this shared premise.[25] This strategy placed his American listeners at a further disadvantage. To argue against Khrushchev meant arguing against venerated American heroes. To discredit Khrushchev required that Presidents Eisenhower, Washington, and Jefferson be discredited.

Khrushchev developed a third strategy to satisfy his communist audiences. For the most part, he rendered an ideological analysis of the causes for world problems. He persistently warned that West Germany had to be feared as an instigator of a new war because the West Germans secretly dreamed about revenging their defeat in World War II. He made no mention of fearing East Germany for the same reason. Obviously, socialist East Germany could harbor no thoughts for starting a new war. His analysis of Soviet-American economic relations bore a distinct ideological stamp. He argued that the lack of trade relations between the two countries was caused by Western politicians who believed that refusing to trade with the Soviet Union would weaken its defensive might. Marxist-Leninism teaches that reactionary capitalism is inherently hostile to socialism and tries to weaken it at every turn. Khrushchev superimposed this ideology on American motives to explain the quiescent state of Soviet-American economic relations. Each cause Khrushchev analyzed, he placed in this ideological context.

A variation on this strategy centered on Khrushchev's boasts about Soviet accomplishments in space, economics, and consumer goods. Only a few days before Khrushchev came to the United States, the Soviet Union sent a rocket to the moon and launched an atomic icebreaker, appropriately named *Lenin*, both of which he continually cited as examples of the great strides the Soviet Union had made in technology. However, he did not credit scientists with these accomplishments. Marxist-Leninism made them possible. In his televised farewell speech Khrushchev recounted many of the advancements the

Soviet Union had made since the Revolution. Each, he contended, sprang from the rejection of capitalism and the superiority of socialism. Thus, Khrushchev paid respects to the demands ideology imposes on politics.

One would expect that this one-sided treatment of world affairs would have offended his American audiences. Considering this possibility, Khrushchev tempered his criticism by praising certain American leaders and certain accomplishments of the working classes. Apparently, he deliberately avoided naming those specifically responsible for what he deemed hostile policies. Instead, he spoke vaguely of "some leaders in the West," and of "some nations" as the culprits. His communist audiences could easily fill in the names, while his Western audiences marvelled at his temperance. Beyond these measures, Khrushchev persistently separated President Eisenhower from reactionary policies and heaped praise on him as a "sincere" man, a "peaceful" man.

When Khrushchev departed from analysis of problems and proposed solutions, he discarded ideological arguments. Instead, he concentrated on practical solutions. His speech to the Economic Club showed him at his best. In introducing the speaker, Herbert Woodman, President of the Club, castigated Khrushchev for thinking about capitalism in nineteenth-century terms. Khrushchev dismissed these arguments: "I know you believe in the capitalist system; and it would be, in fact, a sign of disrespect on my part if I were to try to preach to you. You have . . . the capitalist system; we have the Socialist system . . . ; and let history decide which is the best." Khrushchev continually left ideological contradictions to history. He preferred to concentrate on practical solutions on the carefully chosen issues he discussed.

Khrushchev made clear distinctions between his ideological commitments and his practical proposals. Part of this distinction is apparent only through a study of his esoteric communications.[26] Let me cite only one example. Khrushchev came to the United States as Chairman of the Council of Ministers, not as First Secretary of the Communist Party. Thus, he spoke for the Soviet Union, not the Party. To Western minds this may be insignificant. To him it was not. What Khrushchev did is comparable to what a professor does when he speaks out on a political issue. The professor stresses that he speaks for himself, not the university. Thus, the university is absolved of reponsibility for his statements. Khrushchev used this device to let his communist audience know he spoke for the Soviet Union, not as an ideologue for the communist party. Through this division of political and ideological responsibilities, Khrushchev sought to satisfy both his Western and his communist audiences.[27]

Evading issues

Khrushchev's formal speeches cannot be considered apart from the tough question periods that usually followed them. If the speeches were boring and repetitive, the questioning periods were usually lively and revealed a great deal about Khrushchev as a man. The stale style of the speeches gave way to a pungent, aggressive style of parrying antagonists.

Khrushchev faced another rhetorical problem in these situations. He did not want to answer some questions, especially about Soviet intervention in Hungary in 1956 and the anti-Stalin campaign in Russia. Yet he did not want to antagonize his audiences needlessly. To avoid answering questions, Khrushchev used six distinct diversionary devices:

1. he denied outright that any problem existed and resorted to ideological principles to prove his contention.
2. he said Americans did not have the right to question him about the internal affairs of other nations.
3. he criticized the United States for engaging in the same kind of activity (censorship, in particular) thereby charging that they had little moral right to criticize him.
4. he attacked the motives of those who questioned him by asking if they were treating him properly as a guest of the United States.
5. he avoided questions by posing new questions.
6. he threatened to go home if they continued a hostile line of questions.

By far his most effective method was to threaten to return to the Soviet Union. Invariably, subsequent questions were muted.

These sessions revealed a different side of Khrushchev. Americans saw a quick-witted man who could hold his own with his adversaries. He also showed considerable imagination. When questioned about Hungary, Khrushchev invented his most vivid and repugnant simile: "The question of Hungary has stuck in some people's throat like a dead rat. He feels it is unpleasant and yet cannot spit it out."[28] Answers such as this revealed a more complicated and human man than the dry, prosaic speeches presented.

Summary

Khrushchev tip-toed, albeit heavily, the line between ideology and practical politics, between protecting his own career and seeking rapprochement with the United States. Thus, one looks to the strategies he invented that served to reconcile the various political groups with which he had to contend.

This delicate balancing act was missed by most Westerners because they were more interested in the man. Did he really mean what he said? Did he sincerely desire *detente*? Was this only another Soviet trick? These questions intrigued journalists and men on the streets. People appeared to reserve judgment on his proposals until they had judged the man.

KHRUSHCHEV'S ETHOS

During the trip Nikita Sergeyvich Khrushchev, former shepherd and coal miner, stamped his personality on the world and compelled all who heard him to think about him. What sort of man was this Nikita Sergeyvich? Country bumpkin or shrewd antagonist? Machiavellian Devil or practical man of power?

From his ascension to power in 1955 Khrushchev had astounded, confused, petrified, and amazed those who observed him. A writer for *The New Republic* described him as a "fascinating figure, compounded by such bizarre contrasts as Mayor Fiorello La Guardia, W. C. Fields, Jimmy Hoffa and—oddly enough —Winston Churchill."[29] What struck me as particularly distinctive was that he violated our image of the stereotyped dictator. Think about two other dictators of our times. Joseph Stalin appeared as the silent, ever-menacing paranoid willing to use any deceit to gain his goals. Hitler fitted more into the ancient mold—the hysterical, arm-waving demagogue bent on world rule or world destruction. Khrushchev was entirely different. A preacher of peace and understanding, he looked more like a businessman than a politician. One reporter likened him to "any prosperous, hard-working, penny-pinching farmer who has reached the chairmanship of the local school board by sheer weight of his own toilsome success with the field."[30] Furthermore, he had a sense of humor he displayed publicly and often turned on himself. His wife, Nina Petrovna, added to his image. No Mata Hari she, but rather a kind and gentle-looking matron who moved another American reporter to write: "There was the feeling that anyone who had the good sense to marry her, stay married to her, and bring her over here couldn't be all villain, no matter what he was doing during Stalin's regime."[31]

Prior to Khrushchev's visit most Americans had a picture of him similar to Shakespeare's description of a ruler in IHenry VI: "I'll play the orator as well as Nestor;/Deceive more slyly than Ulysses could;/And like a Sinon, take another Troy." American anticommunist rhetoric of the nineteen-fifties had rested on a "devil-image" of Soviet leaders.[32] Khrushchev realized this. At the Economic Club he remarked that Marshall MacDuffie, once representative of UNRRA, had told him that a trip to the United States would be useful if it achieved no more than letting the American people see that he did not have horns. This new image, perhaps, was the major achievement of Khrushchev's trip. He began to replace the image of the "communist devil" with an image of greater complexity—that of a politician proud of his country, skillful in public debate, experienced in public affairs.[33] His agile and human responses to situations conveyed to the American people a leader who broke the mold of their stereotyped dictator.

The question of his sincerity persists. I believe Khrushchev actually sought *detente* on a limited number of issues so he could achieve domestic objectives and reduce the hostility of the cold war. Furthermore, I believe he honestly wished to avoid the possibility of nuclear war which, whether mistakenly or not, he thought the United States might start.[34]

EFFECTS

Immediate responses to Khrushchev

American journalists seemed to find in Khrushchev's speeches what they were already looking for. Walter Lippmann observed that his speeches revealed a critical weakness in our society, the lack of a public philosophy.[35] David Lawrence found his vitriolic anticommunist stance reinforced.[36] A Soviet journalist saw Khrushchev's appearances before the National Press Club as a triumph and quoted an unnamed American reporter as saying: "This is fantastic! He could make anyone into a Communist."[37]

A writer for *The New Republic* admitted that we will probably never be quite the same again.[38] Gallup Polls support this estimate. They show a marked shift in public opinion from "antagonism" before the trip to "no opinion" after the trip.[39] If Khrushchev did not win converts, he appeared to neutralize some hostility.

Khrushchev's impact on the Chinese

In October Khrushchev went to China to celebrate the tenth anniversary of the revolution. He was given neither a welcoming nor a farewell address. The relations between the two powers had become stiff and strained.

To the Chinese Khrushchev's behavior had been intolerable. Nothing could excuse his tactless eulogies for Eisenhower.[40] The Chinese caught Khrushchev in the web of contradictions his rhetoric had spun. To the Chinese, either the United States is a capitalist nation or it is not. If it is, it is corrupt and imperialistic. Eisenhower, as a product of this decadent socety, cannot be trusted, and imperialists can only be encouraged by thoughts that negotiations would be fruitful.

Furthermore, Khrushchev's speeches carried other problems. Throughout his visit Khrushchev spoke of the need for *Russia* and the *United States* to solve the problems that plague the world. He seldom spoke about the *communist* world and the *capitalist* world, except in the abstract. Thus, he seemed to place national aspirations before communist fraternity. Compounding this problem, Khrushchev seemed to subordinate dogma to crass practical considerations.

The Chinese date the break in Sino-Soviet relations from this visit to the United States. An editorial in *People's Daily* on February 27, 1963, charged that Khrushchev violated the agreements reached at the Moscow Conference during his trip and by the acts that issued from commitments made at that time.[41]

Nikita Khrushchev's visit may have marked a personal triumph for him, but it also signaled the end of the Chinese-Russian alliance. To gain rapprochement with the United States he had to speak in more practical and less ideological terms. To keep Chinese friendship he had to remain true to the Chinese literal interpretation of Marxist-Leninism. These two rhetorics are mutually exclusive.

Khrushchev's impact on ideology

Khrushchev's speeches contained the seeds of ideological change. Although complete assessment of his contribution to ideological development must be reserved for another essay, I can remark on one change that carried rhetorical import.

Khrushchev used Marxism to interpret the advances made by the Russian people. He contended that technological development was caused by adherence to Marxist doctrines. Thus, Khrushchev transformed Marxist-Leninism in this respect into a rhetorical, rather than a political, force. Lenin and Stalin had used ideology as a hammer to slay enemies and transform society. Khrushchev did not "need Marxism to transform the world . . . but in order to make the actual transformation of the world intelligible."[42] In his hands ideology became a method for explaining the world and the changes that occur instead of a political tool with which to forge those changes.

Russia moves toward detente

Soviet propaganda emphasized a change in the cold war. A cartoon published in *Pravda* pictured Khrushchev knocking down a snowman captioned "the cold war." In January 1960 Khrushchev ordered demobilization of 1,300,000 men from the armed forces. That meant money could be transferred from military to domestic budgets. It may also be taken as a symbol of good faith in seeking a limited *detente*.

However, moves toward easing tensions suffered a severe blow when an American U-2 airplane was shot down over the Soviet Union in May 1960. When Eisenhower took personal blame, he destroyed any hopes for the summit conference in Paris and any further moves toward rapprochement during the remaining days of his administration. Khrushchev had placed his hopes for *detente* solely on Eisenhower's popularity in the Soviet Union and throughout the world. By accepting responsibility for the U-2 flights, Eisenhower destroyed those hopes.[43]

CONCLUSION

A politician's rhetoric must be analyzed through the lens of the various audiences who view it. Americans seemed less interested than communists, especially the Chinese, in the content of his proposals. For the most part Americans discarded his proposals, with the exception of stimulating better trade relations, as typical Soviet propaganda. They were far more interested in the man. Perhaps Khrushchev realized that to be taken seriously required that he attack the stereotyped images Americans held of the Soviet Union and him.

Throughout his trip Khrushchev pounded away at the "devil" image many had of him. He blustered, bragged, laughed, clowned, got angry, and talked seriously at various times. With each act he became more human, less Satanic. He said he came to find a new language for Soviet-American relations. The old language of anticommunist ideology prevented fruitful discussions. Khrushchev continually sought to replace it, as well as standard communist language, with a more practical language—the language of businessmen—as a means for talking about world problems. He did not succeed fully. Few changes in Soviet-American relations issued from the visit. However, Americans did begin to realize that they had to deal with a man, not a stereotype, who was just as human as they. That was a remarkable achievement for Khrushchev with his American audiences.

On the other hand, this very rhetoric that caused some changes in American perceptions sowed the seeds for ideological divisions within the communist bloc. The Chinese could not tolerate this ideological sacrilege. They took their own path to communism and denounced Khrushchev as a revisionist.

Soviet communists seemed less concerned about ideological purity. Whether this was due to their hopes for *detente* or to their fears of Khrushchev's power we shall probably never know. What we do know is that in September 1959

Khrushchev's performance marked the zenith of his career. He had carefully balanced ideological concerns with practical matters. He had proved he could talk to leaders of the United States as an equal without betraying Soviet interests. He had handled the Americans better than they had handled him.

In the distant future some historian unencumbered by the pressures of the cold war may record that Khrushchev's trip marked a major change in the hostile attitudes between the United States and the Soviet Union. He may record that the issues discussed were the first concrete proposals for rapprochement.[44] We may hope he will remember that it was Nikita Khrushchev—once an illiterate Russian peasant—who initiated the trip and the ideas.

NOTES

[1] Exchange visits by Chiefs of State have been labelled "prestige" or "personal" diplomacy. It differs greatly in form, content, and expectations from traditional diplomacy. See Harold Nicolson, *The Evolution of Diplomacy* (New York, 1962) and Louis J. Halle, "The Coming Test for Personal Diplomacy," *New York Times Magazine*, August 23, 1959, pp. 7+. For an analysis of Khrushchev's trip in his strategy of prestige diplomacy, see my unpubl. Ph.D. dissertation, "The Rhetoric of Peaceful Coexistence: A Criticism of Selected American Speeches by Nikita Khrushchev" (Ohio State University, 1965), chapter one.

[2] Nikita Sergeyvich Khrushchev. *On the Occasion of His Visit to the United States* (New York, 1959), p. 31.

[3] "Not Everybody Favors Khrushchev's Visit," *U.S. News and World Report*, XLVII (August 17, 1959), 65.

[4] "Nixon: Ike Will Not Be 'Taken In or Bluffed,'" *U.S. News and World Report*, XLVII (September 7, 1959), 67–69.

[5] Later in the trip, the State Department advised Lodge to stop arguing with Khrushchev. See *The New York Times*, September 27, 1959, Sect. 4, p. 1.

[6] Cf. Adam B. Ulam, *Expansion and Coexistence* (New York, 1968), pp. 619–629 and Louis J. Halle, *The Cold War as History* (New York, 1967), pp. 354–371. Even though they differ in emphasis, each writer assumes Khrushchev actually wanted to alter the balance of power in middle Europe. My interpretation directly contradicts both.

[7] Nikita S. Khrushchev, "Speech at Friendship Meeting of Polish People's Republic and the Soviet Union," November 10, 1958, in *For Victory in Peaceful Competition with Capitalism* (New York, 1960), pp. 727–746.

[8] "Proposals of the Soviet Government on the Berlin Question," November 27, 1958, in *ibid.*, pp. 758–771.

[9] For one account of the power struggle, see Carl A. Linden, *Khrushchev and the Soviet Leadership 1957–1964* (Baltimore, 1966), pp. 40–57.

[10] Many Westerners perceived Khrushchev's assumption of the position of Prime Minister as final evidence that he had as much power as Stalin once had. If that interpretation were true, then Khrushchev's pronouncements would carry much greater weight than if he were bound by the limitations political power places on leaders. It is generally recognized now that Khrushchev was not an absolute dictator as Stalin had been.

[11] See the Seven-Year Plan ratified by the Twenty-First Party Congress.

[12] Joel J. Schwartz and William R. Keech, "Group Influence and the Policy Process in the Soviet Union," *The American Political Science Review*, LXII (September 1968), 840–851. The authors concentrate on how Khrushchev had to adjust his programs to the power in Soviet government. The examples cited in notes 13 and 14 support this approach to the study of Khrushchev's policies.

[13] Sidney I. Ploss, *Conflict and Decision-Making in Soviet Russia: A Case Study of Agricultural Policy, 1953–1963* (Princeton, N.J., 1965), pp. 113–183.

[14] Roman Kolkowicz, *The Soviet Military and the Communist Party* (Princeton, N.J., 1967), pp. 135–148 and 192–199.

[15] The propaganda mills went into full cycle after the trip. Movies presented filmed versions of the trip. Khrushchev's speeches were published by the hundreds of thousands. A political beneficial "record" of his visit was published under the title *Face to Face with America*, ed. M. Kharlamov and O. Vadeyev (Moscow, 1960).

[16] David Floyd, *Mao Against Khrushchev* (New York, 1963), pp. 61–77.

[17] *The New York Times* printed translations made by Khrushchev's official interpreter. These texts are a record of what most of the American public heard. The American Broadcasting Company hired its own interpreter, Nicholas W. Orloff. Another translation can be found in *Daily Report Supplement*, published by the Foreign Broadcast Information Service. These texts, slightly edited, are the live replay of speeches as broadcast by Tass or other Soviet agencies. The Soviet Union published official English versions in two books: *Khrushchev in America* (New York, 1960) and *World Without Arms: World Without War Book II* (Moscow, 1959). These translations are also slightly edited. Andrei Shevchenko and G. T. Shuisky assisted Chairman Khrushchev in preparing his major addresses. Both are identified by N. H. Mager and Jacques Katel in *Conquest Without War* (New York, 1961), p. v, as speechwriters for Khrushchev. According to a writer for *Time*, LXXV (April 25, 1960), 28, the two men kept notebooks filled with proverbs and historical material to aid in preparing stock speeches.

[18] Premier Khrushchev's Television Speech, *The New York Times*, September 28, 1959, p. 18.

[19] Nikita S. Khrushchev, "On Peaceful Co-existence," *Foreign Affairs*, XXXVIII (October 1959), 1–18. Cf. George F. Kennan, "Peaceful Coexistence: A Western View," *Foreign Affairs*, XXXVIII (January 1960), 171–190.

[20] Khrushchev's proposal for general and complete disarmament within four years caused most to dismiss his proposals as preposterous. From this point on, reporters paid more attention to his personality than to his ideas.

[21] Joint Soviet-American Communiqué, September 27, 1959, printed in *Department of State Bulletin*, XLI (October 12, 1959), 499–500. Emphasis added.

[22] Premier Khrushchev's speech to the United Nations, *The New York Times*, September 19, 1959, p. 8.

[23] Richard B. Stebbins, *The United States in World Affairs 1959* (New York, 1960), p. 165.

[24] Premier Khrushchev's speech to the Economic Club, *The New York Times*, September 18, 1959, p. 20.

[25] Khrushchev introduced his disarmament proposal by citing a statement by Eisenhower on the need for disarmament and developed his argument from this. At the National Press Club Khrushchev produced a variation on this strategy when he agreed with Eisenhower on the need to protect the freedom of West Berlin. He then argued that Western occupation troops should be removed from West Berlin so that it could become a "free city."

[26] Myron Rush developed the theory of esoteric communication. See his chapter, "The Role of Esoteric Communication in Soviet Politics," in *The Rise of Khrushchev* (Washington, D.C., 1958); pp. 88–94. One can find elaborations in any Kremlinological study of the Soviet politics, especially Ploss, Robert Conquest, and Michel Tatu.

[27] The divisions worked only temporarily. Soon, his practical solutions had to be justified ideologically and opened him to the charge of revisionism by the Chinese.

[28] Premier Khrushchev's speech before the National Press Club, *The New York Times*, September 17, 1959, p. 19.

[29] T. R. B., "Following Mr. K.," *The Faces of Five Decades*, ed. Robert B. Luce (New York, 1964), p. 404.

[30] Joseph Alsop, *Washington Post*, September 18, 1959, p. A13.

[31] *The New York Times*, September 28, 1959, p. 16.

[32] Michael Parenti, *The Anti-Communist Impulse* (New York, 1969), pp. 30–54. In sworn testimony before the Committee on the Judiciary of the U.S. Senate Dr. Stefan

T. Possony compared Khrushchev to Hitler. He remarked that one major difference between the two was that Hitler was "perhaps more honest" than Khrushchev. See Senate Document No. 46, 87th Cong., 1st Sess., "Analysis of the Khrushchev Speech of January 6, 1961" (Washington, 1961), p. 3.

[33] Harrison Salisbury, *The New York Times*, September 20, 1959, p. E5.

[34] The closest the world came to nuclear war was during the Cuban missile crisis. Khrushchev put missiles in Cuba. President Kennedy said they had to be removed. By all accounts it was a nuclear confrontation. The Soviets never went as far down the nuclear road as Americans even though the United States practically surrounded Russia with missiles during the nineteen-fifties.

[35] Walter Lippmann, *Washington Post*, September 17, 1959, p. A25.

[36] David Lawrence, *Philadelphia Evening Bulletin*, September 21, 1959, p. 15.

[37] *Face to Face with America*, p. 75.

[38] T. R. B., p. 405.

[39] Hazel Gaudet Erskine (ed.), "The Cold War: Report from the Polls," *Public Opinion Quarterly*, XXV (Summer 1961), 304.

[40] Donald S. Zagoria, *The Sino-Soviet Conflict 1956–1961* (Princeton, N.J., 1961), pp. 243–244. Cf. Klaus Mehnert, *Peking and Moscow*, trans. Leila Vennewitz (New York, 1963), pp. 395–398.

[41] "Whence the Differences?—A Reply to Comrade Thorez and other Comrades," *People's Daily*, February 27, 1963, trans. and published in Floyd, pp. 374–385.

[42] Hans J. Morgenthau, "Khrushchev's New Cold War Strategy: Prestige Diplomacy." *Commentary*, XXVIII (November 1959), 382.

[43] Western "conventional wisdom" of the cold war places the responsibility for wrecking the Paris Summit Conference of May 1960 on Khrushchev's shoulders. Without concrete evidence they project that Khrushchev intended to wreck it all along and only used the U-2 incident to achieve his purpose. That interpretation does a disservice not only to Americans' intelligence but also to Khrushchev's political goals.

Khrushchev trusted Eisenhower to help ease cold-war tensions during the 1959 trip. Khrushchev could not say publicly that he trusted capitalists or he would have seriously impaired his power base. But he could praise a war-hero President whose wartime acts were still admired in the Soviet Union. Then the U-2 incident occurred. In his public statements Khrushchev had to condemn the United States for the flight, but he emphasized in two different statements that he did not believe Eisenhower knew anything about them. Clearly, Khrushchev was offering Eisenhower a way out of a political crisis. When Eisenhower took full personal responsibility for them, Khrushchev had no choice than to refuse to meet with him in Paris. For a variation on my interpretation, see Michel Tatu, *Power in the Kremlin from Khrushchev to Kosygin*, trans. Helen Katel (New York, 1969), pp. 53–100. See in particular Khrushchev's closing speech to the Supreme Soviet session on May 7, 1960 in *Pravda*, May 9, 1960.

[44] On June 1963 President John F. Kennedy sought to do what Khrushchev tried in 1959. At The American University Kennedy called for new attitudes toward Russians and the cold war. The arguments Kennedy used in his speech are remarkably similar to those Khrushchev used in 1959. Little wonder Khrushchev told Harriman that he thought it was the best speech by an American president since those by Roosevelt.

CHARISMATIC AUTHORITY AND
THE LEADERSHIP OF FIDEL CASTRO

Richard R. Fagen

RICHARD R. FAGEN *received his B.A. in English literature at Yale University, and his Ph.D. in political science at Stanford University. He is currently professor of political science at Stanford University and specializes in Latin American politics. He has held fellowships from the Ford Foundation, the National Science Foundation, and the Social Science Research Council; and he is currently a fellow at the Center for Advanced Study in the Behavioral Sciences. Professor Fagen is author of* Politics and Communication *and* The Transformation of Political Culture in Cuba, *and coauthor of* Enemies in Politics *and* Cubans in Exile: Disaffection and the Revolution.

No part of Max Weber's sociology has been as thoroughly over-worked in discourse about politics as has his concept of charisma. The appellation "charismatic" has been applied to leaders as different as Stalin, Nkrumah, Hitler, and Gandhi, and there has been a general tendency to equate the charismatic in politics with the demagogic, the irrational, the emotional, and the "popular."

This luxuriance of meanings and attention is not, as one commentator has already pointed out, simply a result of intellectual faddism.[1] Rather, it represents in part a very genuine groping about for a conceptual framework which might be of service in the analysis of twentieth-century politics. However, if the concept of charisma is to serve in scientific political inquiry, it cannot refer in blanket fashion to leadership styles as disparate as those mentioned above. There is a need for explication and parsimony. This paper attempts to provide a first step toward that explication and to indicate, by example, how the concept might be used in empirical inquiry.

WEBER'S FORMULATION OF CHARISMATIC AUTHORITY

As conceptualized by Weber, charisma (the gift of grace) referred to "a certain quality of an individual personality by virtue of which he is set apart from ordinary men and treated as endowed with supernatural, superhuman, or at least specifically exceptional powers or qualities."[2] The concept was, of course, taken from the idiom of early Christianity, and in Weber's sociology charismatic authority was one of the three pure types of legitimate authority—the other two being rational-legal and traditional.[3]

There are at least five elements of Weber's formulation of charismatic authority which must be taken into account in any political research using the concept. These elements, stated in propositional form, follow:

Reprinted from *Western Political Quarterly*, 18, No. 2 (June 1965), 275–284 with permission of the University of Utah, copyright holder.

214

1. The charismatic leader is always the creation of his followers. That is, charismatic authority (in common with all other types of legitimate authority) is rooted in the belief system of the followers rather than in some transcendental characteristics of the leader.[4] When no one is disposed or able to believe in the omnipotence, omniscience, and moral perfection of the leader, he cannot be said to exercise charismatic authority no matter how strong, wise, or moral he perceives himself to be.

2. An "individual personality" or leader capable of generating a charismatic authority relationship in one context may fail completely to generate that relationship in some other context. There are no universal charismatics. This is clearly a corollary of the first proposition and suggests that the set of followers is always bounded by at least two factors. There are some who are never reached (physically) by the messages of the leader and thus remain at best what we shall call *potential followers*. And there are others who, although reached, do not for a variety of reasons respond in the prescribed manner. These individuals we shall call the *non-followers*.

3. The leader does not regard himself either as chosen by or as solely dependent on his followers, but rather as "elected" from above to fulfill a mission.[5] He perceives his followers as having obligations and duties toward him and he perceives himself as deriving his morality and legitimation from his special relationship with some more abstract force such as God or history. Furthermore, those who resist or ignore him—the non-followers—are regarded as "delinquent in duty."[6]

4. The behavior of the charismatic leader in power is anti-bureaucratic— "specifically outside the realm of everyday routine and the profane sphere."[7] Daily affairs, whether economic, political or administrative, are treated with disdain by the leader. He surrounds himself with disciples chosen for their devotion rather than a staff selected by more formal means.

5. Charismatic authority is unstable, tending to be transformed (routinized) through time.[8] This "natural entropy of the hero's charisma"[9] occurs in part because his image of infallibility cannot be maintained in the face of inevitable failures, and in part because the demands of ruling cannot be met through time without more rationalized involvement in the mundane affairs of state.[10]

These five propositions serve to direct us toward a set of empirical questions which should prove useful when confronted with a suspected instance of charismatic authority in the real world. The first proposition focuses our attention on the attitudes and perceptions of the followers as crucial determinants of the existence or non-existence of the charismatic relationship. The second proposition suggests that deeper understanding of the relationship will result if we can map these perceptions and attitudes against the distribution of social and personality characteristics in the society. The third directs us to an examination of the leader's perceived relationship both to his mission and to his followers. The fourth and fifth propositions are predictive; the former states that the leader in power will behave in certain ways, and the latter states that the charismatic relationship will inevitably be transformed.

This is clearly a mixed bag of propositions, and any thorough investigation of one or more cases would of necessity have to concentrate on some elements to the partial or complete exclusion of others.[11] Nevertheless in the following examination of the Cuban case, whatever data were at hand—no matter how unsatisfactory—are presented in order to offer at least a brief exploration and discussion of each proposition. This exploratory posture is assumed because it best serves the twin purposes of suggesting investigatory strategies appropriate to the propositions and of organizing what little we actually know about the leadership of Fidel Castro.

THE CUBAN CASE

1. The charismatic leader is the creation of his followers

There is no lack of reports which mention that in the early stages of the Cuban Revolution Castro was regarded by large segments of the population as the heaven-sent savior of the nation.[12] The religious overtones of this relationship have been emphasized by many commentators, and one prominent Presbyterian minister in Cuba published an article in which he wrote: "It is my conviction which I state now with full responsibility for what I am saying, of His reign among men."[13]
that Fidel Castro is an instrument in the hands of God for the establishment

Only one study, however, is actually based on the type of systematic data needed for a more thorough analysis of the charismatic elements in the relationship of Cubans to Castro during the first few years of the Revolution. This is a sample survey conducted by Lloyd Free in Cuba in April and May of 1960.[14] Under the direction of Free, a Cuban research organization interviewed a cross section of 500 residents of Havana and another cross section of 500 residents of other urban and semi-urban centers. The 40 per cent of the Cuban population living in rural areas was not represented in Free's survey.

Free classified 86 per cent of his respondents as supporters of the regime. Of all supporters, one-half (or 43 per cent of all respondents) were sub-classified as *fervent* supporters. In "more-or-less typical quotations from the interviews" Free suggests the articulated content of fervent support: " 'Fidel has the same ideas as Jesus Christ, our protector and guide.' 'I would kiss the beard of Fidel Castro.' '[My greatest fear is:] That some mean person might kill Fidel. If this happens, I think I would die.' "[15]

Now these are clearly responses with charismatic overtones. But it would be an unwarranted inference simply to assume that *all* of the fervent supporters are also charismatic followers. Rather, in the absence of an analysis specifically designed to identify the sub-set of charismatics we can only speculate on how closely it might coincide with the set of all fervent supporters. In any event, two points stand out: First, in the early stages of the revolution Castro was perceived as a charismatic leader by some "sizable" fraction of the Cuban population. Second, in the absence of survey research designed especially for the purpose, it is impossible to determine with exactitude just how sizable this fraction was, or how it might have changed in size and composition through time.[16]

2. The distribution of charismatic followers illuminates important characteristics of the relationship

One striking aspect of the Cuban Revolution is the thoroughness and frequency with which the voice and visage of Fidel Castro have blanketed the island. Through the extensive television system and the mass rallies—which have on occasion drawn as many as one million of Cuba's seven million inhabitants into the plaza of Havana—the messages of the maximum leader have been brought to almost 100 per cent of the population.[17] In our terminology this suggests that there is only an insignificant number of *potential followers* (persons not reached by the leader's messages) in Cuba. We can therefore direct our entire attention to the *non-followers*, those who have been reached but do not respond in a charismatic manner.

Once again we must return to Free's data as the best available for an analysis of the distribution of charismatic followers in Cuba. As before, we cannot identify the sub-set of charismatics from the set of all fervent supporters, but the patterning of fervent support by education, social class, and place of residence is revealing. The tendency for fervent support to be associated with low education, low social class, and semi-urban residence is clear.[18] If rural respondents had been included in the sample, we would expect the associations to emerge even more strongly. Finally, Free found that the distribution of

TABLE 1   Support for Castro in 1959 by Education, Social Class, and Place of Residence* (in percentages)

(N = 1,000)	Fervent Supporters (43 percent)	Moderate Supporters and Nonsupporters (57 percent)
Education:		
Elementary or no schooling	49	51
Secondary schooling	35	65
University training	29	71
Social Class:		
Lowest socioeconomic class	48	52
Lower-middle class	39	61
Upper-middle and upper class	34	66
Place of Residence:		
Outside of Havana	49	51
In Havana	34	66

* Adapted from Lloyd A. Free, *Attitudes of the Cuban People Toward the Castro Regime* (Princeton: Institute for International Social Research, 1960), p. 7.

fervent supporters was sharply skewed toward the lower end of the age continuum—43 per cent of all fervent supporters were between 20 and 29 years of age.[19]

Confirmation of this pattern of support for Castro also emerges from data on a systematic sample of Cuban refugees in Miami—a group which is presently unanimous in its expressed hatred of Fidel.[20] When asked how they *originally* had felt about Castro when he came to power in 1959, 42 out of 191 refugees replied that they thought "he was the savior of Cuba." Since the refugee community represents a highly skewed sample of Cubans, a sample comprised substantially of members of the middle and upper classes, Table 2 is of special interest. Thus, even in this refugee sample the association of strong support with lower education, semi-urban and rural residence, and lower age is found.

But should we expect these particular socio-demographic patterns of fervent support (and the less frequently encountered—though similar—patterns of charismatic support) to be found in all cases of charismatic leadership? That is, whenever a charismatic political relationship is identified will the followers tend to come from among the rural, the younger, the less educated, and the lower classes? There is no simple answer to this question, but at least three points should be noted:

First, as emphasized previously, the communication system of Cuba has brought all members of the society into contact with Fidel, giving them at least the *opportunity* to become charismatic followers. In less developed and less homogeneous societies, it would be precisely the lower classes, the rural, and the poorly educated who would tend to be cut off from the national channels and therefore from the messages through which the leader might establish his claim to legitimacy. Second, both the ideological focus and the actual accomplishments of the Cuban Revolution have come to center on the rural and less privileged sectors of the society.[21] It is natural to assume that those who perceive themselves as the prime beneficiaries of Castro's leadership should also tend to relate most frequently to him in a charismatic manner. However, just as all nations do not have Cuba's well-developed communication system, so all charismatic political movements do not necessarily benefit the rural, the poorly educated, and the lower classes. Finally, the social groupings most likely to relate charismatically to Castro may well contain a disproportionate number of persons who as *individuals* are predisposed to make a charismatic response. Davies, for instance, hypothesizes four characteristics of the "charismatic aspect of personality structure,"[22] and Doob has suggested that the less educated and less westernized members of a society perceive and behave toward authority figures quite differently than do their more educated and westernized countrymen.[23] It is perhaps at this level of "personality in social structure" that the Cuban experience will prove to be most similar to other instances of political charisma.

3. The leader regards himself as elected from above to fulfill a mission

Only a close analysis of Castro's published and unpublished thought could supply the richness of detail which a full investigation of his self-image would

TABLE 2 Refugee Support for Castro in 1959 by Education,
Place of Residence, and Age* (in percentages)

(N = 191)	"Castro was Savior of Cuba" (N = 42)	All other responses (N = 149)
Education:		
High school or less	25	75
At least some college	12	88
Place of Residence:		
Outside of Havana	27	73
Havana	19	81
Age:		
40 or younger	26	74
41 or older	18	82

* All respondents currently in exile in Miami.

require. In the absence of such an analysis, we can only note a few recurring and interrelated themes.

First, Castro perceives the Revolution as part of a greater historical movement against tyranny and oppression. Castro developed this theme long before he became a professed Marxist-Leninist. More recently, of course, capitalism and imperialism have replaced (domestic) tyranny and oppression as the prime obstacles to a revolutionary cleansing of the world's political landscape. Second, the Cuban leadership and Castro in particular are seen as blessed and protected by the larger historical movement of which the Revolution is a part. Castro's famous speech ending, "condemn me, it doesn't matter. History will absolve me," is a classic, early articulation of this idea.[24] Finally, because the leader is seen as acting in concert with larger historical forces not always visible to more ordinary men, he alone retains the right to determine "correct" behavior in the service of the Revolution.

It is important to realize that these overtones of intellectual Marxism and political authoritarianism preceded by many months the introduction of Marxist economic determinism and Soviet block alliances into the vocabulary and practice of Cuban politics. Castro's growing impatience during 1959 with his political opposition was only one early manifestation of this particular self-perception. More recently, as is suggested by his attack on Aníbal Escalante and the "old-line" Havana Communists, he has exhibited much the same determination to maintain his position as chief interpreter of the correct meaning and interrelatedness of events.[25] However, now it is (some) Communists in addition to (all) anti-Communists who are being rudely schooled in what it means to be a follower in Castro's Cuba.[26]

4. The behavior of the leader in power is anti-bureaucratic

Once again we find striking agreement among the various interpreters of the Revolution that Castro is (or at least was) highly disdainful of and uninterested in the routine processes of public administration. Friends and foes of the Revolution differ on whether this disinterest is "good" or "bad," "creative" or "uncreative," but few deny its existence.

This characteristic of Castro is thrown into ironic relief by the immensity and pervasiveness of the bureaucratic structures which have been created to direct the reorganization of Cuban society. For instance, the National Institute of Agrarian Reform (INRA), once headed by Castro and often called the heart of the Revolution, directly or indirectly controls 80 per cent of the farm land on the island.[27] But Castro's behavior, both while chairman of INRA and after, hardly fits Weber's model of rational-legal leadership. On the contrary, his leadership was highly personalized and un-hierarchical, and his choice of second-level administrators was based primarily on ascription (is he a trusted follower from the Sierra?) rather than achievement criteria.

Nowhere is the personalized and un-hierarchical nature of Castro's leadership better drawn than in an episode reported by Jean-Paul Sartre. In a chapter called "A Day in the Country with Fidel," Sartre tells how on a stopover at a rural tourist center Castro became upset because his soft drink was warm.[28] According to Sartre, Castro's ire was not aroused by his personal inconvenience but rather by his generalized irritation with a bureaucratic structure which was created to serve "the people" but which frequently succeeded only in frustrating them. After "rummaging passionately around in a refrigerator that was out of order . . ." and being unable to fix it himself, "He closed with this growled sentence: 'Tell your people in charge that if they don't take care of their problems, they will have problems with me.' " And this, Sartre maintains, was typical of the manner in which the "maximum leader" invested his energies in the administration of Cuba.

5. Charismatic authority is unstable, tending to be routinized through time

Now we come to a set of questions which we have in part glossed over by pretending that the legitimacy of Castro's rule has been relatively stable since 1959. This is not the case, for there have been changes along at least two dimensions. First, there has been some shrinkage of the set of followers, both the charismatic and the non-charismatic. Most simply, Castro's rule is not now as legitimate for as many Cubans as it once was. However, we lack the data needed to document and quantity the extent and distribution of this partial disintegration of legitimacy.

Second—and this bears most directly on Weber's concerns—there has been at least a partial shift as predicted from authority relationships based on charisma to relationships based on rules, law, and a nascent "revolutionary tradition." This shift cannot be adequately described in brief compass, but central to the partial routinization of charisma in Cuba has been a movement away from Castro as the prime popular symbol of the Revolution and a concomitant movement toward a heterogeneity of symbols which includes other leaders, a whole spectrum of martyrs, revolutionary organizations, and achievements. This movement away from Castro as the organizing symbol of the Revolution incarnate is illustrated in Table 3, which compares the frequency with which

TABLE 3   Pictures of Castro in 22 Available Issues of INRA

First 11 Issues	No. of Pictures	Second 11 Issues	No. of Pictures
Vol. I (1960)		Vol. II (1961)	
#1	11	#2	5
2	6	3	1
3	4	4	2
5	8	5	4
6	5	6	8
7	6	7	1
8	7	8	5
9	18	9	4
10	9	10	0
11	6	11	1
Vol. II (1961)			
#1	12	12	0
	Total = 92		Total = 31
	Mean* = 8.36		Mean* = 2.82

* For difference between the means, $t = 3.85$, d.f. $= 20$, $p = .001$.

Castro's picture appeared in two successive sets of *INRA*, the official monthly magazine of the National Institute of Agrarian Reform.[29] Although these data do not constitute a test of Weber's hypothesis, they do suggest that his statement that "in its pure form charismatic authority may be said to exist only in the process of originating. It cannot remain stable, but becomes either traditionalized or rationalized, or a combination of both"[30] may be susceptible to more rigorous investigation than it has hitherto received.

Certainly our understanding of politics and political change in the emerging nations of the world would be much enhanced by systematic research designed to explore the validity of this and other segments of Weber's model of charismatic authority. This paper has attempted to explicate that model in a way which might prove useful for research. A brief look at the leadership of Fidel Castro leads to cautious optimism regarding the usefulness of Weber's ideas for the investigation of charismatic politics. But much work is still needed before we can claim with any confidence to understand the processes by which politicians like Castro bind to themselves and their causes the men and women who as charismatic followers constitute the primary resource of such regimes.

NOTES

[1] Carl J. Friedrich, "Political Leadership and the Problem of the Charismatic Power," *Journal of Politics*, 23 (1961), 3–24.

[2] Max Weber, *The Theory of Social and Economic Organization*, trans. A. M. Henderson and Talcott Parsons (Glencoe, Ill., 1947), p. 358.

[3] Weber's three-part typology of legitimate authority has been discussed so frequently

that there seems to be no need to summarize it here. For a particularly compact and cogent explication of the typology see Peter M. Blau and W. Richard Scott, *Formal Organizations, A Compartive Approach* (San Francisco, 1962), pp. 30–36. The most recent critique of Weber's typology is Peter M. Blau, "Critical Remarks on Weber's Theory of Authority," APSR, 57 (1963), 305–16. Blau's essay contains a useful listing of earlier critical appraisals of the typology.

4 "It is recognition on the part of those subject to authority which is decisive for the validity of charisma." Weber, *op. cit.*, p. 359; see also p. 382. This aspect of the charismatic relationship was stressed in an important article by James C. Davies, "Charisma in the 1952 Campagin," APSR, 48 (1954), 1083–1102. Using data from the Survey Research Center of the University of Michigan, Davies identified and analyzed 32 respondents (out of 1,799), who perceived Eisenhower as a charismatic leader. Davies' insights and approach do not seem to have been followed up by scholars interested in the rapidly changing political environments where the concept would be of more research value.

5 Weber, *op. cit.*, pp. 359–61.

6 *Ibid.*, p. 360.

7 *Ibid.*, p. 361.

8 See H. H. Gerth and C. Wright Mills (eds. and trans.), *From Max Weber: Essays in Sociology* (New York, 1958), pp. 248–50.

9 The phrase is from Immanuel Wallerstein, "Evolving Patterns of African Society," in Immanuel Wallerstein et al., *The Political Economy of Contemporary Africa* (Washington, D.C., 1959), p. 6.

10 Notice that our five propositions say nothing about the social and political conditions conducive to the establishment of charismatic authority. This reflects a gap in Weber's thought structure which has been succinctly pointed out by Blau: "In short, Weber's theory encompasses only the historical processes that lead from charismatic movements to increasing rationalization and does not include an analysis of the historical conditions and social processes that give rise to charismatic eruptions in the social structure. He has no theory of revolution." Blau, *op. cit.*, p. 309. Davies, *op. cit.*, discusses the genesis of the "charismatic phenomenon," but only in the context of politics in the large modern state.

11 Except for the first proposition which cannot be ignored because it is at the core of the definition under which we are operating.

12 Among the book-length studies in English which stress the charismatic elements of Castro's relationship with his followers I would mention the following ten: Teresa Casuso, *Cuba and Castro* (New York, 1961); Jules Dubois, *Fidel Castro* (Indianapolis, 1959); Leo Huberman and Paul M. Sweezy, *Cuba, Anatomy of a Revolution* (New York, 1960); Herbert L. Matthews, *The Cuban Story* (New York, 1961); Warren Miller, *90 Miles from Home* (New York, 1961); C. Wright Mills, *Listen Yankee* (New York, 1960); R. Hart Phillips, *Cuba, Island of Paradox* (New York, 1959); Nicolas Rivero, *Castro's Cuba, An American Dilemma* (Washington, D.C., 1962); Jean-Paul Sartre, *Sartre on Cuba* (New York, 1961); William Appleman Williams, *The United States, Cuba, and Castro* (New York, 1962). These books, which otherwise represent a wide range of interpretations of the Revolution, are in consensus on the charismatic basis of the leader-follower relationship—at least in the first year or two of Castro's rule. For two brief scholarly analyses which make the same point see Russell H. Fitzgibbon, "The Revolution Next Door: Cuba," *Annals*, 334 (1961), 113–122, and George I. Blanksten, "Fidel Castro and Latin America," in Morton A. Kaplan (ed.), *The Revolution in World Politics* (New York, 1962). The two most scholarly sources on the Revolution and its antecedents are Wyatt MacGaffey and Clifford R. Barnett, *Cuba, Its People, Its Society, Its Culture* (New Haven, 1962), and Dudley Seers (ed.), *Cuba, The Economic and Social Revolution* (Chapel-Hill, N.C., 1964). A critical and well-documented treatment of many aspects of the Revolution can be found in International Commission of Jurists, *Cuba and the Rule of Law* (Geneva, 1962).

13 Rafael Cepeda, "Fidel Castro y el Reino de Dios," *Bohemia* (July 17, 1960), p.

110 (my translation). An American observer noted: "In many Cuban homes a picture of Fidel has an honored place; in some of them it is a photograph of a bearded youth who seems to be wearing a kind of halo; the resemblance to potraits of Christ is notable." Irving P. Pflaum, "By Voice and Violence," Part I, *American Universities Field Staff Reports*, Series V, No. 3 (August 1960), p. 16. See also MacGaffey and Barnett, *op. cit.*, pp. 284–85.

[14] Loyd A. Free, *Attitudes of the Cuban People Toward the Castro Regime* (Princeton; N.J., 1960).

[15] *Ibid.*, p. 6. Free makes the point that such expressions of devotion were not dictated by the political exigencies of the open-ended interview situation. If a respondent simply wanted to give a "safe" answer, it would have been quite sufficient simply to express admiration for Castro and the regime.

[16] Of course the problems of conducting survey research in areas undergoing rapid political and social change are immense. Free mentions that the Cuban organization which originally promised to undertake the field work backed out at the last moment when informed by a government leader that it would be "suicidal." The organization which finally undertook the research did so only because it felt its days in Cuba were already numbered. *Ibid.*, p. i.

[17] I have developed and documented this theme of the modernity and pervasiveness of the Cuban communication system in two other papers. See Richard R. Fagen, "Calculation and Emotion in Foreign Policy: The Cuban Case," *Journal of Conflict Resolution*, 6 (1962), 214–21, and "Television and the Cuban Revolution" (Stanford: Dept. of Political Science, 1960), mimeo. For a useful evaluation of Castro's television talents see Tad Szulc, "Cuban Television's One-Man Show," in CBS (ed.), *The Eighth Art* (New York, 1962), 197–206.

[18] Our inabiltiy to isolate the charismatics from the fervent supporters is not too crucial here for it seems safe to assume that, if anything, the charismatics would exhibit these tendencies to a greater degree than the fervent supporters do.

[19] Free, *op. cit.*, p. 8.

[20] This derives from an unpublished study by the author and Professor Richard Brody of Stanford University. As part of the study, a self-administered questionnaire was given to a pre-selected sample of male Cuban heads of household living in Miami (in March 1963). The data in Table 2 are taken from the completed questionnaires. Complete demographic data on the refugees are reported in Richard R. Fagen and Richard C. Brody, "Cubans in Exile: A Demographic Analysis," *Social Problems*, 11 (1964), 389–401.

[21] By actual accomplishments of the Cuban Revolution we refer to such social gains as the educational, health and welfare, and housing facilities which have been built since 1959. For examples of the manner in which the Revoluntary Government uses the themes of egalitarianism and social welfare, see Richard R. Fagen, *Cuba: The Political Content of Adult Education* (Stanford, 1964).

[22] Davies, *op. cit.*

[23] Leonard W. Doob, *Becoming More Civilized: A Psychological Exploration* (New Haven, 1960).

[24] This speech was delivered by Castro at his trial for leading an attack on the Moncada Army Barracks in 1953. It is available in English under the title, *History Will Absolve Me* (New York, 1961). The attack and the trial are well treated in Dubois, *op. cit.* The theme of historical blessedness and protection received popular reinforcement from the circumstances surrounding Castro's return to Cuba from Mexico in 1956 with 82 men and the avowed purpose of overthrowing Batista. Only Castro and 11 others escaped to the Sierra Maestra where they launched the guerrilla action which culminated in the downfall of Batista two years later. All the elements of high drama and miraculous escape were attached to the story of the guerrilla band during these two years. At one time, Castro was reported dead, and subsequently a price of $100,000 was set on his head.

[25] The crucial document here is Castro's television speech of March 26, 1962. This

is available in English under the title *Fidel Castro Denounces Bureaucracy and Sectarianism* (New York, 1962). See also the discussion in Theodore Draper, *Castro's Revolution* (New York, 1962), Appendix Three.

[26] I am simplifying a very complex and poorly understood relationship (between Castro and the old-line Communists) for purposes of emphasis. However, I think that the essential point remains valid; i.e., Castro has fought very hard to maintain his position as the prime interpreter of the larger historical importance and meaning of events in Cuba, and thus he sees himself as a leader who is not obligated to accept the interpretations of others with regard to what his or their political roles should be.

[27] International Commission of Jurists, *op. cit.*, p. 61.

[28] Sartre, *op. cit.*, see pp. 122–3.

[29] *INRA* is a large-format popular magazine of 108 pages. It contains both pictures and text much in the manner of *LIFE*. Although *INRA* concentrates rather heavily in the areas of current events and recent history, it does publish essays, reviews, fiction, and poetry. The original intent was to compare Volume I (1960) with Volume II (1961), but two issues of Volume I could not be located so the 22 remaining issues were split into two equal sets of 11 each.

[30] Weber, *op. cit.*, p. 364.

PARTY CHARISMA:
POLITICAL PRACTICES AND PRINCIPLES
Irving L. Horowitz

IRVING LOUIS HOROWITZ *is professor of sociology at Rutgers University and chairman of its Livingston College Division. He is also editor-in-chief of* Transaction Magazine, *and the author of* Three Worlds of Development: The Theory and Practice of International Stratification. *Long active in developing a social science of Latin American affairs, he has authored and edited* Revolution in Brazil, Latin American Radicalism, *and* Cuban Communism. *He is editor of* The New Sociology: Essays in Social Science and Social Theory in Honor of C. Wright Mills *and* Power, Politics, and People: The Collected Essays of C. Wright Mills.

It is a democratic dogma that the two-party system, with a legally sanctioned change-over of political power, is not simply functional in certain Western cultures, but organic and universal to any definition of democracy. True enough, this is more of a populist than a professional view; yet academic sanction is not lacking. Perhaps the most direct expression of this position was made by Maurice Duverger, when he wrote that "the two party system seems to correspond to the nature of things, that is to say that political choice usually takes the form of a choice between two alternatives."[1] This proposition contains two distinct and not necessarily connected premises. First, that the two-party system is "natural" because contradictory interests tend to polarize. Second, that political choice entails a choice between alternative party organizations.

Since *Political Parties* was written, a great deal has taken place which would indicate that, while politics does indeed involve choice, and while the "myth" of a centrist focus in politics is just that, this offers little warrant for the necessity of a two-party system. In fact, political gamesmanship, and even democracy, is just as adaptable to a single-party apparatus representative of the major interest groups and factional elements as it is to different parties.[2] There is increasingly pointed evidence that even in such a classic two-party nation as the United States there is probably more difference between factions within each party than between Democrats and Republicans as such.[3] Indeed, astute commentators have taken to speaking of the American "four-party" system—with liberal and conservative groupings within each political party.[4]

The number of parties does not necessarily determine the presence or the absence of democracy—the word is being used here simply to denote the extent and impact of public opinion on policy decisions. This asymmetry between democracy and the party system is essential to any discussion of political behavior in Third World nations; in such "one-party democracies" as Mexico (*Partido Revolucionario Institucional*) and India (Congress Party), no less than in such "two-party dictatorships" as Morocco, the Union of South Africa,

Reprinted with permission of Irving L. Horowitz from his *Three Worlds of Development.* Oxford University Press, 1966, pp. 225–246.

and Paraguay.[5] Thus, to examine seriously political principles and practices in the Third World requires a radical shedding of parliamentary preconceptions in the study of democratic and totalitarian processes alike.

Max Weber went far toward anticipating the instability of personal rule, or pure charisma. Because of the caprice of "god-like" rulers, bureaucratic institutions, which represent the routinization of political life, become necessary. While Weber did allow for the charisma of office, he did not apply this concept to political systems, in the present context of bureaucratic regulation and rationalization. For him, there was an ultimate choice between "the sovereignty of the charismatic man" and the "superordination of the institution." While Weber notes that the "conflict between discipline and individual charisma has been full of vicissitudes," the polarities between discipline and individual charisma remain hard and unyielding. Discipline, "like its most rational offspring bureaucracy, is impersonal," while charisma, which often reveals itself in military or semi-military situations, "uses emotional means of all sorts to influence followers through 'inspiration' and, even more, to train them in 'emphatic understanding' of the leader's will."[6] What has become apparent, but thus far remains relatively inexplicit in the literature of political sociology, is how discipline and charisma, rational authority and personal appeal, are fused in the political party which is at the same time the natonal party. This party, which embodies both the charismatic leadership responsible for making the national *revolution of independence* and the bureaucratic directors responsible for guaranteeing the follow-up national *revolution of development*, in effect transforms the Weberian duality into a search for a "higher unity"—into what is herein called party charisma.

There is scarcely a Third World nation which is not caught up in a political bind. This is becoming clear only now, after liberation. On one side, nearly every nation in the Third World exhibits a powerful leader principle, a *Führerprinzip*, in which power is seen to reside first and foremost in the leader, since he contains within his person the sum and substance of the aspirations and sentiments of the whole people. There is thus a powerful tendency in the direction of charismatic authority—particularly since the leader is identified in the minds of the people with liberation from colonialism. But at the same time the people themselves have become greatly interested in participating in the existent apparatus. Socialist rhetoric has only heightened the mass appeal of such participation.

In the light of the tensions produced by these contrary trends, unique political forms have evolved in the emergent states. This new form, however "transitional" it may turn out to be, can be summed up by the phrase *party charisma*. Yet, the number of new states reflecting the crystallization of party charisma would indicate that it is anything but a passing fancy. The single party assumes the "god-like" features of leadership, which in the medieval world belonged to a series of Popes, in the seventeenth and eighteenth centuries belonged to a series of monarchs—some enlightened, but all absolute—and which, in the present century, have been raised to a new level by such secular rulers as Hitler, Stalin, and, on a lesser level, Mussolini and Perón. Nonetheless, in the past charisma was most often lodged in living rulers rather than in the institution per se. Although, as Weber showed, the Catholic Church attempted to lodge charisma in the institution rather than in the person.

I

Every social institution has an ideological rationale. As long as the colonial powers held ultimate power, they could support the growth of European types of institutions against the pressures exerted by the internal society to resist such institutions with stubborn parochialism. The civil service ethos increased steadily under the sponsorship of colonial powers.[7] Indeed, as in India, the bureaucracy is often considered a colonial achievement in the underdeveloped areas. But with the completion of the anti-colonial phase, we find what seems to be a curious political reversion to traditionalist ways of sanctioning public authority. This is especially noticeable in Africa.[8] Thus, the new leaders, who may appear as demagogues to Westerners, are often considered democrats by their own peoples. The Maximum Leader is someone whose authority is permanent, personal, pervasive, and, above all, "legitimized." It is a power not necessarily destroyed by being out of office, as is made clear by the career patterns of men like Patrice Lumumba and Jomo Kenyatta, and to lesser extent by Juan Perón and Getulio Vargas. Indeed, it might be argued that political exile aids resistance to new political leadership and may actually prolong the lifespan of obsolete political institutions.[9]

Recently James S. Coleman has divided party systems into three distinct types—one-party dominant systems, coprehensive nationalistic parties, and competitive party systems—but they seem more academic than real.[10] First, most of the nation-states fall into the category of one-party dominant systems; second, comprehensive nationalist parties are functionally one-party systems, only without the protective gloss of minority parties. Third, even competitive party systems are rarely competitive, since the dominant parties invariably have more than 65 per cent of the total electoral vote, the minority parties rarely more than 25 per cent. Hence, only in rare instances can Sub-Sahara Africa be said to exhibit a genuine two or multi-party system. Thus, party charisma accounts for more fundamental characteristics than can be appreciated by an examination solely of the political doctrines or organizations apart from the men behind them.

It is significant to note that this phenomenon of pseudo-competitive parties is by no means strictly African. The Mapai, ruling party in Israel, has maintained an unbroken rule, despite ostensible "competition" from other parties. More recently, the Mapai has withstood the onslaught of its own charismatic founder—David Ben-Gurion. He was only able to muster small support against an "organization" candidate. The Congress Party in India has clearly become an omnibus ruling party, despite the tolerance of other political parties. The P.R.I. in Mexico encourages the widest differences and divergences of opinion—but only as long as they occur within the party. Hence, the shift from multi-party to one-party domination is a world-wide phenomenon. The end of traditional society, the rise of modernization, has been accompanied by a decline in competitive party politics.

Charisma, however vague a concept it may be, is a factor in the "national liberation struggle." We must satisfactorily explain what takes place after this revolutionary phase. On the whole, the social functions of charisma radically shift after the successful conclusion of the national liberation effort. The revolutionary period is characterized by a heightened personal charisma. The revolutionary leaders take advantage of the weakness of the established social order by intensifying the mass sense of bewilderment and helplessness and by terrifying the population through the specter of innumerable dangerous enemies. In this way the new set of leaders can establish their credentials.[11]

Charisma in the post-revolutionary period must respond to an entirely different set of needs: (a) it entails a response to the need to make order out of revolutionary chaos; (b) it fuses the social sectors rendered antagonistic during the revolutionary period; (c) it must resurrect the distintegrated personality by welding it to a higher collective purpose. Through the process of symbolic identification of the masses with the leadership, the individual can realize his sense of fulfillment. For such reasons, charisma in the new nations of Asia and Africa increasingly takes on depersonalized qualities—with the mystique of charisma residing in the leading office, not in the person. This kind of political charisma makes the fusion of mass aspirations with leadership demands much simpler, if for no other reason than that party charisma is a more stable and reliable guide to action than personal (and inevitably capricious) leadership.

Charismatic authority is not only a stimulus to change; it may also act as a brake on social change. As Hirschman has shown, the idea of change may be a prime obstacle to development.[12] The charismatic leader develops an ego-focused conception of progress which hampers economic development by placing the responsibility for it on the political means rather than the technological. In the United States, development has historically been accomplished in a "human engineering" light, whereas in many of the emerging nations struggles for political popularity tend to reinforce charisma features of rule. To summarize this point, a highly accentuated charisma is dysfunctional in that it puts tremendous weight on fate, fortune, and the skills of leadership to make capital of each, but it underestimates political skills based on use of exact information, and defeats development of a mass educational and political socalization apparatus.

Charismatic leadership often degenerates into personal tyranny because intrinsic to its practices is a heavy reliance on the symbolic value of the ends sought, with little consideration for the means necessary to achieve such ends. The charismatic leader, in order to make good his pledges and promises, is forced to turn to terroristic methods or run the risk that his followers will quickly turn from disillusionment to disaffiliation. Party charisma is a synthesis of practical political considerations and symbolically laden personalist leadership. While it is unappealing to those reared in a culture stressing constitutional norms, it is an outgrowth of pressures to limit the excesses of pure personal charisma. What is more, party charisma can more readily absorb defeat, or a series of defeats, than can the individual leader. The Church long ago

understood that the fallibility of Popes had to be separated from the infallibility of the Papacy if the charisma invested in Catholicism was not to deteri-
orate into sectarianism.

II

Party charisma is hardly a new phenomenon. While it has achieved considerable refinement in African nations, many of its aspects can be seen in the
revolutionary movements of Latin America. Here the "science" and "art" of
leadership are dedicated to moving beyond the legacy of Western parliamentary democracy and socialist centralism. Capitalism and socialism, mass action
and creative leadership, worker and peasant, male and female, etc., are all
summed up in the party of the "whole people." In Argentina it bore the name
Justicialismo under Perón. The party became the "mediating power." The
party is also the "perfect organization." For whatever the defects of the maximum leader may be, such "human defects" (as Perón called them) do not
carry over to tarnish the party. Unlike Africa, however, old and well-established
political parties do exist in Latin America. But the charismatic party claims
that these traditional parties are riddled with self-interest and fraud, and are
too weak to integrate the nation. The "politicos" go nowhere; they lack a
sense of destiny—which is what *Justicialismo* claimed to have. For it is not
simply an "old-fashioned party," but a movement—an activity going somewhere, responsible to somebody, headed by someone.[13]

The extent to which Peronism is a party phenomenon, rather than a simple
charismatic condition, is made clear in the survival of the party, even though
the leader is scarcely likely to resume power, since he has been in exile for a
decade.[14] Personal leadership does not by any means disappear. The Revolutionary *Party* persists even though the Revolutionary *Government* may be
overthrown. And this is a significant fact—since party charisma seems also to
be evident in such diverse conditions as the *Apristas* of Peru and the Brazilian
Labor Party (PTB) of Brazil. Signs of this are now taking place in Cuba,
where despite the monumental personal authority of Castro, the elevation of
the United Party of the Cuban Socialist Revolution (PURSC) to a supreme
place necessarily means that Castro has been willing and able to place himself
under its authority.[15] Perhaps this is the only way to prevent factionalism from
openly breaking out.

Strangely enough, the Peronist movement in the Argentina of the 'forties
is more a prototype of what took place in Africa a decade later, in the 'fities,
than an imitation of fascist Italy of the 'thirties. Peronism was directly linked
to the transformation of a rural society into an urban society; it served as a
catalyst for the industrialization of the nation; it served to give the drive toward economic development a base in a socially revolutionary doctrine and
ideology.[16] But perhaps the most perfect symbol of charismatic authority is
the unique relationship the "leader" is said to have with the "people," a
uniqueness underscored by the "anguish" of the past and the "joys" of the
present. Eva Perón wrote:

The Argentine people does not forget those days of anguish and death. Why should it not celebrate the First of May, now that it can do so without fear and anxiety? Instead of screaming with clenched fists in front of the closed doors of Government House, the Argentine working people now celebrate May Day with a magnificent festival, at which their Leader presides from the balconies of Government House in his character of the first Argentine worker, the title which, without any doubt, Perón appreciates most. And the marvelous thing is that, instead of fearing death on that day, the people are wont to offer their lives, yelling a chorus which always moves my soul: "Our lives for Perón."[17]

The role of the leader is to purify the hearts and cleanse the minds of his followers. There is always much to purify and cleanse! The culture of poverty is difficult to celebrate when it is realized that its asking price is the surrender of the political processes to the benevolence of wealthy classes. Up close, within sight and touch, the culture of poverty evaporates into a poverty of culture. For want of a resistant and sophisticated political system, the mass of the poor is prey to promises of deliverance. For this reason, the leader can be charismatic, can appear god-like in his presentation of self to the undifferentiated mass. But when the poor are newly mobilized, uprooted from older patterns and former life styles, then "working class authoritarianism" becomes a factor. The process of development cannot be judged by whether it avoids charismatic appeals, but only by its achievements. Hence, the real measure of party charisma is, first, in the successful execution of the tasks of social development and, second, in its ability to satisfy the claims of the masses.

This "role confusion," in which the leader identifies with the nation in an almost tautological fashion, has been carried to perfection in Latin America. We have the most "perfect" illustration in the suicide of Getulio Vargas, who in his suicide message[18] declared he would enter history by this act of identification with the "people." "My sacrifice will maintain you united, and my name will be your battle flag. Each drop of my blood will be an immortal call to your consciene and will maintain a holy vibration for resistance . . . I fought against the looting of Brazil. I have fought against the looting of the people. I have fought bare-breasted. The hatred, infamy, and calumny did not beat down my spirit. I gave you my life. Now I offer my death. Nothing remains. Serenely I take the first step on the road to eternity and I leave life to enter history." One can see here, as in the words of Evita Perón, the powerful strain of messianic fervor, a fervor which gives rich substance to the charismatic aspect of this ostensibly altruistic identification of person with nation, and through this identification, with the gods, with immortality.

From the less sacred and more profane side of things, it is evident that this "old-fashioned" Latin American personal charisma is not easily transferred into party charisma. In the case of Perón, through Justicialismo, and in the case of Vargas, through the Partido Trabhalista Brasileiro, the image of the personal leader was a handicap rather than a help to party charisma. In the absence of any authentic social revolution, the mystique of charismatic leadership cannot readily be transferred to a party as the bearer of "principle." Therefore, when personal charisma collapses under such circumstances, there is a return to traditional political processes. This shows that, in Latin America at least, traditional politics may yet house modernist economics—at least until the question of structural reform is pressed to the limit.

Political party leaders often see themselves as the "vessels of universal truth" while manipulating their party machinery "as simple mechanisms with which to gain power."[19] But in fact, this approach is more common to the "old" underdeveloped nations of South America than to the "new" under-developed nations of Africa. In Latin America, the artificial grafting of a liber-tarian political code onto a soft underbelly of feudal socio-economic relations often accentuated pure charisma, just as it also accentuated pure bureaucratic norms. It is precisely the kind of permanent crisis of dependency evident in Latin America which many of the new nations of Asia and Africa have sought to overcome through party charisma. In those cases in Latin America where more or less successful changes in the social structure have been brought about —Cuba, Mexico, Chile, and to a lesser extent Venezuela—the party apparatus becomes the vessel of universal truth, while the leadership draws its inspiration from the claims of the party. Developing nations tend to become the model— replacing that of the most developed "first new nation," the United States, and avoiding the well-advertised problems of the Soviet Russian bureaucratic state.

In Brazil, precisely because its present military leadership is charismatic without party, political parties often follow the ways of United States politics by stressing electoral function and providing bureaucratic careers for popular leaders. In these instances the leadership often turns to the bureaucracy or military to build up power reserves. This intensifies the political character of the bureaucracy and makes it subject to political seizure. Control of the "bu-reaus" at the administrative levels and important alliances with military and other sectors become the real power bases. The direct power relation is between personal leadership and the state machinery. The Brazilian political party is the leader's vehicle, but it does not become enmeshed in government as such or enjoy the mass following of a "movement." It lies outside the state to a greater degree, and control of it is only peripheral. It does not become fused with charismatic dimensions except in revolutionary "movements." Even then, party organization, being essentially "non-ideological," is likely to overpower or modify charismatic party tendencies. It is a commonplace for the Brazilian intellectual to decry the opportunism of Brazilian parties and their lack of solid ideological lineage and loyalty. Because of the tenuous connection between leaders of the party and those of the state, political reorganization may be stifled. Politics may then be fragmented into many parties' representative interests.

III

One of the peculiarities of authority in the Third World is that the party ideology is generally much more inflexible than criteria for party membership. While the ideological features of the political apparatus are often highly cen-tralized, the actual organization allows for a wide variety of ideological types.

Lipset has recently noted that "such parties tend to be loosely structured, more like a *rassemblement* than a party of ideology or interest. They combine a number of interests and strata, either through the charisma of the leader or through the original need for unity in the struggle for independence. Charisma is necessary if the system is to survive in its early stages, and the absence of opposition may prove beneficial if it preserves the often frail mystique upon which authority depends."[20] It is not so much the "frail mystique" which determines the situation, since it rests on the frailties of power, but rather the inability of any one social sector to dominate the political context. The foundations for legal authority are strengthened when one well-defined social-economic sector is in control of the state. The American bourgeoisie in the nineteenth century (notwithstanding the rubrics which may be employed to show the aristocratic tastes of that class) gave legal shape to society because they were able to generalize their class interests so that they became identified with the national interest. Since the emergent nations of Latin America, Asia, and Africa have never witnessed a complete crystallization of modern class relationships, there has not been a properly installed rational-legal superstructure. The irony is that in many nations of Latin America law has been revered rather than obeyed. On the other hand, in those nations where the national movement was initially based on charismatic force, such as Mexico and Cuba, there are strong grounds for anticipating the long-range success of rational authority, as was the case in the United States between 1775 and 1865.

If we take Japan between 1860 and 1940 as typical of the "pre-Third World" developmental process in Asia, we find that disillusionment with multi-party processes does not necessarily resolve itself in party charisma but may result in personal charisma, which in this context meant the emperor.

> Despite growing popular participation in elections and extensive parliamentary experience, a politically mature middle class, with demands and expectations, did not develop. There was not enough time for this adjustment: rather, politicians came to be regarded as corrupt, parasitic, somehow un-Japanese, and "politician" took on a pejorative ring in prewar Japan. Essential power remained entrenched in a small elite, civilian and military, with the latter having direct access to the Emperor and able to use him to sanction its objectives without reference to the wishes of the popularly elected Diet.[21]

The tension between the needs of a mass society and a neo-feudal economy did not have to be resolved by party charisma. Stability was supplied by custom and tradition, the hierarchical rigidity of Japanese poitical leadership, and its close identification with military order and religious sanction.

This sense of hierarchy is precisely what is absent in most Third World natons, where there is extreme fluidity in both the definition and execution of leadership. Charismatic leaders are often under pressure to establish a principle of rule that is based on the political party as such. In Kwame Nkrumah's Convention People's Party (CPP) in Ghana, this transference of charisma from the person to the party is nearly total:

> The party must become at once the symbol and the focus of the national

consciousness towards which loyalty can be directed above and even irrespective of loyalty to particular persons. Thus the agents of the party's authority may be acknowledged to fail or defect and ministerial heads may be seen to roll, but this must never be equated with any failure by the party as such. When the source and agency of authority are successfully separated in this way, it can then become true that *le parti regne mais il ne gouverne pas*. Charisma will become successfully routinized once the separation of the source from the agency of authority immunizes it against the failure which would bring about the collapse of a "pure" charismatic system.[22]

Even where personal charisma is exceptionally powerful, as in Cuba, we find direct appeals to party charisma. In an address delivered in May 1964, Fidel Castro said: "If the imperialists should invade this country, you would have to realize that the majority of the leaders of today would die in the struggle. But the people will remain, and the party would remain. There would be no need to ask for names or for men. Each one of us would do his duty in the way demanded of him and do it well."[23] There is no question of the sincerity of the emotions herein expressed. It is obvious that under stress and duress the appeal to the rank and file is made in the name of the people and the party. The rhetoric does indicate a clear distinction between transient elite and permanent mass. Cuban leadership displays a passionate involvement rather than an Olympian detachment. In this fashion the party serves to solve the succession of leadership without destroying personal charisma. To say that this is simply a clever and modern way of reinforcing personal charisma misses the point that the cult of the party is quite commonplace. If we examine the history of the Soviet Union, it will be found that the extreme cult of personality came, not at the outset of the Revolution, but only at a late stage when the goals of political revolution hardened and became goals of economic development; and only at that point when the fight over control of the party apparatus became uppermost.[24]

One of the chief functional byproducts of charismatic leadership is that traditional economic sectors are made subordinate to state decisions. The kinds of independent class struggles engaged in by trade unions and business associations in the highly developed capitalist nations are intolerable for the Third World. They are viewed as obstructions to the task of social development— and in this way, the conduct of the union or the corporation has to become subordinate to state power. This is perfectly expressed by the African leader Tom Mboya. Speaking of both union and management separatist tendencies, he writes:

> The lesson they have to learn is that if their beliefs are to be respected in our new countries, they will need to show a response to government and nationalistic requirements. If their stand appears to be negative and unnecessarily obstructive, then it is inevitable that, with this sense of urgency in our new countries, they will be overriden and completely set aside. If they show they are cooperative and become partners in the urgent need for development, then they will survive.[25]

This is a way of pointing out that, in the Third World, economic power is not equivalent to political power.

IV

Class competition is replaced by the doctrine of the "whole people." This doctrine makes multiple parties superfluous, since the whole people can obviously be represented by the whole party.[26] Yet, the conception of the whole people, or the myth of the mass, imposes severe limitations on totalitarian possibilitis in the Third World. For any party which is compelled to make appeal by crossing class lines has clearly limited its cohesive potentialities. Yet party charisma is also the product of a relatively unstable equilibrium, an instability created by the fact that the very social forces which contributed to the formal political independence of the emerging nation are not compelled to choose between socialism and capitalism. Since experimental attitudes do prevail, they create a political atmosphere that is far from rigid or totalitarian.

Many Third World countries tend to place great emphasis upon the mobilization of the working classes and union movements in support of the national leadership. In this, the nations of the Third World have incorporated selective features of other radical movements to further consensus between the various classes in the society. Unionism becomes the most powerful bulwark of the nationalist elites. The working classes thus believe they have attained power rather than acted as a mere factor in the power arrangement. This variety of "national socialism" is made possible by the rational division of the economic spoils. Since large-scale capital is held by foreigners, internal economic fissures between classes will be dissolved, or at least drastically minimized. In this form, the *development ideology* of national unity replaces the *socialist ideology* of class struggle.

The formal independence of many Third World nations makes possible greater economic penetration by the older colonial powers. Formal freedom liberates the ex-colonial powers of the necessity of rule, and insures greater productivity, greater output, and greater interaction with foreign powers. The new middle classes which emerge in post-colonial situations move in the direction of the kind of formal authority which characterizes advanced middle-class societies elsewhere; but they are thwarted by the overt sentiments of the revolutionary leadership. More important, middle-class political consolidation stands in contradiction to the stated socialist objectives of many emergent nations. Therefore, the political elite must continue to exercise the special prerogatives of office, lest the middle class and proletariat jeopardize through social conflict the thorough mobilization and integration of the nation.

Party elites are shrewd enough to avoid making exaggerated claims for themselves as purveyors of universal truths; they now prefer to invest such claims in their party. In a new nation like Mali, for example, the Political Bureau of a dozen men make all decisions, and these decisions are binding for all Malians. It is the *Union Soudanaise* party which "holds in its hands the destiny of the country and has absolute power." The danger in this situation is that it fails to "surround the party with guarantees of popular agreement." There is a genuine concern about keeping connections to the mass, and this is resolved by an unnatural consensus—a demand for collectivity as a way to avoiding errors. But this often leads to an avoidance of decision-making.[27]

Party charisma enables the new nation to combine maximum organizational efficiency with the greatest mobilization of the masses. It becomes a way of establishing the paradoxical claims of a consensus built upon mass participation and of a coercive apparatus built upon elitist drives toward development. And to the degree that such paradoxical claims are matters of ultimate interests and are "non-negotiable," then party charisma may turn out to be an unstable and temporary equilibrium. But then again, the entire Third World may be in this position in relation to the advanced industrial-military complexes of the world.

The new nation-states are an extremely fertile area for observing party charisma. The problem might be posed in the following way: Why is there a need for charismatic rather than rationalistic types of political authority? First, there are very few educated people in the new African states; very few whose background and qualifications alone could help create non-charismatic rule. Second, people feel frustrated that development has come so late and been so difficult; party charisma therefore serves as a ready-made tool to accelerate this process. Third, most African states have a long history of acceptance and response to raw power. In both British and French former possessions the lines of authority were clear, however much they were hated.[28] With the departure of the colonialists, this clear demarcation between ruler and ruled also ended. Party charisma thus overcomes the problem of political succession in the most feasible way possible within a context which exhibits a high degree of traditionalism amongst the masses and a no less marked modernism amongst the elites.

In response to the cry of treason which has been heard with increasing stridency from socialist elements in the Third World and Western Europe alike, the leadership of many emerging states has asserted that the national liberation phase has not yet been concluded (at least this is held to be so in Africa); only when nations like Angola and South Africa are liberated from white domination will it be possible or desirable to focus attention on internal imbalances between social sectors within the continent. It is further stated that for relatively advanced nations such as Ghana and Nigeria to intensify the conflict between the new urban proletariat and the new urban bourgeoisie would only postpone a settlement of accounts with the remaining imperial powers. Thus, the spokesmen of these new nations claim that a class struggle would prove to be sectarian and self-defeating—at least at this historical juncture. This concept has come to define not only the whole people, but has been enlarged into one for the whole continent. It seems to underlie the insistence on the unique properties of African socialism.

The growth of party charisma in the Soviet Union was thwarted by two important factors; one practical and the other theoretical. On the practical side, the Soviet Union inherited a relatively complex, if not especially well-organized, bureaucratic apparatus from the Czarist regime. Unlike the post-colonial situation in the new nations of Africa and Asia, the technical functions of this pre-revolutionary bureaucracy were left intact. From the outset, it was a distinctively Russian entity, and not a colonial import which could be expanded or withdrawn at the pleasure of the foreign governing body. It was not necessary for the Bolshevik Party to incorporate unto itself all the features of organizational life. On the theoretical side, the separation of power between Government and Party was a Leninist canon. It represented the Communist Party way of establishing a one-party system of checks and balances. The fact that under Stalin the role of government was profoundly weakened, and federal and party functions combined, made possible the kind of personal charisma which sapped the strength of Soviet organizational life. One may characterize, therefore, the Khrushchev and Kosygin eras as a time of restoration—the re-establishment of lines of authority which are in some measure traditional, while, in other respects, legalistic and ratonalistic.[29] In any event, at no point in past Soviet political history has there been any real unfolding of the party charisma phenomenon.

V

The underlying assumption that "man" will eventually assert his individuality in the face of tyranny takes for granted that people of the Third World share the Western cultural conception of "man against state." There is no evidence that the powerful disposition in favor of constitutionalism exhibited by the British working class in the nineteenth century is a valid guide to action for the recently liberated colonial working classes. To assume that a mobilization system is undemocratic while a reconciliation system is democratic simply turns constitutionalism into an article of religious fath.[30]

Until now constitutionalism, when employed in underdeveloped nations, has not operated to create or broaden the consensual base but became a basic instrument for popular wants and needs. The role of party charisma is therefore to establish a basis of authority which is at one and the same time personal and legal—one that focuses on the party and not on either the individual or the law as such. It should not be assumed that the Third World is one in which personal authority is exclusive and dominant. This is, as a matter of fact, rarely the case. Party authority is not simply a rhetorical device used to disguise the fact of personal power. It is itself a limitation on personal power, though not yet legal or universally acknowledged. The actual transitory character of political parties stands in the way of the complete rationalization of the social systems in the Third World.

Party charisma does not do away with problems of bureaucracy and formal organization. On the contrary, such problems are multiplied to the degree that authority takes on multiple social roles: a portion of power remains with the leader, and another portion with the party directly, and yet a third in the technical requirements of leadership and organization. Historically, a greater measure of power has been invested in the personal leadership *prior* to the revolutionary period and a greater measure of power invested in the technical-professional elite *after* the revolutionary phase. The charismatic party functions as the clearing house for ideologists and technologists alike, deriving its own momentum from the unstable equilibrium they create. The ability to perform a particular task may appear to rest on "rational" grounds, while the choice and allocation of such tasks may appear to rest upon "irrational" political grounds. Actual political interaction is far muddier, since as a matter of course, the line between task and decision is constantly shifting, and it is in the areas between that friction arises.

The problem becomes particularly acute because so many of the new nations have one-party arrangements. All major decisions and tasks must be funneled through this single-party channel. The battle for control of the party apparatus becomes especially bitter. To lose control of this apparatus may mean to lose out in the overall sense, to forfeit the opportunity to move the nation. Thus, the battle for control is not only severe, but invariably subversive.[31] Seen in this way, we can understand how personalism and constitutionalism are tactical responses to an unstable historic situation, and not historical stages in the unfolding of nationhood.[32]

There is a growing literature dedicated to proving that not all of the emergent nations fit this pattern. Sir James Robertson has recently cited Nigerian "exceptionalism" based on the long precedent of compromise, the slow maturation of political responsibilities under the Crown, and the development of three strong parties.[33] This sounds more like an apologia for the superiority of British imperialism than an example of significant differences between Nigeria and other new African states. There is also the literature attempting to prove that constitutional monarchy resolves the problems of Middle Eastern bureaucracy. The argument is that, given the background and context of Middle Eastern history, a cultivated, Westernized notion of democracy can only be brought about by the modern counterpart of the eighteenth-century benevolent despot. This seems to place Middle East nations, like Iran, in a more backward political condition than even that reflected by party charisma. The latter at least has the advantages of depersonalization of the political machinery, and the legalization of the bureaucracy over and above kings and monarchs.[34]

VI

Ideology has become a particularly powerful force of rationalization in the newer African states. It can be seen with striking voice in Sekou Touré's explicit rejection of the classic struggle in favor of the anti-colonial struggle—even after the successful conclusion of the national liberation phase of the revolution. He speaks of unionism in Guinea as "specifically African . . . an authentic expression of African values."[35] This means that European socialist standards of labor relations are to be replaced by the ideology of development as such. Speaking for Senegal, Leopold Sedar Senghor says that this Africanization of socialist ideology will eliminate the "one-sidedness" of European socialism and Communism. Actually, it is an instrument for making socialism and nationalism problems of social development. This development is to take place through "Community Development Centers." In this the Senegalese Party (UPS) is to be the "echo of the popular aspirations" and also the "scientific expression" of peoples' needs. In this apocalyptic vision of socialism and negritude, the party of the whole people may even become the party of the whole race.[36] The Third World has produced a party ideology as well as a political strategy. However mythic the synthesis of European socialism and African nativism may be, it would be foolish at this early stage to assume that the doctrine of the whole people led by the single, unified peoples' party, headed by the knowing and responsive leader, who is furthermore the choice of the whole people and the unified party alike (the two are not always distinguishable), is either transitory or lacking in practical application. For whatever else they are, the leaders of the emergent African states are sharp-eyed and razor-tongued, and above all practical men, concerned with political survival in extremely rugged social-economic circumstances.

Party charisma also represents a response to the division of power between local or tribal units and national units. Speaking of Ghana, Dennis Austin makes precisely this point. "If one asks how such an aim [of resolving the cosmopolitan-local duality] is pursued, the answer is clear—through the party, which dominates the contemporary scene. It remodels the State in its own image—reducing the power of the chiefs, centralizing the trade unions, legislating against tribal and regional parties, and centralizing power within the constitution."[37] According to Kwame Nkrumah: "There must be no stress on local, separatist loyalties . . . in Ghana, in the higher reaches of our national life, there should be no reference to Fantis, Ashantis, Ewes, Dagembas, etc., we should call ourselves Ghanaians—all brothers and sisters, members of the same community, the State of Ghana."[38] We can see that, contrary to present-day European socialist ideology, ethnic heterogeneity through the "self-determination" principle vanishes after the period of national independence.

However reluctant the inherited oligarchical system is to surrender its traditional power, and however desirous the political rulers are to avoid a direct confrontation with these traditional classes, the introduction of an industrial system compels these rulers to fight the oligarchy. The two forms of legitimation inherited from the past—personalism and constitutionalism—are historical and structural at the same time. Personal charisma, while a mechanism of transition from colonialism to independence, is not something which yields automatically to rational authority. While party charisma may be unstable, with the leader having to choose between absolute dictatorship and benevolent despotism, it remains an ongoing force in every Third World nation—long after some system of rational-legal authority has been created. The dialectic of the situation dictates that a charismatic figure must stay in power long enough to permit the crystallizaton of those opposing factions which can debate the character of the legal system. Charismatic parties thus make possible discussions on laws of political succession, divisions in the power structure, and relations between social and economic sectors. The growth of rational authority should allow for the kinds of innovations by the leadership that will not produce rigidly opposed political factions. There should be enough fluidity to permit the existence of highly personalized relations between leaders and followers in the revolutionary movement for national development. This is the proper function of party charisma.

NOTES

[1] Maurice Duverger, *Political Parties: Their Organization and Activity in the Modern States* (second edition). New York, 1959, p. 215.

[2] See on this John H. Kautsky, *Political Change in Underdeveloped Countries: Nationalism and Communism*. New York, 1962, pp. 116–17.

[3] See Hugh P. Williamson, "The Two Party System, Its Foibles, and Follies," *The American Journal of Economics and Sociology*, Vol. 23, No. 1, January 1964, pp. 85–93.

[4] See on this James MacGregor Burns, *The Deadlock of Democracy: Four Party Politics in America*. Englewood Cliffs, N.J., 1963, pp. 280–322.

[5] For a useful discussion of this question of multiple parties and singular dictatorships, see Fred R. van der Mehden, *Politics of the Developing Nations*. Englewood Cliffs, N.J., 1964, pp. 61–2.

[6] H. H. Gerth and C. Wright Mills (editors), *From Max Weber: Essays in Sociology*. New York, 1946, pp. 254–5; also see their introduction, pp. 51–5.

[7] See Irving L. Horowitz, "A Formalization of the Sociology of Knowledge," *Behavioral Science*, Vol. 9, No. 1, January 1964, pp. 45–55. Paul P. Van Riper, *History of the United States Civil Service*. Evanston, Ill., 1958, esp. pp. 533–64.

[8] See on this clash of universalist and particularist political norms, David E. Apter, *The Gold Coast in Transition*. Princeton: Princeton University Press, 1955; and James S. Coleman, *Nigeria: Background to Nationalism*. Berkeley, 1958.

[9] The idea that there is a correlation between the growth of charisma and the decline of colonialism was first put forward to me by my colleague Alvin W. Wolfe. This idea is being further developed by him in a work in progress on African Conceptions of Authority.

[10] See James S. Coleman, "The Politics of Sub-Saharan Africa," *The Politics of the Developing Ideas*. Princeton, 1960, pp. 286–95. It should be noted that Coleman's paper makes explicit reference to sub-Saharan Africa, but he leaves no doubt that his categories can be extended to other regions of the world.

[11] A serious deficiency in the sociological literature is that while "pure" charismatic leadership and bureaucratic structures have been well described, the intermediary, transitional systems have not been appreciated. On pure charisma, see Leo Lowenthal and Norbert Guterman, *The Prophets of Deceit*. New York, 1941, and Erich Fromm, *Escape from Freedom*. New York, 1941; on pure bureaucracies, see Robert K. Merton, "Bureaucratic Structure and Personality," and Alvin W. Gouldner, "Introduction," to *Studies in Leadership*, edited by Alvin W. Gouldner. New York, 1950, pp. 3–49.

[12] Cf. Albert O. Hirschman, *The Strategy of Economic Development*. New Haven, 1958, pp. 16–18.

[13] See Juan Perón, *Conducción Política*. Buenos Aires, 1952, esp. pp. 205–12, 295–7.

[14] See on this dichotomization of Perón and Peronism, Irving Louis Horowitz, "Modern Argentina: The Politics of Power," *The Political Quarterly*, Vol. 30, No. 4, October–December 1959; in this connection see Gino Germani, "El autoritorismo y las clases populares," in *Politica y Sociedad en una Epoca de Transición*. Buenos Aires, 1962, pp. 127–46.

[15] See the report by Richard Eder on Castro's urging of an easing of tensions between Cuba and the United States, in which Castro's plans for a "constitutional regime in Cuba by 1969" are reported. *The New York Times*, July 6, 1964.

[16] For contrasting views of the significance of Peronism as an ideology of development, see Marcos Merchensky, *Las Corrientes Ideológicas en la Historia Argentina*. Buenos Aires, 1961, esp. pp. 215–30; and Jorge Abelardo Ramos, *Revolución y Contrarrevolución en la Argentina*. Buenos Aires, 1961, esp. pp. 435–45.

[17] Eva Perón, *My Mission in Life*, trans. by Ethel Cherry. New York, 1953, pp. 101–2.

[18] Getulio Vargas, "Farewell Message to the Brazilian People," *Revolution in Brazil: Politics and Society in a Developing Nation*, by Irving L. Horowitz. New York, 1964, pp. 132–3.

[19] See Kalman H. Silvert, "The Costs of Anti-Nationalism," in *Expectant Peoples: Nationalism and Development*, edited by K. H. Silvert. New York, 1963, pp. 355–6. Also see his article on "National Values, Development, and Leaders and Followers," *International Social Science Journal*, Vol. XV, No. 4, 1963, pp. 560–70.

[20] Seymour Martin Lipset, *The First New Nation: The United States in Historical and Comparative Perspective*. New York, 1963, pp. 314–15.

[21] Lawrence Olson, "The Elite, Industrialism and Nationalism: Japan," in *Expectant Peoples: Nationalism and Development*, edited by K. H. Silvert. New York, 1963, pp. 409–10.

[22] W. G. Runciman, "Charismatic Legitimacy and One-Party Rule in Ghana," *Archives Européennes de Sociologie*, Vol. IV, No. 1, 1963, p. 159.

[23] Quoted by Dave Dellinger, "Cuba: Seven Thousand Miles from Home," *Liberation*, Vol. IX, No. 4, June–July 1964, pp. 11–21.

[24] See Myron Rush, *Political Succession in the U.S.S.R.* New York, 1965.

[25] Tom Mboya, *Freedom and After*. Boston, 1963, p. 197; also pp. 56–7.

[26] The most impressive study of this phenomenon of the whole people, and its effects on political processes in the new nations, is Emile R. Braundi, "Neocolonalism and the Class Struggle." *International Socialist Journal*, Vol. 1, Number 1, January–February 1964, pp. 48–68.

[27] See on this subject William J. Foltz, *From French West Africa to the Mali Federation: The Background to Federation and Failure*. Unpublished Ph.D. dissertation. Yale University, 1963.

[28] Cf. Aidan Crawley, "Patterns of Government in Africa," *African Affairs*, Vol. 60, No. 240, July 1961, pp. 393–4.

[29] Irving L. Horowitz, "The Second Soviet Revolution," *The Correspondent*, No. 33, Winter, 1964–65.

[30] For a conventional "Western" position on this, see David E. Apter, "Political Religion in the New Nations," *Old Societies and New States: The Quest for Modernity in Asia and Africa*. New York, 1963, pp. 57–104. It is interesting that the very abstracts and quotations Apter uses to prove the existence of personal charisma and "political religion" demonstrate an impersonal or, better, depersonalized charisma lodged in the authority of the party and not the person.

[31] See on this Colin Legum, "What Kind of Radicalism for Africa?" *Foreign Affairs*, Vol. 43, No. 2, January 1965, pp. 237–50.

[32] The various papers in Gwendolen M. Carter (ed.), *African One-Party States*. Ithaca, New York, 1962, provide a solid basis for my judgment that charisma and bureaucracy ought not to be viewed as historical stages in the unfolding of nationhood, but simply as dialectical poles, between which choices are constantly made and unmade.

[33] Cf. James Robertson, "Sovereign Nigeria," *African Affairs*, Vol. 59, No. 239, April 1961, pp. 145–54.

[34] Mohammad Reza Shah, *Mission for My Country*. New York, 1963.

[35] Sekou Touré, *L'expérience et l'unité africaine*. Paris, 1959, pp. 390–91.

[36] Leopold Sedar Senghor, *On African Socialism*, trans. by Mercer Cook. New York, 1964, pp. 154–9, and 165.

[37] Cf. Dennis Austin, "The New Ghana," *African Affairs*, Vol. 59, No. 234, January 1960, pp. 20–25.

[38] Ibid., p. 21. See also Kwame Nkrumah, *I Speak of Freedom: A Statement of African Ideology*. London, 1961.

COMMUNICATION
IN CONFLICT RESOLUTION

In The Presence of the Word, Walter J. Ong writes:

When hostility becomes total, the most vicious namecalling is inadequate: speech is simply broken off entirely. . . . The breakdown to total hostility in international relations is commonly signaled by withdrawal of diplomatic representatives. The hostile nations cease talking directly. For a while, they may resort to intermediaries for diplomatic business. Should matters worsen, the next step is physical attack, war. If noncommunication persists without physical attack, we have a "cold war," which is indeed war, for without communication there is no peace [Ong 1967:194].

The 1960 world summit conference at the United Nations evoked considerable tension between East and West causing Presidents Tito, Nkrumah, Nasser, and Sukarno, and Prime Minister Nehru to offer a resolution urging the Soviet and American heads of governments to renew contacts that had been broken off since the failure of the Paris Summit Conference the spring before. In 1962, after the Cuban missile crisis, President Jorgé Allessandri of Chile reminisced: "The world trembled at the idea that the specter of war might become a reality. Those were days of anxiety and profound anguish" (Allessandri 1970).

While the "words of war" became threatening at the United Nations during both of these situations, physical attack was averted and the two superpowers retained diplomatic relations. Later, however, during the 1967 emergency debates on the Israeli Six-Day War against the Arab states, the war was commonly called the "Israeli Blitzkrieg" by socialist and Arab representatives. Then an actual physical attack did occur: the socialist states severed diplomatic relations with the Israelis, and the Arabs broke diplomatic relations with several Western states. It was widely feared that the hostilities would evolve into World War III. In the first situation, in 1960, threats and the diplomatic language used were highly abstract, as the danger itself had been abstract. In the 1967 crisis, when the danger was very direct, statements by various heads of state and heads of government were harshly pointed and relatively unambiguous. Naturally, one must expect that at every level of diplomatic language, the statesman inherently introduces a certain level of ambiguity to allow flexibility of interpretation and possible escape clauses when the treaty, protocol, or agreement becomes apparently detrimental to his own national interests. Such ambiguity has led American statesmen somewhat naïvely to charge that Soviet oral agreements are worthless, while at the same time President Johnson's ambiguous statements in 1965 about the American Marine incursion into the Dominican Republic "to protect American nationals" on the one hand and, on the other, "to prevent Communism from establishing a second beachhead in the Western hemisphere," or President Nixon's vague statements about American involvement in Cambodia and Laos "as aspects of the continuing Vietnamization of the war in Indo-China and the increasing withdrawal of American military forces and power in the area" leave both American and Soviet analysts in a quandary about the true meaning of American intentions. Prime Minister Nehru once recalled the problems arising from his first meeting with Chou En-lai in which they haggled for hours on the interpretation of certain words and phrases that they were including in their brief joint communique. They had great difficulty in matching the English and Chinese idiom. Additionally, no great reservoir of trust had yet been established between the Indian and Chinese governments (Prosser 1963:130).

In recent years, the United States has spent greatly of its treasure to rehabilitate former enemies such as Japan and Germany. Not only the Americans and Soviets, but other large and medium-sized powers could divert much of their defense budgets to improved conditions for their peoples, if conflicts could be resolved before they reach the final plateau of communication—violence. Conflict resolution is made much easier when governments and their peoples have mutual trust and confidence for potential antagonists. Allies usually are able to solve such problems at an early stage, whereas cold- or hot-war protagonists intensely distrust every statement or action by their counterparts in a conflict. K. J. Holsti (1966) writes about the problems and behavior involved with conflict resolution, which ranges from awards and passive settlement to violence. He distinguishes between disputes, which are generally accidental or are caused by minor provocations, conflicts arising from incompatible collective objectives, which include an increasing number of civil wars that are joined by two or more outside forces, and more general tensions between two or more states, such as those that are caused by cold-war anxiety. He offers figures on procedures and outcomes of international conflicts since 1919 which show that the resolution of most conflicts involves considerable communication through bargaining, usually until accommodation or submission is reached. Holsti argues that despite the general belief to the contrary, conflicts have been solved more frequently through bargaining since the World War II period than through open hostilities. This conclusion offers the slightly hopeful sign that nations and peoples may prefer peaceful coexistence rather than "coexistence at daggers drawn."

In the first essay, Lillian Randolph offers a model of international negotiation that seeks to demonstrate the relationships among elements in the phases of bargaining which are conducive to reaching an enforceable agreement and the elements in bargaining which are helpful in enforcing the agreement. She also believes, as does Holsti, that certain incompatible objectives hinder parties from bargaining. Limited benefits for at least one of the parties to the conflict or dispute; the difficulty of allied opinions, such as the South Vietnamese and American positions, not being mutually accepted before bargaining; the contradiction between perceived and actual benefits and perceived and actual obligations; and the fact that parties that most need to bargain are often least willing, are among the stumbling blocks to the peaceful settlement of disputes and conflicts.

In my essay on the rhetoric of summitry at the United Nations, I have attempted to explore the success of summit diplomacy engaged in at the United Nations by heads of state and heads of government during its first twenty-five years. Special emphasis is given to the three major periods of summit diplomacy, the 1960 world summit conference, the 1967 emergency session of the General Assembly over the Middle East crisis, and the largely ceremonial twenty-fifth anniversary session in 1970. As the United Nations is the legitimizer of states, large and small, more than one hundred fifty state and governmental heads have assumed the United Nations forum to speak to the governments and peoples of the world. Certain general themes recur. The members extol peace, freedom, and progress, and condemn war, colonialism, and the failure of developed countries to prevent the developing states' "revolutions of rising expectations" from becoming "revolutions of rising frustrations."

Two essays discuss the problems afflicting the Middle East. The first, "The Arabs and the West: Communication Gap" by Michael Suleiman, was written slightly before the Six-Day War but treats the long-standing failure of communication between the Moslem Arabs and the Christian West. He finds that among the causes for such a communication gap, the most dominant are the lengthy antagonism between Islam and Christianity, the colonial domination over the Arab states, Arab belief that their status as a developing area has been retarded by Western efforts to exploit their natural resources, the Arab reluctance to join the West in its struggle against Communism, and, most importantly, American support for Israel's creation and maintenance as a state. Suleiman considers it remarkable not that the Arabs have generally turned to the communist governments for alliance and assistance but that they are still able to communicate at all with the West.

The next essay, "The Rhetoric of the Arab-Israeli Conflict" by D. Ray Heisey, was written after the 1967 Six-Day War and concerns itself with the relational, ideological, and situational dimensions of the broad rhetorical transactions between the Arabs and the Israelis during and since the war. Relational dimensions in this conflict include the failure of the Arabs to accept Israel as a state, the relative disparity between the ability of the Israelis and the Arabs to use power as influence in seeking a solution to the conflict, and a relational distance between the participants. Ideological disparities considered by Suleiman are also noted by Heisey. Arab rights concerning Western exploitation, the displacement of Palestinian refugees, and the Arab concept of peace and justice are juxtaposed to Israeli demands that Israel's sovereignty and right to exist be preserved from Arab harassment and legalized by a binding and permanent peace treaty. Heisey believes that the rhetorical transactions between the potential participants to a peace treaty are hindered by an element of noncommunication in which no dialogue is initiated, the participants talk past each other to world opinion, and the propaganda issued by each side is self-deceptive and self-defeating. One could almost utilize Lacouture's postulant that, like the charismatic leader who is self-destructive because he begins to believe his own miracles, so are the participants in the Middle East conflict.

Approaching directly the concept of noncommunication in international relations as game, William Starosta of the University of Virginia offers a model of noncommunication as game, isolates certain strains of communicative behavior as examples of deliberate noncommunication, and indicates when noncommunication as game proves useful in diplomatic situations. His theory relates not only to Randolph's explorations into conflict resolution but also to the noncommunication evident in President Eisenhower's refusal to meet with Premier Khrushchev during the 1960 summit conference at the United Nations, and the continuing situation in the Middle East. At the ultimate extreme, noncommunication or silence isolates. Isolation endangers the peace. It offers a prelude to a stalemate situation that must either be resolved by a renewal of communicative contacts or by moving to the final plateau of communication—violence.

It is this final plateau of communication that the last essay, by Thomas W. Benson, concerns itself. He focuses on a wide number of recent publications dealing with communication or communication breakdown. He questions whether rhetoric is the primary source of enlightened, parliamentary civilization, or is a form of violence itself. Another perspective sees violence as a final form of communication, suggesting that Hiroshima and the bombing of North Vietnam are communicative events to the enemy of the need for a quick end to what is already a larger violence. The essay brings us full circle to consider whether communication offers the resolution to conflict or whether technocracy's monopoly on communication can be broken only by revolutionary violence, which permits communication freely only to the left and denies it to the right, whether viewed on a national level or cross-nationally. This view negates the right of one party to dispute the possibility of receiving either the award or limited benefits from the process of bargaining. It causes the other side to make nonnegotiable demands rather than bargain with the possibility that it might have to compromise. Benson concludes his essay by posing the question: "Can we, as students of communication, understand and contribute to symbolic methods of conflict resolution that will enable us to balance order with real and not merely symbolic change?" It is indeed a sober question. We need to ponder whether communication averts conflict or whether conflict is itself communicative and the only way to achieve progress.

REFERENCES CITED

ALLESSANDRI RODREQUEZ, JORGE
    1970   Peace, prosperity and security are indivisible. In Sow the wind, reap the whirlwind: heads of state address the United Nations. Michael H. Prosser, ed. New York.
HOLSTI, K. J.
    1966   Resolving international conflicts: a taxonomy of behavior and some figures on procedures. Journal of Conflict Resolution 10:272–296.
PROSSER, MICHAEL H.
    1963   Communication problems in the United Nations. Southern Speech Journal 29:125–132.
ONG, WALTER J.
    1967   The presence of the word. New York.

A SUGGESTED MODEL
OF INTERNATIONAL NEGOTIATION
Lillian Randolph

The literature on international bargaining offers many books and articles on how nations come to engage in a bargaining interaction, on the process of bargaining, and on the various kinds of outcomes.[1] Little attention has been given, however, to two aspects of bargaining which are crucial to a successful outcome (an agreement which is implemented). These are: (1) the relationships among elements in the phases of bargaining which are conducive to *reaching* an enforceable agreement, and (2) the elements in bargaining which are helpful in *enforcing* the agreement. These aspects are perhaps more distinct than appears at first glance, but they are also interrelated, since the second depends on the first.

Lack of attention to implementation problems and to stages or phases of negotiation has produced theories of bargaining which are incomplete and often incompatible. If the theorist's emphasis is on elements that are helpful in keeping negotiations moving, he may overlook those qualities which other theorists feel are necessary to reaching an agreement. If he is mainly interested in qualities helpful to concluding an agreement, he may concentrate on methods of consensus-building which are detrimental to what other theorists see as requirements for enforceability.

The first part of this study describes several incompatibilities among the phases of international bargaining which must be resolved if we are to achieve a comprehensive theory of international negotiation, including the successful outcome defined above. The second part contains a model of international negotiation which attempts to resolve the incompatibilities. The aim of the model is to suggest elements in negotiation which aid the movement of the bargaining through all its phases, including the terminal one of enforcing the agreement.

1. SOME MAJOR INCOMPATIBILITIES

A. The dilemma of limited benefits

One purpose of negotiation is to secure for the participants maximum benefits at minimum risk. Yet maximization of benefits involves the appropriation of third-party resources. Great powers have the greatest appropriable resources, but great powers are also the most capable of destroying enforcement efforts. Third parties whose resources are appropriated may not perceive their loss, or they may conclude that a reprisal would be ineffective; in either of those cases they would make no challenges or claims on the gains of the winners. If they do make claims or seem likely to do so, potential winners face the alternatives of (1) claiming less than they want, but with a higher chance of getting the benefit and keeping it over the long term, or (2) claiming what they want (i.e., maximization), but with less chance of realizing it and little chance of keeping it over the long term. The first alternative means dissatisfaction in the present; the second means dissatisfaction in the future.

Thus, in the dilemma of limited benefits, that which helps the parties reach an agreement conflicts with the likelihood of implementation.

B. The problem of singular and plural positions

A group position is more likely to win than an individual position because of the greater power and resources behind it, because of its greater moral legitimacy (one's cause seems more "right" when others support it), and because it is more likely to be a moderate and general position (hence, more amenable to accommodation). Furthermore, the greater the number of positions encompassed by a solution, as when individual positions are kept distinct, the weaker becomes the focus of the solution and the less likely it is that the settlement will answer the problem which inspired the negotiation. Yet when individual goals are partly forsaken in generalizing to a group position, individual dissatisfaction is increased.

Thus, in the problem of singular and plural positions, that which encourages a willingness to negotiate hinders efforts to conclude an agreement and to enforce it.

C. The contradiction between definite benefits and definite obligations

The more certain are the benefits that will accrue from an agreement, the easier it is to reach the agreement; yet receiving benefits in the future depends on accepting definite obligations in the present. The temporal difference tends to make the obligations clearer than the benefits. Agreements that are easy to withdraw from—those with a future focus rather than a present one, those made by experts and needing to be ratified later by political bodies, those which are ambiguous, those with "escape clauses," and those which only create an institution to "solve" the problem later—such agreements are most readily supported by the parties, but their endurance in the implementation phase is uncertain. Agreements to overcome emergencies are readily concluded because the parties are often willing to accept heavy obligations to surmount the perceived threat; but an abatement of the danger, even a temporary one, often prompts the parties to look for ways of withdrawing from their commitments.

In the contradiction between definite benefits and definite obligations, then, the elements helpful to concluding an agreement are at variance with those helpful to implementation over the long term.

D. The dilemma of need

Those parties who most need international negotiation as a means of settling disputes are the parties with the least chance of securing it. Friendly parties rather than enemy parties are more willing to participate in all the phases of negotiation: they are more favorable to accepting negotiation, they undertake more negotiations because of greater opportunities, they find agreement easier because losses in a compromise can be "cashed in" later, and they implement their agreements in order to keep faith with their allies. Negotiations among enemy parties encounter greater difficulty in all of these phases, and there is less certainty of progressing to the next phase even if the prior one has been completed.

E. The problem of settlement

A settlement on the merits of the issue is likely to be an enduring solution; but seeking a settlement on the merits reduces the number of settlements which are acceptable and so decreases the likelihood of reaching a solution. The more that consensus is a means rather than an end, the more likely it is that the issue is a nonvital one about which the parties do not have intense feelings. The more intensely held are the parties' positions, the more likely it is that consensus must become an end in itself if there is to be any nego- tiated solution at all—and the less likely it is that the settlement will be based on the merits of the issue. This suggests that concern with consensus-building may be detrimental to an enduring settlement of the dispute.

F. Willingness to negotiate versus willingness to agree

Several elements which are helpful in starting a negotiation are antagonistic to other elements which are helpful in reaching an agreement once negotia- tions are under way. Willingness to negotiate is greater when punishments are as narrow as possible and benefits as wide as possible (potential parties want to avoid all the punishments or risks they can, and each wants gains). Willing- ness to negotiate increases with the number of parties who can actually par- ticipate (being a participant, rather than an observer or a third party, helps ensure the receipt of gains). Again, willingness to negotiate is greater when changes in the status quo are believed to be minimal (all parties are likely to perceive fewer disadvantages in the status quo when the changes are unde- termined).

Contrariwise, actual agreement is easier to reach when punishments or risks are as wide as possible and benefits as narrow as possible (that is, each party favors gains directed only to himself, while he favors punishments that are distributed evenly among the parties and directed outward also). Agreement is easier to reach when the number of parties is lower (benefits are greater for each party), and when the agreement involves a great change in the status quo (increased opportunity for greater gains).

Thus, concluding an agreement is less likely when the negotiation begins spontaneously, but voluntary participation may be the only way to get the negotiation started.

2. A SUGGESTED MODEL OF INTERNATIONAL NEGOTIATION

The model outlined on the next page sets forth the elements in each phase of international negotiation which are conducive to progression to the next phase, culminating in an agreement which is implemented. The remainder of the paper will explain the entries in the model, except for those which seem self-evident.

I. Prenegotiation phase

"Ability to negotiate" refers to the conditions required if a negotiation is to take place. "Willingness to negotiate" describes the desirable conditions, those which help to guarantee that a negotiation will take place.

Any negotiation requires that there be two or more actors, although one of the actors may predominate. In unilateral diplomacy one actor undertakes all or most of the activities involved in the prenegotiation and negotiation phases,

A Suggested Model of International Negotiation

I. Prenegotiation Phase	II. Negotiation Phase	III. Agreement Phase	IV. Implementation Phase

A. Ability to negotiate:
  1. Two or more actors
  2. Goals achievable by negotiation
  3. A negotiable issue, or several
  4. Resources possessed and desired
  5. Capability to trade resources
  6. Compatible values; communications
  7. Mutual trust
  8. Others: time, noninterference, nonpreoccupation, agents present
 	
B. Willingness to negotiate:
  1. Parties with direct interests
  2. A prior pledge to negotiate
  3. Certainty of obtaining goals or capability to enhance the certainty
	A. The parties:
	  1. Individual parties
	  2. Symmetrical negotiations
	  3. Friendly parties
	  4. Bilateral or polarized multilateral negotiations
	
	B. The proposals:
	  1. Goals desired over the long term
	  2. General proposals
	  3. Moderate change in the status quo
	
	C. The compromise:
	  1. A trade of similar goods
	  2. A future focus
	  3. "Upgrading the common interest"
	
	D. The aftereffects:
	  1. Capability for legitimation to constituencies
	  2. Noncrisis negotiations
		A. The settlement:
		  1. A compromise solution
		  2. All parties got acceptable satisfaction at tolerable risk
		  3. Absence of ambiguity and "escape clauses"
		  4. A settlement on the merits
		
		B. The aftereffects:
		  1. Moderate change in the status quo
		  2. Terms made legitimate to constituencies
		  3. Terms allowing task- and issue-expansion: definite obligations and indefinite benefits
			A. Voluntarism, by use of:
			  1. Symmetrical negotiations
			  2. Casuistry
			  3. Expanding benefits
			
			B. The agreement:
			  1. As one of a series, or one arising by "spillover"
			  2. Conferral of positive benefits (high satisfaction for participants)
			
			C. Postagreement phase:
			  1. Maintenance of optimal pressure on participants
			  2. Absence of reprisals to prevent enforcement
			  3. Nonoccurrence of outside events to prevent enforcement

and the other actor (or actors) is the target for them. "Goals achievable by negotiation" refers to the fact that potential participants perceive and evaluate benefits and risks that will accrue from the negotiation. If they conclude that their goals can be obtained more cheaply by negotiation than by other means— or more efficiently, more fully, more quickly, or more legitimately—their goals are those achievable by negotiation. Not only must the issue be negotiable, but it must also encompass to some degree the goals of the actors who might participate, so that the acceptance of negotiation seems likely to confer gains.

Under "capability to trade resources" in the model, it is helpful to think of two general ways of classifying resources. (1) In terms of the value of the resources, some are primary and others secondary, though the resources in each group may be similar or dissimilar. Primary resources are those wanted for their own sake; secondary resources have instrumental value for winning primary resources. Dissimilar resources may be traded if, for example, A wants friendship from B and B wants economic aid. Or the resources traded may be similar, like friendship for friendship (e.g., the Franco-German Treaty of Cooperation, 1963). (2) In terms of the nature of the resources, some are limited and some unlimited. A limited resource is one of finite quantity, an example being the manpower of a nation. An unlimited resource is one which can be expanded indefinitely, like friendship. Nations contemplating a negotiation are likely to exert greatest efforts to win resources that are *primary and limited*, because they are the most highly valued and the most difficult to secure.

A mutually compatible value system and the ability to communicate values with respect to resources possessed or desired help to promote the occurrence of negotiation, since actors are made aware that they may be better off if they negotiate.[2] Mutual trust allows potential actors to believe that the information they get from others about resources is correct and that the others will keep the commitments resulting from negotiation.

Having time to negotiate (see item A-8 in the prenegotiation phase) influences the type of negotiation which ensues. In a crisis, the urgency of the problem may compel informal and unilateral or bilateral negotiation rather than formal parliamentary negotiation as in the UN. Interference by a third party is illustrated by West Germany's prevention of US efforts to begin serious negotiations with the Soviet Union for an atomic nonproliferation agreement.

"*Willingness to negotiate*" is related to the nature of the goals sought by the potential parties and the degree to which those goals are believed to be obtainable by negotiation. Parties with a direct interest in the disposition of the issue and who have given a pledge to negotiate are more likely to be willing to negotiate than are parties with goals only tangentially related to the issue or parties without negotiating commitments.

Willingness to negotiate is also a function of the degree of certainty of obtaining goals and the ability to enhance this certainty. Higher certainty is related to ability to define the issue and to "size" it; ability to choose the parties and to limit the number to the optimal range; and ability to choose the setting for the negotiation.

When parties can define the issue, they can make it compatible with their goals and thereby increase the chance of attaining their goals by negotiation. The "size" of the issue refers to the degree to which the issue influences the intrrelationships of the potential parties.[3] If the issue is too large, it evokes intense feelings and negotiation or compromise may become impossible. If the issue is too small, it may be nonnegotiable because the risk of neglecting it is negligible. "Sizing" puts the issue in the intermediate range which is optimal for negotiability.

The optimal range for the number of parties to a future negotiation lies between that number having a direct interest in the issue and the highest number of those who believe they could be satisfied with benefits which would not later be seriously challenged by strong third parties. As the reader will notice, this maximum number involves the "dilemma of limited benefits" discussed earlier. As a result, potential participants in a negotiation feel contradictory pressures to maximize and to minimize the number of parties.[4]

Ability to choose the parties to a future negotiation is related to freedom to define the issue and to select the outcome. Some issues have automatic parties (e.g., Alsace–Lorraine 1871–1914, and the Berlin problem today); functional issues frequently define the parties, as when a conference on naval arms is limited to naval powers. Some parties have predictable goals and established negotiating styles, so that their inclusion restricts the possible outcomes. An example is Bismarck, whose alliances were directed toward preventing a French alliance with another major power (Schmitt, 1947, pp. 6–7).

Ability to choose the setting refers to the fact that small powers gain advantages in negotiations within international organizations, where the rule of legal equality often prevails, whereas great powers may find it more advantageous to resort to traditional or unilateral diplomacy.

Even if a party perceives little certainty of obtaining its goals in negotiation, it may still be willing to negotiate if it sees some way of enhancng that certainty: for instance, using military force in conjunction with negotiation; having a unique resource which others want; being able to name a mediator favorable to one's own side; establishing an irrevocable commitment to a particular outcome; obtaining support for one's position from other parties, including world opinion; pleasing the opponent by a prior act, with an eye to reciprocation during the negotiation itself; and being able to choose which parties one begins negotiations with, because beginning with a favorable party may provoke concessions from others later on.

II. Negotiation phase

The first item in this phase of the model expresses the point made above under "the problem of singular and plural positions," namely, that higher goal satisfaction is likely when parties participate as individuals rather than as group members. Several considerations are involved here. (1) The greater the likelihood that the parties can win their positions, the more they will seek to participate as individuals. (2) If individual parties form a group, other parties are impelled to seek group support to counter the power of the group position. (3) The greater the uncertainty of winning the position, the more likely are the parties to negotiate as a group.

These considerations are related to the second item, "symmetrical negotiations." For a great power, symmetrical negotiations offer less certainty of winning goals than do hegemonic negotiations. Thus symmetrical negotiations invoke pressures favoring group positions, while hegemonic negotiations are likely to involve individual participation by the great power(s) and pressures for a group position for the small power(s). There is a tendency, therefore, for hegemonic negotiations to become symmetrical.

The model shows that bilateral negotiations, and multilateral negotiations where positions are or can be polarized, are more likely to result in an agreement which is enforced than are unilateral negotiations or multilateral ones where the positions are not polarized. Unilateral negotiations often involve a coerced settlement and the possibility of reprisals. Polarized positions limit the spread of the potential resolution. The wider the spread of the resolution— i.e., the more positions it accommodates—the lower its strength of direction, which means that the resolution is less likely to be an enduring solution to the problem.[5] Polarized positions make accommodation easier, since fewer distinct positions must be considered, and they help to insure that the resolution answers the problem being negotiated.

Proposals based on long-term goals are more adaptable to compromise than are those based on short-term ones, because parties can accept a compromise involving losses in the hope of making up the loss in later negotiations. When goals are long-term, moreover, proposals can "begin small"—moderate change in the status quo, small gains from the negotiation—in the hope of winning a series of small gains over a protracted period.[6] The fewer the number of units in a proposal, the easier is overall agreement on the units. Proposals calling for moderate changes in the status quo transfer the certainty of the present into the future. Parties can count on doing what they have been doing, with few additional restraints on behavior. Agreement on the status quo often occurs by default, when parties are unable to agree on the nature and degree of changes desired collectively.

A compromise involving a trade of similar goods is an easier basis for agreement than one involving a trade of dissimilar goods, and it is more certain of implementation because the complexities of a two-step compromise are avoided. When dissimilar goods (such as friendship and economic aid) are to be traded, the parties must agree on equivalent values as well as on the overall "volume" of trading.

A compromise with a future rather than a present focus is easier to reach and easier to enforce. Deferring to the future gives greater choice about the settlement, including a settlement on the merits of the issue, and parties may be more willing to accept obligations when these are not immediate. On the other hand it is easier to withdraw from future commitments; this means that attention must be given to ways of making withdrawal more difficult—for instance, by inserting "irrevocable commitment" terms in the agreement itself.

The advantages of a solution which "upgrades the common interest" (item C-3 in the negotiation phase) have been discussed by Haas (1961). This is an enduring kind of compromise because parties who forsake benefits in the present are likely to want guarantees on benefits to be received in the future, and this puts great emphasis on implementation.

Negotiations which are capable of legitimation to various constituencies—in terms of the reason for the negotiation, the proposals advanced, and the resolution—are more likely to result in an agreement which is enforced. Capacity for legitimation implies that the proposals and outcomes are moderate and that constituency desires were influential, so that there will be greater support in the enforcement phase.

As has been noted already, negotiations inspired by a crisis are less likely than noncrisis ones to produce an enforceable agreement. Crisis negotiations may involve a higher common interest in reaching an agreement, but the agreement may involve pledges of large resources from which the parties may want to withdraw later on. Noncrisis negotiations inspire lesser obligations which can remain acceptable throughout the enforcement phase.

III. Agreement phase

There are four possible outcomes of a negotiation: compromise, unilateral solution, nonsolution with a persisting desire for compromise, and failure. A compromise implies that several or all parties influenced the terms of the outcome; it is thus the only outcome which produces satisfaction for the largest number of parties. Where limited benefits are involved, every agreement carries risks because of dissatisfied third parties who receive no benefits; the enduring agreement is one which confers maximum benefits while avoiding reprisals from third parties, since reprisals can preclude enforcement. Agreements can be designed so as to minimize the possibility of reprisals. If the agreement is conditionally open to future signatories, the parties can guarantee their benefits, grant accession later to parties who may claim an interest, and control the identity and number of parties who benefit by accession. If the agreement is closed to future signatories, the present participants have a maximal guarantee of their own benefits, but third parties may be compensated if there are terms specifying a later conference or establishing an institution for future negotiations.

Any agreement, if it is to endure, must continue to confer greater gains than obligations or costs for each participant. Terms which specify task- and issue-expansion allow the possibility of increased benefits in the future to counterbalance the acceptance of present obligations. When the obligations seem onerous, the ability to take on new tasks may encourage continued support from the participants.[7]

IV. Implementation phase

Voluntary enforcement implies that the agreement confers benefits and risks that are favorably balanced for all or nearly all the parties. Coercion is costly and may provoke reprisals. Thus parties may prefer lesser benefits in an agreement enforced voluntarily to greater benefits enforced by coercion.

In an agreement reached by symmetrical negotiations (item A-1 in the implementation phase), each party can grant the others no better or worse concessions than they grant him; all may therefore perceive themselves as gaining equal benefits, though none may be entirely satisfied.

Casuistry is a means by which parties who receive benefits create perceptions of benefits for nonreceivers (see Schelling, 1960, pp. 28–35). It is useful in the short term but may be a disadvantage over longer periods, assuming congruence between perception and reality, because the user of casuistry may be compelled to share benefits in the implementation phase or to agree to a future conference where sharing might materialize. Expanding the benefits, as by task- and issue-expansion, may win the voluntary compliance of parties who are now dissatisfied with their gains. It may also aid enforcement by holding out the possibility of gains to third parties.

When an agreement is only one of a series, the long-term satisfactions of the parties are potentially greater. Each agreement can be moderate and confer small gains, but the long-term effect may be great gains for the parties. Each successive agreement allows the parties to insert terms favorable to enforcement. If the initial agreement was not well designed for enforcement (for example, if it was not based on the merits of the issue, or if it included "escape clauses"), a subsequent agreement could correct these defects.

Similar in effect are agreements which inspire later agreements by "spillover." The parties and the nature of the later agreements may be the same or different from the original agreement, but when "spillover" does happen, the initial agreement was usually a successful one in terms of the benefits for the signatories and the endurance of its implementation. One such success improves the chances for future agreements.

Positive benefits confer gains in resources; negative benefits confer avoidance of punishment. An agreement conferring positive benefits is an easier one both to reach and to enforce, because all parties want to make and keep gains in resources; the problem is how to distribute the gains in a way that satisfies the parties. When an agreement confers negative benefits, all parties want to avoid all the choices; the problem is how to distribute the punishments in a way that is least unsatisfactory to the parties.

The endurance of an agreement depends partly on its ability to maintain optimal pressure on all the signatories.[8] Optimal pressure means that each party feels he is better off with the agreement than without it, despite the obligations involved. Optimal pressure reduces the likelihood that any party will threaten withdrawal from the agreement in order to obtain further concessions from parties with a greater interest in enforcement. Since task-expansion and issue-expansion are methods of manipulating future costs and gains, they may be used to maintain optimal pressure. If implementation solves the problem which inspired the agreement, so that no additional benefits are forthcoming, the agreement will dissolve unless the problem can be redefined, or more broadly defined, to confer additional benefits.

Implementation also depends on the absence of third-party reprisals to preclude enforcement. Open agreements conferring limited benefits typically involve less-than-maximum gains for the signatories, in order to avoid such reprisals from strong third parties. Greater benefits can therefore be conferred if the agreement is kept secret from third parties.

Finally, successful implementation also depends on the absence of those outside events which could prevent enforcement by making enforcement unnecessary, undesirable, impossible, or ineffective. Such an event may remove the problem to which the agreement applies; it may impose considerations unforeseen at the time of the agreement; or it may show up deficiencies in the agreement.

Anyone who attempts to devise a theory of bargaining must make choices among various incompatibilities present in bargaining. The theorist's choices define the predominant concern of the theory. As a result, some bargaining theories are helpful in describing one of the phases but give little information about the other phases.

The present model of international negotiation takes a broad view of bargaining, since attention was given to each phase of the process and to finding elements helpful in reaching an enforceable agreement. The study of these latter elements underscores the possibility that international negotiation is essentially a conservative process, involving constituency participation or support and modest changes in the status quo, at least in the short term.

NOTES

[1] For example, Iklé (1964), Levine (1963), Liska (1962), Schelling (1960), Vatcher (1958), Kertesz (1957), Nogee (1960), and Pruitt (1962).

[2] Kuhn (1964) analyzes the nature of values in international negotiation.

[3] Fisher (1964) describes the "size" of issues.

[4] A parallel analysis is Riker's treatment of the "size principle" (1962, pp. 41–88).

[5] These statements are an application of Downs' analysis of voting ideology (1957, ch. 8).

[6] Levine analyzes "conditional" and "unconditional" positions (1963, pp. 26–33). In the former, the position "begins small" and may or may not be relevant to the ultimate goal desired. In the latter, the position "begins big" and one can more easily predict the nature of the goal to which the negotiating position relates.

[7] Article 2 of the NATO Pact pledges members to mutual economic cooperation. Secretary of State Rusk recently proposed that the NATO members "explore new and broader fields" and mentioned common policies toward Communism, a common monetary system, and new cooperative trade policies.

[8] Liska analyzes the endurance of alliances in relation to the optimal pressure from the external enemy (1962, pp. 97–101).

REFERENCES CITED

Downs, Anthony
  An Economic Theory of Democracy. New York, 1957.
Fisher, Roger
  "Fractionating Conflict," Daedalus, Summer 1964.
Haas, Ernst B.
  "International Integration: The European and the Universal Process," International Organization, 15, 3 (Summer 1961).
Iklé, Fred Charles
  How Nations Negotiate. New York, 1964.

KERTESZ, STEPHEN D.
"Reflections on Soviet and American Negotiating Behavior," *Review of Politics*, 19, 1 (Jan. 1957).

KUHN, ALFRED
"Bargaining Power in Transactions: A Basic Model of Interpersonal Relationships," *American Journal of Economics and Sociology*, 23, 1 (Jan. 1964).

LEVINE, ROBERT A.
The Arms Race. Cambridge, Mass., 1963.

LISKA, GEORGE
Nations in Alliance. Baltimore, 1962.

NOGEE, JOSEPH
"The Diplomacy of Disarmament," *International Conciliation*, 526 (Jan. 1960).

PRUITT, DEAN G.
"An Analysis of Responsiveness between Nations," *Journal of Conflict Resolution*, 6, 1 (March 1962), 5–18.

RIKER, WILLIAM II.
The Theory of Political Coalitions. New Haven, 1962.

SCHELLING, THOMAS C.
The Strategy of Conflict. Cambridge, Mass., 1960.

SCHMITT, BERNADOTTE E.
Triple Alliance and Triple Entente. New York, 1947.

VATCHER, WILLIAM H., JR.
Panmunjom. New York, 1958.

THE ROLE OF SUMMITRY
IN CONFLICT RESOLUTION
AT THE UNITED NATIONS

Michael H. Prosser

MICHAEL H. PROSSER received his B.A. and M.A. from Ball State University and his Ph.D. in 1964 at the University of Illinois. He has taught at the State University of New York at Buffalo, Indiana University and the University of Virginia where he is currently professor of speech and chairman of the Department of Speech and Drama. He has been a visiting faculty member at Queens College of the City University of New York, California State College at Hayward, and Memorial University in St. John's, Newfoundland. He has served as editor of Today's Speech, as executive secretary of the New York State Speech Association, as Chairman of the Council for International Communication Development of the Midwest Universities Consortium for International Activities, and as Chairman of the national Speech Communication Association's Commission for International and Intercultural Communication. Prosser has edited An Ethic for Survival: Adlai Stevenson Speaks on International Affairs, 1936–1965 (William Morrow, 1969); with Thomas W. Benson, Readings in Classical Rhetoric (Allyn and Bacon, 1969); and Sow the Wind, Reap the Whirlwind: Heads of State Address the United Nations (William Morrow, 1970). Prosser is listed in International Dictionary of Biography (London), Writers' Directory (London), Contemporary Authors, Who's Who in American Education, Leaders in Education, Directory of American Scholars, and Community Leaders of America. Prosser is an associate of the Danforth Foundation.

Francis Kaoma Musonda, a reporter for *The Zambia Mail*, stressed that the Third Nonaligned Nations Conference in Lusaka, Zambia, during September 1970 was Zambia's "biggest event since independence in 1964." He described everyone involved with planning the conference or constructing the sixty-two villas for heads of state and other dignitaries as being possessed with "summit fever" (Musonda 1970). Indeed, summit fever has characterized much of the attitude toward high-level diplomatic communication during and since World War II. The autumn of 1970 not only witnessed the Lusaka Conference but also an Arab summit conference and the twenty-fifth anniversary celebrations of the founding of the United Nations at which eighty-five special envoys of member states, including forty-two heads of state and heads of government, were present for some or most of the ten-day celebration in the General Assembly. We are reminded of such multinational peace conferences as that at Vienna in 1815, Versailles in 1919, and Potsdam in 1945.

D. C. Watt suggests that the archetype of all summit meetings is that at which the victorious ruler in classical times dictated terms to the bedraggled and humiliated leaders of the defeated states. He argues that for a summit conference to occur, international tension must be considerable; such a conference is not a meeting of foreign ministers or even of heads of state, though

256

I would disagree with this latter prescription, but heads of government; it must be multilateral instead of bilateral to qualify as a true summit conference; and one recognized leader of each participating government must hold the genuine power of head of government (Watt 1967:495–496). Watt contends that the desire for summit meetings begins either with the liberal-idealist viewpoint, in which world leaders believe that only face-to-face contact with their opposites will restore communication and allay the mutual suspicions that are driving each side headlong into the abyss, or with the professional-realist point of view, in which leaders believe that international contact is a matter of inter-pretation of the standpoint of one partner in contact with the other. Such cross-cultural communication at the highest levels is fraught with high elements of risk, Watt believes, for:

> Firstly, there is the danger that the concern to demonstrate goodwill may lead to the hasty and unconsidered granting of concessions, never subse-quently recoverable. . . . Secondly, it is by no means certain that such meetings deepen understanding; they may as well perpetuate new misun-derstandings. . . . Thirdly, a failure "at the summit" can so embitter and exacerbate public opinion on each side as seriously to compromise and in-hibit the mutual freedom of manoeuvre of the participating governments thereafter (Watt 1967:493–494).

It is clear to me that whereas full summit conferences, so recorded by histori-ans, must be multilateral, summitry such as the meetings at Camp David be-tween Khrushchev and Eisenhower, or in Moscow between Macmillan and Khrushchev, or the Kennedy-Khrushchev meeting in Vienna, or the Johnson-Kosygin meeting at Glassboro State College, as well as the personal diplomacy of a state's highest leader, for example, at the United Nations, merits serious study as well.

A great advocate of open and personal diplomacy, Woodrow Wilson sig-nificantly advanced the concept of summitry and summit conferences in this century. Unfortunately, summitry must bear success not only on the interna-tional level but also at the domestic level. Internationally, Wilson had con-siderable success; but domestically, his international programs have generally been considered failures, for example, the League of Nations. In 1936, Emperor Haile Selassie of Ethiopia, the first head of state to assert his personal diplo-macy in the League, made a plea that the world governments protect his hapless state against the aggressive attacks by the Italians and warned that failure to heed his words could spell the end of the organization as a functioning entity. He drew little response. Prime Minister Chamberlain's mistaken faith that the summit conference in Munich had "given Peace for our times" led Presi-dent Roosevelt to reject the request of Prince Konoye, Prime Minister of Japan in 1941, for a summit meeting because he believed, perhaps rightly, that he would forever be accused of being a party to a "Far Eastern Munich."

During World War II, Churchill, Roosevelt, and Stalin met several times. Prime Minister Churchill wrote enthusiastically in 1944 that "if the heads of the three Governments could meet once a month there would be no problems between us which could not be swiftly and I trust sensibly solved" (Churchill 1952:III, 89). After the Yalta Summit, he assured his countrymen: "I feel that their word is their bond. I know of no government which stands to its obligations even in its own despite, more solidly, than the Russian government. I decline absolutely to embark upon a discussion about Russian good faith" (Churchill 1960:356). Roosevelt's assessment of the Yalta meeting was that "the atmosphere at this dinner was as that of a family, and it was in those words that he liked to characterize the relation that existed between our three countries" (Sherwood 1948:869–870). Stalin was less sanguine:

> Perhaps you think that just because we are the allies of the English that we have forgotten who they are and who Churchill is. They find nothing sweeter than to trick their allies. . . . Churchill is the kind, who, if you don't watch him, will slip a Kopeck out of your pocket . . . and Roosevelt? Roosevelt is not like that. He dips in his hand for bigger coins. But Churchill—Churchill even for a Kopeck [Djilas 1962:73].

Prior to the 1960 World Summit Conference at the United Nations, eighteen heads of state and heads of government utilized their personal diplomacy in addresses at the United Nations. In some ways, the first twenty-five year history of the United Nations has demonstrated a continuous effort at summitry since the world organization has always paid special homage to visiting heads of state and of government, has provided as one of its fundamental services the legitimizing of states, large and small, and has offered a world forum to visiting state leaders. One hundred twenty-nine addresses of heads of state and heads of government have now been collected in *Sow the Wind, Reap the Whirlwind: Heads of State Address the United Nations* in two volumes which cover the first twenty-five years of history of the United Nations (Prosser 1970). In the early years, the statesmen came largely for ceremonial reasons, evoking the principles and ideals of the charter and a united world. President Harry S Truman, newly the successor to Roosevelt, had spoken to the assembled delegates at the San Francisco Conference by direct radio hookup as they began their deliberations to create a charter; and he addressed them in person when they concluded its drafting in June 1965. His addresses and those early speeches of Prime Minister Clement Atlee and President Vincent Auriol of France to the assembled delegates largely represented the symbolic hospitality of countries that were then hosts to the General Assembly. Like the later intention to rotate the summit conferences between the four major capitals of the World War Allies, early plans for the United Nations had been for the major capitals to serve as hosts for different General Assemblies.

Even in 1950, during the height of the Korean War, President Truman's address to the United Nations, in which he discussed "the direct challenge to the principles of the Charter" posed by the invasion of Korea and "the overwhelming response" of United Nations forces, emphasized customary topics of universal morality, faith of men in human values, the charter as a living instrument, progress in human welfare, and the laying of the foundations for peace and disarmament. Truman's statement about the great roles that the United Nations had to play in preventing wars, although no doubt sincere, was similar to the platitudes offered by other world leaders from the rostrum of the United Nations during this period: "First, it provides a way for negotiation and the settlement of disputes. Secondly, it provides a way for utilizing the collective strength of Member nations, under the Charter, to prevent aggression. Thirdly, it provides a way through which, once the danger of aggression is reduced, the nations can be relieved of the burden of armaments" (Truman 1970:56). Corresponding sentiments can be found in the early speeches of the Presidents of Mexico, Ecuador, Panama, and Uruguay, whose states were signatories to the charter and who were state visitors to the United States, as well as in the addresses of King Paul of the Hellenes, President Tubman of Liberia, King Saud of Arabia, Queen Elizabeth of England, and King Mohammed of Morocco. In 1955, variation was added to the traditional themes of peace, freedom, the development of human rights, and progress, when President Castillo Armas of Guatemala urged "peaceful coexistence" among nations, even among nations of different cultural and political systems. American "sabre-rattling" made many people throughout the world fear that the United States was unwilling to accept such a doctrine.

In Eisenhower's address to the United Nations during the fall of 1953 after his election to office, a custom that had already been initiated by Truman in 1949 and was continued by Presidents Kennedy, Johnson, and Nixon, he warned that "the stockpile of atomic weapons exceeds by many times the total equivalent of the total of all bombs and all shells that came from every plane and every gun in every theatre of war in all the years of the Second World War." He urged that governments should jointly contribute from their stockpiles of normal uranium and fissionable materials to an Atomic Control Agency set up under United Nations auspices (Eisenhower 1970a:83–90). Although of interest as an aspect of personal diplomacy, the concept was scarcely new and had been the first order of business that the Americans submitted to the newly created United Nations in what had been called the Baruch Plan. Watt writes that it was Churchill, inspired by the death of Stalin in 1953, and signs of thaw in East-West relations, that initiated the idea of a four-power summit conference which developed into the 1955 Geneva Summit Conference (Watt 1967:498). At the tenth-anniversary celebrations of the drafting of the charter at the San Francisco Opera House, President Eisenhower called the summit conference about to take place "a season of high hopes for the world" and, in the custom of world leaders at the United Nations, pledged his country's "unswerving loyalty to the United Nations" (Eisenhower 1970b:87–102). If Churchill expected the conference to be small, as had been the Teheran, Yalta, and Potsdam summits, the one hundred persons present at the formal meetings were disappointing. Additionally, Watt writes that the Western allies were negotiating beyond the area of their effective reach, especially in relation to the West Berlin and two-Germany questions and because the Americans, in particular, believed that the Soviet system was still basically insecure. Instead, the Soviets were negotiating from a level of strength, and therefore the Americans consistently misjudged their own capabilities and strengths as well as those of the Soviets. Watt contends: "No progress whatever was made at the Foreign Ministerial level, either during the 'summit' conference itself or at the meeting of Foreign Ministers which followed in November" (Watt 1967:498). Nevertheless, President Eisenhower saw as a result of the conference "evidence of a new friendliness in the world." The "Spirit of Geneva" was hailed as a new mark of respect among world leaders (Rogers 1955:147; Davis 1965:190).

At the same time, the Americans were following an ambiguous policy in which they were threatening to "unleash Chiang Kai Shek"; Secretary of State Dulles had told a House Committee on June 10, 1955, that the Soviet Union was "on the point of collapsing"; the Secretary of State had announced that "we have the initiative, very distinctly" in the Middle East and in South Asia; and Eisenhower praised him because they had jointly "conducted the nation three times to the brink of war and then averted catastrophe" (*New York Times*, November 30, 1955, p. 8 and February 24, 1956, p. 1). Gerald P. Mohrmann suggests that Dulles's policy of brinkmanship carried with it the implicit reliance upon the personal confrontation at the highest levels: "This concept is an extension of the belief that a man cannot look another in the eye and lie, which is in turn an extension of the conviction that personal relationships will clearly reveal the motives and attitudes of all parties" (Mohrmann 1967:176).

In 1958, the situations in Jordan and Lebanon caused the General Assembly to hold its Third Special Emergency Session. President Eisenhower made what may be considered his first nonceremonial address to the United Nations to press the point that the United States had not invaded Lebanon as the Soviet Union had charged but had responded "to a call for help. If it is made an international crime to help a small nation maintain its independence, then indeed the possibilities of conquest are unlimited. . . . We will have let loose forces that could generate great disasters" (Eisenhower 1970c:124). He proposed a six-point program: United Nations concern for Lebanon, United Nations measures to preserve peace in Jordan, an end to the fomenting of civil strife from outside, the establishment of a United Nations Peace Force in the troubled areas, a regional economic development plan to assist and accelerate improvement of the living standards of the people in these Arab states, and steps to avoid the development of a new arms spiral in the area.

The personal diplomatic persuasion of American presidents Truman and Eisenhower at the United Nations had become somewhat commonplace; and only the address in 1958 of Prince Norodom Sihanouk, Chief of State of Cambodia, evoked much international interest. During his major substantive speech he lectured the Great Powers:

> Since listening to the debates between the great Powers and hearing them accuse each other of aggression, in the name of totally opposing moral systems, we have realized that the great Powers, encased in the armor of their own pride and bound hand and foot by their own ideologies, will never admit that they may themselves be at fault. . . . In these last three years, I have made friendly visits to most of the countries in the Western Bloc and in the Socialist Bloc, and both points of view have been dinned into my ears. . . . Just as any man needs a mirror to see himself from behind, so do the great Powers sometimes need the neutral countries to point out to them the flaws in their own reasoning [Sihanouk 1970a:133–141].

The tenseness caused by the Jordanian and Lebanese crises in 1958 was coupled with the Soviet pressure that began with Khrushchev's six-month ultimatum on Berlin in November 1958. Watt reflects that it

> marked the opening of a new and more obviously dangerous phase in East-West relations, as with it Soviet policy abandoned the previous policy of conserving the status quo under the "Two Germanies" policy and swung in a new revisionist direction on Berlin. The threat was so direct that it called forth a new outbreak of diplomacy by heads of government, a ploy in which Khrushchev has shown considerable personal skill and enjoyment since his rise to power in 1955 [Watt 1967:499; see also Plischke 1968].

Amazingly, the threat encouraged Prime Minister Macmillan's journey to Russia to seek an easing of tensions. Foreign Minister Mikoyan paid an official visit to the United States, and Vice-President Nixon made his visit to the Soviet Union. Theodore Otto Windt, Jr., in his essay "The Rhetoric of Peaceful Coexistence: Khrushchev in America, 1959," which has been reprinted in this volume, assesses the Khrushchev visit to the United States as the beginning of a major change in the cold-war tensions between the socialist and Western states. He believes that the carnival atmosphere distorted the significance of the visit, which was intended less to serve as the setting for negotiations on major international issues than to establish a new mutual trust from which subsequent discussions between the Soviet Union and the United States could proceed. Khrushchev publicly announced: "It is important to find a common language and a common understanding on the questions we should settle" (Khrushchev 1959:31). The "Spirit of Camp David" encouraged both statesmen to extoll the role of personal summit diplomacy to reduce the cold war. Plans were made gradually to hold a Big Four Summit Conference in Paris between the heads of government of the United Kingdom, France, the United States, and the USSR, and for future summit meetings in the other three capitals, with exchange visits between the four leaders.

As the first socialist head of government to address the United Nations in its first fourteen years of history, and because of the importance attached to his state visit to the United States, Premier Khrushchev's September 18, 1959, address to the United Nations assumed extraordinary significance. President of the General Assembly, Victor A. Belaunde of Peru, introduced him with the words: "At a time when the eyes of all mankind are turned to the United Nations, your Excellency's presence here answers to the universal desire for peace and friendly relations among all nations." A major problem still threatening the world, Chairman Khrushchev observed, was the continuance of the cold war. As a realistic and urgent goal, steps to end the cold war should include a stopping of calls to war, settlement of issues that grew out of World War II, by which he was referring to the settlement of the German problem, broadening of contacts among peoples, admission of states such as the People's Republic of China to the United Nations, increased cooperation between the two major powers, the abandonment of revisionist cliques within national governments, which still attempted to foster the cold-war tensions, the freeing of backward peoples from colonial dependence, and the conclusion of an international treaty regarding disarmament and the reduction of military budgets.

As the title of his address "Let Us Disarm Completely" implies, Chairman Khrushchev devoted the major part of his speech to the concept of total disarmament. The proposals were far-reaching and innovative: the completion of disarmament by all states in four years; the abolishing of land armies, naval fleets, and air forces; the closing of military bases on foreign territories; the destruction of all atomic and hydrogen bombs and military rockets; the preservation only of an internal police force; and the establishment of an international control organ. He argued: "A decision to carry out general and complete disarmament within a short space of time, and the execution of that decision, would mark the beginning of a new stage in international life. . . . We say sincerely to all countries: As against the slogan 'Let us arm!' which still enjoys currency in some places, we advance the slogan 'Let us disarm completely'" (Khrushchev 1970a:157–160).

Neutral delegations especially welcomed the Soviet display of initiative. Shortly after, Khrushchev announced a massive reduction in Soviet troop strength, which seemed to be an indication of his good faith. Certainly, as I have written elsewhere:

> The Heads of State and Heads of Government who address the United Nations consciously choose that rostrum as their world forum. Their action, . . . is not merely a *means* of doing, but rather a *way* of *being* peacemakers. Despite other conflicting motives, their very presence there symbolically hallows their urgent wish with Dr. Sukarno that "a new day has dawned. We dare not fail" [Prosser 1970:17].

Windt points out that the Chinese believed and feared Khrushchev's statements at the United Nations and throughout the United States:

> The Chinese date the break in Sino-Soviet relations from this visit to the United States. An editorial in *People's Daily* on February 27, 1963 charged that Khrushchev violated the agreements reached at the Moscow Conference during his trip and by the acts that issued from commitments made at that time. Nikita Khrushchev's visit may have marked a personal triumph for him, but it also signaled the end of the Chinese Russian alliance [see Windt, this volume].

It is impossible to tell whether his proposal toward complete and general disarmament would have worked. It may be naïve to think that had the American-Soviet detente progressed satisfactorily, without the 1960 reversal or without the Sino-Soviet split, considerable progress could have been made toward fulfilling his proposal.

His address to the United Nations and that of President Sekou Touré of Guinea to the United Nations in November marked a real turning point in personal head of state and head of government diplomacy at the United Nations. With Ghana's independence in 1956, the universal movement in black Africa was toward freedom from the colonial powers. In his address, Touré warned the member states of the United Nations that: "All plans to check Africa's unwavering determination to regain its dignity are being frustrated one by one and the thrilling cry of 'independence' resounds throughout our continent. Thus, Africa, that great question mark, is today in the grip of two irresistible forces—independence and unity—which are releasing its latent energies." He argued that Africa's first goal was to rid itself of all colonial paternalism and exploitation. He called for free and selfless cooperation between the developed countries and those not yet developed so that human misery in Africa could be eliminated while the struggle to preserve peace could be heightened (Touré 1970a:169–183). The striking aspect of the speech was that it served as a sort of manifesto to the world that African states would no longer tolerate colonial dominance. Curiously, whenever a vote in the United Nations was taken that pitted the colonial powers against the African states, the United States delegation typically abstained or sided with their allies, the European colonial powers. Accordingly, Touré's admonition was received with mixed emotions by the Western delegations.

When the U-2 event occurred, plans for the forthcoming Paris Summit Conference appeared seriously jeopardized. On May 12, in an address at the Conference on World Tensions at the University of Chicago, Adlai Stevenson worried about the potential success of the conference in Paris:

> I hope and pray that the prospect for a test-ban agreement at the Summit has not been harmed by this confusing announcement [Eisenhower's statement of May 7 that the United States would resume underground nuclear test explosions] just when everything looked as if there was for the first time a real chance—perhaps a last chance—to bring the development of nuclear weapons under reasonable control before they spread further through the world and before they become still more lethal and versatile [Stevenson 1969, 251].

When the Paris Summit Conference became clearly a failure, Stevenson issued a terse statement saying that although Khrushchev had wrecked it, "Eisenhower had handed him the crowbar and the sledgehammer to wreck it." Windt places the blame more directly on Eisenhower:

> Khrushchev trusted Eisenhower to help ease cold-war tensions during the 1959 trip. Khrushchev could not say publicly that he trusted capitalists or he would have seriously impaired his power-base. But he could praise a war-hero President whose wartime acts were still admired in the Soviet Union. Then the U-2 incident occurred. In his private statements Khrushchev had to condemn the United States for the flight, but he emphasized in two different statements that he did not believe Eisenhower knew anything about them. Clearly, Khrushchev was offering Eisenhower a way out of a political crisis. When Eisenhower took full responsibility for them, Khrushchev had no choice than to refuse to meet with him in Paris [see Windt, this volume].

Following the collapse of the Paris Summit Conference, a period of profound world anxiety occurred. Premier Khrushchev called for a World Summit Conference at the United Nations at the opening of the fifteenth session of the General Assembly to solve problems left unresolved by the failure of the Paris Summit Conference. Since he had proposed a program of complete and general disarmament at the fourteenth session, he urged the most responsible representatives of every state in the world to attend the General Assembly general debate so that jointly they could solve the problems plaguing the world because of a failure to take seriously his urgent plea for complete and total disarmament. During his first address at the United Nations in 1960, Khrushchev warned: "In other words, as I have already once said, we have not much choice: it is either peaceful coexistence, which would promote the highest human ideals, or else coexistence 'at daggers drawn'" (Khrushchev 1970b:269). Twenty-two heads of state and heads of government did journey to New York for the general debate, most of whom were present for much or most of the three-week session. Socialist leaders joining Khrushchev included Marshal Tito of Yugoslavia, President Novotny of Czechoslovakia, Major General Shehu of Albania, First Secretary Gheorghiu-Dej of Romania, First Secretary Gomulka of Poland, Chairman Zhivkov of Bulgaria, and Prime Minister Castro of Cuba, who linked himself with the socialist governments. Other world leaders included President Nkrumah of Ghana, Prime Minister Diefenbaker of Canada, President Nasser of the United Arab Republic, Prime Minister Krag of Denmark, Prince Sihanouk of Cambodia, Prime Minister Macmillan of the United Kingdom, President Sukarno of Indonesia, King Hussein I of Jordan, Prime Minister Nehru of India, President Salaam of Lebanon, Prime Minister Nash of New Zealand, Prime Minister Menzies of Australia, and President Touré of Guinea. None of the twenty Latin American State members besides Cuba sent their governmental leaders, in part because American diplomats urged those states associated with the so-called Western interests to boycott the meeting because they regarded it as a propaganda ploy by Premier Khrushchev and his socialist allies.

Watt probably would not call this meeting a genuine summit conference, despite the fact that a high degree of international tension existed, that it was multilateral in nature, and that those present represented widely divergent and opposing views. Watt has established the following set of variables for a successful summit conference: The participants must genuinely desire a reduction in tension; they must be convinced that their opponents also desire a reduction in tension; all participants must be genuinely and clearly in control of their own domestic political situations; and finally, there must be a genuine assurance of agreement before the summit meeting begins (Watt 1967:499–501). Certainly, all of the twenty-two leaders who used the rostrum of the United Nations to express their views on international issues professed their own desire for peace, cordial relations, and an end to colonial domination of peoples, and a new détente between the Great Powers. It is clear, however, from reading the more than four hundred and fifty pages of speeches uttered at this general debate on substantive matters by the heads of state and heads of government, not to mention the vast number of speeches by other members of delegations and statements made on procedural matters, particularly on whether the seating of the People's Republic of China should be placed on the agenda, that almost everyone doubted the sincerity of some of those involved. For example, after Eisenhower petulantly refused to meet Khrushchev while the two were in the General Assembly together, Nasser, Sukarno, Nkrumah, Tito, and Nehru drafted a resolution simply urging the American and Soviet heads of government to renew contact. Also, angry statements were made by pro-Western sympathizers such as Menzies of Australia, Nash of New Zealand, Diefenbaker of Canada, and King Hussein of Jordan against the socialist states, ideologies, and leaders. The socialist leaders countered these statements by hurling back epithets at the Western states, ideologies, and leaders. Most likely, all the participants, at that time, were clearly in control of their domestic situations, except that the United States was in the middle of a presidential election between Senator Kennedy and Vice-President Nixon. Still, Eisenhower was in charge of the legally constituted government. None of the other participants were forced to stand for elections or were affected by coups in the immediate period after the conference. No previous Foreign Minister level meetings had been held to prepare an agenda, and the participants were guided primarily by statements like that made by Khrushchev in his first speech:

What we have in mind is that at this session of the General Assembly the representatives of the overwhelming majority of States of the world should express their views on the cardinal problems which today agitate public opinion and all the people in the world who are interested in the further development of freedom and democracy and yearn for peace for themselves and their children [Khrushchev 1970b:276].

Certainly, no assurances of success were imprinted upon any of the participants' minds. Still, the situation was so desperate that, as Watt suggests:

Only a mighty effort of imagination, understanding and will on the part of the statesmen on each side with whom the ultimate responsibility for political decision rests, an effort which can only be exerted in face-to-face contact with their opposite numbers, can restore communication, repair the break and allay the mutual suspicions which are driving each side headlong into the abyss. It will be seen that this view is essentially *polemophobic*. War is the ultimate disaster and anything, any sacrifice, is preferable to it [Watt 1967:501].

I would add that a successful summit in this situation was impossible, if, as Watt suggests, it must be a summit only of the Great Powers, though this definition seems too inflexible in principle. I would agree that Eisenhower's absence in the general debate, except for his address as the first speaker after the opening of the General Assembly, made real progress difficult, if not impossible. It is clear to me from my reading of United Nations resolutions and speeches that, except for the Suez crisis and a few other matters, when the Soviet and American delegations are in agreement on a program of action, which surprisingly is more often than most people believe, near unanimous support can be obtained from the other members. In short, the collective agreement of the two Superpowers almost always assures passage on any item, no matter how controversial. The absence of one of them, such as occurred in the resolutions on Korea when the Soviet delegation was boycotting the sessions of the Security Council and thus was unable to use its veto power, does limit any success which the conference might have. After the conference has ended, the absent Superpower must still agree to decisions made during the conference, or the likelihood is that all future related proposals and decisions will be blocked. For example, when the Soviet delegation returned after the Security Council decision, made in their absence, to send United Nations troops to Korea, the delegation stopped all future collective efforts until the matter was taken to the General Assembly through the Uniting for Peace Resolution. Again, when the Soviet Union refused to support actions and resolutions concerning the 1956 Hungarian crisis, the General Assembly was forced to act instead of the Security Council. Additionally, at the 1960 World Summit Conference, DeGaulle, who always had a disdain for the United Nations in my opinion, absented himself. Only Macmillan and Khrushchev of the Great Powers were present for the entire general debate, but of course each of them was joined by a group of friendly state leaders, plus those who considered themselves uncommitted to either the Western or socialist camps. Even if Watt does not agree that small powers can participate in a summit conference, the leaders themselves did not accept such restricting logic. President Nasser asserted strongly: "The big Powers do not alone have the right to speak about peace and war; it is mankind as a whole that has the final word" (Nasser 1970:404).

Absent, also, but much discussed, was the People's Republic of China. During the 1960 World Summit Conference, various statesmen argued strongly for the seating of the People's Republic of China. If we accept the premise that the Great Powers must be represented to assume a successful summit, no contemporary summit would be successful in China's absence. Because of Secretary of State Acheson's insistence that the Asian problem stemmed rather from the vast revolutionary changes blanketing Asia than from failures in American foreign policy, the Republican caucus in the House of Representatives passed a resolution in 1950 declaring that he "had lost the confidence of the Congress and the American people." No single congressman defended his integrity or the soundness of his proposed two-China policy (see Graebner 1961:281–283). The Dulles policy, which threatened to "unleash Chiang Kai Shek," brought the United States several times to the brink of war. When Eisenhower threatened Kennedy that a change in policy toward recognition or admission of the People's Republic of China to the United Nations would bring him into open opposition, Kennedy determined to delay taking innovative action; and the pattern of statements that Stevenson had to make in the United Nations on the China question were contradictory to his own beliefs. Johnson's delay in beginning a policy change was compounded by the Indo-China war and the frenzied Cultural Revolution that Mao initiated. Curiously, it is President Nixon, one of the strongest allies of right-wing Republicans such as Senators Knowland, Capehart, Jenner, and Joseph McCarthy during the Eisenhower Presidency, who is slowly attempting to ease the tension between the United States and the People's Republic of China. The American decision to permit our Ping-pong champions to visit China, where they were received by Chou En-lai, and the invitation for the Chinese champions to visit the United States has led to the widely repeated quip that Nixon was playing "Ping-pong diplomacy." Still, trade restrictions on nonstrategic materials have been reduced, and American diplomats began talking more seriously about a two-China policy in the United Nations. Admittedly, the policy change was slow in coming and was being prompted in part by the fact that annually the United States was becoming more isolated in the United Nations in its attitude toward admission of the People's Republic of China. The October 25, 1971, vote in the General Assembly to seat the People's Republic and to exclude the Taiwan government was overwhelming in its impact despite Nixon's moves toward better relations with the People's Republic through his announced visit to Peking and American diplomatic attempts to save the Taiwan government from exclusion. Whether Nixon's 1972 state visits to Peking and Moscow would further peaceful relations among the Superpowers on a long range basis is still too early to determine.

As both head of state and of government and as the representative of the host state, Eisenhower spoke first at the 1960 World Summit Conference but did not remain longer at the United Nations than his address. He announced that his reason for coming was that "our human commonwealth is once again in a state of anxiety and turmoil." Although he discussed disarmament, he concentrated his remarks on the turmoil in the Congo that had occurred since the July 1960 independence and urged a five-point plan for Africa, which would assure the Africans of self-determination and assistance by the United Nations in areas such as security, development and modernization, and education (Eisenhower 1970d:185–196).

Setting the tone for those who proclaimed themselves neutralists, the second speaker, President Tito of Yugoslavia, warned: "the world has perhaps never at any time since the end of the war gone through such a period of uncertainty as it is going through today." Tito reviewed the colonial situation, especially in the Congo and Algeria, and the need for complete and general disarmament. Unlike some of the socialist leaders present, Tito very carefully refrained from denouncing the United States or its leaders and sought to serve as a bridge between the United States and the USSR (Tito 1970:197–216). When thirteen African states were admitted to the United Nations in 1960, bringing the African total to twenty-two states, the first African leader to speak in the 1960 session was President Nkrumah of Ghana. Most of his primary issues dealt with Africa. Nkrumah urged that a disarmament proposal include a clause that would forever make Africa a nuclear-free zone. He condemned the colonial process of handing independence to Africans "with one hand only to take it away with the other hand" and argued that the Congo crisis was a test case, for as the United Nations was able to succeed with the Congo, it would be able to assist other emerging areas of Africa (Nkrumah 1970:217–235).

Those who proclaimed themselves neutralists during the 1960 summit attempted to bring the Superpowers into dialogue again. The neutralists sought a fragile balance between criticism and praise for both ideological positions and continued to emphasize that although they were caught in the middle of a dangerous potential conflict, they desired only to live peacefully with friendly relations for both sides and wanted freedom and progress for their own states. They urged an end of the strife in the Middle East, the Congo, and Algeria; they condemned the racist policies of South and South West Africa; they praised the Khrushchev initiatives for complete and general disarmament and ending colonialism but rejected his arguments against Dag Hammarskjöld and for changing the functioning of the office of secretary-general into a troika of three secretary-generals representing the three divisions of the world. Prince Norodom Sihanouk of Cambodia observed that the small states were not only interested in the elimination of nuclear weapons but also conventional weapons:

> Some think that the existence of these terrible weapons so frightens the Governments as to prevent them from boldly launching a "hot war," and cause them to fall back on a "tepid" war. This "tepid" war can in fact be waged without risk to the principals instigating it, as it can be carried on through small "interposed" nations in various parts of the world.

He warned also of the dangerous position in which the world would be placed if the world summit conference were a failure (Sihanouk 1970b:471–487). President Sukarno of Indonesia warned that the session could not be considered merely a routine session discussing routine issues but was the most important conference in world history. As Nasser had done, Sukarno rejected the right for the Great Powers to make all the major policy decisions, for "the fate of the world, which is our world, will not be decided above our heads or over our bodies. It will be decided with our participation and our cooperation" (Sukarno 1970:505–535).

As the leader of one of the two Superpowers so directly involved in the increasing tensions, Nikita Khrushchev gave four addresses, two of which dealt with whether or not the Chinese question should be placed on the agenda, and two of a substantive nature. Although he had little direct dialogue with the Western leaders present, except to respond to statements they made in their own speeches or to heckle Prime Minister Macmillan with his famous shoe-pounding, he maintained extensive informal contacts during the general debate with the leaders of the neutral nations. He hosted them at a reception at the Soviet Embassy and paid a special visit to Prime Minister Castro in Harlem after Manhattan hotels had refused his delegation lodging. Since Khrushchev and other socialist leaders were restricted to Manhattan by American security precautions, he had little flexibility of movement and thus made most of his visits with the neutral leaders at the United Nations itself. His tone was considerably different than in the 1959 address to the United Nations, when he had offered his disarmament plan and had avoided attacking specific Western leaders. In his first 1960 address he charged the United States with elevating such violations of international law as the U-2 incident into deliberate state policy and with "fanning the flames of the cold war, for the unrestricted accumulation of armaments and for the destruction of every basis for international cooperation, with all the dangerous consequences which this entails." Chairman Khrushchev proclaimed three Soviet demands relating to the ending of colonialism, which were later widely discussed and applauded by the neutral state leaders. He demanded immediate freedom for all colonial countries and trust and non-self-governing territories so that the colonial system would be completely abolished; all possessions and leased areas in the territory of all states should be eliminated; and the provisions of the charter regarding self-determination should be observed by all states. Such Soviet statements on colonialism have always been well received by neutral states and have enhanced the USSR's reputation among noncommitted nations (see, for example, Hovet 1960). Additionally, Premier Khrushchev urged that since his proposals for complete and general disarmament had been ignored by the Western powers, the world leaders assembled at this World Summit Conference should themselves draw up a treaty for complete and general disarmament (Khrushchev 1970b:237–277).

In his second substantive speech toward the end of the general debate, Khrushchev exercised his delegation's right of reply, which is reserved for answering attacks made against the country's national policies. That this right prevails but is not normally used in reply to the address of a head of government is obvious from the point of order raised by President Touré of Guinea when Ambassador Wigny from Belgium asked to exercise that right after the earlier speech by Chairman Khrushchev on September 23, 1960. Then President Touré had remarked: "We know that our Assembly has always shown and will continue to show strict and impartial courtesy to all Heads of State. My delegation wishes simply to point out the drawbacks of extending the right of reply to the level of the Heads of State who have consented to lend the weight of their presence to our debates. This precedent should be avoided at all costs." Premier Khrushchev's right of reply to what he felt were misinterpretations of his earlier remarks was later responded to by Secretary-General Hammarskjöld. Khrushchev rejected charges by Western leaders that he was trying to wreck the United Nations by changing the office of secretary-general into a troika. Nevertheless, Khrushchev insisted: "I should like to repeat: we do not, and cannot place confidence in Mr. Hammarskjöld. If he himself cannot muster the courage to resign in, let us say, a chivalrous way, we shall draw the inevitable conclusions from the situation. There is no room for a man who has violated the elementary principles of justice in such an important post as that of Secretary-General (Khrushchev 1970c:537–548). Eventually, it was clear to the Soviet delegation that the support for Hammarskjöld from among the neutral nations was very strong and that they were unwilling to accept a solution which would replace a single secretary-general with three men, even if one did represent the neutral position. This was a case in which the Soviets simply misjudged the neutralists, for over a long period of time until Hammarskjöld's death in 1961, the neutral states consistently gave him their support. Nevertheless, the fact that one of the two Superpowers lost all confidence in Hammarskjöld was responsible for a marked decline in his influence as a peacemaker.

Socialist leaders who were present generally developed the Soviet themes that the two most important issues before the world summit were complete and general disarmament and an end to colonialism. They agreed also that the United Nations should be moved from New York, mainly because of the harassment which they and other statesmen had received by the American government and New York City police. The Socialist leaders, with the exception of Tito, attacked the Western leaders, especially Eisenhower's administration, with particular sharpness. Major General Shehu of Albania warned that "reactionary circles in the United States and its allies are clearly antagonistic to the policy of peaceful coexistence and are following a policy that leads to war." President Eisenhower's statement, "unprecedented in the annals of diplomatic history, proclaiming espionage to be the official and legal policy of the United States" led Chairman Shehu to wonder how such actions could be compatible with peaceful coexistence" (Shehu 1970:313–323). First Secretary Gomulka of Poland countered the statement of Prime Minister Diefenbaker accusing the socialist states with exploiting other nations by affirming the socialist policy of friendly relations among peoples in socialist states, and with other peoples. Gomulka cited as continuing reasons for East-West tension the United States' failure to accept Soviet disarmament proposals, German militarism, the American failure to recognize the existence of two German states, and continued colonialist activities sponsored by the American government and its NATO allies (Gomulka 1970:415–443). Chairman Zhivkov of Bulgaria chided the imperialists for their line of armaments buildup, for intensifying the cold war and increasing international tension, and for undermining international understanding under the flag of anticommunism—all of which represented grave threats to world peace and security. Zhivkov urged the member states to join in Bulgaria's efforts to curb the bellicose imperialist circles from their dangerous and adventurous course in international relations so that they could all be saved from a terrible world holocaust (Zhivkov 1970: 445–469).

One speaker of considerable importance was Prime Minister Castro of Cuba. Castro had been subjected to particularly humiliating treatment by Manhattan hotel proprietors, American diplomats, and New York City police. American newspapers had portrayed him as bringing along his own brothel and gave him treatment that was considered shameful not only by socialist and neutral leaders but also by Western leaders. While at the St. Theresa Hotel in Harlem, he made considerable efforts to demonstrate his link with third-world peoples by his association with Harlem blacks and Puerto Ricans. He made the longest address ever given in the history of the United Nations in which he offered a detailed apologia of how his government had moved from repeated attempts at reconciliation with the American government to the point at which the Americans had pushed him more and more firmly into the socialist ideology. Since his delegation had been humiliated more than any other delegation, he pondered: "Can it be that we, the representatives of the Cuban delegation, represent the worst type of government in the world?" Despite American models of revolution, Prime Minister Castro asserted that the Eisenhower government was unwilling to permit a colony such as Cuba to gain its independence: "Like vultures, the monopolies feed on the corpses which are the harvest of war; and war is a business. Those who trade in war, those who enrich themselves by war, must be unmasked" (Castro 1970:325–372). It is my own belief that one of the failures of American governments since that of Eisenhower has been the refusal to normalize relations with the Cubans. The exportation of the Cuban brand of communism and revolutionary nationalism throughout Latin America will lead, I believe, to established communist governments in at least a half-dozen Latin American states by 1975. A freely elected Marxist government in Chile is an initial step in that direction.

In contrast to the socialist leaders, those who were considered strongly pro-Western praised American efforts for peace while denouncing the war-mongering of the socialist bloc leaders. Prime Minister Diefenbaker of Canada called Eisenhower's speech "restrained, wise and conciliatory" in which he "opened the door to international conciliation and world fellowship," whereas Chairman Khrushchev had launched "a major offensive in the cold war" through a "gigantic propaganda of destructive misrepresentation." He wondered: "how many human beings have been liberated by the USSR?" (Diefenbaker 1970:301–311). Prime Minister Macmillan, who was heckled during his speech by Premier Khrushchev and other socialist delegations, argued that Eisenhower's speech would strengthen the United Nations, whereas the proposals of Khrushchev for restructuring the secretariat would permanently freeze the divisions in the world. He warned of the dangers confronting the summit: "If this session of the Assembly is dramatic, it may well be historic. It may mark the beginning of a period of steady deterioration, ending, as far as human intelligence can foresee, in tragedy. Or it may be the beginning of better things." Macmillan defended the British and French policies of liberating former colonies as they prepared themselves for independence and urged that both East and West stop berating each other so that they could join with the developing countries in improving their conditions and in removing the obstacles for full and complete disarmament (Macmillan 1970:489–503). King Hussein I attacked both the socialist efforts to wreck the United Nations and the attempts of the United Arab Republic to destroy the country of Jordan. Alhough Hussein implied that he was speaking for the entire Arab world, his 1960 position scarcely reflects the general Arab attitudes of the 1970s:

> . . . on every vital issue that confronts this body the nations of the world are being offered a choice. And there is no secret about what that choice is. It lies between becoming part of the Soviet Empire, subservient ultimately to the dictates of the Supreme Soviet of the USSR, or standing as a free nation whose sole external allegiance is to the United Nations itself. That is the choice—and it is there for each nation to decide.
>
> And may I say at once—and with all the strength and conviction at my command—that Jordan has made its choice. We have given our answer in our actions, and I am here to reaffirm our stand to the nations of the world. We reject communism. The Arab people will never bow to communism, no matter what guise it may seek to use to force itself upon us. Communism will never survive in the Arab world because if it ever did then it would have replaced Arab nationalism. There would then cease to be an Arab nation, an Arab world [Hussein I 1970:551].

Hussein believed that his country's difficulties with the attacks from the United Arab Republic began when he denounced communism in the Soviet attempts to gain a foothold in the Middle East: "The United Arab Republic, in seeking to dominate our part of the world, has adopted, as part of its policy of 'neutralism,' some of the methods of the country of which it is most fondly neutral. Should it succeed either as a neutral or as an openly avowed communist ally, it will destroy the very basic aims of the Arab nation" (Hussein I 1970a:549–556). Prime Minister Menzies of Australia expressed shock that Khrushchev was threatening aggression by violent verbal aggression and that he had denounced colonialism so hypocritically when "the facts are that the greatest colonial Power now existing is the Soviet Union itself." The dominant fact of 1960, Menzies stressed, was that world peace was threatened by a colossal war of propaganda, by an unwarranted attack on the person of the secretary-general, by the socialist attempt to convert the United Nations into a "dis-United Nations," and by Khrushchev's efforts to increase cold-war tensions (Menzies 1970:601–610).

As the unofficial convener of the world summit, Premier Khrushchev had announced two major themes for discussion, the 1959 Soviet proposal for complete and general disarmament, from which he hoped that the world leaders present would draft their own treaty, and a solemn declaration calling for the immediate end of colonialism in all its forms. Subsidiary issues became the seating of the People's Republic of China, the problems of cold-war propaganda, the removal of the United Nations from the United States, the removal of Hammarskjöld from office and replacement with a troika system of secretary generals, the specific crises in Algeria and the Congo, and the grave international tension that affected the world because of the Soviet and American rift. Partial success can be attributed to the discussions on disarmament in the signing of the Nuclear Test Ban Treaty in 1963, the Treaty on the Non-Proliferation of Nuclear Weapons in 1968, the 1972 SALT agreements signed by President Nixon and Soviet leaders in Moscow, and Soviet and American agreements to discuss the reduction of troops in Central Europe. Nonetheless, any dream of complete and general disarmament has not been reached, nor will it in the near future. The second major issue appeared important enough to President Touré of Guinea that he delayed his departure from New York as the last remaining neutral leader so that he could argue in favor of the Soviet proposal for a proclamation recognizing that self-determination was an inalienable and natural right of all communities (Touré 1970b:643–648). The proclamation was drafted and passed by the regular members of the delegations in December 1960. During the twenty-fifth anniversary celebrations in 1970, a special ceremony was conducted to celebrate the tenth anniversary of the signing of the Declaration on the Granting of Independence to Colonial Countries and Peoples. At that time, Ambassador Nicol, chairman of the Special Committee on the Situation with Regard to the Implementation of the Declaration, remarked that while the United Nations still had a long way to go to fulfill the aims of the declaration, within the ten years nearly thirty new independent countries had been created with a total population of nearly sixty million people. Unfortunately, especially in southern Africa, eighteen million more persons still remained in a dependent status (Nicol 1970:66–72).

Among the subsidiary issues at the 1960 world summit, the war in Algeria later ended with independence; after considerable bloody strife, the situation in the Congo has now stabilized to the point that United Nations troops are no longer required to maintain order; the socialist states withdrew their demands that the United Nations be removed from the United States, and when Hammarskjöld was killed in 1961, the issue of the troika was quietly dropped. Eventually, the United States found itself so isolated that the People's Republic of China was seated. I have argued that the time must come when not only two separate and distinct Chinas should be seated, but also the two Germanies, two Koreas, and the two Vietnams. On a de facto basis, all of the divided states have been separated for fifteen to twenty years. Universality of membership seems to me more desirable than fragmentation. Thus time gives a certain measure of legitimacy, despite the romantic notion that these divided countries will again become united in the near future. Additionally, if we perceive the United Nations in the French sense of "nations uniting" the organization's purpose is to provide a framework and forum so that nations can *begin* to come together and *begin* to establish a commitment to peaceful coexistence under the aegis of the common bond by which the United Nations links all humanity.

I have hypothesized cross-culturally (1970:9) that the more abstract the crisis, the more symbolic the language and the more specific the tension of an actual war threat, the more direct the language. Though the 1960 world summit was a very tense period, the "words of war" were themselves ambiguous, metaphorical, and highly symbolic. The name-calling, although serious, did not degenerate into a complete breakdown of the dialogue as in 1967 when the Six Day War caused diplomatic relations to be broken between Israel and the socialist states, and between the Arab nations and the Western states. The stronger the symbolic language or the use of metaphors, the more language serves to emphasize a point with unusual force or to maintain a special mood. The heads of state and the heads of government who used such strong symbolic language in 1960 were attempting to stir strong cross-cultural responses about the world's unsteady conditions. Dr. Sukarno's "We have grown accustomed to riding the whirlwind" starkly represented the tensions between East and West with the small uncommitted states caught squarely in the middle of the conflict, impotent to end it, except to urge each side to take steps to ease the tension.

The rhetorical use of basic elements of nature—wind, fire, water, the life-cycle of man, and seasonal analogies to sowing, planting, and harvesting—cut across cultural boundaries as analogous themes to allow leaders of radically different backgrounds to transcend these divisive frames of reference with meaningful and timely messages for their fellow leaders. By speaking in this way, while all the critical issues were not immediately solved, the neutral leaders, particularly, did have an impact on the leaders from the Western and socialist states who were so belligerent toward one another, and may have made it possible, at a later date, for the leaders of the Great Powers to approach each other on a saner and more even basis.

With the concept of summitry at the United Nations firmly implanted in the minds of world leaders, no less than sixteen heads of state and of government addressed the United Nations in the nonsummit year of 1961; and thirteen more utilized the world forum in 1962 and 1963. Increasingly, the themes moved more directly to the problems of modernization, development, and freedom for the third-world states, including the racial difficulties inflicted on large segments of the population in southern Africa. As the leaders of the small nations came to the United Nations on the occasion of their country's independence, new leaders reminded the delegates of their own colonial past and the great feeling of expectation for a better life that independence brought them. The importance of the United Nations to the smaller states continued to be stressed, as some of the titles of addresses illustrate: Prime Minister Mamadou Dia of Senegal, "The United Nations Has Become a Theatre of the Cold War," Prince Norodom Sihanouk, "The United Nations Is Our Only Refuge, Our Sole Support, Our Only Comfort," Archbishop Makarios, "The United Nations: The Conscience of Humanity," and Prime Minister Ben Bella of Algeria, "Our Victory Is a Victory for the United Nations." At the same time, a growing pessimism seized many of the world leaders whose personal diplomacy brought them to the United Nations, as is suggested by the addresses of other leaders: General Abboud, Prime Minister of the Sudan, "Despair Is a Bad Counselor," President Tubman of Liberia, "All Mankind Stands on the Threshold of Universal Destruction," Prime Minister Nehru, "We Live Under a Regime of Terror," President Ould Daddah of Mauritania, "The Great Powers Are Deliberately Trapping Themselves in a Vicious Circle," President Khan of Pakistan, "The Shadow of Nuclear Annihilation," Dr. Radhakrishnan, President of India, "Is It To Be Survival or Annihilation?" and President Kennedy, "The Best Generation of Mankind, or the Last?"

American involvement in the Bay of Pigs attack against Cuba in April 1961 left President Kennedy in a highly vulnerable position when he met later that spring with Khrushchev at Vienna. When the Soviet leader discussed the Berlin question with Kennedy, there is considerable evidence suggesting that Khrushchev simply did not believe Kennedy's assertions that the Western Powers would protect West Berlin, no matter what the cost. Thus during the summer of 1961, and for some time after, the Soviet government seriously tested American resolve there and elsewhere on several separate occasions. When Khrushchev exchanged letters with Kennedy and Macmillan in 1962, he proposed that the opening meeting of the Eighteen-Nation Disarmament Conference at Geneva in May 1962 be turned into a summit conference. Kennedy and Macmillan rejected the suggestion as far as the opening meetings were concerned but indicated that they might be willing to attend at the conclusion if the conference itself should proceed well. Macmillan wrote to Khrushchev in February 1962, indicating that the presence of heads of government at such a conference could serve only to consolidate agreements already partially achieved and to take further steps towards its complete consummation. It turned out that no summit was held at Geneva and October of 1962 found Kennedy and Khrushchev "blinking on the brink" over the Cuban missile crisis. An example of the noncommunication about which Starosta speaks in this volume can be seen in Kennedy's reaction to the two letters he received from Khrushchev during the crisis: One was an ultimatum, whereas the other was a reasonable request for negotiation. Kennedy ignored the first and responded to the second. In this way nuclear war of catastrophic proportions was avoided, and Soviet-American relations began to stabilize again. Speaking at the end of the seventeenth General Assembly, President Alessandri of Chile recalled:

When the seventeenth session of the General Assembly opened the tension which was later to culminate in the Caribbean crisis was becoming more acute. The world trembled at the idea that the specter of war might become a reality. Those were days of anxiety and profound anguish. Fortunately common sense prevailed and the world began once again to return to normal and to regain hope despite the disquieting and threatening symptoms which unfortunately persist [Alessandri 1970:919–926].

While the number of world statesmen who traveled to the United Nations to utilize the world forum diminished after 1963, the 1965 visit by Pope Paul VI caused nearly as much interest as the 1960 world summit had, except that he was there but for a single address, entitled "Never Again War." When President of the General Assembly Amintore Fanfani of Italy welcomed Pope Paul to the United Nations, he said: "The Pontiff is greeted, not by frescos heavy with warnings [of the Last Judgment], but by the representatives of 117 states gathered here to express, at this twentieth session of the General Assembly of the United Nations, the most recent anxieties, caused by the imbalances, the oppressions, the perils and the conflicts which still disturb the human family." He hoped that the Pope would influence nations to create the certitude of freedom, justice, and peace. When Secretary-General Thant welcomed Pope Paul, he recalled that, during the year before in Bombay, the Pope had appealed for an end to the armaments race and asked that all nations undertake "a peaceful battle against the sufferings of their less fortunate brothers." The message that Pope Paul gave to the assembled delegates, including a number of foreign ministers who had traveled to New York for the occasion, among them Andrei Gromyko of the Soviet Union, was an example of spiritual summitry, calling upon higher ideals than the common morality of man. He encouraged nations to fight "never again one against another" and to let "weapons fall from your hands." He also asked all nations to labor "here not only to exercise conflicts between States; but to make States capable of working one for another." He concluded:

Never before has there been such a need for an appeal to the moral conscience of man as there is today, in an era marked by such human progress. For the peril comes neither from progress nor from science; on the contrary, properly used, they could resolve many of the grave problems which beset mankind. The real peril is in man, who has at hand ever more powerful instruments, suited as much to destruction as to the highest conquests [Pope Paul 1970:1051–1057].

President of the General Assembly Pazhwak of Afghanistan opened the Fifth Special Emergency Session in June 1967 with the words:

This meeting . . . reflects a situation of very great and increasing gravity involving peace and war. . . . The situation in the Middle East, which is not confined to that area but represents a crisis of world proportions, must be of immediate concern to the United Nations because of the widely recognized and very direct and continuing responsibility of the United Nations in that area. I personally consider the conflict in the Middle East to be a matter solely for the United Nations to solve [quoted in Prosser 1970:1117].

Although the Security Council had effected a cease-fire in the Six-Day War between Israel and other Arab states, representing some measure of success, failure to agree to the Soviet resolution condemning Israel as an aggressor caused the Soviet delegation to request the special emergency session of the General Assembly under the Uniting for Peace resolution first used against the Soviets in 1950 during the Korean crisis.

Chairman Kosygin personally presented the resolution to the emergency session. During his visit to New York, he and President Johnson met at Glassboro State College in New Jersey as a half-way point between Washington and the United Nations. A number of socialist heads of government, King Hussein of Jordan and President Al-Atassi of Syria, and other heads of state and of government joined Kosygin to denounce Israel's actions against the United Arab Republic, Jordan, and Syria. In effect, a second world summit meeting was again being held at the United Nations although the American President was absent from the meeting, thus losing the initiative. Foreign Minister Abba Eban represented Israel in the discussions. As the first speaker on a substantive matter, Premier Kosygin welcomed the cease-fire but deplored the continued Israeli presence on Arab territory. He argued that the United States, which "has been carrying out direct aggression against the Viet Namese people," also was supplying support for the Israeli aggression. Chairman Kosygin believed that, just as other conflicts were not localized, the Middle East crisis included the 1966 Security Council censure of Israel for its "large-scale military action against Jordan," its April 1967 attack on Syria, and its May 1967 military build-up with threats against the United Arab Republic, Syria, and Jordan. Security Council warnings and the severing of diplomatic relations with Israel still had not convinced Israel to halt its hostilities. Chairman Kosygin believed that this action proved "that Israel bears responsibility for unleashing the war, for its victims and for its consequences." He demanded that the General Assembly "Pronounce itself authoritatively in favor of justice and peace" (Kosygin 1970:1117–1131). Exercising his right of reply, Abba Eban stated that the crisis had only one cause: "Israel's right to peace, to security, to sovereignty, to economic development, to maritime freedom—indeed, its very right to exist—has been forcibly denied and aggressively attacked."

As the representative of one of the states attacked by Israel, President Al-Atassi of Syria pleaded with the General Assembly to act swiftly and strongly to force Israel to vacate Syrian territory and to make restitution for its damages. If the assembly failed to condemn Israel and punish it as an aggressor, President Al-Atassi contended that it "would mean the destruction of the Charter of the United Nations and all the lofty principles contained therein" and "would carry in its wake the destruction of the independence of every nation in the world, as their safety would be exposed to invasion at any time" (Al-Atassi 1970:1133–1141). As the representative of one of the other states attacked by Israel King Hussein announced his mission as a most serious one, "to speak to this distinguished group of world citizens on behalf of my Arab nation. I have a simple purpose and a simple objective: to state clearly our case in the present crisis and to urge that the issue be resolved promptly and with justice." King Hussein spoke of the suffering by his nation and his people through armed aggression, the occupation of the west bank of the Jordan, the death of thousands, and the destruction of their cities and homes. He charged the Israelis with the widespread use of napalm and fragmentation bombs, with inhuman treatment of prisoners, with looting, with the destruction of Jordanian towns, with adding to the refugee problem, and with preventing refugees from recrossing the Jordan River to return to their homes. King Hussein warned that while Jordan obeyed the terms of the cease-fire, if the international organization could not live up to its promise of the order cease-fire, "it will never under any circumstances anywhere in the world be allowed to say the words 'cease-fire' again—and be obeyed" (Hussein I 1970b: 1253–1258).

Among the socialist leaders only Chairman Maurer of Romania attempted to strike a balance between the Israeli and Arab positions by urging both sides to solve their problems through rational channels. He called upon other heads of state and of government to refrain from worsening the situation by words or acts that could aggravate the problems there. He argued for exclusively peaceful means of settlement, for elimination of all foreign intervention in the affairs of the region, and for respect for the fundamental interests of each Middle East state, with recognition of its independent and sovereign existence (Maurer 1970:1229–1235). Other socialist leaders, however, strongly denounced the Israelis while praising the Arabs. Such statements as the following are typical. Prime Minister Lenart of Czechoslovakia suggested that Israel had been supported by outside forces: "Israel and its leading circles have again unmasked themselves as the straw men of imperialist and colonialist forces and the tool of their policy in the Near East" (Lenart 1970:1143–1152). Chairman Tsedenbal of Mongolia called the draft resolution offered by the United States delegation a defense of the aggressor and a criminal act in its efforts to reward Israel for its aggression and encourage it to undertake future hostility against the Arab states (Tsedenbal 1970:1199–1202). Chairman Shcherbitsky of the Ukrainian SSR warned that if the Middle East crisis failed to reach a peaceful solution, "we might witness dangerous consequences," particularly because Israel was a servant of the imperialists, especially the United States, which was also waging "the dirty war against Viet Nam" and carrying on "armed intervention in the affairs of Laos and Cambodia" (Shcherbitsky 1970:1203–1210). Chairman Kiselev of the Byelorussian SSR noted that such an attack against the Arab states could have had no hope for success without the "assistance and support of certain Western countries, primarily of the United States. . . . There is no case in the history of international relations when the protector of an aggressor condemned an aggressor" (Kiselev 1970:1221–1228). Chairman Cyrankiewicz of Poland called the attack an Israeli blitzkrieg and blackmail by which the imperialists would be able to support attacks against African, Asian, and European states without impunity: "We will not reconcile ourselves either now or in the future with aggression and territorial annexations. Neither this nor any other aggressor may ever be rewarded. The aggressor must be made to give up the gains of his aggression. Only under such conditions shall the peaceful coexistence among nations become possible" (Cyrankiewicz 1970:1237–1243).

The only Western heads of government present were Prime Minister Krag of Denmark and Prime Minister Moro of Italy. Both attempted conciliation.

Neutralist leaders included Prime Minister Mahgoub of the Sudan and Prime Minister Maiwandwal of Afghanistan. Both of the neutral leaders labeled the Israelis as extremists. Prime Minister Maiwandwal recalled nineteen years of Israeli aggression against the Arabs, and Prime Minister Mahgoub charged that Israel had been guilty of "naked, premeditated and wanton aggression," which had been supported as a tool for certain Great Powers whose influence had dwindled in the Middle East. He declared that it was not Arab fanaticism about whether Israel ought to exist as a state that caused the problem, but Prime Minister Eshkol's statement "that Israel was prepared to risk an all-out war in a military offensive to topple Syria's army regime." Prime Minister Mahgoub argued that Israel had been guilty of so many aggressive acts during the past twenty years that it had no right to "have it both ways. She must not be allowed to defy the authority of the United Nations, to disregard its most solemn resolutions as she has done for the last twenty years, to commit aggressive acts against the Arabs, and then to come to these halls to hurl accusations at those who have suffered her aggression" (Mahgoub 1970:1175–1190).

The importance of this emergency summit meeting can be seen in that a single serious issue was at stake, whether or not the Israeli government was to abide by the terms of the Security Council cease-fire, and whether or not that government should be condemned for its aggressive actions and be forced to return all conquered areas and make restitution for damages. Overtones included attacks upon the United States and other Western states as supporters of Israeli aggression. In addition to the sixteen heads of state and heads of government present, forty-five foreign ministers attended parts of the emergency session. Later in the fall of 1967, eighty-seven foreign ministers attended some or all of the general debate for the opening of the twenty-second General Assembly, making it the largest foreign ministers' conference ever held to my knowledge. Unfortunately, as a summit meeting, the June session was unequally represented in that two of the parties to the crisis, the United Arab Republic and Israel, were not represented by their heads of government, although Eban is generally considered to represent his government very capably. Additionally, no heads of state or government of the Great Powers from among the Western states were present, even though Johnson and Kosygin had held private meetings, which Eisenhower and Khrushchev had failed to do in 1960. Since all the socialist leaders, except Maurer of Romania and the two neutralist leaders, plus the two Arab leaders Hussein and Al-Atassi, had come to condemn Israel and to support the Arabs, the debate and discussion became very uneven. Unfortunately, too, the Israelis then refused to abide by General Assembly resolutions concerning the restoration of lands and restitution for damages. Therefore, the problem still exists today, with the hopes for serious negotiations between the Israelis and the Arab states not yet very bright despite regular statements from both sides about their willingness to negotiate. The death of President Nasser has not aided the situation. While both the Western and socialist states have involved themselves in the conflict in various ways, including the shipment of weapons, both have fortunately avoided allowing, as far as they are able, the conflict to become a crisis of ever widening proportions. Nevertheless, the Middle East continues to be highly explosive; and a new conflict can be set off at any moment either by accident or by planned reprisals by either side, or by the decision by a Superpower to enter the conflict in force.

In his address introducing his annual report to the United Nations at the opening of the twenty-fourth annual session of the General Assembly, Secretary-General U Thant warned: "The nations of the world have what may be a last opportunity to mobilize their energies and resources, supported by the public opinion of all the peoples of the world, to tackle anew the complicated but not insuperable problems of disarmament." Reflecting on the forthcoming twenty-fifth anniversary in 1970, Thant urged: "I feel very strongly that the celebration of the twenty-fifth anniversary should not be ceremonial but substantive. All organs of the United Nations should, in my view, make a special effort to reach specific agreement on such major issues before the world's organization as development, peace-making, disarmament, decolonization, and friendly relations among nations" (in Prosser 1970:1357). As the anniversary drew nearer, more than fifty heads of state and heads of government were expected to attend, including President Nixon and Premier Kosygin, and an excellent representation from among the Western, socialist, and neutral states. Prominent leaders in the 1960 World Summit Conference such as Eisenhower, Khrushchev, Macmillan, Nkrumah, Nehru, Sukarno, Diefenbaker, and Prince Sihanouk would be replaced by a host of new state leaders. The following heads of state and heads of government actually did attend part or all of the ten-day event in October 1970:

Prime Minister Barrow of Barbados,* President Nyerere of Tanzania,* President Bongo of Gabon, Prime Minister Alaini of Yemen, President Figueres of Costa Rica, President Kaunda of Zambia,* President Ceausescu of Romania, President Lamizana of Upper Volta, Chief Jonathan, Prime Minister of Lesotho,* Prime Minister Palme of Sweden, Prime Minister de Jong of the Netherlands, Prime Minister Borg Olivier of Malta,* Prime Minister Ramgoolam of Mauritius,* Prime Minister Shearer of Jamaica,* President Ribicic of Yugoslavia, President Bokassa of the Central African Republic, Prime Minister Chia-Kan of the Republic of China, President Lukas of Panama, Prime Minister Meir of Israel, Prime Minister Busia of Ghana,* Prime Minister Mara of Fiji, President Ould Daddah of Mauritania,* Prime Minister Sato of Japan, President Khan of Pakistan, Prime Minister Laraki of Morocco, Prime Minister Lynch of Ireland, Prime Minister Baunsgaard of Denmark, President Kekkonen of Finland,* Prime Minister Heath of the United Kingdom, Prime Minister Montague of Peru, Prime Minister Gandhi of India,* President Somoza of Nicaragua, Prime Minister Borten of Norway, Emperor Haile Selassie of Ethiopia,* President Nixon of the United States,* President Tombalbaye of Chad,* President Makarios of Cyprus,* President Maga of Dahomey, Cheng Heng, Head of State of Cambodia, Prince Souvanna Phouma, Prime Minister of Laos,* and Prince Makhosini, Prime Minister of Swaziland.

* Starred names indicate those heads of state and of government who had addressed the United Nations in periods before the twenty-fifth anniversary celebration.

Many of the leading statesmen remained for the entire ten-day celebration, especially the third-world leaders, who are among the strongest supporters of the United Nations. Security precautions were so tight that many leaders complained justifiably that they were locked in an impregnable fortress. When General Assembly President Hambro opened the commemorative session, he cautioned: "The eyes of the world are upon us." Various reporters writing of the ten-day celebration wondered if very many eyes at all were on the United Nations. The United Nations was closed to the public, and, therefore, the heads of state and heads of government found themselves speaking to a nearly empty assembly hall. So few heads were present that the concept of dialogue to which the session was devoted seemed a mockery. In his reply to the statement made by Ambassador Tekoah of Israel, Ambassador Baroody of Saudi Arabia responded directly to this problem:

> He [Tekoah] mentioned that the eyes of the world are upon us. Parenthetically, we are conducting this session in a beleaguered fortress and the world has grown tired of us, it seems. We are suffering from a cholera epidemic of speeches, words *ad nauseam*, general debates, platitudinous statements— all this while tension is mounting in the world in general, and in my region, the Middle East, in particular. Truly the eyes of the world are upon us [Baroody 1970:56].

Increasing Soviet-American tension over the Soviet missile build-up in the Suez Canal area and the American decision to supply new weapons and planes to Israel, new Soviet attempts to close the West Berlin air corridor, which were later attributed to the error of a subordinate, and the American fear that the Soviets were building submarine bases in Cuban waters in violation of the 1962 Kennedy-Khrushchev agreements, all led to a lessening of the spirit of American-Soviet détente that both sides had been proclaiming a few weeks before. Premier Kosygin and other socialist leaders who had indicated their interest in attending the celebrations canceled their trips, again seizing the initiative, this time through noncommunication, though President Ceasescu of Romania continued with his plans for a state visit and major address, which was beamed directly by radio satellite to the Romanian people. At the same time, President Pompidou of France proceeded with his plans for a state visit to Russia. Additionally, the recent death of President Nasser of the United Arab Republic had drawn many world leaders to Cairo; and the Arabs decided that the Middle East situation was too unstable to permit them to journey to New York for the occasion. Finally, some of the heads of state and of government who had attended the Third Non-Aligned States Conference in Lusaka, Zambia, a month before felt it impossible to make the second trip. Still, the Lusaka decisions had considerable influence at the United Nations a month later.

A considerable amount of pessimism was evident among the heads of state and heads of government present for the celebration. A large number of them complained that while plans were being laid for a Second Decade of Development beginning with the twenty-fifth General Assembly, the First Decade of Development had been essentially a failure. The richer nations had grown richer without committing themselves to asssisting the poor nations whose populations had doubled but whose per capita income had scarcely changed. Although the declaration concerning decolonization had been passed almost unanimously in 1960, millions of persons, particularly in southern Africa, were still enslaved. Others who had won their independence were forced to live in such impoverished conditions that their condition was little better than slavery. Many statesmen found that "the major components of international security, namely, disarmament, denuclearization, détente and disengagement from the specific conflicts which are raging in the world, are all being tackled outside the coverage of this organization's procedures" (Barrow 1970:11).

Prime Minister Barrow of Barcados had expressed a considerable amount of pessimism in his address to the United Nations in October, 1967, after the emergency session on the Middle East crisis; but it seems to me that his pessimism in 1970 was still more pronounced. His remarks are typical of those offered by many heads of state and heads of government present at the 1970 session:

> It would appear that what has taken place in the past twenty-five years is that the major Powers have been progressively abandoning the United Nations as the main instrument for regulating and harmonizing international affairs. . . .
>
> Our world therefore comprises the rich and the super-rich—and then the rest of us, the conglomeration of small and medium-sized countries which have been labeled "the irresponsible majority." We are the majority, but we do have responsibility. Our first responsibility must be to fend off starvation and disease, to seek human dignity and some measure of material comfort for our peoples. And our only hope of achieving these ends is in meaningful cooperation with all the members of the human family. . . .
>
> The record shows that the role which has been assigned to the General Assembly on the question of disarmament is that of "noting" and "endorsing" a series of faits accomplis. It is not a notably dynamic role. . . .
>
> And what is the role of the United Nations in the Middle East, where one of the gravest conflicts of our time has been raging practically since the foundation of the Organization? Have the permanent members of the Security Council, with their primary responsibility for peace and security, used the Organization as a centre for harmonizing the relations of the nations in that region? No. . . .
>
> Even the Palais des Nations in Geneva has been recently avoided in a most important harmonization exercise; the current talks between the United States and the Viet-Namese, for which we all wish a speedy and successful conclusion, are taking place in Paris; the United Nations might never have existed for all the attention it is paid by the protagonists in this conflict. . . .
>
> And is there no role for the United Nations, even as a tacit observer in the discussions on the limitations of strategic arms? Apparently not. . . .
>
> When we turn to the economic aspects of the aims of the Charter, the solemn decision taken at San Francisco "to employ international machinery for the promotion of the economic and social advancement of all peoples," we see the same syndrome of abandonment. . . .

In this twenty-fifth anniversary year, the question which everyone is trying to answer is: where do we go from here? [Barrow 1970:2–15].

If admittedly utopian, Prime Minister Barrow urged that the organization become not only the center for harmonizing the actions of nations but the only such center; that the nations with major power and, therefore, with major responsibility for preserving international peace should pledge themselves to employ the full machinery provided by the charter; that member governments should give formal assurances of their readiness to the task of preventing outbreaks of armed violence among nations by using fully the machinery of the United Nations, or create new machinery under its auspices; that from 1971 all governments be invited to decrease their expenditure on armaments by an agreed percent and to contribute one-half of their savings to a special development fund under the aegis of the United Nations; and that, finally, the organization commit the international community to a long-term program of international development as provided for in the document proposed by the committee for the Second Development Decade (Barrow 1970:2–15).

Barrow's statements and those proposals which follow by Prime Minister H. L. Shearer of Jamaica demonstrate clearly the issues that most of the speakers during the ten-day celebration found to be critical: (1) Review the charter to make it more responsive to the problems of the present international community, in relation to the absence of political will now permitted in the charter and to raise the Commission on Human Rights to a status equal to the Economic and Social Council. (2) Relieve the United Nations of the burden of responsibility for excluding either the Republic of China or the People's Republic of China by making clear the universality of the organization. (3) Create an effective United Nations Military Force called for by article 43 of the charter so that it could be used to maintain international peace and security. (4) Reactivate and employ the machinery established in Chapter VI of the charter for the peaceful settlement of disputes among nations, including such problems as the Middle East; and employ, also, previously established measures such as the International Court of Justice. (5) In the sphere of decolonization, take steps to recover the United Nations' specially mandated territory Namibia from the government of South Africa, and bring an end to apartheid in southern Africa. (6) Develop the proposed strategy for the Second United Nations Development Decade by committing developed states to improved trade with and aid for developing states. Ask that the developing countries institute programs of economic aid which offer mutual help and that both developed and developing states attend together to problems affecting the human environment which relate directly to the process of development (Shearer 1970:8–30).

In many ways the themes remained the same in 1970 as in 1960, and even shortly after the United Nations was founded. Although many were pessimistic about the United Nations' accomplishments during its first twenty-five years of existence, most leaders agreed with Thant's appraisal that, despite its deficiency, the United Nations still remained the only organization that existed for conflict resolution of a universal nature, except for the settlement of issues by nonpeaceful means. Without negating bilateral and multilateral contacts, as President Tombalbaye of Chad has suggested:

The United Nations is therefore humanistic because it wishes to listen and to understand, to be heard and to make itself understood. It is humanistic because it wishes all men to enjoy the benefits of the common weal and is patiently trying to civilize the world so that it can become an instrument of thought and of human love. It is humanistic because instead of isolating and separating, it wishes to bring people together [Tombalbaye 1970:36–57].

Despite the tensions between the Americans and Soviets, both President Nixon and Foreign Minister Gromyko of the USSR reaffirmed their states' belief in the principles and authentic nature of the United Nations as a harmonizer of peoples. Both called for joint efforts by the major powers with the other member states to promote international security, disarmament, and the progress of peoples (Nixon 1970:22–35; Gromyko 1970:23–55). The United States' invitation to a state dinner of all the heads of state and heads of government present at the anniversary celebration represented, at least symbolically, the "bringing together of peoples" which the United Nations espouses. Assessing the value of the commemorative session, Ambassador Beaulne of Canada stated:

In the last ten days many prominent contemporary figures, Heads of State and Heads of Government, have honoured us with their eloquence and wisdom and have made known the needs, interests and hopes of the people they govern. We now know that the success or failure of the United Nations should not be judged by whether it has overridden those individual interests but by whether it has protected them, not by whether it has lent itself to the purposes of any one Member or group of Members but by whether it has reconciled the aspirations of all [Beaulne 1970:31].

The assembly ended its commemorative session by adopting the Declaration on Principles of International Law concerning the Friendly Relations among States, the Declaration on the International Development Strategy for the Second Development Decade, and the Declaration on the Occasion of the Twenty-fifth Anniversary of the United Nations, while simultaneously, the Security Council defined the goals of the United Nations with relation to southern Africa and the Middle East and its capability to act effectively for the maintenance of international peace and security.

Although we can judge the failures and accomplishments of the 1960 World Summit Conference fairly accurately and can note that the bases of negotiations in the Middle East crisis are the November 1967 United Nations Resolution that developed out of the 1967 summit meeting of those attending the emergency session of the General Assembly, the achievements of the 1970 quasi-summit of the forty-two heads of state and heads of government who gathered to celebrate the jubilee celebration have not yet been assessed. As President of the General Assembly Hambro noted, in proclaiming the ceremony closed at noon on United Nations Day, October 24, 1970:

Speakers have claimed that this is an historic session, but words alone cannot make us merit this epithet. Only the future can show whether this has indeed been an historic session. That will be decided not by the words of today but by the acts of tomorrow. . . . But our task today is to look towards the future. We do it with courage in the face of tremendous difficulties. . . . And do not let us forget that love of our fellow man, compassion and tolerance are the very basis for the solidarity of mankind which must inspire us all in the future [Hambro 1970:42–43].

The summitry that has occurred during the last twenty-five years and more through the personal diplomacy of heads of state and of government, both bilaterially and multilaterally, and especially in the United Nations, has been very mixed, sometimes providing "a war of words" and sometimes offering a ripple of hope for international cooperation toward peace and for development, which Pope Paul has called the new definition of peace. For good or ill, members of the United Nations have sought to communicate and to use their prestige for conflict resolution nearly two hundred times from the rostrum of the United Nations through their heads of state and heads of government who have spoken here. They are attempting to communicate not only to their fellow leaders but often to what they imagine to be the conscience of mankind. In this way, though there have been many failings in this sort of summitry, the summitry itself has been important in world progress and development during the last twenty-five years. The communication of summitry is thus itself a humanizing factor in that our world leaders produce and receive symbols concerning the messages that are vital to human survival and the preservation of the highest values relating to the improvement of the human condition.

REFERENCES CITED

AL-ATASSI, NOUREDDIN
1970   The aggressor is in a state of military intoxication. In Sow the wind, reap the whirlwind: heads of state address the United Nations. Michael H. Prosser, ed. New York.*
ALESSANDRI, JORGE RODRIGUEZ
1970   Peace, prosperity and security are indivisible.
BAROODY
1970   Right of reply. United Nations General Assembly. A/PV. 1870. 16 October.
BEAULNE, YVON
1970   Closing statement in behalf of Western European and other states. United Nations General Assembly. A/PV. 1883. 24 October.
CHURCHILL, WINSTON
1952   The war speeches of Winston S. Churchill. Charles Eade, comp. London.
1960   Quoted in Lewis Broad, The war that Churchill waged. London.
CYRANKIEWICZ, JOZEF
1970   Israeli blitzkrieg.
DAVIS, PAUL C.
1965   The new diplomacy: the 1955 Geneva Summit Meeting. In Foreign policy in the sixties: the issues and the instruments. Roger Hilsman and Robert C. Good, eds. Baltimore.
DIEFENBAKER, JOHN
1970   The United Nations' most formidable threat.

* All citations for 1970 are taken from this source unless otherwise noted.

DJILAS, MILOVAN
1962   Conversations with Stalin. New York.
EISENHOWER, DWIGHT D.
1970a   The new language is the language of atomic warfare.
1970b   The munitions of peace.
1970c   Ballistic blackmail.
1970d   Smaller nations have the greatest stake.
GOMULKA, WLADYSLAW
1970   Peaceful coexistence is a historical necessity.
GRAEBNER, NORMAN A.
1961   Dean G. Acheson. An uncertain tradition: American secretaries of state in
        the twentieth century. New York.
GROMYKO, ANDREI
1970   Statement to Twenty-fifth Anniversary Commemorative Session. United Na-
        tions General Assembly. A/PV. 1877. 21 October.
HAMBRO, EDVARD
1970   Closing statement to Twenty-fifth Anniversary Commemorative Session,
        United Nations General Assembly. A/PV. 1883. 24 October.
HOVET, THOMAS, JR.
1960   Bloc politics in the United Nations. Cambridge, Mass.
HUSSEIN, I.
1970a   No issue is entirely local.
1970b   Jordan, and the Arabs, want peace with justice.
KHRUSHCHEV, NIKITA SERGEYVICH
1959   On the occasion of his visit to the United States. New York.
1970a   Let us disarm completely.
1970b   Misleading the people is like trying to wrap up fire in a piece of paper.
1970c   The seeds of truth.
KISELEV, TIKHON T.
1970   Birds of a feather flock together.
KOSYGIN, ALEKSI N.
1970   The aggressor is in a state of military intoxication.
LENART, JOSEF
1970   Israeli aggression against Arab states.
MAHGOUB, SAYEED MOHAMMED AHMED
1970   This assembly session is sitting in judgment.
MAUER, ION GHEORGE
1970   Are conflicts in the Middle East incurable?
MENZIES, ROBERT GORDON
1970   The dead past should bury its dead.
MOHRMANN, GERALD P.
1967   Blinking on the brink: the rhetoric of summitry. Western Speech 31:172–179.
MUSONDA, FRANCIS KAOMA
1970   For non-aligned nations: Zambia hosts big conference. Daily Herald-Telephone,
        Bloomington, October 8.
NASSER, GAMAL ABDEL
1970   The unity of history is the unity of conscience.
NICOL, DAVIDSON S.H.W.
1970   Statement to the special ceremony to commemorate the Tenth Anniversary of
        the Declaration on the Granting of Independence to Colonial Countries and
        Peoples. United Nations General Assembly. A/PV. 1866. 14 October.
NKRUMAH, KWAME
1970   The raging hurricane of African nationalism.
NIXON, RICHARD M.
1970   Statement to Twenty-fifth Anniversary Commemorative Session. United
        Nations General Assembly. A/PV. 1882. 23 October.

PLISCHKE, E.
1968   Eisenhower's "Correspondence Diplomacy" with the Kremlin—a case study in summit diplomatics. Journal of Politics 30:137–159.
PAUL VI, POPE
1970   Never again war.
PROSSER, MICHAEL H., ed.
1970   Sow the wind, reap the whirlwind: heads of state address the United Nations. New York.
ROGERS, LINDSAY
1955   Of summits. Foreign affairs 34:147.
SHCHERBITSKY, VLADIMIR W.
1970   The black days of Hitler's aggression.
SHEARER, H. L.
1970   Statement to Twenty-fifth Anniversary Commemorative Session. United Nations General Assembly. A/PV. 1875. 20 October.
SHERWOOD, ROBERT
1948   Roosevelt and Hopkins. New York.
SHESHU, MEHMUT
1970   No single people in the world wants war.
SIHANOUK, NORODOM
1970a The time for narrow nationalism is over.
1970b The tepid war.
STEVENSON, ADLAI E.
1969   Full promise of a distracted world. Quoted in An ethic for survival: Adlai Stevenson Speaks on International Affairs, 1936–1965. Michael H. Prosser, ed. New York.
SUKARNO, ACHMED
1970   Riding the whirlwind.
TITO, JOSIP BROZ
1970   The revival of the cold war.
TOMBALBAYE, FRANCOIS
1970   Statement to Twenty-fifth Anniversary Commemorative Session. United Nations General Assembly. A/PV. 1882. 23 October.
TOURE, SEKOU
1970a African freedom is indivisible.
1970b The problem of freedom is the greatest problem in the world.
TRUMAN, HARRY S
1970   Without peace, lasting progress is impossible.
TSEDENBAL, YUMJAAGIIN
1970   We are witnesses of a crime against humanity.
WATT, D. C.
1967   Summits and summitry reconsidered. International Relations.
ZHIVKOV, TODOR
1970   You cannot put out the light that dies not.

THE ARABS AND THE WEST: COMMUNICATION GAP

Michael W. Suleiman

MICHAEL W. SULEIMAN received his B.A. from Bradley University and his M.A. and Ph.D. from the University of Wisconsin at Madison. He is currently associate professor of political science at Kansas State University. He has written on Arab-American relations, the Palestine question, and Lebanese politics for various professional journals, and is the author of Political Parties in Lebanon: The Challenge of a Fragmented Political Culture. He is presently engaged in a study of the political attitudes and behavior of Arab elites.

Arabs—leaders and intellectuals as well as the general public—have since World War I complained of the difficulty encountered in their persistent but unsuccessful attempt to communicate with the West. Basically and simply their grievance pertains to the lack of understanding of, and sympathy for, the Arab point of view on international, regional and local issues. The object of this paper is to probe into the reasons and, in passing, to test the validity of the assertion.[1]

There are several factors which have contributed to the existence of this communication gap. These factors are certainly inter-related and will be isolated here for analytical purposes only.

ARABS AS PART OF THE MOSLEM WORLD

Most Arabs are Moslem—and very proud of their religion. Even those who are not practicing Moslems display a strong attachment to, and great pride in, their membership in the Moslem *umma* (community). Though there are no-Arabs who are also Moslem by religion and there are Arabs who are not Moslem, to be Arab *and* Moslem is truly to "belong." As Ethel Mannin put it, "perhaps if you're an Arab it's better to be a Moslem—it fits better; the difference between the ready-made coat and the made-to-measure. Islam was made-to-measure by the Prophet for the Arabs."[2] W. C. Smith has made the same observation: "Muslim Arabs have never quite acknowledged, have never fully incorporated into their thinking and especially their feeling, either that a non-Muslim is really a complete Arab, or that a non-Arab is really a complete Muslim."[3] The reason is not hard to find: "Islam gave the Arabs earthly greatness; and vice versa, it was the Arabs who gave Islam its earthly success."[4]

The importance of this point is underscored when it is remembered that Islam has been a significant factor in the alienation between the Arabs and the Christian West. Moslems have been so certain that they have the one and only true religion and that their religion will eventually triumph, that no serious attempt on their part has been made to understand other faiths, including

Reprinted with permission of II Politico, 32 (September 1967), 511–529, and the author.

Christianity. The Christian West, on the other hand, has viewed Islam with suspicion and fear. For over a thousand years, Islam presented a serious threat to Christianity, both as a religious institution and as an ideology. "Eventually," as *Time* magazine put it, "the West dispelled the Moslems, but not the mem- ·ory of one thousand years of dread."[5] Part of the Western response to this fear of Islam was expressed in antagonistic and unfavorable writings about Islam and the Moslems, including the Arabs. Religious leaders and thinkers, poets, and even orientalists reviled Islam and the Prophet Mohammed, and ascribed to the Moslems acts of barbarity of which they were innocent.[6] "The price paid for long-standing hostility is the inability to communicate."[7]

ARABS AS PART OF THE COLONIAL WORLD

The Arabs came into contact with the West when the European powers, France and Great Britain in particular, established colonies and disguised colonies euphemistically called mandates or protectorates. As Erskine Childers forcefully expressed it: "In no other part of the Afro-Asian world were new frontiers drawn on maps as late in the epoch of imperialism as in the Middle East. In no other part of the world in 1917 was territory, already inhabited by a people, declared open for mass immigration by aliens known to be seeking a state of their own, while the original inhabitants were denied self-determination (Palestine). In no other part of Afro-Arab-Asia did post-1918 imperial policy require such brutal fully military imposition as was involved in Morocco, Libya, Iraq, and Syria between 1920 and 1930."[8]

From its very beginning, the Arab nationalist movement was severely shaken and frustrated by the very West it had taken to be a helpful ally. When Sherif Hussein of Mecca gathered his Arab followers and declared war on his co-religionists in Ottoman Turkey, the aim was that, with victory, the Asian Arabs would achieve their independence. Despite Woodrow Wilson's fourteen points and his championship of self-determination, and despite the findings of the King-Crane commission, however, the imperialistic interests and secret diplomacy of the United Kingdom and France were allowed to triumph.[9] The Arabs did not attain their independence, and suffered the more serious afflic- tion of a divided homeland. Not only was the Arab homeland dismembered into numerous kingdoms and republics under foreign domination, but the process of differentiation and disintegration was further enhanced by the sub- jection of the Arabs to two alien powers with distinctly different languages, cultures, governments and administrations. France went still further by estab- lishing Greater Lebanon and dividing Syria into several "administrative" units. It was not surprising, therefore, that the Arab intelligentsia began to lose their faith in the West.

This loss of confidence gradually but surely extended to other aspects of Western civilization which had been admired and imitated by Arab intellec- tuals. Liberalism began to lose its luster when so-called liberals confined their liberal policies to England and France. If democracy was a form of government to be enjoyed by the British and the French, if it did not truly represent nor work for the interests of the public in the various Arab countries, then it was useless to adhere to empty formal procedures. And what of Western liberals? What of the Western socialists who spoke of freedom and the dignity of man? They, too, unfortunately, disappointed their Arab counterparts. British Laborites were, after all, not much different from the Conservatives in their dealings with the Arabs. What is perhaps most disappointing of all to the Arab liberals is the almost complete lack of sympathy or understanding on the part of Western liberals of the Arab side in the Palestine issue—a point to which we shall return later.

ARABS AS PART OF THE "BACKWARD" WORLD

There is little doubt that the Arab world is not as advanced economically as the West. Apart from Kuwait whose wealth was discovered only recently, only Lebanon has a per capita income in excess of $200.[10] While the Arab countries share this characteristic with the developing world generally, certain ramifications make the Arabs more sensitive on this issue. The Arabs' strong pride in their past glory and their shame in the present unfavorable conditions intensify their reactions to Western display of power. The frustrations engendered by the inability to hit back with any effectiveness inflame their passions and add to their fury. This explains to a great extent the almost hysterical exuberation among the Arabs over the nationalization of the Suez Canal Company and the concomitant defiance of the West. That single act more than any other perhaps represented the "ideal" Arab response to any Western provocation.

Once the Arabs began to consciously compare their present backwardness with Western superiority, there was no escaping the conclusion that Arab traditions, mores and culture were in part responsible for the present state of affairs. Even though the loudest and most frequent denunciations were aimed at the West and its imperialistic policy, self-criticism, albeit of the current "unnatural" conditions only, and the search for a new Weltanschauung more suitable for the twentieth century began. This process unavoidably cast serious doubts on the suitability of traditional Islam as an organizing force to restore the Arabs' former glory. Since this was viewed by most Moslem religious leaders and much of the public as a conscious and premeditated attack by the Christian West and the misguided Westernized Arab elites on the Moslem community, hatred of the West was intensified and another avenue of communication was blocked.

The West on its part has enraged and continues to enrage the Arabs by its policy of "balance of power" between Israel with its two and one half million people and the Arab world comprising almost 100 million. Regardless of the arguments which the West may present to justify such a policy, to the Arabs, such a set-up is insidious and infuriating. A comparable reaction is generated by the use of such a term as "power vacuum" to refer to the situation in the Middle East after the British-French withdrawal from Suez in 1956.

A sizable number of the new elites in the Arab countries have internalized Western values and now attempt to make their homeland a part of the modern world. This process entails building an industrial complex and, more importantly, changing the attitudes, mores and social norms of what they consider a decadent present. Most of all, they seek the approval of the "modern" West. That is why their feelings are hurt and their pride is deflated when the Westerners focus their attention, as they often do, upon the bedouins and desert-dwellers. Since WW I and the romanticization of desert life by T. E. Lawrence and the huge success encountered by Lowell Thomas (Sr.) in his film lectures and book on *Lawrence in Arabia*, the West has thought of the Arab as a glamorous sheikh or bedouin with flowing robes and embroidered kaffiyek, roaming the peaceful desert.[11] But Westernized Arabs saw nothing romantic in this picture and had nothing but contempt for the desert-dwellers and their distinctive dress—the very sign of backwardness.[12] A new Western image of the Arab, no less unfavorable than the first, was to emerge and almost supersede it after the end of WW II and the intensification of the cold war in particular.

THE COLD WAR AND THE ARABS

When the West began to experience the ire and fury of the new nationalist and Westernized elites in the Arab world, the word "Arab" began to conjure up the image of a dishonest, dirty and inferior individual. First, Britain and France were met with hostility and violence as they attempted to continue or reestablish their hold over the region. Their frustrations and the indignation that an erstwhile colonial people should demand independence and equal status on the international scene were channelled into bitter hatred for the "ungrateful troublemakers," the educated urban Arabs.

Soon, the United States joined Britain and France in holding this view of the Arabs when its own interests in the area were threatened by the Westernized elite.[13] As scheme after scheme for the "defense" of the Middle East had to be abandoned or shelved because of strong Arab opposition in the form of strikes, demonstrations and violence,[14] Americans began to share the sentiments of their European allies regarding Arab intelligentsia and the masses that accepted their leadership. Such a situation was hardly conducive to proper understanding or fruitful communication and interchange of ideas.

CULTURE AND LANGUAGE IN ARAB-WESTERN RELATIONS

Psychologists, anthropologists, and social scientists generally have argued that "rearing in one community limits one's understanding of unfamiliar or contrasting behavior patterns."[15] It is important, therefore, to investigate how language and culture have played a part in limiting the understanding of the Arabs and the West of each other's behavior.

Any person familiar with Arabic culture is quick to recognize that "Arabs speak with assertiveness and exaggeration."[16] This linguistic pattern is so ingrained in the Arab people's thinking and behavior that an Arab speaker is constantly "afraid that the listener may think that he means the opposite" if he does *not* exaggerate and emphasize his point.[17] This is part of a cultural heritage with a long history behind it. Arab writers and poets recognized this exaggerative trait and made ample use of it. It was so evident that it used to be said that the best poetry is that with the greatest amount of "lying" in it. What was meant, of course, was that the more exaggerated the poetry was, the better it was. This exaggerative trait of the Arabs has been observed and commented upon. Dr. Sania Hamady, in her book on the character of the Arabs, gives several examples of the Arabs' love of exaggeration and over-assertion.[18] This exaggeration is not restricted to poetry and literary prose. Arabs exaggerate in all their language communication, poetry or prose, classical or colloquial, romantic or political.

The Arabic language is alleged to contribute to a "general vagueness of thought; overemphasis on the psychological significance of the linguistic symbols at the expense of their meanings; . . . overassertion and exaggeration."[19] Thus, a writer or a speaker does not find it obligatory to be very specific, so long as the reader or listener can "guess" the meaning. On this score, Nasser's speech nationalizing the Suez Canal Company is a masterpiece: "We must always be cautious of the tricks of exploiters, imperialists and the stooges of imperialists. . . . We shall not permit the war-mongers, the imperialists and slave-traders to have a grip upon us,"[20] etc.

Perhaps it is safe to assume that all languages have ways and means of expressing assertion or exaggeration. The English language certainly has some. Yet they hardly compare with those employed in Arabic. Dr. Shouby writes: "The Arabic language abounds with forms of assertion, *tawkid*, and of exaggeration, *mubalaghah*. There is the common ending words that are meant to be emphasized; there is also the doubling of the sounds of some consonants to create the desirable stronger effect; there are also the freqeuent words *inna* and *kad*, used to emphasize a large number of sentences; and there are such forms of assertion as the repetition of pronouns and certain other words to get across their meanings or significance. Besides these grammatical types of over-assertion are the numerous stylistic and rhetorical devices to achieve even further exaggeration. Fantastic metaphors and similes are used in abundance, and long arrays of adjectives to modify the same word are quite frequent. Though gradually developing in the direction of brevity, the style of Arabic prose is still too florid (as judged by the standards applicable to English prose) to be considered factual and realistic."[21] (Emphasis supplied.)

Most of the grammatical types of exaggeration do, of course, lose their effect or significance upon translation to a language having a completely different set of grammatical rules, e.g., English. Nevertheless, we do have the other types of exaggeration which are almost fully retained in an English translation.

One way to demonstrate how Arabs exaggerate far more than Westerners is to compare the speech of President Nasser nationalizing the Suez Canal Company with Prime Minister Eden's speech in response.[22] Table 1 shows the basis on which the comparison is made and illustrates that even what is translatable of the vagueness in word and thought and of the ways of exaggeration and over-assertion in Nasser's speech, is decidedly more than what Eden employed in his own equally tough and important speech. Even if we

TABLE 1   Exaggerations and Qualifications Employed in Nasser's and Eden's Speeches

	Nasser	Eden
Vague Words and Phrases[1]	107	6
Vague Statements[1]	59	9
Words and Phrases Said More than Once	45	2
Repetition of Statements with Same Meaning	25	0
Exaggeration in Speech[1]	24	0
Assertive or Exaggerative Words Used[1]	74	49
Totals	244	66
Symbols of Qualification Used[1]	4	24

[1] Examples of vague words and phrases are: Battles against imperialism, plot, political trap; an example of a vague statement is: We must always be cautious of the tricks of exploiters, imperialists and the stooges of imperialists. Everyone, always, ever, and all are examples of tools of exaggeration; whereas perhaps, may and about are tools of qualification.

Numerals indicate the number of times the particular symbol is used in the speech.

bear in mind that the excerpts from Nasser's speech, upon which this analysis was made, were about twice the length of Eden's whole speech, our conclusion remains valid.[23]

Attention should be drawn to the third column of Table 1. This is certainly strong evidence in support of the assumption of exaggeration in the Arabic language. Indeed, repeating the same word or sentence, or almost the same sentence with a change of one or two words while retaining the essential meaning of what is being conveyed, is one of the most popular devices used by Arab orators. By contrast, no repetition of sentences of equivalent meaning was found in Eden's remarks; whereas some stretch of the truth and some "fantastic metaphors" in Nasser's speech were scattered throughout.

The ratio of the assertive and exaggerative words used in Nasser's and Eden's speeches is a startling 3:2. One is almost tempted to attribute this to Eden's very adequate study and knowledge of the Arabic language. Another explanation could be that Eden was well aware of the "exaggerative nature" of the Arabs, and wanted Nasser to believe that he meant what he was saying. Nevertheless, when we look for qualification in the two speeches, the pattern reverts to "normal" again, with Eden holding the edge 6:1.

If we now concede the exaggerative linguistic behavior of the Arabs, our next question should relate to the relevance or significance of this fact in international relations. Two implications are evident. When Arabs are communicating to each other, they are forced to exaggerate and over-assert in order not to be misunderstood. Yet non-Arabs, not realizing that "the speaker is merely following a linguistic tradition,"[24] are likely to misunderstand his intent and thus attribute a great deal of importance to the over-stressed argument.[25]

Secondly, when non-Arabs speak simply and unelaborately, they are not believed by the Arabs.

Did such a misunderstanding take place during the Suez Crisis, for instance? The evidence seems to indicate that it did. Both Eden and Dulles revealed in public pronouncements their misunderstanding of Nasser's speech nationalizing the Suez Canal Company. Said Secretary of State Dulles: "No one reading the speech can doubt for a moment that the Suez Canal, under Egypt's operation, would be used, not to carry out the 1888 treaty, but to promote the political and economic ambitions of Egypt—what President Nasser calls the 'grandeur' of Egypt."[26]

Mr. Dulles here misunderstood the germinal point of Nasser's whole speech justifying the act of nationalization. To the Arabs in general it was, I believe, obvious that Nasser was returning a slap in the face that the West had given him. The "grandeur" that Nasser was seeking for Egypt was not at this stage political or economic in nature—except as these may accrue from his main objective, namely to get rid of the "imperialists," "colonizers," and the last vestiges of Western or any foreign domination. This explanation is rendered more acceptable if we remember the tremendous popularity which President Nasser enjoyed at this time among the masses of all the Arab countries. These millions had little to gain economically or politically from Nasser's Suez action. In fact, they continued in their unflinching loyalty to the Egyptian President during and after the Suez war when they stood to suffer financially from the blocking of the Canal.

Furthermore, Nasser referred to the income from the Suez Canal operation as being 100 million dollars. This, of course, was the gross income. Yet he was talking of it as though it were the net income, to be taken over and used "for the benefit of Egypt." This could mean one of two things. It could mean that Nasser, the Egyptians and the Arabs in general found a special significance in taking over the foreign company, operating it themselves, and allocating the profits after the expenses are paid. This is the interpretation that I believe the Arabs held or accepted. The other interpretation of Nasser's statement would be to assume that the Egyptian President was planning to take over all the income from the Canal to spend it on the Aswan Dam project—leaving the Canal unrepaired, and unimproved. This would have meant that Nasser was going to kill the hen that was laying the golden eggs for him. Though unrealistic, Sir Anthony Eden seems to have accepted the latter interpretation of Nasser's speech when he said: "If the [Suez] Canal is to do its job, its capacity to carry the traffic must be increased and much money spent upon it. The [Suez Canal] Company has been building up reserves for this purpose, and they'll all be needed. And what does Colonel Nasser say? Oh, he tells us he must take over the company because he wants to use its money to build the Aswan [High] Dam."[27]

Any non-Arab reading or listening to Nasser's speech would have logically come to the same conclusions as those expressed by Mr. Dulles and Sir Anthony Eden. It is possible, of course, that both Dulles and Eden were "fabricating" these excuses. Nevertheless, I believe it reasonable to assume that they were sincere in their concern over what they understood to be the case.

On the other hand, Nasser did not comprehend completely the Western utterances on the seriousness of the situation. He was quite surprised by the British attack on Egypt. His advisers had concluded that neither the economic nor the military situation of Britain would make possible an invasion before three or four months—during which Nasser "would stand back and wait for world opinion to save him."[28] This might have been a calculated risk worth taking, but it also showed that Nasser "didn't understand that the British mean what they say when they call the Suez Canal the lifeline of empire."[29] Nasser himself told us that he did not believe that the British would back up their ultimatum: "When their [the British Government's] ultimatum came on October 30, I had calculated there was no more than a 40% chance they would really take military action."[30] And again: "We were so deceived about British intentions . . . that one of the first things we did after the Israeli attack was to remove the brigade stationed at Port Said and send it to Sinai."[31]

Thus, there seems to be a "language barrier" between the Arabs and other nations—the Anglo-American nations, at any rate. But language is not the only factor. It would be stating the obvious to remind ourselves that the Arabs are quite different culturally from Westerners. In fact, an assertion can be made that most acts based upon accepted Arab mores or norms are judged bad, immoral, quaint, foolish, or stupid; whereas acts based upon accepted Israeli mores are judged good and/or moral by Westerners. Since Israel is the Arabs' most hated and feared enemy, unfavorable comparison with the Israelis hurts Arab pride and alienates the Arabs while at the same time bringing the Israelis and Westerners closer together. In the heat of the Suez crisis, an American wrote in a letter to *Time* magazine: "I would venture to say that we peace-loving Christians are secretly pleased that Sir Anthony [Eden] helped muzzle the mealy-mouthed Muslim [Nasser]."[32]

Although it is not seriously contended that even a slight majority of the American reading public felt as vehemently as the reader quoted above, a study of the "Religion" section of *Time* reveals the close ties of Jews and Christians and, not infrequently, stresses the clash between Judaeo-Christian mores and Moslem ones. Thus *Time* reported that in Nasser's Egypt: "Not only is prostitution outlawed, but a boy who whistles at or flirts with a girl in public is liable to three months in jail, and taxis leave their inside lights on when a young couple gets in. Hand-kissing is frowned on and alcohol is banned from official functions."[33] In another report the disparity is more outstanding: " 'God fight them,' wrote Mohammed in the Holy Koran. 'What liars they are.' Mohammed meant Christians and Jews, whom he had expected to accept his new vision. When they did not respond, he took to the sword."[34]

On the other hand, Israel is reported attempting to link the "busy present with the Old Testament past," searching for the lost mountain of Sinai, even during its short stay there during the invasion of 1956, and attempting to decipher the Dead Sea Scrolls.[35]

Dignity, honor, grandeur, and pride may and do mean something to a Westerner. However, they do not carry the same connotation or arouse the same feelings and passions in him as they do in an Arab. "Worry about external dignity is his [the Arab's] continual concern."[36] So great is this concern that

TABLE 2 Press Reaction to Acts Based on Accepted Arab Mores

Name of Magazine	Dignity, Honor, Grandeur	Loss of Face	Independence, Freedom (from colonization), Sovereignty	Lack of Strong Concern for Human Comfort	Pride, Prestige	Food and Drink	Cutting off Nose to Spite Face
New York Times	$1^1 + 2^2$	$2^2 + 1^3 + 1^1$	$9^2 + 1^3 + 2^1$	0	$5^2 + 1^3 + 1^1$	0	$2^2 + 2^1$
U.S. News & World Report	3^1	4^1	1^1	0	8^1	0	0
The Nation	0	0	1^3	1^1	0	0	0
The New Republic	0	2^3	1^3	0	1^2	1^1	1^1
Life	0	0	1^1	0	0	1^1	0
Newsweek	0	4^3	0	0	1^2	0	0
Time	5^1	0	3^1	1^1	0	1^1	0
Total	$9^1 + 2^2$	$5^1 + 2^2 + 7^3$	$7^1 + 9^2 + 3^3$	2^1	$9^1 + 7^2 + 1^3$	3^1	$3^1 + 2^2$
Kind of Reaction		38^1	22^2	11^3			
% of Total		53.5	31	15.5			

Numerals indicate the number of times the characteristic is mentioned.
[1] Unfavorably judged.
[2] Neutral, no judgment passed.
[3] Favorably judged.

an Arab is often willing to sacrifice his own life rather than suffer a set-back to his honor or self-esteem.[37] As Wilton Wynn wrote of President Nasser: "It is this determination not to accept humiliation, to lift himself and his people to a position of dignity and respect, that forms the great motivation in Gamal Abdel Nasser. . . . His doctrine is simply whatever action is necessary on a given day to protect the dignity of his people, to provide the strength to keep their heads up and knees unbent."[38]

TABLE 3   Press Reaction to Acts Based on Accepted Israeli Mores

Name of Magazine	Common Cultural and Religious Heritage with West	Apology to and Compensation of the Wronged	Helping Co-Religionists
N.Y. Times	3[1]	0	0
U.S. News & World Report	0	0	0
The Nation	0	0	0
The New Republic	1[1]	0	0
Life	0	0	0
Newsweek	1[1]	0	0
Time	5[1]	4[1]	1[1]
Total	10[1]	4[1]	1[1]
	15[1] = 100%		

Numerals indicate the number of times the characteristic is mentioned.
[1] Favorably judged.

Tables 2 and 3 show American reactions to acts based on accepted Arab and Israeli mores. While the editors and reporters demonstrated some understanding of Arab actions, displeasure was evinced by the Arabs' lack of concern for human comfort, the strange Arab cuisine, and the almost suicidal Arab pleasure in cutting off their nose to spite their face. Though no similar study was made of Arab reactions to Western mores, it is likely that the result would be similar. The point is that Arab-Western communication and understanding suffer greatly as a direct result of these cultural differences.

THE PALESTINE PROBLEM AND ARAB-WESTERN ALIENATION

There is hardly any doubt that the most important element in the creation of a communication gap between the Arabs and the West has been Arab-Zionist rivalry and the creation of the state of Israel. It should be recalled that the driving force behind the establishment of a "Jewish" homeland came from Western, particularly European, Jewish nationalists. As a reaction to prolonged persecution, and in direct response to pogroms in eastern Europe and the Dreyfus case in France in the latter part of the nineteenth century, a world

Zionist organization was established with the explicit purpose of eliciting support for the acquisition of territory on which to set up a Jewish state. The basic premise of the Zionist movement has been that a Jew cannot live in dignity anywhere except in a Jewish state. This assumption was challenged by several prominent Jews and the Zionist idea had a slow start in the United States because of the more tolerant treatment and liberal atmosphere.[39]

In 1917, the Zionists succeeded in persuading the British government to promise them help in the establishment of a Jewish homeland in Palestine. This promise, known as the Balfour Declaration, was made two years after the British had concluded an agreement with the Arabs, their allies in the war against the Ottoman Empire, to the effect that the Arabs would be autonomous in their countries. There is continuing controversy as to whether or not the area of Palestine was included in the Arab-British agreement.[40] What concerns us, however, is why the British issued the Balfour Declaration and the consequences of that action for the whole region. Though several reasons have been advanced to explain the British promise to the Zionist leaders, it is relevant for our purposes to emphasize two in particular. The first is the assumption that the West was beginning to feel a strong guilt for the inhuman treatment of the Jewish residents among them and was, therefore, ready to expiate its previous actions by lending a helping hand in the establishment of a Jewish state—especially since it was far away and did not belong to any Western power. Furthermore, it was convenient to assume that the land belonged to no one, since the Western image of the Arabs as wandering nomads came in handy to relieve any pangs to the conscience.

To the Arabs, the biggest blow was the implication on the part of the British that the Arabs were either expendable or unimportant. For how else could they interpret an official British document about Palestine, which was at the time 90% Arab, that refers to them only as "non-Jewish communities"? This, as J. M. N. Jeffries put it, was tantamount to "calling the grass of the countryside the non-dandelion portion of the pastures."[41] From then on, Arab-Western relations were to be plagued by a crisis of confidence, for not only were the Arabs dealt a crippling blow to their self-esteem, but their faith in the Western world, as personified by Great Britain, was shattered. To compound the difficulties still further, a joint Congressional resolution, also signed by President Harding in 1922, affirmed American support of the Balfour Declaration in almost the same language—with one significant exception, namely that Christians in Palestine were here mentioned by name whereas the preponderant majority of the population, the Moslem Arabs, were once more relegated to the category of "other non-Jewish communities."[42]

Perhaps the main factor that has helped Zionism in the West is the presence of a Jewish community in the various Western countries, and the corresponding absence of a significant element of Westerners of Arab origin. The United States and to a lesser extent Canada are the two Western countries with a detectable Arab population. But these Arabs are mostly of Lebanese (Syrian) origin and preponderantly Christian. Since many of them came to the West with the bitter memory of religious rivalry and massacres of Christians by Druze indirectly aided by the Sunni Moslem Ottoman rulers, their support of

Arab causes is less than enthusiastic. Especially since "Christian Lebanon"[43] has had to fight many battles, including a few bloody ones, to retain its independence and limit Arab "encroachments" in attempts to include the country in a greater Arab union, the "Syrians" in the West have tended to champion Lebanese versus Arab stands.

There are still some Arabs in the West who defend Arab causes but their influence is minimal. This is because they are few in number, hold few if any official positions and are composed primarily of diplomatic representatives, Arab Information Center personnel, students and teachers. They are in the main outside the body politic and can, therefore, exert no effective pressure to influence the decision-making processes. In the United States, the public is further made aware of Arab "propagandizing" since any material distributed by official agents of foreign governments has to be registered with the Department of Justice, and a statement to this effect has to appear on all such publications.

What aids the Zionist cause in the West still further is the inability of the public to distinguish among the three separate groups known as Jews, Zionists and Israelis. Not all Jews are Zionists, of course; the American Council for Judaism, for instance, is anti-Zionist. The Zionists, however, see a great advantage in confusing the three categories, referring to Israel as the "Jewish state," and often claiming to speak in the name of world Jewry.[44] But how does this affect Arab-Western relations? The answer is that it affects them very much— and most adversely. Thus, what should be kept in mind when discussing the numerous aspects of this issue is the sympathy and, in the words of Norman Thomas, the "guilt feeling that all Christians should share when we reflect on the treatment of Jews in ages and countries which we call Christian. Hence our reluctance to criticize *Jewish policy*.[45] Furthermore, the stigma of anti-Semitism is often attached to any possible critic of Judaism, Jews, Israel or any actions of Jews or Israel. As Alfred Lilienthal, an American Jew who is anti-Zionist, wrote of the situation in the United States: "Christian would-be critics [of Zionism, Israel or Jews] were speedily silenced with the smear-word 'Anti-Semitism,' and any latent Jewish opposition to Zionist nationalism has been throttled by the fear of being labeled 'treason to Jewry.' Crushed between the smear and the fear is American foreign policy in the Middle East."[46]

Now we come to a discussion of the structures, channels and styles of interest articulation by or on behalf of Israel and the Zionists in the West, and the consequent debarment of the Arab point of view. In systems theory and the structural-functional approach to the study of politics, it is postulated[47] that interests may be articulated by four major pressure groups designated as anomic, non-associational, institutional and associational. In a "modern" political system, interest articulation should be handled primarily by associational groups, but since there is no "pure" system, modern or primitive, even in Western countries the four different groups can be, and often are, utilized to present a particular point of view.

The associational interest groups have the advantages of an organizational base and the general recognition of being legitimate. Especially since no effective Arab associations are present, Zionist organizations of different kinds find that their task is relatively easy. It is made easier still by the important fact that the Arab-Israeli issue is of little or no concern to the average Westerner. When to this is added the popular association of Jew, Zionist and Israeli, the pro-Israel campaign is greatly aided.

Alfred Lilienthal, Freda Utley, Richard Stevens, Christopher Sykes, Harry N. Howard, Harry S Truman, James Forrestal, Moshe Menuhin, Ben Hecht and the U.S. Senate Foreign Relations Committee have all recounted in detail the persistent pressures applied by Zionist and pro-Zionist organizations on behalf of Israel.[48] In democratic societies, public officials need the support of a majority or plurality to be elected. The "Jewish vote," myth or reality, has been effectively employed to elicit pro-Israeli support from political parties and candidates as well as occupants of public office. Especially in the United States where the two major parties are not cohesive, local and regional contests are influenced to a great extent by the powerful, organized groups in the area. In the city of New York, a special case, it would be most difficult, if not impossible, for any anti-Israeli candidate to win an election. Even gubernatorial campaigns in New York state often develop into races as to which of the candidates would do more for Israel. Since New York is a populous state with a sizable number of electoral votes, presidential candidates avoid running the risk of losing the "Jewish vote" and, since there is no corresponding fear of losing the Arab vote, plunge into lavish promises of support for Israel. When Secretary of Defense James V. Forrestal attempted to bring the two major parties to agree not to press the issue of support for Israel too much since it would be detrimental to U.S. interests in the Middle East, he was accused of being anti-Semitic and was subjected to "persistent and venomous attacks."[49]

Political parties, legislatures, bureaucracies and churches constitute institutional interest groups. Here again the Zionists have found relatively easy access to these bodies whereas the Arabs have not. Zionist and prozionist individuals have been represented in all these various institutions. Since recent democratic theory conceives of the public interest as the end result of the interaction of the numerous interests in the state, the Arabs have suffered because their spokesmen have been few and often ineffective. These individuals have had to not only risk losing electoral support at the next election but have found it extremely difficult to make much headway in an atmosphere where it is "proper" and "respectable" to be pro-Israel and anti-Arab.[50] It is not easy to be persuasive when the stand on Arab-Israeli issues is based not on U.S. interests in the region but on whether or not the speaker is a bigot—where bigotry is defined as having an impartial, anti-Israeli or pro-Arab attitude. Consequently, the Arabs' basic frustration at their inability to communicate with Westerners mounts.

Perhaps just as important, if not more so, has been the influence of non-associational interest groups acting on behalf of Zionism and the state of Israel. Personal connection and the "old school tie" are still very important even in the modern political systems of the West. The Arabs have not had the advantage of close contacts with high public officials comparable to the Rothschilds,

Chaim Weizmann, Eddie Jacobson, Rabbi Abba Hillel Silver and many others. President H. S Truman has given us a glimpse of the pressure exerted on him to act in favor of the Zionists: "I do not think I ever had as much pressure and propaganda aimed at the White House as I had in this instance. The persistence of a few of the extreme Zionist leaders—actuated by political motives and engaging in political threats—disturbed and annoyed me."[51] But at the critical moment, it was Truman's old friend and partner in the haberdashery store, Eddie Jacobson, who secured an interview for Chaim Weizmann with the President of the United States, and persuaded Truman to give a de facto recognition of Israel immediately after it came into existence.[52]

The Arabs, denied most of the ordinary channels to communicate with the West, have consequently resorted to the articulation of their interest through anomic groups. Thus, frustrations are released and hostile reactions are communicated through demonstrations, riots and violent attacks against Western embassies, consulates, and information and cultural centers abroad. Needless to say, this is not a healthy situation and does not contribute to an atmosphere conducive to understanding or amity. Even in the Western countries, where freedom of speech is greatly valued, the Arab cause suffers from the stigma of anti-Semitism that is often applied to statements not favorable to the Israeli point of view. At international club exhibitions in England and the United States, there have been instances of unpleasant encounters between Arab and Zionist groups.

CONCLUSION

This paper, beginning with the premise that a communication gap exists between the Arabs and the West, attempted to analyze the causes behind it. Several elements combined to bring about this serious situation. The burden of a historical and long-enduring antagonism between Islam and Christianity; the Arabs' recent subjection to Western colonial rule; the fact that the Arabs belong to the backward regions of the world when their pride in the glorious past increases their awareness of the miserable present and their hostility toward the West, the alleged perpetrator of this backwardness; the consequent reluctance to side with the West in its major battle against the Communist East; and finally, and most importantly, the Western support in the creation of the state of Israel in the midst of the Arab homeland—all these factors combined to limit Arab-Western understanding and communication. Especially since the Arabs' main antagonists in recent years, the Zionists and the state of Israel, have had active and most successful supporters in the West while the Arabs themselves have not, their frustration in not reaching a modus vivendi with the West has been exacerbated. Added to all this are the cultural differences and the difficulty encountered when the flamboyant and exaggerative statements by Arab politicians are translated into Western languages. Under such circumstances, the wonder is not that so many Arabs have turned to the Soviet and Chinese camps for solace, but rather that such a large number of Arabs continue the attempt to communicate with the West.

NOTES

[1] The assertion is accepted as fairly valid. See Michel W. Suleiman, "An Evaluation of Middle East News Coverage in Seven American News-magazines, July–December, 1956," *Middle East Forum*, Vol. XLI, No. 2 (Late Autumn, 1965), pp. 9–30.

[2] Ethel Mannin, *The Road to Beersheba* (Chicago, 1964), p. 47.

[3] Wilfred Cantwell Smith, *Islam in Modern History* (New York, 1963), p. 99.

[4] *Ibid.* See also Albert Hourani, *Arabic Thought in the Liberal Age, 1798–1939* (London, 1962), pp. 296–297.

[5] *Time*, August 20, 1956, as quoted in Erskine B. Childers, *The Road to Suez* (London, 1962), p. 58. Of course, Christianity became a serious threat to Islam from the eighteenth century onward. See Hasan Saab, "Communication Between Christianity and Islam," *Middle East Journal*, Vol. 18, No. 1 (Winter, 1964), pp. 41–62.

[6] For examples, see Childers, *op. cit.*, pp. 36–46.

[7] Smith, *op. cit.*, p. 125.

[8] Childers, *op. cit.*, p. 32.

[9] For a detailed study of the findings of the King-Crane commission, see Harry N. Howard, *The King-Crane Commission* (Beirut, 1963); for Arab reaction to Wilson's famous statement, see George Antonius, *The Arab Awakening* (Beirut, n.d.), and Albert H. Hourani, *Syria and Lebanon* (London, 1946).

[10] Bruce M. Russet et al., *World Handbook of Political and Social Indicators* (New Haven, 1964).

[11] Childers, *op. cit.*, pp. 36–53; Suleiman, *op. cit.*, pp. 12–13. This romantic picture of the desert and its Arab residents elicits Western sympathy and a desire on the part of some observers to maintain the status quo, as if change is bound to be bad. See, for instance, Carleton S. Coon. "The Nomads," in Sydney N. Fisher (ed.), *Social Forces in the Middle East* (Ithaca, N.Y., 1955), pp. 23–42. Daniel Lerner, however, complains against this "misplaced" sympathy. See *The Passing of Traditional Society* (New York, 1958), pp. 73–74.

[12] Needless to say, the educated Arabs vehemently resent the image which Western film companies portray of the Arab.

[13] Here and elsewhere in the paper, reference to interests merely means the interests as viewed by the authorities in office, since a different group could view such interests differently.

[14] See John C. Campbell, *Defense of the Middle East* (New York, 1960). The defense, of course, was against communist penetration of the area, not of Arab lands against their bitterest enemy, Israel.

[15] John J. Honigman, *Culture and Personality* (New York, 1954), p. 224.

[16] *Ibid.*

[17] Sania Hamady, *Temperament and Character of the Arabs* (New York, 1960), p. 227.

[18] *Ibid.*, pp. 59–63.

[19] E. Shouby, "The Influence of the Arabic Language on the Psychology of the Arabs," *Middle East Journal*, Vol. 5 (1951), p. 291.

[20] Excerpts from Nasser's speech were printed in *U.S. News and World Report*, August 17, 1956, pp. 74–77.

[21] Shouby, *op. cit.*, pp. 298–299.

[22] The comparison was made on the basis of the excerpts from Nasser's speech which appeared in *U.S. News and World Report* (footnote 20 above), and Eden's whole speech which appeared in *ibid.*, August 17, 1956, pp. 78, 81.

[23] One could argue that the length of a speech in general is a good indication of vagueness, repetition, and exaggeration.

[24] Shouby, *op. cit.*, p. 300.

[25] Elie Kedourie asserts the opposing point of view that, in the Middle East, "rhetoric is a part of reality and not a substitute for it, and that the Palestine war of 1948 was a

product of rhetoric which—now as then—is the natural habitat of Arab politics." See Peter Calvocoressi, "Suez—Ten Years After," *The Listener*, Vol. 76, No. 1947, July 21, 1966, p. 79. See also Eliahu Sassoon's comments in the article entitled "How to Speak to the Arabs," *Middle East Journal*, Vol. 18, No. 2 (Spring, 1964), pp. 143–162. But even if it is conceded that rhetoric is a part of reality in Arab life, the main point is still valid, namely that such a situation creates a communication gap between the Arabs and the West.

[26] *U.S. News and World Report*, August 10, 1956, p. 59.

[27] Eden, *op. cit.*, p. 81.

[28] Calvocoressi, *op. cit.*, p. 78.

[29] *Time*, August 27, 1956, p. 26. The remark was attributed to a friend of Nasser's.

[30] *Ibid.*, December 10, 1956, p. 36.

[31] *Ibid.*, p. 41.

[32] *Ibid.*, December 31, 1956, p. 4.

[33] *Ibid.*, July 23, 1956, p. 51.

[34] *Ibid.*, November 5, 1956, p. 67.

[35] *Ibid.*, September 3, 1956, p. 61; December 3, 1956, p. 71; October 1, 1956, p. 10.

[36] Hamady, *op. cit.*, p. 35.

[37] See H. R. P. Dickson's remarks concerning *The Arab of the Desert* (London, 1951), p. 55.

[38] Wilton Wynn, *Nasser of Egypt: The Search for Dignity* (Cambridge, Mass., 1959), p. 66.

[39] Alfred M. Lilienthal, *What Price Israel* (Chicago, 1953), pp. 15–23.

[40] See Antonius, *op. cit.*

[41] As quoted in Edward Atiyah, *The Arabs* (Harmondsworth, England, 1955), p. 103.

[42] Oscar I. Janowsky, *Foundations of Israel* (Princeton, N.J., 1959), p. 138.

[43] The term loosely applies to those Lebanese who champion Christian and generally non-Arab or anti-Arab-Moslem interests.

[44] Perhaps the most frequent complaint of the American Council for Judaism is that the Zionists and the state of Israel claim to speak for world Jewry and the "Jewish people." See their publications, especially the quarterly journal, *Issues*.

[45] As quoted in Alfred Lilienthal, *There Goes the Middle East* (New York, 1957), p. 211 (emphasis in original).

[46] Lilienthal, *What Price Israel*, p. 122. Among the well-known persons or institutions that, at one time or another, have been charged with "anti-Semitism" for their impartial, anti-Zionist or pro-Arab attitudes are the following: President F. D. Roosevelt who earned his anti-Semitic label posthumously, Dorothy Thompson, Willie Snow (Mrs. Mark) Ethridge for her book *Going to Jerusalem*, Professor Millar Burrows of the Yale School of Divinity, Dr. Bayard Dodge, one-time president of the American University of Beirut, Harvard Professor and Philosopher William E. Hocking, Dean Virginia Gildersleeve, Kermit Roosevelt, Professor Arnold J. Toynbee, U.S. Secretary of Defense James V. Forrestal, Adlai Stevenson, though to a much lesser extent, and the U.S. State Department. See Lilienthal, *What Price Israel* and *There Goes the Middle East*; and *Time*, September 24, 1956, p. 6.

[47] See Gabriel A. Almond and James S. Coleman (eds.), *The Politics of the Developing Areas* (Princeton, 1960); and Gabriel A. Almond and G. Bingham Powell, Jr., *Comparative Politics: A Developmental Approach* (Boston, 1966).

[48] In addition to Lilienthal's two books already mentioned, see *The Other Side of the Coin* (New York, 1965); Utley's *Will the Middle East Go West?* (Chicago, 1957); Stevens' *American Zionism and U.S. Foreign Policy, 1942–1947* (New York, 1962); Sykes' *Cross Roads to Israel* (London, 1965); Howard's "The Senate Inquiry into Zionist Activities," *Arab Journal*, Vol. 1, No. 1 (Winter, 1964), pp. 30–35, and "The State Department and the Charge of Anti-Semitism," *Issues*, Vol. 20, No. 3 (Autumn, 1966), pp. 1–8; Truman's *Years of Trial and Hope, 1946–1952* (New York, 1965), II, Ch. 12; *The Forrestal Diaries* (New York, 1951) edited by Walter Millis; Menuhin's

The Decadence of Judaism in Our Time (New York, 1965), and "The Stifling and Smearing of a Dissenter," *Issues*, Vol. 20, No. 2 (Summer, 1966), pp. 1–9; Hecht's *Perfidy* (New York, 1961); and *Activities of Nondiplomatic Representatives of Foreign Principals in the United States*, Hearings before the Committee on Foreign Relations, United States Senate, Eighty-eighth Congress, First Session, Part 12, May–August, 1963.

[49] Lilienthal, *What Price Israel*, p. 99. See also James G. McDonald, *My Mission to Israel* (New York, 1951), p. 13.

[50] Among those who have spoken out against the Zionist pressure tactics have been Senators William J. Fulbright and Ralph E. Flanders, and the American Council for Judaism.

[51] Truman, *op. cit.*, p. 186.

[52] See the two-part story on Eddie Jacobson by Sidney L. Willens in *The Kansas City Times* and *The Kansas City Star*, May 13, 1965, pp. 16D, 18B.

THE RHETORIC
OF THE ARAB-ISRAELI CONFLICT

D. Ray Heisey

D. RAY HEISEY received his B.A. from Greenville College, his M.A. from Ohio State University, and his Ph.D. from Northwestern University in 1964. He has also studied at Edinburgh University. He is currently professor of speech and director of graduate studies in the Division of Rhetoric and Communication, School of Speech, Kent State University. He serves as business manager of The Ohio Speech Journal and has published articles in Western Speech, The Southern Speech Journal, The Speech Teacher, Preaching: A Journal of Homiletics, Acta Symbolica, and The Quarterly Journal of Speech. He has contributed original essays to Preaching in American History (Abingdon, 1969) and Sermons in American History (Abingdon, 1971). He was made a research fellow at Yale University, was awarded a grant for research in the Faculty Institute on Middle East Studies by the Regional Council for International Education and a 1969 Summer Research Fellowship by the Kent State University Research Council. He also serves as secretary and member of the Executive Committee of the Kent State University Faculty Senate.

"The rhetoric used in the Western world to describe the Arab-Israeli conflict," writes Abdel-Wahab El-Messiri, "is a prime example of the use of language, not as a means of illuminating reality, but as a way of evading issues and complex historical totalities."[1] That is an Arab point of view. From the Zionist viewpoint, Robert Alter declares, "After the conflict has been swollen and distorted by twenty years of Arab propaganda, no peaceful solution is possible so long as the Arabs continue to act in consistency with their own ideology."[2] Anyone who has followed the Arab-Israeli conflict is fully aware that rhetoric is crucial. The question is: What is the nature of this rhetoric?

The purpose of this paper is descriptive. Rhetoric in this discussion is viewed as a transaction of ideas among people in a unique situation. The dimensions of the rhetorical transaction selected for consideration here are relational, ideological, and situational.[3]

THE RELATIONAL DIMENSIONS

When Abba Eban addresses the United Nations, and King Hussein the National Press Club, they speak not only or even primarily as individuals but for their nations. The international communication taking place may be said to hold the same kinds of relationships as those between individuals.

The first relational dimension is *acceptance*. This dimension raises the question of the degree of acceptance or rejection between the nations who are par-

Reprinted with permission of the Quarterly Journal of Speech, 61 (February 1970), pp. 12–21.

ticipating in the rhetorical act. In this situation we may interpret acceptance as equivalent to recognition of statehood. The Arab rejection of Israel takes the form of pathological hostility which turns into verbal threats of utter annihilation. In Israeli rhetoric the acceptance dimension functions as a primary element. Foreign Minister Abba Eban, in his address before the United Nations General Assembly on June 19, 1967, stated that "the true origin of the tension which torments the Middle East" is the Arab denial of Israel's "very right to exist."[4] This dimension in the international relationship, above all others, Israel would like to see changed.

Power, the second relational dimension, is the capacity to exert influence. Like rejection, power has created a disparate relationship between the parties in the conflict. Three times within two decades Israel has established her military superiority over the Arab states. In the political arena, likewise, Israel has managed to hold the balance by influencing the "right" decision-makers. Because of her manifest superiority of power, Israel is able to demand direct negotiations with the Arab states. On the other hand, Nasser, being weaker, relies heavily on words, perhaps compensating for military weakness with rhetorical "strength." Palestinians, who have practically no bargaining potential since Israel minimizes them as part of the problem, are forced to turn to non-talking situations, such as guerrilla warfare. The power variable in the international relationship has become a critical factor in determining the rhetorical responses made.

There is, however, another kind of power which the Arab states may find developing in their favor. I refer to the weight of world opinion regarding two matters, the first being the increasing awareness of and sympathy for the Palestinian refugees. The Arabs, with considerable justification, point to the injustice of this problem. The second matter is the increasing possibility of rash Israeli retaliation in the face of mounting attacks by the Al-Fatah. Newsweek reports that only a few days after the end of the Six-Day War, Al-Fatah's leaders met in Amman to ponder their next move. They decided on a long guerrilla struggle, says Newsweek, "to force Israel into another war with the Arab states—and another and another, if necessary."[5] Both of these problems, however, Abba Eban dismisses as secondary. In an interview with Alfred Friendly of The Washington Post of March 6, 1969, Mr. Eban says, "I used to think that a solution of the refugee problem would bring about peace. It is my conviction now that the exact opposite is true, that only peace can bring about a solution of the refugee problem." And regarding the guerrillas, he thinks these groups "are still marginal and not central."[6] If subsequent events prove that Mr. Eban has underestimated both of these items, opinion of the total international community might be able to stay Israel's hand. This would force a different rhetorical stance from Israel.

A disparity in the two variables of acceptance and power generally creates a relational distance between the rhetorical participants. This is the third dimension. When it exists, the primary function of discourse may be to establish an appropriate distance. Traditionally, the Israelis have claimed a desire to decrease at least the communicative distance by calling for direct discussions. For example, during the Eban-Friendly interview of March 6, Mr. Eban said:

In proposing in New York in October to try to reach agreement on each of the eight or nine subjects in the Security Council resolution . . . I said it made no matter to me which was discussed first.

I said let's begin with navigation, or the refugee problem, or boundaries, or take them up simultaneously with subcommittees to discuss each of them.

UAR Foreign Minister Riad's answer was to book passage back to Cairo because any response to this would have involved him in a dialogue with us.[7]

On the other hand, the Arabs claim that engaging in direct discussion would be giving in, as victims of aggression, to one of the points that should be negotiable—the status of Israel. In President Nasser's interview with *Newsweek*, Senior Editor Arnaud de Borchgrave asked: "If Israel were to pull back as the first phase of a settlement, would Egypt be prepared to sit down with the Israelis to discuss other issues?" The answer was: "I could not give you an answer about that until they pull out."[8] Inability to find agreement even on the method of closing the distance illustrates just how great that distance is.

The interesting observation about the distance dimension is that the rule in Arab-Israeli relations has always been destructive extremes—both total noncommunication and episodes of violent contact. Mr. Eban would seem to be making a reasonable observation in his extemporaneous speech delivered on the second night of the war: "I have already said that much could be done if the Governments of the area would embark much more on direct contacts. They must find their way to each other. After all, when there is conflict between them they come together face to face. Why should they not come together face to face to solve the conflict? On some occasions it would not be a bad idea to have the solution before, and therefore instead of, the conflict."[9] It is understandable, of course, why the party in the conflict which holds superior power would have a strong motivation to close the distance by direct communication.

THE IDEOLOGICAL DIMENSION

In addition to the relational, or sociopsychological, dimensions of the rhetorical event, there is the ideological dimension. To many this may appear to be the most important ingredient in the conflict. The Arab ideology, shaped by a long history of political and economic subjugation, is greatly divergent from Zionist ideology, created by the resources and value systems of the West. These respective ideologies provide "comfortable homes" for the ideas advocated by each side.

In stating the case for his nation before the United Nations on June 26, 1967, King Hussein said, "What Jordan and the Arabs want . . . is peace with justice."[10] Three primary claims seem patterned throughout the rhetoric of the Arabs.

(1) *There must be preservation of Arab rights against Western imperialism in the Middle East.* These "rights" are defined by President Nasser in his speech at the UAR Advanced Air Headquarters on May 25, 1967, as "our rights and our sovereignty over the Gulf of Aqaba which constitutes Egyptian

territorial waters."[11] In his speech at Cairo University on July 23, 1967, he also seems to be saying that these rights include the right to continue the revolutionary progress in the field of socialist reconstruction and in increasing national wealth.[12]

By Western imperialism Nasser means the Western powers (chiefly the U.S. and Britain), Zionism which "is the main ally of imperialism," and the Islamic alliance (Saudi Arabia, Jordan, and Iran) which, because it doesn't prevent the supply of oil to Israel, must be classed as "an imperialist alliance."[13]

The most recent meaning given to the term "Arab rights" in the face of Western imperialism is a religious one. With the fire that gutted a wing of one of Islam's holiest shrines, Jerusalem's seventh-century Al Aksa mosque, the Arabs now have a highly emotional religious issue. The sacred places must be preserved. This means the call for a "holy war." "In the coming battle," President Nasser proclaimed, "the Arab soldiers will not be soldiers of the Arab nations alone but soldiers of God and protectors of His religions, houses of worship and holy books."[14]

(2) *There must be a regaining of the rights of Palestinian refugees from Israel.* On June 29, 1967, Dr. George Hakim, Foreign Minister of Lebanon, addressed the UN on "The Palestine Problem." He said:

> The creation of the Jewish state by the partition of Palestine was in itself a negation of the right of self-determination of the indigenous Arab majority in favour of an alien immigrant minority. But that was not all. The establishment of Israel resulted in the eviction of the Arabs from their own country and their displacement during the last twenty years by over a million Jewish immigrants gathered from the four corners of the earth. A great injustice was thus inflicted on the Arabs of Palestine who were doomed to live as homeless refugees in misery and degradation.[15]

He later stated that regaining their rights could be accomplished simply by carrying out the UN solution of "giving the refugees the choice of either returning to their homes in Palestine or receiving compensation for their lost property."[16]

Yasir Arafat, now head of Al-Fatah and the Palestine Liberation Organization, stated in what was one of his last interviews before being elected chairman: "We waited and waited and waited for the justice of the United Nations, for the justice of the world and the governments gathering in the United Nations while our people were suffering in tents and caves. But nothing of this was realized. None of our hopes. But our dispersion was aggravated. We have believed that the only way to return to our homes and land is the armed struggle."[17] Arafat represents the militant view of what justice will mean in the situation, and, according to the *New York Times* writer Dana Schmidt, he not only symbolizes the Palestinian nationalist movement, but is rising in importance while President Nasser is declining.[18] It therefore may be that this second Arab claim will eventually eclipse Nasser's, i.e., the right to the Gulf of Aqaba and to an uninterrupted progress in the revolution.

(3) To the Arab mind "peace with justice" means a third thing. *There has been a gross violation of the rule of law, which, if not corrected, can bring*

nothing but continued war. The Arab attitude is that, from the beginning, the conflict has been characterized by defiance of agreements, resolutions, and laws. One of the most cogent statements on this point is the address Dr. Muhammad H. El-Farra, Jordanian representative to the UN, delivered at the Duke University Law School on March 8, 1968. He defined the "Rule of Law" as embodying the "right of every people to self-determination," and traced the failure of world leaders to abide by this law back to 1897 in Basle when the Zionists resolved to establish a Jewish state. In speaking of the failure of the United Nations in 1967 to adopt a resolution calling for a withdrawal of Israel from the occupied areas, El-Farra warned: "International Law today is facing a real test. So is the United Nations which is the organization created to uphold the rule of law and safeguard the values enshrined in its Charter."[19]

In contrast to the Arab rhetoric of calling for "peace with justice," Zionist rhetoric calls for "security and peace." Mr. Eban, in his June 19, 1967, speech said, "Israel waged her defensive struggle in pursuit of two objectives—security and peace."[20] Mrs. Golda Meir, in her address to the Knesset on March 17, 1969, reiterated, "As in the past, the central tasks facing Israel today are, above all, to safeguard the nation's security and to continue to strive for peace."[21] The sequence of these objectives is the same in both statements; it is significant in understanding the Israeli ideology.

(1) First, *there must be a preservation of Israel's existence against neighboring aggression and an end to the belligerency by the Arab states.* Ever since the first act of aggression over the UN partition lines in 1947, Israel argues that, in light of the failure of the UN to guarantee the security of her borders, she must take all measures necessary for her own protection. This meant the first war, the Sinai campaign, and the Six-Day War. In his UN speech on the second night of that war, Mr. Eban said that in those early days in June "there was peril for Israel wherever it looked." He further stated, "Never in the history of nations has armed force been used in a more righteous or compelling cause."[22] More recently, the Israeli military activity in the vicinity of the cease-fire lines is justified on the basis of reciprocity. Prime Minister Meir announced at the meeting of the Knesset on June 30, 1969: "Anybody who fails to honor the cease fire agreement and shoots at us cannot claim impunity from the results of his aggression. Those who attack us should not be surprised if they are hit sevenfold in response, since our main purpose in retaliating is self-defence and deterrence."[23] For Israel, security is a prior condition to peace.

(2) *There must be a recognition of Israel's sovereignty and a permanent peace treaty* "duly negotiated and contractually expressed." Mr. Eban stated in his speech of October 8, 1968: "This principle, inherent in the Charter and expressed in the Security Council resolution of November 1967, is of immense importance. It should be fulfilled through contractual engagements to be made by the Governments of Israel and of each Arab State, to each other, by name. It follows logically that Arab governments will withdraw all the reservations . . . about the non-applicability of their signatures to their relations with Israel or about the non-existence of Israel itself."[24]

The ideological dimension reveals that the disputants in this conflict both share the central goal of ultimate peace; the ego-involvement in each case, however, produces different attitudes regarding the prerequisite for that peace. For the Arabs, it is justice; for Israel, it is security.

THE SITUATIONAL DIMENSIONS

The situational context in which the Arab-Israeli rhetoric occurs is one of noncommunication, in the sense that the climate of discourse does not lend itself to the revelation of reality.

In the first place, the transaction of ideas between the two groups is expressed in an appearance of *irrationality*, that is, it is propagandistic. Dr. Solomon Simonson of Yeshiva University, in studying the propaganda techniques used by both the Arabs and Israelis, hypothesizes that each group is speaking to five national audiences.[25] His description may be summarized as follows:[26]

Audience	Arab Approach	Israeli Approach
1. domestic	instill "hate"	instill "confidence"
2. allies	encourage "bandwagon"	arouse "fear"
3. neutral	evoke "pity" for refugees	cite legal "proof" of right of statehood
4. satellites	"vilification" of Israel	establish ethos of "plain folks"
5. enemy	create image of "old world charm"	create "envy" for opportunities

The propaganda on both sides confuses the rationality of the respective claims and distorts rather than illuminates reality.

Arab-Israeli rhetoric is noncommunicative not only because it occurs in a context of propaganda, but also in a climate of *self-deception*. The Arabs, driven by their "autistic hostility," blindly refuse to recognize Israel's right to survive as a political state. Robert Alter, writing in *Commentary*, suggests that the Arabs are captives of "a collective myth"[27] about the cosmic forces of evil incarnated in Israel, who serves as an agent of colonial Western imperialism. The Arabs, furthermore, apparently feel the need to believe that Israel is expansionist, in order to help justify their military preparedness.[28] It has been argued that they persist in deceiving themselves on this point. Larry Hochman, in a lecture delivered at Columbia University, said that the case against Zionism is strong enough to stand on what can be well-established without putting forth unsubstantiable claims. He continued, "It is held in some quarters that there is some driving force in Zionism that generates continuous expansion and an inherent dissatisfaction with any fixed borders. This is a mystical and less than useful concept. While it is true that Israel has expanded on three occasions, one cannot conclude that this was some inexorable consequence of Zionist elan. Some elements within Israel are ideologically expansionist, but they are, so far, a minority."[29]

Israel, on the other hand, by her own desperate fight for survival, refuses to acknowledge adequately her complicity in the refugee problem and to take appropriate action that would effectively deny her *apparent* expansionism. Israel is also a victim of self-deception in thinking that a directly negotiated peace settlement will dissolve the years of hostility, resentment, and humiliation experienced by the Arab states and the inhumanity endured by the Palestinian refugees. A piece of paper may change one's legal relationship but not one's feeling relationship.

Moreover, the situational context is noncommunicative in that there is an atmosphere of *misperception*. Both sides perceive collusion between the "enemy" and a Big Power. The two most comprehensive addresses given by Arab-Israeli spokesmen on the Six-Day War were Nasser's Revolution Anniversary speech on July 23 and Eban's UN speech on June 19. A careful examination of these two addresses reveals a remarkable symmetry in their structure and approach. Both speakers commence with an attempt to clarify the historical origins of the conflict, then give their explanation of the 1967 war in particular, and claim that there was nothing else to do but what was done. Finally, in typical "bad boy" fashion, both men spend considerable time and detail describing the demon role of the "real" trouble-maker. Mr. Nasser, for example, says that the United States' role, though vague, was a deception in the interest of the Israeli aggression. He cites the delaying diplomatic efforts of the U.S. in late May, the 6th Fleet near Egyptian shores, the espionage ship *Liberty*, the presence of U.S. aircraft over Arab front lines, U.S. endorsement after the war of the Israeli point of view, and the "appalling difference" between the U.S. attitude of 1956 and 1967. When, in 1956, he says, the U.S. was surprised by the tripartite aggression, it took a stand against it. However, in 1967, when the U.S. was not surprised, it supported Israeli aggression. Therefore, he concludes, there was collusion between the U.S. and Israel.[30] Mr. Eban, in the UN speech, describes the Soviet role as follows: It has changed from a balanced friendship to one of encouraging the Arab states in their effort to conquer Israel; efforts to get Soviet agreement to reduce arms met with no avail; this forced Israel to waste economic energy on arms; alarmist and incendiary reports of Israeli intentions were circulated; on five significant occasions the Soviets used their veto against Israel; the veto has thus denied Israel a just and equitable treatment in the Security Council.[31]

Both of these demon descriptions are based partially on fact; this is what makes them so dangerous as rhetorical weapons. But the fallacies that evolve from the facts could, as Eugene Black says, "raise the temperature of the Middle East to a new flash point—one which could even spark World War III."[32] Speaking before the Middle East Institute in October, 1968, Eugene Black said these fallacies are believing that the policies of Tel Aviv are made in Washington, and believing that the Arab policies are or can be made in Moscow. The realities are that neither Israel nor the Arab states would ever permit such violation of their independence.

A second example of situational misperception is given by Mr. El-Messiri in *The Arab World*. He cites six concepts of the situation held by Israel and the Western world that result in moral and ideological confusion.[33] Probably the best example is the use of the term "Arab terrorists" instead of "Palestinian freedom fighters." Other examples are "Arab-Jewish" conflict when the Arabs have no complaints against the Jews as such, the Arab "holy war" when it is purely a political issue, the analogue between the present situation and ancient Israel, Arab "antisemitism" when antisemitism is a Western phenomenon, and "the fact" of Israel when, in other situations, the logic of the jungle is repudiated and changed. Mr. El-Messiri's examples are from an Arab point of view. Those concepts held by Arabs that are likewise distorted rhetorical formulations might include "driving Israel into the sea" instead of "freeing Arabs and Jews from Zionism," or even the term "Arab" in the phrase "Arab-Israeli" conflict distorts the reality of the situation. The Arabs would like to perceive themselves as having solidarity, but there is more than one "Arab" point of view as to what the problem is and as to what the solution is. This indeed has been one of the difficulties in the Middle East conflict.

SUMMARY AND CONCLUSION

The purpose of this paper has been to examine the nature of the rhetoric of the Arab-Israeli conflict. Considerable disparity in the relational dimensions of acceptance, power, and distance was found. Exploring the ideological dimension of the transaction indicated obviously a wide divergence in priorities. The Arabs call for *justice* and peace; Israel wants *security* and peace. The situational dimension was shown to be characterized by a climate of noncommunication, i.e., a galaxy of distorted formulations of reality. Descriptively, the rhetoric of the Arabs is *juridical*. It is a rhetoric that demands justice in the court of world opinion and in the marketplace of world action for the rights of the Arab peoples, the Palestinian refugees, and the enforcement of international law. The Israeli rhetoric is *justificatory*. It is a rhetoric that seeks to justify after-the-fact. In attempting to obtain secure borders, Israel has had to wage offensive action and then sit back to wage a rhetorical battle, justifying its behavior.[34]

The nature of the rhetoric of the Middle East conflict, in its structure and strategy, suggests two concluding observations. Perhaps these observations would be applicable more broadly to the rhetoric of confrontation where potential violence exists between the parties.

(1) *Both sides in the conflict will need to de-escalate the dysfunctional rhetoric.* This means that the use of propaganda techniques and provocative threats and accusations should be reduced. One of the elements in the Six-Day War was the dramatic speed of the escalation and the significance of the verbal factor (the threats and the boastings on both sides) in the escalation. Georges Tamarin has pointed out that two lessons to be learned from the 1967 crisis are that no verbal violence should be underestimated and demogoguery for "internal consumption" as a legitimate rule of the game should not be tolerated.[35]

De-escalating the dysfunctional rhetoric will also mean eliminating the distorted formulations of realities. Both sides will have to stop building facts into fallacies regarding the roles of the U.S. and the Soviet Union in determining policies. Both sides will have to adopt a revisionist policy with respect to the identity and designs of the opponents. The Arabs will need to perceive the best intentions of Israel, stripped of their expansionist appearances, and see her as she is, an independent, sovereign state in the heart of the Middle East. Israel, on the other hand, will need to perceive the legitimacy and morality of the Palestinian position, stripped of its annihilistic facade.

(2) *Both sides will need to accept the minimal conditions for communication and conflict resolution.* These conditions are mutual acceptance, gestures of trust, agreement on what issue is in conflict, and agreement on the method of resolving the conflict. Observe that included in this list is no mention of improved agreements or more substantial proof for one's case. As Edward Hoedemaker suggests in his article "Distrust and Aggression: An Interpersonal-International Analogy," offers of proof and persuasion are unavailing in relationships, whether person-to-person or nation-to-nation, where one is distrustful and aggressive.[36]

It is unfortunate that Israel responded to the overtures by King Hussein last Spring [1969] with the charge that his address at the National Press Club was merely "pious words" and "exercise of propaganda."[37] This would have been an excellent opportunity for Israel to respond with a mutual gesture of trust, as indeed Hussein's speech may be interpreted to have been. If the trust barrier could be broken, even in a small degree, the chance for a functional rhetoric would be improved.[38] But when Mr. Eban immediately underlines all the negative aspects of the Russian peace plan, denounces Nasser's five "concessions" he was willing to make in order to achieve peace,[39] and official sources call Hussein's peace plan a "two-phrase tactic to end Israel's nationhood,"[40] one is led to believe that Israel's long-standing claim that the Arabs do not want peace may, in fact, be losing some of its credibility. These recent Israeli responses are not examples of "coolness in rhetoric and discussion" which Eugene Black spoke of at the Middle East Institute in Washington.

Moreover, the Arab response to the Al Aksa fire that it was an act of deliberate and premeditated Israeli arson is certainly an unjustifiable exploitation of an unfortunate situation. If the Arab world had been genuinely interested in reducing the conflict, they would not have played into Israel's rhetorical hands in this way. Mr. Eban, in the opening statement of his press conference on August 24, 1969, after announcing that justice could take its due course with regard to the criminal who set fire to the mosque, strategically spent over half his time denouncing the Arabs for committing a crime that "takes us back to the Middle Ages."

> There has been committed and there is still being committed a crime on an international scale by Arab Governments and spokesmen who instead of joining humanity in shock and grief and in hope of repair are attempting to extract political advantage by a campaign with very few parallels in the history of our age. . . . There is need for the human conscience to sit in firm judgement of all those who have tried to exploit this grievous affair for purposes of incitement and hatred, as though there are not enough existing causes of tension so that there has to be a manufactured tension entailed upon the fidelity and belief of millions throughout the world.[41]

An analysis of the rhetoric of the Middle East conflict suggests that it is a rhetoric of divergent ideas held by hostile groups in a context of noncommunication. If this rhetoric continues, it can only create an escalation of the conflict.

But if it can be modified, either by the will of the disputants themselves, or by the overwhelming moral force of world opinion, perhaps there is a ray of hope for a functional rhetoric that would assist in a resolution.

NOTES

[1] "Rhetoric of the Arab-Israeli Conflict," *The Arab World*, XIV (May–June 1968), 15.

[2] "Rhetoric and the Arab Mind," *Commentary*, XLVI (October 1968), 65.

[3] The dimensions selected for use in the essay are adapted from Wayne Brockriede's "Dimensions of the Concept of Rhetoric," *QJS*, LIV (February 1968), 1–12. Mr. Brockriede's article offers "a contemporary concept of interrelated interpersonal, attitudinal, and situational dimensions of a broadly conceived rhetorical act," and suggests that these dimensions may, among other things, provide a framework for critical analysis. My intent has not been to apply Mr. Brockriede's comprehensive model; rather, it has been to select certain dimensions from his framework that seem to be particularly relevant to the Mideast rhetoric and explore their usefulness as a contemporary concept for a contemporary rhetorical situation. For the purpose of this essay, it was considered useful to sketch broad patterns in order to emphasize the dimensional and interrelated nature of the variables constituting the rhetoric of the Arab-Israeli conflict. It doesn't need to be pointed out that this conflict consists of vast and complex dimensions which reach back into history. This study is limited to rhetorical documents and pertinent materials relating to the Six-Day War in 1967 and events since then.

[4] Abba Eban's Speech at the Special Assembly of the United Nations, 19 June 1967," in Walter Laqueur, *The Road to Jerusalem: The Origins of the Arab-Israeli Conflict 1967* (New York, 1968), p. 336.

[5] "Pawns No More," *Newsweek*, LXXIII (January 20, 1969), 38.

[6] "Text of Interview with Israel's Foreign Minister Eban," *The Washington Post*, March 6, 1969, pp. E22–23.

[7] *Ibid.*, p. E23.

[8] "A Talk with President Nasser," *Newsweek*, LXXIII (February 10, 1969), 34.

[9] "Not Backward to Belligerency," in *Under Fire: Israel's 20-Year Struggle for Survival*, ed. Donald Robinson (New York, 1968), p. 350.

[10] *Vital Speeches*, XXXIII (August 1, 1967), 610.

[11] In Laqueur, p. 300.

[12] Nasser's Revolution Anniversary Speech at Cairo University, 23 July, 1967, in Laqueur, p. 326.

[13] Nasser's May 25th speech, in Laqueur, p. 300.

[14] "A Cry for a 'Holy War,'" *Newsweek*, LXXIV (September 8, 1969), 37.

[15] "The Palestine Problem at the United Nations," *Middle East Forum*, XLIII, Nos. 2 and 3 (1967), 30–31.

[16] *Ibid.*, 31.

[17] "Fatah Leader Stresses Militancy," *New York Times*, December 3, 1968, p. 6.

[18] *New York Times*, February 14, 1969, p. 14.

[19] "Role of the U.N. vis-a-vis the Palestine Question" (xeroxed copy of typed manuscript), p. 12.

[20] *Vital Speeches*, XXXIII (August 1, 1967), 619.

[21] "Safeguarding Nation's Security While Striving for Peace Remain Central Tasks of New Government" (mimeographed "Policy Background" paper), The Embassy of Israel, Washington, D.C. (March 18, 1969), p. 1.

[22] In Robinson, p. 344.

[23] "Highlights from the Address of Prime Minister Golda Meir in the Knesset, June 30, 1969" (mimeographed "Policy Background" paper), The Embassy of Israel, Washington, D.C. (July 2, 1969), p. 2.

[24] Abba Eban, "Forward to Peace" ("Text of the Address by Mr. Abba Eban, Israel

Minister for Foreign Affairs, in the Twenty-third Plenary Session of the General Assembly of the United Nations, Monday, 8 October, 1968") (printed pamphlet), Embassy of Israel, Washington, D.C. (October 1968), p. 13. The nine principles for peace, as seen by Israel, are here outlined and discussed.

[25] "An Analysis of Arab and Israeli Propaganda," Vital Speeches, XXXIV (June 1, 1968), 494–497.

[26] Professor Simonson's conclusions, though suggestive, are somewhat misleading. For example, where he says that the Arabs use a "hate" campaign with their domestic population, this writer finds in Nasser's major 1967 speeches—to the National Assembly, to the Advanced Air Headquarters, to the Arab Trade Unionists, and to Cairo University—that the general approach is one of building confidence, courage, and determination. Before the Six-Day War, he said: "It is the greatest honour for us to defend our country. We are not scared by the imperialist, Zionist or reactionary campaigns. We are independent and we know the taste of freedom. We have built a strong national army and achieved our aims" (in Laqueur, pp. 300–301). After the war, he stated, "Brothers, perhaps Almighty God wanted to test us to judge whether we deserve what we have achieved, whether we are able to protect our achievements, and whether we have the courage to be patient and stand firm against affliction" (in Laqueur, p. 327). Moreover, considerable evidence could be cited to show that for the neutral audience the Arabs likewise appeal to the historical and legal aspects of the issue, just as the Israelis do. The Arabs do more than simply evoke pity for the refugees.

[27] Alter, p. 64.

[28] For example, the Arab Information Center reports that there is a widespread feeling "that Israel might launch a pre-emptive strike against the United Arab Republic." The article continues: "Dayan's 'get-tough' speeches—stating that Israel must prepare for war on the Egyptian front, that considerable portions of the west bank would be retained in a peace settlement, that the Golan Heights now constitute an integral part of the State of Israel, and that the retention of Sharm El Sheikh means keeping half of Sinai— leaving the U.A.R. no choice but to prepare militarily," "Gun Diplomacy Escalates at Suez," Arab News and Views, XV (July 1969), 2.

[29] "Israel and the Arab Revolution," The Arab World, XV (June 1969), 17.

[30] Nasser's Revolution Anniversary Speech, in Laqueur, p. 332.

[31] Eban's speech at the Special Assembly of the UN, in Laqueur, pp. 349ff.

[32] Eugene R. Black, "Settlement or Solution in the Middle East?" U.S., Congressional Record, 90th Cong., 2nd Sess., October 21, 1968, CXIV, E9422.

[33] El-Messiri, 15–17.

[34] Compare the rhetoric of black power as described by Robert Scott in Robert L. Scott and Wayne Brokriede, The Rhetoric of Black Power (New York, 1969), pp. 132–145.

[35] He cites two examples of the consequences of verbal violence. Nasser's "strategic threat system," perhaps originally intended for internal consumption, evoked countermoves from the Israelis to such an extent that he was trapped by his own liberation of forces and became no longer a decision-maker. In Israel, when Eshkol gave his so-called "stammered speech," a surprising consequence occurred. Though he was trying to show restraint in the situation, his activist opponents reacted by leading a disloyal campaign against him. The "colorless" address had a "catastrophic effect on the overtense public, generating a feeling of having no real leadership." The strong personalities of Ben Gurion and Dayan were evoked and an aggressive tone was adopted by part of the press. See Georges R. Tamarin, "Israeli-Arab Conflict in Terms of Non-Communication," New Outlook, XI (February 1968), 18–19.

[36] The Journal of Conflict Resolution, XII (March 1968), 75.

[37] See "King Hussein and the Question of Peace in the Middle East" (mimeographed "Policy Background" paper), The Embassy of Israel, Washington, D.C. (April 14, 1969), for an Israeli analysis and response to the Hussein speech.

[38] "How to Break the Trust Barrier?" Newsweek, LXXIII (January 20, 1969), 36–37.

39 Arnaud de Borchgrave, "Pride, Fear, Suspicion," *Newsweek*, LXXIII (February 24, 1969), 42–43.

40 "King Hussein and the Question of Peace in the Middle East," pp. 2–3.

41 Abba Eban, "Opening Statement by the Minister for Foreign Affairs at the Press Conference, Jerusalem, 24 August 1969," Israel Information Services, New York, pp. 4 and 6.

NONCOMMUNICATION AS GAME
IN INTERNATIONAL RELATIONS
William J. Starosta

WILLIAM J. STAROSTA received his B.A. from Wisconsin State University at
Oshkosh where he spent his junior year in India studying parliamentary debate in
the Lok Sabha. He received his M.A. at Indiana University and his Ph.D.
there in cross-cultural communication. He received a CIC Summer Fellowship
to study advanced Hindi at the University of Michigan. He has published
articles in Southern Speech Journal and Today's Speech. He is assistant to the
editor of Intercommunication Among Nations and Peoples. During 1971–1972 he
was a Fulbright Scholar in Ceylon engaged in dissertation research into intercultural
communication and innovation in the villages. Starosta is presently an assistant
professor of speech and director of forensics at the University of Virginia.

For slightly over twenty years, since the formulation of Lasswell's
model of the communication process, communication students have
used as a point of departure for further study the formula: Who says what to
whom in what channel with what effect? (Lasswell 1948). In the intervening
years, alterations have naturally been made in order to encompass the study
of communication context (Thayer 1961), noise (Shannon and Weaver 1949),
intent (Berlo 1960) and the semantics of understanding (Perelman 1963).
Until the writings of Kenneth Burke (Burke 1945) were applied to the study
of the communication process, however, where scene was studied as influential
to shaping act by agent through agency for purpose, little or no attention
was given to normative considerations in communication,[1] nor were communicative models used to predict those circumstances under which one might
logically expect communication to occur or to break down.

To facilitate the location of those points where communication will most
probably occur, the present analysis has three interrelated goals. First, a view
of communication as game is offered. Then the model is applied to examples
of international political communication to isolate certain strains of communicative behavior that may, in a broad sense, be viewed as examples of
deliberate noncommunication. Finally, the game model of communication is
used to predict perimeters within which noncommunication would seem
profitable.

I

The examination of communication as game does not begin with the present
writer. One of the better treatments of the game aspects of international
communication is advanced in the writing of Thomas Schelling in the discussion of the risks that one undertakes in trying to influence the actions of

Printed with permission of the author. This essay was written for this volume.

another nation (Schelling 1960; 1966). Also, certain political decisions are now influenced by game theory (Rapaport 1962; Braithwaite 1955; and Goffman 1970), through which possible policy alternatives of a probable opponent are examined in terms of gain and loss, relative probability, and likely reward to the initiator of the action. When the sum of positive factors appears to override considerations of risk, a venture such as the Cuban missile blockade may be undertaken. Such a view of games, however, becomes more concerned with material considerations than with psychological ones, and, as an example of communication, it is at least once-removed from the model of concern in this paper.

The communication game, or any other game, can seldom be played in conditions of absolute certainty. A master chess player has been known to lose to lesser players, and a strong communication player must always guard against the possibility of loss. If the odds in favor of one player were absolute, the game would not continue. At most the one player might wish to maintain the appearance of choice. But the situation would clearly be reducible to terms of direct coercion. For this reason, a weak player remains in the game only so long as he sees a possibility of gain, even though to do so might result in his ultimate defeat. A characterizing feature of communication is that a message cannot be "transfused" into the mind of a receiver, and no absolute certainty may be expressed that the message will have its intended effect. At most, communication is a process or a result that must necessarily be expressed in terms of probability. Henry Johnstone, Jr., relates: "To argue is inherently to risk defeat. An argument we are guaranteed to win is no more an argument than a game we are guaranteed to win is a real game" (Johnstone 1965). Those nations with a common world outlook (Boulding 1966), a common goal (Van Nieuwenhuijze 1963) or a common cultural heritage (Hymes 1967) maximize their chance of communicating.

If communication is a process aiming at a probable outcome, a number of factors inhere in the communication circumstance that reinforce or weaken the chances of "success," however defined. Among the more significant factors are the knowledge of risks involved, a recognition of the magnitude of the stakes, an awareness of relevant rules, some concept of the relative status and ability of the players, a factor of awareness that a message has been initiated and a continuing commitment to play. If the various factors, taken in sum, seem to favor the process of communication, communication will then surely be strengthened. If the factors are lacking, singly or collectively, communication will suffer distortion.

Risk is a factor in all communication. In an abstract sense the party that communicates risks being given a response. Consideration of the response risks a change in the perception of the communicator. As a result, personality, belief, and action may be altered because of communication. Moreover, instead of receiving an answer in some overt channel, the communicator risks being ignored, denounced, or threatened in return for his offering of a message. As put by Burke, in communicating " 'Thou shalt not' there is implicit 'what would happen if' . . ." (Burke 1941). India attempted repeatedly to communicate through the organs of the United Nations that it would accept a plebiscite to determine the status of Kashmir, but the risk was in this case that the offer might be accepted and pressed by the Security Council. A gambit offered by the USSR to remove the Secretary General of that organization in favor of a *troika* arrangement met with the consequence that the Afro-Asian group decidedly turned against the proposal. In short the assessment of risks leads to the formulation of appropriate tactics. Tactics "represent those rule-bound behavioral options designed to make the game end appropriately" (Rosenfield 1968). The choice of tactics serves to increase or to decrease the chance of success in meeting the purpose of the communication.

Several factors are important in assessing risk and in formulating tactics for play. Of these the most important may be to consider the stakes of the game. If there is nothing to be gained, and no negative consideration such as loss of "national honor" at stake, concessions may be easy to grant. Minor freedom of the press may be granted in an otherwise closed society. Little worry need be shown if a nation or delegate does not vote as expected in the case of a relatively minor measure in an international assembly, so long as the appropriate messages are initiated when the measure is of greater importance. Or, if a nation is in a clear position of dominance, it may initiate propaganda without fear of reprisal by the recipient nation. The stakes are too great for the recipient to respond in kind. Stakes are largely accessible to calculation in terms of wealth, property, or substantive gains and may actually be measured in many cases.

Less concrete are odds. To a great extent odds may be largely subjective, calling into play factors of incentive, commitment, dedication, public opinion, prediction of an opponent's values, and political climate. Propaganda may in one case bring no response at all, whereas in another it may cause the broadcast of counter-propaganda, the initiation of threats and troop movements, or the seizing of some objective by an opponent using the message as a pretext for a retaliatory damaging measure. To begin to understand the odds of receiving a predictable response, the communicator need know not only those features that distinguish the recipient's culture from his own, but he must also know the style of his opposing decision maker under conditions of varying stress. To this extent the calculation of odds is the assessment of relative intangibles. Underlying these considerations are others concerning the projection of a communicator's image: "In addition to what the leadership of a country says, the capabilities of a country, as well as its past and present action, influence the enemy's credibility of that country's intentions" (Halperin 1966). There-fore, "The rational man plays the odds; he bets on the greater probability as he sees it from the available evidence. . . . In a dispute, the odds (or probability) may be the same, but the importance of a win or loss (the stakes) may be drastically different" (Ray and Zavos 1966). Accordingly, when the stakes are high, a nation may play the game regardless of odds, which leads to the con-clusion that odds are dependent on stakes as a motivating factor, not stakes on odds.

A fourth factor that determines the outcome of a communication is the nature of the game. Some games are played to make communication a sub-stitute for action. Such a game is played from a position of inequality of opponents, when either a stronger player need not concede a just solution or when a weaker player cannot take the object of his communication by more direct means. As opponents approach relative equality or are backed by secondary players, a second type of game ensues, and communication often tends toward establishing an actual solution to the dispute. After World War II, there has been a distinct tendency to solve those disputes which were backed by stronger players of relatively equal strength (Holsti 1966). In these cases the rules of the game include an injunction that communication means the most in a stalemate situation, and may be seen as a gambit in positions of great inequality. Status considerations are all part of the game.

Players vie for position within a matrix of communicative rules of behavior. Major powers may communicate by proxy. Nonrecognition of one or more of one's opponents may be put as a condition of further communication. Or parties to a solution may make efforts to present themselves as "eager to continue to look for a solution" in order to satisfy noncommunicating observers. In effect these factors, in addition to physical items such as the shape of the bargaining table and credentials of the delegates, become fixed rules of play. In certain stages of communication, these factors are given more attention than the fact that a situation of war exists between parties to the communication. Depending upon the style of play, rules may be open or secretive. In the latter case: "At the same time as knowing ourselves, we must prevent our adversary in the game from knowing us, our strength and our intentions, our style of 'play'" (Aranguren 1967). Otherwise, we and our game plan become calculable. If a strategy is too openly presented, a weaker opponent has "queen's odds" toward victory in communication. The stronger player of course still may win, but the outcome is less predictable, such as the position of the United States in the Paris talks over Vietnam.

Two other conditions for play that were noted earlier, that is, awareness and a commitment to play, are better discussed by posing the possibility of deliberate noncommunication by at least one party to the conversation as it relates to the game formulation of communication.

II

A counterpart to communication is silence. In its simplest form, silence isolates the parts of a message. It emphasizes, shows approval or disapproval, condemns, conveys uncertainty, marks the assertion of superiority or of defeat, or perhaps is used to mark time while strategy is formed. Whereas communication proceeds from the breaking of a symbolic code by the receiver, silence permits no ready deciphering. Meaning is drawn almost exclusively from the mental set of the observer and more or less corresponds to the concept that occupies the mind of the observed. When employed tactfully, silence serves a purpose for the communicator. It is a "scene" within which interpretation occurs.

At the same time as silence supplements communication, it may also signify the breakdown of communication. Diplomatic recognition is a promise that governments will abandon a policy of political silence with another nation in order to establish political exchange. By contrast the United Nations may issue a resolution that nations should use "whatever means necessary" to effect a change of South Africa's racial policies. Embargo or "stern measures" may be threatened to alter that policy. The very ambiguity of the threat is a form of silence, which is used to maximize the scope of possible action. If the directive would state the outline for very specific action the case would be communicative by contrast. The directive is explicit or silent. It may communicate or it may deliberately be phrased to avoid communication of an explicit action step. Noncommunication has supplemented communication as a means of making a threat more compelling.

I have earlier suggested that the use of noncommunication is likely to be most frequent between unequals. Here the stronger party can safely neglect the pleas of the weaker for as long as a stronger power fails to side with the weaker party. The varieties of noncommunication open to such a party are legion: A message may be communicated to help outside parties from a desired impression of events with little attempt at communicating with the party in question (Starosta 1971). In the Middle East, nations address the world in order to justify their positions, while at the same moment failing to communicate directly with each other. Whereas the United States retains a choice on the issue of being diplomatically silent with Mainland China, those neighboring nations within China's sphere of influence can afford no such luxury. By contrast, diplomatic ties have been retained with the Soviet Union, a relative equal to the United States. In this way silence is manipulated to suit national ends.

Likewise the silence of inequality terminates military exchanges between parties. When the Indian government was faced with repeated protest from Pakistan about the accession of Kashmir, a very limited amount of arms buildup occurred. India at this moment promised to honor her pledge of offering a plebiscite to the people of Kashmir. Little attempt was seriously made to reach a settlement with Pakistan, however, because of the position of inequality after the British withdrawal from both countries. When China threatened to open up a second front against India at the same moment as India was fighting against Pakistan, India was led to consider (1) bargaining in earnest with Pakistan, (2) seeking outside support, and (3) returning to the United Nations to seek a political settlement. Such moves recognized the altered situation as necessitating a need either to communicate seriously or to gain a position of rhetorical (and actual) dominance. Contrarily, Pakistan to this day ritually protests the Indian measures, much as the West still protests the Soviet action in Hungary and Czechoslovakia, to no avail. The message appeases those who wish to make a display of their resolve but who are in no position to make good their words. Silence once more was generated by a position of inequality. By the same token it will terminate when Mainland China becomes an equal to the West, when Pakistan again receives outside support, or when a counterthreat is again posed to neutralize the rhetorical advantage of the stronger opponent. The question comes down to stakes and odds. Silence is a luxury that equals cannot afford, whereas the powerful gain policy and communication options, including the ability to employ noncommunication.

A second aspect of noncommunication is seen in the propaganda line of China toward the West. Sinologists comb the available Chinese wall posters and newspapers for changes in the wording of the official line. If one day the United States were no longer to be categorized as imperialistic, the observer would be led to begin speculation on the reason for that change. Perhaps this could be taken as a sign of entente or rapprochement, or it could be a way of bargaining for Western support in China's dispute with the Soviet Union. Two factors are again the key to interpreting the message. First, Western observers must be aware of the change in line. Without such an awareness, noncommunication cannot communicate. Silence would go unnoticed. The second point to note is that the propaganda silence is no more than a sign, a clue or an indicator of policy change. Silence, in such a case, is laden with ambiguity. Perhaps China merely wished to change her example of imperialist to Russia and has no changed stance toward the West. Or perhaps we would be reading in meaning where none was intended. China's silence may have been completely unintentional, and this particular communication game would be a conjuring up from our own mind. Of course we would lack a valid response for such an eventuality. Schelling carries this analysis one step further (Schelling 1966). He views the line of China as an example of stylized irrationality through which China makes every action ambiguous. In this way other countries are forced to allow an extra margin of safety when dealing with China. Because of the noise factor, which distorts an ambiguous message, the message is never communicated in its entirety. Silence, in addition to being ambiguous, demands the constant attention of an observer. If that attention were to lapse, the silent message would effectively cease to exist.

Some rhetorical situations automatically assure the attention of another party. When Warsaw Pact members begin troop maneuvers within the boundaries of a member state that has been liberalizing its press and educational system in recent months, action communicates. No supplementary message is needed to suggest that such liberalization is not a desired course of action. Even when the drills are accompanied by a joint statement of solidarity between the Soviet Union and the country in question, a silent message is read between the lines. It is understood only in conjunction with an interpretation based upon scene or message circumstance. In all probability the message is simply another example of noncommunication. As such it takes its meaning only in the mind of an observer who can penetrate the wall of silence and noise around the message. The landing of American marines in a foreign country to "preserve American lives and property," the cancellation of a track meet between cold-war powers for some trivial excuse, the delivering of a United Nations address by a second-rank member of the diplomatic staff when protocol would demand that the speech be given by a high-ranking ambassador, or the movement of ships into the Mediterranean for drills when the Middle East situation becomes more intense all serve to communicate. The precise message may be a result of context, trust or mistrust, current political conditions, or the personality of the actor or observer. The message is to some degree ambiguous and calls for a full measure of keen observation and the sorting out of possible interpretations.

A special case of diplomacy through silence and noncommunication is explored by Schelling (1966) and Morton H. Halperin (1966) as the process of influence. Influence uses threat, intimidation, irrationality, nuclear stockpiles, and silence in an effort to change behavior of an opponent by building an appearance of inequality. Whereas the nation that is strong will simply take, a relative equal resorts to influence. Influence, according to Schelling, is likewise a game. It is a process aimed at enforcing a solution that is minimally acceptable to an opponent and its chief agency is the credible threat of damage or reward. Even in war such communication exists, with the end in mind that the combatant should see some advantage to coming to terms:

> War appears to be, or threatens to be, not so much a contest of strength as one of endurance, nerve, obstinacy and pain. It appears to be, and threatens to be, not so much a contest of military strength as a bargaining process —dirty, extortionate, and often quite reluctant bargaining on one side or both—nevertheless a bargaining process.

At this point the present analysis has come a full circle. Action is viewed as an imprecise means of communication. Refraining from action or lapsing into silence is an alternative form of communication. When an act is deliberate, it may be studed by rules that define noncommunication as a discrete game. Even when nondeliberate, action may be construed as a communicative act. Actions are observed and interpreted. Allowance must be made for the fact that silence is ambiguous, remembering that ambiguity may legitimately be used to advance the process of bargaining and diplomacy. Pervading all acts and their interpretation is the element of stylization, which imparts meaning to the message.

III .

Thus far I have delineated a view of communication as game. I have attempted to sketch boundaries for communication as it merges into more ambiguous forms of perceived and real noncommunication. In the one extreme communication is largely direct and unambiguous, whereas in the other it merges with the study of behavior. The continuum connecting the two points stretches from the clear to the unclear, from the intended to the unintended and from the understood to the misunderstood. A brief summary of the contrasts in the extremes of this continuum will provide clues for the prediction of when noncommunication will occur or, at a minimum, ought to occur. Criteria thus suggested include the need for candor, considerations of status, awareness, the need for precision of meaning, whether or not an act calls for additional verbal interpretation, a noise factor, whether or not a need is perceived for dialogue or whether rules, stakes, risks and odds are clear. A stylistic element occurs as well, but is resistant to analysis.

Candor becomes a communication variable when nations are traditionally friendly or hostile with each other. Presumably, more exchanges will be noncommunicative between avowed enemies than among friends. If a difference arises between the Soviet Union and Cuba, attempts at communication between the two will predictably be open. If both nations are neutral, communication will also be likely. As nations become more hostile, they leave more room for ambiguity in their exchange. Noncommunication serves the end of downplaying candor and emphasizing the need for indirectness or even feigned disinterest in a possible solution.

Status considerations include an estimate of the actual strength of the communicators and also imply a summing up of potential support for the communicator. Unequal agents may not communicate. If they do so, they may communicate at the expense of the stronger. If a weaker nation does not communicate, it may do so as a concession to the strength of the stronger. When the stronger does not communicate, it may choose this alternative in order to consolidate some previous gain that it made at the expense of the weaker.

Awareness is a third factor in communication. The easiest way to communicate is to ask for the attention of the recipient of the message. To neglect to do so may mean that the message goes unobserved. At one point, President Kennedy sought to alert the Soviets to the fact that a United States scientist was going to deliver an important paper at an international conference. The paper gave background information necessary for the construction of a safeguard for nuclear missiles. While Kennedy chose an indirect means of communication, he realized the need to assure Russian awareness for his message. Given the hostility of the communicators, the message was sent through indirect channels with an artificially stimulated interest.

A fourth game factor is the need for precision of meaning. Red China stylizes messages by making them irrational, whereas in some particular case the need for clarity would call for a very open and precise meaning. In Korea the habit of China's irrationality may have meant that cues were missed to the effect that Chinese troops were about to enter the war zone. If the value of one's communication is undermined, it may be hard to restore the lost credibility factor when precision in fact becomes necessary.

Fifth is the consideration of whether an act deserves interpretation. By itself it may be clear, unclear, or all too clear. Words may be needed to supplement a favorable meaning that was attached to an act or to counterbalance attempts to discredit an act. Here one need only consider foreign aid as an altruistic or as a utilitarian act, with or without strings and given from surplus or essential commodities. Recent history, for example, shows that China has contributed the largest amounts of aid to recent world relief efforts after natural calamities. Debate will ensue as to China's motives. In explaining an act, noncommunication is unlikely. When an expected act is not performed, noncommunication may defy accurate analysis. In this case noncommunication cannot be accurately forecast.

Sixth is the perceived need for dialogue. In a sense, dialogue is a composite term and encompasses many of the factors already surveyed. Certain difficult problems, however, may only be accessible to dialogue and by a drawn-out, fairly straightforward exchange of positions. In such an instance, silence could well be construed as an act of war.

Finally, stakes, rules, odds, and risk help to determine if a nation will communicate, on the one hand, or is engaged already in some form of noncommunication, on the other. Certain stakes and circumstances almost demand the initiation of a message. Silence, in such a case, is probably communication. When the odds are against the communicator, further empirical study should help to suggest whether a nation will communicate, not communicate, or show no preference.

IV

The criteria that I have chosen are not definitive in a strict sense, nor are they in fact comprehensive. They are intended (1) to suggest the predictive capacity of selected communicative indicators, (2) to call for an empirical study of the precise functioning of such indicators, (3) to call attention to the widespread use and misuse of noncommunication, and (4) to aid in the interpretation of such a choice of message.

The criteria are further selected to suggest the utility of studying negotiation and communication as a game played, as any other game, to maximize one's gains and an opponent's losses, and to reach a satisfactory termination. The most valuable application of the model may very well be in the study of the stalemate situation, since this seems to be a point where messages ought to be initiated. This is the point where negotiations, in all likelihood, begin.

NOTE

[1] For example note Richard Fagen's variation of Lasswell's model: Who *should* be able to say what, in what channels, to whom, for what purposes? *Politics and Communication* (Boston, 1966), p. 6.

REFERENCES CITED

ARANGUREN, J. L.
  1967 Human communication. New York.
BERLO, DAVID
  1960 The process of communication. New York.
BOULDING, KENNETH
  1964 Organization and conflict. In American national security: a reader in theory and practice. Morton Berkowitz and P. G. Bock, eds. New York.
BRAITHWAITE, R. B.
  1955 Theory of games as a tool of the moral philosopher. Cambridge, Mass.
BURKE, KENNETH
  1941 Philosophy of literary form. Baton Rouge.
  1962 A grammar of motives. Cleveland.
FAGEN, RICHARD R.
  1966 Politics and communication. Boston.
GOFFMAN, IRVING
  1970 Strategic interaction. Philadelphia.
HALPERIN, MORTON H.
  1966 Contemporary military strategy. New York.
HOLSTK, K. J.
  1966 Resolving international conflicts: a taxonomy and some figures on procedures. Behavioral Science 11: 1–17.

HYMES, DELL
1967 The anthropology of communication. Human communication theory: original essays. Frank E. X. Dance, ed. New York.
JOHNSTONE, HENRY, JR.
1965 Some reflections on argumentation. *In* Philosophy, rhetoric and argumentation. Maurice Natanson and Henry Johnstone, Jr. eds. State College, Pa.
LASSWELL, HAROLD
1948 The structure and function of communication in society. *In* The communication of ideas. Lyman Bryson, ed. New York. pp. 37–48.
PERELMAN, CHAIM
1963 The idea of justice and the problem of argument. New York.
RAPAPORT, ANATOLE
1962 The use and misuse of game theory. Scientific American December: 108–118.
RAY, JACK, and
HARRY ZAVOS
1966 Deduction and induction. *In* Perspectives on argumentation. Gerald R. Miller and Thomas R. Nilsen, eds. Chicago.
ROSENFIELD, L. W.
1968 A game model of human communication. Proceedings of the University of Minnesota Spring symposium in Speech-Communication. David H. Smith, ed. May 4:26–41.
SCHELLING, THOMAS
1966 Arms and influence. New Haven.
SHANNON, CLAUDE, and
WARREN WEAVER
1949 The mathematical theory of communication. Champaign.
STAROSTA, WILLIAM J.
1971 United Nations: agency for semantic consubstantiality. Southern Speech Journal. Spring: 243–254.
THAYER, LEE O.
1961 Administrative communication. Homewood, Mo.
VAN NIEUWENHUIJZA, C.A.O.
1963 Cross cultural studies. The Hague.

VIOLENCE: COMMUNICATION BREAKDOWN? FOCUS ON RECENT PUBLICATIONS

Thomas W. Benson

THOMAS W. BENSON is a rhetorician, film maker, and critic who has taught at Cornell University, the State University of New York at Buffalo, the University of California at Berkeley, and is currently associate professor of speech at Pennsylvania State University. He edited, with Michael Prosser, Readings in Classical Rhetoric. His articles and reviews have been published in the Quarterly Journal of Speech, Speech Monographs, Today's Speech, Southern Speech Journal, Theatre Design and Technology, and Film Society Review. In 1970 he was a participant in the National Developmental Project on Rhetoric.

> We, who seven years ago
> Talked of honor and of truth,
> Shriek with pleasure if we show
> The weasel's twist, the weasel's tooth.
>
> > William Butler Yeats
> > "Nineteen Hundred and Nineteen"

The nation's sudden concern for the damaging results of domestic violence has led to the publication of an enormous diversity of books on violence and related topics. In the context of this journal's announced concern for communication breakdown, I propose to examine a sample of these books from the premise that the second most important fact about violence in contemporary society is its connection to communication. The first fact about violence, needing little elaboration here, is that someone gets hurt.

When violence and communication are examined in a static, analytical model, they present a variety of points of contact which must be understood before the dialectical interplay of the two forces can be appreciated. Let us first tentatively elaborate the various interfaces of violence and communication, and then explore issues raised by the analysis and by recent works relevant to the subject.

A conventional approach to the communication-violence interface is to see communication as an alternative to violence. In this traditional view, the processes of persuasion and negotiation are seen as democratic substitutes for the use of force in settling disputes and maintaining law and order with consent. The ethical claims made for this position place rhetoric as a primary source of enlightened, parliamentary civilization. The legal system reinforces the distinction by elaborating rules of procedure for verbal behavior and by maintaining a distinction between talk and action that allows for considerable non-

Reprinted with permission of Today's Speech (Winter 1970).

conformity in advocacy so long as it stops short of action. Those who theorize that books, plays, and movies featuring violence purge us of violent impulses are also classifying communication as an alternative to violence.

Another approach, one which reinforces the distinction between the two forces but provides a dynamic link, sees communication as the cause of violence. Rap Brown, the Chicago conspirators, and the leaders of the People's Park movement in Berkeley are all descendants of a long line of men accused of speaking or plotting to cause violence.

It is also common to see communication as a form of violence. The British executed Lord Haw Haw primarily for his activities as a broadcaster in aid of the Nazi cause, and his opposite number, Sefton Delmer, created "black radio" as a weapon of war against Germany. (See *Black Boomerang*, 1962.) World War II prompted studies of ideas as weapons (see, for instance, Daniel Lerner's 1951 anthology, *Propaganda in War and Crisis*), and scholars in communication must now increasingly recognize the importance of communication as an auxiliary to violence (see David Kahn, *The Codebreakers*, 1967). Even more frequently, this identification of communication as violence is metaphorical, as when the newsmen at Chicago described the debate over the Democratic platform plank on Vietnam as a "floor fight," incidentally undermining the ethical superiority of talking to fighting every time they did so. And in a remarkable speech in 1967, Martin Luther King, Jr., apostle of non-violence, peppered his language with references to non-violence as "the most potent weapon available to the Negro in his struggle for justice in this country," which "in assault after assault . . . caused the sagging walls of segregation to come tumbling down" (quoted in Scott and Brockriede, *The Rhetoric of Black Power*, 1969). Was King hedging on the moral superiority of non-violence, or emphasizing to listeners who might abandon him for advocates of violence that non-violence could generate the same power as violence? One wonders if there were not side effects in this tactic.

Seen from another perspective, violence is a form of communication. Institutional violence such as war and police action is usually not carried to the ultimate extreme of massacre and salted earth, but is used until the enemy is convinced to halt resistance. Even Clausewitz, the advocate of total warfare, could ask: "Do the political relations between different peoples and governments ever cease when the exchange of diplomatic notes has ceased? Is not war only a different method of expressing their thoughts, different in writing and language?" (Quoted by H. Rothfels, "Clausewitz," E. M. Earle [ed.], *Makers of Modern Strategy*, 1943.) Granted, the dead soldier has not been convinced of anything, but, according to this theory, his living colleagues may read his death as a warning, and surrender or retreat. Advocates of the death penalty occasionally defend it on the grounds that it acts as a deterrent to crime.

What is lacking in the set of categories I have proposed is a sense of how they depend for their usefulness upon a fundamental agreement that violence and communication are not the same thing, and at the same time an appreciation for the constantly shifting relation between the two. In every work I have examined, one term is seen to do the work of or gradually merge into the other.

A theoretical and abstract account of the merging of communication and violence may be offered by noting that, like other human behaviors, both can be described in terms of syntactics (structure), semantics (meaning), and pragmatics (effect). Violence is not pure act, but possesses structure and meaning as well as effect. Communication is not pure symbolism, pure meaning, but also has effect.

To illustrate one dimension of the interweaving of action with communication, let us take as an example the response of the legal establishment to protest. Originally, those seeking expanded protection for dissent worked to draw a firm line between speech and action, thus insuring a free zone of dissent. The law resisted the expansion, maintaining its right to punish both action and many forms of speech. But the liberated zone of free speech was established and began to grow, until dissenters have now begun to claim free speech protection for some varieties of action, on the grounds that they are really "symbolic speech." And so we are now in a period when dissenters, having sanctified dissenting speech as beyond the law, are defining actions as speech, while the law, in the face of mounting dissent, struggles to maintain its power to punish action, and in many cases tries to roll back the theory so as to punish speech behaviors on the ground that they are acts.

A practical demonstration of the logical dilemma produced by these opposing movements of legal theory is provided by Abe Fortas' *Concerning Dissent and Civil Disobedience*. Fortas tries to hold the line against expanding the zone of permissible symbolic action by arguing that when speech and non-speech elements are combined in an act, the government can regulate the act. It will simply not do, for instance, to excuse assassination on the grounds that it is an expression of political opposition, or to defend bank robbery as a protest against the crime of property. So far, so good. But when the doctrine is applied in an actual case, we encounter a problem. The doctrine for which Fortas was reaching in his book matured a short time later in the Supreme Court's decision to uphold the conviction of a draft card burner, in the case of United States v. David Paul O'Brien. The Court found that the statute prohibiting the destruction of draft cards "could not properly be attacked on the ground that the purpose or motive of Congress was to suppress freedom of speech," since the burning of a two-by-three inch piece of paper was indeed an overt act. O'Brien certainly requested too sweeping a ruling in arguing that because his act contained symbolic elements it was therefore protected. But does this force a reasonable man to agree that Congress had no motive to suppress freedom of expression? The Court failed to recognize further evidence. Surely the Congress can punish the destruction of a small piece of paper. But when O'Brien is sentenced to six years of restraint (for "supervision and treatment," says the record), are Congress and the Court punishing the act as pure act, or are they punishing the symbolic importance of the act? The strong sentences handed down for such acts as O'Brien's are out of all proportion to their existence as acts. A six-year sentence for burning a piece of paper can be justified only by admitting that it is the symbolic dimension of the act that is being punished. The prosecution is thus caught in a contradiction. When the case is being tried, the burning is an act. When the defendant is being sentenced, the burning is a symbol.

For a response to Fortas, the radical has typically turned to Herbert Marcuse, whose One-Dimensional Man outlined the apparatus enabling post-industrial elites to control society by co-opting sexual and critical impulses, and whose essay on "Repressive Tolerance" claims that where the technocracy has a monopoly on communication, tolerance of all points of view leads to a closed circle of domination. To replace this repressive tolerance, Marcuse, in an excess of verbal manipulation worthy of the Orwellian opponents he so convincingly describes, suggests a policy of selective tolerance, which is not tolerance at all but the employment of revolutionary violence. "Liberating tolerance," he says, "would mean intolerance against movements from the Right, and toleration of movements from the Left."

Marcuse ends his essay with a statement about violence that precisely parallels a remark of Fortas' regarding what he considered legitimate civil disobedience: "If they use violence, they do not start a new chain of violence but try to break an established one. Since they will be punished, they know the risk, and when they are willing to take it, no third person, and least of all the educator and intellectual, has the right to preach them abstention."

Both Fortas and Marcuse seem to agree that in certain circumstances the willingness to take one's punishment for direct action sanctifies the protester and places him at a moral level which transcends mere debate. It requires only a slight broadening of perspective to see that this leads to an analysis of social violence in terms of its effect on the person who uses it. Where might this lead?

Frantz Fanon, writing of the Algerian struggle, says that for the native, violence is not only a means of terrorizing and driving away the colonial master, but also a form of therapy. "At the level of individuals, violence is a cleansing force. It frees the native from his inferiority complex and from his despair and inaction; it makes him fearless and restores his self-respect." Although Fanon has been invoked by American revolutionaries, especially in the black community, which with increasing frequency describes itself as a colony needing to drive out its oppressors, no significant American group seems yet to have reached the point where violence must be used as a purgative. But there is no guarantee that we will not move further in that direction, since even non-violent confrontational tactics are often defended not only for their efficacy as tools of bargaining, but also as agents of self-improvement.

The most important black writers of the decade have spoken of the need for strengthening the images of Negro manhood, and have dealt with the question of violence, though they have not, as critics often charge, indissolubly linked the two together. Indeed, one finds in the works of Malcolm X and Eldridge Cleaver a remarkable restraint and serenity whenever the question of violence is raised. Violence is held in reserve, it is threatened. But, one fears, it may eventually become sanctified as the only route to manhood and redemption. Once that happens, violence will be beyond bargaining. Violence will no longer be something to be settled by negotiation, since the only thing the victim will have to offer will be his death. At the conclusion of Cleaver's "The Allegory of the Black Eunuchs" appears this speech:

"Yes!" replied the Eunuch. "I'm thirsty for blood—white man's blood. And when I drink I want to drink deeply, because I have a deep thirst to quench. I want to drink for every black man, woman, and child dragged to the slaughter from the shores of Africa, for every one of my brothers and sisters who suffered helplessly in the rotton holds of the damned slave ships —for your friend who bashed his own brains out in the nuthouse—I want to drink the white man's blood for every ounce of my flesh and blood that he crushed and broke in the Caribbean Islands, for all the souls of black folk mangled in the fetid fields of the Old South and for every one slaughtered and lynched in the mire of the New South—and in the North, East, and West of the hells of North America! Only the white man's blood can wash away the pain I feel. You shrink from shedding the white man's blood, you old Lazarus, but I say to you that the day is here when I will march into the Mississippi legislature with a blazing machine gun in my hands and a pocketful of grenades. Since I will be going to die, I definitely will be going to kill."

In the face of such an implacable blood lust, still only hypothetical at the writing of Soul on Ice, we might consider ourselves lucky that violence can be legitimized as a form of communication.

And even in his most recent collection, Post-Prison Writings and Speeches, Cleaver, while bowing to the inevitability of violent revolution, holds out hopes for reconciliation, and falls short of condemning all of white society to the bloodbath. Though he now embraces Fanon as the founder of an ideology adaptable to a black colony within the mother country, violence, for Cleaver, is still rhetorical and selective. Revolutionary violence can be headed off by honest negotiation; therapeutic violence cannot.

But a train of reasoning which concentrates exclusively on the violence of dissenters leads in a direction not borne out by recent literature on the subject. The current national agitation about violence arises from violence committed against the establishment. And yet in the confrontations that have been studied, by far the largest share of violence was committed by the Establishment itself, and frequently it is not meaningful to accuse the anti-Establishment forces of violence at all.

Time after time government commissions, founded when there seemed to be a threat of violence to the power structure, have reported that, for instance, "The overwhelming majority of the persons killed or injured in all the disorders were Negro civilians" (Kerner Report). The Walker Report refers to "unrestrained and indiscriminate police violence," which was "made all the more shocking by the fact that it was often inflicted upon persons who had broken no law, disobeyed no order, made no threat." The Skolnick Report finds that "a segment of the movement has been drifting towards 'confrontationism'; physical injuries, however, have more often resulted from the actions of authorities and counter demonstrators." In one of the few exceptions to this pattern, described in Shoot-Out in Cleveland, Commission consultants were unable to ascertain who started the violence, but tended to undermine court findings which assigned guilt to black militant Ahmed Evans, sentenced to death for his part in the battle. The team studying the San Francisco State College strike of 1968–1969 withheld detailed comments on police activity, trying to strike a balance between student provocation and police over-reaction.

But the Commissions' reports go unheeded. When the Commissions strongly condemn police-state tactics in a desperate attempt to maintain the system of government they are serving, the government which appointed them nevertheless continues to arm for short range conflict in the streets, continues to jail the leaders of protest, even in some cases trying leaders on felony charges of conspiring to commit a misdemeanor.

In their refusals to respond to, or even recognize the legitimacy of Constitutional dissent in speech or action, government leaders play into the hands of those in the protest movement who see no alternative to violence. From the beginnings of the protest movement that arose in 1956 with the Montgomery Bus Boycott, so-called responsible leaders have condemned as excessive the tactics and demands of the day's demonstrations. The Establishment is never ready for the demands of social reformers, and is all too ready to label creative leaders as violent and revolutionary, hoping to keep the lid on, but in fact undermining the moderates and encouraging the prophets of violence and despair. As late as 1963, a group of bishops and other ministers issued a call for law and order, which they coupled with charges that Martin Luther King, Jr.'s Birmingham movement was inciting "hatred and violence." King responded with the celebrated "Letter from Birmingham City Jail." (Both documents are included in Bosmajian and Bosmajian, *The Rhetoric of the Civil-Rights Movement*.)

The position of the protesters themselves is not only in transition, it is undergoing complexification in several directions at once. Analyses of current agitation describe or evaluate protest on the basis of its place along several continua. The most important conceptual polarities are between Symbol and Act, Violence and Non-violence, Self-improvement and Social Change. Choose one from each pair in any combination, and you will have the basic disposition of at least one group in the movement.

Current questions asked among protesters and their interpreters illustrate the interaction of these pairs. Is non-violence to be employed merely for its tactical advantages, or because of its moral superiority? Is the resort to militant direct action most important as an act of conscience, or as a force for change? Does a truly non-violent protester have to sit still while a policeman beats him, or should he escape to protest another day? Is it hypocritical to advocate opposition to the war and yet submit to the draft?

While one element of the protest movement defends its acts in court on the grounds that they are "symbolic speech," another element exhorts dissidents to action on the grounds that mere speech, without action, is hypocritical.

The theme of individual salvation runs throughout radical movements to arrive at quite different conclusions. Fanon described salvation through violence. King defended non-violence on the grounds that "unmerited suffering is redemptive."

In American radical protest movements, the effect of action has generally been symbolic. By a curious twist, it becomes necessary to shock the audience into responding by stepping across the ever-shifting line between speech and action. But it is the shock, and the response, both symbolic reactions, that are sought. When Thoreau refused to pay his taxes, he depended upon a complex, but stable reaction. He took action, an act of moral courage proving he was not a hypocrite, and provoked a measured response which considerably embarrassed the government. A more violent action would have created more response but less embarrassment. A less militant action might have produced neither embarrassment nor response. In this example, both Thoreau and the government accepted the legitimacy of the government and its response, despite Thoreau's plea to the contrary. Thoreau took, indeed welcomed, his punishment. The government jailed, but then released Thoreau when Emerson paid the tax.

But we are now in a period when we must, hypothetically at least, pose another set of problems. What is to happen when legitimacy itself becomes an issue? When demonstrators are not content to influence but wish to supplant the established order? (See Scott and Smith "The Rhetoric of Confrontation," Quarterly Journal of Speech, LV [February 1969], 1–8.) On the other hand, what happens when the government refuses to accept the legitimacy of militant but non-violent dissent?

When a government either attacks or co-opts all dissent, the dissenter can choose between impotence and revolution. Similarly, when dissent turns to revolution, the government must choose between repression and retreat. Many of the books here reviewed seem to be saying that we are perilously close to the line. In the ongoing dialectic of protest and response, we may be edging closer and closer to a rhetorical stalemate, after which our symbolic patterns may offer no new moves short of taking the actions both sides have been until now merely rehearsing in the streets.

We are free to hypothesize a more pleasant possibility consistent with the terms of our argument. If symbolic processes have delivered us to this point, they can take us back. A premise of the argument is the utter inseparability of symbol and act. Until now, every move of one element has forced a redefinition of the other. In a culture bound by the dialectical interplay of these forces, we can hope that the dialectic itself is inescapable. This is not a utopian view, but at least it provides an alternative to cataclysm.

Which prediction to choose? I have no answer except to say that faith in an automatic natural or historical process has often been used to excuse violent excesses against people and institutions, conducted in the assurance that when the play at hand was over the stage would, after all, be ready for the next performance.

Meanwhile the drift toward violence continues. Those who in 1960 read Thoreau and Gandhi now read with attention and approval, and also with a romantic longing for direct action, the works of Fanon, Debray, Guevara, Mao Tse-tung, and Giap.

Some in the movement argue that violence is the only means left to create change. They do so on several grounds. They can show that the forces of the system themselves respond with violence to non-violent protest, often using as their excuse that protesters are using methods which are equivalent to violence. Hence, ask the advocates of violence, why stop short of real violence, if that is the language of the system and one is going to be attacked in any case? Will it work? American students have not had the success of French students in constructing alliances with workers; but student revolutionaries can be partly credited with having removed Johnson and De Gaulle from power.

In a recent article in an underground newspaper, the Berkeley *Tribe*, Frank Bardacke and Tom Hayden propose a scenario for victory in Berkeley which features general strikes and guerrilla war spreading from Berkeley throughout California, resulting in liberated zones from which the revolution could be carried foward throughout the country. As the authors admit, this is a fantasy, but it is a fantasy consistent with the mood of this city, which has known the Free Speech Movement and the People's Park struggle, in which the city of Berkeley has been occupied by troops firing on demonstrators and spectators alike, and making wholesale attacks with clubs and gas upon campus and community areas deemed to be within "enemy hands."

But the revolution sought by the white youth movement need not, its leaders make clear, come about through violence. Among the best of the current books dealing with revolution as a change in consciousness are Abbie Hoffman's *Revolution for the Hell of It* and Theodore Roszak's *The Making of a Counter Culture*. Hoffman, a co-defendant at the Chicago conspiracy trial, founder of the Yippies, whose slogan might well be "make news not war," has shown himself to be a master at manipulating the media. Quite openly basing his campaign on the works of Mailer, Maslow, Marcuse, and McLuhan, Hoffman has produced a book which is itself a put on. During the Democratic Convention other movement leaders were inventing disguises that would allow them to work in Chicago without being filmed by the media. But Hoffman hit upon the simple solution of writing "fuck" on his forehead, thus becoming instantly invisible to the network cameras. Hoffman understands that in order to make his way in the revolution, he needs to sense the current balance of symbol-act, self-society, violence-non-violence, and give them each a quarter turn in either direction, thus upsetting everyone's equilibrium and gaining leverage for himself.

Theodore Roszak attempts a defense and an analysis of the current movement, which he describes as a general assault on technocracy. Part advocate, part intellectual historian. Roszak explores the contributions of Marcuse, Norman O. Brown, Allen Ginsberg, Alan Watts, and Paul Goodman to the formation of a utopian, even magical, response to what he calls the "myth of objective consciousness." Although there are passages where he sounds like an angry young academic using mysticism as a stick to beat his straight colleagues, Roszak also touches deftly on the dangers of anti-intellectualism contained in the new sensibility.

Scholars in rhetoric and communication have consistently maintained that deliberation is morally superior to violent confrontation, both existentially and because deliberation actually aids in the formation of wise policy. But as the books reviewed here make clear, every defender of parliamentary social process and non-violent bargaining must ask himself some tough questions. Have we entered an era of technocracy in which rhetoric means not deliberation by citizens but monopoly propaganda by experts? Is our defense of non-violent talk simply a timid refusal to accept social change? Our unique concern for the process of communication must not blind us to the unanimous conclusion of the works here reviewed that there exist substantive evils in the status quo which cannot be papered over by improved methods of social control, or by appeals to demonstrators to abide by consensus politics. Can we, as students of communication, understand and contribute to symbolic methods of conflict resolution that will enable us to balance order with real and not merely symbolic change?

BOOKS REVIEWED IN ESSAY

Here is a listing of major recent works drawn upon in the preceding review. It is meant as a sample. For theoretical foundations, consult the writings of Kenneth Burke, Norman O. Brown, Ernst Cassirer, Régis Debray, Hugh Dalziel Douncan, Jacques Ellul, Erving Goffman, Ché Guevara, Kenneth Keniston, Marshall McLuhan, and works cited in the bibliographies of the books listed below. Among the rapidly expanding literature in academic and intellectual journals, see especially the recent work in *Quarterly Journal of Speech* and *Philosophy and Rhetoric*.

The Rhetoric of Our Times. Edited by J. Jeffery Auer. New York, 1969.
   [Contains indispensable essays by Burgess, Griffin, and Haiman.]
The Rhetoric of the Civil-Rights Movement. Edited by Haig A. Bosmajian and Hamida Bosmajian. New York, 1969.
   [Documeints by King, Farmer, Malcolm X, Wilkins, Carmichael, and McKissick.]
Malcolm X Speaks. Edited by George Breitman. New York, 1966.
Post-Prison Writings and Speeches. By Eldridge Cleaver. Edited by Robert Scheer. New York, 1969.
   [A selection of Cleaver's rhetorical prose from the appearance of *Soul on Ice* in 1967 to his flight and exile in late 1968. An analysis of violence and the question of land for America's "black colony" in "Babylon."]
Soul on Ice. By Eldridge Cleaver. New York, 1968.
   [In *Sympathy for the Devil*, Jean-Luc Godard locates the essence of black rhetoric in readings from Charles Keil's *Urban Blues*; in a speech by Stokely Carmichael at a 1968 rally for Huey Newton in Oakland, California; and in *Soul on Ice*. After spending most of his adult life in prison for rape, Cleaver won parole largely on the basis of this autobiography of a black imagination, and soon became an important interpreter and agent of black revolution.]
The Wretched of the Earth. By Frantz Fanon. Translated by Constance Farrington. New York, 1968.
Concerning Dissent and Civil Disobedience. By Abe Fortas. New York, 1968.
Rebellion and Repression. By Tom Hayden. New York, 1969.

[Hayden's testimony before the National Commission on the Causes and Prevention of Violence and the House Committee on Un-American Activities, probing the Chicago disorders. In an introduction, Hayden briefly defines the priorities for the movement as of June, 1969.]

Revolution for the Hell of It. By Free [Abbie Hoffman]. New York, 1968.

Violence in America: Historical and Critical Perspectives. By Hugh Davis Graham and Ted Robert Gurr. A Report to the National Commission on the Causes and Prevention of Violence. New York, 1969.

Law & Disorder: The Chicago Convention and Its Aftermath. Chicago, 1968.

[An ACLU-oriented collection of articles and photographs on Chicago, 1968.]

Look out Whitey! Black Power's Gon' Get Your Mama. By Julius Lester. New York, 1968.

The Agitator in American Society. Edited by Charles W. Lomas. Englewood Cliffs, New Jersey, 1968.

The Armies of the Night. By Norman Mailer. New York, 1968.

Miami and the Siege of Chicago. By Norman Mailer. New York, 1968.

[I have recorded elsewhere my views of Mailer's contribution as a rhetorical critic. These two works are required for an understanding of contemporary demonstrations.]

One-Dimensional Man. By Herbert Marcuse. Boston, 1964.

[A portrayal of the apparatus of repression in which tolerance replaces terror as the chief instrument of social control.]

The Black Panthers. By Gene Marine. New York, 1969.

Shoot-out in Cleveland. By Louis H. Masotti and Jerome R. Corsi. A Report Submitted to the National Commission on the Causes and Prevention of Violence. New York, 1969.

Political Violence: The Behavioral Process. By H. L. Nieburg. New York, 1969.

[This is a revision and expansion of work originally done for the Commission on the Causes and Prevention of Violence. Nieburg views violence as one rational element in the process of political bargaining, if a deplorable one. A "value-free" theoretical analysis is followed by an impassioned plea for creative response to protest. Useful bibliography.]

Shut It Down! A College in Crisis. By William H. Orrick, Jr. A Report to the National Commission on the Causes and Prevention of Violence. Washington, D.C., 1969.

The Almost Revolution: France 1968. By Allan Priaulx and Sanford J. Ungar. New York, 1969.

Report of the National Advisory Commission on Civil Disorders [The Kerner Report]. New York, 1968.

The Making of a Counter Culture: Reflections on the Technocratic Society and Its Youthful Opposition. By Theodore Roszak. New York, 1969.

"Robert F. Williams: A Rhetoric of Revolution." By Diane H. Schaich. Unpublished M.A. Thesis, State University of New York at Buffalo, 1970.

[In 1968, Cleaver said, "Today Malcolm X is dead and Robert Williams is still alive. Now in China, the guest of the Prophet of the Gun, Mao Tse-tung, Williams is coming into his own because his people have at last risen to his level of consciousness and are now ready for his style of leadership." In 1969 Williams returned to the United States.]

Arms and Influence. By Thomas C. Schelling. New Haven, 1966.

["The power to hurt—the sheer unacquisitive, unproductive power to destroy things that somebody treasures, to inflict pain and grief—is a kind of bargaining power, not easy to use but used often."]

Violence: America in the Sixties. By Arthur Schlesinger, Jr. New York, 1968.

No One Was Killed. By John Schultz. Chicago, 1969.

[One of the best reports to come from the disorders of Chicago in August, 1968. Schultz gives vivid eye-witness reports combined with a novelist's reflections on what he sees, from a point of view sympathetic to the demonstrators. He disputes the Walker Report's view that there was a police riot, charging instead that the police violence was the result of direct orders from the political hierarchy. For visual evidence to support his point, see Haskell Wexler's *Medium Cool,* which shows Chicago police marching in file, clubs swinging, into crowds of panicky demonstrators.]

The Rhetoric of Black Power. Edited by Robert L. Scott and Wayne Brockriede. New York, 1969.

Red Flag/Black Flag: French Revolution 1968. By Patrick Seale and Maureen McConville. New York, 1968.

The Politics of Protest. By Jerome H. Skolnick. A Report Submitted to the National Commission on the Causes and Prevention of Violence. New York, 1969.

Rights in Conflict. By Daniel Walker. A Report to the National Commission on the Causes and Prevention of Violence. New York, 1968.

A Sign for Cain. By Fredric Wertham. New York, 1969.

["When individuals fully communicate with one another they do not use violence. But if we cannot get a response to our egos by communication of words and feelings, we are tempted to evoke in fantasy a response by violent means. When violence does erupt, it comes from a breakdown of communication." Wertham follows this analysis with an indictment of the mass media for their celebration of violent attitudes.]

A Critique of Pure Tolerance. By Robert Paul Wolff, Barrington Moore, Jr., and Herbert Marcuse. Boston, 1969.

The Autobiography of Malcolm X. By Malcolm X, with the assistance of Alex Haley. New York, 1966.

[A devastating social critique that exists as both rhetoric and myth, in which Malcolm repeats the cycle of innocence-initiation-corruption-salvation-disillusion-redemption-death, and, ultimately, vindication.]

COMMUNICATION AS AGENT
AND INDEX OF SOCIAL CHANGE

Y. V. Lakshmana Rao in Communication and Development defines development as "the complicated pattern of economic, social, and political changes that take place in a community as it progresses from a traditional to a modern status. These changes include political consciousness, urbanization, division of labor, industrialization, mobility, literacy, media consumption, and a broad general participation in nation-building activities" (Rao 1966:7). Similarly, Karl Deutsch defines social mobilization as "the process in which major clusters of old social, economic and psychological commitments are eroded or broken and people become available for new patterns of socialization and behavior" (Deutsch 1961).

Social change occurs both in developed and in developing or preindustrial states. Except for revolution, the change that is seen in developed countries is more evolutionary than swift, more deliberate than dramatic. The same condition exists to a certain extent in the developing countries, but the distance that they must travel toward literacy, urbanization, and indusrial progress makes social change in these countries seem more sudden and sometimes erratic. The appeal of the charismatic leader is that his goals appear revolutionary. M. N. Srinivas in Social Change in Modern India indicates that although westernization became greatly intensified after India's independence in 1947, the most critical step had been the establishment and maintenance of British influence, a Pax Britannica, over a one hundred fifty year period before independence. Though the communications revolution has increased considerably since independence, it, too, was initiated by a British injected press, which served as a sort of inspector general and teacher of westernized manners and customs (Srinivas 1969:61).

Richard Fagen argues that there are three general categories of events in developmental change, as it relates to the role of communication, which serve as a model: (1) socioeconomic changes with important communication concomitants in channels, content, style, opportunities, and so forth, lead to (2) new ways of perceiving the self and the world, which in turn lead to (3) behaviors that, when aggregated, are of consequence to the function of the political system. Historically, the events tend to occur together or to overlap. Where there is urbanization, there tends to be change from agricultural occupations to increasing literacy, rising per capita income, and similar developments. The processes tend to reinforce one another in a mutually supportive way (Fagen 1966:109–110). The alternates to the model "Urbanization-Education-Communications-Democratic Political Development" offered by McCrone and Cnudde (1967) agree with the supportive and overlapping nature of development suggested by Fagen. Fagen admits that his model, which implies the customary labels of a "communication revolution" and the "revolution of rising expectations," presumes generally that change is seen as a result of developments that occur exogenously, or outside of the political system, which in turn comes to be affected by the new patterns of communication. Deutsch's formulation makes social mobilization, treated as a set of social and economic transformations, the cause rather than the consequence of changes in the political system. The communication transformations that give rise to nationalism in colonial areas, in this view, are the by-products of social, economic, and political developments of exterior origin (Fagen 1966: 111).

Fagen offers another model that involves endogenous change. In this model, the starting point of change is within the political system itself: (1) political strategies and forms of organization that directly or indirectly imply changes in communication patterns are selected. These patterns, once in operation, lead to (2) new ways of perceiving self and the world, and politics that in turn contribute to (3) changes in the functioning of the political system, although these changes are not always anticipated or planned by those who implemented the new strategies and forms of organization. The exogenous and endogenous models differ mainly in the locus of the primary stimulus to change in communication patterns. In the latter model, a purposefully directed leader seeks to rectify current situations by creating new political resources or by exploiting existing resources in an innovative and sometimes revolutionary manner. Fagen argues that communication changes in this model are both the instrument and the consequence of this policy-oriented leadership. We can add that the charismatic leader is thus dramatically involved with communication, both as he urges the adoption of his own social programs and as he articulates the changes that he has effected to his own people and to other leaders and peoples. When the charismatic leader becomes routinized, assassinated, or deposed, communication continues to serve as the initiating catalyst for the emerging leader and as an index of the former leader's loss of power and the new leader's current or evolving power. As Fagen suggests, communication changes accompanying authoritarian stabilizations—the increased control over the mass media, the silencing of the elite dissent, the burgeoning motivational and informational campaigns directed toward the masses—may all serve to contribute to the political transformation of a state (Fagen 1966: 117).

The process of convincing a preliterate or traditionally oriented populace that social change is inevitable, necessary, and beneficial is at best difficult. Wilbur Schramm (1967) indicates that before people can be convinced to participate in social change, often they must be persuaded that they belong to a community or nation. The Nepalese mountaineer who is asked about Nepal or its capital Katmandu may perceive that both are far away and have no relation to his own community, that is, his immediate village or family. The same example can be multiplied almost infinitely. If nationness can be perceived, the villager or peasant must be convinced that he can raise his own social aspirations for his family. If he has seen no beneficial changes in his lifetime or is too deeply imbedded into caste rigidity, as many Hindus are, upward mobility appears conclusively out of his reach. If that barrier can be surmounted, the individual must perceive the importance of learning new skills so that he can participate in the planned social change (Schramm 1967: 18–19). S. C. Dube postulates that communication is gradually coming to be recognized as a key factor in the process of directed change, which is leading to more systematic and organized efforts at the formulation of communication policies for the developing society. Still, many difficulties lie in the way of effective use of communication to facilitate social change: Communication policies are time-bound and unsystematic; communication networks are inadequate; wide gaps exist between the small modernizing elite and the large mass of tradition-bound people; mass communications are limited chiefly to the elite; traditional communication networks are little used; there is little scientific knowledge of the situation in which communication is expected to function; mass communication is little tried and its workings not entirely understood in developing societies; and, most important, the developing societies often have only the vaguest notion of the modernity that they are trying to achieve (Dube 1967:93–97).

It is important to remember that communication as an agent of change offers no panacea and that communications as an overlying aspect of development may need to be budgeted as Harry T. Oshima suggests in a strategy of selected growth, within a framework of balanced development for the society. In selective growth, where the society determines which specific goals can be brought to a successful conclusion and thereby serve as models whose innovative influence ripples outward, communication itself serves as a multiplicative, leavening medium. Communication networks are established on a selective basis, increasing as the economic or social growth itself expands. Oshima warns that programs like the Big Push, Takeoff, and the Great Leap Forward normally cannot sustain permanent growth of percentages as high as 10 percent annually and that the use of communication as an agent of social change should be programmed to the actual development that can be realistically achieved. For most developing societies this growth may be as low as 2 to 3 percent annually (Oshima 1967:77–99). Taking natives from the most primitive tribal state to a period of relative modernity in a decade or two and sustaining that kind of advancement ignores the fact that the developed nations have been progressively developing for a very long time. Despite modern technology, new nation-states are unable to advance as rapidly endogenously without massive exogenous support. Such support often means domination from outside.

Nevertheless, if we accept the reality that most social change is painfully slow rather than dramatically swift, the conclusions that Rao has drawn about the role of communication in development from his study of two Indian villages, one progressively modern and the other traditionally backward, are useful for the analyst looking at communication as an agent and index of social change:

In the economic sphere, communication
helps a person find alternative ways of making a living,
reduces the pressure on land by opening new opportunities,

helps raise the family's economic status,
creates a demand for goods,
motivates local initiative to meet rising demands,
broadens the entrepreneurial base,
and helps economic development become a self-perpetuating process.
In the social sphere, communication
aids in the process of status change from heredity to achievement,
motivates the illiterate to become literate,
helps shift influence from age and traditional status to knowledge and
    ability,
forces traditional leaders to compete for status retention and motivates
    them to acquire knowledge and adapt to changes,
helps in inducing parents to send their children to school,
helps people find new norms and achieve a balance during a period of
    rapid change,
helps bring about greater equality and a greater respect for human dignity,
and makes cultural and social change a self-perpetuating process.
In the political sphere, communication
helps in the process of power change from heredity to achievement,
motivates traditional leaders to defend their power by raising their informa-
    tion level,
helps the masses recognize their own importance in the power structure and
    acts as a stimulus to political participation,
helps the government learn of the needs of the public and plan its programs,
helps the public know the government plans and programs,
helps a nation or community achieve power,
brings about greater equality and respect for human dignity in the political
    arena,
and makes political growth self-perpetuating [Rao 1966:98–110].

In "Towards a Communications Theory of Democratic Political Development:
A Causal Model," Donald J. McCrone and Charles F. Cnudde (1967) suggest communications development as a variable around which democratic
political development can be built. Both normative and empirical theory
point to communications as a prerequisite to a successfully operating political
democracy. Phillips Cutright finds that communications developments is by
far the strongest socioeconomic correlate of political development. Daniel
Lerner theorizes that communications development is the final prerequisite
for a successfully functioning democratic political system. Based on these
findings, McCrone and Cnudde build a developmental sequence including
four variables: urbanization, education, communications, and democratic
political development. The argument can also be made, I believe, that such
a model would fit an autocratic or totalitarian political system equally well,
though this is beyond the scope of the McCrone and Cnudde argument.
Their argument does not take into account that communications serve not
only as an agent of change, as they claim, but also as an index of change.
However, they do offer a series of alternative models and conclude that communications are present at every level in the political system in which progressive development is occurring.

In the first essay, "Social Change and the Mass Media," Thelma McCormack hypothesizes that mass communication can and must act as a counterforce to the totalitarian tendencies of mass society. Judgments about the media are based on the indices of its content, influence, and power, in relation to its protest against the alienation of the individual and as an agency to restore identification in activities that check or break up monolithic concentrations of political power. These two elements serve as a model, which includes two dichotomous pairs of independent variables: social change and social stability, class society and mass society. The intervening variables are the relationships between communication and political institutions, and between communication and political roles. Though totalitarian control of the mass media is common and therefore self-perpetuating, the best service that the mass media can perform is to keep its critical capabilities without allowing them to become totally subverted to mass society.

John T. McNelly, in his essay "Mass Communication and the Climate for Modernization in Latin America," offers a specific case study about the availability of the mass media as an index of change in Latin America. McNelly suggests that to work efficiently as an index of change, communications must be available, they must have content relevant to modernization, they must have the attention of mass audiences, and the content must have real effects on the knowledge or attitudes of audiences, predisposing them to modern ideas, methods, or products. The last condition is not only the most difficult to actualize but also the most difficult to test. As van den Ban and others have cited, face-to-face communication is still the most effective means of changing attitudes or getting an individual to take social action that will affect his own life. McNelly cites the authors of an Ecuador study who concur in such a judgment but agree that massive influence becomes impossible on a face-to-face basis, making the use of mass communication methods essential. He concludes that mass communication may best be conceived as neither a simple "injection" operation on an entire population nor a neat two-step flow from media to opinion leader to general public, but rather as a multistage, multidirectional process with possibilities for both direct and indirect effects.

Turning from the influence of the mass media in social change, Bruce M. Borthwick discusses the Islamic sermon as a channel of political communication. One of the most effective ways of communicating to the people a new-world outlook and new images of how life can be improved is to utilize media that are familiar. In the Middle East the mediators between the new and the old must have sympathy for the traditions of Islam in the Arab world and for the modernizing influences of the West. As Daniel Lerner indicated, the Western model is not exclusively Western, and may in fact be socialist, but is distinctly modernizing (Lerner 1967:114). Since World War II the training of Muslim preachers has been extended, so that many of them have become the mediators between old and new. In the Friday sermon, which all male Muslims are obligated to attend, the preacher can speak about the problems Muslims face in the modern world and about the nation in which they live. New elites in the Arab states have assumed control over the sermon, requiring the preachers to propagate elite policies while at the same time supporting their statements with traditional Islamic concepts. Occasionally, a revolutionary leader ascends the pulpits of the Mosques. Assuming the role of preacher, he offers a heavily political sermon in which he advocates social, economic, and political changes in keeping with his own revolutionary goals and programs. Nationalism becomes a prominent topic in the sermons and, by a careful weaving of Arab history and Islamic principles, the sermon becomes one of the most important channels of political communication in the Middle East.

Two essays, one by A. W. van den Ban and the other by Satadal Dasgupta, concern the diffusion of innovations. In a 1964 essay, van den Ban challenged the two-step flow hypothesis, which postulates "Ideas often flow from radio and print to the opinion leaders and from them to the less active sections of the population." Katz discovered (1957) that despite the greater exposure to the mass media, most opinion leaders are still primarily affected not by the media but by other people. In his 1964 study, van den Ban concluded that the mass media play an important role in the early stage of proposed adoption of a new idea; but later, personal contacts become especially influential. Now, van den Ban expands this theory by suggesting that interpersonal communication between opinion leaders and their followers plays an even more substantial role in the decision to adopt innovations. Differences between villages in the effect of personal influence on the adoption of new farm practices can be caused by differences in group norms, specialization and concentration in opinion leadership, and mutual confidence among the villagers. Thus, van den Ban concludes that attitude change among individuals and social development is significantly more complicated than the original two-step hypothesis suggests.

Whereas van den Ban applied his case study to farmers in the Netherlands, Satadal Dasgupta investigates the sources of information about farming practices used by the West Bengalese in India. He questions how the differences in culture and the level of education between Western and non-Western cultures influence the flow of communication regarding improved practices. Like van den Ban, Dasgupta finds that early innovators are more likely to use institutionalized sources than are later adapters, who are more likely to use noninstitutionalized sources. The relationship was tested by interviewing 246 farm families of the Baraset region about their sources of information for nine improved agricultural practices.

REFERENCES CITED

Deutsch, Karl W.
  1961 Social mobilization and political development. American Political Science Review 55:493–514.
Dube, S. C.
  1967 A note on communication in economic development. In Communication and change in the developing countries. Daniel Lerner and Wilbur Schramm, eds. Foreword by Lyndon B. Johnson. Honolulu.
Fagen, Richard R.
  1966 Politics and communication. Boston.
Katz, Elihu
  1957 The two-step flow of communication: an up-to-date report of an hypothesis. Public Opinion Quarterly 21:61–78.

LERNER, DANIEL
  1967 International cooperation and communication in national development. *In* Communication and change in the developing countries. Daniel Lerner and Wilbur Schramm, eds. Foreword by Lyndon B. Johnson. Honolulu.
McCRONE, DONALD J. and
CHARLES F. CNUDDE
  1967 Toward a communications theory of democratic political development: a causal model. American Political Science Review 61:72–79.
OSHIMA, HARRY T.
  1967 The strategy of selective growth and the role of communication. *In* Communication and change in the developing countries. Daniel Lerner and Wilbur Schramm, eds. Foreword by Lyndon B. Johnson. Honolulu.
RAO, Y. V. LAKSHMANA
  1966 Communication and development: a study of two indian villages. Minneapolis.
SCHRAMM, WILBUR
  1967 Communication and change. *In* Communication and Change in the Developing Countries. Daniel Lerner and Wilbur Schramm, eds. Foreword by Lyndon B. Johnson. Honolulu.
SRINIVAS, M. N.
  1969 Social change in modern India. Berkeley.
VAN DEN BAN, A. W.
  1964 A revision of the two-step flow of communications hypothesis. *Gazette* 10: 237–249.

SOCIAL CHANGE AND THE MASS MEDIA*

Thelma McCormack

THELMA MC CORMACK received her B.A. from the University of Wisconsin, did graduate work at Columbia, and is at present associate professor of sociology at York University, Toronto, Canada. She has done research for the United States Department of Agriculture and the United States Air Force, and taught sociology at Northwestern University, McGill, and the University of British Columbia. She has published articles in The Public Opinion Quarterly, American Journal of Sociology, Social Research, British Journal of Sociology, American Behavioural Scientist, Studies in Public Communication, and others. She has been awarded a Canada Council Fellowship to complete a book called Social Theory and the Mass Media of Communication.

It has been suggested that the general function of the mass media is social, to organize a Gestalt from the partial disassociated fragments of insight and knowledge which characterize perception and understanding in contemporary societies.[1] Our technology and division of labour, our specialization and individualization—fruitful, efficient, and desirable as these are—create a chronic state of poor communication, the effects of which can be seen in a drift toward individual isolation, toward a condition of "pluralistic ignorance" when one does not know or cannot assess correctly the views of others.[2]

Pluralistic ignorance may be pluralistic bliss. At times we should be grateful that social action has been averted or postponed until cooler heads could prevail. But the "quest for community," to use Nisbet's phrase, persists whether the particular form it takes is to our liking or not.[3] And it persists under the most improbable circumstances. Whether it succeeds is the issue. When people are unable to communicate, the collective action they contemplate may suffer so severely from misjudgment that its outcome is a matter of chance. The synthesis of experience the media create, then, is instrumental to social action. Far from lulling us into a state of dogmatic slumber, it is an active force in the resolution of problems, expediting social change by eliminating some of the risk.

It is one thing to say that the mass media have a pragmatic social function, and another to say that the mass media can meet the responsibilities of democratic social change. Most critics of the media hold otherwise. They see the media as reactionary, obstructing social change by idealizing the status quo. In the extreme, the media are blamed for debasing culture, forcing social change into counter-revolutionary channels, furthering the anonymity of individuals,

Reprinted from the Canadian Review of Sociology and Anthropology,: (1964), by permission of the author and the publisher.

* This is a revised version of a paper presented to the annual meetings of the Canadian Political Science Association, Laval University, Quebec, on June 7, 1963.

and thus, from a number of different directions, increasing the danger of totalitarianism.[4]

Political journalists, however, are a proud profession. In their way, they are as idealistic as their critics. And it is more than self-interest when they claim that the media have a critical function which can serve the interests of democracy in the twentieth century, taking over the essential functions of the democratic social movement characteristic of the nineteenth. The problem is one of means. On this point, however, they lapse into a picture of society as a small town, and of the journalist as a rugged individualist. An illustration is the current furor over "news management." Some of our most distinguished journalists equate the present policies of news management by the Pentagon with those of old-line politicians trying to conceal petty corruption in the county court house. Accordingly, the cure for it is a tougher, more aggressive approach to government officials by Washington reporters, many of whom have, according to their own confessions, grown soft and lazy on a diet of press releases.[5] In the context of mass society, confidence based on these romantic but obsolete assumptions is unwarranted.

Somewhere between the indictments of critics and the *mea culpas* of journalists there is an hypothesis to be examined, the hypothesis that the mass media can act as a counterforce to the totalitarian tendencies of mass society. This hypothesis is different from that of the social critics; there is no assumption that the mass media intrinsically favour totalitarianism, or that popular culture is inherently undesirable in terms of Political Man. It differs also from the Protestant Ethic of journalists since the emphasis is on a social process and the interaction of institutions rather than on the work habits of journalists. It does *not* assume that the mass media are the *only* anti-totalitarian force in the social matrix but it does assume that they are uniquely qualified to serve this purpose, better adapted for it than the traditional social movement. What follows here is a proposed model for analysis.

The crux of the problem is the changing relationship between the media of communication and political institutions; specifically, and in operational terms, the relationship between political journalism and politics as two separate but related social systems; between political journalist and politician as independent but interdependent roles.[6] What is the impact of mass society on these relationships? How is it different from class society? Above all, how do these changes affect the political process of the media?

The political process of the media is essentially a creative one. It involves information, criticism, and interpretation, but like any configurational process, it is greater than the sum of its parts. For practical as well as for research purposes, we have selected for this discussion the most obvious dimension, the critical one. In theory, however, the critical activities of the media are only part of a much more subtle, complex process. And it is well to keep in mind that media (like the tabloid press) which rate high on a critical index but low on other dimensions are a parody of the process.

But whatever dimension is chosen for analysis, judgments about it are based on what the media say, how receptive audiences are, and how far the media can go; in short, *content*, *influence*, and *power*. These are separate but overlapping concepts, and their variations are, as I shall suggest later, related to each other and to social structure.

Our concern here with the critical function of the media is in the context of mass society. By mass society I mean twentieth-century society. Its triumph and its glory have been to solve without civil war or political revolution some of the worst social and economic inequities of the nineteenth century. New problems, however, now plague us, two in particular: the alienation of the individual and the mass movement.

"Alienation" refers to attitudes of indifference, helplessness, distrust, or apathy which result when the individual has no sense of identification with the organizations on which he is dependent.[7] These and similar attitudes appear to be the result of large-scale organization which removes the citizen further and further from the source of power and decision making; of a new technology which is beyond either the comprehension or control of most people; and of the decline of the market mechanism through which individual preferences, opinions, and attitudes were registered. The patterns of spontaneous identification by an individual with smaller, more informal and intimate forms of association fade and must be artificially restored as he perceives that his efforts and those of the organizations in which he participates are of little or no consequence.

He may continue to participate in voluntary associations. Indeed, voluntary associations seem to thrive and proliferate in mass society, largely on account of increased leisure.[8] But these activities, however pleasurable and socially useful in a limited sense, do not touch upon the primary structure. In other words, it is erroneous to assume that the number of voluntary associations available to the individual is a measure of political pluralism. And while there is some truth in the proposition, "I join, therefore I am," alienation and integration *in the political sense* depend on what one joins and how effective it is in the larger political structure. If the critical function of the media is, then, to resist the totalitarian tendencies of mass societies it must, first, reduce the sense of political alienation, and, second, restore identification in activities which check or break up monolithic concentrations of political power.

Third, it must act as, or on behalf of, the democratic social movement.[9] In mass society the vehicle of social protest is typically the mass movement in which people from all backgrounds, having limited association with each other, are brought together out of a sense of frustration.[10] Extreme measures must be used to maintain discipline; internal dissidence becomes intolerable. And members do not have the collective resources behind them to resist manipulation by a leadership clique or by a charismatic personality. It is, then, the mass movement that is the adversary of the media in the hypothesis proposed here. Difficult as it may be to define operationally, the media must then offer an alternative to the mass movement.

To summarize: that the mass media can serve as a buffer against the totalitarian tendencies of mass society is an hypothesis that can be tested. The model involves two dichotomous pairs of independent variables: social change and social stability; class society and mass society. The intervening variables are the relationships between communication and political institutions, between communication and political roles. These are influenced by the larger social structure, and, in turn, they influence the dependent variable which we have described here as the critical function of the media. Variations in the critical function are ascertained through separate and combined measurements of content, influence, and power; roughly the same indices that would be used in ranking or comparing the effectiveness of an insurgent social movement. The final effects that one must examine, however, concern the individual's identification with and involvement in meaningful rational political activity. This requires both an atmosphere and a social system in which the critical function of the media is institutionally secure.

In the remainder of this article, I shall discuss in more detail certain aspects of the model. First, I shall clarify the three indices of the critical function, content, influence, and power. Second, I shall compare class and mass societies with respect to the position of the media vis-à-vis political institutions. In Part III, I shall attempt to locate the line which differentiates democratic and totalitarian systems with respect to the media. Finally, I shall indicate how the critical function of the media can be maintained given the conditions of mass society.

Most of the evidence cited will be drawn from the United States. Part III will be based on material from the U.S.S.R. It is hoped that by clarifying some of the concepts and developing further the theoretical model, the experience of other countries may be usefully examined.

I

The proposition that the media of communication are instrumental to social action does not account for the *variations* in content, influence, and power. It does not specify under what conditions media content is a rationalization of things as they are and under what conditions media content is partisan and provocative. Similarly, variations in influence range from being negligible and therefore of little importance for social change to being so high that the issue is whether censorship is self-imposed or imposed by others. Nor does the proposition account for differences in media power, in relation to the power of other institutions.

These variations are a matter of commonplace observation, but they are generally interpreted as the concomitants of the personalities and social positions of the people who control the media. Raymond Williams, for example, observes that popular culture is "anti-culture" begot by "speculators who know how to exploit disinheritance because they themselves are rooted in nothing."[11] This particular theme, that media personnel are drawn from marginal groups in society, is very old, going back at least as far as Marx and Engels who once described journalists as the déclassé "dregs of the Bourgeoisie."[12]

Without dismissing this connection, it is a fact that media outlive the people who earn their living by working for them. And if it is true that journalists are regularly recruited from disaffected groups in society, it must be noted that the values and social composition of marginal groups change too. In short, the media have, like any social institution, a flexibility and capacity for adaptation, so that the explanation of variations whether in content, influence, and power must be sought in terms of social structure more generally.

1. Content. By and large, the content of the media is conservative. It affirms the rightness and truth of conventional values; it looks back toward a simpler past rather than ahead toward a more complex future. Psychologically, media content is a mirror, a mirror in which we see ourselves as the fairest of them all, a mirror which reinforces a collective Ego. Socially, media content is a gentle reminder to honour rules and obligations accepted by earlier generations; it thus ensures conformity and historical continuity.

Within this framework, however, the media may be more or less sensitive to social problems, more or less ready to take sides in any controversy. In a period of social stability, media content is sweetness and light. At times following a drastic upheaval media content emphasizes unity and reconciliation. To do otherwise would be dysfunctional. But in a period of crisis or social instability, media content reflects the moods of dissatisfaction and the conflicts of interest. As the situation deteriorates and choices must be made, media content becomes less and less neutral and more and more exhortative, ultimately capable of inciting total submission or civil disobedience.

Thus the media have a dual function, passive and active. Both are legitimate; both are subject to abuse. But in theory there is nothing inherent in a system of mediated communication to interfere with the normal social oscillation between permanence and change. Like a clock, the media may run fast or slow, and the social consequences of this inaccuracy may be considerable. The people who wind and set it may be responsible for the error, but the mechanism itself does not necessarily distort reality. And even when the clock is most accurate, the reactions of people reading the time may vary within certain limits, depending on the social angle from which they are looking at it.

2. Influence. Content is one way of measuring the critical function of the media, but it is not always a reliable one. It needs to be supplemented by the amount of influence the media have, that is, the extent and intensity of their impact on audiences.

In a national election, for example, the influence of the media on the voter is slight, indirect, and related to other indices of political behaviour such as interest and participation.[13] Indeed, it has become almost axiomatic to say that the media do little more than activate a latent predisposition or reinforce a decision already made. Coleman found that so far as local community conflicts were concerned even this was too strong a statement.[14]

However, the story is different in societies undergoing a major social revolution. In many of the underdeveloped nations, for example, it appears that the influence of the media must be regarded as a major force.[15] Similarly, in a national crisis the influence of the media increases to a point where even popular sentiment favours some sort of regulation. In the United States during the 1930's, for example, newspapers were probably less conservative than they were in the 1920's, yet the situation in the 1930's was more desperate, and the bias of the press was felt to be a more serious matter.

There is no mystery about why the influence of the media increases with social instability. The indices of instability are much the same the world over, though the sequence and salience of each item may be different in each case. Primary group relations are weakened, inter-generational continuity is disrupted, authority figures cease to be respected, former traditions are repudiated, old group ties are dissolved. In short, all of the controls—social and psychological—that normally limit the influence of, or compete with, the media in the persuasion process are rendered ineffectual. A partial vacuum is created so that general receptivity to the media increases.

Various factors may lessen the potential impact at any given time: the ineptness of media personnel, poor distribution, rivalries among the different media, and above all the degree of trust which citizens have in the media. But the point I should like to emphasize is that the view, which one hears quite often, that influence is a bundle of manipulative tricks and essentially exploitative, reflects an ideology rather than a social fact. The last vestiges of Manchester Liberalism seem to have found their way to discussions of the mass media where it is assumed that "that influence is best which influences least."

3. Power. Power is distinct from the influence of the media, though it goes without saying that unless the media have some influence they do not have power. But power, here, refers to the relation of the media to other institutions. It is measured by the ability of the media to dominate other institutions or to resist domination by them. An underground radio, for example, may have a small audience but be able so effectively to harass an administration that it is regarded as an independent political power comparable to a conspiratorial social movement. General de Gaulle was no more prepared to let the French press question his Algerian policies[16] than Dr. Adenauer's government was to tolerate the exposées of *Der Spiegel*, to cite two recent examples of censorship.

Censorship alone is not a measure of power. Stouffer and later Lazarsfeld[17] found in studying the McCarthy period that efforts to suppress free communication may reflect anxiety rather than any real danger. Censorship battles are the stage where the power of the media may be tested. But it is in the day-to-day interactions of the two institutions, communication and political systems, that one must look for measurements of power.

People who claim that the power of the media has increased in relation to political institutions are usually thinking of the political campaign where the media have gradually replaced the "whistle stop." This trend began long before television, but radio and television, by providing national audiences, have given it a boost. And it is not surprising that some media personnel develop delusions of grandeur. Richard S. Salant, President of CBS News, in reviewing the experience of the 1960 Kennedy-Nixon debates, urged broadcasters to use all their "persuasive powers to avoid the curtailment of debates during the last two weeks before Election Day—as happened in 1960 at the insistence of one of the candidates who wanted to control his appearance during the crucial two weeks before Nov. 8."[18] More revealing is the fact that the TV networks persuaded the Federal Communications Commission to suspend its "equal time" ruling, thus denying smaller or dissident parties the same access to the public as the two giants. In the long run, the power to handicap minority parties may be the most decisive effect and serious aspect of the media's power with respect to political processes.

Campaigning, however, is only part of a political process. Behind it is the political organization with other duties. One measure of the political power of the media is the extent to which political personnel are displaced by media personnel. At the lower ranks of American political parties—the level of precinct captains and city bosses—there has been a steady decline in power. As political issues have become more national in scope, as patronage has declined, as urban life has become more transient, these functionaries have become steadily less important and less effective. The editor of a neighbourhood press may be more familiar with the constituency than a precinct captain.[19] The latter may defect completely, creating what Janowitz has called a state of "social absenteeism," but more generally local political leaders continue to operate although their wings have been clipped.[20] The increasing power of the media then reflects the automation of the political process. And as with automation elsewhere, it hits the unskilled and semi-skilled workers first.

At the level of the skilled workers, especially the Chief Executive, the media may have more power than they have had in the past, but not necessarily in relation to political power, which has increased much faster. A case in point is the Presidential press conference. In the modern state its function is, as Rossiter suggests, to enable a President to reach the public and persuade it to accept government policies.[21] Many of these policies, based on highly technical scientific data or on considerations of military security, are not debatable. But even if this were not so, a national government with extensive administrative responsibilities is bound to try to use the media as part of its information service. Thus the televised press conference turns national political journalism into Journalism of the Absurd.

Still another clue to the power of the media is the proportion of media personnel employed directly by the government. These people, like their "agit-prop" counterparts in the U.S.S.R., are not likely to criticize the regime. Finally, one must also consider the distribution of personnel within the media, especially with respect to the number of reporters who ask the questions and the number of analysts who interpret the answers.[22]

To summarize, attempts to measure the critical function of the media using content, influence, and power as the three major indicators, present difficulties to the empiricist. The chief difficulty lies in the fact that there is no static line against which to measure performance. Therein lies the strength of the media: their content varies, their influence rises and falls, and their power shifts. But we can, by reference to social structure, arrive at a range of expected values against which we can measure deviations in any given case and at any given time. These deviations constitute measures of dysfunction.[23] Hence the media cannot be branded as dysfunctional until the broader context is known.

II

The critical function of the media in mass society is neither greater nor less than one would expect depending on the degree of stability or instability in the social structure. The context, however, is different. The autonomous relationship between the media and political institutions, characteristic of class society, becomes a contingent relationship. And it is within this contingency pattern that the lines must be drawn between the media in a democratic society and a totalitarian one.

Class society is what we have been. Mass society is what we are becoming. Between these two points of reference is the completion of the industrial and urban revolutions. Among the results are a high standard of living, increasing leisure, the extension of leisure to all classes, universal suffrage, and an almost universal consumption of some form of the mass media. Mass society is distinguished by centralized planning, bureaucratic organization, leadership by experts, and the emergence of a substantial group of white-collar wage-earners. Older forms of stratification—regional, ethnic, social—become less important in the conduct of political life. Economic stratification, the keystone of class society, similarly declines as public measures close the gap between rich and poor, insuring the worker against unemployment, the family against illness, and children against educational discrimination.

In class society, especially the open class society which developed in the United States during the latter half of the nineteenth century, the media of communication and political institutions, much as they may have co-operated or collaborated with each other, were not fundamentally dependent on each other. The media were concerned with other institutions, while political machines depended for support on personal service rather than ideology. The fact that the press was financially independent as well was a manifestation of the autonomy rather than a causal factor, but it helped create a tradition within which the media trained themselves in political dissent. The song is ended, but the ideology which links free enterprise with political independence lingers on.

Despite the autonomy of the two institutions, there were certain parallels between them. Both, for example, were class oriented. In the case of the media, this bias did not mean that they were always in favour of the "Haves." Newspapers frequently championed the underdog. And at the turn of the century, the Muckrakers, writing chiefly in magazines, gave this populist sentiment a social conscience without being doctrinaire. Muckraking journalism was Fabian research without Fabian socialism and without the Fabian Society. But it was not the mainstream of American journalism. And the class bias of the media was most evident in connection with industrial conflict. With few exceptions, the media were not mass media but class media: written by the middle class, for the middle class, opposing whatever threatened the middle class, supporting whatever furthered it; expressing the ethos of the middle class and the sectional or other divisions within it.

The major political parties followed the same general pattern. Their differences, too, were differences within the middle class. And it was not until the Great Depression of the 1930's that an open conflict developed between party and press along class lines. Radio, the new electronic medium, was used to break through the class bias of the press.

Both journalist and politician had their roots in the local communities they served. They shared with each other and with their publics a common social experience that gave them insight into what would win votes and what would build circulation. Neither journalist nor politician was an expert or subject-matter specialist. Each learned his craft on the job, and although city editors, like city bosses, were sometimes college men, both went to great lengths to disassociate themselves from intellectuals, intellectualism, and cultural affectations.

Provincials and amateurs, both politicians and journalists were also individualists. By that I mean that they were not incumbents of a standardized role within a large organization. Their assignments reflected a personal or organizational loyalty within which they defined their own responsibility. If it was an era of "personal journalism," it was also an era of "personal politics."

With mass society the autonomy, the class bias, the local orientation, the amateurism and individualism—these and other characteristics of the two institutions changed. Class media became mass media; class politics became mass politics. The major sources of news were increasingly national rather than local; the major sources of political power were increasingly in the national government rather than the local community. Journalism and politics both became more standardized so that they could be taught formally, thus cutting down the time spent on apprenticeship. At the same time, they became more specialized. The enormous growth of special-interest media created a demand for journalists who had a subject-matter specialization, for instance, agriculture, finance, sports, travel, home economics, medicine, and so on. Government created a similar demand for politicians who not only were able to win elections but also understood the intricacies of monetary theories, scientific development, social security, and so forth.

These, of course, are only trends. Despite centralization, for example, journalism and politics both retain local commitments. But as the focus of attention shifts from local events to local issues, some of the indigenous colour is lost. Fluoridation controversies, to take just one illustration, are local, but the pattern is much the same from Maine to California. The more "issue-oriented" local journalism and local politics are, the more "local look" becomes secondary, although it still sells newspapers and it still wins votes.

All these separate trends are part of a much larger change which places the media and political institutions in a closer, more contingent relationship. The modern state cannot operate without political journalism. It must collect information to formulate policies and afterwards ascertain the impact of those policies; it must explain and interpret policies, and it must make efforts to win approval for and conformity with the policies. If it cannot do this with private journalism, it is prepared to create its own. For want of a better term, this can be called "administrative journalism."

Administrative journalism involves the collection of information as well as interpretation; it is concerned with policies rather than personalities, with trends rather than events. Thus, it has one foot in traditional political journalism, the other in modern social science. It is part house organ, for purposes of internal use only, part political organ, for export only; it is part private, part public; it can be as dull as the census publications or as controversial as a policy paper. It can reveal more facts than most people want or can digest, or fewer.

Out of administrative journalism has come the development of "prestige" journalism and the prestige political journalist. Prestige journalism tends to be national journalism, professional journalism, and subsidized in such a way that public interest is not sacrificed to profit. But it has many of the characteristics of "administrative journalism." Some of this is suggested by Murray Kempton's comparison of the New York Times with the New York Daily News:

> The Times protects privacy while the News invades it. . . . The Times attempts to describe the public world unfortunately too often in the language the public world uses to protect itself. The News violates the private world. It is thus local where the Times is global; its goal is entertainment where the Times's goal is information. The News suffers from cynicism where the Times being impersonal and cosmic suffers from innocence. The Times reveres institutions because they are institutions; the News distrusts them for no better reason.[24]

This comparison of two extremes comes very close to differentiating traditional journalism in class society from administrative journalism in mass society. Long live the tabloid, but the essential distinction that must be made in terms of the hypothesis under discussion is between prestige journalism and administrative journalism.

III

One way of locating this line is to examine the position of the media in totalitarian countries. In the U.S.S.R. the function of journalism is entirely administrative, that is, to ensure that national government policies are understood and carried out. It is not uncritical journalism, but criticism is confined to local malpractice.[25] There is no criticism of the Party. To paraphrase Kempton, Pravda reveres the Party Line because it is the Party Line.

In the U.S.S.R. the journalist is a role within an institution. His personal views and his personal interpretation of his responsibilities are subordinate to the institution he serves. He is most usually an expert in some subject area. The Tass correspondent, for example, is chosen for his background in history and languages, a background that would qualify him to serve in a foreign embassy, and for many Tass correspondents this is the career line.[26] Soviet journalists who stay at home are no less qualified. They, too, must be subject-matter specialists, and increasingly they are graduates of schools of journalism, thus combining specialization with professionalization.

Although the media in the U.S.S.R. are centrally controlled and not competitive, there is very considerable decentralization. Every effort is made to reach every person, primarily through his place of work and in terms of his work, but also in terms of age, language, and geographical location.

These similarities are perhaps enough to indicate that "administrative journalism" in totalitarian countries is not too different from "administrative journalism" in democracies. It is the journalism of mass society. No one would be deceived by the similarities. Administrative journalism in the U.S.S.R. has other functions. It is intended to suppress any ideological differences; it is a technique of surveillance; it is a part of a system of intimidation. But the similarities suggest that the traditional basis for protecting the critical function of the media is not likely to be of much avail. Journalists will still carry their battles into court and win sometimes. The media will continue to seek other sources of financing outside of government. Journalists will continue to use their increasing professionalization as a bargaining point. But none of these measures does more than plug a hole in the dyke. In any real showdown between private and public journalism, there is no question about which could survive.

IV

Any hope for securing the media's critical function lies in forming alliances with other social groups who have a similar vested interest to protect. Reference was made earlier to the fact that public or administrative journalism has one foot in modern social science. By virtue of the same set of circumstances, academic freedom is challenged. If one looks closely at the position of the social sciences vis-à-vis the state, many of the same points made here about political journalism apply. For administrative journalism, read "administrative research." The counterpart of the government information officer is the government social scientist. Prestige journalism corresponds to prestige science, financed often by government but free—within certain well known political limits—to explore bizarre paths. Both journalist and social scientist find it difficult to resist being consultants and Presidential confidants. Neither is above dubious strategies that might yield information, and data that can give them a professional scoop and better their bargaining power with their superiors. Both have a great deal to lose. Apart, they are whiners; together they constitute a viable form of pluralism.

I do not reject the proposition that the mass media increase the danger of totalitarianism in mass society. What I have tried to suggest is that a reasonable case can be made for the alternative proposition, namely, that the function of the mass media is to check the totalitarian tendencies of mass society through the exercise of a critical function. A critical function, however, must be implemented. In mass society, this involves something more concrete than pious resolutions on the part of political journalists. It involves power, and in this case, assistance from outside must be sought.

One laments, therefore, the traditional hostility between media personnel and academicians. Over the years it has been thawing, especially as the educational standards of journalists have been raised. But the chronic anti-intellectualism of the media—not entirely a bad thing—and the chronic elite mentality of the academician—not entirely undesirable, either—suggest that this partnership will not be easily achieved. Unless it is achieved, the critical functions of both may be sacrificed, and with them the opportunity to reconstruct pluralism within mass society.

NOTES

[1] Thelma McCormack, "Social Theory and the Mass Media," *Canadian Journal of Economics and Political Science*, XXVII, no. 4, 1961, 479–89.

[2] Warren Breed and Thomas Ktsanes, "Pluralistic Ignorance in the Process of Opinion Formation," *Public Opinion Quarterly*, XXV, no. 3, 382–92.

[3] Robert A. Nisbet, *The Quest for Community* (New York, 1953).

[4] Criticisms of the media which suggest that they increase the danger of totalitarianism have been made on the basis of media content, both factual and fictional. Since the purpose of this article is to construct a model that lends itself easily to empirical investigation, we will restrict comment to content least debatable in its political implication, i.e., information and editorial interpretation.

[5] "The News Management Issue: A Symposium," *Nieman Reports*, March, 1963.

[6] Although the model presented here is intended to apply to all media, the focus of attention is on newspapers, the oldest and most pervasive medium. This permits an examination of the system in different phases of institutional development.

[7] Melvin Seeman, "On the Meaning of Alienation," *American Sociological Review*, XXIV, December, 1959, 783–91. See also Arthur G. Neal and Salomon Retting, "Dimensions of Alienation Among Manual and Non-Manual Workers," *ibid*. XXVIII, no. 4, 599–608, for a major step forward in clarifying and isolating the different dimensions of the concept of "alienation." For our purposes, however, it is enough to agree that there is something which can be called "alienation" differentiated from "integration" and that it is related to the structural properties of mass society.

[8] Deniel Bell. "America as a Mass Society: A Critique," *The End of Ideology* (Glencoe, Ill., 1960), 21–36.

[9] Democratic social movements are movements which have as their goals greater equalization of opportunity, social and economic, through the extension of economic planning and greater diffusion of political power. Historically, these have been class movements though often built around ethnic, regional, occupational homogeneity. Although the internal organization of such movements varies with respect to the participation of members and other indices of democracy, the rank and file of such movements have, by virtue of their common backgrounds, a potential resistance to manipulation by leaders which they may or may not use.

[10] William Kornhauser, *The Politics of Mass Society* (Glencoe, Ill., 1959).

[11] Raymond Williams, *Britain in the Sixties: Communications* (Harmondsworth, 1962), 75.

[12] Quoted by Max Nomad, *Aspects of Revolt* (New York, 1959), 160.

[13] There is considerable literature on voting, based on empirical research. See in particular Bernard R. Berelson, Paul F. Lazarsfeld, and William N. McPhee, *Voting* (Chicago, 1954); Joseph T. Klapper, *The Effects of Mass Communication* (Glencoe, Ill., 1960); Eugene Burdick and Arthur Brodbeck, eds., *American Voting Behavior* (Glencoe, Ill., 1959); William N. McPhee and William A. Glaser, eds. *Public Opinion and Congressional Elections* (Glencoe, Ill., 1962); Angus Campbell, Philip E. Converse, Warren E. Miller, and Donald E. Stokes, *The American Voter* (New York, 1960).

[14] James S. Coleman, *Community Conflict* (Glencoe, Ill., 1957).

[15] Daniel Lerner, *The Passing of Traditional Society* (Glencoe, Ill., 1958).

[16] Martin Harrison, "A Lesson on the Freedom of the Press," *The Listener*, June 14, 1962, LXVIII, no. 1733.

[17] Samuel A. Stouffer, *Communism, Conformity and Civil Liberties* (Garden City, N.Y., 1955); Paul F. Lazarsfeld and Wagner Thielens, Jr., *The Academic Mind* (Glencoe, Ill., 1958).

[18] Richard S. Salant, "The Television Debates: A Revolution that Deserves a Future," *Public Opinion Quarterly*, XXVI, No. 3, Fall, 1962, 350.

[19] Morris Janowitz, *The Community Press in an Urban Setting* (Glencoe, Ill., 1952).

[20] *Ibid.*, 214.

[21] Clinton Rossiter, *The American Presidency* (New York, 1960).

[22] I am indebted to Mr. Mark Gayn of the *Toronto Daily Star* for calling this to my attention.

[23] The terms "functional" and "dysfunctional" as used here can be defined as follows. "Functional": media content with the probable impact of increasing rational collective behaviour, i.e., action based on analysis of causal factors that are neither supernatural nor absolute imperatives of social organization, a consideration of alternative courses of action, and a final selection based on judgments of the appropriateness of means to ends. "Dysfunctional": media content with the probable impact of increasing non-rational behaviour either in the form of spontaneous disorganized action—such as riot or panic—or passivity and withdrawal.

[24] Murray Kempton, "The N.Y. Daily News," *Commentary*, Sept., 1961, 243.

[25] Alex Inkeles, *Public Opinion in Soviet Russia* (Cambridge, Mass., 1950).

[26] Theodore E. Kruglak, *The Two Faces of Tass* (Minneapolis, 1962).

MASS COMMUNICATION AND
THE CLIMATE FOR MODERNIZATION
IN LATIN AMERICA*

John T. McNelly

JOHN T. MC NELLY is *professor of journalism and mass communication at the University of Wisconsin. He came to the field of communication research following a decade of journalistic experience in the United States and England. His first two academic degrees were in journalism, from the University of Wisconsin. He received his doctorate in communication at Michigan State University and served there on the journalism and communication faculties before moving to Wisconsin in 1966. Research on the role of mass communication in development has taken him to more than a dozen Latin American countries, and he has lived in Costa Rica and Peru. He is a coauthor of* Communication and Social Change in Latin America: Introducing New Technology. *He has also served as a visiting professor at the Berlin Institute for Mass Communication in Developing Countries and has served as communication consultant for governmental and international agencies. At Wisconsin he is a member of the Ibero-American Studies Program, the Center for International Communication Studies, and the Center for International Urbanization and Population Research.*

A mounting number of studies have shown striking relationships between mass communication development and various economic, political and social aspects of national growth.[1] Although these studies generally have been based on available data from countries throughout the world, similar relationships also can be found within regional groups of countries. Among the twenty Latin American countries, we find newspaper circulation per capita correlated .89 with urbanization, .82 with literacy, .80 with per capita income, and a negative .88 with percentage of population employed in agriculture.[2]

Such studies, of course, do not establish causal relations. Is mass communication merely a reflection of other more basic factors of development such as urbanization and industrialization, literacy and political participation? Or does mass communication play a functional role in the development process: can the communication of facts and opinions through the mass media actually influence people to move to the cities, take up new skills, learn to read and write, and become involved in politics?

A growing tendency among social scientists and others to assign an impor-

* The author acknowledges the support of the International Communication Institute of Michigan State University for the preparation of this article and some of the research upon which it is based. Some of the other research cited was done with support from Michigan State University International Programs—Ford Foundation grants and from the Programa Interamericano de Información Popular, San José, Costa Rica. This article is based in part on a paper presented at the 1964 convention of the Association for Education in Journalism at the University of Texas.

Reprinted with permission of the *Journal of Inter-American Studies*, 1966, pp. 345–357.

358

tant role to mass communication has been exemplified in some of the work of UNESCO. A report of a UNESCO conference held in Santiago, Chile, a few years ago contained many recommendations for building and improving the mass media in Latin America.[3] Because little mass communication research had been done in the region up to that time, the recommendations were based largely on untested assumptions and long-range hopes regarding media effects on economic and social development.

Since publication of the UNESCO report, however, a number of studies have been undertaken in Latin America which provide evidence of the impact of mass communication on several development fronts. These studies will be cited in this article and various implications drawn from them. These implications may have relevance to the role of mass communication not only in Latin America but also in other developing regions of the world.

At the outset, it can be assumed that in order for mass communication to influence the climate for modernization in Latin America, several conditions must be met: (a) mass communication media must be available; (b) they must contain content relevant to modernization; (c) they must have the attention of mass audiences; and (d) the content must have effects on the knowledge or attitudes of audiences, predisposing them to accept modern ideas, methods or products. We shall consider these conditions briefly in that order but give more attention to the final one, which is the most difficult to establish.

AVAILABILITY AND CONTENT

The over-all diversity of Latin America is reflected in the availability of mass media. The differences are tremendous, not only between but also within the countries. In the big cities we find the full-range of media readily obtainable, both print and electronic, except in a few cities still without television. In the hinterlands there are often few if any media to be found. In general, Latin America is better off in terms of mass media than most of Asia or Africa. It was reported in 1961 that for every 100 inhabitants of Latin America there were 7.4 copies of daily newspapers, 9.8 radio receivers, 3.5 cinema seats and 1.5 television receivers.[4] Several of these figures, especially those for the broadcast media, have undoubtedly risen considerably since then. In brief, it can be said that the mass media are available to a fairly large and increasing proportion of Latin Americans, especially in the cities.

Systematic content analyses of the mass media in Latin America are scarce, but even a casual reader of Latin American newspapers can note the remarkable proportion of news stories dealing with plans for housing projects, dams, industries, new schools and governmental reorganization and other aspects of modernization. The papers also contain much news of political, economic and social change in other countries; Markham has shown that Latin American metropolitan newspapers carry a much higher proportion of foreign news than do their North American counterparts.[5] Much of the content in the other media available to Latin Americans—magazines, books, radio, television and movies—is obviously designed to inform or persuade people about various kinds of modernization.

ATTENTION

It is not enough for mass media to be available and to carry content relevant to development; people must be able to use them. In Latin America much of the population cannot use the mass media because of illiteracy (although this is being changed rather spectacularly in some countries through mass literacy campaigns resulting in increasing media). The electronic media, leaping the literacy barrier, are now reaching millions who were virtually insulated from the outside world a few years ago. It is far more difficult and costly to obtain data on media attention than on availability. Nevertheless, drawing on a number of studies, we can assemble figures which give some glimpses of the extent to which attention is being paid to mass media in Latin America.

Some figures on the use of the individual media on a typical day (based on interview responses referring to "yesterday") by different kinds of Latin Americans are presented in Table 1 for comparative purposes. The first column gives the percentages for adults in Midwest cities of the United States. We can see that newspapers lead the list in terms of daily use, followed by television, radio, magazines and books. The second and third columns show USIA figures on media used "yesterday" by adults in Buenos Aires and five provincial cities and by adults in some rural districts. The Argentine urbanites are very close to the North Americans in the use of radio and books, somewhat behind on magazines, considerably behind on newspapers and far behind on television. The rural Argentinians are less regular users of all the media except, significantly, radio. Television has practically no penetration into the rural areas represented in the Argentine sample, but in some parts of Latin America television has begun to reach some rural people. The fourth and fifth columns give some USIA figures for Brazil showing striking differences between persons who have had primary schooling and those who have had none. Those with a primary education are users of the mass media, though not to the extent of Argentine urban adults. The urban Brazilians with no education are clearly light users of all the media except radio. Here again radio is shown to be exceptionally effective in reaching segments of the population inaccesible to other forms of mass communication. The sixth column gives the figures for male heads of households who live in well-to-do neighborhoods of San José, capital of Costa Rica. Media use by these men clearly is comparable with or higher than that of a cross-section of North Americans, as are their living standards in general. More than half of these men, many of them professionals and executives who use English-language reference books in their daily work, said they had read a book "yesterday," a much higher proportion than was found in the United States. The next to the last column shows that professionals and technicians in eleven Latin American countries also are heavy users of the mass media. The last column also puts Costa Rican university students in the category of heavy media users. It can be noted that all three of the last groups mentioned rank slightly higher on newspaper use "yesterday" than the North American urban sample. (The USIA study, incidentally, found

TABLE 1   Percentage Who Used the Mass Media "Yesterday"

	Adults in six midwest U. S. cities (a)	Argentina urban adults (b)	Argentina rural adults (b)	Brazil urban primary education (b)	Brazil urban no education (b)	San José high status men (c)	Latin American profession-als and technicians (d)	Costa Rica university students (e)
Newspapers	92%	65%	40%	35%	6%	95%	95%	97%
Magazines	40%	30%	20%	12%	2%	59%	45%	37%
Books	17%	19%	10%	8%	1%	56%	71%	39%
Radio	58%	59%	61%	56%	47%	45%	76%	74%
Television	70%	32%	1%	16%	8%	39%	51%	29%
Movies	—	6%	5%	5%	3%	14%	12%	15%
(N)	(700)	(2,000)	(300)	(1,033)	(357)	(66)	(214)	(280)

(a) Inland Daily Press-Midwest Universities Research Committee, *Images of Six Inland Daily Newspapers: A Summary Report of the Attitudes of Six Communities Towards Their Newspapers.* Michigan State University (May 1964).

(b) United States Information Service, *The General Pattern of Exposure to Mass Media in Seven Latin American Countries,* Washington, D.C., November 1961.

(c) John T. McNelly and Paul J. Deutschmann, "Media Use and Socioeconomic Status in a Latin American Capital," *Gazette,* IX (1963), 1–15.

(d) Paul J. Deutschmann, John T. McNelly and Huber Ellingsworth, "Mass Media Use by Sub-Elites in Eleven Latin American Countries," *Journalism Quarterly,* XXXVIII (Autumn 1961), 460–472.

(e) John T. McNelly and Eugenio Fonseca, "Media Use and Political Interest at the University of Costa Rica," *Journalism Quarterly,* XLI (Spring 1964), 225–231.

levels of media use in several Latin American countries rising with socio-economic status and education, except that this trend is frequently reversed in the case of radio. The San José study also showed higher use of radio by lower socioeconomic groups; however, the opposite trend with respect to radio was reported in a survey of media use in Santiago, Chile.[6])

It is clear that among professional, technical and well-to-do urban groups in Latin America, media use is roughly comparable to and in some cases higher than among similar groups in the United States. Furthermore, the poor and less educated are moving rapidly into several of the Latin American mass media audiences and already provide a major share of the radio listeners. Television is taking hold fast, particularly in the cities.

Any discussion of media use in Latin America should mention the remark-able consumption of foreign magazines, especially by higher socioeconomic groups. The USIA reported high readership of Latin American editions of *Life,* the *Reader's Digest, Time,* and of the Brazilian magazine, *O Cruzeiro.*[7] For example, thirty-two per cent of a sample of Peruvian urbanites reported reading *Life* magazine. Twenty per cent read *Selecciones* of the *Reader's Digest,* ten per cent *O Cruzeiro,* and three per cent *Time.* Even in a sample of rural districts in Peru, fifteen per cent of the adults reported reading *Selecciones* and nine per cent read *Life.* In the study of urban professionals and technicians in eleven Latin American countries, readership of *Life* was found among about half of the sample, closely followed by the *Reader's Digest* in either its Latin American or United States editions, and then by *Time* magazine.[8]

EFFECTS

Assuming on the basis of the foregoing that the mass media are available, have content pertinent to modernization and reach massive audiences, we turn now to the final condition to be met in order for mass communication to contribute to development: that the messages have effects on the audiences.

In his recent book on the mass media's role in national development, Schramm stated that the research literature on Latin America contained no major study in which economic and communication development were the chief variables.[9] However, Schramm did cite a study on social change in which communication was obviously important. That study, by Holmberg, deals with the well-known experiment conducted by Cornell University in a rural community high in the Peruvian Andes. Holmberg's comments on the importance of bringing new information to the people of Vicos and the possible future role of the mass media in that task are quoted by Schramm. But one of the quotations concludes that "in the early stages, only patient face-to-face explanation and demonstration can provide effective channels of communication."[10] The clear implication is that mass communication is ineffectual in the early stages of development in such a community.

On the other hand, evidence has arrived from another part of the Andes that mass communication can indeed play a direct and effective role in introducing new ideas to the people of extremely underdeveloped rural areas. In an experimental study of the introduction of health practices in four rural communities of Ecuador, it was found that radio programs beamed in with special mobile transmitters were clearly effective in influencing villagers to adopt such health practices as vaccination and the building of latrines.[11] Other audiovisual media, such as films, also were found to be effective. In the communities which received the radio treatment, radio was reported by the inhabitants as the most influential medium in their decisions to participate in the health practices. Face-to-face communication, education, literacy, and other factors also were related to adoption of the practices, but the influence of the mass media was strikingly evident.

The authors of the Ecuador study concede that ideally, perhaps, the communication so necessary to social development should occur in face-to-face situations, but they continue:

> Obviously, face-to-face communication is impractical where there are many potential participants, as in most developmental projects of the U.S. Agency for International Development, or other public and private organizations. Even if enough skilled development technicians were available, the cost of using them as personal instructors to the millions of people involved would be prohibitive.[12]

In still another part of the Andes, Deutschmann also found evidence of mass media effects on rural people. He found that household heads in a small Colombian village who had high media exposure opportunities also tended to know more about, have more favorable attitudes toward, and be more likely to have adopted modern agricultural practices.[13]

Five farm communities in the foothills of the Colombian Andes provided the setting for a study by Rogers in which he explored the proposition that exposure to the mass media leads the campesinos "down the road to modernization."[14] Using an index of media exposure made up of regular consumption of radio, television, newspapers, magazines, and film, he found significant relationships between exposure and empathy (defined as ability to place oneself in the role of community, national or other leaders), agricultural innovativeness, political knowledge, achievement motivation, and aspirations for education of children. Analysis of zero-order and partial correlations provided evidence that the exposure to the mass media was an intervening variable between the above-mentiond consequent variables and such antecedents as literacy, education, size of farm and social status.

In a small community in Guatemala, Deutschmann found mass media exposure related to knowledge and adoption of food and drug products by the largely illiterate female heads of households.[15] (Among the products were a brand of aspirin, a soft drink, coffee, and a food supplement.) The data showed that the mass media were an infrequent first source of information about these products, in comparison with interpersonal channels; however, "early adopters" accounted for the majority of media first-source events, underlining the significance of mass communication as a means of reaching such persons.

Another kind of modernization, participation in industrial development, has been studied by Waisanen and Lassey in Costa Rica.[16] There a group of entrepreneurs recently started a new cement plant and, in a demonstration of "enlightened capitalism," offered shares to the public on a first-come, first-served basis. In addition to personal contacts by company representatives, they used an extensive mass media campaign to sell shares. Several thousand Costa Ricans bought them. Using a national sample of more than 1,000 Costa Ricans, plus a special smaller sample of persons who bought stock in the company, the investigators undertook a study to compare characteristics of the two groups. In both they found the expectable relationships between mass media use and such variables as urbanization, income, education and occupation. And persons who bought stock in the cement company scored considerably higher on use of the print media than did non-buyers of the stock. Controlling for factors like income, education and urbanization did not eliminate the relationship. (Non-buyers, incidentally, listened to the radio more than did stockholders; again, as in several of the media consumption studies cited earlier, radio was particularly popular among less modernized members of the population.) A majority of the actual decisions to buy stock were taken on the basis of personal contacts, but the relation between stockholding and print media use is suggestive of the role of mass communication in establishing a favorable attitudinal climate for such behavior.

Levels of mass media use by Latin American professional and technical people shown in Table 1 would suggest that they make heavy use of what they learn from the mass media in their work and in their daily lives.[17] This we found to be the case as we interviewed these people in countries from Mexico to Argentina. Many of them had on their desks or in nearby bookcases the latest texts, manuals and technical or trade journals in their various fields. Their replies to questions about kinds of useful information they obtained from the media covered a broad range and included not only technical but also popular media offerings.

Since data for that study were gathered in 1961, the governments of six of the fourteen countries involved have toppled in military coups, with resulting disruption of development programs. The establishment of political stability is gaining recognition as an essential condition for the modernization of Latin America. Political progress is closely linked with economc progress in the region.[18] A few recent studies have produced some evidence of the role of mass communication in the political education of Latin Americans.

Civic information was a variable in Deutschmann's previously mentioned study in a rural Andean village of Colombia.[19] It included an index of political knowledge made up of ability to name the president, the governor of the department, and local leaders. Mass communication exposure was found to be highly correlated with this index. For illiterates the correlation was even higher than for literates, and Deutschmann suggested that this was due to literate persons in the family receiving information through the media and passing it on to other members of the family. In this village, many illiterate persons had their children read newspapers to them, a behavior not unknown in the past history of the United States. Nearly half of the illiterates said they purchased newspapers occasionally or regularly and more than one-fourth said that they had listened to the radio during the past six months. This village was in the early stages of political development process. Four of every ten individuals interviewed had no knowledge at all on the political index.

The Rogers study in Colombian villages, as mentioned earlier, showed a correlation between the media exposure index and levels of political knowledge.[20]

Moving to a more advanced urban setting in the capital of Costa Rica, McNelly and Deutschmann found mass media exposure related to knowledge of a number of news topics, including some involving international politics. Some, but not all, of this relationship was traceable to the antecedent variable of socioeconomic level.[21]

An even more advanced stage of political development is represented in the universities of Latin America, where student maneuvering and agitation can determine the fate of national governments. As Table 1 shows, University of Costa Rica students studied by McNelly and Fonseca were found to be heavy users of the mass media. Exposure to the print media was found to be highly related to knowledge of world affairs as indexed by responses to questions on political personalities and events. The relationship held up when we controlled for socioeconomic status. In addition, print media exposure was found to be closely related to participation in politics, a relationship that also held when socioeconomic status was controlled. Thus exposure to the news through the print media was closely linked to the development of political awareness and participation among these young people.[22]

Further analysis of the University of Costa Rica data has probed into some of the dynamics of this relationship between media use and political awareness. At Deutschmann's suggestion we included questions about the acquisition of knowledge and the adoption of attitudes on international political-economic topics in order to obtain data comparable to that traditionally obtained in the study of diffusion of agricultural and other innovations. One of the concepts used was the Alliance for Progress. We asked the students how long ago they had first heard of the Alliance (about four out of five students said they had heard of it). The results, plotted in cumulative fashion, produced the familiar S-shaped curve commonly found in diffusion studies. The foot of this curve, however, was made up of a small proportion of the students who erroneously named times of first knowledge before President Kennedy originally launched the Alliance. Following the heavily publicized Kennedy speech, the diffusion curve ascended rapidly and later tended to level off as the information reached all but a minority of the students. As predicted, the curve for students who made heavy use of the print media was considerably ahead of that of students who made little use of the print media. This relationship remained when we split the students into high and low socioeconomic groups. The times of adoption of a favorable or unfavorable attitude toward the Alliance also were earlier for students who had heavy exposure to the news through the print media, and this relationship, too, held up when socioeconomic status was controlled. Additional analysis of the Costa Rica data and further studies in other Latin American universities are planned to help throw additional light on the role of mass communication in the political socialization of students.

SUMMARY AND DISCUSSION

Evidence has been cited from a number of recent studies of the role of mass communication in the creation of a favorable climate for modernization in Latin America. It has been shown that mass media carrying content relevant to modernization are available and being attended to by large and increasing numbers of Latin Americans, especially in the cities and among the higher socioeconomic groups. Media effects have been cited in a variety of fields—health practices, food consumption, agriculture, industrialization, political socialization.

But any attempt to pinpoint media effects on specified cognitions, attitudes or behaviors can at best tell only part of the story. Media messages do not necessarily perform their functions in strict accordance with neat theoretical models. A particular message may indeed change a particular attitude as predicted, but it may also affect other attitudes which impinge on that attitude. For example, a message or series of messages influencing a Colombian farmer favorably toward chemical fertilizer may at the same time affect his attitudes toward other agricultural innovations and even have side effects on his feeling about education or other aspects of the modernization process (as cognitive balance theories would lead us to expect). As a matter of fact, such generalized media effects may be far more important in the long run than specific effects singled out in individual studies.[23]

Just as it can be extremely difficult to limit media-effect studies to a single *dependent* variable, so it may be hazardous to attempt precise specification of the *independent* variable. For example, as Hyman has pointed out, certain parts of the mass media content may have manifest functions for political socialization while other parts, such as news of the world in general and all kinds of entertainment and commercial content which surround the political content, may also influence the attitudes of receivers in a kind of Gestalt effect.[24]

Thus, not only can one media message have effects on an unspecified number of different attitudes, but a particular attitude may be affected by an unspecifiable number of different messages—and all of these different messages may in turn be affecting other attitudes or groups of attitudes among the same or different individuals in the mass media audiences.

The situation is complicated still further, of course, by the fact that media message effects outside of laboratory experiments take place in social situations which may muffle, amplify, deflect or alter them in unpredicted ways. Indeed, such mediation of mass messages has become a central concern of some researchers, a concern which may stem at least in part from the fact that group and interpersonal channels are more readily investigated given the conceptual and methodological tools traditionally used in the social sciences. The two-step flow notion that mass communication has only indirect effects through the good offices of opinion leaders has won wide acceptance among social scientists partly as a reaction against the idea of all-powerful media.[25]

But a simplistic interpretation of the two-step hypothesis is inadequate in accounting for some of the evidence cited in this paper. Mass media influences appear to have reached down to persons other than just opinion leaders. And this in no way implies that personal influence did not play a part at all levels.[26]

Mass communication phenomena must be investigated, then, in all their endless complexity, with multiple effects from many possible kinds of cognitions, attitudes and behaviors in one, two or more stages and even in different directions through social structures. Mass communication may best be conceived neither as a simple "injection" operation on an entire population nor as a neat two-step flow from media to opinion leader to general public—but rather as a multi-stage, multi-directional process with possibilities for both direct and indirect effects.

The studies cited have provided glimpses of various aspects of this kind of enormously complex process at work in the modernization of Latin America. They support a conception of mass communication as not only accompanying economic, political and social factors in national development but also affecting such factors and having the potential of being used creatively to accelerate all aspects of development.

NOTES

[1] Among the relevant studies are: Daniel Lerner, "Communication Systems and Social Systems: a Statistical Exploration in History and Policy," *Behavioral Science*, II (October 1957), 266–275; Raymond B. Nixon, "Factors Related to Freedom in National Press Systems," *Journalism Quarterly*, XXXVII (Winter 1960), 13–28; Richard R. Fagen, "Relation of Communication Growth to National Political Systems in Less Developed Countries," *Journalism Quarterly*, XLI (Winter 1964), 87–94; Paul J. Deutschmann and John T. McNelly, "Factor Analysis of Characteristics of Latin-American Countries," *American Behavioral Scientist*, VIII (September 1964), 25–29; Phillips Cutright, "National Political Development: Measurement and Analysis," *American Sociological Review*, XXVIII No. 2 (April 1963), 253–264; Everett E. Hagen, "A Framework for Analyzing Economic and Political Change," in Robert E. Asher, et al., *Development of the Emerging Countries* (Washington, D.C., 1962), 1–38; Wilbur Schramm, *Mass Media and National Development* (Stanford, Calif., 1964); Dick Simpson, "The Congruence of the Political, Social, and Economic Aspects of Development," *International Development Review*, VI, No. 2 (June 1964), 21–25.

[2] Deutschmann and McNelly, *op. cit.*

[3] UNESCO, *Los medios de información en América Latina* (Paris: UNESCO, 1961). For views of a variety of social scientists on the development role of the media see Lucian W. Pye (Ed.), *Communications and Political Development* (Princeton, N.J., 1963); and Schramm, *Mass Media and National Development*.

[4] UNESCO, *Mass Media in the Developing Countries* (Paris, 1961), pp. 24–28. The minimum UNESCO target for the developing countries per 100 inhabitants is 10 newspapers, 5 radio receivers, 2 cinema seats and 2 television receivers.

[5] James W. Markham, "Foreign News in the United States and South American Press," *Public Opinion Quarterly*, XXV (Summer 1961), 249–262.

[6] Roy E. Carter, Jr., and Orlando Sepúlveda, "Some Patterns of Mass Media Use in Santiago de Chile," *Journalism Quarterly*, XLI (Spring 1964), 216–224.

[7] Report cited in note (b) of Table 1.

[8] Deutschmann, McNelly and Ellingsworth study cited in note (d) of Table 1.

[9] *Mass Media*, p. 53.

[10] Quoted in Schramm, *op. cit.*, p. 56, from Allan R. Holmberg, "Changing Community Attitudes and Values in Peru: A Case Study in Guided Change," in Council on Foreign Relations, *Social Change in Latin America Today* (New York, 1960), p. 105.

[11] Paul Spector et al., *Communication and Motivation in Community Development: An Experiment* (Washington, D.C., November 1963).

[12] *Ibid*, p. iii.

[13] Paul J. Deutschmann, "The Mass Media in an Underdeveloped Village," *Journalism Quarterly*, XL (Winter 1963), 27–35.

[14] Everett M. Rogers, "Mass Media Exposure and Modernization among Colombian Peasants," *Public Opinion Quarterly*, XXIX, No. 4 (Winter 1965–66), 614–625.

[15] Paul J. Deutschmann and Alfredo Méndez D., "Adoption of New Foods and Drugs in Choleña: A Preliminary Report," San José, Costa Rica, 1962.

[16] F. B. Waisanen and William R. Lassey, study to be published in forthcoming monograph by Programa Interamericano de Información Popular, San José, Costa Rica.

[17] Deutschmann, McNelly and Ellingsworth, *op. cit.* in Table 1. Further data on mass media use and the attiudes and technical change activities of these people will be included in a book manuscript now in preparation.

[18] Hagen, *op. cit.* in note 1, pp. 2–6.

[19] See note 13.

[20] See note 14.

[21] Study cited in footnote (c) of Table 1.

[22] Cited in footnote (e) of Table 1.

[23] On the basis of his review of the diffusion literature, Rogers has suggested that perhaps change agents should seek to alter their client systems' norms on innovativeness in

general, rather than to promote single innovations. Everett M. Rogers, *Diffusion of Innovations* (New York, 1962), pp. 279–281.

[24] Herbert Hyman, "Mass Media and Political Socialization: The Role of Patterns of Communication," in Pye (Ed.), *Communications and Political Development*, pp. 128–129.

[25] Hyman has noted that social scientists greeted the two-step flow hypothesis with enthusiasm because it "reinstated the human factor in what at first appeared to be too impersonal and mechanical a process of communication." But he goes on to question the easy assumption that mass communication can be defined as impersonal. He points out that the apparent disadvantage of the mass medium when not combined with interpersonal links "may be simply an illusion fostered by our own analytical distinctions." In traditional cultures, he says, and for that matter even in our own, a mass medium may well take on human features and be seen as the "vital embodiment" of some well-known entertainment personality or well-known writer. *Op. cit.*, pp. 144–146. Judging from what the present writer was told in Ecuador by staff members of the previously mentioned study of the introduction of health practices (Spector *et al.*, *op. cit.* in n. 11), radio became a personal medium there in just such a sense. Some of the programs were in the form of serialized dramas, in which leading characters achieved considerable local fame as they acted out health lessons. The villagers were reported to have taken keen personal and even emotional interest in the radio project.

[26] A Dutch researcher, on the basis of a recent study of three farming communities in the Netherlands, suggests replacing the two-step hypothesis by a more complicated set of hypotheses—in which both opinion leaders and followers are said to be influenced by the mass media as well as by other people, but at different stages of the adoption process. A. W. van den Ban, "A Revision of the Two-Step Flow of Communications Hypothesis," *Gazette*, X (1964), 237–249.

THE ISLAMIC SERMON
AS A CHANNEL
OF POLITICAL COMMUNICATION*

Bruce M. Borthwick

BRUCE M. BORTHWICK was born in 1938. He studied at the American University of Beirut and received his B.A. at Syracuse University in 1959. His M.A. and Ph.D. were earned in near eastern studies and political science at the University of Michigan. While a graduate student at the University of Michigan, he was a recipient of the National Defense Foreign Language Fellowship for the study of Arabic. He is a fellow of the Middle East Studies Association and a member of the American Political Science Association, the International Studies Association, and the Society for Iranian Studies. He is currently an associate professor of political science at Albion College.

Today the modernizing ruling élites in the Middle East are trying to promote social change, build nations and legitimize their rule. These men of the new middle class—using the term of Manfred Halpern[1]—are communicating to the people a new outlook on the world and new images of what life can be. If the trauma of change is to be lessened, the ruling élites must communicate new messages to the people without producing "crippling tension and deep psychological frustrations and anxieties."[2] They must amalgamate the new messages with the habits, ways of thinking and social processes of the people, so that they can identify emotionally with the messages and feel that they are indigenous to their culture. This amalgamation will reduce the gap between the modernizing ruling élites and the traditionally oriented masses, and will increase the stability and viability of the Middle Eastern political systems.

Mediators[3] who are well grounded in both the traditional and modern cultures and institutions are essential to this process of change. They must have one foot in the world of the traditional Arab Middle East and the other in the modern world of the West.

In the period since World War II some Muslim preachers have become

* This paper is extracted from the author's Ph.D. dissertation, "The Islamic Sermon as a Channel of Political Communication in Syria, Jordan and Egypt" (University of Michigan, 1965). The dissertation is a study of the content of 41 sermons in 1960 and 1961 over Radios Damascus, Amman, and Cairo, which were recorded and transcribed in the original Arabic in Beirut by Naf'at Nasr and 'Abd al-Rahman Bitar, graduate students at the American University of Beirut and by Professor Ralph Crow of the Department of Political Studies and Public Administration of the same university. The recording and transcription was made possible by a Rockefeller Foundation research grant from the research committee of the Faculty of Arts and Sciences of the American University of Beirut. Professor Crow kindly allowed the author to use these transcripts. The author translated the sermons with the assistance of Dr. Fu'ad George Massah.

Reprinted with permission from *The Middle East Journal* (Summer 1967), pp. 299–213.

such mediators. Prior to World War II the "*ulamā*," of which the preachers are a part, were educated solely in the traditional Islamic studies and were known for their conservatism and parochialism. After World War II, particularly in Egypt, their education was changed so that now they study science, modern foreign languages and other modern subjects in addition to traditional subjects such as Qur'ān commentary and Islamic jurisprudence.[4] This grounding in traditional and modern subjects enables them to be mediators.

There are two types of Islamic sermons: the homily (wa'z) given any time during the week when a member of the "*ulamā*" can gather around himself a group of listeners on the floor of the mosque, and the Friday sermon (*khutbat al-jum'ah*) delivered from the pulpit during the Friday noon worship service which all adult Muslim males are obligated by the *Shari'ah* to attend. This article deals with the Friday sermon only.

Prior to World War II the Friday sermon was stylized and pedantic. Often the preacher simply memorized and recited sermons which were hundreds of years old.[5] But in the postwar period several members of the "*ulamā*" have advocated a reform of the sermon. They have urged preachers to speak about the problems Muslims face in modern life and about the nations in which Muslims live. The reform in the education of the "*ulamā*" and the reform of the sermon have enabled the preachers to become mediators between the traditional and modern cultures.

During the same period when some preachers have become mediators and when a reform of the sermon has taken place, the new élites in some Arab states have assumed control over the sermon. They now require the preachers to propagate their policies; however, the preachers are also required by the *Shari'ah* to support everything they say with verses from the Qur'ān and *hadith*. As a result, the sermon in some Arab states is now an amalgamation of traditional Islamic concepts with the policies of the contemporary ruling élites and is a channel of communication of the state.

THE SERMON THROUGHOUT THE HISTORY OF ISLAM

Islamic history has provided the precedents for the sermon serving as a channel of political communication. The sermon has been a means whereby the ruling élite has informed the public of its policies, programs and ideas. The political content of the sermon has varied, but at least in theory it has always been considered a channel of communication of the state. During the lifetime of Muhammad and for approximately one hundred years after his death this political content was quite high; then it disappeared from the sermon almost entirely until the twentieth century.

The fusion of state and religion in Islām caused the sermon and related religious institutions to have social and political functions. Muhammad was a "prophet and statesman"[6] and the community he left behind was both political and religious. This fusion of religion and state and the fact that the sermon and related institutions have performed social and political functions in the past have made it easier for contemporary political leaders in the Arab world to give an Islamic coloring to themselves, their programs to modernize the society and the economy, and their policies of nationalism.

THE POLITICAL AND RELIGIOUS ROLES OF THE PREACHER

From the beginning of Islām the responsibilities of the preachers have been religious and political. At least in theory, and often in practice, they have been representatives of the state charged with exhorting the "believers" to uphold Islām and with informing them of the policies of the government. Today, the preachers continue to carry out these dual functions.

Muhammad was the first preacher, and when he preached, he acted in two capacities: the leader and spokesman of the Islamic community, and the Prophet, or Messenger, bringing the revelation of God to man. Sometimes one rôle predominated, sometimes the other. Muhammad's successors, the caliphs, inherited these secular and religious rôles, as symbolized by two of the appellations given to them: amir al-mu' minin, "the commander in chief of the believers," and imām, "the leader of prayer."

Not only did this unity of political and religious office exist at the very top, but also down through the hierarchy of the Islamic empire. The caliph was the chief preacher. He formally assumed office by ascending the pulpit of the principal mosque in the capital, receiving the homage of the community, and by delivering his first sermon.[7] In each province the governor was the chief preacher. The caliph appointed him ruler "over the prayer and the sword," and commissioned him to administer "justice among the people" and to lead the prayer.[8] Sometimes it was even said that the governor had "the province and the sermon" under him.[9] He formerly took office in a manner similar to that of the caliph. He ascended the pulpit of the principal mosque of the provincial capital, said a few words glorifying God and the Prophet, read the letter from the caliph announcing his appointment, and delivered a sermon which frequently was interspersed with crude threats against the enemy if a war was in progress.[10] He, in turn, appointed the preachers in the various cities and towns of the province.

In the early years of Islām it was the practice that the general who commanded an army would also lead it in the communal prayer and deliver the Friday sermon. No special imām-preacher traveled with the army in order to fulfill this function. Indeed there existed no profession of imāms or preachers because the duties of leading the prayer and preaching the Friday sermon were part of the responsibilities of the caliph, governor or local ruler.

Under the 'Abbāsids the caliphs, governors and lesser officials ceased to lead the prayer and deliver the sermon, except on special occasions, such as the month of Ramadan.[11] The responsibilities were then transferred to men learned in religious matters, the "ulamā"; in the larger mosques one or more men served as imām, but only one as a preacher; in the smaller mosques the two duties were assumed by one man, an imām-preacher. The imāms and preachers were appointed by the ruler, either the caliph, the governor or a lesser official, and they led the prayer or preached in the name of the ruler. The preachers acknowledged the source of their authority by asking God in the sermon to bless the caliph, the heir-apparent and the governor or king of their province or country. Because of his political responsibility the preacher was more important than the *imām* in the Friday service.[12] If the preacher failed to mention the caliph's or governor's name in the sermon, it was the signal of a revolt against the ruler's authority.[13] Even after the governor ceased to lead the prayer and to deliver the sermon, he was still appointed "over the prayer."[14]

The tradition that preachers are appointed by the ruler has made it easier for modern Muslim states to exercise control over their preachers, while the early practice of the caliph acting as the Friday preacher has served as the precedent for contemporary political leaders to preach on Friday.

The movement to reform the sermon

During the first centuries of Islām the preachers developed the rhymed prose in the sermons into a high art,[15] but at the same time the sermon became very stereotyped, and increasingly preachers did not write their own sermons and instead selected them from anthologies. As preachers fell into the habit of reciting prepared sermons, the sermons became increasingly irrelevant to the times of the listeners. Political messages disappeared and the sermon became a dry exposition of theological doctrines. The only vestige which remained of the former high political content of the sermon was the invocation asking God to bless the caliph, the heir-apparent and the governor.

After World War I members of the "ulamā" in Egypt began to criticize these dull archaic sermons. Their criticisms were that the preachers spoke about the problems of former ages which only the "ulamā" knew about and ignored the problems the Muslim faced in the modern world;[16] they spoke in a very learned Arabic about rather esoteric subjects, and therefore their ideas were incomprehensible to most of their listeners;[17] they were very prone to derogate this world "and cause the people to love poverty and indigence,"[18] and they did not practice what they preached.[19] Under these conditions the average Muslim lost interest in the sermon. Some critics went so far as to say that one of the greatest causes of the decline of the Arabs and Muslims was the decline in preaching.[20]

These critics pointed out the tremendous influence that the sermon could have on Muslims. It could rouse souls, stir hearts, kill widespread evil, "sow virtue and the love of good" and "plant glory, honor, vigor, courage and the spirit of sacrifice in the hearts of their countrymen.[21] They pointed out that Islām was "a religion of politics, economics, sociology and literature" and therefore the sermon could touch on any of these subjects.[22] In short, the sermon could be an instrument of social reform and political liberation in the contemporary world, but instead it was a dead, lifeless instrument which had no effect on the believers.

The reformers urged their fellow preachers to write their own sermons and to make them relevant to the times in which they lived. They wrote "how-to-write-sermon" books, in which they included several of Muhammad's sermons, because they were considered to be models of how to make sermons relevant to the times in which one lives, and contemporary sermons to illustrate how this could be done today.[23] The contemporary sermons included such topics as: "The Influence of the Mosque on Reforming the Nation,"[24] "The Way to True Independence,"[25] "Quickening the Battle Against the Boll Weevil,"[26] and "The Promotion of the Industrial Development of the Nation."[27]

Maulana Muhammad Ali stated the reformers' concept of the modern sermon:

> Any subject relating to the welfare of the community may be dealt with in the [sermon] . . . [It] is for the education of the masses, to awaken them to a general sense of duty, to lead them into the ways of their welfare and prosperity and warn them against that which is a source of loss or ruin to them . . . it is meant, in fact, to throw light on all questions of life. . . .[28]

As a result of this reform movement, the sermon has been revitalized in style and content, and restored as a channel of political communication which characterized it in early Islām.

Reassertion of state control over the mosque and the sermon

Over the centuries governments in Islamic countries have had at least nominal control over the mosque and sermon. Today in Egypt this control is much more than nominal. In the twentieth century, Egypt has followed the policy that political, social and economic questions may be dealt with in sermons as long as they support the state. Under the old régime which was overthrown in 1952, the government controlled the content of the sermons, and confined the topics to loyalty to the existing order, satisfaction with one's lot, the sacredness of property, and the defense of capitalism, "in order to give the people the idea that the huge differences between the classes were sanctioned by Allāh."[29]

Under the revolutionary régime the contents of the sermons have likewise been controlled by the government, but now the preachers advocate social and economic reform, rather than the preservation of the status quo. All religious institutions, mosques and "ulamā" are under the strict control of the state.[30] Every week each preacher receives a written directive from the Ministry of Religious Affairs telling him the topic of the week's sermon. He can either write his own sermon on that topic or use a sermon written by the Ministry of Religious Affairs.[31] In Jordan prior governmental approval is required of all sermons.[32]

Some of the new revolutionary leaders have ascended the pulpits of Cairo mosques on Friday and preached. Prior to 1952 modern government officials had not been in the habit of doing this. Anwār al-Sādāt in 1953 was the first member of the Revolutionary Command Council to preach. Majallat al-Azhar ("The Magazine of al-Azhar") noted this and pointed out that in early Islām the military leaders had preached; therefore it was appropriate for Anwār al-Sādāt to do likewise. His sermon, which was described as being of a new order, affirmed that liberation was not merely evicting the oppressor and terminating tyranny, but was the liberation of the souls of men from selfishness and all of the remaining influences of the old régime.[33]

Jamāl 'Abd al-Nāsir, during the tripartite invasion of Egypt in 1956, fused in the office of the President of the Egyptian Republic the dual rôles of imām and amir al-mu'minin, which the caliphs in early Islām had possessed. On November 2 and 9, 1956, he went to the mosque of al-Azhar, the "national cathedral" of Egypt, listened to the Friday sermon, performed the congregational prayer, and then ascended the pulpit and delivered a speech, which was similar to the other speeches he gave during this national crisis. It contained such statements as: "Egypt will be a graveyard for the invaders," "From the aggression Egypt will emerge stronger then she was before." Although technically this was not a sermon—a member of the "ulamā" had already delivered the formal sermon—Nāsir did deliver a speech during the Friday worship service from the pulpit of the principal mosque of Egypt and one of the country's oldest. His choice of time and place was sufficient to identify himself as the defender of the nation and the faith. It was sufficient to demonstrate that Egypt was being invaded by infidels and imperialists, and that Islām as well as Egypt was being threatened.[34]

State control over the mosque and the sermon is described here only for Egypt and Jordan because there is adequate written evidence only for these countries. However, there seem to be varying degrees of state control over the sermon and mosque in other Islamic countries, because without such control they could be used to stir up sentiment against the government.

MEDIATION IN CONTEMPORARY SERMONS

In order to illustrate that the preachers are now acting as mediators between the ruling élites and the traditional masses, there follows an examination of some radio sermons dealing with three different aspects of contemporary Arab "nationalism": Arab history, the desire of the present day Arabs for political unity, and the Algerian war for independence. We will see that the preachers are amalgamating the ancient message of Islām with the modern message of nationalism. The thesis is that this nationalism which the ruling élites advocate and support more easily penetrates the minds of the masses when it is wrapped in the tradition and "truths" of Islām.

Arab history: the battle of Badr

At the Battle of Badr, on Ramadān 17 of the second year of the Hijrah (624 A.D.), 300 Muslims led by Muhammad defeated a force of about 950 Qurayshis (Meccans). The preachers speak about this battle because it is one of the most important in early Islām. They also feel that the weak position of the Arabs at that time is analogous to the weak position of the Arabs relative to their adversaries, the Israelis and their supporters, and that God will grant eventual victory to the contemporary Arabs, if they "believe," just as he granted victory to Muhammad and the first Muslims.

The preacher from Amman on March 3, 1961/Ramadān 16, 1380, declared that "economic warfare" was a weapon successfully used by Muhammad at the Battle of Badr, and by implication justified the present Arab economic boycott of Israel. The caravan trade was the basis of the Meccan economy. By attacking at Badr the richly laden caravan returning from Syria to Mecca, the Muslims struck at their adversaries' source of wealth and supplies. The preacher showed that the patient, long suffering Muslims found in this attack on the caravan a successful alternative to a frontal attack on Mecca; he suggested that similar patience and indirection today might achieve the same results against the Israelis who are likewise dependent upon outside sources of supply:

> God sent his Messenger as compassion for all beings, and the Messenger did not like to shed blood. When injury to the Muslims increased, they looked more intently to Heaven, and waited for permission to defend their Call and themselves. Permission to fight was granted.
> After granting the permission to fight, and promising victory, God asked them to pray in order to find a bloodless way to stop the raids of the Quraysh. Muhammad saw that destruction of their economy would be better than destruction of their military strength, for when the economy collapses, the nation collapses. This is known today as "economic warfare."
>
> . . .
>
> O men! It becomes clear that the immediate cause for God's permitting the Muslims to fight at Badr was that they had been persecuted and driven from their homes. This is what happened to the Arabs of Palestine. They were persecuted as much as anybody can be persecuted, and were driven from their homes under the most frightful conditions. But the day is coming when the flag of the jihād will rise—God willing.

While not mentioning the Battle of Badr, the Cairo sermon of May 13, 1960, also draws the parallel between the present day "plight" of the Arabs and the predicament of Muhammad and the first Muslims. It states that Muhammad's life is "the best example and model." Muhammad "faced the entire world alone, and went to Heaven alone."

> His only power lay in his "belief in God" and in his confidence in His truth and in the power of His will. There was no place behind him to which he could retreat or seek protection, except the promise of his Lord to aid him and grant him victory. . . . He did not perceive the difficulties which would block his way, nor the hardships he would face, nor the injuries and suffering he would meet, nor the ostracism, abuse, treachery and conspiracies that would be hatched for him. Nevertheless, none of these lessened his determination.
>
> . . .
>
> O Muslims! How many present-day events confirm the fact that treacherous intrigues and conspiracies surround our Nation. The hearts of the weak are confused and afraid. But those who are proud of their Lord and secure in their belief are firm before them.

Arab history: the crusades

The nineteenth and twentieth century military, economic and cultural invasion of the Middle East by the West has resurrected the Crusades in the minds of the Arabs.[35] The Crusades are the chief historical evidence for the Arabs' belief that their society is still under attack from the West. The Arabs picture the Crusades as "imperialistic" attacks seeking to destroy their military power, dominate their economy, and wipe out their civilization. The religious basis of the Crusades is considered a ruse to conceal the "imperialistic" motives.

The preachers say that victory came to the Arabs fighting the Crusaders because they "believed in God." They picture the Crusades as a "battle between truth and falsehood," a struggle between the "righteous servants" and the infidels, and as a *jihād* against an aggression "camouflaged in faith and a holy war." They say that the Arabs were the agents of God distributing His retribution to the unbelievers and that the Arab victory was the result of the will of God in support of the believers.

In contrast to this religious interpretation of the preachers is the secular-nationalist interpretation of Nāsir. He, in his speeches, has said that the "fundamental cause of the aggressors' defeat" was "Arab unity, Arab nationalism, and Arab solidarity."[36] The preachers have a religious education and are only speaking to Muslims. They state that "belief" was the cause of the Arab victory over the Crusaders, a religious interpretation which they also mix with nationalism. Nāsir has a secular education and is speaking to Muslims and Christians in the United Arab Republic (Syria and Egypt at that time); therefore, he gives a solely nationalistic interpretation. Since the masses are more oriented to Islām than to Arab "nationalism," the preachers' religious-nationalist interpretation probably has a greater impact, because it has the imprimatur of religious legitimacy.

The Cairo sermon of May 6, 1960, which was given in commemoration of the withdrawal from Egypt in 1250 of King Louis IX of France after the total failure of the Seventh Crusade, is illustrative of the contemporary use of the Crusades by preachers. After an introduction about "evildoers," "unbelievers," "truth," "falsehood," and the reward believers receive for bearing hardships, the preacher says:

O Muslims! In the Middle Ages this nation faced one of its harshest trials: the mad march, whose waves followed one after the other for two centuries, which wanted to destroy the distinguishing characteristics of this nation, to demolish its pillars, obliterate its mission, and tear up its roots. It was a march blazing with fire and mad with hatred. It was driven by greed camouflaged in faith and a holy war. It was just a struggle for spoils and worldly things.

Our forefathers were surprised by the first waves of this attack. Some were fighting for power among themselves . . ., but God sent to Egypt men who took matters firmly in hand and prepared for the encounter with the enemy. Everywhere the believers shouted, "Come to the *jihād*". . . .

Fat lay in wait for them. Led by the French King, Louis IX, they landed at Damietta and took the road to the capital. The people rallied behind their government, which displayed "belief in God and His Messenger." This "be-life" permeated the ranks of the people and made them one voice. The battle started between the brave defenders and the ancestors of the modern imperialists. We were as God described in His Book:

33:23 Among the believers are men who were true to their covenant with God; some of them have fulfilled their vow by death, and some are still awaiting, and they have not changed in the least. . . .

The battle between truth and falsehood showed some faces in a good light and some in a bad light. The covetous invaders fell into the trap which the nation laid to punish them for their aggression. The Europeans learned that covetousness was their ruin, and that the Muslim Arabs, when united in voice and ranks, can not be conquered. . . .

Arab unity

A further example of the preachers' amalgamation of nationalism and Islām is their viewpoints on contemporary Arab "unity." They espouse the general thesis that "belief" will bring an end to the Arab internecine disputes, and will bring about some sort of large unity encompassing all the Arabs. This thesis proceeds from the historical fact that it was the spirit of Islām and the diplomatic skill of Muhammad that united the warring tribes of the Arabian Peninsula and made them into a power that conquered the Middle East. Likewise, say the preachers, Islām is an indispensable foundation for a contemporary united Arab nation state.

The year 1960 was filled with some bitter inter-Arab disputes. Relations between the UAR and Iraq, Jordan and Tunisia were particularly strained and the radios of these countries were hurling invectives at each other. In this climate two Damascus preachers declared that dissension and disunity were unislamic. The āyahs and hadiths with which they substantiated their position were appeals to peace, which God or Muhammad had intended for the warring factions and tribes of Arabia.

On January 29, 1960, the preacher over Damascus radio said:

[Almighty God reminded the "believers"] that it is required by their belief that they all be brothers, living together with no factions hating one another. For the true belief unites the hearts, strengthens the ties of love between souls, and eliminates divisions among them, which lead to dissension, strife, hostility and hatred.

God said:
3:98/103 And you hold fast to God's bond, together, and do not scatter; remember God's blessing upon you when you were enemies, and he brought your hearts together, so that by His blessing you became brothers.

The Messenger of God—Peace and blessings of God be on him, his relatives and descendants—said in the true hadths:

'The relationship of a believer to another believer is like a building, one part of which supports another.
'The believers in their friendly relations, mutual understanding, and mutual assistance are like a body, which, should a part of it have pain, the rest of it will respond with sleeplessness and fever.

O brothers! These passages show that belief creates in the believers a spiritual unity.

[Spiritual unity] brings into existence the bigger unity which eliminates the motives and artificial obstacles dividing individuals and communities. Some of the lackeys of the imperialists and the agents of evil tried, and are still trying, to make these artificial obstacles into a tool of division to enclose every country within a narrow circle and within artificial boundaries so nobody will think some day of erecting a bigger unity, which protects the rights of all and which gives us a voice heard by the powerful nations.

On March 4, 1960, the preacher from Damascus continued the theme of cooperation and unity among the believers:

[The believer and his fellow citizen] are one hand against the enemy of the country. They are one hand, one heart and one force against those who want to destroy the unity, weaken the power and lessen the determination. This is what belief dictates and requires of the believer. The greatest virtues which the believers must practice are mutual aid, unity, cooperation and adherence to the factors which bring high rank and power.
. . . The tenets of the believer's faith call on him to erect a shield which does not violate the unity. . . . As to your power; in the past people have not been stricken by division or enmity, nor have the imperialists succeeded except after the ranks were divided and the seeds of division were planted between the people of two Arab-Islamic nations.

An even more Islamic interpretation of Arab unity is expressed by the preacher from Amman on January 20, 1961:

All of us desire to unite. We desire that our Nation unites. We desire to restore the unity of our Nation. But on what basis? Say: 'There is no deity but God.' Read the entire history of the Arabs. Did we have a united society before Muhammad? Did the Arabs reunite after the Prophet without Islam? Why? Because these Arabs innately can not unite without having one belief and mission.

The Algerian war for independence

The Algerian war was viewed by the preachers as being both a nationalistic and a religious struggle. They felt that Algeria was a part of the greater Arab nation, and that Arabs in Syria and Jordan should support the struggle there out of a feeling of loyalty to their fellow nationals. They used a phrase such as "nationalism, Arabism, blood, the soil, suffering, hope, one common history" to evoke support for the war. But the preachers also intermixed with the nationalistic appeals, appeals to the religion of Islām. The war was a "jihād for the cause of God" and a battle between truth and falsehood. The religion called the listeners "to volunteer for the cause of the defense of Algeria." But fighters for this cause were assured that "every battle for truth ends in victory and every battle for falsehood ends in shattering defeat." Both Islām and Arab nationalism were used to communicate the message urging support of the Algerians against the French.

The Provisional Government of the Republic of Algeria named its official newspaper al-Mujāhid, which means one who fights in a jihād. Thereby they undoubtedly sought to use the tradition and myth of the jihād to mobilize support for their movement. Parenthetically, "holy war" is a misleading translation of jihād. It has this connotation in contemporary Arabic, but it is also used in exactly the same manner as crusade is sometimes used in English, i.e., a struggle carried on with moral fervor, e.g., "The Crusade for Freedom," or Barry Goldwater's "crusade" in the 1964 campaign. In the sermons that follow we see that the preachers are exploiting both meanings of the word.

In response to a request from the Algerian provisional government for volunteers, the preacher from Damascus on March 15, 1960, said:

> O believers! O noble friends! O proud fighters! *Jihād* for the cause of God with all of your power and all of your soul. Join the *jihād* which was established by the religion. Join the battle against the imperialists, till they leave our country censored and routed.
> O believers! O Arabs! O Muslims! The religion calls you to volunteer for the cause of the defense of Algeria. The nation watches you. Belief unites the believers wherever they may live. . . .
> Nationalism, Arabism, blood, the soil, suffering, hope, one common history, all call you to *jihād* for the cause of God and to fight for your country, for the home of your forefathers, for the home of your conquests, for the home of cultural brilliance, for the entire world of Arabism and Islām. All call you to *jihād* for the cause of Algeria, O Arab believer.

In commemorating the beginning of the Algerian Revolution, the preacher from Amman on October 28, 1960, said:

> With the zeal of Arabs and with self assurance the *mujāhids* in Algeria undertook the risk of this blessed revolution, which foretold a bright future, the victory of truth and the defeat of falsehood . . .
> O Muslims! Every day the radio and press bring us the news of those bloody battles between truth and falsehood, between justice and injustice, between the right of the Algerians to freely decide their own fate and the wrong of France's imperialism and its false claim that Algeria is a part of France . . . Every battle of truth ends in victory, and every battle for falsehood ends in shattering defeat. Every day the political and military leaders of France receive the news of shame and humiliation in these glorious battles. The sixth year of the Algerian Revolution is now drawing to a close, and the awakening of glory, respect and honor is now near its noble goal.
> 26:228/277   . . . And those who do wrong shall surely know by what overturning they will be overturned.

CONCLUSIONS

Since World War II the demands for economic development have forced the Middle Eastern ruling élites to mobilize the entire population of their countries into a modern economy and polity. Economic and political development cannot be carried on by an élite alone. They demand the active participation of all sectors of the society. In order to fulfill this objective the modernizing élites must bridge the communications gap between themselves and the traditional masses. The Islamic sermon promises to be such a bridge.

The twentieth century reformers of the sermon took the first step in making the sermon a bridge across the communications gap. Prior to their reforms, the sermon was only a channel of communication among the "ulamā." Ancient sermons, which only the "ulamā" could understand, were usually recited. The reformers of the sermon established communication between the "ulamā" and the Muslim masses by writing their own sermons, by simplifying their language, and by preaching on topics which concerned their listeners. These reforms connected the traditional Muslims to the output end of the sermon.

After World War II the ruling élites connected themselves to the input end. They realized that if they did not control the sermon, it could be a powerful weapon in the hands of their political enemies. For example, in Egypt the Muslim Brethren used the sermon to attack Nāsir. He therefore censored the sermon and allowed only "ulamā" who supported his policies to preach. Censorship of sermons is imposed in Jordan and probably in other Middle Eastern countries also. The result of this government control is that the preachers now attempt to amalgamate the modernist nationalist policies of their governments wih the Qur'ān, hadith and Islamic tradition.

The legitimizing impact of the sermon

Through the sermon the modern nationalist messages of the ruling élites are clothed in the legitimacy myths of the Islamically oriented masses. For the traditional Muslim the sermon is legitimate because it is a regular and established part of the Islamically molded society in which he lives. The sermon is as old as Islām. Muhammad created it, and he was the first to use it to communicate political messages. This use of the sermon remained a tradition, if not always a practice, in Islamic society. The sermon is preached in the midst of traditional Islamic rituals and in the setting of the mosque whose architecture evokes memories of the great Islamic past. The sole sources which the shari'ah permits the preachers to use to justify their arguments are the Qur'ān and hadith, books which the traditional people have memorized to some extent. The preachers are members of a traditional social and occupational group, the "ulamā," and are usually of humble birth. They have usually been educated in part at a traditional school (the kuttāb), where only the Qur'ān is taught. They usually wear the traditional dress, have a modest standard of living, and live close to the traditional people.

The legitimacy of the sermon makes the traditional people more willing to listen to it and comply with the modern messages now being communicated in the sermon.

Why is nationalism such a prominent topic?

Nationalism offers the transitional man the easiest way to participate in modern society without giving up his attachments to traditional society. Nationalism requires only a minimal participation in the modern world—a simple affective expression of loyalty to the nation. Full participation in the political processes is not required. The individual does not have to form or join an interest group, articulate governmental policy, reconcile conflicting interests or perform any of the other multifarious activities of citizens in a modern nation.[37]

While the individual can participate to a minimal degree in the modern world through nationalism, he still does not have to give up his traditional Islamic heritage, because all of the elements of Arab nationalism are in some way associated with Islām. The Arabic language reached its peak of perfection in the Qur'ān. Arab history began with Muhammad. Arabic culture has been predominantly influenced by Islām.

Also, Arab nationalism fits naturally into the style of the sermon. The sermon is an exhortation to the Muslim faithful, primarily intended to arouse them to greater diligence in the practice of their religion. The preacher uses the beauty of the Arabic language and rhetoric to give the sermon a stirring tone. Because of the close affiliation between Islām and nationalism, this rhetoric and exhortation can also be used to arouse nationalism without being out of place in the sermon.

The Islamic sermon is a channel of communication which is well suited to the needs of contemporary Middle Easterners. It is an old Islamic institution with a high degree of legitimacy among the traditional people. Yet the modernizing ruling élites can control it and feed into it modern messages which the preachers wrap in the legitimacy myths of the traditional people. Thus the sermon is one way by which the ruling élites can communicate across the communication gap to the traditional people.

NOTES

[1] Manfred Halpern, The Politics of Social Change in the Middle East and North Africa. Princeton, N.J., 1963.

[2] Lucian W. Pye, ed., Communication and Political Development. Princeton, N.J., 1963, p. 13.

[3] See Dankwart A. Rustow, Politics and Westernization in the Near East. Princeton, N.J., 1956, pp. 25–8.

[4] See Bayard Dodge, Al-Azhar: A Millennium of Muslin Learning. Washington, D.C.; 1961, pp. 157–8, 166–8.

[5] See 'Ali Rifa'i, Al-Anwar al-Muhammadiyah fi al-Khutah al-Minbariyah. Cairo: 1954, pp. 6–7.—, Waby al-Nahdah al-Wataniyan fi al-Khutah al-Minbariyah. Cairo; 1956, p. 7. Muhammad 'Abd al-'Aziz al-Khawli, Islah al-wa'z al-Dini (5th Printing) Cario; 1961, pp. 4–5.

[6] William Montgomery Watt, Muhammad: Prophet and Statesman. London, 1961.

[7] The Encyclopaedia of Islam (1st ed.) Leiden: E. J. Brill, "masdjid," Vol. 3, pp. 347–8. Hereafter The Encyclopaedia of Islam is abbreviated El(1) or El(2), according to whether it is the first or the second edition. Reuben Levy, An Introduction to the Sociology of Islam. London, 1930, Vol. 1, p. 295.

[8] El(1), "masdjid," Vol. 3, p. 347.

[9] Ibid.

[10] Ibid., p. 348.

[11] Ibid., p. 372.

[12] Hamilton A. R. Gibb and Harold Bowen, Islamic Society and the West: A Study of the Impact of Western Civilization on Moslem Culture in the Near East. London, 1957, Vol. 1, Part 2, p. 96.

[13] Levy, op. cit., Vol. 1, p. 307. El(1), "khutba."

[14] El(1), "masdjid," Vol. 3, p. 372.

[15] El (1), "khutba," Vol. 2, p. 982.

[16] Al-Khawli, op. cit., p. 14.

[17] Ibid.

[18] 'Ali Rifa'i, Kayfa Takunu Khatib (4th Printing) Cairo, 1958, p.4.

[19] Al-Khawli, op. cit., p. 14.

[20] Ibid., p. 7. Also see, The Muslim World, Vol. 43 (Oct. 1953), pp. 308–9.

[21] Rifa'i, Kayfa . . . , op. cit., p. 8.

[22] Rifa'i, Wahy . . . , op. cit., p. 7.

[23] The works of al-Khawli and Rifa'i, op. cit., and 'Ali Rifa'i, Al-Tarbiyah al-Asasiyak fi al-Khutab al-Minbariyah. Cairo, 1962, Diwan al-Khutab lil-Juma' wa al-A'yad. Damascus, 1948.

[24] Al-Khawli, op. cit., p. 95.

[25] Ibid., p. 98.

[26] Ibid., p. 170.

[27] Rifa'i, Kayfa . . . , op. cit., p. 100.

[28] Maulana Muhammad Ali, The Religion of Islam: A Comprehensive Discussion of the Sources, Principles and Practices of Islam. Lahore, 1960, pp. 434–5, passim.

[29] James Heyworth-Dunne, Religious and Political Trends in Modern Egypt. Washington, D. C.: published by the author, 1950, pp. 50–1.

[30] Nadav Safran, Egypt in Search of Political Community: An Analysis of the Intellectual and Political Evolution of Egypt, 1804–1952. Cambridge, Mass., 1961, p. 255. Al-Ahram (Cairo), Sept. 13, 1954, p. 6.

[31] Interview with Dr. 'Abd al-Halim al-Najjar, former director of the Islamic Center in Washington, D.C.

[32] Cashiers de L'Orient Contemporain (Paris), Vol. 31 (1er Semestre 1955), pp. 76–7.

[33] Majallat al-Azhar, Sha'ban 1372, p. 1030.

[34] Al-Ahram, Nov. 3, 1956, p. 1; No. 10, 1956, p. 3. Panayiotis J. Vatikiotis, "Dilemmas of Political Leadership in the Arab Middle East: the Case of the U.A.R.," International Affairs, Vol. 37 (April 1961), pp. 195–6.

[35] Wilfred Cantwell Smith, Islam in Modern History. Princeton, N.J., 1957, p. 106, note 13.

[36] Gamal Abdel Nassar, Speeches and Press Interviews. Cairo, April–June 1960, pp. 82, 86.

[37] See Halpern, op. cit., pp. 197, 208.

INTERPERSONAL COMMUNICATION
AND THE
DIFFUSION OF INNOVATIONS*

A. W. van den Ban

A. W. VAN DEN BAN studied agricultural economics and rural sociology at the Agricultural University of Wageningen, Netherlands. After his graduation, he worked for eight years in research for the Dutch Agricultural Extension Service at the Department of Rural Sociology of this university. During this period, he studied for one year in the Department of Rural Sociology at the University of Wisconsin. In 1964 he was given a professorship in the new Department of Extension Education in Wageningen, and in 1966 he worked in the Michigan State University Diffusion of Innovations Project at the National Institute of Community Development in Hyderabad in India.

1. INTRODUCTION

Many studies show that the mass media do not result in important changes in human behaviour unless they are combined with inter-personal communication (Klapper, 1960; Rogers, 1962; Luthe, 1968). Some of the advantages of interpersonal communication over the mass media are that (1) it is more casual and therefore less inclined to attract only persons already sympathetic to the view expressed, (2) it is more flexible in countering resistance, (3) it provides immediate personal rewards for compliance, and punishment for non-compliance, being itself capable for expressing social pleasure and displeasure, and (4) the receiver can ask questions to the sender in order to decrease his uncertainty on the effects of the new behaviour. (See: Lazarsfeld, Berelson and Gaudet, 1948.) The relative importance of these and perhaps other factors is unknown.

The decision to adopt or not to adopt agricultural innovations usually in-volves a considerable amount of uncertainty. The situation of every farmer is somewhat different and frequently it is not known what the results of the innovation will be on his land with this year's weather. It is unknown how soon this innovation will be replaced by a better innovation. Also prediction of prices is difficult. Laboratory experiments by Sheriff and others indicate that in such a situation interpersonal communication can have considerable influ-ence on the perception of the effects of an innovation. Social scientists will have to help extension officers to decide how they can take this influence into account in their attempts to stimulate the diffusion of good agricultural inno-vations.

* Revision of a paper presented at the Second World Congress of Rural Sociology, Workshop on Extension Research, Drienerlo, the Netherlands, August 5–8, 1968.

Reprinted with permission of Sociologia Ruralis: Journal of the European Society for Rural Sociology 10 (1970), 199–219, and the author.

We shall discuss the processes of interpersonal communication at three different levels:

1. the individual level: what are the characteristics of the opinion leaders?
2. the two-person level of the seeker-sought dyad: who influences whom and in which way?
3. the village level: how do villagers differ in interpersonal communication?

In each case we will try to raise some questions for further research. This is also done in a last section concerning the way in which change agents can use the research on interpersonal communication processes. In addition we will raise some doubts about the two-step flow of communication hypothesis.

2. CHARACTERISTICS OF OPINION LEADERS

A considerable number of research workers have investigated the characteristics of those farmers who have much influence on the decisions of their colleagues to adopt agricultural innovations. Several studies have tried to summarize the findings from this research by following Homans's (1950) assumption that the opinion leaders follow the group norms more closely than their followers. However, Homans himself has left no doubt that this assumption is incorrect (1961, ch. 16). Now he says that a man of high status provides rare and valuable services to the other group members. An important service is to select which changes should be adopted by the group. The leader is the man who introduces new ideas in such a way that others follow him and not the man who only conforms to the old established group norms. Naturally, most of these ideas will be in agreement with the group norms, but in some situations he will take the initiative to change these norms.

Research has also shown that there is no clear distinction between leaders and non-leaders, but there are different degrees of leadership. The result is that many farmers exert some influence on the behaviour of their colleagues.

Nearly all studies have found that adoption of agricultural innovations and contact with change agencies are positively correlated with opinion leadership (Rogers and Stanfield, 1968). Some studies found that this correlation is higher in high adoption communities with favourable norms towards change than in low adoption communities (Marsh and Coleman, 1954; van den Ban, 1963; Yadav, 1967). It is not hard to explain this if one accepts Homans's theory that opinion leaders are the group members who are able and willing to provide rare and valuable services to the group. In groups with favourable norms towards change the members with most experience with and information about new farm practices are best able to help the other members with their decisions whether or not to adopt these practices. However, especially in cultures where leadership is ascribed, it is also possible that the explanation runs in the other direction: in villages where the opinion leaders have a high adoption level and many contacts with reliable sources of information about innovations, new farm practices are diffused rapidly (Yadav, 1967).

On the basis of Homans's theory one could expect to find rather low correlations between opinion leadership and the adoption of new farm practices or the contact with change agencies in developing countries. However, in some studies high correlations have been found (e.g., Sen and Roy, 1967, table 16).

This problem has been studied carefully by Sen and Bhowmik (in process) on the basis of data gathered in the Michigan State diffusion of innovations project in 8 to 20 villages in Brazil, India and Nigeria. They found that the degree of opinion leadership of an individual depends on three sets of variables:

1. a higher socio-economic status (farm size, income, caste rank, number of wives, and level of living);
2. formal positions;
3. external links (knowledge of extension agent, extension agent contact, political knowledge, newspaper exposure, and literacy).

Probably in these developing countries ascribed status as reflected, for example, in formal positions held, is a much more important factor than in industrialized countries.

When the research workers ranked the villages according to innovativeness they found that the difference in the innovativeness of leaders and the followers was relatively small in the villages which were low and high in innovativeness, and larger in the villages with a medium level of innovativeness. The explanation is perhaps that in the villages with a low level neither the leaders nor their followers are interested in the adoption of innovations. In the medium villages the leaders feel secure concerning their social position and therefore free to deviate from the group norms. Furthermore, the extension officers might feel that their position depends on the opinion of these formal leaders about their work and therefore try to help, especially the leaders, as much as possible. In the high adoption communities the leaders might feel less free to deviate from the group norms, because their social position is less secure, whereas their followers can be more inclined to follow their example as soon as possible.

In addition, one might wonder whether the group norms expect the same behaviour from all people in the community, or whether one expects the powerful leaders to be the first to try new ideas. Perhaps, in the analysis of opinion leadership, especially in developing countries, the power dimension has been neglected by rural sociologists. In order to study this dimension sociometric methods might have to be combined with anthropological methods.

The need for research on the changes in the leadership pattern in developing countries is also important. The introduction of agricultural extension and other forms of systematic economic development requires new leadership roles. To what extent are these roles fulfilled by the old leaders? From where is new leadership developing? What kind of tensions are there between the old and the new leaders? Does the extension officer arouse the opposition of the old leaders against his programme by stimulating the development of new leaders? Some research on these questions has been done, but a satisfactory answer to all these questions is certainly not yet available. A longitudinal study of some communities could help to answer them.

Barnett (1953) said that innovations are first adopted by the marginal members of the community, because they look for outside contacts to compensate their lack of acceptance in their community. However, he does not substantiate this statement. Many studies show that the leaders of a community are more cosmopolite and adopt agricultural innovations earlier than the low status members. Perhaps this is not true for other innovations which endanger the position of the leaders.

Coleman, Katz and Menzel (1966, ch. VII) found that well integrated doctors, who received many sociometric choices, adopted a new drug soon after its release to about the same extent as the less integrated doctors. However, their adoption rate was much higher and therefore, after 10 months, their adoption level was much higher than of the less integrated doctors. Van den Ban (1963, p. 188) could not confirm this finding in a study of the adoption of artificial insemination among Dutch farmers. From the first year onward the adoption level of the integrated farmers was much higher and the difference remained about constant.

3. WHO INFLUENCES WHOM, AND IN WHICH WAY?

To study social relationships one can analyze the dyads of the man who makes a sociometric choice and the person he has chosen. This makes it possible to study the similarities and the differences in magnitude and in direction between the seeker and the sought. Such a study can only be made if both the seeker and the person he has sought fall in the sample of interviewees. This is usually the case if one interviews all farmers in a rather closed community or if one uses snowball sampling, that is a two-stage sampling procedure in which one interviews in the second stage the people who have been chosen on sociometric choices in the first stage. In such studies one finds a differentiating effect, that is a tendency to select farmers who are different from the respondent, and a segregating effect, that is a tendency to select farmers who are similar to the respondents (Blau, 1962). Which tendency is strongest depends probably on the kind of relationship to which the sociometric question refers. One can ask questions regarding an:

1. *evaluative-instrumental* relationship, that is whom one values for the way in which he does his work, e.g.: which two farmers do you consider as good farmers?
2. *interactional-instrumental* relationship, that is with whom one prefers to interact regarding his work, e.g.: from which two farmers would you most probably ask advice regarding a decision whether or not to adopt a new farm practice?
3. *evaluative-sociable* relationship, that is whom one values for social contacts, e.g.: which two farmers do you like most?
4. *interactional-sociable* relationship, that is with whom does one most frequently interact on a social basis, e.g.: with which two farmers do you drink a glass of beer most frequently? (Yadav and Rogers, 1966, p. 15).

Several research workers have asked: "With which other farmer do you talk most frequently?" Probably this mainly gives an indication of the interactional-sociable relationship, but to some extent also an interactional-instrumental relationship.

For the evaluative-instrumental and the interactional-instrumental relationships the studies show a differentiating effect. There is clearly a tendency to choose as good farmers, and to a lesser extent as advisers, other farmers who have adopted more new farm practices and who have more contact with change agencies and other information sources. This might be a result of the correlation between these factors and social status, at least the differentiating effect with regard to social status (judge rating) is even stronger (van den Ban, 1963, pp. 182–3).

With regard to the question concerning with whom one talks most frequently there is some of this differentiating effect, but also a tendency to choose people who are similar in adoption level, contact with change agencies, and social status. Recent studies by Chou and Rogers (1966) in Colombia, and by Yadav in India do not confirm the hypothesis of a stronger differentiating effect for an interactional-instrumental relationship than for an interactional-sociable relationship. I cannot explain why their findings contradict the results from previous studies.

If this hypothesis is correct it could explain the difference in the findings of Katz and Lazarsfeld (1955) and of Lionberger and Coughenour (1957). The first authors found the opinion leaders to be at about the same status level as their followers, whereas Lionberger and Coughenour found them on a higher level of status and technological competence. They asked farmers from whom they obtained useful farm information. As they depend for their livelihood on the quality of information it is understandable that they look for a competent source. The choice of the movie to which one will go is much more a social activity and therefore it is understandable that Katz and Lazarsfeld found opinion leaders who are quite similar to their followers with questions of this kind.

In accordance with this explanation one can expect that farmers who are looking for information about a problem will get this mainly from farmers with a higher level of technological competence than they have themselves. In addition they will obtain a great deal of information, which they use in their decisions on the adoption of new farm practices, from other farmers at about their own level of competence in a more or less accidental way. An explanation for this phenomenon is given in Homans's valuable book, *Social Behaviour*. He sees human interaction as an exchange in which one does not get something for nothing. People at about the same level of technological competence can exchange information, because each of them will have valuable information which the other does not yet have. A farmer, however, who asks for information from a much more competent colleague cannot give him valuable information in return, for the simple reason that he does not have much information which the other does not yet have. Thus, he has to repay for the information he receives by admitting the other's competence and in this way increasing his status. This also decreases his own status. He will only be willing to pay this cost if he is aware that he needs this information to make a good decision. Perhaps this is a reason why Hruschka and Rheinwald (1965) found that in discussions between pilot farmers and their neighbours in 80 per cent of the cases the pilot farmer had to introduce the new farm practices he had adopted, whereas in only 20 per cent did other farmers ask him for information about his experience. They also found that farmers are more inclined to follow the example of influential pilot farmers than of less influential. An attempt by the extension service to use a not very influential farmer as an example for his colleagues introduces a change in the social structure of the community, which is resisted. With regard to a new brand of coffee Arndt (1968, p. 463) found that among Harvard student wives "leaders and non-leaders often exchanged transmitter and receiver roles." In a case like this technical competence is much less important than with new farm practices with which only the pilot farmers have any experience.

(This theory might also help to explain why the farmers who are, objectively speaking, most in need of help from the extension service usually ask for this help least frequently. For them, asking for advice implies that they are not able to cope with their own problems, whereas experience of the best farmers is necessary for the extension officers in order to discover how new research findings can be applied in their area. Therefore, the best farmers can exchange valuable information with the extension officer.)

Very few studies have not been restricted to the study of dyads, investigating also the effects of sociometric chains (e.g. Singh, Arya and Reddy, 1966) or sociograms (Rahim, 1965; Yadav, 1967). Further studies of this kind might help the extension officers to find a few key leaders, with whom they can cooperate to introduce certain innovations. These sociograms could also be used to study whether one is influenced by the cliques to which one belongs or by the individuals whom one has chosen on sociometric questions. It is possible that different cliques in one village have different group norms and that these norms influence individual behaviour.

In a number of rural societies one is inclined to rely more on government help for village improvement than on their own efforts. Thus, one needs leaders who have connections with government officials which enable them to bring a road, a school, a job for a village boy or whatever one needs to their village. In this situation one usually does not consider new knowledge as an important resource for village development. The "clients" will help their "patron," who often does not live in their village, in elections and by providing services for him, and in return they expect him to bring a somewhat larger share of the scarce resources of the society to them (Galjart, 1968, ch. 6). It is not yet known in which circumstances such a patron can help with the diffusion of agricultural innovations. Perhaps the patron is only willing to help the extension officers if he gets something in return for his help, e.g., the assistance of the extension officers in the next election campaign. In general, the role of the leaders in relating their village to the larger society deserves more attention in extension research. Sociometric methods will not be sufficient to study this role. Perhaps anthropological methods are more valuable for this purpose.

Many adoption studies are implicitly based on the assumption that the farmer, who has responded in the interviews, takes the decisions regarding the adoption of new farm practices, although we know that other family members share in the decision-making. Wilkening (1958) has shown that the farmer's wife has most influence on decisions, which can have considerable influence on their life, either because she participates in the farm work or a decision to invest money in the farm involves that less can be used in the house. Probably customs regarding financial management also affect the relative influence of husband and wife. In the Eastern and Southern part of the Netherlands, where subsistence farming was still prevalent less than a century ago, it is the custom that the wife keeps the purse because she is usually at home when someone comes with a bill. In recent years, most payments have been made through the bank. This probably has decreased the considerable influence the wife had on many farms in decisions to adopt new practices. Previously she had to solve the difficulties if, as a result of investments in new farm practices, not all bills could be paid immediately. Now her husband has to arrange this with the bank.

Unfortunately there is not much research on the roles of father and son in the decision-making process regarding new farm practices. Wilkening (1953, pp. 31 and 43) and Herzog et al. (1968, p. 34) found no correlation between an index of father-centered decision-making or patriarchalism and the adoption of new farm practices. Also, the communication between the farmer and his labourers on agricultural innovations can be an important topic for research. This communication is probably difficult where there is a large gap in status between both categories and where the labourers do not have confidence that the farmer is trying to serve their interests. Frequently, these labourers can see to it that the adoption of an agricultural innovation is not profitable to their boss.

Sociometric research techniques can tell us who influences whom, but not how they influence each other; these techniques give very little information on the content of the communication. Cartwright (1965, pp. 28–31) noticed that a person may yield to the influence exerted on him, because

1. he hopes for some kind of reward,
2. he fears some kind of punishment,
3. he likes to identify himself with the person who exerts this influence,
4. the person who exerts influence has a legal right to influence him because he is his superior,
5. the person who exerts influence is perceived to be more competent in this field than the person he influences.

It is not known to what extent each of these factors plays a role in interpersonal influence concerning agricultural innovations. In fact, rural sociologists have not given much attention to the content of interpersonal communications, but recent surveys have used two different techniques to analyse this content.

Arndt (1967 b and 1968 b) asked whether the comments which one had received on a new brand of coffee were favourable or unfavourable for its use. The answers were clearly related to the use of the product. He also showed nicely that the impact of this communication depends on the social position of the receiver and on her interest in the information transmitted.

Lionberger and Francis (1969) used a semantic differential technique to analyse how farmers see different information sources. They found that the farmers who are considered to be innovators are seen as more up-to-date and scientific than the farmers who influenced the decisions of the respondents to adopt certain new practices directly. This latter category is seen as more trust-worthy, considerate and dependable than the innovators. Obviously, each technique has its limitations, and therefore both need attention in future research.

It is also possible to study the leadership roles with projective techniques, as has been done on a small scale by Srivastava (1965), who used sentence completion tests, and by Rogers and Beal (1958) with stimulus pictures.

Anthropologists have shown that in many societies religion and belief in supernatural power have much more influence on the technology of the people than in the industrialized countries (e.g. Mair, 1965, chs. 13 and 14). This may be because these people have not much confidence that they can master the world around them with scientific methods. In order to influence the outcome of their efforts in agriculture and elsewhere they turn to other methods. Frequently, magical rituals are performed in order to influence supernatural powers to give good crops, rain at the right moment, to prevent illness, etc. The way in which a farmer should grow his crops can be prescribed fairly precisely by these rituals and religious beliefs. These support orderly behaviour which usually is in accordance with natural conditions. This can have advantages, but also disfunctional effects. It might make it more difficult to adopt scientific agricultural methods which deviate from the prescribed methods, especially if one believes that a deviation from the prescribed rules might not only bring harm to the person who deviated, but also to other members of his group. Unfortunately, there is not much research in this field. Anthropologists have not been interested in the first place in economic change whereas rural sociologists, working in developing countries, have frequently neglected the influence of religion on economic life because they were not used to studying this factor in the industrialized countries. In order to study the influence of religion and magic on the adoption of agricultural innovations it seems to me that new research methods have to be developed. For these problems rural sociologists might have to use depth interviews, whereas anthropologists should quantify their information as much as possible.

Witchcraft is partly a social control technique. Some people are believed to have the capacity to harm others, e.g., with sickness. If someone becomes ill or is overcome by some other kind of evil, which cannot be explained as a correction by some supernatural power for his own faults, a witch is believed to have used his powers to harm somebody he does not like. This may be because he envies him for his success, but also for many other reasons. In some parts of Africa the fear of witches and of the accusation of being a witch is widespread. Persons who are considered to be able to detect and destroy or cure the witches or their evil deeds as a rule have considerable influence. It is not known whether or not this belief in witchcraft influences the diffusion of agricultural innovations.

4. VILLAGE STRUCTURE OF INTERPERSONAL COMMUNICATION

Many adoption studies have correlated the characteristics of individuals, e.g. their innovativeness with their social status. Partly on the basis of the correlations found in these studies most sociologists believe that human behaviour is influenced to a large extent by the groups to which an individual belongs. In order to test this hypothesis there is a tendency in recent years, in several fields of social research, to study the structural effects, that is to study whether individuals with the same characteristics differ in behaviour if they belong to different groups (e.g. Likert, 1961). Attempts to apply these methods in adoption research give the impression that individual levels can be predicted just as well from the characteristics of the group to which the individual belongs as from his individual characteristics (van den Ban, 1960; Rogers and Burdge, 1961).

It is not yet known with a high degree of certainty how the group influences the behaviour of its members. Some studies have found relatively large differences between villages in their group norms towards innovativeness, which can be measured by questions such as: "What is the general opinion in this village about a farmer who is always one of the first to try some new farm practices?" (van den Ban, 1963). One possibility is that these group norms influence the social status of high and low adopters in the community. As there is a tendency to prefer interactional-instrumental relationships with persons of higher status than one has oneself, one may expect that in villages with group norms favourable towards innovativeness the high adopters interact frequently with other farmers, and in this way influence their adoption behaviour. A study of the factors influencing the college plans of American high school seniors found this pattern of influence. No effects of the school norms about college plans could be found if the plans of the friends of the students were kept constant (Campbell and Alexander, 1965–1966).

Another possibility is that the group norms result in some form of social control by which the group as a whole influences the behaviour of its members. It is my impression that this has been the case in Western European peasant societies. In these societies, the neighbourhood used to have a strong influence on the behaviour of the people. The families were very open to each other. It was usual for everybody to enter the house of the other members of his neighbourhood without knocking on the door. He merely came in, took a seat and was able to participate in any discussion. This made the people relatively closed in two ways. In the first place they were closed to outsiders, especially to city people with a different set of values and interests, and in the second place to each other. Husband and wife were not much inclined to show that they loved each other if at any moment one of the neighbours might step into the house.

During the frequent discussions the neighbours had usually developed a general agreement on the group norms about the way one should behave. If somebody deviated from these norms it would certainly be discussed extensively in the neighbourhood. In extreme cases, the boys of about 20 years of age, on behalf of the neighbourhood, might show quite clearly their dissatisfaction concerning this behaviour, e.g., by hanging a puppet of the person who deviated in the neighbourhood centre. In such a situation it was more or less the neighbourhood as a whole which influenced the behaviour of its members, although there were naturally some leaders who had much influence on what the neighbourhood would do.

In some traditional societies the leaders can have considerable influence, because the other villagers accept their decisions, in many fields, as binding to them. In other traditional societies, however, it seems to be more difficult to find the leaders than in modern societies (van den Ban, 1963, p. 78; Rogers and van Es, 1964, p. 18). A further study of the factors which determine the influence traditional leaders have in developing societies seems necessary.

In a modern rural society the situation is quite different. Here, one does not frequently interact with everybody in the community, but selects a few friends from a much wider geographical area. These friends give each other much more privacy than do neighbours in the traditional society. The group norms do not precisely prescribe how one should behave, but are much more concerned with which criteria one should choose one's behaviour (Germani, 1960). Here, social influence is exerted much less by the community as a whole and much more by the group of friends. It is not quite clear how much influence these friends exert. It is not fully acceptable to admit that one is influenced by one's friends, but these friends do have an opportunity to exert influence which neighbours in a more traditional peasant society do not have. These neighbours are supposed to interact with all the members of their neighbourhood except when they have misbehaved quite seriously. In a modern society one is free not to select somebody whom one does not really like.

The way in which these interaction patterns influence the diffusion of agricultural innovations has not yet been studied carefully. In two villages with traditional interaction pattern we asked how much time it takes for the majority of farmers in the village to know that one of them has tried something new. Six per cent said that they already knew this before he had tried it. A farmer in these traditional communities may complain, as may happen nowadays, that one sees that one of the neighbours has bought a new manure spreader. Previously one used to discuss for months with his neighbours before one adopted such an innovation. The same question asked in a modern community showed quite clearly that it takes much more time before the news that somebody had adopted an innovation was spread by word of mouth (van den Ban, 1963).

Perhaps the picture that one interacts frequently with all other members of one's neighbourhood is not always correct. In European peasant societies factions are not unknown. They might have been started during a fight over the division of an inheritance, but can continue for quite a long time. Sometimes these factions become so serious that members of opposite factions hardly talk to each other. In developing countries, such as India, one gets the impression that these factions are much more prevalent. This might be partly due to the patron–client relationship discussed earlier. If each of the different patrons tries to obtain as great a share of the limited government resources as possible for his followers, it is understandable that factions develop easily between the different groups of followers. In other words, serious factionalism can be expected if the available resources are limited for the needs of the people and if one is inclined to rely on outside help rather than on one's own efforts to satisfy these needs.

Research on the effects of factionalism on the diffusion of agricultural innovation is again limited. Fliegel et al. (1967) found only a weak negative correlation between severity of faction disputes and the diffusion of agricultural innovations in 108 villages, but they admit that their measure of the severity of faction disputes was rather weak.

Villages may differ in the amount of interpersonal influence, just as Likert (1961, p. 56) found that departments in a company can differ in this respect. It is not yet sure under which conditions considerable interpersonal influence is exerted. Favourable factors might be an atmosphere of mutual confidence and a high level of willingness to consider new ideas (Yadav, 1967), because one perceives that one has the resources to try these ideas and to be able to continue in the competition with other farmers only if one rapidly adopts good new ideas. In a number of peasant communities, where the people are exploited for a long time by landlords and powerful urban people, anthropologists have found very little mutual confidence among the peasants. Lopreato (1967, ch. IV) reports, for instance, from Southern Italy that everybody is expected to serve his own interests, if necessary at the expense of his neighbours' interests.

Another difference between villages can be in the extent to which the leadership is specialized, that is the extent to which leaders in one field are also leaders in other fields. Perhaps the most serious study of this problem has been made by Singh, Arya and Reddy (1966). In two Indian villages they used sociometric methods to find four kinds of leaders: traditional (ascribed), political, opinion making (advice on work) and decision-making (consult in daily life and act upon their advice). The average correlation coefficients for the two villages were:

traditional	—political	.21
traditional	—opinion maker	.93
traditional	—decision maker	.97
political	—opinion maker	.43
political	—decision maker	.33
opinion maker	—decision maker	.96

In these villages there is little specialization in leadership, except for the new role of political leader. There are indications that in modern societies the leadership is more specialized (Yadav, 1967), partly because a good deal of the leadership activities are exerted in specialized associations. The effects of the specialization in leadership on the adoption of new farm practices are not well-known.

There are also differences between communities in the concentration of leadership; there might be a few very powerful leaders, or a much more diffused pattern of leadership. Herzog et al. (1968) found that, with an increasing level of development of communities, the concentration of opinion leadership decreases. Two studies found indications that the concentration of opinion leadership in agriculture is positively related to village level adoption of agricultural innovations (Fliegel et al., 1967, p. 171 and Hursh, Röling and Kerr, 1968, pp. 99 and 108), but one found a negative correlation coefficient of —.67 (Herzog et al., 1968). The reason for these contradictory findings is not yet clear.

In villages where the leaders have frequent contacts with change agencies the rate of adoption of innovations and the adoption level are usually high (Coughenour, 1964; Fliegel et al. 1967; Yadav, 1967). The main reason is probably that modern leaders stimulate the adoption of innovations by their followers.

5. THE TWO-STEP FLOW OF COMMUNICATIONS HYPOTHESIS

A well-known hypothesis on the process of interpersonal communication is that, "ideas often flow from radio and print to the opinion leaders and from them to the less active sections of the population" (Lazarsfeld, Berelson and Gaudet, 1948, p. 151). It is doubtful whether this hypothesis is correct. The opinion leaders indeed use the mass media more than their followers, but at least in one study it was found that this is also true for personal sources of information (van den Ban, 1964, p. 241). Adoption research has shown that people become aware of new ideas from the mass media, but they usually do not adopt these ideas themselves before they have been able to use personal sources of information. Probably this holds true for the opinion leaders just as much as for their followers. The major difference between the opinion leaders and their followers is that the first use information sources of a higher quality. They read more, and more specialized papers, have more contacts with technical experts and with innovators among the farmers in other villages, at least in modern villages. Whether or not these opinion leaders influence their followers, directly or indirectly, depends on the need these followers feel for their information. As we discussed previously, low status farmers will only turn to farmers with a high status directly if they feel a serious need for this information. Otherwise, they will restrict their discussions mainly to their friends, who have only a little higher status than they have themselves. In that case it may take some time before the innovation trickles down through the whole community. Also the opinion leaders will not simply pass on the information they receive, but they will give their own interpretation to this information (Arndt, 1968a), taking into account what they expect their followers would like to hear.

6. IMPLICATIONS FOR EXTENSION EDUCATION

Perhaps in adoption research we have not sufficiently asked what the implications of our research are for extension education. An indication is given in Sanders's (1966) recent textbook on extension education, which makes very little use of the numerous studies on the adoption of new farm practices. Therefore, let us briefly discuss how extension officers can use the research summarized in this paper, and which of their questions cannot yet be answered by this research.

It has been found that personal communication is usually required before new farm practices are adopted, but that there is some resistance to asking advice from other farmers. Therefore, it seems desirable to make more use of group discussions in extension education in order to create a situation where the information from one farmer to the other flows easily. Levêsque (1961) found indications that such a discussion group can decrease the mutual distrust among farmers and, if the extension officer participates, the distrust in him also. If we accept that human behaviour is influenced to a large extent by the norms of the groups to which one belongs, another advantage of these group discussions is that it is often easier to change the norms of a group as a whole than to let a person deviate from the norms of his groups. Group discussion can be the best way to change group norms. If one likes to work through groups one can work through existing groups or try to establish new groups. What are the advantages and disadvantages of both methods?

What can the extension officer do in communities where the group norms do not favour the introduction of new ideas? Probably the informal leaders there are not much interested in co-operating with the extension officers, whereas most farmers who are interested in this co-operation have not much influence. Can the extension officer build new leaders out of this last group or can he gain the co-operation of some of the established leaders? In which way is this possible? What can be done with a discussion group where the extension officers use counselling methods in order to help the group to discover its own problems and stimulate them to try to solve these problems?

In order to develop rural leadership the extension service, folk high schools, farmers organizations and others frequently give courses in which the participants can discover that the society as a whole is changing and that they have to adjust themselves to these changes. What is the effect of these courses? In which circumstances are the participants accepted as leaders? Does it perhaps happen that they become outsiders in their own group, because of their participation in these courses?

What are the effects of working with extension committees? Under what circumstances does this stimulate co-operation among the people, and between the people and the extension service? In which circumstances does it stimulate factionalism? How effective is the application of social action theory? How can an extension officer work effectively in a community where there are serious tensions between different factions?

Extension officers do not have sufficient time to work intensively with all farmers. Research shows that by working with the local leaders they will often be more effective than by working with the farmers who are most interested in co-operating with the extension service. The informal leaders are frequently more important than the formal leaders, but how can an extension officer find them? Research on leadership characteristics can help to make the extension officers sensitive to the kind of people among whom they would probably find the informal leaders. What is the best way to find them? Sociometric methods are usually out of the question, because asking these kinds of questions directly does not fit in with the role expectations for the extension officers, and the analysis takes too much time. Can one use a judge's rating of the influence of different farmers? Can the extension committee make the selection, or do they make their selection on the basis of factors other than or different from informal leadership? Can the village itself select the farmers through whom they get the information from the extension service, as is done in the "animation rurale"? Is it true that in poor villages the leaders are often more inclined to hoard the information they have rather than to pass it on to other villagers?

Lionberger and Coughenour (1957) studied a community where they found a clear tendency to select persons of higher social status and technological competence as sources of farm information, whereas status differences did not serve as serious barriers to the selection of high status persons as information sources. If this also holds true for an interactional-sociable relationship the extension educator may reasonably expect to influence those at the bottom indirectly, in due time, by working with those at the top of the scale. In other situations, however, status differences do serve as a serious barrier to communication. It even happens that small farmers select large farmers as a model for their farm management, and therefore do not farm intensively enough to make a reasonable income on the small acreage of land they have (van den Ban, 1963, pp. 164–5). How does the extension officer know in which situation he is working if he does not have the resources to make a full-scale sociological study? What should he do if there are serious status barriers? Starting a discussion group for small farmers only might also cause some resistance.

A well-known principle for introducing change is, "if the group is to be used effectively as a medium of change, those people who are to be changed and those who are to exert influence for change must have a strong sense of belonging to the same group" (Cartwright, 1961). On the basis of this principle it has been advocated that the extension officer should try to decrease the status difference between him and the farmers. Is this indeed the best way in developing countries with a tradition of large status differences? Is not an extension officer of high status, who has presumably also much power, more effective?

There is no doubt that research on leadership and interpersonal communication is useful for extension officers. However, even after all the research which has been done many important questions in this field of extension can only be answered on the basis of common sense. The same holds true in the field of marketing (Arndt, 1967a).

REFERENCES CITED

ARNDT, J.
  1967a Word of Mouth Advertising (New York).
  1967b Role of Product-related Conservations in the Diffusion of a new Product, Journal of Marketing Research, 4, pp. 291–295.
  1968a A Test of the Two-step Flow in Diffusion of a new Product. Journalism Quarterly, 45, pp. 457–465.
  1968b Selective Processes in Word of Mouth. Journal of Advertising Research, 8, (3) (Sept.) pp. 19–22.
BAN, A. W. VAN DEN
  1960 Locality Group Differences in the Adoption of New Farm Practices. Rural Sociology, 25, pp. 308–320.

1963 Boer en landbouwvoorlichting; de communicatie van nieuwe landbouw-methoden (Assen).
1964 A Revision of the Two-step Flow of Communications Hypothesis. Gazette, 10, pp. 237–249.
BARNETT, H. G.
1953 Innovation, the Basis of Cultural Change (New York).
BLAU, P. M.
1962 Patterns of Choice in Interpersonal Relations. American Sociological Review, 27, pp. 41–55.
CAMPBELL, E. Q. and
C. N. ALEXANDER
1965/ Structural Effects and Interpersonal Relationships. American Journal of
66 Sociology, 71, pp. 284–289.
CARTWRIGHT, D.
1961 Achieving Change in People, in: W. G. Bennis, K. D. Benne and R. Chin (editors), The Planning of Change (New York). pp. 698–710.
1965 Influence, Leadership and Control, in: J. G. March (ed.), Handbook of Organization (Chicago).
CHOU, I. K. M. and
E. M. ROGERS
1966 Homophily in Interpersonal Communication Patterns in the Diffusion of Innovations: An Illustration from three Colombian Villages (East Lansing).
COLEMAN, J. S., E. KATZ and
H. MENZEL
1966 Medical Innovation; A Diffusion Study (Indianapolis).
COUGHENOUR, M. C.
1964 The Role of Technological Diffusion among Locality Groups. American Journal of Sociology, 69, pp. 325–339.
FLIEGEL, F. C., P. ROY, L. K. SEN and
J. E. KIVLIN
1967 Innovation in India, the Success and Failure of Agricultural Development Programs in 108 Indian Villages (Hyderabad).
GALJART, B. F.
1968 Itaguai, Old Habits and New Practices in a Brazilian Land Settlement. Agricultural Research Reports, 712, Wageningen.
GERMANI, G.
1960 Secularización y desarollo economico, in: Resistèncias à Mudanca. (Rio de Janeiro).
HERZOG, W. H. et al.
1968 Patterns of Diffusion in Rural Brazil. (East Lansing, Mich.).
HOMANS, G. C.
1950 The Human Group (New York).
1961 Social Behavior: Its Elementary Forms (New York).
HRUSCHKA, E. and
H. RHEINWALD
1965 The Effectiveness of German Pilot Farms. Sociologia Ruralis, 5, pp. 101–111.
HURSH, G. D., N. R. RÖLING and
G. B. KERR
1968 Success and Failure of Agricultural Programs in 71 Villages in Eastern Nigeria (East Lansing, Mich.).
KATZ, E. and
P. F. LAZARSFELD
1955 Personal Influence, The Part Played by People in the Flow of Mass Communications (Glencoe).
KLAPPER, J. T.
1960 The Effects of Mass Communication (Glencoe, Ill.).

LAZARSFELD, P. F., B. BERELSON and
H. GAUDET
1948   The People's Choice. 2nd ed. (New York).
LEVESQUE, A.
1961   Etude sur le Marché de la Vulgarisation (Paris).
LIKERT, R.
1962   New Patterns of Management (New York).
LIONBERGER, H. F. and
C. M. COUGHENOUR
1957   Social Structure and the Diffusion of Farm Information. Missouri Agr. Exp.
       Station Research Bull. 631, Columbia.
LIONBERGER, H. F. and
J. D. FRANCIS
1969   Views Held of Innovator and Influence Referents as Sources of Farm Infor-
       mation in a Missouri Community. Rural Sociology, 34, pp. 197–211.
LOPREATO, J.
1967   Peasants No More (San Francisco).
LUTHE, H. O.
1968   Interpersonale Kommunikation und Beeinflussung (Stuttgart).
MAIR, L.
1965   An Introduction to Social Anthropology (Oxford: Clarendon Press).
MARSH, C. P. and
A. L. COLEMAN
1954   Farmers' Practice Adoption Rates in Relation to the Adoption Rates of
       Leaders. Rural Sociology, 19, pp. 180–183.
RAHIM, S. A.
1965   Communication and Personal Influence in an East Pakistan Village (Comilla:
       Academy for Rural Development).
ROGERS, E. M.
1962   The Diffusion of Innovations (New York).
ROGERS, E. M. and
G. M. BEAL
1958   Reference Group Influence in the Adoption of Agricultural Technology
       (Ames, Iowa).
ROGERS, E. M. and
R. J. BURDGE
1961   Muck Vegetable Growers: Diffusion of Innovations among Specialized Farm-
       ers (Columbus, Ohio).
ROGERS, E. M. and
J. C. VAN ES
1964   Opinion Leadership in Traditional and Modern Colombian Peasant Communi-
       ties (East Lansing, Mich.).
ROGERS, E. M. and
J. D. STANFIELD
1968   Adoption and Diffusion of New Products Emerging Generalizations and Hy-
       pothesis, in F. M. Bass et al. (eds.), Application of the Sciences in Marketing
       Management (New York).
SANDERS, H. C. et al. (eds.)
1966   The Cooperative Extension Service (Englewood Cliffs).
SEN, L. K. and
D. K. BHOWMIK
(in process) Opinion Leadership and the Diffusion of Innovations, in: E. M. Rogers,
       Diffusion of Innovations in Brazil, Nigeria and India, Ch. V (East Lansing,
       Mich.).
SEN, L. K. and
P. ROY
1969   Awareness of Community Development in Village India (Hyderabad).

SINGH, S. N., H. P. ARYA and
S. K. REDDY
  1966 Different Types of Local Leadership in two North Indian Villages, in: Pareek,
        U. (ed.), Studies in Rural Leadership (Delhi). pp. 1–12.
SRIVASTAVA, S. K.
  1965 Directed Social Change and Rural Leadership. In India in Emerging Patterns
        of Rural Leadership in Southern Asia (Hyderabad).
WILKENING, E. A.
  1953 Adoption of Improved Farm Practices as Related to Family Factors. Wisconsin Agr. Exp. Station Research Bull. 183, Madison.
WILKENING, E. A.
  1958 Joint Decision-making in Farm Families as a Function of States and Role.
        American Sociological Review, 23, pp. 187–192.
YADAV, D. P.
  1967 Communication Structure and Innovation Diffusion in two Indian Villages
        (East Lansing, Mich.).
YADAV, D. P. and
E. M. ROGERS
  1966 Interpersonal Communication in Innovation Diffusion (East Lansing, Mich.).

COMMUNICATION AND INNOVATION IN INDIAN VILLAGES

Satadal Dasgupta*

SATADAL DASGUPTA *is research officer in the Socio-Economic and Evaluation Branch* of the Department of Argriculture for the Government of West Bengal, Calcutta, India.

The study of communication and the adoption of improved farm practices has received much attention from rural sociologists during the last 20 years. Most of these studies have been made within the Western cultures, especially in the United States.[1] Few studies carried out in non-Western cultures have been reported. In this study the sources of information about farming practices used by farmers in India are investigated. It was considered useful to investigate and ascertain whether, in a traditional society like India, a similar situation, as found in Western cultures, prevailed. There are differences of culture and level of education between Western countries and India. How do they influence the flow of communication regarding improved practices?

An attempt has been made in this study to find answers to the following questions relating to farm practices: What are the different sources of information which are generally utilized by the farmers? What is the comparative importance of institutional and noninstitutional sources of information? Is there any relationship between socioeconomic status of the farmers and their utilization of different sources of information? To what extent do sources of information vary with the type of practices for which information is sought? For this purpose a series of hypotheses have been set up with the background of knowledge of similar studies in Western cultures. These hypotheses have been systematically tested.

METHOD

The field work was carried out in four villages of Baraset region in 24 Parganas district of West Bengal.[2] Baraset region covers an area of 384 square miles and is near the city of Calcutta. There are only two small towns in this region with a total population of 22,546. The rest of the population of 371,434 is distributed in 594 villages. Farming is the principal occupation of two-thirds of the population and the remaining population depends on transport, business, trade, production, etc. Farming is carried on in a comparatively conservative pattern, each family owning an average of only 3.5 acres of crop land. The area has close connections with the city through the people working in

* The author is indebted to Professor S. P. Bose for his suggestions in preparing this paper and also to Mr. Bibhas Sasmal for his kind assistance in the statistical analysis of data.

Reprinted with permission of *Social Forces* 43 (March, 1965), 330–337.

the city and through radios and newspapers. There are seven Blocks under the National Extension Scheme. Each Block consists of 100 villages and is served by ten village level workers, two agricultural extension officers, one veterinary surgeon, one cooperative inspector, and two social educational organizers, headed by a Block Development Officer.

The four villages were selected from the list of 25 villages, which, in turn, were selected at random from 594 villages of Baraset region. These selected villages were in different parts of Baraset to include diverse areas, economic levels, religious groups, castes, and topography. All 246 farm families of these four villages were interviewed. Each head of the family, who was responsible for decision-making in farming matters, was asked (1) how many years he had been following a practice, (2) how he became aware of the practice, (3) from whom he got the information about the practice, (4) whether he discussed the utility, applicability and advantages of the practice with anyone, (5) and what was his relationship with the person from whom he sought information?[3] He was also asked whether he applied the practice to the entire part of his farm when he first adopted it, or gradually increased it during successive years. Besides these items of information, his religion, caste, occupation, education, size of farm owned, size of farm operated, number of houses, and other items of living were also noted.

TYPE OF SOURCES

The various types of sources may be dichotomized into two groups: (a) institutional and (b) noninstitutional sources. An institutional source may be defined as a group organized for the purpose of communication of information. Such an organization is primarily expected to disseminate knowledge and ideas about the improved agricultural practices to the farmers. Extension agents such as agricultural extension officers, village level workers, food production assistants, and impersonal sources such as newspapers, bulletins, and radios are institutionalzed sources. The noninstitutionalized sources include neighbors, relatives, friends and commercial dealers. These noninstitutionalized sources are not formally organized for the purpose of dissemination of information although they act as important sources of information.

It may be seen in Table 1 that neighbors and relatives (both inside and

TABLE 1 Number and Percent of Replies Given by All Farmers Relating to Different Sources of Information for Nine Improved Farm Practices

Type of Source	Number	Percent
Total	755	100.0
Neighbors and Relatives	542	71.8
Other Farmers (Outside Village)	34	4.5
Commercial Dealers	82	10.9
Extension Agencies	94	12.4
Newspapers	3	0.4

outside the villages) were very important sources of information for all the 246 farmers interviewed. About 72 percent of the total replies specified that neighbors and relatives were sought as sources for information. The next two important sources were extension agencies and commercial dealers. Twelve percent of the total number of replies were for the extension agencies and the corresponding percentage figures for the commercial dealers was 10.9. A comparatively smaller number of respondents sought information from the other farmers outside the village. A very insignificant number specified newspapers as a source for information. This shows that noninstitutionalized sources of information are very important for the Indian farmer. The village as a social system is an effective universe for the dissemination of information. Information is generally disseminated through personal interaction between the neighbors and relatives within the village. This is emphasized by the data showing that more than 70 percent of the replies indicated neighbors and relatives as sources of information, and comparatively fewer replies indicated outside formal and informal sources i.e., extension agencies, commercial dealers and other farmers outside the village, respectively. The reason for a very insignificant number of replies indicating the use of newspapers may be attributed to the extreme illiteracy of Indian farmers and the poor coverage by Indian newspapers of agricultural subjects. Not a single respondent, however, gave bulletins or pamphlets published by the agriculture department of the state as a source of information nor were there any users of the radio as a source of information.

ADOPTER CATEGORIES AND SOURCES OF INFORMATION

To understand the role of institutionalized sources like extension agencies and newspapers etc., and their comparative importance in disseminating information about improved farming practices among farmers, further probing into the problem is necessary. For this purpose the farmers were divided into three broad categories—innovators, early adopters and late adopters.[4] It should be stated that the categories are somewhat arbitrary. Working with American data, Rogers was able to distinguish five distinct categories of adopters—innovators, early adopters, early majority, late majority and laggards (or late adopters).[5] This categorization has now become somewhat standard in the United States, but an effort to identify these categories did not meet with immediate success in the villages under investigation. The two categories of early majority and late majority could not be effectively distinguished.

Taking each village as an effective social unit for dissemination of information it was found that when any new practice was introduced in the village a very small number of farmers came forward first and adopted the practice. After these farmers adopted the improved practice, they influenced and disseminated information to another group of farmers. This second group of farmers became interested in the improved practice after the first group adopted it, and sought information from the latter. They discussed with the first group of farmers the utility, applicability and advantages of the new practice and ultimately adopted it. The first group of farmers has been designated as innovators and the second group as early adopters. The number of farmers in the second group, however, was larger than the innovators although much smaller than the farmers who were yet to adopt the practice. After these first two groups of farmers adopted the new practice, the rest of the farmers gradually became interested, sought information from the farmers of both earlier groups, and when they were convinced of the utility of the new practice, they adopted it. These farmers were called late adopters. This was precisely the process in which the farmers of the villages under investigation were found to adopt an improved farming practice. Since this adopter categorization is entirely arbitrary and one can classify the adopters into a large number of categories according to the time of adoption, it was thought useful to restrict the classification into three broad categories to avoid complexities.

Lionberger found that there was a higher correlation between the use of personal sources and adoption than between the use of impersonal sources and adoption.[6] From this he concluded that personal sources were more effective than the impersonal sources.

Rogers and Beal found that personal sources of information were more important for the late adopters, while the impersonal sources were greatly utilized by innovators and early adopters.[7]

By modifying Lazarsfeld's "two step flow of communication"[8] theory (because this was developed on the basis of the study of voting behavior) Rogers and Beal maintained that "Technological farming ideas often flow from the impersonal sources to the innovators and early adopters and from them to late majority and laggards." With this background the first hypothesis of the present study was constructed and tested in the Indian situation.

Hypothesis 1. Innovators and early adopters are influenced more by certain sources of information than are the late adopters

As indicated in Table 2, neighbors and relatives were most frequently reported as sources of information by the late adopters. Comparatively fewer of the innovators and a larger percentage of the early adopters reported them as sources of information. The difference between the late adopters and early adopters, and between early adopters and innovators in the utilization of neighbors and relatives as sources of information were found to be significant after the application of a proportion test. A greater proportion of the replies of the late adopters attached greater significance to neighbors and relatives as sources of information than the early adopters and the innovators. A greater proportion of replies of the early adopters, however, attached greater significance to these sources than the innovators.

Extension agencies were an important source of information to the innovators and early adopters, while a very few late adopters utilized them for the purpose. About half of the total number of replies of the innovators and about one-third of the total replies of the early adopters specified extension agencies as a source of information. But less than five percent of the late adopters utilized the extension agencies as a source of information. The difference between the innovators and early adopters, and between the early adopters and late adopters in utilizing the extension agencies as a source of information were

TABLE 2   Percentage Distribution of Replies Given by Innovators, Early Adopters and Late Adopters Relating to Different Sources of Information for Nine Improved Farm Practices

Type of Source	Adopter Categories			Significance of Difference		
	(1) Innova-tor	(2) Early Adopter	(3) Late Adopter	(1-2)	(1-3)	(2-3)
Total Number	57	128	570			
Total Percent	100.0	100.0	100.0			
Neighbors and Relatives	14.0	35.2	85.8	2	3	3
Other Farmers (outside the village)	15.8	10.9	1.9	x	1	2
Commercial Dealers	15.8	21.9	7.9	x	1	2
Extension Agencies	49.1	32.0	4.4	1	1	2
Newspapers	5.3					

Note: Significance of difference has been determined by the "test for the difference between proportions" [see Croxton & Cowden, *Applied General Statistics* (London, 1956,) pp. 679–680]. The "x" indicates no significant difference while a number indicates a significant difference and identifies the adopter category of the comparison in which the greater proportion of the replies attaches a greater importance to the corresponding source.

found to be significant. Here, as can be seen in Table 2, a greater proportion of the replies of the innovators favored the extension agency as a source of information than early and late adopters. A greater proportion of the replies of early adopters were for this source than the late adopters.

Comparatively few replies of the late adopters favored commercial dealers as a source of information. Commercial dealers were, however, reported more by the early adopters as a source of information than the late adopters. While the difference between innovators and early adopters in the utilization of commercial dealers as a source of information was found to be insignificant, the differences between the innovators and later adopters, and early adopters and late adopters were found to be significant.

While about 16 percent of the replies of the innovators indicated "other farmers outside the village" as a source of information, the least number of replies of the late adopters specified "other farmers" as a source of information. In the utilization of "other farmers" as a source of information the innovators and early adopters did not differ between themselves significantly, but the differences, both between the innovators and late adopters, and early adopters and late adopters, were found to be significant.

None of the early adopters and late adopters reported newspapers as a source of information for any of the farming practices they adopted. Only five percent of the innovators used newspapers as a source of information.

To see further to what extent the different adopter categories varied in the utilization of institutional and noninstitutional sources the various sources of information were lumped into two groups as such. Such sources as extension agencies and newspapers were grouped into institutionalized sources, and neighbors and relatives, commercial dealers, and "other farmers" were grouped into noninstitutionalized sources. It was found (Table 3) that the innovators re-

TABLE 3 Distribution of Replies Given by Innovators, Early Adopters
and Late Adopters, Relating to Institutionalized and Noninstitutionalized sources for Nine Improved Farm Practices

Source	In-novator	Early Adopter	Late Adopter	Total
Noninstitutionalized sources	26	87	545	658
Institutionalized sources	31	41	25	97
Total	57	128	570	755

$\chi^2 = 166.35$, d.f.$=2$, P$<.001$

ceived information from the institutionalized sources more than the other two adopter categories. The late adopters, on the other hand, got more information from the noninstitutionalized sources than the other two adopter categories. The position of early adopters was, however, intermediate. The association was found to be significant by the application of chi-square test ($\chi^2 = 166.35$, df $= 2$, $p < .001$).

The above findings can be summarized as follows:

1. Institutionalized sources of information such as extension agencies were utilized more by the innovators and early adopters than by the late adopters.
2. Noninstitutionalized sources of information, such as neighbors, relatives etc., were more frequently reported as sources of information by late adopters than by the early adopters and innovators.
3. Innovators and early adopters obtained information more frequently from the farmers of the other villages than did the late adopters.
4. Commercial dealers were reported as a source of information more by the early adopters and the innovators than by the late adopters.
5. Newspapers were reported a source of information by only a few of the innovators. Neither of the other two adopter categories reported them as a source of information.

Thus, these findings support Hypothesis 1. They are consistent with the findings of Rogers and Beal[9] who also found that impersonal sources (which were obviously institutionalized) were used more by early adopters and innovators, and late adopters utilized personalized sources (which were mainly noninstitutional or informal personal sources). In the light of this, Lazarsfeld's "two step flow of communication" theory, which has been modified by Rogers and Beal, can also be applied here—that the improved farming ideas flow from institutionalized sources to the innovators and early adopters and from them on to late adopters.

VARIATION OF SOURCES BY SOCIOECONOMIC STATUS

The next objective of the study is to show if the type of sources varies with the socioeconomic status of the farmer. Wilkening found that farmers of higher socioeconomic status utilized formally organized sources of information while those of lower socioeconomic status utilized personalized sources of information.[10]

In India the farmers of higher socioeconomic status are comparatively educated, generally come from high castes, own comparatively larger farms, have high social participation, and because of these characteristics, they are more rational in their approach to farming. Due to their greater contact with the outside world they develop a more scientific attitude to farming and become more business-minded. Bose has shown that the farmers who are rational, scientific, and business-minded adopt more improved practices.[11] Similarly it was thought useful to see whether the farmers with high socioeconomic status and having rational motivation towards farming utilized institutionalized sources more than the farmers of lower socioeconomic status. With this end in view the second Hypothesis was constructed and tested.

Hypothesis 2. Farmers of higher socioeconomic status utilize institutionalized sources and those of lower socioeconomic status utilize noninstitutionalized sources

The farmers here have been classified into three socioeconomic status groups using a composite index of socioeconomic status. This index included the following factors: caste, education, tenure of land, size of farm owned, acres of land operated; condition of house, and level of living.[12] It was found (Table 4) that extension agencies were reported more frequently as a source of information by the farmers of highest socioeconomic status than by the farmers of status groups II and III. The importance of extension agencies as sources of information decreased in order from status group I to status group III. Very few of the farmers of the lowest status group reported them as a source of information, with group II in between. A greater proportion of the innovators used "extension agencies" as a source of information than the early and late adopters. The proportion of early adopters using extension agencies as a source of information was greater than the late adopters. Neighbors and relatives were most frequently reported as the source of information by the farmers of the lowest socioeconomic status group. While the neighbors and relatives were important sources of information for all the status groups, their relative importance decreased sharply as status increased. In ultilizing neighbors and relatives as sources of information the farmers of status groups I and II, I and III and the farmers of status groups II and III differed significantly. A greater proportion of the farmers of status group III used "neighbors and relatives" as a source of information than the farmers of status groups I and II. However,

TABLE 4   Percentage Distribution of Replies Given by All Farmers Classified by Three Socioeconomic Status Groups Relating to Different Sources of Information for Nine Improved Farm Practices

Type of Source	Socioeconomic Status Groups			Significance of Difference		
	(I)	(II)	(III)	(I-II)	(I-III)	(II-III)
Total Number	130	380	245			
Total Percent	100.0	100.0	100.0			
Neighbors and Relatives	53.8	71.0	82.4	II	III	III
Other Farmers (outside village)	6.2	5.0	2.9	x	x	x
Commerical Dealers	6.9	12.1	11.0	x	x	x
Extension Agencies	30.8	11.9	3.7	I	I	II
Newspapers	2.3					

Note: Significance of difference has been determined by the test for the difference between proportions [see Croxton & Cowden, *Applied General Statistics* (London, 1956,) pp. 679–680]. The "x" indicates no significant difference while a number indicates a significant difference and identifies the socioeconomic status groups of the comparison in which the greater proportion of the replies attaches a greater importance to the corresponding source.

the proportion of the farmers of status group II using "neighbors and relatives" as a source of information was greater than the farmers of status group I. In the utilizing of commercial dealers as a source of information the farmers of different status groups did not differ significantly. In the utilization of "other farmers" also the status groups did not differ very significantly although a comparatively larger number of farmers of the highest socioeconomic status group looked more to the "other farmers" outside the village as a source of information than did the other two groups, due to their greater outside contact. Only the farmers of high socioeconomic status made any use of newspapers as a source of information.

The data were further analyzed to see to what extent the farmers of different socioeconomic status groups differed in the utilization of information sources when these are lumped into two groups—institutionalized and noninstitutionalized sources. It was found that the farmers of status group I got information from the institutionalized sources more than the farmers of other two status groups. The farmers of status group III depended more upon the noninstitutionalized sources for information than the farmers of the other two status groups. The position of the farmers of status group II was intermediate. This association was found to be significant after the application of chi-square test ($\chi^2 = 66.27$, d.f. $= 2$, P $< .001$).

Thus, Hypothesis 2 is supported by findings that the farmers of higher socioeconomic status depend more on institutionalized agencies while the farmers of lower status utilize noninstitutionalized sources—friends, neighbors and relatives—although there is almost equal use of "other farmers" and commercial dealers by all status groups.

TABLE 5   Distribution of Replies Given by All Farmers Classified
by Three Socioeconomic Status Groups Relating to
Institutionalized and Noninstitutionalized Sources for
Nine Improved Farm Practices

	Socioeconomic Status Groups			
Source	I	II	III	Total
Noninstitutionalized sources	87	335	236	658
Institutionalized sources	43	45	9	97
Total	130	380	245	755

$\chi^2 = 66.27$, d.f. $= 2$, P $< .001$

VARIATION OF SOURCES BY TYPE OF PRACTICE

Wilkening hypothesized that noninstitutionalized sources like neighbors, relatives and commercial dealers would be utilized as sources for the practices which were associated with older farm enterprises.[13] It is our purpose here to see to what extent this hypothesis is correct in the Indian situation. For these purposes the third hypothesis was constructed and tested:

Hypothesis 3.   Information for the new farm practices which are associated
with older farm enterprise are sought from noninstitutionalized sources
and information for improved farm practices which are entirely new
to the farmers' experience are sought from institutionalized sources

The use of ammonium sulphate for fertilizer and the use of pumping plants for irrigation have been practiced by the farmers for some time in this region. These practices are not foreign to the farmers because ammonium sulphate or fertilizer mixture is congruent with the older practice of fertilizing fields with farm yard manure. Pumping plants simply replaced an indigenous process of irrigation by primitive tools. However, such practices as the Japanese method of rice cultivation (which is an improved method of rice cultivation), drilling of jute, and improved rice seed are foreign to the farmers. The Japanese method of rice cultivation threatens to replace the entire old method of rice cultivation and contains complexities; drilling of jute is also comparatively new, involving mastery of operation; and so far as rice seed is concerned the farmers feel insecure in replacing their indigenous seeds.

Our expectation is that for the former practices mentioned above, which are associated with older farm enterprises, noninstitutionalized sources will be utilized and for the latter practices, which are entirely new, institutionalized sources will be utilized for information.

In Table 6 it may be seen that our findings support the hypothesis. However, the number reporting information on newer practices is too small to permit great confidence in the results. Nevertheless, the data indicate a positive relationship between newer practices and institutionalized sources of informa-

TABLE 6 Percentage Distribution of Replies Given by All Farmers Relating to Different Sources of Information for Six Improved Farm Practices

Type of source	Ammonium Sulphate	Fertilizer Mixture	Irrigation Pump	Improved Rice Seed	Japanese Method of Rice Cultivation	Drilling of Jute
Total Number	191	86	87	21	5	3
Total Percent	100.0	100.0	100.0	100.0	100.0	100.0
Neighbors and Relatives	68.6	57.6	75.8	47.6	40.0	33.3
Other Farmers (outside village)	4.7	—	11.5	4.7	—	—
Commercial Dealers	15.7	28.1	3.5	—	—	—
Extension Agencies	10.0	14.3	9.2	47.7	60.0	66.7
Newspapers	1.0	—	—	—	—	—

tion. Neighbors and relatives were utilized by the farmers as sources of information for ammonium sulphate, and irrigation pumps. But for the Japanese method of rice cultivation and drilling of jute, extension agencies were greatly utilized for information. In the case of improved rice seed the maximum number of replies (47.7%) specified extension agencies as the source of information although when the noninstitutionalized sources like neighbors, relatives and other farmers are considered together the figure exceeds that of the extension agencies.

SUMMARY AND DISCUSSION

The main theme of this investigation was to test the findings in Western culture in similar fields in India. Literacy among Indian farmers is extremely low, their attitude to farming is comparatively traditional and there is a considerable paucity of means of communication, especially mass media. Naturally, one can expect some differences in information seeking habits and patterns of adoption of improved farming practices in India. But the findings of the investigation tend to show some similarities with the finds in Western countries. Indian innovators and early adopters seek information from the institutionalized sources like their American counterparts (as found by Rogers and Beal) and disseminate knowledge to the late adopters through informal personal interaction. The innovators and early adopters in India also come from higher socioeconomic strata, which is consistent with Wilkening's findings in the United States that the farmers seek information from institutionalized sources for improved practices is also supported by Indian data.

NOTES

[1] See Herbert F. Lionberger, Adoption of New Ideas and Practices (Ames, Iowa, 1960) and E. M. Rogers, Diffusion of Innovations (New York, 1962).

[2] All these villages were exposed to extension for some time. Before independence there was one agricultural graduate with two or three demonstrators for every 2,000

square miles. After independence in 1947, the area of the agricultural graduate was decreased to 700 square miles and he had about six assistants to help him. Each of these assistants worked with ten to 15 villages. They set up demonstrations and arranged supplies of improved seeds, fertilizers, plant protection chemicals, etc. This pattern is, however, being replaced by development blocks under the National Extension Service Scheme.

[3] The following practices recommended by the Agricultural Extension Service were included as improved practices: ammonium sulphate, fertilizer mixtures, plant protection chemicals, improved jute seed, improved rice seed, Japanese method of rice cultivation, drilling of jute, use of pumping plant for irrigation and artificial insemination of cattle.

[4] For characteristics of farmers of different adopter categories in India, see S. Dasgupta, The Innovators (Research Bulletin I, Socio-agroeconomic Research Organisation, Department of Agriculture, Government of West Bengal) and "Innovators and Innovation in Indian Villages," Man in India, 43: I (March 1963).

[5] Everett M. Rogers, "Categorizing the Adopters of Agricultural Practices," Rural Sociology, 23 (December 1958).

[6] Herbert F. Lionberger, Sources and Use of Farm Information by Low Income Farmers in Missouri, Missouri Agricultural Experimental Station Bull. 472 (May 1951).

[7] Everett M. Rogers and George M. Beal, "The Importance of Personal Influence in Technological Change," Social Forces, 36 (May 1958), p. 329.

[8] Paul F. Lazarsfeld and others, The People's Choice (New York, 1948).

[9] Rogers and Beal, op. cit.

[10] Eugene A. Wilkening, "Sources of Information for Important Practices," Rural Sociology, 15 (March 1950).

[11] S. P. Bose, "Peasant Values and Innovation in India," American Journal of Sociology, 67 (March 1962).

[12] In measuring the socioeconomic status of the farmer, W. B. Rahudker's A Scale for Measuring Socio-economic Status of India Farm Families, Nagpur Agricultural College Magazine, 34:1–2 (1960), was used after a slight modification.

[13] E. A. Wilkening, 1960, op. cit.

PROPAGANDA

The dissemination of a systematically planned and widely addressed presentation of a particular set of values or policies, which has come to be called propaganda, dominates nearly all the sections of this volume of studies. Its use can be seen in the development of opinion, in efforts at social change and control, as utilized both by the routinized and the charismatic leader, as an important aspect of conflict and its resolution or expansion, and as it effects the tightening or liberalizing of communication rights within nations and among nations. For example, Arthur Larson (1966:439) argues that one of the best illustrations of propaganda's potential impact, not only for its enormous consequences for a great war but for a whole era of conflict, is the period leading up to World War I. From 1900 to the outbreak of war, an intensive campaign of irredentist propaganda was conducted by Serbia in Bosnia and Herzegovina. As early as 1909, Serbia agreed to renounce its opposition to the annexation of Bosnia and Herzegovina and promised to live on good-neighbor terms with Austria-Hungary. The Serbs carried on agitation both by clandestine means and by open efforts in their mass media, which led to the exclusion of more than eighty-one Serbian publications from Austria-Hungary on the grounds that they flagrantly violated the domestic criminal code. The 1914 Austrian ultimatum demanded that the Serbian government officially control all propaganda directed against the monarchy and make an agreement to suppress all criminal and terroristic propaganda. Larson reasons that "as scholars look back upon the explosive situation in the summer of 1914, they are inclined to conclude that, as a result of nationalistic propaganda, a peaceful disposition of the controversies had already become virtually impossible" (Larson 1966).

Clark C. Havighurst (1966:437) argues that if control of propaganda between nations poses a serious practical problem, the idea of regulating communications between a government and its domestic population seems utterly unworkable and outside the usual province of international law as well. Unfortunately, that type of propaganda, most likely to exacerbate tensions and result in war, is least amenable to international control. Arguing against general international control or censorship of propaganda, Havighurst offers an interesting alternative:

> Perhaps it is paradoxical that one remedy for government monopoly or domination of news and opinion is international propaganda, sometimes even of a sort that might be fairly characterized, from the target government's point of view at least, as warmongering, subversive, or defamatory. One may therefore easily prefer not to close off channels of communication that may serve to keep domestic sources of information in the target state relatively honest. By extension of this thinking, an issue may even be raised . . . about the constitutionality of a hypothetical United States effort to "jam" a foreign political broadcast. And a broad conclusion seems

411

at least possible that would keep all communication channels open, would avoid inhibiting free expression by attempting to distinguish—except perhaps in the most extreme and obvious case—between truth and falsehood or between harmful and beneficial propaganda, and would tolerate serious and admittedly dangerous types of propaganda as a necessary concomitant of an international "marketplace of ideas" [Havighurst, 1966:438].

With the development of the radio particularly, which is still the most easily available method of mass communication in developing countries, and currently with the development of communications satellites, international as well as domestic propaganda penetrates nearly every cultural and national boundary. It is estimated, on the level of information exchange, that more people in the world knew almost instantly about the assassination of President John F. Kennedy and the first American moon-walk than almost any previous events in history, except for the 1941 American declaration of war and the 1945 dropping of the first atomic bombs on Hiroshima and Nagasaki. All of these events became the subjects of immediate efforts at national and international propaganda of various sorts. Even the simple statement made during the first moon-walk, "We came in peace for all mankind" became the subject of intense propagandistic efforts on the part of the American government to convince the world of its peace lovingness and on the part of the People's Republic of China to convince its people that the moon-walk was an example of American duplicity and warmongering.

Arthur Larson cites three kinds of international propaganda as illegal according to generally recognized international law: warmongering, subversive, and defamatory propaganda (Larson 1966:439–451). Warmongering is expressly forbidden both by the United Nations Charter and the Nuremberg trials, which established aggressive war as an international crime. The universally accepted principle is that incitement by words to commit aggressive war is itself illegal. Although the illegality of warmongering propaganda is of relatively recent origin, since until recently aggressive war itself was not illegal, subversive attempts by an outside power to overthrow the government of a friendly power have been considered illegal during most of the period when international law has been enforced. The 1949 Essentials of Peace resolution in the United Nations General Assembly called on all nations "to refrain from any threats or acts, direct or indirect, aimed at impairing the freedom, independence, or integrity of any state, or at fomenting civil strife and subverting the will of the people in any state." Treaties forbidding defamatory propaganda are numerous, such as the 1948 Bogota treaty for the Latin American States or the 1954 resolution of the General Assembly revising the 1936 "Convention Concerning the Use of Broadcasting and the Cause of Peace." Despite the international agreements and protocol regarding defamatory propaganda, particularly that aimed at the high officials of states, they are honored mostly in the breach. For example, in Premier Castro's 1960 address at the United Nations, the president of the General Assembly felt it necessary to call upon him to refrain from abusing verbally American Presidential candidates John F. Kennedy, whom he called "an illiterate and ignorant millionaire" and Richard M. Nixon "who lacks in political sense."

Assuring the President that he had no intention to offend anyone, Prime Minister Castro was again admonished by the President for his attacks on American President Eisenhower: "The Chair does not think it is in keeping with the dignity of the Assembly, or the decorum that we like to preserve in our debates, that references of a personal nature should be made to the Heads of States or the Heads of Governments of States Member of the United Nations, whether present here or not" (Castro 1970:325–372).

In the first essay in this section, "International Propaganda and Minimum World Public Order," William V. O'Brien, chairman of the Institute of World Policy at Georgetown University, contends that meaningful legal regulation of international propaganda is so difficult at best and so inconceivable in the presently divided world, that international law is not well served by encouraging the belief that substantial progress in this problem area is imminent. Still, he believes that certain normative imperatives and practical necessities exist for directing statesmen to their responsibilities and opportunities to contribute to patterns of behavior leading to greater international control of propaganda. He appraises current international law and summarizes the basic obstacles to the more successful enforcement of the existing law and the problems in developing additional law. O'Brien thinks that there is no consensus about what world public order consists of. He concludes that the path to progress is slow and lies in understanding the realities of a divided world and the need not only for international but also enlightened unilateral contributions to a minimum world public order in so far as international propaganda and the broader ideological instrument are concerned.

Yuri Bobrakov, in his essay "War Propaganda: A Serious Crime Against Humanity," takes the position that if we intend to work out ways of dismantling the most dangerous weapons of physical destructtion, we should struggle also to work out ways of dismantling the psychological warfare of war propaganda. Bobrakov recognizes that, until recently, war had commonly been an instrument of national and international policy. In 1957 the Soviet government labeled war-propaganda ideological aggression. This was the culmination of a whole set of Soviet acts against aggressive war and aggressive propaganda. Bobrakov urges other states to adopt national policies to outlaw the propaganda of war as important contributions to the cause of peace and lessening of world tensions.

Larson (1966:449) speaks not only of state propaganda but also of the problems of private propaganda, in which no clear guidelines for state responsibility under international law are normally imposed on the individual members of the state. Identifiable exceptions largely center on individual propaganda directed in a warmongering, subversive, or defamatory way against foreign states or high officials of those states. A general view also prevails, despite some noted disagreement, that it is illegal to allow the territory of one state to be used to emit radio signals with these kinds of propaganda which are aimed at another state. Soviet jurists have long argued that signals emitted from Voice of America and Radio Free Europe violate the international protocol concerning propaganda.

The final two essays in this section treat private propaganda. The first, by M. Broman, assesses the role of the big character wall poster as an instrument of conflict and mass communication during the recent Chinese cultural revolution. As a traditional feature in Chinese life, the tatzepao took on new significance as the Red Guards, with Mao's encouragement, began making extensive personal attacks against the anti-Maoists for being lackeys of Western imperialism. These attacks were met with more posters by anti-Maoists. One Maoist source credited the posters with having "blasted the lid off the struggle between the proletarian revolutionary line and the bourgeoisie headquarters (i.e. the anti-Maoists) which had existed in the party for a long time." Broman establishes a model to demonstrate the workings of the Red Guard communications network designed to "reflect the thought of Mao Tse-tung." The network originated with messages from the Maoist leadership, which were transmitted to the Red Guard leaders either orally or through secret messages. The leadership then transmitted the messages to their Red Guard followers through newspapers, who in turn produced tatzepao for the masses. In response to the tatzepao, the people made their own wall posters, thus creating an effective form of feedback to the Maoist leadership. Although an interim force, the tatzepao were produced in the tens of millions and thus had a profound propagandistic influence before the cultural revolution dissolved into an anarchist rabble, which Mao finally had to end by calling in the army to restore order.

In the last essay, "Protest Movements: Class Consciousness and the Propaganda Song," R. Serge Denisoff discusses the private propaganda of the protest song. Although he does not discuss protest songs aimed at the Vietnam War, "Hell, no, we won't go," "Hey, hey, LBJ. How many kids have you killed today?" "All we are saying is give peace a chance," and "Knee deep in the Big Muddy, and the old fool says, 'Push on,' " all have had profound propagandistic impact not only on successive American governments, but also for pro- and anti-American groups abroad. Naturally, propaganda songs are not limited to war protests or to Americans; and they can treat subjects favorably or negatively. Songs about the drug culture, ecology, and civil rights have played an important part in spreading widely a specific point of view. Denisoff defines the propaganda song as being either magnetic—that is, seeking to attract followers to a movement—such as songs of Marxist or Western ideologies—or as being rhetorical—that is, pointing out social conditions without trying to offer ideological solutions. Although Denisoff believes that the period 1957–1964 was the last genuine phase of protest songs which are folk oriented, a reading of current musical and political history indicates that the protest songs clearly have not disappeared as an important aspect of domestic and international propaganda.

REFERENCES CITED

CASTRO, FIDEL
   1970   The Problem of Cuba. In Sow the wind, reap the whirlwind: heads of state address the United Nations. Michael H. Prosser, ed. New York.

Havighurst, Clark C.
1966 Foreword to issue on propaganda. Law and contemporary problems. 31:437–438.
Larson, Arthur
1966 The present status of propaganda in international law. Law and contemporary problems. 31:439–451.

INTERNATIONAL PROPAGANDA AND MINIMUM WORLD PUBLIC ORDER

William V. O'Brien

WILLIAM V. O'BRIEN *was born in 1923 in Washington, D.C. He received his B.S. and M.S. in foreign service from Georgetown University and his Ph.D. from there in government. He was a Fulbright fellow on the Faculty of Law at the Sorbonne in Paris. In 1963 he was a visiting research professor at the Max Planck-Institut in Heidelberg. He is former president of the Catholic Association for International Peace, was an International Expert for the Third World Conference of the Lay Apostolate at Rome in 1967, and was a member of the White House Committee on Arms Control during 1966. Presently, he is chairman of the Institute of World Polity at Georgetown University and professor of government there. He is associate editor of World Justice published at Louvain University and is associate editor of World Affairs published in Washington. With Ulrich S. Allers, he has coauthored Christian Ethics and Nuclear Warfare (1961), with Walter H. E. Jaeger, International Law; Cases, Text-Notes, and Other Materials (1959), and with J. R. Leguey Feilleux, International Law (1967). He has authored World Polity IV: Intervention in International Law and Relations (1967) and War and/or Survival (1969). He has edited The Law of Limited International Conflict (1965), World Polity: A Yearbook of Studies in International Law and Organization (1957 and 1960), World Polity III: The New Nations in International Law and Diplomacy (1965). Professor O'Brien has contributed to The Georgetown Law Journal, The Military Law Review, Worldview, The Yale Law Journal, America, Commonweal, and Social Order.*

The author's original mandate was to prepare "A Case for Unlimited Propaganda," to oppose "A Case for Controlled Propaganda" in a "debate" with Professor von Glahn. However, the author found it impossible to reconcile a case for unlimited propaganda with existing international law and responsible foreign policies. This paper will not support unlimited propaganda because it is impossible to reconcile such a concept with existing international legal obligations binding on all states. Nor will it attempt to make a case for maximum freedom of international propaganda based on some theory of the desirability of a competition of ideas from which greater truth and understanding might result. Likewise eschewed in this paper is any notion of "just" propaganda which, in virtue of some higher rights, should prevail over the ordinary positive international law. Rather it will be the author's contention that meaningful legal regulation of international propaganda is so difficult at best and so inconceivable in the present divided world, that international law is not well served by encouraging the belief among its supporters that substantial progress in this problem area is imminent. On the other hand, it will

Reprinted with permission from a symposium, "International Control of Propaganda," appearing in *Law and Contemporary Problems*, 31, no. 3 (Summer 1966) published by the Duke University School of Law, Durham, North Carolina. Copyright 1966 by Duke University.

be argued that there are normative imperatives and practical necessities for directing the attention of statesmen to their responsibilities and opportunities to contribute to patterns of behavior leading to greater international legal control of propaganda.

This position will be substantiated, first, by an appraisal of existing international law relevant to international propaganda and, second, by a brief summary of the basic obstacles to more successful enforcement of the existing law and to the development of additional law. In the discussion which follows stress will be placed upon the view that "the international law of propaganda" is most profitably treated not as a separate chapter of law but in the context of broader factual and legal categories.

First, as a phenomenon of international politics, propaganda will be treated as a part of McDougal's "ideological instrument" which together with the diplomatic, economic, and military instruments, constitute the principal means utilized in international politics.[1] The ideological instrument has been defined as follows:

> The use of the ideological instrument commonly involves the selective manipulation and circulation of symbols, verbal or nonverbal, calculated to alter the patterns of identifications, demands, and expectations of mass audiences in the target-state and thereby to induce or stimulate politically significant attitudes and behavior favorable to the initiator-state. It includes, in combination with other instruments, all the techniques of propaganda, infiltration, subversion, and *coup d'état* which have been refined and developed to such high efficiency as to have given rise to repeated proposals to condemn their use for certain objectives as a distinct form or mode of aggression.[2]

It is believed that both the differentiation of instruments within the over-all arsenal of instruments of foreign policy and the identification of the use of propaganda as an integral element within the broader concept of the ideological instrument properly indicate the importance and complexity of efforts to bring propaganda under international legal regulation.

Second, as a subject treated by international law, propaganda falls within the following categories:

1. the law regulating the threat or use of force;
2. the law governing dictatorial intervention (to the extent that such intervention does not fall within the first category);
3. the law of international responsibility for acts injurious to sovereign states originating with another state's jurisdiction; and
4. the corpus of positive legal obligations to promote world law, order, and justice.

It is believed that existing functional international law relating to various means of spreading propaganda—international communications law, for example—is most usefully treated within the foregoing categories. It is artificial and comparatively irrelevant to isolate the subject matter in primarily functional legal categories.

I

Existing legal limitations on international propaganda

There is no dearth of legal limitations on international propaganda. The hard questions concern their meaning and their effectiveness. First, use of propaganda as part of the ideological instrument is limited by the prohibition against the threat or use of force embodied in article II (4) of the U.N. Charter and supported by an overwhelming consensus expressed in legal documents since the time of the League Covenant. Determination that use of warmongering propaganda[3] violates the prescription prohibiting the threat or use of force against the territorial integrity and political independence of a state will presumably be made in the broader context of a finding that some of the other instruments—diplomatic, economic, military—are also being used in a coordinated pattern of aggression. This brings us to one of the central and seemingly insoluble problems of international law. Two things, however, are clear:

> *First*, the illegality of aggressive recourse to force in violation of article II (4) is established beyond dispute. So great is the consensus on this point that it remains the foundation for the existing minimum world public order despite all violations of that order.
>
> *Second*, the definition of aggression has thus far not been the product of the application of formulae systematically arrived at in advance by authoritative decision-makers. Rather, aggression has been defined case by case, primarily through the process of claims and counterclaims predominantly by national entities interacting either bilaterally or through the processes of international organizations. Efforts at more systematic and generally acceptable definitions of aggression have, notoriously, been thwarted by, among other things, ideological and political differences and the reluctance of states to agree in advance to definitions of aggression which might restrict them inordinately to the detriment of their vital interests.[4]

In these circumstances, it would seem that students of international law and relations should now turn to detailed studies of some of these cases wherein there was a substantial consensus that aggression occurred and that use of the ideological instrument constituted an important component of the aggressive behavior—for example, the struggles in the Middle East and Malaysia, and Castro's machinations in Latin America. It would seem that "practice" in the sense of international agreements, resolutions, *voeux*, unilateral declarations, and the like, as it relates to the problem of international propaganda has been substantially collected and analyzed by Professors Whitton and Larson.[5] What they have done in essence is to collect all of the more formal evidences of states' practice on this subject much in the way that Brownlie has surveyed this kind of practice with respect to the broader law regulating resort to force.[6] What appears to be needed now is a closer and deeper look at that more subtle "practice," the patterns of actual behavior emerging from the international political process.

Next we must turn to the problem of indirect aggression, a necessarily vague category which straddles the line between the law regulating recourse to armed coercion and the law relating to essentially nonmilitary dictatorial intervention. The ideological instrument usually assumes commanding importance in indirect aggression. Indirect aggression is so termed because of ambiguity as to the relationship of the alleged indirect aggressor to attacks by primarily nonmilitary or subconventional military means against the territorial integrity and political independence of another state and because of uncertainty as to whether the means employed, even if they are traceable to the alleged indirect aggressor, constitute "the threat or use of force." Despite obvious problems of definition and interpretation, it is clear that international law presently recognizes and prohibits indirect aggression. It is equally clear that subversive propaganda falls within this prohibition. Subversive propaganda may therefore constitute an important element in the crime of indirect aggression and contribute to a state of affairs warranting enforcement action by the United Nations or, more likely, measures of individual and collective self-defense. Following the logic of the concept of self-defense, a victim of indirect aggression would have the right if it so desired to engage in otherwise prohibited propaganda against the indirect aggressor.[7]

As in the determination that aggression has occurred, judgments about the propriety of self-defense measures against alleged indirect aggression are usually made on a case-by-case basis through the decentralized process of claims and counterclaims by interested international persons. If more universal sources such as resolutions in the U.N. or at regional conferences are persuasive authority that there is a crime of indirect aggression, they are generally not too helpful in determining the content in specific instances of the prohibited act. It again appears to be necessary to study the evolving law on this subject through the collection and analysis of cases about which interested parties and third parties have expressed an opinion. From such studies guidelines for the evaluation of allegedly subversive propaganda and of countermeasures of self-defense may emerge. Our experience with efforts to define "aggression," "indirect aggression," and "intervention" suggests that this approach may be more useful than that of attempting scientific codification of prescriptions regulating indirect aggression generally and the international propaganda components thereof.

Moving down the spectrum of international coercive measures as viewed from a legal perspective, we come next to impermissible dictatorial intervention not amounting to "the threat or use of force." The general principle of international law prohibiting dictatorial intervention, reinforced by general and particular conventional international law, as well as customary international law, prohibits dictatorial interference in the internal or external affairs of a state even when such interference does not amount to the use or threat of force. A great part, perhaps the bulk, of international propaganda of a patently unfriendly character falls into this category.

Legal regulation of propaganda of this kind presents a problem which thus far has baffled international lawyers and statesmen. To an even greater extent than in the case of the law regulating recourse to force, the universal agreement that dictatorial intervention is illegal is vitiated by the problems of defining this delict and of providing remedies for victims of illegal intervention.[8] What little relief is available to victims of illegal intervention seems generally to be of a political rather than a legal character. The conviction that this is true leaves the author very skeptical about the practical importance of the various ingenious suggestions of Professors Whitton and Larson and others concerning the identification and legal condemnation of technically illegal international propaganda.[9]

Closely related to the foregoing is the general international law of international responsibility. It is clear that all states have an obligation to prevent the commission of acts within their jurisdictions which endanger the territorial integrity and political independence of sovereign states with which they are at peace. The rule goes far in its requirements for responsibility for private as well as public acts originating in its jurisdiction. A particularly well-established corollary of this rule requires suppression of, and responsibility for, revolutionary expeditions and so-called terrorist plots and activities aimed at another state. Given the well-known importance of propaganda in modern international relations, it is as illegal for a state to condone or encourage warmongering, subversive, and, in some cases, defamatory propaganda against another state as to contribute bases and materiel to an aggressive invader. Having said this, however, we must face the same problems of enforcement already mentioned. Responsibility for delictual propaganda is clear; practical remedies must depend upon the more or less fortuitous functioning of international organization and the possibilities for permissible measures of self-help.

Moreover, the rifts and conflicts of our era have notoriously eroded the traditional concepts of "peace" and "friendly" relations. The facts of the several existing cold wars collide head-on with the underlying assumptions and goals of the traditional law of international responsibility. For this reason and in view of the difficulties of obtaining enforcement of the law regulating international conflict and intervention, this paper will not examine in detail the functional law relating to international communications and other subjects touching international propaganda which are well set forth by Professors Whitton and Larson in their book.[10]

Last, we must acknowledge that in addition to the prescriptions limiting the use of propaganda as part of delictual recourse to force or dictatorial intervention there are equally important obligations on all nations to promote the goals of peace, cooperation, pacific settlement of disputes, international economic and social justice, and disarmament. These obligations both reinforce the prescriptions against warmongering, subversive, and defamatory propaganda and oblige states to make positive contributions to the realization of these goals through, inter alia, the propaganda policies they pursue.[11]

In summary, therefore, no state or individual purporting to respect international law could contend that there is an unlimited right to engage in international propaganda. It should be emphasized that this in itself is a sign of progress. The same statement could not have been made with equal confidence in, say, 1914. In any event, the issue is not whether international law should regulate propaganda but how. One's answer naturally is determined by one's picture of the international law-making process. Some international law writers, confronted with the widespread violation of the norms summarized above, see the problem as one of codification and development of relevant rules and legal institutions. Without discounting the importance of such efforts, it is the contention of this paper that the more realistic and ultimaely more fruiful approach to the problem is to proceed in the following manner:

1. study the claims, counterclaims, and third-party judgments of controversial instances of recourse to propaganda as part of the ideological instrument;
2. seek points of consensus, however modest, with respect to the customary law relevant to international propaganda and the ideological instrument;
3. study the degree of effectiveness of controversial uses of the ideological instrument in order to determine forms or circumstances of its use that appear to have been ineffectual or disproportionately mischievous and hence the more indefensible in that they involved violation of the law without a commensurate selfish gain. It is always useful to buttress arguments based on normative obligation with utilitarian arguments of self-interest and there is reason to believe that, in the tricky field of propaganda, law and self-interest properly perceived may be much closer than proponents of dubious forms of psychological warfare would have us believe.[12]
4. seek to convince decision-makers that their policies concerning the use of the ideological instrument should be based, first, on an awareness of their legal obligations and their opportunity to contribute to the development of international law rather than on their knowledge that sanctions underlying the law relating to propaganda are virtually nonexistent and that violations of the law can be expected to continue. Second, proponents of international law should seek to persuade decision-makers that there are grave dangers in irresponsible recourse to the ideological instrument and positive benefits in responsible policies with regard to propaganda.

To the extent that such efforts are successful in nations such as the United States, international practice tending to produce customary international law will improve. To the extent that such practice may educate other states which presently indulge in unlimited propaganda and, possibly, induce more responsible behavior, the basis may be laid for more systematic efforts for codification and development of rules and institutions for control of international propaganda. As indicated at the outset, however, it is believed that the prospects for meaningful progress in this field are modest and that a very conservative attitude should be taken in appraising the scope and effectiveness of universal and even regional international law as it bears upon the problem of international propaganda. Let us, then, examine some of the reasons which support this conservative analysis.

II

Obstacles to the development of meaningful international legal regulation of international propaganda

The most fundamental obstacle to regulation of international propaganda results from philosophic-ideological rifts which divide the world. Men differ profoundly on the definition of ultimate reality and, consequently, on the interpretation of human events. Granted that the problems of international propaganda relate as much to its effects as to its truthfulness, truthfulness is still the starting point in any evaluation of propaganda. But we know that there exist a number of fundamentally different approaches to the quest for ultimate truth. Two have particularly influenced contemporary history, the Judaeo-Christian and the Marxist-Leninist worldviews. As we know, these differences are far from academic since they influence the thoughts and actions of governing elites and substantial portions of the citizenry in the world's major powers. If we add the factor of missionary zeal which is present in both camps we have a situation that would seem to deny efforts to obtain global consensus on regulation of propaganda which is vital to the propagation of each side's version of "truth."

For example, even if we remove the traditional communist words of scorn (for examples, "feudal oppression," "exploiters," "warlords," and "lackeys") from the communist propaganda attacks quoted by Professors Whitton and Larson,[13] the underlying core of the message is "true" when viewed from a communist perspective. To predict the collapse of the present political system in Iran would appear, from a Marxist-Leninist viewpoint, to be as scientific and objective as a prediction by a psychiatrist that an individual was destined for mental illness. On the other hand, one need not be a Kremlinologist or Pekinologist to predict that conspicuous representatives of the Judaeo-Christian worldview will probably not fare very well under Marxist-Leninist regimes and that serious threats to their lives, property, and human rights are a distinct possibility. Propaganda reflecting this point of view is certainly "true," but it may also be "warmongering," "subversive," or "defamatory." The same can be said of Western propaganda of a positive kind which asserts that man can only prosper in societies that conform to God's law—or perhaps to the secular principles of a free society.

At this point, of course, the proponents of control of international propaganda turn to their municipal law analogies of libel, slander, treason, and the like and remind us that such limitations on free expression arise not solely or even primarily out of a concern for truth but out of the need to suppress breaches of the public order that may result from the exercise of the right of expression. Thus the truthfulness of a statement may not redeem its antisocial or illegal effects. We might then conclude that, drawing by analogy from this concept, states holding different views about the meaning of "truth" should restrain themselves from expressing these views in ways that patently disturb the world public order.[14]

The difficulty here is that these fundamentally different views of reality divide nations in their attitudes toward the world public order. The law-makers and acquiescing citizens who decide that in certain circumstances the national public order is a higher value than freedom of expression obviously agree sub stantially that the existing order is desirable and worth protecting. Do we have anything like this consensus with respect to the world public order? Most authorities seem to think not. Increasingly we encounter expressions such as "the law of minimum world public order"[15] or "the international law of co existence" which is contrasted with " 'universal' and 'regional' law of coop eration."[16]

The well-known conclusion that such modern authorities reach is that, de spite the obstacles to a true world public order, a minimum world public order can and in fact does exist. It is based, in effect, on a tacit agreement to dis agree but to avoid expressing the disagreement in ways that would be disad vantageous if not ruinous for all. This means in practice that the form of the world public order and the content of universal international law is deter mined more or less pragmatically and often informally or tacitly rather than by systematic agreement from a basic consensus. Consequently, the value at tached to this minimum world public order and to any particular rules relating to its maintenance tends to be variable. Whereas judgments about the com parative value of a domestic public order and freedom of expression taking forms that threaten that order would presumably lead toward protection of the domestic order, the same assumption cannot necessarily be made with respect to the relationship between the world public order and international propaganda.

It would appear, then, that the normative imperative requiring some limita tion on international propaganda arises not from a consensus over what natural law thinkers call "the international common good" but from the pragmatic necessities of coexistence in a dangerous world of conflict. Thus, propaganda that threatens to incite World War III would be judged impermissible—in deed, criminal—by all responsible members of the minimum world public order, whatever their ideological persuasion. But less dangerous propaganda which thwarted progress in arms control and disarmament and pacific settle ment of disputes might be considered permissible because its alleged truth and its ideological-political necessity outweighed the propagandists' concern for the minimum world public order.

A second obstacle to significant legal regulation of international propaganda arises from the fact that the deep-rooted differences just discussed, along with other causes, produce persistent and widespread international conflict. Conflict and drastic change are endemic to the contemporary world society and to most national societies. Separate from, even though often arising out of or influ enced by, the fundamental rifts just discussed, there is an ethos of change in most of the world. This ethos encourages "ends-justify-the-means" attitudes which have little or nothing in common with the attitudes of law-makers and citizens in advanced legal orders which place sophisticated limitations on free dom of expression in the interests of the commonweal.

The intermingling of political and ideological activity both within and be tween existing states that characterizes our time clearly diminishes respect for public orders at all levels—from local to national to global. The statesmen who developed rules of international law prohibiting hostile acts originating within a state's jurisdiction and having effect within the jurisdiction of a friendly power were content with their own public order and sufficiently content with the public orders of most of the other states so that they could support a norm that valued order and stability over violent change. Mutual respect, protection of vital interests, and nonintervention were the rule in that world. Thus the British representatives at the Alabama Claims Arbitration came to see that a mischievous source of revolutionary change ought to be discouraged by a rule prohibiting even tacit encouragement of support to those in rebellion against a friendly power.[17]

But the revolutionary elite that establishes a new state or takes over an old one is generally not at all disposed to respect the rights of other, quite differently organized and oriented, public orders. Indeed, such revolutionaries often fear, detest, and seek to destroy their neighbors' public orders. In any event, for these revolutionary elites order, stability, and mutual respect of sovereigns are all values that are subordinate to the highest of all values, rapid and decisive change. Since propaganda is the most important and most available instrument of such elites there is (from their standpoint) both a normative and practical right and duty to use propaganda in their assaults on "unjust" public orders—local, national, regional, global.

In addition to these fundamental forces working against respect for order in our age, there is the resultant impact of psychological and sociological characteristics of individuals and groups which bring about conflict and change. Attitudes and habits of expression and behavior are developed which are shocking to the supporters of the *status quo*. Thus, as we view the attitudes, language, and tactics of various advocates for change in *American* society we are not encouraged to believe that the world community is ready for an early return to a public order based on mutual respect and good manners. Nor are we likely to find more genuine enthusiasm for legal restraints on propaganda than exists within domestic activist groups for stricter rules regulating strikes, sit-ins, boycotts, and demonstrations in defiance of public order.

There are, then, in the new or transformed nations, many elites—some enjoying strong popular support—who believe that they have an unlimited right to lash out against all that they see as wrong in the world. They further assume the necessity and rectitude of preserving their own systems and of advancing their political interests and ideological causes through the use of the ideological instrument, their strongest instrument of foreign policy.

III

International law relating to international propaganda and the practice of states

In the light of the foregoing considerations it is not surprising that, despite widespread adhesion to conventions explicitly or implicitly condemnng warmongering, subversive, and defamatory propaganda,[18] despite extensive formal and informal discussions of the problems some of which have produced draft conventions and codes on the subject,[19] and despite the tremendous volume of charges and protests which specifically acknowledge the relevant legal prescriptions and apply them to the policies of other states,[20] all states appear to engage in propaganda activities which could be termed legally impermissible. To the extent that it is normatively binding, international law ultimately rests upon a feeling of obligation on the part of its subjects to obey it. Or, to use McDougal's formulation, international law rests upon the "expectations" of authoritative decision-makers about the behavior of states that purport to be acting legally.[21] As one deduces obvious corollaries concerning international propaganda from relevant functional international law, from the law regulating recourse to force, dictatorial intervention, and international responsibility, and from the law enjoining states to support world public order, what are one's expectations?

It is submitted that expectations are, first, for only intermittent, variable and marginal observance of these legal prescriptions. But, perhaps more important, one anticipates that the states as they violate these norms do not appear to be conscious of doing wrong. In many instances, on the contrary, states manifestly engage in technically illegal propaganda with a feeling of rectitude ranging from a conviction that they have a right to disseminate their propaganda to the belief that they have a duty to do so in the interests of mankind as well as for their own interests. Until this kind of attitude is altered it would seem impossible successfully to deal with the problems of international legal regulation of propaganda.

There is a further aspect of this problem, moreover, that is more difficult to prove. One wonders whether, notwithstanding the repeated acknowledgments in this century of the potency and dangers of international propaganda (so well catalogued in Professors Whitton and Larson[22]), the widespread tendency to ignore prescriptions limiting propaganda may result in part from a failure of statesmen to take the problem seriously. Have the words that statesmen have uttered, written, and endorsed with binding adhesions really penetrated their consciences so as to have effect when those statesmen make their policy decisions? Does the very subtlety of propaganda as a means of coercion result in its use without the kind of crisis of conscience which presumably would precede a decision to employ more direct forms of coercion, such as the economic or military instruments of foreign policy?

Concern over this possible explanation for the gap between law and practice relating to international propaganda is obviously particularly acute among those of us whose hopes for the development of a minimum world public order rests more with responsible decision-makers who contribute good examples and potential precedents than with drafters of codes and participants in international conventions. The point of hope is not the outraged victim for whom little remedy other than retaliation in kind is presently available. Rather, hope for improved state practice in the matter of propaganda lies with potential senders of propaganda who must be made aware of the importance and legal implications of the use that they make of propaganda. But the first requirement of this approach obviously is a clear recognition by responsible decision-makers that there is both a practical and a legal problem.

At the risk of inviting charges of parochialism, it must be submitted at this point that United States decision-makers seem, on the whole, to have understood that there is a problem. The protests of Americans who would have the United States take the ideological offensive are a measure of the reluctance of this country to engage in propaganda that could be termed impermissible under international law. Yet this is a never-ending problem, and a good record to date does not preclude the possibility that a nation as sorely tested as the United States has been and will be might be tempted to experiment with the potent and dangerous possibilities of legally impermissible propaganda. Those who advocate restraint in the use of the ideological instrument, therefore, should constantly urge upon their government the necessity of keeping this problem in mind and of dealing with it responsibly.[23]

For the problems of international propaganda will not, it is believed, be substantially alleviated in the foreseeable future as a result of clearer definitions of crimes, rights, and duties or by new legal rules or ingenious attempts to provide sanctions to enforce the old ones. The essence of the problem is that, on the one hand, the ideological instrument is too valuable to contemporary international actors and too complex and that, on the other, community consensus is too lacking for the successful employment of sophisticated approaches borrowed from advanced legal orders. The path to progress—and it promises to be very, very slow—lies in studying the realities of our divided world and in seeing how they can be gradually influenced and alleviated by enlightened, generally unilateral, contributions to minimum world public order in so far as international propaganda and the broader ideological instrument are concerned.

NOTES

[1] Myres S. McDougal & F. P. Feliciano, Law and Minimum World Public Order 27–36 (1961).

[2] *Id.* at 29.

[3] For a definition and discussion, see John B. Whitton & Arthur Larson, *Propaganda Towards Disarmament in the War on Words* 10, 62–82 (1964).

[4] McDougal & Feliciano, *op. cit. supra* note I, at 61–62; see generally Julius Stone, *Aggression and World Order* (1958).

[5] Whitton & Larson, *op. cit. supra* note 3 [hereinafter cited as Whitton & Larson].

[6] Ian Brownlie, *International Law and the Use of Force by States* (1963).

[7] On indirect aggression, see Paul W. Blackstock, *Strategy of Subversion* (1964); Manuel R. Gracia-Mora, *International Responsibility for Hostile Acts of Private Persons against Foreign States* (1962); I Daniel P. O'Connel, *International Law* 328–31 (1965).

[8] Burke, "Legal Regulation of Minor Coercion" in *Essays in Intervention* 97 (Stanger ed. 1964).

[9] Whitton & Larson 183–273.

[10] Larson, *The Present Status of Propaganda in International Law*, pp. 439–51 supra; Whitton, *The Problem of Curbing International Propaganda*, pp. 601–21 infra.

[11] See U.N. Charter arts. 1, 2, for the fundamental basis for these international obligations.

[12] See Blackstock, *op. cit. supra* note 7.

[13] Whitton & Larson 91–92.

[14] *Ibid.*

[15] McDougal & Feliciano, *op. cit. supra* note 1.

[16] Wolfgang G. Friedmann, *The Changing Structure of International Law* (1964).

[17] Thomas A. Bailey, *A Diplomatic History of the American People* 409 (5th ed. 1955); Percy E. Corbett, *Law in Diplomacy* 153 (1959).

[18] See, e.g., the International Convention Concerning the Use of Broadcasting in the Cause of Peace, Sept. 23, 1936, 186 L.N.T.S. 301(H) (1936) (effective April 2, 1938), 32 Am. J. Int'l L. Supp. 113 (1938).

[19] See, e.g., Draft Code of Offences Against the Peace and Security of Mankind, adopted by the International Law Commission in 1951, U.N. Doc. No. A/1858, A/CN.4/48, ch. 4, 45 Am. J. Int'l L. Supp. 123, 128 [arts. 2(5), 2(6)]; Draft Convention on Freedom of Information, U.N. Office of Public Information, Everyman's United Nations 185 ff. (U.N. Pub. Sales No. 1952.I.9), and Draft Convention on the International Right of Correction, 1952 U.N. Yearbook 463–65 (U.N. Pub. Sales No. 1953.I.30.

[20] See Whitton & Larson 12–180 *passim*; Whitton, *Propaganda and International Law*, 72 Hague Recueil 545–59 (1948); I O'Connell, *op. cit. supra* note 7, at 329–31.

[21] See, e.g., McDougal, *International Law, Power and Policy: A Contemporary Conception*, 82 Hague Recueil 137, 170–71 (1958) McDougal & Feliciano, *op. cit. supra* note 1, at 45–49.

[22] Whitton & Larson 1–52.

[23] Two of the most persuasive conservative views on this subject are L. John Martin, *International Propaganda* (1958), esp. 107–08, and Julius Stone, *Legal Controls of International Conflict* 318–23 (1954).

WAR PROPAGANDA:
A SERIOUS CRIME AGAINST HUMANITY
Yuri Bobrakov

YURI BOBRAKOV, born in Leningrad in 1928, graduated from the Moscow State
Institute of International Relations in 1950. He took a postgraduate course in
economics and received his Ph.D. in economics. He served as a professor of economics
and an economic press observer until 1963. From 1963 to 1967 he was the press
attaché of the Embassy of the USSR in Washington, D.C. Since 1968, he has been
the Head of the Economics Department of the Institute of the USA in the
Academy of Sciences of the USSR at Moscow. Professor Bobrakov is the author
of several books, his most recent being The Federal Reserve System and Economic
Regulation, published by Nauka Publishing House of Moscow in 1971.

The term propaganda has rather a broad meaning, implying dissemination, or, more specifically, purposeful dissemination, of certain information that is to produce upon its recipient a certain reaction which from the viewpoint of the disseminator is desirable. In a broad sense it can be interpreted as dissemination of political and economic conceptions, natural science knowledge, musical culture, art, aesthetics, and so on. Propaganda, as such, has been in existence since the time human society came into being; it has always been most closely associated with social and political aspects of the development of nations.

Throughout history, different social groups, political parties, and governments, in pursuit of their political and economic aims, have thrust their ideas and conceptions forward—that is, they were involved in propaganda. Historical records of any country bear witness to that. For example, the inscription "A Lesson to Arbitrary Kings and Wicked Ministers" on the four-dollar bills issued by North Carolina in 1778, at the time of the Revolutionary War, was doubtlessly of a propagandist flavor and reflected political struggles of the period.

Propaganda, which bears influence on the relations between nations, quite understandably is supposed to be among the objects of discussion in the international law field.

The most urgent problem of modern times is that of safeguarding peace, of eliminating war from the repertoire of Man. It is from this direction that I am discussing the issue of "the international control of propaganda." Professors Whitton and Larson in their book, Propaganda,[1] emphasized that propaganda could be a threat to peace. As they put it, it is "over the line"[2] propaganda that tends to produce a breach of peace. As Professors Whitton and Larson quite rightfully underline it, war propaganda has much in common with armaments, and, no doubt, if we mean to work out ways of dismantling the most

Reprinted with permission, from a symposium, "International Control of Propaganda,"
appearing in Law and Contemporary Problems, 31, no. 3 (Summer 1966) published
by the Duke University School of Law, Durham, North Carolina. Copyright, 1966, by
Duke University.

dangerous weapons of physical destruction, we should also be struggling to work out ways of dismantling psychological weapons used to exacerbate the causes of war.[3] Those psychological weapons constitute war propaganda.

The multi-century history of mankind bears the record of thousands of bloody battles, which took the toll of millions and millions of human lives. It is difficult to imagine how our planet might appear had humanity not been haunted by wars through thousands of years of its existence. There is an estimate, made with electronic computing techniques, that through the last five thousand years, the peoples of our planet had only 292 peaceful years. For the rest of the time there took place 14,513 large and smaller wars, which took the lives of 3,640,000,000 human beings, more than the whole population of the world at the present time.

The twentieth century, with its great scientific and technical progress, has experienced the most devastating wars in human history. In the European wars of the seventeenth through nineteenth centuries, human losses were fourteen million. The First World War alone carried away ten million lives and left another twenty million wounded and crippled. The Second World War took an even greater toll: about thirty-two million soldiers died on the battlefield, twenty-five million helpless civilians perished in the cities and villages, and about ninety million were wounded. It is possible to rebuild a city out of ashes, but by no means can one resurrect the tens of millions of people whose lives were lost in war.

With the creation of atomic and hydrogen weapons, the prospect of a new war breaking out became a hundred times more awesome. Accordingly, the problem of safeguarding the peace became more vital than ever before.

The Soviet Union has always been most sincere and resolute in the pursuance of measures to ensure peace in the world. Vladimir Lenin, the founder of the Soviet state, said, "Disarmament is an ideal of socialism." The Soviet Union contributed greatly to the introduction into modern international law of the principle of defending the peace and that of responsibility for aggressive wars.

Modern international law prohibits war as a means of solving disputes between states and/ as a lever of governmental policy. It terms such wars "aggressive" and as "representing the gravest crime against humanity." All international disputes, according to international law, should be settled peacefully. That prohibition (of aggressive wars) and its definition as the gravest international crime were established in international law only a short time ago.

In the "Decree on Peace," adopted on the second day of the existence of Soviet power, the Soviet Government elevated to the level of state policy the idea that aggressive war is criminal. Before that time, the right to resort to war, irrespective of its aims, was considered by international law to be an inalienable right as a chief expression of state sovereignty. This right was meticulously guarded by all the systems of international law for hundreds of years. Neither the first (1889) nor the second (1907) Hague Conference questioned the right of a state to resort to any kind of war. It was mentioned only that before resorting to war the conflicting nations should try to settle their dispute by peaceful means. Thus, in the Decree on Peace, aggressive war was termed as the gravest crime against humanity for the first time.

Prohibition of aggressive war has as its immediate consequence the issue of the aggressor's responsibility. Before the Second World War, this problem was practically a nonexistent factor in international law. When joining the Briand-Kellogg Pact of 1928,[4] the Soviet Union pointed out one of its worst shortcomings: it did not provide for sanctions against aggression. Where there is crime, there should also be punishment. War propaganda, as the whole historical experience testifies, is a means of preparing for aggressive war, and consequently is also a crime. The International Military Tribunal in Nuremburg, which tried major war criminals of the Hitler regime, established that war propaganda is one of the means of promoting war, thus confirming the criminal nature of war propaganda. This issue was specifically emphasized in the United Nations General Assembly's resolution of November 3, 1947, denouncing war propaganda:[5] "The General Assembly condemns all forms of propaganda, in whatsoever country conducted, which is either designed or likely to provoke or encourage any threat to the peace, breach of the peace, or act of aggression."

According to the Soviet definition of aggression, presented to the twelfth session of the General Assembly in 1957,[6] propaganda of war was termed an ideological aggression. By this definition the state is considered to have committed ideological aggression if it

(a) encourages war propaganda;
(b) encourages propaganda of using atomic, bacteriological, chemical, and other kinds of mass extermination weapons; or
(c) stimulates propaganda of fascist-nazist views, racial or national superiority, hatred and disdain for other peoples.

So as to practically implement the idea of prohibiting propaganda of war, the Soviet parliament, the Supreme Soviet of the Union of Soviet Socialist Republics, on March 12, 1950, passed a law on the defense of peace:

The Supreme Soviet of the Union of Soviet Socialist Republics, guided by the high principles of the Soviet peace policy, which seeks to strengthen peace and friendly relations between the peoples, recognizes that the (human) conscience and concept of right of the peoples, who during one generation, suffered the calamities of two wars, cannot accept that the conduct of war propaganda remain unpunished, and approves the proclamation of the Second World Congress of the Partisans of Peace, who expressed the will of the entire progressive mankind concerning the prohibition and condemnation of criminal war propaganda. The Supreme Soviet of the USSR decrees:

1. To recognize that war propaganda under whatever form it is made, undermines the cause of peace, creates the threat of a new war and is the gravest crime against humanity.
2. To bring to court persons guilty of war propaganda and to try them as having committed a most grave criminal offense.

In other socialist countries, as is known, legislation against war propaganda was also adopted.

At the eighth session of the General Assembly in 1953, the Soviet Union made a proposal to denounce war propaganda and to call upon all the countries to take measures aimed at curbing such propaganda as incompatible with the principles of the United Nations. Although the proposal was fully in compliance with the U.N. Charter, which makes it a duty of the member nations to uphold peace, it was not passed by the General Assembly because of opposition on the part of certain Western powers. Thus, although modern international law recognizes the criminal essence of war propaganda, in fact only a small number of nations, until now, have taken practical measures to outlaw it on a national basis through domestic legislation.

In the discussion that took place at the Duke International Law Society's annual conference in February 1966, some speakers expressed the opinion that it is not possible to adopt legislation against war propaganda, because such legislation will "run counter to the constitutional principle of freedom of speech."[7] In my opinion, such arguments bear little logic. Since certain action is recognized as representing a danger to society (and war propaganda is recognized as such a threat), it should be dealt with as such, and should not be thought of as having to do with "freedom of speech." I find it quite strange that war propaganda, considered a crime internationally, could, at the same time, go unpunished nationally.

There is no task more vital and urgent than that of preserving peace on earth. This task has been set before the peoples of our planet by the very course of historic development, in which means of waging war have become more and more destructive and threaten to claim larger and larger tolls of human lives. And, of course, never has war been so dangerous, so devastating, and so inhuman as it might be today, when Man has learned to use the immense power of nuclear energy. It is estimated that the total stockpiles of nuclear explosives in the world are now equal to 12,500,000 bombs of the yield of the first atomic bomb dropped over Hiroshima, or to 250 billion tons of TNT. This makes more than eighty tons of TNT for every man, woman, and child now living on our planet. One can imagine what it means by recalling the words of the late President Kennedy: "A full scale nuclear exchange, lasting less than sixty minutes, could wipe out more than 300 million Americans, Europeans, and Russians, as well as untold numbers elsewhere."

It is the nature of man to draw experience from the past. The tragic experience of the Second World War, unleashed by Nazi Germany, demands that nations take all necessary steps to prevent the horror of a third world war. Unfortunately, people sometimes tend to have a very peculiar interpretation of the tragedies of the last war. The following excerpt, from an article by an American journalist, deals with such a peculiar interpretation of the past, in this case, with the treatment that Nazis accorded prisoners of war:

> In "Hogan's Heroes," a current hit, the setting is a World War II prisoner-of-war camp in Germany. The camp head, a burlesque of the Prussian officer, obviously is no Nazi—in fact he's scared of them. And the guard is a low-comedy dumkopf with a vaudeville accent—and he is positively lovable.
>
> The prisoners of war themselves, led by a jaunty Air Force colonel, lead as

comfortable and fun-filled lives as one could imagine. In fact, one of the big jokes of the show is that people try to break into, not out of, the camp.[8]

It is difficult for a thinking person to accept such "humor." To illustrate my point, I cite a letter from an American reader of the magazine *Soviet Life*, in which he comments on the publication by the magazine of materials on Nazi atrocities:

> This is what you should repeat, this is what should be read by every free person in this world. This is a tragedy which cannot happen again—as long as the rotten nazi is watched and stopped from repeating his beastly crimes. I suggest that you continue to feature such articles to remind the complacent and indifferent people of today that perhaps TOMORROW it will be their fate to fall under the lash and the extermination of the still alive nazi, who is planning again his next great campaign.[9]

The Nazi concentration camps are hardly a subject for comedy or vaudeville.

The issue of curbing war propaganda is closely connected with the struggle for strengthening peace, for peaceful coexistence between states with opposite social systems. Peaceful coexistence, as Alexei Kosygin, Soviet premier, emphasized recently, is increasingly becoming an objective requirement in the relations between countries of opposite economic and social views. Ideological struggles of today reflect the existence and competition of two opposite social systems. It means that ideological differences, being an objective factor, cannot be ruled out.

Although we cannot ban the conflict of ideologies, the forms and methods of ideological controversy should be under control. The debate based on the truthful portrayal of the merits and objective criticism of the failings and deficiencies of this or that system is one thing. It is altogether compatible with peaceful coexistence. Any reasonable person will understand that adherence to opposite ideologies is not an obstacle to peaceful relations and international cooperation.

But if there is resort to cold war tactics, it only undermines peaceful coexistence. Some people in the West say that ideological differences make peaceful coexistence between states of opposite systems impossible. I find no truth in such statements. There are, on the other hand, real, and not imaginary, threats to peaceful coexistence—such as further accumulation of armaments, violations of principles of international law, interference in domestic affairs of other countries and peoples—war propaganda being among them. I believe that adoption of measures by each nation to prohibit propaganda of war would be an important contribution to the cause of peace and to the lessening of international tension.

NOTES

[1] John B. Whitton & Arthur Larson, *Propaganda: Towards Disarmament in the War of Words* (1964).
[2] *Id.* at 9.
[3] *Id.* at 1.
[4] Treaty Between the United States and Other Powers Providing for the Renunciation

of War as an Instrument of National Policy, Aug. 27, 1928, 46 Stat. 2343, T.S. No. 796.

[5] U.N. Doc. No. A/428.

[6] U.S.S.R. draft definition of aggression, U.N. Doc. No. A/AC.77/L.4.

[7] See Newhouse, *The Constitution and International Agreements or Unilateral Action Curbing "Peace-Imperiling" Propaganda*, pp. 506–26 infra; Van Alstyne, *The First Amendment and the Suppression of Warmongering Propaganda in the United States: Comments and Footnotes*, pp. 530–52 infra.

[8] Lowry, *Is this the War That Was?*, The Sunday Star T.V. Magazine (Washington, D.C.), Feb. 13, 1966, p. 65.

[9] Letter by M. Labrie, Soviet Life, Sept. 1965, p. 5.

TATZEPAO: MEDIUM OF CONFLICT IN CHINA'S "CULTURAL REVOLUTION"

Barry M. Broman*

BARRY M. BROMAN wrote this essay when he was a first lieutenant in the United States Marine Corps, serving in South Vietnam. He received an M.A. in Southeast Asian studies at the University of Washington.

One of the oldest forms of communication in China is the *tatzepao* or wall poster (sometimes called the big-character poster). Dating from imperial times when royal edicts were posted on village walls, *tatzepao* have played a variety of communication roles in China.[1] Under the Communists *tatzepao* became an efficient medium of mass persuasion guided by the Propaganda Department of the Central Committee of the Chinese Communist Party (hereafter, the Propaganda Department). In the summer of 1966, as the conflict within China's highest political echelon reached crisis proportions, a new and radically different function was assigned to *tatzepao*.

This paper examines the phenomenon of *tatzepao* as an instrument of conflict during the so-called Proletarian Cultural Revolution. It looks at *tatzepao* as a unique form of mass communication which helps to explain the nature of the recent struggle inside Communist China.

Intimately linked with any decision of *tatzepao* must be a discussion of the active agents in the cultural revolution, the Red Guards. The study focuses on a critical period of the cultural revolution beginning in June 1966, when Red Guard units began to appear and *tatzepao* emerged as their primary weapon, until early 1967, when the Red Guards were dispersed and the cultural revolution entered a new phase. The source material incorporates translations of Chinese publications and *tatzepao*. English-language materials are drawn largely from eyewitness accounts by correspondents in Peking. Most commonly, however, these observers were concerned with the content or "news" function of *tatzepao* rather than with the medium as an instrument of conflict.

Broadly speaking, the cultural revolution was a struggle for the reins of leadership at the apex of the political pyramid. The conflict centered on two rival factions, with Mao Tse-tung heading a Leninist-Stalinist minority faction. Supported by a small circle of intimates,[2] Mao managed to survive through the aid of Lin Piao and a substantial segment of the army—and the Red Guards, an organization Mao created in 1966 to prosecute the cultural revolution. Opposed to the Maoists was a diverse group of party faithful which foreign observers have united by the term "anti-Maoist." Under the nominal leadership of Liu Shao-ch'i this group, which is believed to include the majority of

* The author wishes to thank Professor Alex S. Edelstein of the School of Communications and Henry G. Schwartz of the Far Eastern and Russian Institute for their assistance and comments.

Reprinted with permission of *Journalism Quarterly*, 46 (Spring 1969), 100–104, 127.

party leaders, sought to follow a policy line toward modernity that the Maoists branded "revisionist."

At issue was not only who were to be the architects of China's future but also basic policy divergences. Deep ideological differences created an internecine situation in which the struggle for control of mass media was of central importance. Whoever controlled the official media controlled the only means of mass communication. In this respect the anti-Maoists were in a position of strength, for they incorporated many high-level propaganda and communications personnel. As early as 1961 anti-Mao articles began appearing in influential publications with no overt efforts seemingly made to stop their production. Thus, while the official start of the cultural revolution is taken from the appearance of an editorial condemning the play "Hai Jui Dismissed from Office" in November 1965, it should be noted that the play dates from early in the decade.

Wu Han, the play's author, along with Teng T'o and Liao Mo-sha were three important anti-Maoist writers whose prominence resulted from the publication of their "Notes from the Three-Family Village" articles (appearing between 1961 and 1964). Teng T'o, considered to be the leader of the trio, had himself published more than 150 articles in a series called "Evening Chats at Yenshan" in 1961–1962. These were cleverly disguised attacks at the policies of Mao Tse-tung. Overt pressure was not brought to bear against the "Three-Village Gang," however, until 1965 with the attack on Wu Han's play.

With large segments of the official media "captured" by anti-Maoists, Mao Tse-tung faced a difficult task in attempting to reach the masses whom he considered the crucial link in effecting his "revolution." The monolithic structure of the Propaganda Department further frustrated the Maoists since the department functioned hierarchically down to the village level through millions of cadres making up a "closed"[3] communications network. The system oriented all provincial propaganda departments toward Peking whence every important policy message originated. This structure was of critical political importance. Maoist attempts to regain control of the Propaganda Department apparently failed, necessitating the creation of a rival apparatus. The Red Guards emerged as the counterpart to the official propagandists, in function if not in form, and tatzepao became their primary medium.

Tatzepao brought the power struggle into the open on May 25, 1966, when, symbolically, the "first" wall poster of the cultural revolution was written. Its primary author was Nieh Yüan-tzu, a woman teaching assistant in the philosophy department at Peking University who, acting apparently on Mao's personal instructions, attacked the University's president and others. Among the indictments was a charge that University officials had discouraged support for Mao and discouraged the writing of tatzepao:

> To counter-attack the sinister gang which has frantically attacked the Party, socialism, and Mao Tse-tung's thought is a life-and-death class struggle. The revolutionary people must be fully aroused to vigorously and angrily denounce them, and to hold big meetings and put up big-character posters is one of the best ways for the masses to do battle.[4]

This poster signaled a deluge of *tatzepao* and set the stage for the pattern of conflict to follow. Mao Tse-tung personally was credited with having "discovered (this) the first Marxist-Leninist big-character poster in the country and approved its publication for the country and the world."[5]

Soon more posters appeared attacking anti-Maoists by name. Typical of these was a poster entitled "Important Directive Given by Chairman Mao at the Central Committee Cultural Revolution Meeting on 8 September (1966)" in which two powerful anti-Maoists were attacked:[6]

> This man T'ao Chu was introduced to the Party Central Committee by Teng Hsia-p'ing. I said in the beginning that T'ao Chu was not an honest man. Teng Hsiao-p'ing said T'ao Chu was all right.
> I have not solved the problem of T'ao Chu and you have not solved the problem of T'ao Chu. (When) the Red Guards arise, it will be solved.[7]

Unlike the official media which referred vaguely to "those persons in authority who are taking the capitalist road," *tatzepao* attacked the anti-Maoists by name, frequently citing "crimes" of doubtful authenticity. The hapless T'ao Chu, for instance, was condemned for "corrupting" the people.

> In 1960, T'ao Chu personally led Hei Hsien-nu (a former Hong Kong opera actress originally known as Hung Hsien-nu) and Ma Shih-tseng, together with actors from Hong Kong . . . to attend a ceremony marking the completion of the Shumchun Reservoir and Shumchun Theater. . . . Workers, peasants and soldiers were shut out. Besides, he permitted the Pao-an Hsien Party Committee to import from Hong Kong obscene, reactionary films made by capitalist countries. . . . As a result, the people of the Shumchun border defense area were profoundly corrupted by the capitalist ideas. The poison was widespread.[8]

The conflict thus was brought into the open through *tatzepao* in a manner that left those condemned defenseless against the relentless and often anonymous charges. T'ao Chu spoke for many party leaders when he cautioned in an August speech: "Wall posters may be put up in the streets as long as they benefit the cultural revolution. You people [i.e. Red Guards] have to do so openly and do what is helpful and desist from doing what is of no help."[9] As if in answer to T'ao, *Hung Ch'i*, the theoretical journal edited by Mao aide Ch'en Po-ta, taunted:

> True, when the masses are aroused the big-character posters may name some of the middle elements: This is scarcely avoidable. But no harm can come to them if these big-character posters are not published in the press and those named are allowed to put up big-character posters to defend themselves; instead this can stir them into making progress.[10]

Confident that the Red Guards were effective in their "purge by poster," the Maoists further baited their opponents:

> Are you a revolutionary? Then you are bound to welcome these posters, stand up for them, take a lead in writing them and encourage the masses to write them freely and freely reveal the problems.

Are you a royalist? [i.e. an anti-Maoist] Then you are bound to be scared to death of such posters. . . .[11]

The choice of tatzepao by Mao as the medium through which to "reveal" his enemies to the people is understandable. Eight years earlier he had expressed his faith in the utility of the medium as an instrument of conflict:[12]

> The big-character poster is an extremely useful new type of weapon. It can be used in cities and the countryside, government and other organizations, army units and streets, in short, wherever the masses are. Now that it has been widely used, people should go on using it constantly.[13]

Accordingly, on August 5, 1966, as the battle lines of the conflict were being drawn at the Eleventh Plenary Session of the Central Committee of the Chinese Communist Party, a wall poster bearing Mao's own signature appeared. Entitled "Bombard the Headquarters—My Big-Character Poster," according to a Maoist source, it "blasted the lid off the struggle between the proletarian revolutionary line and the bourgeoisie headquarters [i.e. the anti-Maoists] which had existed in the party for a long time."[14]

As Red Guards poured into Peking in August 1966, the number of tatzepao attacking anti-Maoists rose sharply. On September 1, less than two weeks after the public debut of the Red Guards,[15] Premier Chou En-lai announced that there were already five hundred schools throughout China with Red Guard organizations.[16] Emboldened by the cultural revolution group led by Chiang Ch'ing and Chen Po-ta and by guarantees that "no measure would be taken against students . . . because of problems that arise in the movement,[17] the Red Guards were exhorted by Maoist appeals for further action through tatzepao:

> The big-character poster is a powerful weapon which these young leaders use to attack those overt and covert factions in power who follow the capitalist road, and all demons and freaks. Their big-character posters, like swords and daggers, hit the vital part of the enemy and make his sore spot hurt.[18]

The Maoists hoped that the pressures brought about by the tatzepao and Red Guard violence would reduce the effectiveness if not the will of the anti-Maoists, but the degree to which the leaders of the cultural revolution could control the Red Guards decreased rapidly as schools closed and millions of youths surged forward to wage "revolution." In short, the campaign got out of hand.

Apart from the small group that was charged with directing the cultural revolution there was little direct control by Maoist forces over the Red Guards. What controls that existed were rapidly dissipated in the days following the massive August rallies as the ranks of the Red Guards expanded faster than the Maoist organization could assimilate them. At this point Red Guard newspapers emerged in an attempt to give direction to the increasingly ill-disciplined youths who roamed throughout China leaving havoc in their wake. The appearance of these newspapers signaled the institutionalization of the cultural revolution.

The newspapers became the internal control medium for the mobilization of youths and as a link between the Maoist leadership and the rank-and-file Red Guards. They enjoyed a wide geographical distribution and established policy for the Red Guards. The small-circulation publications were circulated by hand to cadres and to a lesser extent to the Red Guard masses.[19]

By the end of 1966, with the aid of tatzepao, over 250 leading editors, propagandists, and leaders of the arts had been removed from their posts,[20] including men who had held key positions within the party since the hard days in Yenan before the Second World War.

A THEORETICAL FRAMEWORK

It can be deduced that the Red Guard communications network functioned to reflect the "thought of Mao Tse-tung." (See Figure 1.) The network originated with messages from the Maoist leadership, (A) in Figure 1. These

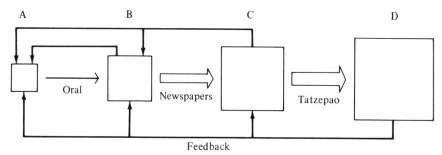

Figure 1. The Red Guards' communication network.

basic policy statements were transmitted orally or possibly through secret directives to the Red Guard leadership (B). This strategically located group, in turn, transmitted the policy statements downward through Red Guard newspapers to the mass of the Red Guards (C). This group then produced tatzepao, which completed the chain of information from the Maoist leadership to the Chinese population (D).

In response to tatzepao the population would produce tatzepao of their own, serving the purpose of feedback. Similarly, the activities of the Red Guard hierarchy generated feedback toward the Maoist leadership.[21] As the cultural revolution progressed, the model tended to break down and the Red Guards were reduced to a fragmented, anarchist rabble. From December 1966 until the army was called in to restore order in the spring of 1967, the Maoist leadership seemed to have lost effective control of the Red Guards.

Definitive assessment of the effectiveness of the Red Guard communications must wait until the cultural revolution has run its course. In June 1968 the fate of the "revolution" was still in doubt. Since the spring of 1967, when Red Guard activities were virtually ended, there has been a move toward the re-establishment of Maoist control over the official media.

As a medium of conflict there can be little doubt of the utility of *tatzepao*. Millions of youths were mobilized and tens of millions of *tatzepao* were produced promoting the cultural revolution.

Tatzepao was an interim force, essentially remedial in character, that Mao Tse-tung utilized to fill a vacuum in his struggle for the propaganda machinery in China. The Red Guard "purge by poster" campaign toppled many prominent anti-Maoists while effectvely forestalling anti-Maoist activity in the official propaganda apparatus until major personnel changes could be effected by the Maoists.

NOTES

[1] For a discussion of communications in imperial China, see James Markham, *Voices of the Red Giants* (Ames, 1967). For a treatment of *tatzepao* under the Communists prior to the cultural revolution, see Vincent King, *Propaganda Campaigns in Communist China* (Cambridge, Mass., 1965) and Frederick T. C. Yu, "Campaigns, Communications and Change in Communist China," in Daniel Lerner and Wilbur Schramm (eds.), *Communications and Change in the Developing Countries* (Honolulu, 1967).

[2] Besides Lin, Mao gathered around him Chiang Ch'ing (Mao's wife) and Ch'en Po-ta (Mao's former secretary) both of whom held key posts in the special group that was charged to direct the cultural revolution.

[3] This term is used with reference to the special training and vocabulary required of cadres in interpreting messages of the Propaganda Department. See Franz Schurmann, *Ideology and Organization in Communist China* (Berkeley, 1966), p. 58.

[4] Quoted in *Peking Review*, Sept. 9, 1966, p. 20.

[5] *Peking Review*, March 10, 1967, p. 5.

[6] T'ao Chu was the short-lived director of the Propaganda Department between June–Nov., 1966. Teng Hsiao-p'ing, Party Secretary-General, is considered one of Mao's most influential opponents.

[7] Quoted in *Samples of Red Guard Publications*, Vol. 1 (Washington, D.C., 1967), p. 5.

[8] "T'ao Chu Actions in Shumchun Border Area Condemned," a handwritten *tatzepao* dated 13 Jan., 1967 quoted in *Samples, op. cit.*, pp. 59–60.

[9] "Comrade T'ao Chu's Speech at the CCP Central Committee's Propaganda Department" (Aug. 25, 1966), quoted in *Current Background* (Hong Kong: U.S. Consulate-General, March 10, 1967), p. 15.

[10] "The Programmatic Document of the Great Proletarian Cultural Revolution," *Hung Ch'i*, Oct. 1966, quoted in *The Great Socialist Cultural Revolution* (Peking, 1967), p. 8.

[11] *Hsinhua* (New China News Agency), June 20, 1966, quoted in *Current Scene*, Hong Kong, May 31, 1967, p. 4.

[12] It is interesting to note that Mao's first public writing was in the form of a *tatzepao*. The poster was written when Mao was about seventeen and it proposed that Sun Yat-sen be made President of China. Mao later described it as "somewhat muddled." Edgar Snow, *Red Star Over China* (London, 1963), p. 136.

[13] Mao Tse-tung, "Introducing a Co-operative," April 15, 1958, quoted in *Peking Review*, Sept. 11, 1967, p. 16.

[14] *Peking Review*, Sept. 11, 1967, p. 8.

[15] The August 18, 1966 rally in Peking is accepted as the debut of the Red Guards. Some reports, however, cite Red Guard units in operation as early as May. See K. S. Karol, *China: The Other Communism* (New York, 1967) and "Five Red Guard Leaflets," *China News Analysis*, Nov. 11, 1966, p. 1.

[16] "Chou En-lai Speech to Red Guards in Peking," quoted in *Current Background*, March 10, 1967, p. 17.

[17] Chün-tu Hsüeh, "The Cultural Revolution and Leadership Crisis in Communist China," *Political Science Quarterly*, June 1967, p. 180.

[18] *Hung Ch'i*, August 1966, quoted in *Current Scene*, May 31, 1967, p. 2.

[19] A Japanese journalist, Miss Chie Nishio, reports that the only Red Guard newspapers she saw during an extensive tour of China in early 1967 were at Peking University but that she was not permitted to read them. Personal communication.

[20] For a description of the pattern of purge, see "The Cultural Revolution Broom," *China News Analysis*, Nov. 18, 1966.

[21] For a more detailed model which develops the forms and functions in the abstract, see Bruce Westley and Malcolm S. MacLean Jr., "A Conceptual Model for Communications Research," *Journalism Quarterly*, 34:31-38 (Spring 1957). Cf. the model for the opinion-making process in James N. Rosenau, *Public Opinion and Foreign Policy* (New York, 1961), p. 22.

PROTEST MOVEMENTS:
CLASS CONSCIOUSNESS
AND THE PROPAGANDA SONG*

R. Serge Denisoff

R. SERGE DENISOFF is associate professor of sociology at Bowling Green State University. Denisoff is the author of numerous articles and books dealing with social movements and music. He is the author of Social and Political Movements (with Gary B. Rush), Great Day Coming: Folk Music and the American Left, and Sing A Song of Social Significance: A Sociological View of Protest Songs. Professor Denisoff is also the popular music editor for the Journal of Popular Culture.

The purpose of this paper is to examine the relationship of propaganda songs to social movements. The role and function of the propaganda song has in the past received little attention from sociologists and social scientists as a whole. The primary usage of the propaganda song is to create political or social consciousness favorable to the position of the movement or individual using the propaganda song. The original interpretation of the concept "political consciousness" connotes a predisposition for social change.[1] Lenin derived the concept of political consciousness from Marx who viewed class consciousness as the subjective means of facilitating change in the social structure. For Marx, class membership was originally an aggregate of persons in a given economic strata or "a class in itself." Class consciousness emerges when members of a class (the proletariat) identify themselves with the class (the protelarian class) and their position in the stratification system and when the members of the class are aware of their historical role in the Marxian theoretical scheme or a change-oriented "class for itself." Mills correctly defines three elements essential for class consciousness to exist:

(1) a rational awareness and identification with one's own class interests;
(2) an awareness of and rejection of other class interests as illegitimate; and
(3) an awareness of and a readiness to use collective political means to the collective political end of realizing one's interest.[2]

Lenin made explicit this postulate in What Is To Be Done by suggesting that the proletariat was not and could not be conscious of the irreconcilable antagonisms of their interests. Workers, according to Lenin, are singularly engaged in "outbursts of desperation." Therefore, an organization must be formed and maintained to "take up the political education of the working

* I am indebted to Andrew P. Phillips, Thomas J. Duggan, and especially Delfo Giglio for their suggestions, assistance, and critiques of the original version of this paper.

Reprinted with permission of the Sociological Quarterly, 9 (Spring 1968), 228–247, and the author.

class, and the development of political consciousness."[3] Lenin, hereby, injected the factor of a mobilizing force—social movements—generally ignored in the structural-psychological tenets of class consciousness as perceived by Marx. One means of creating class consciousness, especially by political and social movements familiar with the writings of Marx and later Lenin, has been the use of the propaganda song performed or composed in the folk idiom, that is, songs performed employing the instrumentation and presentational techniques traditionally manifested by nonprofessional folk singers.[4] Few folklorists consider contemporary propaganda songs as being folk songs. Although there appears to be some disagreement among observers as to the elements constituting the definition of a folk song, the following characteristics are consensually submitted: (1) the author of the song is anonymous; (2) the songs are orally transmitted from one generation to the next; and (3) the song must experience verbal alteration during generational transmission. Generally propaganda songs of the twentieth century have not met the definitional criteria. The vast majority of these songs suggest the following properties in varying degrees as being present: (1) the author of the song is publicly identifiable; (2) song transmission is through audio-visual aids, such as the printed page, e.g., songbooks, or in contemporary times, records; and (3) few propaganda songs survive beyond their historical genre or organizational milieu. This truncated comparison of the characteristics of folk and propaganda songs indicates that generally propaganda songs are not folksongs in the definitional sense, and, therefore, the two terms cannot be employed interchangeably.

A propaganda song or "song of persuasion" in the folk idiom can be defined as a song which functions to communicate an idea, a concept, or a total ideology to the listener, employing the structure of a folk song.[5] Propaganda songs function to achieve six goals: (1) the song solicits and arouses outside support or sympathy for a social movement or attitudinal orientation; (2) the song reinforces the value system of individuals who are a priori supporters of a social movement or ideology; (3) the song creates and promotes cohesion and solidarity in an organization or movement supporting the singer's or composer's ideological position; (4) the song attempts to recruit individuals to join a specific social movement; (5) the song invokes solutions to real or imagined social phenomena in terms of action to achieve a desired goal; and (6) the song directs attention to some problem situation or discontent, generally in emotion laden terminology.[6] These six usages of the propaganda song are to be achieved by two categories of songs of persuasion.

The first type of song of persuasion is the magnetic song. The magnetic propaganda song is defined as a song written by a "folk entrepreneur"[7] which appeals to the listener and attracts him to a specific movement or ideology within the ranks of adherents by creating solidarity in terms of the goals expressed in the propaganda song. Two essential factors are contained in this definition: the song persuades, both emotionally and intellectually, individuals into supporting or joining the movement or goals of the writer and of the organization for which the song is written; and the ballad creates social cohesion or a feeling of solidarity among the membership or supporters of a given movement or ideological set. The definition dichotomizes the concept

Merton and Lazarsfeld report as "reciprocal reinforcement," that is, the involvement of the individual in a movement or ideology beyond the intellectual
level (canalization) and his feeling of belonging to others in the group who
have similar ideological orientations (supplementary).[8] The concept of a
magnetic propaganda song may be operationalized as the Marxian view of a
"class for itself" or Lenin's view of political consciousness. The magnetic song
contains the three elements of class consciousness, that is, an awareness of class
position, a differentiation from others, as indicated in the content of the songs,
and further, a desire or willingness to join a movement as suggested in the
lyrics of the propaganda song. In Lenin's terms left-wing political consciousness
encompasses the two dominant characteristics of the magnetic song, that is, the
creation of solidarity and attraction and recruitment of new members to a
social movement.

The other category of propaganda song is the rhetorical song defined as a
song written by a folk entrepreneur and is designed to point to some condition
and describe the condition, but offers no ideological or organizational solution
such as affiliating with a social movement. The rhetorical song poses a question
or a dissent in relation to the institutions of the social system, e.g., Wall Street.
The rhetorical song may point to an event which is endemic to its geographical
or historical content and may require little commitment of the listener. This
type of song can be as useful as the above category in promoting cohesion
within the membership of a social movement, but may have little effect on non-
members and in some circumstances may negatively affect nonparticipants.[9]
Rhetorical songs can also be divided on a historical continuum as being universal or specific. For example, "Kevin Barry" transcends time and geographic
boundaries and political movements, whereas propaganda songs dealing with a
specific event such as a strike may not transcend the historical context of the
song, i.e., "Pretty Boy Floyd" or "Dreadful Memories." The latter category
associates or correlates with the Marxian stage of "a class in itself" in that
only a question or a protest is suggested within the context of the songs and
the organizational solution of class unity and action is omitted. Rhetorical songs
are thus defined as "outbursts of desperation" rather than mobilizing factors
or problem solving devices in the historical sense of consciousness as delimited
by both Marx and Lenin. These definitions suggest that the political or class
consciousness of a social movement and its membership, to the degree that
they support the leadership, may be indicated in terms of the propaganda songs
produced by a social or political movement. The structure of these songs indicates organizational trends in the Marxian sense and a unity of collectivity,
therefore, making propaganda songs operational vis-à-vis class and political
consciousness. In this work, the former conceptualization will be treated.

In the present century four periods have manifested a significant amount of
propaganda song acivity: (1) the period of 1905–15 dominated by the Industrial Workers of the World; (2) the period of 1935–43 dominated by the
C.I.O. and the American Left-wing; (3) the period of 1945–50 dominated by
the People's Songs, Inc.; (4) the period of the so-called folk song revival,
1957–64. These periods of historical spectrums represent the peak years of
heightened propaganda song activity employing the folk idiom. Also, the selec-

tion of these periods on a historical continuum allows a presentation of a representative sample of propaganda song content.

HISTORICAL BACKGROUND

Period I

The Industrial Workers of the World (IWW) was formed in 1905 to introduce industrial unionism or syndicalism during this period into the United States; the "one big union" would in turn bring about a socialist economic system. The occupational composition of the membership primarily included lumberjacks and miners in the West, wheat and stockyard workers in the Mid-west, and textile workers in the East. The movement attained a maximum membership in 1910 of 100,000 adherents and from this points declined after the beginning of the First World War due to several factors: (1) the repression of the movement by governmental agencies and vigilante groups, such as the American Legion; (2) the transference of support by IWW members.

Period II

In the mid-thirties John L. Lewis withdrew from the American Federation of Labor and formed the Congress of Industrial Organizations (CIO). This labor reorganization created various tactical difficulties which Howe and Coser define:

> . . . there was precious little glory and still less comfort in organizing for the CIO, and as a rule, only men moved by a conviction that unionization of mass-production industries was a step toward a larger social end were willing to take the risks that came with the job.[10]

One group willing to undertake the deprivations of the role, labor organizer, was the American Communist Party, which was accepted by some of the leadership of the CIO anxious to have organizers.[11] The Lewis element of organizers—mine workers with a rural tradition—and the personnel from the Left injected or reintroduced the propaganda song employing the folk structure. The Party used similar songs of persuasion in its recruiting drives. Songs advocating participation in the Spanish Civil War, urging nonintervention in the European conflict, and espousing a greater effort in defeating the Axis were utilized by the Stalinists to communicate a specific interest orientation.[12]

Period III

The People's Songs, Inc. (PSI) was formed from the ashes of the prewar activities of the labor movement and the political Left. The major function of the group was to provide propaganda songs to the labor movement and left-of-center movements such as the Progressive Party of 1948. The substantive differentiation of this organization, and others like it, from the above was that PSI was to provide and perform propaganda songs for other social movements rather than to recruit members for the PSI. People's Songs disbanded in 1949, after achieving a peak membership of two thousand adherents, because of a lack of funds, the change of attitude in the CIO as to the type of tactics and organizers the labor movement desired to have, and attacks upon the group by several legislative committees.

Period IV

The final period under consideration saw the disappearance of the cited movements from the realm of functional significance. The CIO was legitimized and institutionalized, the CPUSA and other Marxist groups had declined into political oblivion, and the IWW consisted of several small offices maintained by a handful of members, remnants of the 1910's. However, the folk music revival, the emergence of the New Left, and intensive civil rights activity in the South renewed interest in "protest songs," originally those of the cited periods. This rebirth of interest evidenced itself in the form of folk entrepreneurs who composed and performed material dealing with specific events and perceived grievances. These songs are representatives of Gusfields' "expressive politics," that is, political expression without a function, e.g., protest for the sake of protest.[13] The civil rights movement employed songs in a traditional pattern with several contemporary adaptations, specifically in the Southern states.

These four periods may be "idealized" in the Weberian sense according to the dominant traits, structures, and ideologies of the social movements of these eras. Periods I and II are characteristically "structure-directed" in that social discontents were frequently defined within the confines of nineteenth-century "grand cosmic schemes." The latter two periods are typically "event-oriented," that is, they evidence topical concern or free floating protest aimed at specific problem situations such as racial discrimination or recently the Vietnam War. For example, the IWW and the CPUSA viewed system change, based on the ownership of the means of production, as the remedy for their consciousness of dysfunction. In juxtaposition, the New Left desires specific outcomes of conflict situations, which differ from one ad hoc protest group to another.

METHODOLOGY

In this work different songs are typologized and utilized as indicators of class consciousness, i.e., the songs have been categorized in terms of the extent to which they reflect the Marxian conceptualization, through a content analysis of the songs of the periods under consideration. This index will then be applied to the above historical periods during the twentieth century where songs of persuasion were used by social movements left of the relative political center.[14] Magnetic songs, therefore, are operationalized as being indicators of class conscious social movements. Conversely, rhetorical songs are associated with the absence of change-oriented entities. The magnetic song reflects a high degree of class consciousness as opposed to the rhetorical ballad. It is, therefore, expected that there will be a greater than chance association between social movements exhibiting working class orientations and songs that reflect a high degree of class consciousness than between those movements and songs that reflect a lesser degree of Marxian consciousness (see Table 2).

SAMPLE

In 1906, the IWW during a Seattle membership campaign adapted the techniques of the propaganda song from the movement's religious rival, the Salvation Army. One observer visualized the competition in this manner:

the revolutionary philosophy that Walsh (an IWW organizer) was peddling conflicted with the principles of religious complacency being preached simultaneously up the street by the Salvation Army and the Volunteers of America, and the two bands marched down, surrounded Walsh and proceeded to drown him in a cacophony of coronets and tambourines. Walsh . . . retired long enough to organize a brass band of his own. . . .[15]

From this encounter, according to Greenway, emerged the *Little Red Song Book* with the preamble "to fan the flames of discontent." The pocket-sized book featured parodies of "Starvation Army" songs which subsequently have been transmitted into thirty editions as of May, 1962. This latter edition indicates the manifestation of class consciousness in the IWW.[16] Table 1 suggests that the IWW was primarily concerned with recruiting new adherents and maintaining cohesion in the movement. The number of cases in the rhetorical song classification of the table indicates a small percentage (.29) of propaganda songs outside the magnetic category. In the subcategory of rhetorical songs the majority of songs dealt with a specific strike situation or a martyred hero in the movement, e.g., the execution of Joe Hill. The majority of propaganda songs are indicative of class consciousness in that the supplementary variable present in the songs correlates with the Marxian typology.

To cite all of the magnetic and rhetoric songs found in the IWW song book is outside the scope of this paper, however, we offer one example of each classification and subcategory:

Magnetic Songs/song to recruit outsiders:

Workers of the world, awaken!
Break your chains, demand your rights
All the wealth you make is taken by
exploiting parasites . . .
Join the union, fellow workers,
Men and women, side by side . . .
("Workers of the World Awaken.")

song to promote solidarity:

Fierce and long the Battle rages
But we will not fear,
Help will come when 'er it's needed
Cheer my comrades, cheer.
("Hold the Fort.")

song to achieve both new members and solidarity:

Come and join in the fray
Come and join us today
We are fighting for Freedom and Bread
("Now Awaking.")

Rhetorical Songs/specific event:

High head and back unbending—fearless and true
Into the night unending; why was it you?
Heart that was quick with song, torn with their lead;
Life that was young and strong, shattered and dead.
("Joe Hill" by Ralph Chaplin.)

universal theme:

They go wild, simply wild over me
I'm referring to the bedbug and the flea—
They disturb my slumber deep and I murmur in my sleep,
They go wild, simply wild over me.
("The Popular Wobbly.")

A like pattern of propaganda songs occurred during the recruiting drives of the thirties and early forties as employed by the labor movement, especially the CIO and the American Left-wing. Both movements were greatly affected by the organizational methodology of the IWW in part because discontented members of the IWW who left the movement in the late twenties joined the Communist Party; and other dissidents, as well as integrated Communist Party members, served as organizers for the newly formed CIO. The transmission of techniques that occurred between the Salvation Army and the IWW was replicated in terms of the IWW and the CIO and the American Left.

A total differentiation of segments of the American Left and the CIO during the late thirties and early forties is a difficult task due to the fact that the CIO, especially in the person and staff of John L. Lewis, welcomed all support and personnel into the industrial workers union, thus increasing the influence of the left-wing vis-à-vis the so-called labor song of protest.

The Communist Party in the late thirties published the Songs of the People which was employed extensively at Party rallies.[17]

The content analysis of the Songs of the People suggests that the movement conformed to the Marxian definition of a class conscious movement. The composition of the song book in relation to rhetorical songs indicates a specific orientation toward the Loyalist movement in Spain during the Civil War and the CIO. The increase of rhetorical songs points to the issue orientation of the Party in contrast to the movement orientation of the IWW or Wobblies. The following verses are representative of the typology suggested in this paper:

Magnetic Songs/song to recruit members:

So, workers, close your ranks
Keep sharp and steady
For Freedom's cause your bayonets bright
For worker's Russia, the Soviet Union
Get ready for the last big fight.
("Red Army March.")

song to promote solidarity:

Lenin is our leader
We shall not be moved
Lenin is our leader

We shall not be moved
Just like a tree that's standing by the water
We shall not be moved.
   ("We Shall Not Be Moved.")

song to achieve both new members and group solidarity:

Young comrades, come and join us,
Our struggle will endure
Till ev'ry enemy is down
And victory is sure.
In struggle and in valiant fight
We're marching to the workers might.
   ("Youthful Guardsmen.")

The rhetorical songs found in the *Songs of the People* deal primarily with the Spanish Civil War. For example:

Spain darkens under a cloud
Where sun should light the land
Spain thunders out clear and loud
To stop the fascist band.
   ("Spain Marches.")

The function of the *Songs of the People*, as noted, was that the Party during this period was primarily oriented to maintain its membership while recruiting neophytes to the movement. The rhetorical songs included in the song book deal primarily with events in which the Party had an interest, e.g., the Loyalist movement in Spain. Similarly, the Party's preoccupation with the labor movement was a dominant theme in the *Songs of the People*.

In 1939 the CPUSA, while continuing in its support and activity in the labor movement, shifted emphasis with the signing of the von-Ribbentrop-Molotov Pact and concentrated its efforts to keep the United States out of the European conflict. In this historical context two forms of propaganda songs were brought to the fore, the labor union song and the anti-intervention song (see Table 1).

In the first magnetic sub-category two songs are specially designed to recruit new members—"All I Want" and "Talking Union." The former includes the following excerpt:

Take the two old parties, mister
No difference in them I can see
But with a Farmer-Labor Party
We could set the people free.

"Talking Union" (spoken words put to music) contains these verses to illustrate the role of a magnetic song:

If you want higher wages let me tell you what to do
You got to talk to the workers in the shop with you
You got to build you a union, got to make it strong
But if you all stick together boys, it won't be long
You get shorter hours . . . better working conditions . . .

The internally directed song is found in the lyrics of "The Union Maid" and "Get Thee Behind Me, Satan":

> Get thee behind me, Satan
> Travel on down the line
> I am a union man
> Gonna leave you behind.
> ("Get Thee Behind Me, Satan.")

and:

> Oh, you can't scare me,
> I'm sticking to the union,
> I'm sticking to the union,
> I'm sticking to the union.
> ("Union Maid.")

Ballads which encompass the joint characteristics are "Which Side Are You On," "The Ballad of Harry Bridges," and "The Union Train." The latter propaganda song, representative of the magnetic song, contains the following verse:

> It [the union] has saved many a thousand, etc.
> It [the union] will carry us to freedom, etc.
> ("Union Train.")

In the appeals directed at industrial workers and members of labor unions, the Almanac Singers employed magnetic songs, as Table 1 suggests; however, in their political and issue presentations the reverse was the case. In the anti-intervention campaign of 1939–41, the Almanacs recorded the album "Songs For John Doe," which contained six songs whose basic thesis was that the United States should remain neutral vis-à-vis the European conflict; all of the ballads included in this collection were rhetorical and specific. Two verses from "Washington Breakdown" and the "Ballad of October 16th" are illustrative:

> Wendell Willkie and Franklin D.
> Seems to me they both agree
> They both agree on killing me.
> ("Washington Breakdown.")

and:

> Oh, Franklin Roosevelt told the people how he felt
> We damned near believed what he said
> He said, "I hate war and so does Eleanor, but
> we won't be safe 'till everybody's dead."
> ("Ballad of October 16th.")

In this type of song the goal is to elicit tacit support or establish an attitudinal set on the part of the listener by raising questions in the receiver's mind, rather than attempting to recruit the individual to a movement, that is, to make the listener aware of his position, but not to invoke collective action as defined by the concept of class consciousness.

In 1941 the type of propaganda songs performed by the Almanac Singers changed in relation to the events in Europe (the invasion of the Soviet Union by the German Army); subsequently, the non-involvement orientation of the songs also changed. In 1942 the Almanacs released an album titled "Dear Mister President," which advocated support for the war. The majority of these songs were parallel to the propaganda songs described; however, the function of these war songs was more to promote solidarity and increase commitment to the war effort than to convince the listener of the righteousness of the cause or of commitment to a movement. Pearl Harbor had already accomplished this task.

The propaganda songs of the war period, be it from either pole of the political spectrum, urged national unity and greater devotion or commitment to the international conflict. One song designed to further labor union support for the war production program is illustrative:

> There'll be a union label in Berlin
> When the union boys in uniform march in
> And rolling in the ranks
> There'll be UAW tanks
> Roll Hitler out and roll the union in.
> ("UAW-CIO.")

Another propaganda song frequently performed on the Columbia Broadcasting System was Woody Guthrie's "Round and Round Hitler's Grave" put to the tune of an old square dance melody:

> Round and round Hitler's grave,
> Round and round we'll go.
> Gonna lay that poor boy down
> He won't get up no more.
> ("Round and Round Hitler's Grave.")

Another form of war propaganda song in the folk idiom is that invoking the concept of duty or social responsibility:

> I'm gonna cross the ocean wide
> With a Springfield rifle by my side
> When Hitler's beat you can be my bride
> And I told her not to grieve after me.
> ("Sally, Don't You Grieve.")

These songs of the "duration" evidence the national ethos of consensus during the war and mobilization, where patriotism transcends organization goals, i.e., radical political movements supported the war effort.

A comparison of the material from the People's Song Book with the above illustrates the rise of the rhetorical song with organizational (magnetic) songs remaining relatively constant; however, if we calculate only the songs written by the People's Songs which appear in the songbook we find a decline of the magnetic song and a significant rise in the rhetorical propaganda song.[18]

Magnetic-rhetorical songs in the "People's Song Book" (1948)

Magnetic songs	25
songs to recruit outsiders (external)	9
songs to promote cohesion (internal)	6
songs to achieve both new members and cohesion (both)	10
Rhetorical songs	18
specific	15
universal	3
	—
	43

Magnetic-rhetorical songs written by PSI in "People's Song Book"

Magnetic songs	6
external	3
internal	0
both	3
Rhetorical songs	14
specific	12
universal	2
	—
	20

Similarly, in the *People's Song Bulletin Reprints*—a collection of songs from the *People's Songs Bulletin* over a three year period—the material supports the original finding, if songs not written by PSI are held constant. (Writer's note: examples of songs from periods III and IV are excluded due to the fact that the structure of songs is identical to the above.)

Magnetic-rhetorical songs by PSI members in "Reprints"

Magnetic songs	7
external	1
internal	3
both	3
Rhetorical songs	15
specific	11
universal	4
	—
	22

An analysis of the PSI songbook indicates that a decline of class consciousness in the Marxian sense had occurred and that an organizational decline was in progress. Historically, the failure of the Progressive Party and the decline in left-wing membership during this period suggests this hypothesis of class consciousness is correct. In 1949 the PSI disbanded and was partially incorporated into the People's Artists.

The latter part of the fifties witnessed the folk music revival, the emergence of a militant Southern civil rights movement, and ad hoc protest "publics." The propaganda songs popular in the initial stages of this period were those most frequently noted.[19] The injection of the propaganda song into a sector of the mass media, outside of the civil rights milieu, altered the traditional transfer of material process. Urban, northern, protest publics, while sporadically employing traditional songs of persuasion, placed predominant emphasis on the compositions of successful folk entrepreneurs of the revival, e.g., Dylan. Recent "teachins" and rallies have featured singers such as Phil Ochs, Joan Baez, and others to communicate rhetorical indignation to an audience. Ochs' rendition at a Vietnam Day demonstration at the University of California is illustrative:

> Here's to the land you've torn out the heart of,
> Mississippi find yourself another country to be part of.
> ("Here's to the State of Mississippi.")

Another sampling of this trend is provided by a piece popular in the underground Top Ten of protest organizations several years ago by Bob Dylan:

> I hope that you die and your death will come soon,
> I'll follow your casket by the pale afternoon,
> and I'll watch while you're lowered down to your death bed,
> Then I'll stand over your grave 'till I'm sure that you're dead.
> ("Masters of War.")

The two examples of rhetorical songs index the ethos of the New Left, in that they express individual dissatisfaction or alienation in relation to the social structure, while lacking an ideological or organizational alternative.[20] The New Left outside of the context of marches has almost totally abandoned propaganda songs for the symbolic protest material of rock and roll as performed by the Beatles, Rolling Stones, Bob Dylan in his post protest song period, and groups such as Moby Grape, the Fugs, and the Jefferson Airplane.[21]

The Southern civil rights movement, musically annexed to its northern counterparts, functionally utilized propaganda material from periods I and II. Labor songs such as "We Will Overcome," and "We Shall Not Be Moved" were adapted to the cohesive needs of the movement.[22] Other songs, generally alterations of Negro religious hymns, were incorporated into conflict situations. While some interaction and transfer of songs between the North and South do take place—the use of civil rights ditties such as "We Shall Overcome" in northern marches and in the repertoires of folk entrepreneurs—propaganda songs in the main appear endemic to organizational and geographic boundaries.[23]

Broadside magazine was established to report and circulate propaganda songs in the fashion of the People's Songs Bulletin emphasizing the material of northern song writers and songs from the "Freedom" movement. A sampling from twenty-five issues of the magazine reflects a diminution of class consciousness and an organization decline in social movement oriented propaganda songs, .77 of which are rhetorical. Of these rhetorical songs .81 are specific as contrasted with that of the IWW where .29 of the propaganda songs fit the rhetorical classification .57 of which are specific.

The sample shows a specific issue orientation rather than organizational prerequisites. Twenty songs connoted the theme of world peace, while the civil rights question, a dominant concern of this period, was treated rhetorically in a majority of the songs, 38.

Rhetorical songs treating the topic of civil rights as contrasted to those emanating from the movement are to be differentiated. The rhetorical ballads of the northern folk entrepreneur such as "Here's to the State of Mississippi" functionally point to the composer's view of the plight of the Negro in America, whereas civil rights songs are generated from Negro musical tradition and actual protest activities.[24] "Ain't Gonna Let Nobody Turn Me 'Round" is an adaptation of a spiritual by Rev. Ralph Abernathy of SCLC during the Albany demonstrations. The song has subsequently been utilized in a myriad of protest situations. In Albany, Georgia (1962):

Ain't gonna let Chief Pritchett, Lordy turn me 'round . . .

In Selma, Alabama (1964):

Ain't gonna let Sheriff Clark, turn me 'round . . .

and Chicago, Illinois (1966):

Ain't gonna let mayor Daley, turn me 'round . . .

The genesis of Southern civil rights songs has rendered the selection of a representative collection of this type of material difficult to amass due to the number of versions existent and the spontaneity of composition endemic to specific protest milieu.[25] The only anthology of these propaganda songs, at present, is *We Shall Overcome*, compiled for the Student Non-Violent Coordinating Committee (SNCC).[26] This songbook was functionally edited for use in conflict situations.[27] As a result, .90 of the songs are magnetic, stressing solidarity and cohesion. However, only .05 of this category are overtly structured to appeal to outsiders. Three songs (.05) of the rhetorical style are found in this collection, one of which is a popular song written by two urban folk entrepreneurs, "The Hammer Song." The functional role of propaganda songs was underlined by Martin Luther King in a television interview:

> they invigorate the Movement in a most significant way. . . . These freedom songs serve to give unity to a movement, and there have been those moments when disunity could have occurred if it had not been for the unifying force of freedom songs and the great spirituals. The Movement has also been carried on by these songs because they have a tendency to give courage and vigor to carry on. There are so many difficult moments when individuals falter and would almost give up in despair. These freedom songs have a way of giving new courage and new vigor to face the problems and difficulties ahead.[28]

The utilization of magnetic songs by the movement, however, is not comparable to that of periods I and II due to the absence of recruitment or external direction as suggested by the definitional criteria of consciousness as summarized by Mills or treated by Lenin. Therefore, the songs are limited to "Public Witness" phenomena, rather than a specific racial or class orientation.[29]

TABLE 1 Magnetic-Rhetorical Song Distribution by Percentages

	Total (N)	Magnetic					Rhetorical			
		Percentage	(N)	External	Internal	Both	Percentage	(N)	Specific	Universal
1. I.W.W.	(48)	70.8	(34)	35.2	26.4	38.2	29.1	(14)	56.8	42.5
2. Songs of the People	(46)	67.3	(31)	28.8	14.7	28.8	32.6	(15)	60.0	40.0
3. Almanac Singers 1941	(7)	100.0	(7)	28.5	28.5	42.8	0		0	0
4. People's Song Book I 1948	(43)	58.1	(25)	35.9	23.9	39.9	41.8	(18)	83.6	16.4
5. People's Song Book II 1948 (control)	(20)	30.0	(6)	50.0	0	50.0	70	(14)	85.4	14.2
6. PSI Reprints 1946–48	(22)	31.7	(7)	14.4	42.8	42.8	68.2	(15)	73.0	26.3
7. Broadside 1962–64	(138)	23.1	(34)	28.1	28.1	43.7	76.8	(106)	81.1	18.8
8. We Shall Overcome, SNCC songbook 1964	(80)	95.0	(57)	5.0	50.8	49.9	5.0	(3)	33.3	66.7

As Table 1 suggests, a percentage increase in rhetorical songs has occurred with an inverse decline in magnetic songs. This is with the exception of the material from the SNCC songbook. However, these songs are primarily internally oriented. This decline is found to be associated with the fall of so-called working class social movements, as noted.

A chi-square test was made in order to distinguish the differences between the periods exhibiting activity by working, leftist class social movements and the two periods in which they were on the decline. The rationale for the usage of χ^2 is that this measure of association indicates whether or not the degree of association between these variables departs significantly from an association that might be expected on the basis of chance alone. Thus, the greater the difference between the theoretical (expected) number of types of songs from the actual (observed) number of songs associated with each type of social movement—the more significant the relationship will be.

TABLE 2   Songs

Movements	Magnetic (External, Internal, and Both)		Rhetorical (Specific and Universal)	
structural	72° (52.2)^t		29° (50.1)^t	101
event	102° (121.8)^t		138° (116.9)^t	240
	174		167	341=N

χ^2=23.53

As this table suggests, we can conclude that the association of working class movements to magnetic songs is highly significant, since the probability of obtaining a χ^2 value this large may be attributed to chance only one out of 100 times.

Also a greater than chance association is to be expected between social movements that are class oriented and songs that reflect a high degree of class consciousness (magnetic) and that are designed to appeal to listeners outside the movement than between those movements and songs that exhibit a high degree of class consciousness (magnetic) and that are not designed to appeal to receivers outside the movement.

As the table suggests, the findings are significant at the .05 level of significance. A derived χ^2 of 4.83, as against a tabled value of 3.84 could have been obtained only five times out of a hundred on the basis of chance alone. However, given $4.83 < 6.635$, the results are not significant at the .01 level, i.e., a χ^2 of 4.83 could have been expected on the basis of chance alone at this level.

FINDINGS

The survey of propaganda songs as manifested in the four periods of maximum song activity suggests the following: (1) there has been a marked decline in the magnetic propaganda song and a rise in the rhetorical song; (2) propaganda songs have become increasingly specific in terms of issues and events; (3) propaganda songs as an indicator of class consciousness find a decrease in the class orientation of social and political movements; (4) the usage

TABLE 3   Songs

Movements	Magnetic		
	External	Internal	
Structural			
(IWW to Almanac Singers)	23° (17.6)^t	24° (29.4)^t	47
Event			
(PSI to SNCC)	16° (21.4)^t	41° (35.6)^t	57
	39	65	104=N

$\chi^2=4.83$

of propaganda songs suggests a sharp decline in working class or proletarian movements in the United States.

CONCLUSION

The change in emphasis in propaganda songs on a longitudinal scale suggests several fundamental changes in the polis and the degree of class orientation or class consciousness in social movements considered left-of-center on the American political continuum. The change of orientation from the magnetic song to the rhetorical song correlates with the decline or virtual extinction of numerous ideological movements. The Industrial Workers of the World, the militant industrial unions of the thirties, and the sectarian Left, that is, ideological movements adhering to the philosophies of Lenin and Trotsky, have all experienced their influence and membership peaks and have been dissolved into radical political obscurity. The labor movement appears to have been legitimized into a "respectable" social institution. The sectarian Left today has little if any political import, even amongst the members of the so-called "new left." The decline of these social movements, in the sense of significance, correlates with the reduction of class consciousness found in the content analysis of the songs. The data suggest that class consciousness in relation to radical social movements has tended to point in the inverse direction from the Marxian model, that is, from the second phase of a "class for itself" to "a class in itself." This phenomenon may be approached from two directions: (1) the decline of class conscious movements; (2) the lack of success of class oriented movements due to the false class images found in the United States by students of social stratification. The material or song content implies a correlation with a reduction of ideological movements, e.g., the Broadside sample contains 5 labor songs.

The emergence of contemporary "protest publics" and reformist move-ments, such as the civil rights movement, does not alter the fundamental po-sition of this examination. Songs identified with the "new left" are predomi-nantly reflective of individual rather than collective consciousness. Further, following the lead of several folk entrepreneurs—Bob Dylan, Joan Baez—rhe-torical songs are rapidly being replaced by songs of symbolic introspective pro-test, rock and roll. The songs of the civil rights movement are internally di-rected to adherents, emphasizing the unity function of "we shall overcome" as contrasted to class fur sich.

In sum, this work suggests that propaganda songs might be used as sugges-tive indicators of the organizational and ideological orientations of social move-ments. However, the overall results of songs as tools of mobilization are diffi-cult, if impossible, to ascertain at this writing.[30]

NOTES

[1] V. I. Lenin, "What Is To Be Done?" in Collected Works (New York, 1929), IV, 113–54.

[2] C. Wright Mills, White Collar (New York, 1956), p. 325.

[3] Lenin, op. cit., p. 139.

[4] Harold D. Lasswell and Dorothy Blumenstock, World Revolutionary Propaganda (New York, 1939), pp. 89–94; Arlene E. Kaplan, "A Study of Folksinging in a Mass Society," Sociologus, 5:19 (1955).

[5] This definition in the context of the paper refers to those propaganda songs dealing with sociopolitical ideologies and events in the framework of the polity. See R. Serge Denisoff, "Songs of Persuasion: A Sociological Analysis of Urban Propaganda Songs," Journal of American Folklore, 79:581–89 (1966), for a further discussion of the defini-tions and criteria of propaganda songs.

[6] Ibid., pp. 582–84.

[7] The term "folk entrepreneur" is employed here rather than folk singer to distinguish the performer from traditional folk singers from a folk community. The term can be defined as a composer or performer of songs in the folk idiom employing and utilizing the style and method of a folk song for purposes other than self-entertainment, e.g., economic or ideological goals.

[8] Robert K. Merton and Paul F. Lazarsfeld, "Communication, Taste, and Social Action," in Communication of Ideas, ed. Lyman Bryson (New York, 1948), p. 115.

[9] In 1941 the Almanac Singers recorded "The Ballad of October 16th," critical of President Roosevelt. The basic theme of the song indicated FDR would not be happy until "everybody's dead." Several years after the song's appearance the Almanacs were publicly sanctioned and discharged from the Office of War Information due in part to this song. "OWI Plows Under the Almanac Singers," New York Times, Jan. 5, 1941, p. 9.

[10] Irving Howe and Lewis Coser, The American Communist Party: A Critical History (Boston, 1957), p. 371.

[11] Ibid., pp. 372–73.

[12] Peter Seeger, "People's Songs and Singers," New Masses, July 16, 1946, p. 9; also Woody Guthrie, "People's Songs," The Worker, Mar. 13, 1946, p. 7.

[13] Gusfield defines this phenomenon in these terms: "Expressive movements are marked by goalless behavior or by pursuit of goals which are unrelated to the discontents from which the movement had its source." Joseph R. Gusfield, The Symbolic Crusade (Urbana, Ill., 1963), p. 23.

[14] By "relative" is meant that the political climate of a given period is not identical to another, e.g., the labor movement.

[15] John Greenway, *American Folksongs of Protest* (New York, 1960), p. 174.

[16] The pocket songbook employed by the IWW was of the model employed at revival meetings in the nineteenth century. This propaganda technique was also emulated by the CPUSA, CIO, and later the AFL-CIO. The songs contained in the book are frequently introduced in a fashion to place them in ideological context. These introductions have been held constant in this analysis. One factor accounting for this transference of artifacts and techniques has been the mobility of members from one movement to another, e.g., IWW to CPUSA; see John S. Gambs, *The Decline of the IWW* (New York, 1932), pp. 82–91.

[17] *Songs of the People* (New York, 1937).

[18] The tables include only songs employed by PSI in a propagandistic manner in their songbooks, excluding songs which may deal with a proletarian situation, but which outside of an ideological context are not propagandistic, i.e., Negro spirituals of symbolic protest such as "Let My People Go." Many of these songs contained introductions placing them in a proletarian context; however, the songs themselves were not propaganda songs in terms of the definitional criterion.

[19] One observer indicated that "Union Maid" is far better known on college campuses than it is in the average union hall. Peter Seeger, "Whatever Happened to Singing in the Unions," *Sing Out* (May, 1965), p. 31. A similar phenomenon occurred in the civil rights movement. See Anne Braden, "Highlander Folk School—The End and the Beginning," *Sing Out* (Feb.–Mar., 1962), pp. 30–31; and Josh Dunson, *Freedom in the Air: Song Movements of the 60's* (New York, 1965), pp. 33–43.

[20] Jack Newfield, "The Student Left," *Nation* (May 10, 1965), pp. 491–95; Michael Munk, "New Left: The Ideological Bases," *National Guardian* (Sept. 25, 1965), pp. 3–4; and for a sociological treatment, R. Peter Lewis, "The New Left: A Political Movement?" (unpubl. paper, San Francisco College, 1966).

[21] R. Serge Denisoff and William F. Segen, "The Haight-Asbury Sub-Culture: A Descriptive Analysis of a Contemporary Bohemia" (mimeograph; San Francisco State College, 1966), pp. 63–68.

[22] Dunson, *op. cit.*, p. 29.

[23] *Ibid.*, p. 29.

[24] Peter Seeger, "You Can't Write Down Freedom Songs," *Sing Out* (July, 1965), p. 11; and Sam Clark, "Freedom Songs and the Folk Process," *Sing Out* (Feb.–Mar., 1964), pp. 13–14.

[25] *Ibid.*, p. 11.

[26] Guy Carawan and Candie Carawan, *We Shall Overcome* (New York, 1963).

[27] Josh Dunson, "Freedom Singing Gathering in the Heart of Dixie," *Sing Out* (Sept., 1964), pp. 34–35.

[28] National Educational Network, "Freedom Songs," 1964.

[29] See Myrdal's discussion of race and class consciousness in Gunnar Myrdal, *An American Dilemma* (New York, 1944), pp. 676–83.

[30] R. Serge Denisoff and Carol Denisoff, "Interpretations of Propaganda Songs in the Mass Media" (unpublished paper, Simon Fraser University, 1967).

FREEDOM: COMMUNICATION RIGHTS AND CENSORSHIP

The theme of freedom and human rights is scarcely new. Rather, it is as old as man himself. In the story of the creation in Genesis, God could have kept primeval man untouched by evil. Instead, God endowed man with free will. Thereby, Adam and Eve protested what they thought was a denial of their most fundamental human right—the pursuit of a knowledge equal to God's. Or they sought, as the Greek Protagoras postulated and men of the Enlightenment echoed, to make man the measure of all things. Man's urgent quest for his human rights and basic freedoms has not abated through the centuries. His great human documents and convenants: the Mosaic law, the Twelve Roman Tables, the Christian promise, the Magna Charta, the American Declaration of Independence, and, most recently, the Universal Declaration of Human Rights and the Universal Declaration Against Colonialism have all attested to man's longing to be free. These rights have come to mean not only John Lock's "inalienable rights to life, liberty, and the pursuit of happiness," including the freedoms of speech, worship, information, assembly, press, self-rule, and the overthrow of a despotic government, as we in the West traditionally view these rights, but also freedoms from fear, hunger, human bondage, and oppression of whatever sort. Under Moses, captive Israel voted "with their feet" when they fled en masse from their Egyptian captors, using the only form of protest available to them. The same protest has been used extensively in massive flights from tyranny of all sorts, including recently the Nazis, the communists, and the African Portuguese colonies. A large number of young Americans have fled to Canada to avoid the draft.

The 1968 Tehran Proclamation on the Universal Declaration of Human Rights said that it "states a common understanding of the peoples of the world concerning the inalienable and inviolable rights of all members of the human family." The World Council of Churches in its 1968 World Assembly at Uppsala, Sweden, affirmed: "Nations should recognize that the protection of fundamental human rights and freedom has now become a common concern of the whole international community, and should therefore not regard international concern for the implementation of these rights as an unwarranted interference."

In the first of his addresses to the United Nations, Sekou Touré, President of Guinea, challenged the assembled delegates:

At a time when the United States and Soviet peoples are striving to widen man's domain and extend it to the moon, Africa is surely justified in asking why colonialism persists in its effort to maintain its domination over Africa's

461

people and wealth. Can human progress conquer outer space and reach the moon without first being able to give the colonial peoples freedom and dignity?

Now, in 1959, all but one of the continents are completely free; the exception is the fifth—Africa. . . .

While mankind is progressing towards a truly unified society with all the benefits of opportunity, experience and human resources, Africa seems like an imprisoned land, excluded from human achievement, deprived of its most fundamental rights and of its most valid reason for existence.

. . . Guinea prefers freedom in poverty to opulence in slavery, we believe it also our duty to declare before the members of this Assembly that, with the prospect of a rapid and democratic development of Africa, we, the national leaders of the Republic of Guinea, prefer to be the last in a united Africa than first in a divided Africa [Touré 1970a:169–183].

Consistently, Touré and other third-world leaders have since reminded their audiences at the United Nations of the steady march of men toward freedom. In 1960 he recalled his 1959 statement that "the liberty of Africa is indivisible and indissolubly bound up with the liberty of the whole world." He repeated his urgent pleas for "Members of the United Nations to remember that a world divided cannot stand, and that a state of affairs can no longer be tolerated in which one half of the world lives in bondage and misery while the other half enjoys liberty and plenty." Unfortunately, he argued, a year later the colonialist forces had strengthened their oppression and exploitation. Still, he believed that a central theme of the United Nations Charter "is that peace cannot be safeguarded if oppression, injustice and economic exploitation persist in the world, if peoples are deprived of the barest minimum and, finally, if certain Governments are free to impose on other peoples systems of tyranny and violence conducive to the perpetuation of their own privileges" (Touré 1970b:611–642).

When Premier Khrushchev presented a draft resolution granting immediate independence to all colonial peoples, President Touré delayed his departure from New York at the end of the 1960 Summit Meeting to represent the African and Asian heads of state and heads of government who had already left:

Every age has its own imperatives. The fundamental imperative of our age is respect for the freedom of all peoples and the establishment of world peace, for the progressive development of all nations. . . . There can be no doubt that the problem of freedom is the greatest problem in the world. No people and no thinking person can think that freedom is divisible or that it belongs to a single people, race, or religion. . . . Freedom, both from a moral and philosophical and from a historical point of view, is not the concern of colonial or former colonial peoples alone. When a colony is freed, the metropolitan country is made free [Touré 1970c:643–648].

During the 1970 twenty-fifth anniversary celebrations and the Tenth Anniversary Celebrations of the Declaration on the Granting of Independence to Colonial Countries and Peoples, speaker after speaker recognized that although twenty-six new nations had been granted indepependence since 1960, twenty-eight million persons were still under colonial domination, eighteen million of whom lived in southern Africa. A major topic of concern was the apartheid policies of South Africa and Rhodesia. In his essay, "The U.N. and Human Rights," published a year before the anniversary in Foreign Affairs, Morris B. Abram (1969:363–374) stresses that although the General Assembly's Special Committee on Apartheid focused energetically on the Union of South Africa, with a few other exceptions, the United Nations bodies have failed to give detailed attention to other charges involving the denial of human rights. He argues that governments avoid criticizing other governments for fear of alienating them or for fear of retaliation. Criticism thus is voiced as an adjunct to a military or political conflict. He reflected:

> At the last session of the Human Rights Commission, one representative of a "nonaligned nation" told me candidly: "We'd like to condemn the Soviet Union for its repression of intellectuals; we'd like to condemn the United States because of Viet Nam. We cannot afford to do either, so we'll support a condemnation of Israel for reprisals against Arab sabotage" [Abram 1969:366].

Abram believes that:

> Although Americans have long cherished the concept of free speech, press, religion and assembly, they were unaccustomed to, and seriously questioned, the notion that individuals also had the "right" to a job, to leisure, education, medical care, housing and social security. Despite the "Four Freedoms," which included "freedom from want," some Americans still do not understand that the Universal Declaration's economic and social rights like our own Constitution's political safeguards, are not luxuries, but necessities for a free and viable society. . . .
> The Universal Declaration of Human Rights proscribes distinctions "of any kind, such as race, colour, sex, language, religion, political or other opinion, national or social origin, property, birth or other status. . . ."
> This places a grave responsibility on the major powers, and especially the United States, which has always been the most vocal spokesman for human rights in the international arena. Unless we succeed in solving our own racial and other problems of human rights—and unless we speak the same language in the U.S. Senate that we use in the Human Rights Commission and other international forums—we will find we are forfeiting the leadership and respect we once enjoyed [Abram 1969: 369–374].

In the first essay in this section, "Fredom, A Neglected Area for Social Research," Charles W. Hobart concludes that freedom of self-determination seems to be an especially crucial issue today, as a potentiality because of the nature of man and as an opportunity and a necessity because of the nature of contemporary society. Because of the confusion of values in Western culture, Hobart contends that man is forced to actualize his own uniqueness, which is his potential, by choosing his own value commitments when there is no authority to do it for him. If freedom is the opportunity to express oneself, Hobart suggests that it involves knowing oneself and choosing between real alternatives. The case can be made for the newly emerging nation or culture, that the basis of its freedom is in knowing its own nationhood or

culturehood and then expressing itself by making conscious choices between
values of one ideological system and another or by accepting those values of
each system that lead to the self-fulfillment of the nation or the culture.
Touré's conscious choice between being last in a united Africa rather than
first in a divided Africa, and living in freedom in poverty rather than living
enslaved in opulence are among the defining characteristics that he as an
African nationalist wishes his people, and the people of Africa, to adopt as an
aspect of determining their own destiny.

The Soviet author A. P. Chermenina is the writer of the second essay
included in this section, "The Concept of Freedom in Marxist-Leninist
Ethics." She takes issue with the Western concept of self-determination as an
aspect of freedom, in that in Western philosophy, self-determination constitutes
the limit to which one can go in recognizing the dialectics of freedom and
determinism, external and internal, objective and subjective. She regards the
concept of self-determination as evidence, on the one hand, of the dissatisfaction of the most serious students of ethics with metaphysical extremes
in solutions to the problems of freedom and, on the other hand, as proof
of their incapacity to counterpose to Marxism any idealist treatment of the
problem that is at all persuasive. The distinctive feature of Marxist reflections
on freedom, Chermenina believes, is that the psychological foundation of
freedom is examined in a context of societal relations which affect the
individual. Thereby, the Marxist perceives the creative activity of the individual,
the nature of the individual creativity, and the influence of the individual's
creativity on the world outside himself, which questions why he chooses one
alternative over another and in what sense he is free. Chermenina concludes
that true freedom assumes that individual personal freedom depends upon the
freedom of the class or society as a whole and thus social freedom determines
the framework, limits, and opportunities pertaining to the creative activity of
the individual, that is, to his own freedom.

Considerable criticism has been leveled at the socialist governments of
Eastern Europe for alleged repressions of individual freedoms. The Soviet
trials of such authors and scholars as Siniavsky, Daniel, Khaustov, Bukovsky,
Ginzburg, Galanskov, Dobrovolsky, and Lashkova (Smith 1968:151) have
not only attracted world-wide attention but also received a great deal of
exposure in the Soviet Union. In May 1967, Alexsandr Solzhenitsyn, the
author of such novels as One Day in the Life of Ivan Denisovich, originally
acclaimed by Premier Khrushchev when he accelerated the period of de-
Stalinization, and The First Circle and Cancer Ward, sent an open letter to
the Fourth USSR Writer's Congress demanding that the Soviet Constitution
be honored by making a total and unqualified abolition of literary censorship
in the Soviet Union. He received much support from a number of fellow-writers
in publicly signed petitions supporting his "Open Letter," but the secretary
of the Union of Writers left his letter unanswered until September 1967,
when the first of several meetings was held with Solzhenitsyn at which he was
generally berated for failing to develop positive heroes as prescribed by Socialist
Realism (see, for example, Monas 1967: 44–56) and for an offensive tone
against Soviet morality, customs, and ideology. In June 1968, Literaturnaia

Gazeta denounced him for his "demagogic behavior," for "attacking the fundamental principles that guide Soviet literature," and for "maliciously slandering the Soviet System," and warned him to cease his anti-Soviet activities. The 1968 trials of four young Soviet citizens "for anti-Soviet agitation and propaganda" earned them labor-camp sentences of from one to seven years. Four hundred intellectuals signed public petitions in their behalf.

Solzhenitsyn's experiences with mental institutions, house arrests, and trials, and the widely unauthorized publication of his works abroad, without the privilege of copyright, since the Soviet Union has never joined the International Copyright Convention, coupled with his receiving the Nobel Prize for Literature have made him, like Pasternak, one of the most widely known Soviet authors outside of the Soviet Union. It is curious that when One Day in the Life of Ivan Denisovich was first printed in 1962 in Novyi Mir, which was subsequently unable to publish Cancer Ward because of adverse pressure from the government and the Writers' Union, the historical novel of the Stalin labor camps was acclaimed by Premier Khrushchev and widely praised in Soviet literary magazines. When Khrushchev fell from power, such writing quickly became no longer acceptable. I suspect that Solzhenitsyn would have had no disagreement with the idea consistently proposed to him by members of the secretariat of the Writers' Union that Socialist Realism demanded that the Soviet people and government be portrayed in a favorable light, nor with the concept of individual freedom that is moulded by the context of social freedom as postulated by Chermenina. However, it seems clear from his "Open Letter" and subsequent letters and his transcripts of hearings by the secretariat of the Writers' Union, as well as from the cases of other writers and intellectuals who were tried for anti-Soviet activities and propaganda, that he considered statements made against him by government officials and fellow writers slanderous and that he believed he was being deprived of his legally established rights as provided by the Soviet Constitution (see Weiner 1968; Friedberg 1968; "Writers and Censors" 1968; and Smith 1968). Because of the interest that his "Open Letter" aroused both within the Soviet Union and abroad, and its relevance to the study of communication rights and censorship as aspects of freedom, I am presenting the letter in its entirety.

Without attempting to balance the Soviet and American theory and practice concerning communication rights and their denial, the essay by Haig Bosmajian, "Speech and the First Amendment," nevertheless demonstrates clearly that except for speech which forms a clear and present danger to those involved in the situation, whether as speakers or audience, or speech which seeks the forcible overthrow of legally constituted government, or speech which is inherently obscene (O'Neil 1966), speech in various forms in the United States is protected by the First Amendment of the Constitution. Even these three traditional restrictions have been challenged consistently in various legal cases recently before the courts. One of the critical problems that Bosmajian feels the scholar and those who use speech in America, as well as the courts, must face is the role of symbolic action as a communicative event. He places the onus of protecting the freedom of speech in America less on the courts and more directly on the ordinary citizen who is responsible for electing a congressman such as F. Edward Hebert, who proposed that "we forget about the First Amendment" in order to prosecute antiwar and civil-rights spokesmen, or who is responsible for decisions initially to censor or not to censor, to ban or not to ban, or to grant or deny others their constitutionally protected rights to free speech (see also, for example, Goldberg 1968 on freedom of information as a basic human right).

Freedom of the press has generally been acknowledged throughout the world at least as a concept. Raymond Nixon, in his 1965 study of "Freedom in the World's Press: A Fresh Appraisal with New Data" (1965), indicates that every government in the world (117 countries were rated in his study) now pays at least lip service to the principles of press freedom, which is significant; for though the guarantee of freedom may be counter-weighted by controls, the very presence of the word "freedom" stresses that even dictators acknowledge its wide appeal. Further, Nixon believes that as the level of literacy and education increases and as communication among the world's peoples accelerates, the difference between the symbol and the reality of freedom should diminish still more. His study suggests a correlation between press freedom and economic development, literacy, and growth of the mass media. Because the data was often gathered from official government sources, the discrepancy between the actual and stated situation might be considerable, for example, in the case of Paraguay where the official adult illiteracy rate is only 34 percent, whereas the unofficial figures suggest a rate as high as 80 percent. Additionally, GNP measures accepted by Western economists are not accepted by socialist economists, and thus no comparable measures are standardized. Nixon concludes that economic and social development favor the development of freedom in every sphere, including freedom of the press. Thus one can assume that, even in dictatorial states, internal and external pressure will force the leaders to permit more freedom than less.

A former reporter of the Cape Times, Trevor Brown, in his essay "Free Press Fair Game for South Africa's Government," assesses the situation for the press in South Africa. The press may oppose government policies but cannot expose practices and policies that it finds undesirable. A key problem both for the English and the Afrikaans press is that they consistently are forced to operate in an ambiguous state, without knowing clearly whether any specific item has violated a specific but vague regulation wihch the government has set up as "prejudicial to the interest of the Republic." Brown cites George Oliver, president of the South African Society of Journalists, who complained that the South African press had entered a "new dark era in which the normal means of communication enjoyed elsewhere in the enlightened world will be sacrificed for secrecy, acute apprehension and ever-present peril." Brown concludes that despite the fear which the government has tried to instill in the press and the continuing government domination of the Afrikaans' press, English journalists are beginning to examine their performance with an eye toward introspective improvement, and the Afrikaans journalists are beginning to question their press ideology. Both of these actions offer hope that the presses may become respected adversaries rather than partisan opponents.

Tony Vinson and Arthur Robinson, in their essay "Censorship and the

Australian Public," attempt to assess public tolerance of criticism of organized religion, the monarchy, and censorship as samples of contentious issues about which "dangerous" views are sometimes expressed. The study demonstrates the actual sensitivity of the majority of Australians to critical assessments or satirical treatment of controversial issues over the mass media. Three of every four persons questioned in Sydney and Melbourne supported the idea of public discussion in the mass media of critical opinions of the monarchy, organized religion, and censorship. However, the authors agree that the public interest in open discussion of controversial questions is at odds with official government positions that have been very restrictive of what subjects can be discussed in public meetings, on radio and television, and through the print medium.

The final essay, "The Quasi-Theory of Communication and the Management of Dissent" by Peter M. Hall and John P. Hewitt, stresses a preoccupation with communication, its presence or absence, its process, and its style in the Nixon handling of events surrounding the 1970 introduction of American troops into Cambodia, the massive American student involvement throughout the United States in protest of the Cambodian incursion, and the deaths of American students at the hands of National Guardsmen. The management of dissent is often more subtle than outright denial of human and civil rights. Still, Hall and Hewitt believe that the American government found itself unable to communicate with a whole young generation whose ideological and cultural values were different from those of President Nixon and his key advisers. The authors explore the cultural and situational bases from which the administration tried to manipulate and manage the dissenters and the failures that occurred on both sides. Hall and Hewitt discovered that an important attempt was made on the part of the administration to offer symbolic assurance of right intentions, both to American and foreign publics and also to the young American dissenters. Unfortunately, these assurances were offered too late or appeared superficial to the dissenters and may have served to further polarize conflicting opinions about American involvement in Indochina (see also Benson and Johnson 1968).

REFERENCES CITED

ABRAM, MORRIS B.
   1969   The U.N. and human rights. Foreign Affairs 47:363–374.
BENSON, THOMAS W. and
BONNIE JOHNSON
   1968   The rhetoric of resistance: confrontation with the warmakers. Today's Speech 16:35–42.
FRIEDBERG, MAURICE
   1968   What price censorship? Problems of Communism 17:18–23.
GOLDBERG, ARTHUR J.
   1968   Freedom of information, a basic human right. Department of State Bulletin April 1:452–455.
MONAS, SIDNEY
   1967   In defense of socialist realism. Problems of Communism 16:44–56.
NIXON, RAYMOND B.
   1965   Freedom in the world's press: a fresh appraisal with new data. Journalism Quarterly 42:3–14, 118–119.

O'NEIL, ROBERT M.
1966 Free speech: responsible communication under law. Indianapolis.
PROBLEMS OF COMMUNISM
1968 Writers and censors 17:37–58.
SMITH, PAUL A., JR.
1968 Protest in Moscow. Foreign Affairs 47:151–163.
TOURÉ, SEKOU
1970a African freedom is indivisible. *In* Sow the wind, reap the whirlwind: heads of state address the United Nations. Michael H. Prosser, ed. New York.
1970b The real path for Africa is a path of freedom and dignity, a path of peace. *In* Sow the wind, reap the whirlwind: heads of state address the United Nations. Michael H. Prosser, ed. New York.
1970c The problem of freedom is the greatest problem in the world. *In* Sow the wind, reap the whirlwind: heads of state address the United Nations. Michael H. Prosser, ed. New York.
WEINER, STEPHEN
1968 Socialist legality on trial. Problems of Communism 17:6–13.

FREEDOM, A NEGLECTED AREA
FOR SOCIAL RESEARCH

Charles W. Hobart

CHARLES W. HOBART was born in 1926 in Swatow, China of American-born
Baptist missionary parents. Graduating summa cum laude with a B.A. in sociology
from the University of Redlands, he took his M.A. in sociology at the University
of Southern California and completed his Ph.D. in sociology at Indiana University.
Originally interested in social organization theory and social psychology, with
special reference to the substantive area of courtship and family, he has more recently
developed an interest in urban sociology and minority-group relations. He has
taught at the University of Redlands, as a visiting professor at Pomona College,
and is currently a professor at the University of Alberta. He has received grants from
the Social Science Research Council and the Haynes Foundation in the United
States and grants from the Canada Council, the Canadian federal and the Alberta
provincial governments. The Royal Commission on Bilingualism and Biculturalism
is publishing his book Italian Immigrants in Edmonton: Adjustment and Integration,
and the University of Toronto Press is bringing out his Adjustment of
Ukrainians in Alberta, which he coauthored with J. T. Borhek, A. P. Jacoby,
and W. E. Kalbach. His Eskimo Education in Residential Schools, a Descriptive
and Comparative Report will be forthcoming. He has also published articles in the
Journal of American Indian Education, Canadian Review of Sociology and
Anthropology, The American Journal of Sociology, the Journal of Existentialism,
Canadian Social Problems, Marriage and Family Living, the Journal of Social
Psychology, Social Forces, and the Pacific Sociological Review.

A discipline, like a man, may be known by what it ignores as well
as by what it investigates. Like a man, also, the areas which it as-
siduously avoids may reflect unresolved infantile conflicts, refusal to acknowledge relationship to a parent where the struggle for emancipation has been a
recent and desperate one. The studied ignoring of ESP phenomenon by American psychology is a case in point.[1] Equally remarkable is the extent to which
American sociology has ignored love, one of the more common of "interpersonal relationships," and freedom.[2] This paper seeks to demonstrate that
"freedom" does exist in several senses which are meaningful to behavioral
science, that it is amenable to empirical inquiry, and that it is an important
area for investigation.

THE CASE FOR FREEDOM

The explanatory model subscribed to implicitly or explicitly by most sociologists and social psychologists is a deterministic one: A man is as he is because

Reprinted with permission of Ethics: An International Journal of Social, Political, and
Legal Philosophy, 75 (April 1965), 153–165.

of the interaction of his genetic and cultural heritages. Given these determinants, he could not be other than he is: he cannot escape his past, cannot jump out of his socializational skin. He can continue to learn, but what he learns is a result of the interaction of the situations he encounters and his response to them, which is a function of his past. The system here described is largely a closed system. Perhaps it is prematurely closed.

If behavioral scientists continue to ignore, and thus to avoid attempting to make sense of, the concept of freedom, many questions about human behavior which are important both theoretically and practically must go unanswered.

A. H. Maslow has noted that "practically every serious description of the 'authentic person' extant implies that such a person, by virtue of what he has become, assumes a new relation to his society, and indeed, to society in general. He not only transcends himself in various ways; he also transcends his culture. He resists enculturation. He becomes more detached from his culture and from his society. He becomes a little more a member of his species and a little less a member of his local group."[3]

How can man, if determined by his culture, come to transcend his culture? It would seem to be an impossibility. But before Maslow's statement is dismissed as the wishful thinking of an existential psychologist, let us consider some parallel assumptions by sociologists. The most widely known is Riesman's characterization of the autonomous man in The Lonely Crowd. "The 'autonomous' are those who on the whole are capable of conforming to the behavioral norms of their society . . . but are free to choose whether to conform or not."[4] Erich Fromm distinguishes "negative freedom," freedom "from all bonds that once gave meaning and security to life"[5] from "positive freedom" which "consists in the spontaneous activity of the total, integrated personality."[6] He further says that "spontaneous activity" is not the activity of the automaton, which is the uncritical adoption of patterns suggested from the outside" but "is free activity of the self . . . of one's free will."[7] The title and the description on the dust jacket of Winston White's book Beyond Conformity—"A bold attack on the view that the growing complexity of American life is leading to conformity and cultural decline . . . and an exploration of new chances and challenges for individual development"—clearly presume some way of "transcending" conformity. Winston White does not even include the word freedom in his index, although he does write of modern man's "freedom to make a greater variety of choices,"[8] freedom to ask "Who am I?" But he has nothing to say concerning the circumstances under which man is able and is not able to "handle" this freedom. At one level, Émile Durkheim's answer was clear enough: Freedom, or anomie, leads to suicide, and it is thus important to find ways to reduce anomie.[9]

Philosophical and literary treatments of man's ability to transcend his culture, his society, his own earlier "self" are numerous. I shall make reference to only three. Peter Viereck's The Unadjusted Man protests against a "Procrustean and rather ga-ga normalcy, determined by a continuous secret plebiscite to which inner spontaneity is continually sacrificed."[10] Viereck describes the unadjusted man as, in the eyes of the majority, "a laughable Quixote, too unadjusted to settle down with a steady, productive windmill," whose values are not determined by a plebiscite. He may "even be arrogant enough to retort, 'One man and God make a majority,' when accused of being undemocratic for not joining the majority in filtering his reading through the roughage-removal machinery of the digest magazines."[11]

Colin Wilson describes *The Outsider* as "a man who cannot live in the comfortable, insulated world of the Bourgeois, accepting what he sees and touches as reality. 'He sees too deep and too much,' and what he sees is essentially chaos."[12] Thus the outsider—one such as Nietzsche, Van Gogh, T. E. Lawrence, Nijinsky, or Kierkegaard, for example—seeing too deeply, sees through society's thin but orderly grid over reality, awakens to chaos, and can never again experience the world as the same straightforward place. He can no longer accept society's definitions of reality, order, meaning, purpose, value, or of his own identity.

Morse Peckham describes what he conceives to be the only possible solution to the outsider's problem in his conclusion to *Beyond the Tragic Vision: The Quest for Identity in the Nineteenth Century.*

Value arises when identity creates itself by symbolizing itself in aesthetic structure, but these new values must themselves, since they are but instruments, be continually restructured. . . . Once the artist has created a style which symbolizes his identity . . . it threatens to degenerate into a mannerism . . . his identity begins to fade . . . continuous transformation (of style) meant a continuous renewal of identity. It was an endless . . . transvaluation of aesthetic values, for it was a continuously renewed encounter of the structuring mind with reality. . . .
Nietzsche discovered that the true dialogue of the mind lies in the eternally transvaluating encounter between the mind's instrumental constructs and reality in a continuous restructuring of orientations. Further, in that dialectic process between reality and the mind's instruments lie identity, order, meaning, and therefore value, constantly being lost as the instruments dull and break on reality's contradictions, and constantly being renewed as the mind forges new instruments . . . to renew the struggle to master the world. The world is nothingness; the midnight bell wakes us from that nothingness to struggle with nothingness, and in that struggle we forge, and continuously reforge, our identities.[13]

An adequate sociology of freedom would make possible the bridging of the gap between the "humanities," with their emphasis on man as free, creative, and responsible, and the behavioral sciences with their approach to man as conditioned and determined. This would be highly desirable but is currently impossible. It would begin to reverse the situation, which has worried Christian Bay, C. Wright Mills, Robert MacIver,[14] and many others, where the activities of sociologists and psychologists tend to sabotage democracy and jeopardize the future of human freedom and dignity by increasing the ways of manipulating human behavior. "It is about time, I submit," Bay writes, "that behavioral scientists pay more attention to the opposite side of the manipulation problem: How can increased insights into human behavior be employed in the service of sheltering the growth of individuality and freedom in modern society?"[15]

And, more narrowly, an adequate sociology of freedom would probably help to explain some of the "failures of conditioning" which sociologists have traditionally been interested in: the non-delinquent who grows up in the high delinquency area; the "rebel without a cause" from a "good" middle-class background; spontaneity, innovation, creativity, which are perhaps among the hardest of behaviors to explain sociologically. Moreover, such a sociology of freedom is needed to complement and to round out a rather impressive if somewhat "far out" psychology-of-freedom literature which includes Allport's *Becoming*, Rogers' *On Being a Person*, Maslow's *Toward A Psychology of Being*, and Royce's *The Encapsulated Man*.[16]

THE LITERATURE ON FREEDOM

A number of books make a helpful contribution toward the formulation of a sociology of freedom. Malinowski defines freedom as "the conditions necessary and sufficient for the formation of a purpose, its translation into effective action through organized cultural instrumentalities and the full enjoyment of the results of such activity."[17] This leads him to emphasize throughout that freedom presupposes the structuring of a cultural system that includes the existence of law, an economic system, political organization, and people endowed with cultural motives, implements, and values.

Dorothy Lee characterizes freedom as "the opportunity for spontaneous functioning," "awareness of the unique tempo of the individual," personal autonomy, absence of coercion.[18] She points out that even primitive, homogeneous cultures characterized by very narrowly structured avenues of expression may permit a great deal of autonomy to the individual. "Actually," Lee notes, "it is in connection with the highest personal autonomy that we often find the most intricately developed [cultural] structure; and it is this structure that makes autonomy possible in a group situation."[19] She cites examples of societies in which a baby's hair is not cut until he asks to have it cut, in which the child is permitted "to explore and discover for himself, without any attempt to influence him." She concludes that "the individual, shown absolute respect from birth and valued as sheer being for his uniqueness, apparently learns with every experience to have this same respect and value for others; he is 'trained' to be constantly sensitive to the beginnings of others" and to refrain from infringing on their autonomy, thus granting a freedom completely foreign to our society.[20]

But it is only in a heterogeneous society that freedom itself becomes a consciously formulated issue. As a self-conscious issue it takes on a new dimension. Not only is it a matter of freedom to respond or not to respond, to do or not to do, as it is in a homogeneous society; it is a matter of the content of the response, *what* to do. There are choices between alternatives to be made.[21]

Most recent discussions of freedom, such as Felix Oppenheim's *Dimensions of Freedom*, have been concerned with its political aspects: freedom from coercion of arbitrary police power, economic power, personal influence.[22] These discussions are highly relevant for the sociology of institutions and political sociology, but they are not relevant to the crucial question: "*Can* man transcend determinism?"

Perhaps the most valuable single work available today, remarkable for its comprehensive, systematic, integrated, and well-informed discussion of many of the issues of freedom, is Christian Bay's *The Structure of Freedom*. Having defined freedom as "self-expression, or the individual's capacity, opportunity, and incentive to express whatever he is or can be motivated to express,"[23] Bay goes on to distinguish three main variants: psychological freedom, social freedom, and potential freedom. Psychological freedom he characterizes as "degree of harmony between basic motives and overt behavior" or, negatively, as the absence of defensiveness.[24] This definition is sensible of depth-psychology investigation of conscious and unconscious motives or needs and controls and may have fruitful implications for research in view of the "steady progress [that] has been made over the last decades, in finding ways to study both basic motives and conflicts between motives and behavior."[25]

Social freedom "means the relative absence of perceived external restraints on individual behavior," where restraint refers "to all the potential obstacles that limit the possibilities of individual choice or put penalties on alternatives,"[26] including both rewards and punishments. All of the traditional discussions of coercion, institutions, authority, power, and anomie are relevant to social freedom.

Potential freedom "means the relative absence of unperceived external restraints on individual behavior"[27] or, more poetically, it "means floodlighting the world in which the individual lives, making him aware of his resources, trends that affect his interests, alternative goals, and means he might strive for, alternative dangers he might wish to avoid."[28] The problem here posed, negatively, is freedom from unperceived manipulation, and, positively, it is the maintenance of conditions under which man can develop into what he has it within himself to become. Thus potential freedom means the sheltering of individuality against institutional and reformist pressures. Tocqueville's apprehension about extreme majoritarianism in the United States reflected his concern for potential freedom when he wrote that "the majority possesses a power that is physical and moral at the same time, which acts upon the will as much as upon the actions and represses not only all contest, but all controversy. I know of no country in which there is so little independence of mind and real freedom as in America."[29] Potential freedom presumes the ability to resist manipulation whenever the individual is pushed toward behavior detrimental to his own interests. It presumes some incentive to act unconventionally when the time comes, regardless of inconvenience or other consequences.[30]

In Bay's definition of freedom as "self expression, of the individual's capacity . . ." all three variants—freedom from defensive inhibition within oneself, from external coercion, and from subtle manipulation—are interrelated and integrated, without "stretching" the definition.

Mention must be made of another, monumental, work: Mortimer Adler's two-volume *The Idea of Freedom, a Dialectical Examination of the Conceptions of Freedom and the Controversies about Freedom*.[31] This work summarizes and analyzes twenty-five centuries of recorded thought on freedom.[32] Several definitions from this work are of interest. Adler's synthetic definition of freedom is: "A man is free who has in himself the ability or power whereby he can make what he does his own action and what he achieves his own property."⁵⁵ This definition seems less satisfactory than Bay's conception of self-expression because it does not imply awareness of the range of limitations of freedom as Bay's conception does.

Adler's analysis leads to the identification of three variants of freedom, "self-realization," "self-perfection," and "self-determination," which have some interesting implications. "Self-realization" refers to "an individual's ability to act as he wishes for the sake of the good as he sees it,"³⁴ which is dependent upon circumstances and is thus analogous to Bay's social and, to some extent, to his potential, freedom.

"Self-perfection" is "being able to will (and to live) as one ought."³⁵ Adler goes on to say: "The man who is able to will or live as he ought is one whose intentions or plan of life expresses his *higher or better self*. When that part of his makeup dominates his lower nature, or is at least not thwarted by a kind of inner coercion or constraint that arises from forces within himself, what he *ought* to will becomes identical with what he himself . . . desires to will."³⁶ The freedom of self-perfection is thus quite similar to Bay's psychological freedom. It is similar also to Maslow's distinction between the compulsive behavior of the deficiency-motivated person and the freer behaviors of the growth-motivated person.³⁷

"Self-determination" refers to an individual's "ability to determine for himself what he wishes to do or to become."³⁸ In elaborating on this conception Adler writes: "The decisions or plans a man makes are his own only if they are made *by him*, not just *in him* or *for him*. Even if nothing outside compelled him to make them, they are not initiated by him if their formation and adoption resulted from processes beyond his control. In order for his decisions or plans to be an instance of self-determination, they must be determined *by himself and nothing other than himself*."³⁹ This freedom is also clearly related to Bay's "psychological freedom," and it points to the fact that Bay does not clearly distinguish, as Adler does, between a person's ability to execute a projected self-concept he thinks he wants, or ought to do, and his ability to hammer out his own unique self-concept, to determine for himself what he is to become.

FREEDOM OF SELF-DETERMINATION

In the remainder of this paper I shall restrict my consideration to self-determinative freedom, for several reasons. The primary one is that the existence of social and potential freedom and the modes of attainment of these freedoms are non-problematic: There is little difficulty in envisaging absence of external coercion and manipulation, or in conceiving how these freedoms might be increased. However, psychological freedom, especially self-determination, is far more difficult for a behavioral scientist to conceive. How does one whose course of development is conditioned, determined, become self-determinative? It is the thesis of this paper that there are determinants of self-expressive freedom, of self-determination, which are compatible with the assumption of determinism. I shall sketch what I believe to be a theory of freedom of self-determination which is entirely compatible with what behavioral science knows about human behavior, and I shall suggest some of the research implications and applications of this theory.[40]

The character typologies developed by David Riesman in *The Lonely Crowd* provide a helpful way of organizing the remainder of this paper. Riesman describes four types of unfreedom as found in tradition-directed, inner-directed, other-directed, and anomic man; and one type of freedom as found in the autonomous man.

Of the tradition-directed pattern Riesman writes: "the type of social order we have been discussing is relatively unchanging [and] the conformity of the individual tends to reflect his membership in a particular age-grade, clan or caste; he learns to understand and appreciate patterns which have endured for centuries and are modified but slightly as the generations succeed each other. The important relationships of life may be controlled by careful and rigid etiquette. . . . Little energy is directed toward finding new solutions of the age-old problems."[41] "Conformity," he writes, is largely given in the "self-evident" social situation.[42]

Here freedom is not a conscious issue; only in a complex, heterogeneous society does the presence of alternatives shatter the single image of the way life is lived, its meaning, and its value. Only here is man at all generally confronted with the terror and the guilt of life-shaping decision.

The price of awareness of the broad range of alternatives available in heterogeneous society is anxiety, inescapable because of the extent to which the basic orientation to life is threatened with disruption. Unlike fear, anxiety is a diffuse feeling of uncertainty and helplessness. It is objectless because it is the object classification or value orientation of the person which is jeopardized. Rollo May's description of anxiety makes this clear: "In fine, the objectless nature of anxiety arises from the fact that the security base itself of the individual is threatened, and since it is in terms of this security base that the individual has been able to experience himself as a self in relation to objects, the distinction between subject and object also breaks down."[43]

Perhaps the easiest way to deal with this anxiety is through repression. Both the inner-directed and the other-directed man are characterized by a repression defense against anxiety and thus control the potentially disorienting consequences of open awareness of alternatives. One possibility is to internalize a value orientation, refuse to consider alternatives seriously, and ignore the fact that choice of the value orientation to be internalized was made by the accident of birth into his particular family, rather than some other. This is the solution of the inner-directed person who narrows the field of alternatives by a rigid value orientation and sense of self given him by others, usually parents. The stability of this commitment is probably most easily maintained by repressing awareness of other possibilities of commitment. The inner-directed man has the freedom of "self-perfection," but he is incapable of "self-determination."

The other-directed person is not value oriented and has a diffuse sense of self. His adjustment is that of chameleon-like adaption to the cues of others in the situation at hand. He is highly aware, in the sense of having "an exceptional sensitivity to the actions and wishes of others."[44] He sees alternatives; he experiences freedom of choice, the terror of decision. But the right decision for him is the *approved* decision not the decision in line with any consciously formulated value system. Hence his repression lies in his unawareness of the values involved or threatened by the manipulative and self-manipulative actions of his peers and himself. Although he is highly self-conscious, he tends to lose a unified sense of self, since it is an ever latent anxiety that keeps him open to the dictates of his peers.[45] Thus his *orientation* is never *established*, and his security is always threatened. Rollo May has stated this relationship as follows: "Mounting anxiety reduces self awareness. In proportion to the increase in anxiety, the awareness of one's self as a subject related to objects in the external world is confused."[46] Note that the other-directed person is capable of neither the freedom of "self-perfection" or of "self-direction."

Reisman's anomic category is a heterogeneous one. He describes anomic types as "maladjusted": "Those constitutionally and psychologically unable to conform or feel comfortable in the role . . . a society assigns."[47] More specifically, he is Colin Wilson's outsider: disoriented, immobilized by the chaos of alternatives. He discerns no authoritarian basis of choice, and he cannot escape into the changing adjustments of the other-directed person. As noted above, he is incapacitated because he sees too deeply. He sees beyond society's thin but orderly grid over reality; he has "awakened to chaos." He is the alienated man, aware of his differentness from other men, who is thereby made unable to relate to them.[48] And so he too is lacking in freedom of "self-perfection" because he has no sense of what he *ought* to will, and of course he too is unable to be "self-determinative." But if he is unable to become a "self-made man" he is at least not an "other-made man" as are both the inner- and the other-directed persons. Since he is free of the need to conform either to the expectations of others or to the dictates of a conscience fashioned for him by others, the way is open for him to be free if he can orient and motivate himself.

The free person is Riesman's autonomous man,[49] Adorno's non-authoritarian,[50] Rokeach's open-minded person.[51] He is, like the anomic, aware of alternatives but he is able to orient and reorient himself in their midst. An open, integrated, but evolving sense of value and of self provides a basis for choice.

There are four crucial characteristics which distinguish the free person. (1) He is able to tolerate the awareness of orientations different from his own, with their implied threat that his own orientations may be "wrong." (2) He is able to tolerate the awareness of the accidental nature of his value commitments, awareness that their origins are capricious since they were determined by his being born into *this* family, social class, region, nation, and age rather than into some other. He can tolerate the renewed threat that his orientation, dictated as it is by chance, may be wrong. (3) He is more able to stand alone: He does not need an authority figure, perhaps in the form of a rigid conscience, or a peer reference group as a constant source of assurance that he is right. (4) He is able to change his commitments; his orientation is dynamic. He is able to confront fully new alternatives, to evaluate them free of compulsive tendencies to accept or to reject, and, when he feels justified, to commit himself to them.

This is the essence of his freedom: He is able to move away from the early and chance socializational identifications of prematurity, is able to confront and choose between new value alternatives and so to be self-determinative, to choose and make himself.

There are two crucial questions suggested by this formulation: (1) How is the person able so uncommittedly to confront value alternatives that he can freely, of himself, choose between them, rather than choose on the basis of standards acquired from others, which are thus not "his own?" (2) If he is able to confront these value alternatives, how can he tolerate the anxiety intrinsic to the resulting shaking of the value foundations upon which his existence as a person is predicated?

The answer to the first question seems to be that this person has to some extent awakened to chaos: The values into which he was socialized, which were unquestioned, must become problematic for him. His earlier orientation must to some extent fall apart. It is Gibbs' contention that there are important pressures in contemporary American society which make for the value disorientation of people.[52] These can be thought of merely as value anomie, on the one hand, but they have social structural manifestations. They are tensions to which people may be exposed at different stages of the life cycle. The child, for example, may be caught between inner-directed parents and an other-directed school system, or between both and an other-directed peer group. As Miller and Swanson demonstrate in The Changing American Parent, bureaucracy-employed families tend toward other direction, but the impact of the church tends yet, in many ways, to encourage inner direction.[53] There appear to be a number of these institutionally channeled and structured stresses in contemporary American life. The consequences of these stresses for the value identifications and the awareness tolerances of people have not been studied by sociologists. There appears to be a variety of kinds of evidence (including not only that cited in The Lonely Crowd and The Changing American Parent but also works such as Orrin Klapp's Heroes, Villains, and Fools: The Changing American Character)[54] that there may be frequent repression of awareness, as in the inner- or other-direction modes of adjustment. There is need for more study of the unadjusted or the outsider, who, as both Viereck and Wilson stress, is maladjusted but not neurotic, and of the autonomous man in Riesman's sense of "those who are . . . capable of conforming to the behavioral norms of their society . . . but are free to choose whether to conform or not."[55]

It would appear that to become somewhat anomic, to sustain deterioration of one's value commitments, is a necessary condition for freedom. But the sufficient condition presupposes an answer to the second question posed above: How does one avoid becoming incapacitated in the process? How can a person tolerate the anxiety of awakening to chaos and move on to restructure the chaos into a new orientation which can serve as a basis for living but is not seen as final, to which commitment is not rigid? The broad outlines of the answer to this question are provided by Carl Roger's philosophy of psychotherapy. Key concepts in his position are permissiveness, acceptance, nondefensiveness, and genuineness of response in a relationship. A person may learn to dare to be free, to tolerate the anxiety which awareness of alternatives imposes, by coming to experience a valid self in a particular kind of interpersonal relationship.

The valid self cannot emerge in isolation. Mead has shown that the self can emerge only in society, that only through the other does one find the me. A critical consideration, however, is whether the other functions to *dictate* the self in accord with his expectations for the person or functions to *validate* the self he discovers in the person. Laing writes "the sense of identity requires the existence of another by whom one is known."[56] To be known, not to be told what to do but to be validated as one is, is the foundation for the individual's sense of security and is thus prerequisite to the toleration of anxiety. This sense of security is a matter of experiencing in another the recognition of one's existence and right to exist. It is the validation and acceptance of one's existence regardless of *what* one is. The fact that one is and is accepted is not threatened by how one is. Without this kind of security the individual is stranded, isolated, and he can only escape this isolation by being engulfed by others: other authority figures for the inner-directed, other peers for the other-directed.[57] These relationships were clearly expressed by one of Laing's patients whom he calls Joan:

> Everyone should be able to look back in their memory and be sure he had a mother who loved him, all of him . . . otherwise he feels he has no right to exist. . . . No matter what happens to this person in life, no matter how much he gets hurt, he can always look back to this and feel that he is lovable. He can love himself and he cannot be broken. If he can't fall back on this, he can be broken.
> You can only be broken if you're already in pieces.[58]

An interesting corroboration comes from May's study of anxiety in unwed mothers. He found that neurotic anxiety was usually associated with lack of acceptance of validation in the home. In those cases where this relationship did not hold true he found that rejection in the home did not threaten the basic security of the child because this security was grounded and validated elsewhere.[59]

Carl R. Rogers too has come to the same conclusion. He writes that in order for a person to be able to face a reorienting experience openly he must be provided with "psychological safety" and "psychological freedom." These are created, he contends, by a quality of relationship. Psychological safety includes:

1. Accepting the individual as of unconditional worth. . . . This attitude can probably be genuine only when the teacher, parent, etc., senses the potentialities of the individual and is thus able to have an unconditional faith in him, no matter what his present state. . . .
2. Providing a climate in which external evaluation is absent. When we cease to form judgments of the other individual from our own locus of evaluation, we are fostering creativity. For the individual to find himself in an atmosphere where he is not being evaluated, not being measured by some external standard is enormously freeing. Evaluation is always a threat, always creates a need for defensiveness, always means that some portion of experience must be denied to awareness.

3. Understanding empathetically. It is this which provides the ultimate in psychological safety, when added to the other two. If I say that I "accept" you, but know nothing of you, this is a shallow acceptance indeed, and you realize that it may change if I actually come to know you.[60]

·Rogers characterizes psychological freedom as follows: "When a teacher, parent, therapist, or other facilitating person permits the individual to a complete freedom of symbolic expression, creativity is fostered. This permissiveness gives the individual complete freedom to think, to feel, to be, whatever is most inward within himself."[61]

The openness to experience which ensues is: "the opposite of psychological defensiveness, when to protect the organization of the self, certain experiences are prevented from coming into awareness except in distorted fashion. . . . It means lack of rigidity and permeability of boundaries in concepts, beliefs, perceptions, and hypotheses. It means a tolerance for ambiguity exists. It means the ability to receive much conflicting information without forcing closure upon the situation."[62]

It appears that the critical variable in predisposing the individual at various stages of childhood to inner direction, other direction, anomie, or freedom is a quality of relationship. These predispositions have varying impacts on successive stages of development, but it would seem that the inner-directed person is least likely to change his orientation once it is set, although his vulnerability to becoming anomic is enhanced by the fact that he lives in an increasingly other-directed society. The other-directed person is much more precariously oriented and is potentially anomic.

This paragraph suggests a variety of theoretically and practically significant research problems. Can indexes be devised for identifying inner-directed, other-directed, anomic, and free types? What are the experiences which awaken one to the chaos of seeing too deeply? How genuinely free are the "free" in the sense of low levels of anxiety and tension? Are the experiences which freed them those which Rogers and others have described?

There may be questions about how these people distribute themselves through society, occupationally, in terms of voluntary association memberships, the exercise of leadership, etc. Medical sociology would be interested in their susceptibility to stress diseases and to emotional disorders. There are questions about how they rear children, about their adjustment to old age. Are they appreciated by their fellows, or do their fellows find their unconventionality threatening, their openness a disturbing reminder of their own inability to meet them halfway?

CONCLUSION

Freedom, in the sense of freedom of self-determination, seems a crucial issue today as potentiality, as opportunity, and as necessity. It is potentiality because of the nature of man; it is an opportunity and a necessity because of the nature of contemporary society. It is intrinsic to the nature of man that all men, excepting only monozygotic twins, are genetically unique, unprecedented, endowed with the potential for distinctiveness. To some extent, socialization inevitably involves the shaping of man in violation of this distinctiveness by ethnic group, social class, and regional subculture, irrespective of whatever he might be uniquely suited for with his peculiar combination of potentials.

But a culture does not have to serve as a mold or strait jacket. A culture can function as a cafeteria, providing in our day a vast diversity from which each might choose his own involvements and so fashion his own distinctive way of life, peculiarly appropriate to his own unprecedented uniqueness. The heterogeneity of contemporary culture signifies an opportunity for Everyman to select from the diversity available in order that he may become more what only he might become.

It is intrinsic to contemporary Western society that universally accepted values are virtually non-existent. Since "God is dead," at least in the traditional absolutistic sense, there remains no dependable resource for the sacralization of new universalistic values. Children are socialized by parents, peers, school, church, into some initial value identifications. But these are identifications which, given the value confusion of our society, will almost inevitably be challenged and quite possibly will be broken down in adolescence or early adulthood. Since there is no absolute authority (disregarding the compulsive authority of the "true believer") to point the way surely to new "ultimate" values, man must somehow choose his own values out of the contradictory sets which confront him. Thus it would seem that man today is *forced* to actualize the uniqueness which is potential to him by self-determinatively choosing his value commitments, for there is no authority which can do it for him.

The characterization and analysis of freedom here presented appear to be compatible with and relevant to the model of man which is generally accepted in the behavioral sciences. To recapitulate briefly, it begins with Bay's definition of freedom as the opportunity to express oneself. But, whereas in a homogeneous society one may express oneself primarily by responding to a narrow range of demands or expectations, in a hetergeneous society self-expression becomes a conscious and a self-conscious experience. Here it involves not only responding but determining who one is and choosing how to respond and what to do, *because one must choose between alternatives*. When choices and the basis for them—value commitments—are conscious, they may become an expression of the self. But it is only a largely already-*formed* self which is able to choose, and this self, reflecting on its origins, must awake to its "accidental nature"—accidental to having been born here, in this Protestant family on this street, rather than there, in the Catholic family next door. Awareness of one's accidentally acquired nature and of the variety of alternatives which are readily at hand *means* anxiety. The individual who is "known," accepted, validated, can tolerate the anxiety of awareness of the accidental nature of his value identifications which have become his by chance association. Because he is aware of his limitations, he can take steps to transcend them. Since he has no need to ascribe absolute authority to accidental associations, he is open to change in value commitment along lines which may permit a greater realization of his potential, which permit greater self-consistency, integration, and reintegration. Originally guided by external authority, he becomes guided by a selective, integrated sense of self. He is not at this point completely independent of others. His need to be validated, "confirmed" by some sort of reference group continues, but he is now able to deal consciously with this need and to seek associations which will meet this need.

NOTES

[1] Throughout its thirteen years of publication the Annual Review of Psychology has never mentioned J. B. Rhine or his work on ESP. Nor is there any mention in the series on Psychology: A Study of a Science, edited by Sigmund Koch, although it might have appeared in Volume I, which deals with Sensory, Perceptual and Physiological Formulations (Paul R. Farnsworth [ed.], Annual Review of Psychology [Palo Alto, Calif: Annual Reviews Inc., 1950–1962]; Sigmund Koch, Psychology: A Study of a Science [New York, 1959]).

[2] In nine years of the Sociological Abstracts for which index supplements are available there are no more than six references to sources dealing with "psychological freedom," in contrast to freedom from external coercion. In Sociology Today the only references to freedom are a brief discussion of Fromm's thesis in Escape from Freedom and a passing allusion to Weber's pessimistic views of the effects of growing bureaucratization on freedom. Gittler's Review of Sociology does not include any references to freedom in the index. Parsons' The Structure of Social Action makes three historical references to the concept of freedom in the German idealistic tradition, but includes no discussion of the relevance of "psychological freedom" to the structure of social action (Robert K. Merton, Leonard Broom, and Leonard S. Cottrell, Jr. [eds.], Sociology Today [New York, 1959]; Talcott Parsons, The Structure of Social Action [2d ed.; Glencoe, Ill., 1949]).

[3] "Existential Psychology—What's in It for Us," in Rollo May (ed.) Existential Psychology (New York, 1961), p. 55.

[4] David Riesman, Nathan Glazer, and Reuel Denney, The Lonely Crowd (New York, 1953), p. 278. (Italics added.)

[5] Erich Fromm, Escape from Freedom (New York, 1941), p. 256.

[6] Ibid., p. 258.

[7] Ibid.

[8] New York, 1961, p. 165.

[9] Suicide: A Study in Sociology, trans. J. A. Spaulding and G. Simpson (Glencoe, Ill., 1951).

[10] Boston, 1956, p. 4.

[11] Ibid., p. 5.

[12] Boston, 1956, p. 15.

[13] New York, 1962, pp. 367–68.

[14] C. Wright Mills, "Types of Practicality" in The Sociological Imagination (New York, 1959).

[15] The Structure of Freedom (Palo Alto, Calif., 1958), p. 3.

[16] Gordon Allport, Becoming (New Haven, 1960); Carl R. Rogers, On Becoming a Person (Boston, 1961); Abraham H. Maslow, Toward a Psychology of Being ("An Insight Book" [Princeton, N.J., 1962]); Joseph Royce, The Encapsulated Man ("An Insight Book" [Princeton, N.J., 1963]).

[17] Bronislaw Malinowski, Freedom and Civilization (New York, 1944), p. 25.

[18] Freedom and Culture ("Spectrum Books") (Englewood Cliffs, N.J., 1959), pp. 5, 6.

[19] Ibid., p. 9.

[20] Ibid., p. 7.

[21] Ibid., p. 53.

[22] New York, 1961.

[23] Op. cit., p. 83.

[24] Ibid., p. 83.

[25] *Ibid.*, p. 86.
[26] *Ibid.*, pp. 88, 89.
[27] *Ibid.*, p. 95.
[28] *Ibid.*, p. 122.
[29] Alexis de Tocqueville, *Democracy in America* (2 vols.; New York, 1954), I, 273.
[30] Bay, *op. cit.*, p. 99.
[31] Garden City, 1958, 1961.
[32] *Ibid.*, I, xix.
[33] *Ibid.*, I, 614.
[34] *Ibid.*, I, 171.
[35] *Ibid.*, I, 251.
[36] *Ibid.*, I, 420.
[37] *Op. cit.*, chap. 3, "Deficiency Motivation and Growth."
[38] Adler, *op. cit.*, I, 168.
[39] *Ibid.*, I, 421.
[40] In developing this theory I am indebted to an unpublished paper by Janet Gibbs, "The Determinants of Freedom: An Inquiry into Socialization" (Redlands, Calif., 1962).
[41] Riesman *et al.*, *cit.*, p. 26.
[42] *Ibid.*, p. 25.
[43] Rollo May, *The Meaning of Anxiety* (New York, 1950), p. 193.
[44] Riesman *et al.*, *op. cit.*, p. 38.
[45] *Ibid.*, p. 42.
[46] *Op. cit.*, p. 192.
[47] *Op. cit.*, p. 280.
[48] A few recent titles in the growing literature on alienation in modern man include "A Symposium on Alienation and the Search for Identity" (*American Journal of Psychoanalysis*), XXI (2) (1961); Eric and Mary Josephson, *Man Alone, Alienation in Modern Society* (New York, 1962); Fritz Pappenheim, *The Alienation of Modern Man* (New York, 1959); and Allen Wheelis, *The Quest for Identity* (New York, 1958).
[49] *Op. cit.*, Part III, "Autonomy."
[50] T. W. Adorno, Else Frenkel-Brunswik, D. J. Levinson, and R. N. Sanford, *The Authoritarian Personality* (New York, 1950).
[51] Milton Rokeach *et al.*, *The Open and Closed Mind* (New York, 1960).
[52] Gibbs, *op. cit.*, pp. 104–105.
[53] Daniel R. Miller and Guy E. Swanson, *The Changing American Parent* (New York, 1958).
[54] "Spectrum Books" (Englewood Cliffs, N.J., 1961).
[55] *Op. cit.*, p. 278.
[56] R. D. Laing, *The Divided Self* (London, 1960), p. 151.
[57] *Ibid.*, p. 45.
[58] *Ibid.*, p. 188.
[59] May, *op. cit.*, p. 241.
[60] *On Becoming a Person* (Boston, 1961), pp. 357–58.
[61] *Ibid.*, pp. 358–59.
[62] *Ibid.*, pp. 353–54.

THE CONCEPT OF FREEDOM
IN MARXIST-LENINIST ETHICS

A. P. Chermenina

The problem of freedom is becoming ever more pressing in our day, as the effectuation of real and complete freedom for all people who work is one of the principal objectives of the social morality of communism set forth in the Program of the CPSU. On the other hand, capitalism and its ideological defenders in the struggle against the world communist movement seek to turn the idea of freedom to their own ends, distorting and limiting this concept so as to prove the unprovable, to wit, that the capitalist social system is the "free world," while socialism and communism constitute a violation and destruction of freedom. In so doing they recognize the fundamental opposition of the Marxist and bourgeois conceptions of freedom, while holding, naturally, that their standpoint represents truth and the Marxist, confusion. Here, for example, are the words of a bourgeois theoretician: "The Marxist concept of freedom as recognition of necessity changes the meaning of freedom so as to make it unrecognizable. It pays formal respect to free will, while accepting determinism in its entirety" (S. R. Mukherji, "Is Moral Responsibility a Myth?", *The Philosophical Quarterly*, Amalner, India, 1962, Vol. 35, No. 2, p. 127).

While criticizing the Marxist concept of freedom, bourgeois theoreticians are compelled, however, to grant its wide influence and practical effectiveness. Herbert Read, for example, writes that the Marxist theory of freedom has demonstrated its superiority over idealist systems which serve the purposes of the bourgeois world. Therefore, he continues, "we cannot resist Marxism and expect to overcome it until we have a philosophy of equal force" (H. Read, *Existentialism, Marxism and Anarchism*, London, 1949, pp. 19–20).

The major forms taken by this "overcoming" of Marxism are identifications of Marxism with Freudianism (the only difference between them is held to be that Marxism sees the source of human acts in social laws, while Freudianism traces them to the depths of the subconscious) (see R. Peters, "The Contemporary Malaise: Freud, Marx, Responsibility," *The Listener*, 1957, Vol. 57, Nos. 1474–1476). Marxism is also identified with the mechanical determinism of the 18th century (see E. Kamenka, "Philosophy in the Soviet Union," *Philosophy*, London, 1963, Vol. 38, No. 143). Thus, both the building of communism and the demands of the struggle against bourgeois ideology necessitate serious attention to the problem of freedom. A number of interesting writings by foreign and Soviet Marxists—R. Garaudy, I. Kendzyuro, G. Mende, Y. N. Davydova, and others—have been devoted to this problem. However, they all deal primarily with the social aspect of freedom, leaving its moral aspect undeveloped. But study of this question is very important inasmuch as it

Reprinted from *Filsofskie nauki*, No. 6 (1964).

is directly associated with those moral tasks that are presently being resolved by Soviet society, first among them that of developing a new communist man.

All morality takes its origin from the fact that, under identical conditions, an individual may behave variously, depending upon his own choice and decision. Proceeding from the assumption that free will exists, a system of requirements—moral standards—of individual behavior is established and the individual's deeds are subjected to moral evaluation. This is why the problem of freedom has been studied in ethics from earliest times, and continues to be studied. Moreover, in the opinion of certain investigators, the philosophical problem of free will arose as the result of the search for a real standard of human responsibility. Its goal was to determine a scale of punishment for crimes and, consequently, of guilt, a standard for measuring the personal participation of the individual in predetermining the final event (see G. de Tarde, Penal Philosophy, Boston, 1912). This opinion is well founded. The theory of the responsibility of the individual for his behavior with respect to others and to society as a whole truly does require a search for means of reconciling freedom and determinism in philosophy. This philosophical problem cannot be solved without first solving that of the relationship between the voluntary and the involuntary in behavior. This is because all responsibility, on the one hand, is associated with ascertaining who was the cause of the given phenomenon or event and, on the other hand, it assumes that man bears responsibility only if he committed the deed himself, of his own free will.

In connection with the fact that it is the individual who is the subject in moral freedom, bourgeois ethics has to this day considered primarily only the psychological aspect of freedom. Such an attitude has a basis, inasmuch as the moral nuances of freedom may be seen only if we turn to analysis of the motives for the behavior of a given individual. In this sense, the freedom of a person's behavior expresses the dynamic character of the situations in which he exists. Moral freedom is an integral part of the moral influence of the individual upon the world of social relationships around him, a manifestation of his philosophy, views, habits, and of the system of moral values and ideals he has adopted.

Possibilities for change in a situation and the possibility of purposive response are concentrated, accumulated, in the will. Freedom is the possibility of not mechanically returning or transmitting impulses coming from without, information received from without, but of determining the nature and mode of response oneself. Therefore one may conclude that the essence of freedom, understood in its moral aspect, is creative activity in accordance with the moral convictions of the individual.

No one actually places in question the relationship between freedom and a determination proceeding from the subject. For creativity is the making, and predetermination is the determination in advance, of that which does not yet exist. The subject is the originator of new lines of determination. And it would be false to deny, on the excuse of struggle against idealism, any role to the subject and his consciousness in the manifestation of his freedom. It is no accident that, from the very beginning of ethics, the nature of freedom has been sought and is still being sought in the mind of man, in that creative laboratory in which plans and projects for the future behavior of the subject are born. Man's behavior is called free in the sense that he himself has been the cause of an act, regardless of anyone's will or influence. Therefore, in bourgeois ethics, the basic theory of freedom has become the problem of the self (selbst, ipse).[1]

The spread of the influence of determinism and, in particular, of the theory of psychoanalysis, led to the posing of the question, in bourgeois philosophy, as to whether the activity of the individual is also determined by the influence of the environment, heredity, the subconscious, etc. But the theory of psychoanalysis, which is a consistent development of mechanical determinism, denies the existence of freedom. Therefore, seeking to escape this extreme and at the same time refraining from recognizing determinism, contemporary bourgeois philosophers give preference to the theory of "self-determination." According to this theory, the decisive role in behavior is played not by the influence of the environment, heredity, and so forth, but by man himself, his own ego. It must be stated that there are numerous varieties of this theory, from the affirmation of the absoluteness of self-determination (Sartre) to efforts to combine recognition of the determination of the will from without and within with so-called "partial self-determination."

In seeking to define the very concept of "self," the proponents of "self-determination" contend that the "self" is nothing more than the nature of man. It is either the integrated result of the interweaving of physical and mental influences which combine in themselves the ability to create, or it constitutes something, some essence, inherent in man and independent of all influences. But this essence is considered only from the psychological viewpoint, only as a reflex activity, as something sovereign, sufficient unto itself, related to the world but capable internally of rising above it, having communicated the beginning of a new line of causal relationships.[2] The theory of self-determination constitutes, for bourgeois philosophy, the limit to which it can go in recognizing the dialectics of freedom and determinism, external and internal, objective and subjective. It may be regarded as evidence, on the one hand, of the dissatisfaction of the most serious bourgeois students of ethics with metaphysical extremes in solution of the problem of freedom and, on the other hand, as proof of their incapacity to counterpose to Marxism any idealist treatment of this problem that is at all persuasive.

That which is distinctive to the Marxist conception of freedom is the fact that, here, reflex acts—the psychological foundation of freedom—are examined in a context of societal relations which affect the individual. Therefore the problem of the subjective nature of creative activity is not at all omitted from the Marxist concept of .freedom, but acquires a new meaning, a scientific explanation. From the Marxist standpoint, the question of the creative activity of the individual has two aspects:

1. In what does the nature of creative activity lie; what determines and directs the behavior of the individual? This aspect requires study of the process whereby the individual obtains information as the result of his relations with

his environment, i.e., influence from without to within. It includes questions of the psychological foundation of free will and of the correlation between the objective and the subjective in the internal world of the subject.

2. The second aspect is investigation of the functioning of creative activity, i.e., influence from the individual to the world without. It includes the questions as to why the individual chooses one and not another form of purposive response and what impels him to choose precisely this and not another variant; what the freedom of choice of the individual consists of; in what sense he is free. This aspect includes the theory of motivation, choice, decision, will, and action.

Both of these aspects of the problem were brilliantly solved and elaborated in the writings of the founders of Marxism-Leninism: the first as the theory of the concreteness of truth and knowledge of objective laws, the dialectics of the objective and the subjective, and the second as the theory of the transforming role of the individual in history, and of his active consciousness. It is necessary to refute, as utterly at variance with the facts, the various assertions of bourgeois sociologists and moralists to the effect that, in the Marxist concept, man must be "submerged in the historical process" in order to emerge from it a free personality, "reduced to an object" in order to gain freedom in the future (see W. Rotenstreich, "Historical Inevitability and Human Responsibility," *Philosophy and Phenomenological Research*, Philadelphia, 1963, Vol. 23, No. 3), that Marxism makes only formal acknowledgement of free will, etc.

On the contrary, no other theory so honors the personality, with its capacity to create, as the theory of the founders of scientific communism. It is another thing that Marxism does not elevate to an absolute the concept of individual personality, and examines it not in isolation from society but as a totality of societal relations.

The subjective—the self—the creative principle—is shaped and determined under the influence of the objective: circumstances, the environment, i.e., external factors and heredity, and the specifics of the psychological set, i.e., internal factors of motivation. The objective becomes the subjective upon refraction through the prism of the individual—consciousness, senses, will, character. From this it can be understood that it is not only a matter of purely external determination, but also of internal determination which, in turn, rests upon external circumstances and is brought about through determination from without. From this explanation it may appear to some that freedom of the will has been eliminated. This may perhaps be why certain bourgeois theoreticians, in their effort to defend individual freedom, seek to prove that, in the determination of deeds, in motivation, there is, independent of all other factors, an innate undetermined, personal expression of the ego, the selfhood of the individual.

Marxism rejects these inventions. At the same time it is far removed from any reduction of the subjective to a purely mechanical expression of the objective. The self is not merely a transmitter of determinations. The objective is reworked and transformed into the subjective in accordance with the individual peculiarities of the ego, as shaped by circumstance.

The relationships between the objective and subjective (after the latter has already gone through the process of formation) are always contradictory. But that which is most important they have in common. All that is "internal," subjective, and unique in the individual is brought into being and has meaning only for his acts in the outside world, as an individualized and at the same time interdependent part of a social whole, intimately associated with its other parts. Marxism, recognizing determinism to be universal, does not seek in man's mentality and behavior anything that is his own in an absolute sense, anything that is outside of and above causal connections, applying to determination both of the subject and by the subject. Freedom in such an absolute sense, we hold, does not exist. But Marxist dialectical determinism—the conception of necessity in both its general philosophical and sociological aspects—makes it possible to provide a theoretical foundation for the freedom of the individual in another sense.

That everything must be causally conditioned is not absolutely necessary. Necessity is the principal tendency of motion, of development. But it is manifested through accidents that are determined but are not inevitable for the given tendency. Therefore necessity determines the framework, the limits, within which various variations are possible. In other words, the sphere of necessity is the "spectrum of possibilities" for the individual's freedom. Moreover, the fact that reality exists on many planes and is contradictory leads to collisions among various types of necessities, and this further increases the role of individual choice and decision. But if we examine the individual in isolation from social conditions, from social possibilities, it becomes exceedingly difficult to determine what is necessary and what is accidental in his behavior, which of the necessities is most pressing, what has been done voluntarily and consciously, and what under the pressure of circumstances, inasmuch as motivation and deed are the results of the interweaving of so many lines of determination, direct and mediate, that neither the individual himself nor, to an even greater degree, those around him are able properly to consider and evaluate all the pertinent factors. Therefore, if the standard of individual freedom be sought only in the mind, the result will be an interminable discussion over whether the individual could or could not have acted otherwise (and discussion of this order never ceases in the bourgeois press). Marxist ethics approaches the decision of this most complex question by another path.

We give consideration to the "thresholds" of man's psychological possibilities, basing ourselves upon the findings of psychology and the physiology of the higher nervous system. But the essence of the phenomenon of freedom and a standard for measuring its possibilities is something we locate not in an invented absolute independence of the subject from the environment, but in the socially objective possibilities for matching the requirements of objective circumstances with subjective interests. Moreover, these very interests also depend—but now only in the ultimate analysis—upon the position of the individual in society and upon other factors that are in many respects not dependent upon him. Thus, instead of an attempted analysis of phenomena of an individual's responses which are not subject to direct control, we propose a sober assessment of the objective factors which form the properties of the individual, factors which are entirely within the range of our control.

The psychological foundation for freedom is, in the first place, the capacity to react, to produce a response to the influence of stimuli, and to establish an intimate connection with the environment. Secondly, it is the capacity to react selectively. The variety and diversity of the manifestations of the reality by which man is surrounded have developed in him the capacity to evaluate possible alternatives with the aid of reason, to acquire supplementary information, to think, compare, trace possible consequences in his mind, project various courses and, finally, having made his choice, to take a decision. But one cannot choose from among the unreal, the objectively impossible. The basis of freedom, if we are discussing the freedom to act and not the freedom to wish, is the diversity of tendencies in processes objectively occurring. These tendencies may be studied, selected among, given preference to. Within this diversity it is possible to manifest one's self utterly and completely. The entire diversity of human acts, of the manifestations of individual personalities, is embodied in this principle.

Both the connections with the environment and the possible feedback and response to external influences acquire a social and, in particular, a moral character within society. In his thinking about, and evaluation of, possible consequences and in his motivation and choice of a line of behavior, the individual gives consideration to the influence of his actions upon other individuals, i.e., he takes into account the possible response by those around him to the act he has in mind.

The basic contradiction between materialism and idealism in resolving the problem of freedom lies in the fact that the former recognizes and the latter denies, in actuality, the dependence of individual, personal freedom upon the freedom of a class or of society as a whole. Therefore, unlike the idealist position, the materialist makes it possible to see and consider not only the millions of individual wills, sovereign and capable of changing existing circumstances, but entire groups of identical wills, whose possibilities of implementation are many times greater than that of the individual, since a group of individuals is of course more powerful than one individual taken alone. It is precisely social freedom that is the prime determinant of the framework, limits, and opportunities pertaining to the creative activity of the individual, to his freedom.

The fact that necessity will find its way to realization in any case does not mean that it functions independently of the will of the individual. That which is distinctive in the human attitude toward reality lies in the fact that the individual is capable of choosing, as the goal of his actions, what is most valuable to him and the most effective means for attaining it under the conditions of possibilities constituting necessity. The behavior of an individual may be passive or active; therefore, the degree to which opportunities may be utilized differs. Inasmuch as the necessary consequences take shape out of the actions of individuals, it is the attitude of these individuals to the given conditions that is of decisive importance.

However, free will does not consist solely of freedom of choice. It is not only the choice that is important, but the conscious direction of one's own activity. Choice, as the result of thought, consideration, and the weighing of possible consequences, is only the first step in free will. In addition, a subordination is needed of acts and deeds to the goal posed, the attainment of a result, a change in the situation or state of affairs in accordance with a plan. In other words, free will as a whole is control over the process, over the form of one's own activity and its results.

Inasmuch as the laws of societal development operate as tendencies, they permit not only choice within the confines of necessity, but conscious influencing of necessity. Of course, the individual does not by himself determine the course of history, cannot individually thwart certain trends of historical development and open the door to others, but in unity with other members of his class and of his people he can carry out such processes. The individual is the freer, the broader the range of those who support him. The individual is free to the degree that he makes use in his activity of the opportunities open to a class, i.e., to the degree to which he, in his own activity, expresses what is necessary for that class. The degree of freedom for the individual is the degree of conscious and voluntary utilization of the opportunities presented by the patterns of necessity on various planes.

When we evaluate whether the individual is capable of acting differently, voluntarily, consciously, or whether he has been compelled to do something, we proceed not only from the characteristics of the given individual, not only from his "self" but—and above all—from his "type essence," the objective possibilities of the given situation in the given epoch for a member of a given class, group, or the like, to act in a given fashion. Such an approach to the problem of freedom provides us with an objective criterion for evaluation of the degree of freedom of a given individual.

If other members of a group, class, or the like, have acted and are acting differently under similar circumstances, we are in a position, by giving consideration to all the specifics of the situation and the level of development of the given individual, to evaluate his behavior as free or not free. In turn, this solution of the problem provides an objective criterion for determination of the responsibility of the individual. The individual is responsible to the degree that he is free. He is responsible for those possible initiatives that are or were open to him. This explains the fact that a man is responsible not only for a deed, for an act performed, but for non-utilization of opportunities, for inaction when he might have done something. This is why, as freedom increases in the course of the building of socialism and communism, the moral demands made by society upon the individual and the moral responsibility of the individual also increase.

The classification of morality into three spheres has already become well established in our literature. Certain variations in definition do not do away with the differences between morality as a set of standards of conduct or demands upon the individual, morality as the internal attitude of the individual to standards of conduct, and morality as a particular aspect of individual behavior, practical morality or morality as practiced. The sphere of standards is the sphere of that which is obligatory for the individual and determined by society—the sphere of moral necessity. It presents itself as a demand differentiated into numerous specific directives covering all the variety, and the many planes, of the individual's life. Moral standards, being an approximately true expression of social necessity, provide a further means for social organizations to influence the behavior of the individual. Moral necessity is the need to commit moral acts, to consider moral prohibitions and solutions; it is a system of moral values and ideals adopted by society, i.e., it is the framework that gives to the individual's behavior the character of that which is necessary, essential to existence and to the development of society.

Moral necessity, that which is obligatory in an individual's behavior, the requirements an individual must meet, is moral duty rendered specific in a system of obligations pertinent to all spheres of the life and activity of the individual (his attitude toward work, toward property, toward government, toward politics, toward his homeland, his class, his social group, to other nations and races, to his family—parents and children—to the aged and the weak, to problems of everyday life, to creativity, to ideology, etc.). But if, for example, legal order is enforced regardless of the attitudes of individuals to the codes addressed to them, then a negative or neutral attitude toward duty, toward necessity in morality, will lead to immorality and not to moral behavior. That is, morality requires internal acceptance—an understanding and conviction of the correctness of the demands, the transformation of external obligations into internal convictions.

Moral freedom is morality, that is, control over one's own behavior, over oneself, because it is based upon understanding of the morally necessary, upon acceptance of duty; it is the transformation of this into the primary stimulus of behavior.

But inasmuch as moral necessity and a system of standards comprise a phenomenon in the sphere of social consciousness, it may lag behind changing social relationships and behind the socially obligatory. Therefore moral freedom is also expressed in the ability to see the contradiction between existing standards and societal necessity and actively to promote the growth of new moral standards and new moral values. In this sense there is a significant difference between the social and moral aspects of freedom. Certain individuals may morally overcome the system of outdated attitudes that exist in society and rise above them. Although this possibility is limited, it is extremely important, particularly at turning points in the development of society.

It must be emphasized that moral freedom is not only an attitude toward other persons, to societal relationships, but to oneself, not only to that which is essential for oneself, but to one's own capacities. Moral freedom is the conscious direction of one's own desires, the guidance and cultivation of them in such fashion that they, becoming based upon societal necessity, promote the maximum expansion of the possibilities inherent in man.

Consequently, freedom presupposes self control, but not at all "self suppression," violence to one's own will; it presupposes not a passive subordination of desires to necessity, but a rational and humane evaluation of a man's desires and interests. And this requires that the structure of the personality correspond to those social attitudes and values in which the tendency of society to develop in a progressive direction is most completely expressed in the given concrete circumstances.

All this indicates that the attitude of Marxism to free will is by no means one of "formal recognition." Moral freedom, expressed in the moral responsibility of the individual, will in the future become one of the principal factors of social progress.

In demonstrating the necessity and reality of the societal liberation of the individual, Marxism provides a foundation for the possibility of complete and all-encompassing freedom of man, but at the same time places upon him full responsibility for his attitude toward these opportunities. Therefore one is fully justified in saying that it is precisely Marxism which is the theory fundamentally rendering full respect to the free will of the individual, and that communism is the social order which will finally establish the conditions for his real freedom.

NOTES

[1] Examining the essence of the problem of freedom as a whole, the authors of a volume titled *The Idea of Freedom*, New York, 1958, conceive of three types of freedom, which have divided all philosophers from Socrates to the present into three groups. The first treats freedom as self-realization, the second as self-determination, and the third as self-perfection. (The classification and distinctions are such that one philosopher may be found in two or even all three groups.)

[2] The theory of self-determination is defended, albeit in different forms, by Barrett, Baylis, Campbell, Garnet, Ayer, Ewing, Nowell-Smith, Hook, Blanchard, and others.

SOLZHENITSYN TO THE FOURTH
CONGRESS OF SOVIET WRITERS

A. I. Solzhenitsyn

ALEKSANDR I. SOLZHENITSYN, winner of the 1970 Nobel Prize for Literature, has been called by his contemporary Russian author Yevgeny Yevtushenko "our only living classic." Solzhenitsyn was born in 1918 in Kislovodsk, Caucasia, and grew up in Rostov-on-Don, USSR. He received his education at the University of Rostov and the Moscow Institute of History, Philosophy, and Literature. When imprisoned at Mavrino, near Moscow, and later at the labor camp in Kazakhstan, he wrote The First Circle. He was released on the day of Josef Stalin's death in 1953 but was exiled to Dzhambul Oblast in Siberia until 1956. The next year he was "officially" rehabilitated. Soviet officials did not permit him to accept the Nobel Prize and most of his major works have not been published in the Soviet Union. His writings include One Day in the Life of Ivan Denisovich, published originally in Novyi Mir and as a book in Russian during 1962 and 1963; For the Good of the Cause, also published originally in Novyi Mir and in book form in Russian during 1963; We Never Make Mistakes, also first published in Novyi Mir in 1963; The First Circle, never published in Russia, but published in unauthorized versions in English in 1968; Cancer Ward, never published in Russia, but published in unauthorized versions in English and Russian in 1969; and several plays and poems, some of which Solzhenitsyn has renounced. Solzhenitsyn first attracted world-wide notice in May of 1967 when he sent an open letter to the Union of Soviet Writers, a meeting he was not permitted to attend, stating that his country's literature had been enduring censorship for decades and calling for the abolition of all censorship, overt or hidden, of all fictional writing. He charged the Soviet government with canceling his public readings, adding: "My work has thus been finally smothered, gagged, and slandered." The Writers Union officially denounced him in June 1968 in an editorial in Literaturnaya Gazeta.

 To the Presidium and the delegates to the Congress, to members of the Union of Soviet Writers, and to the editors of literary newspapers and magazines:

Not having access to the podium at this Congress, I ask that the Congress discuss:

I. The no longer tolerable oppression, in the form of censorship, which our literature has endured for decades, and which the Union of Writers can no longer accept.

Under the obfuscating label of Glavlit, this censorship—which is not provided for in the Constitution and is therefore illegal, and which is nowhere publicly labeled as such—imposes a yoke on our literature and gives people unversed in literature arbitrary control over writers. A survival of the Middle Ages, the censorship has managed, Methuselah-like, to drag out its existence

Reprinted from "Writers and Censors," Problems of Communism (September 1968), pp. 37–39.

almost to the 21st century. Of fleeting significance, it attempts to appropriate to itself the role of unfleeting time—of separating good books from bad.

Our writers are not supposed to have the right, are not endowed with the right, to express their cautionary judgments about the moral life of man and society, or to explain in their own way the social problems and historical experience that have been so deeply felt in our country. Works that might express the mature thinking of the people, that might have a timely and salutary influence on the realm of the spirit or on the development of a social conscience, are proscribed or distorted by censorship on the basis of considerations that are petty, egotistical, and—from the national point of view—shortsighted. Outstanding manuscripts by young authors, as yet entirely unknown, are nowadays rejected by editors solely on the ground that they "will not pass." Many members of the [Writers'] Union, and even many of the delegates at this Congress, know how they themselves have bowed to the pressures of the censorship and made concessions in the structure and concept of their books— changing chapters, pages, paragraphs, or sentences, giving them innocuous titles —just for the sake of seeing them finally in print, even if it meant distorting them irremediably. It is an understood quality of literature that gifted works suffer [most] disastrously from all these distortions, while untalented works are not affected by them. Indeed, it is the best of our literature that is published in mutilated form.

Meanwhile, the most censorious labels—"ideologically harmful," "depraved," and so forth—are proving short-lived and fluid, [in fact] are changing before our very eyes. Even Dostoevsky, the pride of world literature, was at one time not published in our country (still today his works are not published in full); he was excluded from the school curriculum, made unacceptable for reading, and reviled. For how many years was Yesenin considered "counterrevolutionary"?—he was even subjected to a prison term because of his books. Wasn't Maiakovsky called "an anarchistic political hooligan"? For decades the immortal poetry of Akhmatova was considered anti-Soviet. The first timid printing of the dazzling Tsvetaeva ten years ago was declared a "gross political error." Only after a delay of twenty to thirty years were Bunin, Bulgakov, and Platonov returned to us. Inevitably, Mandelshtam, Voloshin, Gumilev and Kliuev will follow in that line—not to mention the recognition, at some time or other, of even Zamiatin and Remisov.

A decisive moment [in this process] comes with the death of a troublesome writer. Sooner or later after that, he is returned to us with an "explanation of [his] errors." For a long time the name of Pasternak could not be pronounced out loud; but then he died, and since then his books have appeared and his verse is even quoted at ceremonies.

Pushkin's words are really coming true: "They are capable of loving only the dead."

But the belated publication of books and "authorization" [rehabilitation] of names does not make up for either the social or the artistic losses suffered by our people as a consequence of these monstrous delays and the suppression of artistic conscience. (In fact, there were writers in the 1920's—Pilniak, Platonov, Mandelshtam—who called attention at a very early stage to the beginnings of the cult [of personality] and the peculiar traits of Stalin's character; but these writers were silenced and destroyed instead of being listened to.) Literature cannot develop in between the categories of "permitted" and "not permitted," "about this you may write" and "about this you may not." Literature that is not the breath of contemporary society, that dares not transmit the pains and fears of that society, that does not warn in time against threatening moral and social dangers—such literature does not deserve the name of literature; it is only a facade. Such literature loses the confidence of its own people, and its published works are used as wastepaper instead of being read.

Our literature has lost the leading role it played at the end of the last century and the beginning of this one, and it has lost the brilliance of experimentation that distinguished it in the 1920's. To the entire world the literary life of our country now appears immeasurably more colorless, trivial and inferior than it actually is—[or] than it would be if it were not confined and hemmed in. The losers are both our country—in world public opinion—and world literature itself. If the world had access to all the uninhibited fruits of our literature, if it were enriched by our own spiritual experience, the whole artistic evolution of the world would move along in a different way, acquiring a new stability and attaining even a new artistic threshold.

I propose that the Congress adopt a resolution which would demand and ensure the abolition of all censorship, open or hidden, of all fictional writing, and which would release publishing houses from the obligation to obtain authorization for the publication of every printed page.

II. The duties of the Union towards its members.

These duties are not clearly formulated in the statutes of the Union of Soviet Writers (under "Protection of copyrights" and "Measures for the protection of other rights of writers"), and it is sad to find that for a third of a century the Union has not defended either the "other" rights or even the copyrights of persecuted writers.

Many writers have been subjected during their lifetime to abuse and slander in the press and from rostrums without being afforded the physical possibility of replying. More than that, they have been exposed to violence and personal persecution (Bulgakov, Akhmatova, Tsvetaeva, Pasternak, Zoshchenko, Platonov, Aleksandr Grin, Vassili Grossman). The Union of Writers not only did not make its own publications available to these writers for purposes of reply and justification, not only did not come out in their defense, but through its leadership was always first among the persecutors. Names that adorned our poetry of the 20th century found themselves on the list of those expelled from the Union or not even admitted to it in the first place. The leadership of the Union cravenly abandoned to their distress those for whom persecution ended in exile, labor camps, and death (Pavel Vasilev, Mandelshtam, Artem Vesely, Pilniak, Babel, Tabidze, Zabolotsky, and others). The list must be cut off at "and others." We learned after the 20th Party Congress that there were more than 600 writers whom the Union had obediently handed over to their fate in prisons and camps. However, the roll is even longer, and its curled-up end cannot and will not ever be read by our eyes. It contains the names of young prose-writers and poets whom we may have known only accidentally through personal encounters and whose talents were crushed in camps before being able to blossom, whose writings never got further than the offices of the state security service in the days of Yagoda, Yezhov, Beria and Abakumov.

There is no historical necessity for the newly-elected leadership of the Union to share with its predecessors the responsibility for the past.

I propose that all guarantees for the defense of Union members subjected to slander and unjust persecution be clearly formulated in Paragraph 22 of the Union statutes, so that past illegalities will not be repeated.

If the Congress does not remain indifferent to what I have said, I also ask that it consider the interdictions and persecutions to which I myself have been subjected.

1) It will soon be two years since the state security authorities took away from me my novel, *The First Circle* (comprising 35 authors' sheets [*avtorskie listy*]),[1] thus preventing it from being submitted to publishers. Instead, in my own lifetime, against my will and even without my knowledge, this novel has been "published" in an unnatural "closed" edition for reading by an unidentified select circle. My novel has [*thus*] become available to literary officials but is being concealed from most writers. I have been unable to obtain open discussion of the novel within writers' associations and to prevent misuse and plagiarism.

2) Together with this novel, my literary papers dating back 15–20 years, things that were not intended for publication, were taken away from me. Now, tendentious excerpts from these papers have also been covertly "published" and are being circulated within the same circles. The play, *Feast of the Conquerors*, which I wrote in verse from memory in camp, where I went by a four-digit number—and where, condemned to die by starvation, we were forgotten by society, no one outside the camps coming out against [such] repressions—this play, now left far behind, is being ascribed to me as my very latest work.

3) For three years now, an irresponsible campaign of slander has been conducted against me, who fought all through the war as a battery commander and received military decorations. It is being said that I served time as a criminal, or surrendered to the enemy (I was never a prisoner-of-war), that I "betrayed" my country and "served the Germans." That is the interpretation being put now on the eleven years I spent in camps and in exile for having criticized Stalin. This slander is being spread in secret instructions and meetings by people holding official positions. I vainly tried to stop the slander by appealng to the Board of the Writers' Union of the RSFSR and to the press. The Board did not even react, and not a single paper printed my reply to the slanderers. On the contrary, slander against me from rostrums has intensified and become more vicious within the last year, making use of distorted material from my confiscated papers, and I have no way of replying.

4) My novel, *Cancer Ward* (comprising 25 author's sheets), the first part of which was approved for publication by the prose department of the Moscow writers' organization, cannot be published either by chapters—rejected by five magazines—or in its entirety—rejected by *Novyi mir*, *Zvezda*, and *Prostor*.

5) The play, *The Reindeer and the Little Hut*, accepted in 1962 by the Sovremennik Theater, has thus far not been approved for performance.

6) The screen play, *The Tanks Know the Truth*; the stage play, *The Light That Is In You*; [a group of] short stories entitled *The Right Hand*; the series, *Small Bite*—[all these] cannot find either a producer or a publisher.

7) My stories published in *Novyi mir* have never been reprinted in book form, having been rejected everywhere—by the Soviet Writer Publishers, the State Literature Publishing House, and the *Ogoniok* Library. They thus remain inaccessible to the general reading public.

8) I have also been prevented from having any other contacts with readers [either] through public readings of my works (in November 1966, nine out of eleven scheduled meetings were cancelled at the last moment) or through readings over the radio. Even the simple act of giving a manuscript away for "reading and copying" has now become a criminal act (ancient Russian scribes were permitted to do this five centuries ago).

Thus my work has been finally smothered, gagged, and slandered.

In view of such flagrant infringements of my copyright and "other" rights, will the Fourth Congress defend me—yes or no? It seems to me that the choice is also not without importance for the literary future of several of the delegates.

I am of course confident that I will fulfill my duty as a writer under all circumstances—even more successfully and more unchallenged from the grave than in my lifetime. No one can bar the road to truth, and to advance its cause I am prepared to accept even death. But may it be that repeated lessons will finally teach us not to stop the writer's pen during his lifetime?

At no time has this ennobled our history.

A. I. SOLZHENITSYN

May 16, 1967.

NOTE

[1] "Author's sheets" are printed pages, each containing 40,000 typographical characters, used in the Soviet Union for computing the author's fee.—Ed.

"SPEECH" AND
THE FIRST AMENDMENT

Haig A. Bosmajian

HAIG A. BOSMAJIAN *is an associate professor in the Department of Speech at the University of Washington. His publications include* The Principles and Practice of Freedom of Speech *(Houghton Mifflin),* The Rhetoric of Nonverbal Communication *(Scott, Foresman),* Readings in Speech *(Harper & Row),* The Rhetoric of the Civil Rights Movement *(Random House),* The Rhetoric of the Speaker: Speeches and Criticisms *(Raytheon/Heath), and* This Great Argument: The Rights of Women *(Addison-Wesley). His articles on rhetoric, language, freedom of speech, and dissent have appeared in* School and Society, College English, Journal of General Education, Etc., Folklore, Today's Speech, Quarterly Journal of Speech, Western Speech, The Dalhousie Review, The Christian Century, *and other periodicals and academic journals.*

In his Areopagitica: A Speech for the Liberty to Unlicensed Printing, To the Parliament of England, John Milton, well versed in rhetoric and recognizing that men communicate in diverse ways, wrote in 1644 that ". . . whatever thing we hear or see, sitting, walking, travelling, or conversing, may be fitly called our book, and is of the same effect that writings are. . . ."[1] Milton devoted several lines to a discussion of the futility of censorship and the regulation of printing unless men were prepared to regulate other activities which had communicative functions and might corrupt the minds of men:

> If we think to regulate printing, thereby to rectify manners, we must regulate all recreations and pastimes, all that is delightful to man. No music may be heard, no song be set or sung, but that is grave and Doric. There must be licensing dancers, that no gesture, motion, or deportment be taught our youth, but what by their allowance shall be thought honest; for such Plato provided of.[2]

Three hundred and twenty years later, the courts of California were grappling with the question of whether topless dancing was a form of communication, a form of expression, protected by the First Amendment. In 1965, Miss Kelley Iser, a topless dancer, and Mr. Albert Giannini, the manager of the nightclub in which she danced, were found guilty by a municipal court jury of violating California's Penal Code section 314, subdivision 1 (wilful and lewd exposure) and section 647, subdivision (a) (lewd and dissolute conduct). The case reached the California State Supreme Court which considered first, the communicative functions of the dance, and second, the obscenity question. In deciding that Miss Iser's topless dance was a form of communication, the Court said:

> . . . the performance of the dance indubitably represents a medium of pro-

Reprinted with permission of *Today's Speech*, 18 (Winter 1970), 3–11, and the author.

tected expression. To take but one example, the ballet obviously typifies a form of entertainment and expression that involves communication of ideas, impressions, and feelings. Similarly, Iser's dancing, however vulgar and tawdry in content, might well involve communication to her audience. In fact, the Attorney General basically argues that Iser's dance violated the statute because it communicated improper ideas to her audience. This implicit admission of the Attorney General undermines his preliminary contention that the dance does not enjoy at least a prima facie protection of the guarantees of the First Amendment. Precisely because, as the Attorney General points out, the performed dance primarily constitutes a form of expression and communication, it potentially merits First Amendment protections.[3]

Having decided that Miss Iser's dance was a form of communication and expression, the Court then went on to discuss the question of obscenity and stated that "we conclude the convictions must be set aside because the prosecution failed to introduce any evidence of community standards, either that Iser's conduct appealed to prurient interest or offended contemporary standards of decency."[4] In considering the question of whether distinctions are to be made between political speech and entertainment and whether one deserved more First Amendment protection than the other, the Court said in a footnote:

> . . . the life of the imagination and intellect is of comparable import to the preservation of the political process; the First Amendment reaches beyond protection of citizen participation in, and ultimate control over, governmental affairs and protects in addition the interest in free interchange of ideas and impressions for their own sake, for whatever benefit the individual may gain. . . . In any event, the apparent lack of relevance of the dance here at issue to any political decisions is immaterial; . . . the dance potentially merits First Amendment protection. Thus the First Amendment cannot be constricted into a straitjacket of protection for political expression alone. Its embrace extends to all forms of communication, including the highest: the work of art.[5]

A work of art which did not get First Amendment protection in 1970 consisted of "constructions," similar to sculptures, by artist Marc Morrel and displayed for sale at Mr. Radich's art Gallery on Madison Avenue in New York City, "constructions" in which the flag of the United States was used in the following manner:

> 1—in the form of a male sexual organ, protruding from the body of form, in the anterior portion of the body of the form and depicting the erected male penis, protruding from a form of a cross. 2—the flag of the United States of America, wrapped in a chained bundle. 3—the standard of the United States on the form of an alleged elephant. 4—the Union of the flag of the United States of America, depicted in the form of an octopus. 5—the American flag attached to a gas meter. 6—the American flag wrapped around a bundle attached to a two wheeled vehicle. 7—the American flag in the form of a body, hanging from a yellow noose.[6]

Mr. Radich was convicted for violation of a New York penal provision which said, in substance, that any person who shall publicly mutilate, deface, defile, or defy, trample upon, or cast contempt upon the flag of the United States of America, either by words or act, shall be guilty of a misdemeanor. Mr. Radich, testifying in his own behalf at his trial, explained that the "constructions" were protest art and when he was asked about the use of the flag for the purpose of protest ". . . he said that the object extending from the vertical member of the cross and wrapped in a small flag was representative of a human penis; that tassels at the base of this protrusion represented 'probably * * * decorative or pubic hair, depending on what one decides it looks like to him.' "[7] Mr. Radich was then asked as to the particular expression and protest intended to be conveyed and he replied "that perhaps the penis represents the sexual act, which by some standards is considered an aggressive act; that organized religion is also symbolized by the figure, which seems to suggest that organized religion is supporting the aggressive acts suggested."[8] In upholding the conviction, the New York Court of Appeals said: "The defendant may have a sincere ideological viewpoint, but he must find other ways to express it. Whether defendant thinks so or not, a reasonable man would consider the wrapping of a phallic symbol with the flag as an act of dishonor; he would consider the hanging effigy a dishonor; and to a lesser and more debatable extent it might be found that wrapping the flag in chains, attaching it to a gas meter, and fashioning the other representations involved, were acts dishonoring the flag."[9] Judge C. J. Fuld, however, did not agree and said in his dissenting opinion: ". . . in the absence of a showing that public health, safety or the well being of the community is threatened, the State may not act to suppress symbolic speech or conduct having a clearly communication aspect, no matter how obnoxious it may be to the prevailing views of the majority."[10]

The protest art displayed by Radich and the topless dance by Iser are only two cases among many others of the past decade during which the courts have had to decide on the communicative functions of symbolic behavior such as wearing black armbands to school to protest the Vietnam war,[11] burning the flag of the United States to protest the shooting of James Meredith,[12] burning draft cards to protest the war and the draft,[13] wearing a jacket bearing on it the words "Fuck the Draft,"[14] sit-ins to protest racial segregation,[15] demonstrations for civil rights,[16] heckling a Congressman delivering a Fourth of July speech,[17] and cutting up an American flag to have it made into a vest worn in public.[18] The symbolic behavior and the rhetorical strategies of the dissenters of the past decade have made it necessary for the courts to decide questions related to the communicative aspects of these strategies and behavior. Up to the middle of the twentieth century, when the courts dealt with freedom of speech issues, they were for the most part dealing with oral and written discourse: pamphlets, speeches, literature of various kinds.[19] This is not to say that the courts did not on occasion consider the communicative features of such activities as picketing,[20] flag salutes,[21] and displaying of a red flag.[22] But in the 1960s, with the coming of the civil rights movement, with its sit-ins, boycotts, picketing, demonstrations, and other symbolic behavior, the courts more than ever were required to make decisions on what constituted "speech." Following the civil rights sit-ins and demonstrations there came the anti-war protesters and their diverse rhetorical strategies and behavior. The problems faced by the jurists in deciding what constitutes "speech" and "communication" are problems which nonjurists interested in speech, rhetoric, or communication cannot ignore any longer. What jurists and legal scholars have had to say in the past decade (and earlier) about speech and communication indicates that nonjurists would do well to pay attention to them in their attempts to arrive at definitions and interpretation of "speech."

Before turning to some of those definitions and interpretations, it is appropriate here to look at another freedom guaranteed by the First Amendment, the freedom of assembly, for without this freedom much of our speech would be sterile and the freedom to petition the government for a redress of grievances would be meaningless. Historically, the right of assembly has long been closely connected with the right of petition.[23] It is not without reason that one of the first acts of a totalitarian regime is to restrict or do away with the freedom of assembly. Yet this freedom, so important in a free society and so closely related to freedom of speech, has been conspicuously ignored by scholars interested in speech and communication. Freedom of assembly, the right to organize and conduct meetings are so taken for granted, it would appear, that little need be said about them. Yet without freedom of assembly, we might as well be talking to ourselves when we speak orally or through symbolic behavior. Without the right to freely assemble together, we would soon recognize the dependency of communication on community. In a speech delivered in 1963 at Brown University, Justice William O. Douglas pointed out that "joining a lawful organization, like attending a church, is an associational activity that comes within the purview of the First Amendment. 'Peaceably to assemble' necessarily involves a coming together, whether regularly or spasmodically. A coming together is often necessary for communication—for those who listen as well as those who speak. . . . Joining a group is often as vital to freedom of expression as utterance itself."[24]

On several occasions the United States Supreme Court has emphasized the importance of freedom of assembly and its close relationship to freedom of speech. In 1937, Chief Justice Hughes said in De Jonge v. Oregon: "The right of peaceable assembly is a right cognate to those of free speech and free press and is equally fundamental. . . . The greater the importance of safeguarding the community from incitements to the overthrow of our institutions by force and violence, the more imperative is the need to preserve inviolate the constitutional rights of free speech, free press, and free assembly in order to maintain the opportunity for free political discussion, to the end that government may be responsive to the will of the people and that changes, if desired, may be obtained by peaceful means."[25] In 1944, the United States Supreme Court, after asserting that freedom of assembly could be limited only under the gravest abuses, endangering paramount interests, said that "it is . . . in our tradition to allow the widest room for discussion, the narrowest range for its restriction, particularly when this right is exercised in conjunction with peaceable assembly. It was not by accident or coincidence that the rights of freedom of speech and press were coupled in a single guarantee with the rights of the people peaceably to assemble and to petition for redress of grievances. All these, though not identical, are inseparable. They are cognate rights, and therefore are united in the First Article's assurance."[26]

The person who wants to communicate his thoughts and feelings and grievances usually wants an audience, a group of people who will hear his message, all of which implies the right of people to assemble together to hear the communication. To prohibit the citizenry to gather together for meetings can isolate them from each other and in effect restrict their speaking and acting in concert. Freedom of assembly is particularly relevant to the dissent of the 1960s and 1970s since without this freedom demonstrations, sit-ins, parades, and related rhetorical strategies of the dissenters would have been and will be prohibited. Much of the message in the dissenter's communication is in the symbolic activities which bring together a number of people; where the verbal communication would not create unity and group cohesiveness, the demonstration and parade would; where verbal communication would not inspire determination and commitment, the sit-in and public draft card burning would. And all of this symbolic rhetorical behavior of the dissenter presumes a right to freely assemble together.

The nexus between communication, the dissenters' symbolic behavior of the past decade, and the First Amendment has been recognized and commented upon by various judges and legal scholars. Their observations indicate that much remains to be done in this crucial area of communication and the law. A lengthy "Note" in the June 1968 issue of the *Columbia Law Review* begins with a recognition of the need to grapple with the questions and problems which have been raised with the increased uses of this type of symbolic conduct as a means of communication. The "Note" begins: "Symbolic conduct is an exceptionally vivid means of communication. It is more intensely emotional than the spoken or written word or the traditional cool art forms. Its dramatic effect is a substitute for the protester's lack of access to the more traditional mass media. The illegal act of burning draft cards, done at mass rallies in a city park, creates news and assures press and television coverage for the 'speaker's' views. The same voice would be lost in obscurity if its only outlet were mimeographed pamphlets."[27] Two important reasons why First Amendment claims of symbolic communication cannot be slighted are presented in the "Note." First, there is the matter of assuring that the freedoms in the First Amendment will remain alive, relevant, and a significant force in our society. This can happen ". . . only if the methods of communication actually employed in our complex world are afforded substantial protection. . . . In today's society symbolic conduct is a widely practiced form of communication and may, in fact, convey a thought more effectively than sophisticated oratory. To the extent we accord inadequate protection to symbolic conduct, we place fetters on expression and in some small way clog the channels of communication."[28] Secondly, there is the matter of silencing and alienating those persons who do not possess verbal skills: "Implicit in the notion that the first amendment gives a man the right to say what he wants is the idea that a man must be able to form his own beliefs and opinions, that he is to be allowed to express his thoughts and beliefs in his own way, and that any suppression of either the formation or the expression of these beliefs and opinions is an affront to his dignity. Perhaps the artist in *People v. Radich* who wrapped a construction resembling a dead body in an American flag had not the eloquence to express in words his disgust and revulsion with America and its participation in what he believed to be an unjustified war."[29] While recognizing the need to provide First Amendment protection to symbolic conduct, the "Note" concludes with an acknowledgment of the problems we face in according that protection:

> There can be no doubt that a commitment to free expression is a strain on any society and its legal system. It is very tempting to cut corners with our civil liberties when the facts are ambiguous. The burden of tolerating symbolic speech is even greater than that of protecting verbal expression. Once we acknowledge the existence of symbolic speech, we find that otherwise valid laws may be broken and the lawbreakers left unpunished. We may find some who violate a statute are to be penalized, while others may go free if they intended to communicate. Statutes which have been on the books for many years must be reassessed in light of new times, when the conduct which they restrict becomes a popular form of protest. Symbolic speech, however, must be recognized by the courts, for there can be no doubt that nonverbal expression is speech, both in fact and in law.[30]

Not only must symbolic speech be recognized by the courts, it must also be recognized by laymen and scholars interested in "speech" in our society. The relationship between what the public will accept in this area and what the jurists will decide is commented on by political scientist Theodore Denno when he writes about the *Tinker* decision and the Court's equating the wearing of black armbands by students (to protest the war in Vietnam) with "pure speech": "Rather than moving to define symbolic speech and/or action, the Court chose to interpret pure speech beyond a simply verbal expression. As a matter of tactics in legal maneuvers there may be reasons to prefer one move over the other, but the accomplished results are the final test. Expanding on speech is moving from known solid ground to unexplored territory rather than plunging directly into the unknown. Public acceptance, of course, is always a question in the justices' minds."[31] That public acceptance is somewhat dependent on how we treat symbolic behavior as an area of study in our institutions of learning.

As I have pointed out elsewhere,[32] we need to better understand and appreciate the communicative functions of the symbolic "speech" of dissenters and non-dissenters. The "advances" of contemporary society have brought with them the feeling so many Americans have of utter helplessness to propose, to alter, to support or oppose political and social programs and policies by the traditionally accepted means of discussion, debate, and voting. The further the people get away from their government, the less influence they have on their representatives, the diminishing possibility of being heard through the monopolistic mass media, the more likely the people will turn to other means of expressing and communicating their grievances. Justices Douglas, Warren, Brennan, and Fortas, in a case dealing with the convictions of black student protesters demonstrating at a Florida county jail, said in their dissenting opinion:

> The right to petition for redress of grievances has an ancient history and is not limited to writing a letter or sending a telegram to a congressman; it is

not confined to appearing before the local city council, or writing letters to the President or Governor or Mayor. . . . Conventional methods of petitioning may be, and often have been, shut off to large groups of our citizens. Legislators may turn deaf ears; formal complaints may be routed endlessly through a bureaucratic maze; courts may let the wheels of justice grind very slowly. Those who do not control television and radio, those who cannot afford to advertise in newspapers or circulate elaborate pamphlets may have only a limited type of access to public officials. Their methods should not be condemned as tactics of obstruction and harassment as long as the assembly and petition are peaceable, as these were.[33]

How was a Negro living in Brooklyn, New York supposed to express his deep-felt protest to the shooting of James Meredith on a Mississippi highway? Who would have heard the protest if he had written his congressman? What television time or newspaper space was available to him? How was this angry and grieved citizen to communicate his dissent? Mr. Sidney Street, living in a Brooklyn apartment, on June 6, 1966, hearing a radio news account of the shooting of James Meredith, took from his chest of drawers a neatly folded, 48-star American flag which he on occasion displayed on national holidays. He took the flag to a nearby street intersection where he lit the flag with a match and dropped the flag to the pavement when it began to burn. A police officer arrived, found the burning flag and heard Mr. Street say, "We don't need no damn flag." The officer asked Mr. Street if he had burned the flag and the reply was: "Yes; that is my flag; I burned it. If they let that happen to Meredith we don't need an American flag." Sidney Street was charged and convicted of having committed "the crime of Malicious Mischief in that [he] did wilfully and unlawfully defile, cast contempt upon and burn an American flag, in violation of 1425-16-D of the Penal Law, under the following circumstances: . . . [he] did wilfully and unlawfully set fire to an American Flag and shout, 'If they did that to Meredith, we don't need an American Flag.' " Mr. Street's conviction was appealed and in 1969 the United States Supreme Court reversed the lower court's decision.[34] Here is a situation of a black American citizen protesting through symbolic behavior the shooting of another black American citizen who was himself attempting to communicate, through his own symbolic behavior of walking alone down a Mississippi highway, the idea that a black American could walk safely and unmolested along the highways of the South.

The importance of studying and understanding the dissenters' symbolic behavior, its rhetorical functions, and relationship to the First Amendment, is made evident also by the misunderstandings about the differences between this activity and revolutionary action. Throwing balloons filled with red paint at a Federal building or burning an American flag or sitting-in to desegregate a lunch counter may be symbolic acts which have rhetorical functions, but they are not acts of revolution. Unfortunately, too often both the dissenters and their critics see such acts as revolutionary. And as far as some critics are concerned, such behavior must be suppressed inasmuch as the symbolic behavior has been labeled "revolutionary."

Revolutionary actions, actions which themselves are intended immediately to bring "the System" tumbling down are one thing. Symbolic behavior, violent or nonviolent, intended to persuade the "audience" to change attitudes and behavior is something else. Writing about the communicative aspects of the violence in the black communities in the 1960s, Professor Robert Fogelson has pointed out that ". . . the riots were attempts to alert America, not overturn it, to denounce its practices, not renounce its principles. They were not insurrections, and not because the Negroes lacked the numbers, power, and leaders, but because they wanted a change in norms, not in values."[35] Professor Harry Kalven, Jr., discussing the arrests and convictions of some black students for their demonstrations in South Carolina and Louisiana, comments on their styles of dissent: "These are structured ceremonials of protest; they are not riots. The demonstrators were not . . . trying to bring government to a halt; rather they were expressing the concern of the young Negro about his situation. What was symbolized was a deep grievance, not a break with the society. They prayed, they pledged allegiance to the flag, they sang 'God Bless America,' and —in Cox—they even stopped for a red traffic light. Whatever the power, pressure, and anxiety generated by such huge numbers, the demonstrations showed a tact, a grace, a patience, and a distinctive rhetoric of their own."[36]

Distinctions between the various kinds of symbolic speech need to be made. Unfortunately, too many Americans fail to make the distinctions and are eager to punish and imprison dissenters who choose to communicate their grievances through such symbolic behavior as sit-ins, demonstrations, picketing, flag burnings, draft card burnings, flying the American flag upside down, et cetera. This in itself would indicate that there is a need to study the dissenters' rhetorical strategies so that we can arrive at clearer distinctions between the various types of symbolic behavior, and as a result avoid blanket condemnation of all such behavior. Once these distinctions are made, then the decision about which of the strategies, as "speech," merit First Amendment protection, can be based on a knowledge that the strategies differ, take various forms, appeal to diverse motives and senses, evolve from a variety of grievances and circumstances, affect people differently, are intended to achieve various goals, and result sometimes in failure, sometimes in success.

We are faced with the task of distinguishing between revolutionary actions and symbolic rhetorical behavior; once the distinctions are made, we then face the task of distinguishing between symbolic behavior which is "speech" and that which is not; finally, we have to distinguish between that symbolic "speech" which warrants First Amendment protection and that which does not. In upholding the conviction of O'Brien for burning his draft card, the Court said in 1968: "We cannot accept the view that an apparently limitless variety of conduct can be labeled 'speech' whenever the person engaging in the conduct intends thereby to express an idea."[37] Three years earlier, the Court stated in Cox v. Louisiana that it rejected the notion "that the First and Fourteenth Amendments afford the same kind of freedom to those who would communicate ideas by conduct such as patrolling, marching, and picketing on streets and highways, as these amendments afford to those who communicate ideas by pure speech."[38]

While the courts have said that there are varieties of conduct which could not be labeled "speech" and that conduct and "pure speech" are different enough from each other not to warrant the same kind of First Amendment protection, they have at the same time spoken of the civil rights demonstrations in *Edwards* as an example of "an exercise of these basic constitutional rights [First and Fourteenth Amendments] in their most pristine and classic form."[39] Further, the Court said in *Tinker* that the problem of deciding whether students have the right to wear black armbands to school to protest the war in Vietnam was a problem involving "direct, primary First Amendment rights akin to 'pure speech.' "[40] So one question (among others) we are faced with is, to use Professor Denno's words, "What is there about parading, picketing, soliciting, demonstrating, distributing pamphlets, sit-ins, burning draft cards, wearing armbands, displaying a red flag, burning an American flag, hanging clothes on a front lawn, sitting on a sidewalk, or wearing a vest made out of a flag, that characterizes some of these acts as expressive and others as just plain conduct?"[41] The answer to this question needs to come not only from the jurists of our society, but also from students and professors studying and writing in the areas of speech, rhetoric, and communication.[42]

There are many other communication and law problems and controversies which require ongoing inquiry. Reoccurring bans on the appearances of speakers, especially at our colleges and universities, are to be contended with.[43] Censorship questions, especially as related to television broadcasting and programming, remain unresolved.[44] Drama and film productions periodically become the objects of the censors.[45] The duties and responsibilities of an audience listening to a speaker become subjects of court decisions deciding the rights of the heckler.[46] In 1970, a Federal District judge had to decide the constitutionality of a rule that required that a man salute the flag as a condition of letting him speak at a public meeting.[47] In 1970, there were scores of cases before the courts dealing with the desecration of the flag.[48]

If the First Amendment freedoms are to be significant and vital forces in our society, jurist and layman alike must examine and re-examine the definitions and grounds upon which those freedoms are based. Without this ongoing inquiry, as with opinions generally held by mankind, the freedoms may become dead beliefs, maxims to be uttered at appropriate occasions. What John Stuart Mill said about vital religious doctrines degenerating into dead dogma which people mouth but do not make a part of their everyday conduct applies equally to our First Amendment guarantees: "They are not insincere when they say they believe these things. They do believe them, as people believe what they have always heard lauded and never discussed. But in the sense of that living belief which regulates conduct, they believe these doctrines just up to the point to which it is usual to act upon them. The doctrines in their integrity are serviceable to pelt adversaries with."[49] In the end, the vitality of our First Amendment freedoms and the breadth of these freedoms are determined by the citizenry.

Too often, however, we have relied on the courts to protect our freedom of speech, when the citizenry should have been doing the protecting by seeing to it that suppressive measures never were legislated in the first place. We cannot always expect the courts to do for us what we should do for ourselves, that is, guard our First Amendment freedoms from overzealous men who are afraid of freedom and who, being afraid, attempt to restrict the expression of others. As Professor of Law Daniel Pollitt wrote in the *North Carolina Law Review*: "Although the courts have held fast to democratic traditions, and in some instances have extended first amendment freedoms to new fields, the pressures of uncertainty and confusion have pushed other public agencies, and private citizens, to extreme action. Pacifists have been beaten by toughs, the Georgia legislature attempted to deny an elected seat to Julian Bond because of his anti-war expressions, highschool students have been suspended for wearing black armbands in mourning for the Viet Nam dead."[50] The American people, says Professor of Law Thomas I. Emerson, ". . . have frequently been warned that they must not count too heavily upon the legal system for the preservation of democratic liberties."[51] But it seems to me that the warning has not been heeded for we have counted largely on the courts, the judges, and legal scholars to define and defend our First Amendment freedoms.

Under our system, the citizenry and their representatives initially make the decisions to censor or not to censor, to ban or not to ban. It is this citizenry which must be taught in our institutions of learning the implications, definitions, and utility of the freedoms of speech, assembly, and petition. It was, after all, a jury of laymen who initially denied Miss Iser's dance First Amendment protection. Protesters communicating through heckling their dissatisfaction with Congressman Tunney's Fourth of July speech were convicted by a jury of laymen. Laymen demanded that a person must salute the flag before he could speak at a public meeting. Laymen originally ruled that black armbands could not be worn by students to protest the war in Vietnam. Laymen ban from the libraries *Soul on Ice*, *Brave New World*, *Catcher in the Rye*, and scores of other books. Laymen elect representatives like Congressman F. Edward Hebert who proposed that "we forget about the First Amendment" in order to prosecute anti-war and civil rights spokesmen. The May 6, 1967 *New York Times* reported: "Members of the House Armed Services Committee demanded today that the Justice Department disregard the First Amendment right of free speech and prosecute those who urged young men to defy the draft law. 'Let's forget about the First Amendment,' Representative F. Edward Hebert, Democrat of La., told Assistant Attorney General Fred M. Vinson, Jr., in a loud voice during hearings on the draft." One congressman wanted to know why Stokely Carmichael had not been prosecuted for leading students at Hampden Institute in chanting, "We ain't gonna go. Hell no." The Assistant Attorney General replied that his department could not prosecute Mr. Carmichael because of the First Amendment and he cited a decision going back to Oliver Wendell Holmes that utterances were protected by the First Amendment unless they constituted a "clear and present danger" to the country. Congressman Hebert's reply revealed that he was ready to deny First Amendment rights to more people than Mr. Carmichael. "We have been made aware of that in the past year," Mr. Hebert replied to the Assistant Attorney General. "How can the Carmichaels and Kings stand before the American people and incite violation of the law while the Justice Department stands idly by?" "No one," Mr. Vinson said, "has been prosecuted because the department felt no one has violated the law." Could the law be amended to "get around the First Amendment?" asked Mr. Hebert. "Any law that deals with utterances must be read in the light of the First Amendment," said Mr. Vinson. It was then that Congressman Hebert said, "Let's forget about the First Amendment."

We cannot, however, "forget about the First Amendment." In the words of Learned Hand: "[The First Amendment] presupposes that right conclusions are more likely to be gathered out of a multitude of tongues, than through any kind of authoritarian selection. To many this is, and always will be folly; but we have staked upon it our all."[52] If we have staked upon it our all, then our folly would be not to give it our all.

NOTES

[1] John Milton, *Areopagitica and Of Education* (New York, 1951), p. 26.

[2] *Ibid.*, p. 23.

[3] *In re Giannini*, 72 Cal. Rptr. 655, 660, 446 P.2d 535, 540 (1968).

[4] *Ibid.*, at 663, 446 P.2d at 543.

[5] *Ibid.*, at 660, 446 P.2d at 540.

[6] *People v. Radich*, 26 N.Y.2d 114, 117, 308 N.Y.S.2d 846, 848 (1970).

[7] *Ibid.*, at 118, 308 N.Y.S.2d at 848.

[8] *Ibid.*

[9] *Ibid.* at 123, 308 N.Y.S.2d at 852.

[10] *Ibid.* at 127, 308 N.Y.S.2d at 856.

[11] *Tinker v. Des Moines Ind. Community School District*, 393 U.S. 503 (1969).

[12] *Street v. New York*, 359 U.S. 576 (1969).

[13] *United States v. O'Brien*, 391 U.S. 367 (1968).

[14] *People v. Cohen*, 81 Cal. Rptr. 503, 1 Cal. App.3d 94 (1969).

[15] *Garner v. Louisiana*, 368 U.S. 157 (1961); *Brown v. Louisiana*, 383 U.S. 131 (1966).

[16] *Edwards v. South Carolina*, 372 U.S. 229 (1963); *Cox v. Louisiana*, 383 U.S. 131 (1966); *Adderley v. Florida*, 385 U.S. 39 (1966).

[17] *In re Kay*, 83 Cal. Rptr. 686, 464 P.2d 142 (1970).

[18] *People v. Cowgill*, 78 Cal. Rptr. 853, 274 Cal. App.2d 174 (1969).

[19] *Schenck v. United States*, 249 U.S. 47 (1919); *Abrams v. United States*, 250 U.S. 616 (1919); *Gitlow v. New York*, 268 U.S. 652 (1925); *Whitney v. California*, 274 U.S. 357 (1927); *Herndon v. Lowry*, 301 U.S. 242 (1937); *Cantwell v. Connecticut*, 310 U.S. 296 (1940); *Chaplinsky v. New Hampshire*, 315 U.S. 568 (1942); *Terminiello v. Chicago*, 337 U.S. 1 (1949); *Feiner v. New York*, 340 U.S. 315 (1951).

[20] *Thornhill v. Alabama*, 310 U.S. 88 (1940); *Milk Wagon Drivers Union, Local 753 v. Meadowmoor Dairies, Inc.*, 312 U.S. 287 (1941); *Giboney v. Empire Storage and Ice Co.*, 336 U.S. 490 (1949).

[21] *West Virginia State Board of Education v. Barnette*, 319 U.S. 624 (1943).

[22] *Stromberg v. California*, 283 U.S. 359 (1931).

[23] David Fellman, *The Constitutional Right of Association* (Chicago, 1963), pp. 3 ff.

[24] William O. Douglas, "The Right of Association," *Columbia Law Review*, 63 (December 1963), 1374.

[25] *De Jonge v. Oregon*, 299 U.S. 353 (1937).

[26] *Thomas v. Collins*, 323 U.S. 516 (1945).

[27] "Symbolic Conduct," *Columbia Law Review*, 68 (June 1968), 1091.

[28] *Ibid.*, pp. 1106–1107.

[29] *Ibid.*, p. 1107.

[30] *Ibid.*, p. 1126.

[31] Theodore Denno, "Mary Beth Tinker Takes the Constitution to School," *Fordham Law Review*, 38 (October 1969), 45.

[32] See especially Introductions to my *Dissent: Symbolic Behavior and Rhetorical Strategies* (Allyn and Bacon, in press) and *The Rhetoric of Nonverbal Communication* (in press).

[33] *Adderley v. Florida*, 385 U.S. 39 (1966).

[34] *Street v. New York*, 394 U.S. 576 (1969).

[35] Robert Fogelson, "Violence as Protest," in *Urban Riots: Violence and Social Change*, ed. Robert H. Connery (New York, 1969), p. 35.

[36] Harry Kalven, Jr., *The Negro and the First Amendment* (Chicago: Phoenix Books, 1966), pp. 178–179.

[37] *United States v. O'Brien*, 391 U.S. 367 (1968).

[38] *Cox v. Louisiana*, 379 U.S. 536 (1965).

[39] *Edwards v. South Carolina*, 372 U.S. 229 (1963).

[40] *Tinker v. Des Moines Ind. Community School District*, 393 U.S. 503 (1969).

[41] Denno, p. 189.

[42] See for instance, Franklyn S. Haiman, "The Rhetoric of the Streets; Some Legal and Ethical Considerations," *Quarterly Journal of Speech*, 53 (April 1967), 99–114.

[43] *Brooks v. Auburn University*, 280 F. Supp. 188 (1969); *Dickson v. Sitterson*, 280 F. Supp. 486 (1968); *Snyder v. Board of Trustees of University of Illinois*, 286 F. Supp. 927 (1968); *Egan v. Moore*, 14 N.Y.S.2d 775, 199 N.E.2d 842 (1964); *Buckley v. Meng*, 230 N.Y.S.2d 924 (1962); *American Civil Liberties Union v. Board of Education of City of Los Angeles*, 55 Cal.2d 167, 359 P.2d 45 (1961); *McLaurin v. Oklahoma State Regents*, 339 U.S. 637 (1950); *Danskin v. San Diego Unified School District*, 28 Cal.2d 536, 171 P.2d 885 (1946).

[44] See Goodman Ace, "The Dirty Five-letter Word," *Saturday Review*, 53 (January 24, 1969), p. 10, comments by Miss Judy Collins on Dick Cavett show blipped out by network (see *New York Times*, March 31, 1970); Joan Barthel, "The Panic in TV Censorship," *Life*, 67 (August 1, 1969), 51–54; David Dempsey, "Social Comment and TV Censorship," *Saturday Review*, 52 (July 12, 1969), 53–55; Nat Hentoff, "Who Controls TV?" *Look*, 33 (June 24, 1969), 27–29; Nicholas Johnson, "The Silent Screen," *TV Guide*, 17 (July 5, 1969), 6–13; "Listener's Right to Hear in Broadcasting," *Stanford Law Review*, 22 (April 1970), 863–902; Richard Marks, "Broadcasting and Censorship: First Amendment Theory After Red Lion," *The George Washington Law Review*, 38 (July 1970), 974–1005; Marilyn Zack, "F.C.C. and the Fairness Doctrine," *Cleveland State Law Review*, 19 (September 1970), 579–594; "ABC and NBC Agree to Pastore Censorship Plan," *Censorship Today*, 2 (June–July 1969), 50–53.

[45] *Hair, Che!, The Beard, Oh! Calcutta!*, and *The Slave* all have been recent targets of the censors. For instance, see "All 7 in 'Che!' Guilty of Obscenity," *New York Times*, February 26, 1970; for *Hair* controversy in Boston, see *New York Times*, May 7, 1970 and May 23, 1970; *Oh! Calcutta!* controversy reported in *New York Times*, December 19, 1969; *I am Curious—Yellow*, as of March 1970, was the subject of obscenity cases in twenty-three cities in thirteen states (see *New York Times*, March 24, 1970); "Maryland Librarians Condemn Film Censors," *Library Journal*, 95 (June 15, 1970), 2212; David Merrick, "Must Smut Smother the Stage?" *Reader's Digest*, (March 1970), 103–105. See also *United States v. A Motion Picture Entitled "I Am Curious—Yellow,"* 404 F.2d 196 (1968) and more recently, a Federal appeals court overruled a lower court jury verdict and held that *Language of Love*, a Swedish motion picture, was not obscene and must released by Customs officials (*New York Times*, September 16, 1970).

[46] See especially *In re Kay*, 83 Cal. Rptr. 686, 464 P.2d 142 (1970).

[47] See *New York Times*, September 9, 1970.

[48] See *Civil Liberties*, September 1970.

[49] John S. Mill, *On Liberty* (New York, 1947), p. 41.

[50] Daniel Pollitt, "Free Speech for Mustangs and Mavericks," *North Carolina Law Review*, 46 (December 1967), 39–40.

[51] Thomas I. Emerson, "Toward a General Theory of the First Amendment," *The Yale Law Journal*, 72 (April 1963), 893.

[52] *United States v. Associated Press*, 52 F. Supp. 362 (1943).

FREE PRESS FAIR GAME
FOR SOUTH AFRICA'S GOVERNMENT

Trevor Brown

TREVOR BROWN, a South African, was a Rhodes Scholar to Oxford University, where he received a B.A. and M.A. in Modern History. He worked on a Cape Town daily newspaper, then received an M.A. in journalism at Stanford University. He was a junior lecturer in English literature at the University of Cape Town for two years before returning to Stanford University to work on his Ph.D. in public affairs communication. In January 1972, he took a post as assistant professor in the Department of Journalism at Indiana University.

"I see South Africa as having a Government and an Opposition. But this Opposition is not the United Party. It's the newspapers. I see this as a very healthy state of affairs," said Nationalist Member of Parliament Val Volker in an interview with the Natal Mercury January 22, 1970. His is an exceptional view in South Africa's ruling National party. It is also inaccurate.

Restricted by government legislation and threat, restrained by cautious owners, read but seldom revered by the public, South Africa's press is far too vulnerable to act as an effective opposition. Significant sections of the press, moreover, either do not believe in or cannot risk an oppositional stance to government—the Afrikaans press is essentially the handmaiden of the National Party; non-white newsmen suffer under apartheid as second class citizens and as employees of white owners. Mr. Volker must refer then to the dominant section of the press, the English-language newspapers, and his conception of their role emerged in his next breath.

He saw little merit, he said, in a newspaper exposé of government malpractice or unethical behavior in the medical profession. Too much such knowledge might shatter public confidence in institutions of this nature and lead to instability. "There are no real alternatives for these things," he concluded, "and you don't have anything to replace them with if you destroy them."

The press may oppose; it may not expose. This is to confine South African newspapers to a form of political party debate, a function they have not always transcended.

> Instead of being an arbiter it [the South African press] has become, through varied historical, political and economic causes, the vehicle of one section. It stands for non-partisanship but is, in fact, politically partisan. What it pronounces good is immediately branded by the opposing section as bad. There is thus, even in the small white minority, no moral judge of public affairs, but only instruments of endlessly contending parties.[1]

English-language newspapers have dared to practice the libertarian ethic they profess, but at the expense often of professional perspective. The tendency has

Reprinted with permission of Journalism Quarterly (1971), 120–127.

been less to watch over government than to catch out the Nationalist Government, a distinction which has blurred largely because journalists receive little or no professional training. Brilliant and courageous as some have been in defense of press freedom, most are inadequately prepared for its responsibilities. Perceptible shifts in journalists' attitudes lighten the gloom of this situation but the dead weight of ideology and legislation frustrates significant change.

Six months before Mr. Volker observed a very healthy state of affairs, the Nationalist Government had virtually secured a press-government relationship in conformity with his conception.

In late June 1969, the Newspaper Press Union (NPU), the association of South African newspaper owners, sent a deputation to Deputy Minister of Justice G. F. van L. Froneman. Section 29 of the 1969 General Law Amendment Act had created the Bureau of State Security (labeled BOSS by the opposition) and empowered certain State officials to prevent a court from receiving evidence considered by any of these officials as prejudicial to the interests of the State or public security, and the NPU was worried that newspapers might be liable for unwittingly reporting on security matters. Mr. Froneman quieted their fears. Innocent publication would not incur prosecution, he said, "there would only be a contravention if the publication of security matters was prejudicial to the interest of the Republic and such publication was wilful." He assured the NPU he would always be prepared to discuss the reporting of security matters with the press.[2]

The South African Society of Journalists (SASJ)[3] was not as comforted. It issued the following statement:

> As long as this law remains in force, never again will the public of South Africa have any means of knowing how much information is being suppressed and whether the Government—through the Prime Minister, his nominees or his Ministers—is acting genuinely in the interests of the State, or whether secrecy is being resorted to for other reasons. . . .[4]

The SASJ asserted that the act's effect on newspapers was far worse than that of direct censorship. Newspapers would be "forced not to publish news on certain spheres without their being able to ascertain what these spheres encompass," a situation which would "stop free inquiry by the Press in many important fields, and the public will no longer have access to full and authoritative information to which it might otherwise be entitled." George Oliver, president of SASJ, said the South African press had entered "a new dark era in which the normal means of communication enjoyed elsewhere in the enlightened world will be sacrificed for secrecy, acute apprehension and ever-present peril."[5]

CASE OF THE RAND DAILY MAIL

The day after the Rand Daily Mail reported the SASJ's statement, a classic confrontation between press and government ended in a Johannesburg court. On July 10 after an 89-day trial in which the issues of press freedom and performance had been ominously defined, the Mail was convicted of violating the Prisons Act; specifically, of failing to take "reasonable steps" to verify information in its exposé of prison conditions published in June 1965. The fines were negligible. The owners, South African Associated Newspapers (SAAN), paid $420; editor Laurence Gander $280; and senior reporter Benjamin Pogrund, author of the articles, was given a six-month jail sentence suspended for three years.

Details of the Mail's violation of the law obscure the underlying struggle; the paper's real offense, and that of the entire English language press, emerged as different points in senior state counsel Liebenberg's address to the court. Cyril Dunn reporting the trial for the London Observer of July 13, 1969, wrote:

> . . . he had made it clear that in the opinion of the State there could be no such thing as a freedom which allowed the Press to be anything but subservient to the interests of the Government, with which Mr. Liebenberg plainly identified the interests of the country. . . .
> . . . besides insisting that a newspaper must not attack Government officials, Mr. Liebenberg had also said that a newspaper must not cause "stirs or rumpuses," must not arrogate to itself rights it did not possess, and must serve the interest, not of small sections of extremists, but of the majority of its readers.

Gandar responding in the Mail, July 12, 1969, with a front page editorial headed "A Free Press," concluded:

> . . . the obvious disadvantages of Press freedom—sensationalism, bias, invasion of privacy, and so on—are far outweighed by the incalculable advantages to society of the fullest possible disclosure of information, access to a variety of opinions, exposure of malpractices and the promotion of public discussion of matters of importance. Without this democracy would die.

Democracy wasn't dead after the trial, but it was less alive. Yet confusing events not long before the Mail's conviction hed held out some hope. On June 21 the Mail had reported the banning of the May edition of the African paper Drum (it had been selling for a month). Why? Was an article, "Love Without Fear," by sex education expert Dr. Eustace Chesser the cause? Drum editor G. R. Naido said he had no idea. The same issue of the Mail reported that the Publications Control Board had passed the controversial film "Katrina," awarding it an "A" rating (suitable for general audiences). Emil Nofal, producer of this first local film about interracial love, proclaimed that "a new era in South African film making had been started."

Oliver's vision of a dark era for the press and Nofal's era then were strikingly contradictory, even for a country dazzling in its ability to rationalize and balance contradiction. "Katrina's" rating, however encouraging, nevertheless ran counter to a trend consistent for 20 years during which beleaguered journalists have defended a press philosophy inadequately understood and less and less tolerated in South Africa.

The libertarian theory of the press is predicated on the separation of press and government and, to sustain democracy, approves an adversary relationship between them. In defiance of the British Cape Colony government Thomas

Pringle introduced this Anglo-American journalistic ethic to South Africa in 1824. The Republic's Nationalist Government is concerned less with democracy, however, than with the survival of white South Africa. It is intolerant of any such separation, and its authoritarian ideology concedes no conflict of interest when press and government are one.

The involvement of the National Party in the Afrikaans press is total.[6] Dr. D. F. Malan, leader of the victorious National Party in the 1948 election, had been editor of Die Burger and with his successor as Nationalist prime minister, Johannes Strydom, had formed the Voortrekkerpers company to publish Die Transvaler as an organ for the Party in the Transvaal. First editor of this Afrikaans daily was Dr. Hendrik Verwoerd, prime minister after Strydom's death in 1958, and a major shareholder in the Voortrekkerpers and in the Afrikaansepers (publishers of Die Vaderland and Dagbreek). Johannes Vorster, Vervoerd's minister of justice, was chairman of the boards of both the Voortrekkerpers and Afrikaansepers in 1966, posts he resigned when he became premier after Vervoerd's assassination that year. Minister of Bantu Administration and Development M. C. Botha took over the chairmanships from him.

National Party leadership dominates the boards of all the Afrikaans newspaper companies and is irritated by the modicum of editorial independence which does exist, rigidly contained though it is within the aspirations of Afrikanerdom. In October 1965, for example, when the Nasionale Pers launched a new Afrikaans Sunday paper, Die Beeld, in competition with the Afrikaansepers's Dagbreek, Dr. Vervoerd, then chairman of both companies, responded anxiously: "It would be a great pity if this should diminish the power of existing National media which are such a valuable aid to our cause." (News/check, July 15, 1966)

The unity of Afrikaans press and government in service of that cause pervades the administrative structure of much governed South Africa. Attack on any institution of government is attack on all. The Mail's exposé of prisons, therefore, was a form of treason, and before the series was complete the security police raided the Mail's offices, seizing Gandar's and Pogrund's passports. Leading journalists on other English language papers have suffered similar harassment.

The government has used this tactic of intimidation mainly because the Press Commission failed to complete its task and recommend legislation directly to curb the press. Appointed two years after the Nationalists came to power, the Commission sat for 13 years, and its voluminous report was essentially an indictment of the English press, whose "crimes" are suggested by the title of a pamphlet based on the 1964 report: "How They Hate Us: South Africa, and in particular the Afrikaners, their church, culture, leaders, under fire in the world press."[7]

Government attacks on the English press are echoed by the South African Broadcasting Corporation (SABC), a state monopoly. As a public corporation maintained by public funds, it should, theoretically, be above political partisanship. Yet Dr. Denis Worrall, a political scientist at the University of South Africa, in an analysis of an SABC program, "Current Affairs," counted six attacks on the Mail, four on the Star, three on the Cape Times, and three on the English press as a whole between June 1966, and July 1967.[8] Accused in Parliament of using the SABC as a propaganda machine for the National Party, Dr. Albert Hertzog, then minister of posts and telegraphs, now leader of the Herstigte (Reconstituted) Nasionale Party, and a "flat earthist if ever there was one,"[9] replied that the English press had over the years published "slanted news." "Current Affairs," he said, "could bring home to the English-speaking South Africans the true facts in regard to the news."[10]

LEGISLATION AND PRESS RELATIONS

But the true facts are difficult to obtain because of legislation inhibiting the press. Horace Flather, former editor of the *Star*, has said this legislation makes editing a newspaper in South Africa "like walking blindfolded through a minefield." Most formidable is the Suppression of Communism Act which, like the 1969 General Law Amendment Act, can be widely interpreted— virtually all reform advocated in South Africa by critics of the government can be equated with some of the aims of communism.[11] Difficulties multiply for reporters seeking information in non-white areas. The mass of apartheid legislation forbids them access without permit, and the black world is largely closed to whites.

The main African political organizations, the African National Congress and Pan African Congress, are banned, their leaders in exile or in jail. Such African founded and owned papers as *Ilange Lase Natal* and *Imvo Zabantsundu* have been bought by the Bantu Press, a white financed company which published the largest African newspaper, the *World*. This is now owned by the Argus Company, an English press group which also owns the *Cape Herald*, organ for the Cape Coloured community. In 1951 Jim Bailey, son of gold mining millionaire, Sir Abe Bailey, bought the most famous African paper, *Drum* (which ran an exposé of prisons back in 1953), and in 1955 founded the *Golden City Post*. The *Post*'s spectacular success (circulation in July 1968, was 250,000) seems to have reduced *Drum*'s popularity, and in 1965 it became an insert in the *Post*. Under a watchful government and white ownership, non-white editors have, understandably, muted political reporting and commentary, preferring to serve their readers a rich diet of sex and violence.[12]

White editors, however, maintain critical focus on politics despite an emasculated relationship with government. Reporters can rarely confront authority in person. Press conferences are almost never held; interviews with officials are difficult to secure.[13] Reporters must rely either on the Department of Information or on the Afrikaans press for news, which, because of government press ideology and its intimate involvement in Afrikaans newspapers, is often indistinguishable from propaganda.

The inadequacy of this relationship may in part explain the English newspapers' poor credibility with the public and the anomalous situation in which they find themselves. Although over half the white population is Afrikaans, the English press overwhelmingly exceeds the Afrikaans press in number of newspapers and in circulation. There are 13 English dailies and five Afrikaans. English newspaper circulation is roughly 680,000 to 215,000 Afrikaans.[14] But despite this dominance, uniformly anti-government English editorials are apparently ignored by readers, for since 1948 Nationalist electoral majorities have, until April 1970, steadily increased.[15]

Sensitive to these numbers, newspaper owners have diluted the idealism professed in Gandar's editorial. Morris Broughton, after 30 years of editorial experience in South Africa, most of them on Argus papers, is adamant:

> Freedom became secondary to the necessity of commercial and financial stability . . . The outcome has been that the balance of power rests to this day with the owners, through their instruments, the business managers and directorates. . . . There is no genuine editorial power of decision, only and fundamentally of conformity.[16]

South African Associated Newspapers has a reputation for greater flexibility but it is difficult to avoid the conclusion that management is concerned more with material self-interest than morality. Gander's stand doesn't sell newspapers; in South Africa principle costs.

The Prisons trial, for example, cost SAAN an estimated $280,000 in legal fees and precipitated a threatened merger. On November 11, 1968, 10 days after the trial began, a consortium of shareholders in SAAN, citing rising production costs and the need to diversify their investments, offered the Argus group an option to buy a 65.9% shareholding in SAAN, thereby giving the Argus Company control of 60% of all daily newspapers, English and Afrikaans; 70% of English language weekly circulation; and 77% of English language daily circulation. The English press protested. "Corder [Clive Corder, chairman of SAAN] and his associates have made it abundantly clear that as trustees, they are not interested in politics or the public interest, but only in money," commented the *Fnancial Mail* (in which SAAN has a 50% interest) on November 22, 1968. The takeover was in the interests neither of press freedom nor of journalists (since the Argus group would then control 74% of all employment opportunities), said the SASJ. Management ignored journalists' protests. The Argus took up the option, to be stopped instantly by Prime Minister Vorster: "The Cabinet feels that newspaper takeovers to this extent and which so obviously conflict with the public interest are not in the interests of the country."[17] After clearing its offer with the government, a smaller group led by the independent East London *Daily Dispatch* made a bid for the Argus option. The consortium rejected it and the question of merger was shelved.

Management took another slap from government that same month. In 1962, anticipating the criticisms of the Press Commission report, the NPU had drawn up its own code of conduct. A Board of Reference, composed of two managerial nominees under the chairmanship of a retired judge, was to try to insure that newspaper reports were accurate and not offensive to decency. Under the code the Board may reprimand any editor or journalist found guilty of an infringement of the code; and such reprimand will be published in other newspapers. The ambiguity of the code's final clause reveals the subtle modification of the libertarian tradition Thomas Pringle brought from Britain. It reads as follows: "Comment by newspapers should take due cognizance of the complex racial problems of South Africa and should also take into account the general good and the safety of the country and its peoples."[18] Implicit in the clause is power for the owners to suppress criticism of government. The Gander trial suggests why they might want to do so, why the creation of BOSS made them nervous.

But their caution and the Board's hearing of some 15 complaints in six years has not satisfied the government. On November 8, 1968, Minister of the Interior Lourens Muller announced that the government did not regard the NPU's code of conduct as sufficient guarantee against "sensational reporting and sex," and had decided to act. The English press was predictably loud in protest. If Mr. Muller intended "stuffing newspaper offices with censors," said the *Mail* (November 11, 1968), then the government "will have dropped the last remnant of pretended devotion to democratic principles."

Mr. Muller has not yet carried out his threat, and the last remnant still survives. With justification the English press, particularly the *Mail*, may claim some responsibility for the preservation of whatever democratic principles exist in South Africa and their courage has won the admiration of the Western democracies from which their traditions derive. Virtually ignored, however, has been the small but significant dissent of a few Afrikaans editors and newsmen.

DISSENT IN AFRIKAANS PRESS

Mr. Muller's threat, for example, provoked a timid plea from the Afrikaans Sunday paper, *Dagbreek en Landstem* (November 10, 1968): "No one would take it amiss if the Government decided to act against excessive sex and sensation. But the Government had to be careful not to create the impression that it actually wanted to get at the press itself." Afrikaans editor Schalk Pienaar was more outspoken. As the Cabinet debated whether to stop the Argus takeover of SAAN in November 1968, Pienaar warned: "This is a problem for the English Establishment—basically it is an English prickly pear which they should handle themselves. In any event, the National Government, for all its other virtues, has never yet distinguished itself in the handling of newspaper matters—except on that one occasion when it decided to leave newspapers alone to run their own affairs" (*Die Beeld*, November 24, 1968).

And in an article headed, "Thus Have the Afrikaans Newspapers Failed," Dirk Richard, editor of *Dagbreek*, asked his colleagues how well they had run their own affairs. At one time, he said, it was necessary for Afrikaners to stand together in politics, cultural affairs and in the Press. But because of this, after 1948 the Afrikaans press had backed every governmental action "when it could sometimes, very fruitfully for South Africa and the National Party, have come forward with constructive criticism." (*News/check*, January 26, 1968).

As the government has escalated its attack on the press, so increasingly a murmur has been heard from comparatively independent Afrikaans newspapers like the *Burger*, *Beeld* and *Dagbreek*. A vital participant in the development of the Afrikaans language and culture and in the political struggle with English-speaking South Africans, the Afrikaans press faithfully reflects the internal tensions of Afrikanerdom. After 20 years in power the National Party is rent by squabbles between the *verkrampte* (extreme conservative) and *verligte* (enlightened) factions, culminating last year in Dr. Hertzog's dismissal from the party and his formation of the Herstigte Nasionale Party. Though the HNP was crushed in the April 1970 elections the breach in Afrikaner ranks has not healed. The crack in the monolith has to some extent freed critical voices in Afrikaans newspapers, and the government, which often flies its kites in the Afrikaans press to test the response of the people, now apparently has a less passive instrument at its disposal.

If Afrikaner voices continue to rise in defense of press freedom, if they come to share that burden, then English newspapers may be freed for self-appraisal. "South Africa possesses some of the most readable daily newspapers in the world," says Douglas Brown.[19] In tense multiracial South Africa, however, newspaper readability may have more to do with an atmosphere of crisis and controversy than with journalistic talent. A social system which protects the privileges of a white minority and a lack of competition between newspapers and from other media dull aspirations to excellence, although television's introduction, expected within a few years, should disturb newsmen's complacency. Increasingly the quality of their performance is being questioned. *News/check*, South Africa's only newsmagazine, commented on June 17, 1966:

> There is . . . too little in-service training, a lack of concerted action in implanting the basic technical requirements of reporting, and a shirking of some much needed professional soul searching. Reporters cry about the freedom of the press, but do little to gain the expertise that brings confidence from their information sources.

South Africa universities have been slow to recognize their responsibilities in journalism education, newspaper owners have been reluctant to pay for theirs, and the public is not only uneducated about the standards and performance of a free press but increasingly socialized to reject them. A free press voices a conscience whites prefer to quiet. Initiative for improvement, therefore, has been left to journalists themselves and proposals now before the SASJ for more militant unionization are motivated by a desire mainly to protect employees against management, party to raise journalists' ethics and standards of performance.[20]

The battle for press freedom will continue. "Fear has and will shut out much but it will not silence South Africa's opposition press. They will speak out, they will still expose the iniquities where they find them anew," wrote a South African newsman on the Prisons trial for the British *Guardian* (July 17, 1969). That stance has flattered journalists' egos and retarded professional appraisal, but as newspapers prepare to confront the technological and economic mass media problems of the 20th century, journalists are growing more critical. Some Afrikaans journalists seem tentatively to be questioning their press ideology, many English journalists are examining their performance and such introspection may produce a healthier state of affairs in South Africa, a press-government relationship between respected adversaries rather than partisan opponents.

NOTES

[1] Morris Broughton, *Press and Politics of South Africa* (Cape Town, 1961), p. 5.

[2] *Rand Daily Mail*, June 20, 1969.

[3] The SASJ, whose membership (about 700) represents 80% of the editorial staff of English language newspapers, is "a sort of journalists' trade union negotiating with employers for wage increases, running its own educational trusts, and letting off at the government now and then. It has no counterpart among Afrikaans journalists, nor have Afrikaans journalists on any scale ever been keen to join the SASJ." (*News/check*, May 20, 1966).

[4] *Rand Daily Mail*, July 9, 1969.

[5] *Ibid.*

[6] Opposition politicians have also been involved in newspapers. Sir de Villiers Graaff, leader of the United Party, whose supporters are mainly English-speaking, was a minority shareholder in the Afrikaans weekly *Landstem* until the Afrikaanse Pers took it over in November 1967. At the same time the Argus group announced the closure of its Afrikaans Sunday paper, *Sondagstem*, and with these two events "non-Nationalist newspapers have been eliminated from the Afrikaans Press field altogether" (*News/check*, Dec. 1, 1967).

[7] H. M. Moolman, *How They Hate Us* (Pretoria, 1965).

[8] Denis Worrall, *New Nation*, July 1967.

[9] Stanley Uys, " 'No' to Arthur Ashe," *New Republic*, Feb. 14, 1970, p. 18.

[10] Muriel Horrell, *A Survey of Race Relations in South Africa* (Johannesburg, 1967), p. 63.

[11] Edgar H. Brookes and J. B. Macaulay, *Civil Liberty in South Africa* (Cape Town, 1958), pp. 72–88 discuss the legislation affecting the press. See also Richard L. Friedman, "Press Restrictions in South Africa," Freedom of Information Report No. 227, September 1969, and Peter B. Orlick, "Under Damocles' Sword—the South African Press," *Journalism Quarterly*, 46:343–8 (Summer 1969).

[12] Clive Kinsley, general manager of Rhodesian Printing and Publishing Company and the first general manager of the *World*, has a different view. "The immediate acceptance of the *World*," Kinsley said, "showed that it had met a widespread demand. Editorially, it concentrated on news of the Bantu townships, and avoided politics, because there was apparently very little interest in it among the Bantu" (*News/check*, Nov. 3, 1967). *News/check* (Dec. 22, 1967) itself commented that "If *Post* is so full of saucy sex and sudden death, so are the lives of its readers. And if it avoids dealing with high-sounding political, economic and social topics, this is because its readers are more involved in the elemental struggle to survive in a new urban environment."

[13] Minister of Information Dr. C. P. Mulder announced in Parliament in September 1970 that press conferences for the Prime Minister as well as special briefing sessions on important events would in future be held. Attendance of the conferences will be by invitation; local political correspondents and other senior editorial staff and accredited members of the foreign press corps will qualify. The creation of two senior posts—Press Liaison Officer and Assistant—had been approved, Dr. Mulder said (*News From South Africa*, Oct. 2, 1970).

[14] This estimate is compiled from figures listed in *Editor and Publisher International Yearbook 1970* (New York, 1970), p. 548, and Fritz Fenereisen and Ernst Schmacke, *Die Presse in Afrika* (Munchen-Pullach, 1968), pp. 174–91.

[15] In 1948 the Nationalists won by five seats with 40% of the vote; in 1953 they increased their representation from 79 to 94 seats and won 45.5% of the vote; in 1958 they won 103 seats and 49% of the vote; in 1961, 105 and 53.5%; in 1966, 126 and 58.6%; in 1970, they lost 9 seats and won 54.4% of the vote. This drop is largely explained by the candidacy of many Herstigte Nasionale Party members. The HNP won 3.56% of the vote but no seats.

[16] Broughton, op. cit., pp. 21–2.
[17] Rand Daily Mail, Nov. 20, 1968.
[18] Horrell, op. cit., 1963, p. 59.
[19] Douglas Brown, Against the World (New York, 1968), p. 153.
[20] Proposals to SASJ by Tim Muil, May 1970. Draft in author's possession.

CENSORSHIP AND
THE AUSTRALIAN PUBLIC

Tony Vinson and Arthur Robinson*

TONY VINSON *holds the degrees of M.A. from the University of New South Wales, with a Dip. Soc. and B.A. with a Dip. Soc. Stud. from the University of Sydney, Australia. After working as a psychologist and then parole officer in the New South Wales Department of Prisons, he gained further experience in industry while completing postgraduate studies in sociology. Appointed to the teaching staff of the School of Sociology of the University of New South Wales in 1963, he has been associated with the university's social work program since its inception in 1965.*

ARTHUR ROBINSON, *A.I.D.A., is a design consultant to the National Library of Australia. He is past president of the Industrial Design Institute of Australia and for some years has been engaged in a study of biological, psychological, and sociological aspects of design.*

In recent years Australia has witnessed lively discussion on the merits and disadvantages of its system of censorship. One facet of the controversy has been the questioning of the right to discuss publicly or present satirically conflicting viewpoints on topics considered taboo by some sections of the community, such as religion, politics and certain moral issues.

There has been little sound evidence available to help clarify the extent to which people generally oppose the presentation of "dangerous" opinions through mass media. Debate has usually centred on the largely emotional ideas of various spokesmen, who claim to represent the views of significant proportions of the public.

It has been demonstrated in a number of overseas studies that attitudes towards the open discussion of controversial issues lend themselves to objective study. For example, Stouffer (1963), an American researcher, developed a number of techniques for assessing public tolerance of minority viewpoints.[1] One form of questioning tested peoples' willingness to give to a hypothetical visitor the opportunity for speaking publicly in their community on various controversial issues.

In explaining his approach Stouffer pointed out that issues of civil liberty were not, and never had been, the preservation of absolute rights of freedom, but rather of how and where people set their limits. He illustrated his point of view in the following way: "Most business leaders can scarcely be expected to endorse the views of a man who advocates government ownership of . . . all

* Recently the authors with the assistance of a research grant from the Sebel Company of Australia, carried out a study of attitudes and held by sub-groups within Australian society. One of the topical issues investigated was the desirability of censorship of the mass media. The results of this section of the inquiry, based on a questionnaire administered to 1,455 adults in Sydney and Melbourne, are presenttd in this article.

Reprinted with permission of the *Australian Journal of Social Issues* (1968), pp. 63–74.

519

big business. Neither presumably does the rank and file of the population in an American community. But should the views of a socialist be suppressed? Should he be allowed to make a speech in one's community?"[2]

Stouffer formulated a number of questions to assess public tolerance of open expression of viewpoints like the one mentioned above, but before presenting examples of his approach some further comment on arguments employed in the discussion of censorship is warranted. A penetrating intellectual investigation of these arguments has been carried out by three distinguished authors: McKeon, Gellhorn, and the sociologist R. K. Menton (1957).[3] Asked to outline the problem and explore whatever questions seem relevant from the viewpoints of philosophy, sociology and law, their report provides a comprehensive framework within which to consider the contributions of other spokesmen on various detailed issues, including the extent and acceptability of censorship practices in Australia. The report of McKeon et al. will therefore be examined in some detail before returning to a closer examination of Stouffer's methods and their adaptation in the present study.

The three authorities have identified three sets of interrelated arguments used in discussion of censorship today:

". . . (1) basic philosophic arguments. These proceed from principles found in the nature of man and freedom, they provide the grounds and the frame for (2) political arguments. These proceed from principles found in the nature and responsibilities of state and society; they establish the political and social mechanisms for (3) moral and legal arguments. These are applied to secure specific ends."[4]

Two opposed philosophic views have been crucial in the enduring debate on censorship; on the one hand, freedom has been understood to consist in the ability to do as one pleases, whether or not one does as one ought, while on the other, it has been conceived as consisting in the ability to do as one ought, whether or not one wishes to.

Arguments for and against censorship have at one time or another been based on both of these conceptions of freedom, but in contemporary society, attitudes towards censorship have been linked with a choice between the two views of freedom. Today, the expressed purpose of censorship is to protect the individual and the community, ". . . the individual from the formative influences which might lead him into immorality or error and inspire actions harmful to himself and to others, the community from corruptive influences that might undermine its security, lessen respect for its institutions and confidence in its government, or pervert its values and traditions. . . . If knowledge and virtue are grounded and grow in freedom, the general argument against censorships runs, the contents of knowledge, the precepts of virtue, the canons of taste, and the judgements of prudence cannot be set down in advance. They are tested in free competition, and the individual is formed by the active exercise of freedom. Passive acceptance and conformity lead to the degradation of values and the enslavement of man."[5] These two formulations have usually been presented as irreconcilable in public debates on censorship.

McKeon et al. argues convincingly that the case against censorship derived from both of the conceptions of freedom already outlined is sound. Censorship (of the Hobbesian variety) based on the concept of freedom to do as you please, and of the Platonic variety, based on the concept of freedom to do as one should, depend ultimately on the exercise of power. There is no practical way to distinguish the considered judgement of officials who are wise and good from the arbitrary judgement of officials who are unwise and bad. However, the authors acknowledge that the outcome of the censorship issue depends on more than the cogency of abstract argument. It depends also on the preservation of a political framework which permits full development of such arguments and therefore requires "reasonable communication" among people who do not necessarily hold identical philosophic, religious or political convictions.

This general position has not gone unchallenged in the literature. For example, Berns,[6] after reviewing Supreme Court decisions on censorship, riots, Communists, and related topics, found the court deficient in not according priority to "virtue" as the end of government. He believes that a government properly engaged in raising the moral quality of the community must judge and limit public discussion according to the "moral quality" of speaker or speech. The major difficulty in his approach, reaching agreement on the meaning of "moral quality," is overcome by an appeal to "rational common-sense morality." Citizens who can properly claim a citizen's privileges must be decent, loyal, and peaceful.

Meiklejohn (1965)[7] has persuasively argued the insufficiency of such a simple concept of virtue. How, for example, does one demonstrate loyalty? Meiklejohn is convinced that any participant (for example, a Communist) in public speech demonstrates loyalty in the fundamental sense. Such a speaker offers ideas concerning the public for public consideration. Still, argues Lippman, "there can be no right to destroy the liberal democratic state."[8] The crucial question is what "destroying the liberal democratic state" means. The exclusion of Marxist doctrines may be a contribution to its destruction and in itself a source of encouragement to angry minorities.

We are reminded by McKeon et al. that little clarity can exist about the meaning of a term like "censorship" until it is given a concrete meaning in terms of the institutions by which it operates. Differences of opinion cannot be reduced to a simple ideological opposition of independent choice versus control or of freedom versus licence. "Problems of censorship are neither purely philosophic nor purely political: they are problems of both values and power."[9]

It is argued that in totalitarian regimes, criteria of values and use of power are not separate. "Art and science, the pursuit of truth and the cultivation of morality are all defined and used by the state."[10] On the other hand, in democratic regimes, choice of values and use of power are separate: "freedom of thought and expression are preserved to provide a plan both for individual judgement in art, science and religion and for common discussion of the exercise of power, including its effects on the preservation of rights and the advancement of values."[11]

Two main threats to a democracy are seen to be posed by censorship: first, although undertaken in the interests of cultural values, the richest sources of inspiration and enlightenment are banned along with the trivial, and second, censorship has not been successful in achieving its alleged objectives. "Morality" defined in terms of conformity to the professed decencies of a particular era diverts attention away from values "universal to all times and all cultures."

The immediate pressures for censorship arise from the practical problems characteristic of periods of crisis and change. However, the arguments advanced in support of censorship usually derive not from these problems but the "interrelated dangers of immorality, treason, irreligion and error."[12] McKeon and his collaborators draw upon examples from Ancient Greece and Rome and the Christian era to illustrate the tacit assumption that none of these dangers needs to be defined independently, since each implicates the others. Political and social objectives have been used to define impiety, immorality and error and have in turn been defined by them. On this basis it has seemed reasonable to suppose that a political crisis may be caused or be influenced by irreligion, immorality or error, and that current practices exemplify those disorders and should be suppressed. Their analysis of the arguments for censorship has convinced McKeon et al. that the basic fallacy of censorship can be traced to the confusions between the arguments and that the single most important contribution to clarification would come from separating questions of irreligion, error and immorality from questions of danger to the state. Moreover, the real issues are not dealt with directly, the issue posed being whether one is "for or against" obscenity, violence and subversion without regard to the actual effects of the "objectionable" communication. (The difficulties of establishing a connection between exposure to pornography and subsequent behaviour has been amply described by Bates (1967) who comments: ". . . we expect juries and magistrates to decide in a period of changing norms, on a question about which science has not . . . a scrap of experimental evidence to offer."[13])

While acknowledging their personal aversion to pornography and sadism, the authors are convinced that attempts to make such material inaccessible simply stimulate curiosity and have no other clear consequences so far as interest in obscenity or immoral behaviour is concerned. They believe that a widespread taste for good books, for example, can be cultivated. Where it is felt necessary to have censorship then it should be kept within limits by carefully drafted laws and alert use of procedures provided by law. Books cannot be assessed by semantic tests or topical lists of shocking themes. The judicial method of assessing these traits only in the context of the work as a whole affords a minimum corrective.

A recent study by Campbell and Witmore (1966) examined censorship practices as part of the overall picture of ". . . the freedom of the individual under the law and government in Australia."[14] The inquiry reached conclusions similar to those of McKeon et al. However, the evidence presented in the Australian study amply supported an earlier judgement of Donald Horne's: "Throughout the century, where other democracies have censored badly Australia has censored worse."[15]

Campbell and Whitmore draw attention to the many formal and informal methods of censorship, the official attitude which regards institutions of government as "sacred cows" and the conferring of almost unrestricted powers on boards, ministers and other authorities to restrict individual freedom. The authors are in complete agreement with McKeon *et al.* in stressing the positive value of controversy and debate in preserving ideals of democracy and justice. Where some restriction is felt to be necessary, they also emphasize the importance of clearly defined regulations, standardized review procedures and the conferring of power only upon persons competent to exercise it. "We feel that legal restraints upon individual liberty should be tolerated only where they are absolutely necessary to prevent infliction of harm or to secure the liberties due to others. A more or less remote possibility that someone will be harmed or that the stability of society will be undermined is not, we think, sufficient justification for any legal prohibition."[16] The evidence Campbell and Whitmore present on the censorship of radio and television suggests a marked discrepancy between their ideal and the present reality.

Television and radio are controlled by the Postmaster-General and the Australian Broadcasting Control Board, which exercise powers conferred by the Commonwealth Broadcasting and Television Act. Parliament has placed no limitations on the standards which may be imposed by the Board, or the Minister's powers to prohibit programme matter. "So far as the Act is concerned, the Board and the Minister are masters of the situation."[17]

Campbell and Whitmore refer to the example of the "Bidault Affair" in 1963 to show that prohibitions on the broadcasting or televising of programmes may be imposed for purely political reasons. A B.B.C. interview with M. Bidault, leader of the Council of National Resistance to General de Gaulle, was considered by the Postmaster-General to be "an affront to France, a friendly nation" and its presentation on Australian television was prohibited. In the controversy that developed around the issue, it was revealed that the Postmaster-General had taken action only after consultation with the Prime Minister.

All broadcasting and television stations are subject to an absolute prohibition against the dissemination of blasphemous, indecent or obscene material. No programme should deride or otherwise discredit the law or significant social institutions. Serious presentation of religious issues is to be encouraged, but attacks on established religious faiths should not be permitted. Recently the chairman of the Broadcasting Commission acknowledged an "error of taste" when a senator drew his attention to insulting references to the Queen during a panel discussion.[18] The Broadcasting and Television Act places severe limitations on the broadcasting or televising of political material. Theoretically, no dramatization is permitted of any political matter which is current or was current at any time during the preceding five years.

Official policies are supported by the threat of prosecution against individuals involved in their violation or, as occurred in 1964, requests that station management take disciplinary action against offending announcers.[19] More devious means of control include the threat that programmes will need to be prerecorded and insistence that only "experts" should discuss social and moral problems. Ultimately, there is the fear of losing a broadcasting licence and the considerable financial profits which accompany it.

In similar fashion to several of the arguments discussed earlier in this article, Campbell and Whitmore's analysis of the political and social implications of television and radio censorship in Australia converges on the question of the necessary limits to individual freedom on the one hand, and the positive value of criticism, conflict and debate within a democracy on the other. They believe that overall control of the two media is approved by the great majority of the public but consider it doubtful that this approval extends to all of the areas in which it is currently exercised. "A policy of avoiding offence to all Governments and institutions is incompatible with a responsibility to present news, comment and ideas."[20]

Stouffer (1963) has developed survey techniques which could help clarify the attitude of Australians towards public criticism of major social institutions. To illustrate Stouffer's method, reference must again be made to an issue mentioned in the earlier discussion of his work, namely the rights of a socialist to advocate government ownership of all big business. In a national survey intended to assess public acceptance of the socialist's right to air his opinions, Stouffer posed the issue in the following terms: "If a person wanted to make a speech in your community favouring government ownership of all the railroads and big industries, should he be allowed to speak, or not?"

The results were as follows:

TABLE 1

	Yes	No	No Opinion Or Not Answered
National Cross-Section	58%	31%	11%	(Sample 4933)

Another topic of relevance to Stouffer's inquiry was the issue of the right to criticize the institution of religion. Stouffer found, in fact, that for many people protection of the rights of atheists was a more difficult problem than protection of the rights of socialists.

In the following table, answers are tabulated to his question, "If a person wanted to make a speech in your community against churches and religion, should he be allowed to speak or not?"

TABLE 2

	Yes	No	No Opinion
National Cross-Section	37%	60%	3%	(Sample 4933)

As a lively public interest in certain controversial Australian television programmes developed concurrently with our study, it seemed appropriate to adopt Stouffer's approach in the phrasing of some items in our Australian questionnaire. To assess the degree of tolerance shown to the local instances of "non-conformity" it was decided to select three topics, the satirical presentation of which had prompted hostile retaliatory comments from spokesmen for various organizations. The three topics were religion, the monarchy and censorship. The following remark prefaced questioning about these three issues. *"There are some television programmes which are considered bad or dangerous by some people. For instance, some organizations opposed to all churches and religion have expressed their views during television programmes."*

Respondents were then asked the first of three related questions, "Should an organization opposed to all churches and religion be allowed to express its views to the general public through television?"

The combined Sydney/Melbourne results and the separate results for each city were as follows:

TABLE 3

	Yes		No		Other		Total Number
Combined	1088	(74.7%)	350	(24.1%)	17	(1.2%)	1455
Sydney	579	(76.5%)	167	(22.1%)	9	(1.4%)	755
Melbourne	509	(72.7%)	183	(26.1%)	8	(1.2%)	700

The total sample of 1,455 persons comprised 51.7 per cent Sydney people and 48.3 per cent Melbourne. The samples in both cities were based on the area probability method. After dividing the metropolitan areas into census collectors' blocks and after randomly selecting a number of such areas, a number of households were drawn according to the population within each block. The work of each of the paid interviewers was checked in the field. A supervisor examined the interview records and observed several interviews conducted by each field worker.

Sixty-five per cent of the sample identified themselves as Protestants, 26 per cent said they were Catholics. Respondents were also rated for "occupational prestige," a six-fold classification being used.[21] Six hundred and twenty-one (42.6 per cent) of those interviewed were men, 834 (57.4 per cent) women. The age and status distributions were as follows:

TABLE 4   Age Distributions (two cities)

	Number	Percent
Respondents in their twenties	288	19.8
Respondents in their thirties	310	21.4
Respondents in their forties	323	22.2
Respondents in their fifties	242	16.6
Respondents over 60 years	292	20.0
	1455	100.0

TABLE 5   Occupational Status
            Distribution (two cities)

Status Groups	Number	Percent
A (high)	67	4.6
B	84	5.8
C	137	9.4
D	208	14.3
E	386	26.5
F	573	39.4
	1455	100.0

There was no significant difference in the attitudes of men and women towards this issue. There was, however, a trend in relation to age, in that older people were less tolerant of public criticism of religion. The trend was far more pronounced in the case of Melbourne.

TABLE 6   Percentage Answering "Yes"

	Sydney	Melbourne	Combined
Respondents in their twenties	81.8	84.4	82.9
Respondents in their thirties	77.9	83.2	80.5
Respondents in their forties	76.7	72.0	73.8
Respondents in their fifties	77.6	70.0	74.2
Respondents over 60 years	71.6	56.6	64.2

In both Sydney and Melbourne people at the upper end of the prestige continuum were more accepting of public opposition to religion; in the case of Sydney, however, the trend was not a uniform one:

TABLE 7   Percentage Answering "Yes"

	Sydney	Melbourne	Combined
Occupational Group A (higher)	88.9	88.0	88.5
Occupational Group B	85.0	81.5	83.5
Occupational Group C	78.7	81.0	79.8
Occupational Group D	73.6	76.2	74.7
Occupational Group E	82.4	77.0	80.4
Occupational Group F (lower)	70.4	67.1	68.5

The two major religious groupings were equally tolerant of their critics.

THE MONARCHY

The second question asked was, "*Should an organization opposed to the monarchy be allowed to express its point of view through a television programme?*" Sixty-nine per cent of the combined city sample answered this question in the affirmative. There was virtually no difference between the overall results in Sydney and Melbourne but women were slightly less inclined to accept the idea of public opposition to the monarchy:

TABLE 8   Percentage Answering "Yes"

	Sydney	Melbourne	Combined	Total Number
Men	79.4	71.3	75.5	620
Women	64.3	65.1	64.7	835

There were substantial differences of opinion between the youngest and the oldest age groups. In the Sydney sample, increasing age was associated with decreasing tolerance of public opposition to the monarchy. The trend was not uniform in the case of Melbourne, but the difference between the extreme age groups was more pronounced:

TABLE 9   Percentage Answering "Yes"

	Sydney	Melbourne	Combined
20-year-old group	76.9	77.8	77.3
30-year-old group	75.4	78.5	76.9
40-year-old group	73.2	65.8	70.7
50-year-old group	67.9	71.0	69.3
Respondents over 60 years	60.1	45.4	52.9

There was no difference of opinion between the two major religious groups. People of higher occupational prestige were again inclined to take a more liberal view on the question of censorship than that adopted by the group lowest in prestige. There was no clear trend in the results for the intervening groups:

TABLE 10   Percentage Answering "Yes"

	Sydney	Melbourne	Combined
Occupational Group A	77.7	88.0	82.0
Occupational Group B	70.0	81.5	75.6
Occupational Group C	69.7	62.0	66.1
Occupational Group D	72.7	73.7	73.1
Occupational Group E	74.1	69.6	72.4
Occupational Group F	67.3	65.6	66.4

CENSORSHIP

The third question in the series was, "*Should an organization opposed to censorship be allowed to express its point of view through a television programme?*" Approximately four out of every five people (81.6 per cent) in the total sample said yes, there being no difference in the results for the two capital cities. A comparison of the results for men and women showed no major difference of opinion, nor did the analysis in terms of religious and occupational groupings reveal any significant trends. In Sydney, younger people were slightly more inclined to favour opposition to censorship; in Melbourne the difference of opinion between the youngest and oldest age groups was more pronounced but there was no uniform pattern in the results for the intervening age groups:

TABLE 11   **Percentage Answering "Yes"**

	Sydney	Melbourne	Combined
20-year-old group	84.2	90.1	86.7
30-year-old group	83.6	89.2	86.3
40-year-old group	80.8	82.2	81.6
50-year-old group	80.6	85.9	83.0
Respondents over 60 years	75.6	70.6	73.2

CONCLUSION

An attempt was made in the present study to assess public tolerance of criticism of organized religion, the monarchy and censorship. These three subjects represented only a small sample of the contentious issues about which "dangerous" views are sometimes said to be expressed. The questions dealing with these three selected topics may, however, be considered broad indices of the acceptability of critical comments on established institutions.

Without assuming too fine a precision of measurement with the techniques used, the results of the survey place in reasonably clear perspective the often alleged sensitivity of the majority to critical assessments or satirical treatment of controversial issues over the mass media. Three out of every four people questioned in Sydney and Melbourne supported the idea of public ventilation of opinions critical of organized religion, the monarchy and censorship. There was no appreciable difference in the results for the two capital cities but older people, especially in Melbourne, seemed less appreciative of the role of the social critic. There was a tendency for people of higher occupational prestige to be more likely to support use of television for the expression of "dangerous" views but the overall pattern was not a clear one. There was no difference of opinion between Catholics and Protestants on the three issues discussed.

NOTES

[1] Stouffer, S. A., *Communism, Conformity and Civil Liberties*, Gloucester, 1963.

[2] Ibid., p. 26.

[3] McKeon, R., Merton, R. K., Gelhorn, W., *The Freedom to Read*, New York, 1957.

[4] Ibid., p. 2.

[5] Ibid., pp. 5–6.

[6] Discussed in Meiklejohn, D., *Freedom and the Public*, New York, 1965, pp. 118–119.

[7] Ibid., p. 119.

[8] Ibid., p. 120.

[9] McKeon, et al., op. cit., p. 14.

[10] Ibid., p. 16.

[11] Ibid.

[12] Ibid., p. 20.

[13] Bates, A., "The Sad History of Censorship," *Humanist*, Vol. 82, No. 9, September, 1967, p. 270.

[14] Campbell, E., Whitmore, H., *Freedom in Australia*, Sydney, 1966, p. (vii).

[15] Horne, D., *The Lucky Country*, Victoria, 1964, p. 186.

[16] Campbell, E., Whitmore, H., op. cit., p. 270.

[17] Ibid., p. 121.

[18] Ibid., p. 123.

[19] Ibid., p. 129.

[20] Ibid., p. 130.

[21] Congalton, A. A., "Occupational Status in Australia," *Studies in Sociology No. 3*, School of Sociology, University of New South Wales, Sydney, 1963.

THE QUASI-THEORY
OF COMMUNICATION AND
THE MANAGEMENT OF DISSENT

Peter M. Hall and John P. Hewitt

PETER M. HALL received his B.A. and M.S.W. from the University of California, Berkeley, and his Ph.D. from the University of Minnesota in 1963. He has taught at the University of Iowa and the University of California, Santa Barbara, and is currently an associate professor at York University in Toronto. He has published articles in Sociometry and Social Problems and is currently working on a book that is to be a symbolic interactionist analysis of politics.

JOHN P. HEWITT received his B.A. from the State University of New York at Buffalo in 1963, and his A.M. (1965) and Ph.D. (1966) in sociology from Princeton University. He has taught at Oberlin College and at York University (Canada), and is now in the Department of Sociology at the Amherst campus of the University of Massachusetts. His interests lie in the areas of social psychology, social stratification, and social problems. He is the author of Social Stratification and Deviant Behavior (Random House, 1970). He is currently collaborating with Ely Chinoy on an introductory text is sociology and is also working on a book-length analysis of the impact of mass society upon the self.

On April 30, 1970, President Richard Nixon announced that he was sending U.S. troops into Cambodia to clear out enemy sanctuaries in order, he said, to protect the lives of U.S. servicemen and to guarantee the success of his program of "Vietnamizing" the war. On May 8, the President held a press conference in which he adopted an apparently conciliatory attitude toward student dissent and attempted to link his actions with the goals of the student war protesters. In the dawn hours of May 9, in fact, the President left the White House to talk to some demonstrators at the Lincoln Memorial, an act that contrasted sharply with his studied avoidance of the moratorium demonstrations in the Fall of 1969.

In the days between these Presidential actions there occurred a number of dramatic and unusual events. The Cambodian action revived the moribund student anti-war movement. May 1 saw the renewal of rallies, demonstrations, bitter rhetoric, anger, frustration, and outrage. There were strikes, confrontations, building burnings, tear gas battles, and arrests, and law enforcement agencies were mobilized on numerous campuses. Also on May 1, the President visited the Pentagon, where he contrasted the actions of American GI's with those whom he characterized as "bums" who blow up campuses, a phrase that was taken to reflect on all student dissenters. On Monday, May 4, four Kent State University students were shot to death by Ohio National Guardsmen. The verbal responses of President Nixon and of Vice President Agnew linked

Reprinted with permission of Social Problems, 18, No. 1 (Summer 1970), 17–27.

the shootings with campus violence and student dissent. The response on the campuses was swift, widespread, and unified in its opposition to the administration. Together with previous anti-war students, moderate students were now being mobilized. In addition, faculties and administrations supported the student strikes and protests. College presidents wrote the President, and some held a conference with him to indicate their concern and to inform him of the consequences of his actions and of administration rhetoric on the campuses. Such actions represented a significant escalation of the campus opposition. Also, and quite significantly, a surprising letter from Secretary of Interior Walter Hickel to the President, which was leaked to the press, criticized the administration for consciously alienating the young, for not being sensitive to or informed about the mood and thought of the campuses.

On Saturday, May 9, there was a demonstration of 75,000 to 100,000 war protesters, mainly students, who came to Washington to be seen, heard, and heeded. The main response of the administration was to cool its own rhetoric, establish lines of communication, appoint a consultant, send aides to meet with groups of protesters for discussion, make a symbolic appearance in the person of the President, and lend verbal support to the right to dissent.

Much of the concern shown by the President, by members of his administration, and by the working members of the media, dealt with matters of communication. A comment made by a spokesman for the Department of Health, Education, and Welfare, in describing arrangements his department had made to meet with students, was typical: "There is a feeling in the country that no one is listening," he said, "and we want to show we are listening" (New York Times, May 9, 1970, p. 9).* And in his press conference, the President was asked such questions as the following: "Do you believe you can open up meaningful communications with this college-age generation and how?"; "Mr. President, what do you think these students are trying to say?"; "Mr. President, will you see the demonstrators tomorrow in the White House?" The President also appointed Chancellor G. Alexander Heard of Vanderbilt University as his advisor on academic community affairs in order to insure that he, the President, was fully and regularly informed as to the thinking of the academic community. He asserted that ". . . this is a time for communication rather than violence and above all mutual understanding" (New York Times, May 9, 1970, p. 1). It might reasonably be argued, in fact, that there was a preoccupation with communication (its presence or absence, its process, and its style) that deflected and obscured the basic issue of the war, perhaps intentionally, by defining the situation in terms of a quasi-theory of communication breakdown, barriers, or failures. This quasi-theory is strongly rooted in our political culture and is, at the same time, a means or device for cooling controversy and managing discontent (cf. Gamson, 1968).

Underlying the emphasis upon communication as a tool for conflict resolution is an American myth of common values—a widely shared belief that

* In this, and subsequent references to news events, citations are provided for direct quotes, but not for generally reported events.

there is a set of values upon which all Americans ultimately agree (cf. Strauss, 1963:154–5; Williams, 1960:415–470). While none can point with precision to the exact nature of these values, the faith in their existence provides the means by which a great variety of particular goals and actions can be rationalized. Thus, in the political sphere, it is culturally possible to treat conflicting points of view and conflicting goals as merely manifestations of disagreements on how to go about realizing the values (unspecified) that we all share.

But the importance of communication does not lie solely in the degree of cultural emphasis it receives. For it is a principal component of all *social action;* indeed, for many purposes it *is* social action. Because communication is tied intimately to action, the emphasis laid upon it generates expectations about the effects of communication.

Max Weber (1947:88), in defining social action, asserted that "Action is social insofar as, by virtue of the subjective meaning attached to it by the acting individual (or individuals), *it takes account of the behavior of others and is thereby oriented in its course* (emphasis ours). This view is further expounded by Shibutani (1966:166–7) in his explication of society as a communicative process: "The mark of society, that which differentiates a social group from a mere aggregate of individuals, is the capacity of the participants to engage in *concerted action.* . . . *Coordinated action* requires that participants make *reciprocating adjustments* to one another." Joint action flows from the alignment of individual lines of action through symbolic interaction or communication. The end product of the communication process is *action,* action that is affected by the meanings ascribed to the content of the communication.

Thus, people will feel that they have communicated when they see the *results* of their verbal exchanges, when they see that their desires, needs, interests, and perspectives have been taken into account. They will believe that they have communicated when the course of action they have requested, demanded, or defended is forthcoming. Communication, to be realized and to be defined fully as communication, must result in alteration, effect, and action. In concrete terms, those who have protested a war for six years, or racial conditions for fifteen years, will not be content merely to speak out with only token response. They will want to be heeded, at least by seeing their opponents move toward their positions and, at best, by full exhibition of their "called-for" actions.

In the early phases of social interaction, participants may be content to make representations to others and to await responsive action. They may be willing to engage in discussion or dialogue, for a time, but they fully expect in the long run that dialogue will lead to actions on the part of others that will differ from the actions they might have expected had no dialogue taken place. Again in the concrete terms of the present crisis, dialogue between students and the administration concerning the war will not in itself prove satisfying to either. For its part, the administration will expect to make some converts and, at the very least, to cool some of the dissent. For their part, students will expect dialogue to be followed by action in accord with their views.

We belabor these points in order to set the stage for an analysis of the Presidential response to the current situation as a means of "cooling the mark out" (Goffman, 1952). The force of his action is directed to the transformation of a substantive issue into a technical problem, so that basic conflict comes to be denied and, in its place, communication failure becomes the definition of the situation. The goal is to achieve *cooptation* of student protest by appearing to link the students into the political order without relinquishing any power or in any way altering the course of events.

The Presidential strategy depends upon the existence in American culture of a commonsense notion of what gives rise to organizational and interpersonal problems and how these can be resolved. This notion stresses that problems (failures, errors, conflicts, controversies, and crises) are due to breakdowns in channels of communication. Such breakdowns are held to prevent the flow of information and explanation, and as a result, promote disagreement and misunderstanding. The possibility of substantive differences, real disagreements, or basic conflicts of interest is denied by this perspective. Conflict and differential interest are denied because they are held to separate people from one another, to disturb social tranquility, to lend plausibility to the spectre of manipulation, exploitation, and evil intent, and, in fact, to threaten the social order itself.

Moreover, such a perspective assumes a unity of community, purpose, and values. We are held all to be one, all part of the same social order, ultimately committed to the same goals, values, and beliefs. We are an integrated, consensual society. Americans are tenaciously faithful, it seems, to a Parsonian vision of society that proclaims a transcending, unitary, homogeneous, conscious social order and identity. And because of this vision, any differences that exist among us *must*, it is held, be more apparent than real; once we see behind the facade of difference, we will find that our difficulties can be explained by ignorance or misunderstanding.

It is also assumed within this Weltanschauung that the leaders share in this unity and reflect this fact by being system representatives in the achievement of collective goals. They demonstrate their unity of purpose with us by constantly and visibly striving for those ends desired by *everyone*, and they show their striving by earnestly, conscientiously, diligently, and responsibly *acting*. Indeed, frequently the evidence of their unity with us is to be found in the personal and moral qualities of the leader, which are read into the way in which he does things. What he does is *assumed* to be right (Edelman, 1967:73–94).

This attitude rests upon a faith in the President that depends upon the fact that he *is* the leader, the symbol of national unity. This can best be examined if we assume the opposite and examine its implications. If the leader cannot be trusted, if it cannot be assumed that he is striving first, foremost, and always for *our* goals (not his or theirs), then we are indeed in a situation that is provocative of great and widespread anxiety, but which fails to provide institutional ways of managing that anxiety. This is brought home most dramatically in reference to internal responses to external conflict, a situation over which we as individuals have the least information and control. If it is not possible to trust the President, then whom can we trust? Thus the assumption is widespread that the President, because he *is* the President, is doing "the right thing," that he has the information and the wisdom on which to act, and that everything will turn out well if we are patient. Speaking in this vein to protesters at the Lincoln Memorial the morning of the demonstration, President Nixon implored them to "try to understand what we are doing" (New York Times, May 10, 1970, p. 1, emphasis ours). Allied to this view of the leader, especially in times of external conflict, is the belief, often stated in the most explicit terms, that disagreement and disunity will impede his actions and give aid and comfort to the enemy (cf. Coser, 1956:95–104; Hall, 1965). When it seems, therefore, that we are not in agreement with the President, he is not to be pressed hard, since he is busy and the fault is probably ours. Of course, if the apparent disagreement should persist, then we are to engage in dialogue, so that questions may be voiced and explanations given, ambiguities cleared up, and reassurance given by the calming, knowledgeable voice of the President.

Underlying this benevolent and benign view of values, community, and leaders is a commonsense notion about the common sensibility of men (Berger and Luckmann, 1966:23). Members of the community are deemed to be men of good will, which is to say they are capable of understanding. As they are human, they are defined as rational and reasonable, sensitive and sensible. Men who share a common identity are assumed also to share a common culture—a common set of meanings—which they are able to articulate and understand. This culture embraces a set of presumptions about individual behavior—that men will be fair-minded, logical, sane, discriminating, and reasonable—as well as the belief that by means of such behavior men will be able to work together, to listen to one another, to avoid extreme and excessive demands upon one another, and to make their common sense govern the resolution of any differences that might separate them, differences that are by definition quite minor.

Such a view of rationality and reasonableness denies the place of emotion, anger, and raised voices; and it emphasizes the desirability and logic of acquiescing to the collectivity or its representatives. American society equates emotion with irrationality and passion with lack of control. Both commonsense and "scientific" characterizations of the distinctive qualities of adults (cf. Smith, 1968) emphasize rational control of behavior, whereas uncontrolled outbursts are regarded as childish. The display of intense feelings invariably calls forth the cultural caution against losing self-control, against immaturity.

This line of reasoning may be extended to attitudes toward authority. Maturity is frequently taken to connote obedience, so that to disagree with or disobey authority is to show a fit of childishness. The parallel between the bad boy who says "no," stamps his foot, and throws a temper-tantrum and student protesters of the war or other issues is frequently drawn, by laymen and social scientists alike (e.g., Feuer, 1969). The collective wisdom of the community is reflected in authority, it is believed, and average members of the community should defer to it. To act counter to this belief is to risk being called immature and emotional.

Moreover, men are held to be sensitive beings, and in their relations with others they are urged to be appreciative of their feelings and experiences. They assume that others will not give offense unnecessarily nor disturb the quality of encounters. To cause such disturbances of interaction is regarded as embarrassing and as requiring an apology (cf. Goffman, 1967:10–11; Gross and Stone, 1964:12–13). Thus, because of the innate characteristics of people and their given sensibility, the expectation is that the everyday life of the community will follow a normal and expected course—because people are people who trust and accept one another as they cooperate in community. In essence this is what is meant by being sensible: exhibiting a sense of thought and a sense of community.

Thus, American culture fosters a number of widespread assumptions about the nature of social reality and of permissible political behavior: 1) we are all part of the same community; 2) our leaders represent that community; 3) we are all rational and reasonable men; 4) our troubles and disagreements are fundamentally caused by misunderstandings or lack of information about values and goals that we, as a community, hold in common; 5) consequently solutions to political and social problems lie in their open discussion.[1]

The foregoing discussion leads us to conclude that American culture provides fertile ground for the strategy of transforming substantive issues into technical problems of communication and understanding. The cultural matrix of assumptions about the nature of men and the relations between them makes it possible for at least some dissent to be dealt with by means of the communications strategy. On one hand, many men may find their anger cooled by such appeals. On the other hand, Presidents and their "silent majorities" will find in such appeals a means of exerting moral pressure on dissidents and deviants (Coleman, 1957:12).

However, only part of the effectiveness of such a strategy rests upon the cultural matrix we have described; the strategy also depends upon the very structure of the setting in which discussions between opposing sides take place, in which the advantage is typically in the hands of the incumbent (cf. Edelman, 1967:95–113). If we imagine where most such encounters take place, we see a rectangular table in the office of the official beseeched. The territory is clearly his; and the setting invites awe, quietude, reverence, and respect for his authority. It is not the setting of the picket line, the smoke-filled room, the mass rally, or the living room. The symbolism and effect are clearly that of lower-status people requesting an audience, so that deference is owed the leader. At the same time, the spokesman for the group is often unfamiliar with the setting and appears ill at ease and discomforted. While the leader often attempts to put his audience at ease, he in turn captures center stage and dominates the encounter. He has and uses the authority of his office to set the stage, fix the agenda, and turn it on and off.

The physical setting of such encounters also limits the movements and emotions of the participants. The conference table—the mark of bourgeois democracy and rationality—is a setting in which it is clearly out of place to raise voices too much or to gesticulate wildly. In current idiom, the setting and style serve up a cool image: the soundproofing effect of the carpet, the solidity of the chairs and table, the weight of the office and its authority, and the solemn call for rational discussion, all lead to the withholding of expressions of feeling and intensity. The tightness of the setting imposes self-control on the participants, and the opening gambit of the official places him as a person clearly interested in *talking* and discussing. Since he has invited the participants or accepted their request to meet, he has demonstrated his sincerity and goodwill. Given all of this, participants cannot be other than controlled, rational, low-keyed, appreciative, and respectful. Thus, in the present crisis, the President (in his press conference) indicated he intended to bring representatives of the academic community to *his* office to engage in dialogue. And newspaper reports of his pre-dawn visit to the Lincoln Memorial indicate that even in that setting there was less dialogue than monologue, with the President capturing and dominating the scene (*New York Times*, May 10, 1970, p. 1).

Given such cultural definitions of the causes and solutions of problems and the settings in which "discussions" are likely to take place, a number of questions are crucial: 1) What evidence is there that the quasi-theory of communication breakdown is invoked and that it underlies Presidential strategy? 2) To what extent is the experience of being heard, having an audience, and taking part in discussions sufficient to cool the interest and disagreement of participants? 3) What is the utility of symbolic reassurance in holding the political system together? 4) What are the consequences of the use of such strategies for the political system and for American society as a whole?

What evidence supports our belief that a quasi-theory of communication breakdown is used by the President as the basis for cooling dissent? Basically, we note from newspaper reports the following points: (1) the appointment of Chancellor Heard as a campus/administration liaison charged with keeping the President fully informed about the campuses; (2) the President's statement at the time of the appointment that "this is a time for communication rather than violence, and above all for mutual understanding" (*New York Times*, May 9, 1970, p. 9); (3) the response of Press Secretary Ziegler, following the meeting of the President with the governors, that *formal* networks of communication with students be established; (4) the advice of the President and Attorney General to students to engage in *responsible* dissent; (5) the President's early morning visit to the Lincoln Memorial; (6) his dictum that "when the action is hot, the rhetoric should be cool" (*Toronto Star*, May 9, p. 5); (7) the suggestion for a Presidential telethon with students; (8) the meetings of cabinet members and presidential aids with students; and (9) the Vice President's advice that we not allow "the emotional attacks or the rigid mythology of liberal ideologues to drown out objective discussion and analysis of the events of recent weeks in the Vietnam war" (*New York Times*, May 9, p. 9). All of these responses place a major emphasis upon the form and means of communication and relegate the key issue of the Indo-China war to a secondary position.

Indeed, it is in regard to the issue of the war itself that the President's own words seem most clearly to reveal the assumptions underlying the communications breakdown perspective. In his press conference, the President asserted that "What I have done will accomplish the goals *they* want." He said, "They are trying to say that they want peace. They are trying to say that they want to stop the killing. They are trying to say that they want an end to the draft. They are trying to say that we ought to get out of Vietnam. *I agree with everything that they are trying to accomplish*. . . . I believe that this decision (to go into Cambodia) will serve that purpose, because *you can be sure that everything they want is what I stand for*" (*Toronto Star*, May 9, 1970, p. 5 (emphasis ours)). We agree on goals, the President says clearly, and, therefore, it must be only upon the means to attain them that we disagree. In order for this to be made clear, the President seemed to say, the rule of reason must prevail and his voice must be audible above the dissent. The conclusions to which we are led hardly seem to require stating: if we disagree only on means, not ends, then responsible men will not jeopardize Presidential acts by protesting excessively. Instead, they will listen to explanations, understand more fully the basis for the President's actions, and behave sensibly and rationally in their public conduct.

How successfully can such a strategy be employed? We have already elaborated the underlying cultural basis—the myth of common values—for the faith in communication. That faith seems easily documented, and to the extent that it is, the strategy may indeed prove effective. Much has been made, for example, of communication gaps in the society—between races, between generations, between married couples, and even between nations. The youthful concern with doing one's own thing draws its inspiration partly from a desire to open up repressed communication. Psychiatric therapy, sensitivity training, and encounter groups all serve to establish communication links and allow people to express their "true" natures. Nondirective therapy makes a prime virtue of simply having someone with whom to talk. Industrial relations psychological counsellors and personnel engineers are aware of the practices which allow employees to sound off to a sympathetic listener as a means of tension release. Bureaucratic machiavellians know well the utility of the process of "consultation," in which groups and individuals are asked for their opinions and advice—which is typically not followed. But the membership is made to appear as if it took part in the decision-making process.

For some, therefore, and perhaps for many, the ability to talk with a cabinet member or administration aide, or to take part in a mass demonstration close to the White House that is seen on national television, *is* sufficient to reduce pressure and to make the individual feel he is a respected, effective, and responsible member of a democratic society. The President himself asserted there would be no revolution in the United States because protest would operate as a safety valve, although he clearly saw such protest as a means of cooling down dissent rather than as a means of cooling out dissenters. The emphasis here has been on the idea that going through the motions and making use of the forms of communication translate the nature of the situation. By establishing or accepting the appropriate forms of communication, the authorities can exploit popular myths of common goals, appear to act responsibly, reaffirm the values of the society, and ride out the storm without altering the course.

The major stumbling block to the success of the strategy is the existence of a large and growing movement of protest whose members are beyond the reach of the theory of communication breakdown and misunderstanding. For them, the President's alignment of his position with that of the students represents a distortion of his goals and theirs. For in his speeches on the war, most recently in his April 30 announcement of the planned withdrawal of troops, President Nixon has consistently invoked the "hawk" theory of the war (Communist aggression and the "domino theory") which the bulk of the anti-war movement rejects. Consequently, his announced road to peace (Vietnamization and partial troop withdrawal), and his view of Cambodia as a step on that road, do not accord with the reality of the war as it is perceived by protesters. They regard as an illusion his attempt to say that all Americans seek the same goals.

The persistence of the anti-war movement is itself a social problem that demands Presidential response. Edelman's concept of "symbolic reassurance" provides a tool for understanding part of his response (1967:1–21). To most individual members of the society, the political scene is unknowable and threatening. Through the actions and especially the use of symbols by political figures, anxieties can be alleviated. Thus not only the war itself, but the phenomenon of student protest (which is regarded by most Americans as unprecedented), and death and violence on the campuses, aggravate the sense of threat and anxiety. The evidence for widespread anxiety is quite clear: opinion polls (as reported in the New York Times, May 10, 1970, p. 87 and on CBS Evening News, May 10) show that the "decisive action" in Cambodia did not generate the amount of increased support for the President that might have been expected, and that the "silent majority" is somewhat uneasy about administration attitudes toward students. Secretary Hickel's letter reflected this basic concern about the possibility of consciously alienating the young. In this context then, the actions of the President, previously documented, served as symbolic reassurance to the American public. They reaffirmed the rules of democracy and the legitimacy of dissent; they appeared as positive steps to cool dissent, defuse the conflict, and bind the society; they relegitimized the image of the student as a good American—the President referred to the students he talked to at the Lincoln Memorial as "fine kids" (New York Times, May 10, 1970, p. 25); they showed him to be "President of all the people;" they established his sincerity as a listener and as a voice of the people; and they showed him in a position of taking responsibility for, but also explaining, his decisions as President.

The importance of the President's response to the public uneasiness about the turn of events in the war and the protest those events generated thus lies in its symbolic reassurance of the public. But there are more serious, perhaps ominous, implications in the sequence of events and responses that have taken place. For if the tone of the Presidential response was reassuring and conciliatory, it also served notice that any further discord in the country could and would be attributed to the President's critics. We have responded sensibly and responsibly to crisis, the President seemed to imply; and we now expect that our critics will be persuaded, if not that our actions are correct, then at least that it is necessary to confine protest to symbolic forms. The stage is thus set for conflict of even more bitter and violent dimensions.

One consequence of the President's efforts at symbolic reassurance and of the emphasis laid upon communications will be that many members of the public will feel that the administration *has* acted responsibly, and that it will, therefore, be justified in the use of severely repressive tactics if the protest continues. In their view *the* social problem to be dealt with will be *protest*. In his actions, intentionally or not, the President has clearly set the stage for the legitimization of whatever actions against protesters may later be deemed necessary. For his actions not only invite protesters to join in the process of democratic debate; they also offer a clear warning that if they do not join on the President's terms, the "appropriate conclusions will be drawn," to use the language of diplomacy.

Another consequence of the President's actions and words may be to further embitter members of the anti-war movement, for whom *the* war continues to be defined as *the* social problem. For those already in that movement, President Nixon's response must seem cynical in its lip service to the principle of open debate and its simultaneous resolution to remain on course. For those not previously engaged, the call to dialogue and to participation within the rules of democratic society can generate expectations about the success of their participation that will collide with the administration's intended course. The result may well be their radicalization.

Thus, we conclude that the attempt to attribute social conflict and social problems to failures of communication and to deal with it by creating dialogue and by means of symbolic reassurance may well have the intended effect for many Americans. But its long run effects may be to exacerbate the polarization of opinion. Dissent is likely to continue and to grow as long as the war continues in its present course; and the stage has been set for the suppression of such dissent. The road ahead may well be paved with both revolution and repression.

NOTE

[1] In the words of Isaiah, as quoted by Lyndon Johnson, "Come now, and let us reason together." Men of goodwill, it is felt, need only to sit down and discuss their common problems and they will become aware of their consensus, their sincerity, and the real unity that transcends their apparent differences. Because of their unity of ends and identity, they will be reasonable men who can achieve agreement on means toward those ends. Because men are rational and sensible, their discussions will take place in an atmosphere of calm and decorum. Solutions will flow naturally out of this process. The essential honesty of all participants will be reaffirmed, and they will be found willing to moderate positions and to accept positions they had previously rejected. Misunderstandings will be cleared up and information gaps closed by the disclosure and exchange of information, so that participants become aware of the intent and meanings of misperceived or unseen acts. Men will quickly be disabused of any notions that their opponents have malicious or evil intent.

REFERENCES CITED

Berger, Peter, and
Thomas Luckmann
   1966   The Social Construction of Reality. Garden City.
Coleman, James S.
   1957   Community Conflict. New York.

COSER, LEWIS
1956 The Functions of Social Conflict. New York.
EDELMAN, MURRAY
1967 The Symbolic Uses of Politics. Urbana, Ill.
FEUER, LEWIS S.
1969 The Conflict of Generations. New York.
GAMSON, WILLIAM
1968 Power and Discontent. Homewood, Ill.
GOFFMAN, ERVING
1952 "On cooling the mark out: Some aspects of adaption to failure." Psychiatry
15 (November): 451–463.
1967 Interaction Ritual. Garden City.
GROSS, EDWARD and
GREGORY STONE
1964 "Embarrassment and the analysis of role requirements." American Journal of
Sociology 70 (July): 1–15.
HALL, PETER M.
1965 "The symbolic mobilization of support for external conflict." Paper presented
at annual meetings of the Society for the Study of Social Problems, Miami
Beach, Fla.
SHIBUTANI, TAMOTSU
1966 Improvised News. Indianapolis, Ind.
SMITH, M. BREWSTER
1968 "Competence and socialization." Pp. 270–320 in John A. Clausen (ed.),
Socialization and Society. Boston.
STRAUSS, ANSELM et al.
1963 "The hospital and its negotiated order." Pp. 147–169 in Eliot Friedson (ed.),
The Hospital in Modern Society. New York.
WEBER, MAX
1947 The Theory of Social and Economic Organization (Translated by A. M.
Henderson and T. Parsons). New York.
WILLIAMS, ROBIN
1960 American Society, 2nd ed. New York.

THE INTEGRATIVE ROLE
OF INTERCOMMUNICATION

In Modernization Among Peasants, Everett M. Rogers (1969, 360–361) suggests that although there have been hundreds of development studies by anthropologists, economists, psychologists, sociologists, political scientists, and communication analysts, their full contribution to the identification and solution of development problems in emerging countries has been minimal. Although the sociocultural aspects of development often spell the success or failure of a project, these researchers have, to date, failed to focus adequately on the social aspects of development while emphasizing economic factors. No matter how economical or rewarding innovations may be, if they counter the cultural values of a people, they will not be accepted. Early American Peace Corps workers in the Philippines reported:

> Principals and teachers in the barrios do not really understand why we are here; they do not know how to make the best use of us; we feel inadequately trained with respect to job skills; we feel uncomfortable teaching English to children who will never use it; there are needs in our barrio which seem at least as severe as those at school; we wish we had some clearcut jobs to do, and finally, and pleadingly, how can we introduce changes in the schools, even if Manila wants them, when values are so different here? (Fuchs 1967:240).

Rogers protests that although the social sciences are broadly based, there has been little cooperation between researchers of different disciplines, or between researchers in developed and developing countries, or even between the foreign researchers and the host peoples whose development needs are being studied. Researchers often mine data, which includes collecting, taking home, and publishing the data, but fail to involve themselves in institution building, even when host governments or people want and need specific help, and leave behind inficiently trained local researchers whose resources are limited. Rogers also argues that researchers from the developed states have culture-bound research methodologies, which they expect to serve as models for whatever cultural system they enter.

Numerous examples have been offered by contributors to this volume to demonstrate communication problems that arise between two different cultural or subcultural groups because of entirely different cultural ethics. It is doubtful that Americans would fill the streets of Washington, despite the massive protest marches there, the day after an American President has been defeated at the polls with placards reading "President Nixon is no longer our Messiah" or even "is no longer our President." It is inconceivable that the day before his defeat very many would fill the streets with signs reading "President Nixon is our Messiah." A phenomenon such as this did occur in Accra and is peculiar to Ghanaian cultural values and perhaps the values of similar emerging systems. On the other hand, the extreme distrust that black American ghetto youth have developed toward "Whitey" was fostered because the black youth became convinced that "Whitey" was making stooges of them by trying to persuade them that their cultural systems were similar.

A single instance from my own discipline, speech, probably exemplifies the problems that other uniquely American disciplines have when they try to export their fields abroad. For several years, we have been exporting speech education programs to friendly foreign universities, especially in Canada, Germany, Japan, Korea, and the Philippines, usually with the strong Midwestern influence that is so prevalent in American speech education (see Casmir and Harms 1970). The International Christian University in Tokyo now has one hundred speech majors, one-tenth of the university's student population. Partly because of a continuing commitment by American educators, a journal of international communication has been founded in Japan; and the American and Japanese have held two international joint conferences. But the goals of the two sets of educators still differ considerably. To a Japanese individual, still somewhat typically shy and one "who takes in but does not give out," the American emphasis on logical persuasion through public speaking is strange. The Japanese speech educator is much more interested in the importance of phonetics than his American counterpart, in part, because his emphasis often is placed on what we might call "good oral English." Additionally, although the Japanese are becoming rapidly Westernized, many of them retain the Oriental philosophical concept of contradiction. The Japanese "illogic" becomes frustrating and confusing to an American, whereas the American system, which still is generally accepted, of reasoned discourse with carefully thought-out arguments and developed evidence, is just as confusing to the typical Japanese.

My own Japanese student, a graduate of Tenri University, entered Indiana University with virtually no background in the field of speech, except that some of the American enthusiasm for public speaking had reached his university, where he had been known both as an excellent public speaker and as a "god of English," and that he had developed an almost worshipful attitude toward the writings of Marshall McLuhan. During his first semester here, he learned to his dismay that the "god of English" had to take advanced English for foreigners (to him, remedial English) from a woman professor (his first such experience), who was sharply critical of him and who insisted on calling him by his first name (a custom in his family reserved to his mother and father, and not even extended to his younger brothers). He also found that no public speaking courses are offered at the graduate level in American universities and that Marshall McLuhan was studied in some detail only in a second year graduate course, and then not with the appreciation he felt for McLuhan. Additionally, the student was enrolled during his first year in such courses as classical and medieval rhetoric, which are standard for beginning graduate students but which presuppose at least an undergraduate background in Western civilization and basic speech theories; the history of American public address, which presupposes at least an undergraduate background in American history and literature; and research methods in speech for which the student must prepare a prospectus for a master's thesis. Other graduate students who happen to be American also expect to take such courses as the history of British public address, Renaissance, modern and contemporary theories of rhetoric, communication theory, experimental studies in persuasion, and problems in speech education. Normally, these students have an undergraduate background that includes a major or minor in speech, courses in history and literature, and courses in the social, behavioral, and physical sciences. I hasten to add that much of the bad advice that my Japanese student received was mine, perhaps because I attempted to position him within the context of the regular American graduate studies. He might have been better served if he could have been allowed initially to receive undergraduate background in history, literature, and so forth, lower level speech courses in which public performance was a major part, and guided independent study. Fortunately, despite our own sets, he eventually integrated the various courses he had received and was rewarding to us in our classes, where we gained new perspectives because of his presence. For example, in our cross-cultural communication classes, he often broke his traditional silence to give us an Oriental point of view about the subject under discussion, thus making a study about cross-cultural communication a cross-cultural communication experience in itself. I am reminded of the difficulties that would be placed before me if I suddenly entered a graduate program in a Japanese university without much background either in a new discipline or in Japanese history, philosophy, literature, and culture. Hopefully, my student has returned to Japan without feeling obliged to duplicate exactly the information he learned in an American program but will take the models that best serve his teaching needs and the needs of his own Japanese students, whose frame of reference will be Japanese and Oriental instead of American and Western.

Indeed, this principle is the core of Lerner's argument (1967:120) that the process of international development cooperation is essentially a communication process:

> In the perceptive words of Karl Marx, the more advanced country presents to the less developed country "a picture of what it may become." This is precisely the function of the Western model [that is, according to Lerner, the generality of a developmental model formulated in an already highly developed state, such as the western states]—to convey to the developing Eastern nations a heuristic model (or "picture") of "what they may become." It is the developing nations that will then determine which aspects of the picture suit their self-image, which components of the model they wish to adapt and transform, and which plan of action will best accomplish this transformation in terms of indigenous conditions. This is international communication on the highest level. It involves nothing less than intercommunication between countries and continents of ideas about the ends and means of social organization—the shaping and sharing of human values according to a common model that emerged in the Western past and may be transformed and improved in the Eastern future. . . . Had he [Marx] given adequate scope in his theoretical framework for his

insight that a "picture" can be intercommunicated between the most remote regions of the earth, he would have foreseen more accurately our global situation today and established his right to be known as "the father of international communication" [Lerner 1967:120].

The integrative role of intercommunication must be explored both from the perspective of varied researchers or communication analysts and from the different viewpoint of the international and intercultural communicators, who may or may not be the same persons. Frank E. X. Dance (1967:293) refers to the joint efforts of the contributors to his volume Human Communication Theory:

> Human Communication is an area of multidisciplinary concentration rather than an area existing in isolation from life, social sciences, arts, humanities, or other areas of study in their pure form. The contributors seem to be saying that even though individual scholars choose to dedicate themselves exclusively to the study of communication ipse, they must be aware that assistance in their study can come from almost any source—that, in fact, information concerning human communication, like human communication itself, may be found anywhere within individuals, societies, or the study of either.

In the first essay in this final section, "Toward a Theory of the Intercultural Transfer of Ideas," C. D. W. Goodwin and I. B. Holley, Jr., an economist and a historian at Duke University, agree to the importance of a multidisciplinary study of communication and state that "research on the transfer of ideas has been relatively uncoordinated among disciplines, and barriers have remained to interdisciplinary co-operation." They argue that the phenomenon of cross-cultural transfer of ideas falls within the scope of "communications science" no matter how broad a definition is used as a starting point. Their objective is to demonstrate how advances in certain fields, and particularly in communications theory, can be useful to the historian and how he can also stimulate theoretical advances of his own. Goodwin and Holley isolate three elements in the process of intercultural transfer of ideas: (1) the source of an idea in one culture, (2) the agent through which the idea is transferred, and (3) the receiver of the idea in the second culture. As a student of the communication process, the historian draws upon the skills of the psychologist by determining the characteristics of behavior of the principal participants in both cultures. If mass communications are involved as agents, the historian turns to the skills of analysis of the journalist or mass communication theorist to determine the role of gatekeepers, the channel capacity, and the flow of messages. The linguist may aid his insights about the perception of messages in either culture. The historian then turns to the assistance of the sociologist, the economist, the political scientist, and his own skills to study the total social, economic, political, and cultural environment in which the transfer of ideas takes place. Without becoming too simplistic, nor presenting a task which is too formidable, the authors rightly believe that the efforts of varied disciplines can contribute to a more realistic study of the communication process between cultures than has been made in the past.

Hanno Hardt and Brian Goodey have applied the interdisciplinary model and concluded that communication is the key to regional integration. In their essay "A Term-Teaching Approach: Communication and Integration in Western Europe," they discuss their efforts to team-teach a university course in which they and their students examined the means by which interpersonal and mass communication could aid in the political and cultural integration of a region such as Western Europe. They believe that the same model can be extended and proven effective in other regional areas where political and cultural integration has taken place. Presumably, a converse argument might be made that where political and cultural regional integration has failed, the failure stems partly from the inability of participant states to communicate effectively with one another.

In the essay "International Cooperation in Telecommunication for Educational and Cultural Purposes," Robert K. Woetzel is less concerned with the study of intercommunication and more concerned with how the actual interchange of ideas can take place across cultural boundaries by the expanded facilities for telecommunication that have been made available through the new technologies of communication satellites. If literacy is the sine qua non for social and economic development, information exchange is an indispensable requirement for greater freedom and dignity for the world's people. Woetzel believes that radio and television primarily assist in raising educational and cultural standards. Thus he devotes the bulk of his essay to a discussion of how space technology can assist particularly in the overcoming of the obstacles to effective international cooperation through the use of television. Where radio has been the chief instrument for the diffusion of innovations, Woetzel argues that television will eventually be dominant. A major solution to the ideological problems of the present international communication satellite systems would be the creation of a specialized agency under the aegis of the United Nations entitled Space Educational, Scientific and Cultural Organization, in which each state partner would have an equal voice and would assume responsibility for planning and programming transmissions by way of a global system in which each state government can contribute both programs and financial assistance and receive whatever programming it feels is useful to its people. Naturally, although this solution does not provide people within a state the opportunity to receive information that their government does not approve of, the information channels are open to almost all ideologies, and each government has a much wider range of choice than the present satellite systems, which more clearly present a specific ideological point of view.

The final essay, "Thoughts on the Relevance of the 'Communication Explosion' to the Future of World Order," is written by communication pioneer Colin Cherry. Because Cherry's early writing on the development of human communication theory alerted us to the importance of cross-cultural communication, it is appropriate that this volume end with his cautiously optimistic discussion of the role of communication and communications in world order. He contends that all the media of communication have a common characteristic in that they offer the "power to organize" various forms of social institution:

The inventions of money, of telegraphy, or telephony, data-transmission, computers and all the media pouring in from the cornucopia of modern communication technology, all offer one essential thing—the power to relate one set of activities, at one place, to other sets at other places, i.e. to organize. In this sense, all may be thought of as extending the values of the principle of the division of labour, over whole countries and, increasingly, internationally.

Finally, Cherry believes that

The real values to future world order that communication media may contribute will come, not from their power to attack other countries' faiths or traditions or to seek to make them "more like us," but almost wholly from their great powers for organization, giving the conceivable possibility of new forms of institution, especially international institutions, including those of Law, whch are actually seen to work.

The contradiction between local autonomy or identity and international or intercultural cooperation is best resolved by recognizing, as Cherry says, "that we are never, any of us, members only of one community at one time."

That intercommunication must occur among men, whether they will it or not, has been eloquently attested to in recent times by Prime Minister Julius K. Nyerere on the occasion of Tanganyika's admittance to the United Nations in 1961: "We believe that all mankind is one, that the physiological differences between us are unimportant in comparison with our common humanity. We believe that black skin or white, straight or curly hair, differences in the shape of our bodies, do not alter or even affect the fact that each one of us is a part of the human species and has a part to play in the development of mankind" (Nyerere 1970:824–825). Long ago, John Donne said very well: "No man is an island, entire of itself; every man is a piece of the continent, a part of the main."

REFERENCES CITED

CASMIR, FRED and
L. S. HARMS
    1970   International studies of national speech education systems: vol. I. Current reports on twelve countries. Minneapolis.
DANCE, FRANK E. X.
    1967   Toward a theory of human communication. In Human communication theory: original essays. Frank E. X. Dance, ed. New York.
FUCHS, LAWRENCE H.
    1967   The role and communication task of the change agent—experiences of the Peace Corps volunteer in the Philippines. In Communication and change in the developing countries. Daniel Lerner and Wilbur Schramm, eds. Foreword by Lyndon B. Johnson. Honolulu.
LERNER, DANIEL
    1967   International cooperation and communication in national development. In Communication and change in the developing countries. Daniel Lerner and Wilbur Schramm, eds. Foreword by Lyndon B. Johnson. Honolulu.

NYERERE, JULIUS K.
1970 All mankind is one. *In* Sow the wind, reap the whirlwind: heads of state address the United Nations. Michael H. Prosser, ed. New York.
ROGERS, EVERETT M., in association with
LYNNE SVENNING
1969 Modernization among peasants: the impact of communication. New York.

TOWARD A THEORY
OF THE INTERCULTURAL TRANSFER
OF IDEAS

C. D. W. Goodwin and I. B. Holley, Jr.*

C. D. W. GOODWIN, born in Montreal, Canada, in 1934, received his Ph.D. in economics from Duke University in 1958. He has held a Duke University Commonwealth Studies Center Post-Doctoral Fellowship, a Canada Council Fellowship, a Guggenheim Fellowship, and a Smuts Visiting Fellowship at Cambridge University. He taught at the University of Windsor and York University in Canada and was an honorary research fellow at the Australian National University. In 1962 he joined the Duke University faculty and has also served Duke University in the capacity of secretary of the university and director of international studies. Since 1968 he has been a professor of economics and vice provost at the university. He has done research in Canada, England, Australia, and Jamaica and has served as a consultant to the Ford Foundation on American Studies in the Western Pacific and Far East. He is the author of Canadian Economic Thought: The Political Economy of a Developing Nation 1814–1914 (1961) and Economic Enquiry in Australia (1966); he is the coeditor and contributor to A Decade of the Commonwealth 1955–1964 (1966), and The Transfer of Ideas (1968). He has contributed chapters to Economic Systems and Public Policy: Essays in Honor of Calvin Bryce Hoover (1966) and Libraries at Large (1969). He is editor of a new journal published by the Duke University Press entitled History of Political Economy. He is presently on leave from Duke University as program officer in charge of European and international affairs, the Ford Foundation.

I. B. HOLLEY, JR., is a professor of history at Duke University, where he has taught since 1947. He received a bachelor's degree from Amherst College in 1940. He took his M.A. at Yale University in 1942, where, after five years in military service, he received his doctorate in 1947. Professor Holley is the author of Ideas and Weapons (1953) and Buying Aircraft (1964), a volume in the official history series, The United States Army in World War II, as well as several other collaborative efforts. He has written articles and reviews for various journals, including Military Affairs, Air University Review, Technology and Culture, Science, and American Historical Review. He is currently writing a study of General John M. Palmer and the concept of the citizen

* Editor's note: Professors Goodwin and Holley edited a Symposium on the Intercultural Transfer of Ideas for The South Atlantic Quarterly, 67 (Spring, 1968), pp. 203–380. The articles included: Paul Clinton Echols, "The Examination of the Transfer of a Structural Idea"; W. B. Hamilton, "The Transmission of English Law to the Frontier of America"; Hans J. Hillerbrand, "The Spread of the Protestant Reformation of the Sixteenth Century: A Historical Case Study in the Transfer of Ideas"; John Raphael, "Workers' Councils from Russia to Germany in 1918"; Robert S. Smith, "English Economic Thought in Spain, 1776–1848"; Craufurd D. W. Goodwin, "Economic Ideas in the Development of Jamaica"; and C. D. W. Goodwin and I. B. Holley, Jr., "Toward a Theory of the Intercultural Transfer of Ideas."

Reprinted with permission of South Atlantic Quarterly, 67 (Spring 1968), 370–379.

soldier in the United States. Among his various professional activities, Professor Holley includes membership in the History Committee of the American Institute of Aeronautics and Astronautics, where he chairs the subcommittee on historical publications. Appointed by the undersecretary of the Air Force, he has served as a member of the Committee on Air Force History and is a member of the editorial board of the South Atlantic Quarterly. He has been a member of the Advisory Board of the Society for the History of Technology and has for many years been associated with the Army Research Office.

What can we learn from the foregoing papers? Can these studies be used to enlarge our understanding of how formulated bodies of thought have passed from one cultural orbit to another in significant periods of history? We shall attempt to place insights gathered from them within the larger context of the work of scholars of the communication process. Section one contains suggestions of the contributions to an understanding of the transfer of ideas which may come from communications theory. In section two we present a tentative model, or framework of analysis, as a guide for future investigators in the history of transfer.

I

When the members of this symposium first began to give serious consideration to their specific topics, they were immediately impressed with the multiplicity of approaches which may be taken to the general subject. One has only to consult a standard reference tool such as the Library of Congress compilation of the subject headings to discover the great variety of approaches which have been taken toward the question, and consequently, the wide range of literature which is relevant to its examination. "Intercultural transfer" leads to "communication," which in turn leads to "information theory," "language," "mass media," and so on. In addition to works on the process of transfer there are also innumerable studies of the transfer of specific ideas and institutions— economic, social, political, and cultural. However, it became evident in the discussions of the symposium that research on the transfer of ideas has been relatively unco-ordinated among disciplines, and barriers have remained to interdisciplinary co-operation. An important objective of this paper is to suggest how advances in certain fields, and particularly in communications theory, can be useful to the historian. A by-product of the symposium may be to indicate that the historian can stimulate some theoretical advance on his own.

The phenomenon of cross-cultural transfer of ideas falls within the general scope of "communications science," no matter which definition one accepts for this term.[1] For example, Warren Weaver's definition of communication as "all the procedures by which one mind can affect another" obviously includes the flow of ideas.[2] Similarly, the definition of Wilbur Schramm applies, that communication is "when two corresponding systems, coupled together through one or more non-corresponding systems, assume identical states as a result of signal transfer along the chain."[3] Even the most general definition of communication as the transfer of information by signals through space covers the subjects examined by this symposium. If there is a difference in the meaning of such terms as information and idea when used by communications theorists and contributors to this collection, it is one of complexity only and not of kind.

Most progress in understanding the communications process has come in three disciplines: mathematics, linguistics, and psychology. Mathematicians in the last few decades have made great headway in explaining the physical aspects of communication and have provided the theoretical tools needed to advance such devices as the telephone, television, and the electronic computer. Linguists and linguistic anthropologists have explored the character of, and relationships among, messages in communication. Social psychologists have investigated human participation in communication through the study of group dynamics. The question must arise, then, of the place of the historian in the study of communications. The answer is that the historian may contribute as an expert in handling types of data unfamiliar to the other students of the subject. A common characteristic of the three disciplines in which the greatest advances have been made is the search for technical and social behavior patterns of communication through analysis of empirical data. Hypotheses are formulated and tested either by direct laboratory experiment or by their conformity to social data which can be readily collected and easily measured.

Where this symposium differs from the mainstream of research in communications is in its focus on historical experiences selected because they are of special significance in the course of human development rather than solely as evidence to confirm or disprove a hypothesis, and some of the data examined are not easily susceptible to rigorous empirical treatment. The true historian is not concerned with historical incidents exclusively for their own sake (for then he becomes a mere antiquarian), nor does he abandon the scientific method and ignore the insights gained from scientific progress (for then he is a poor craftsman). Nevertheless, the task of the historian is different from that of a pure physical or social scientist because the materials he studies encompass the full range of recorded experience and therefore are more diffuse; his approach must be compounded both of science and of art. In a sense, this symposium, and more particularly this article, is an attempt to bridge parts of the proverbial two cultures and to indicate the potential usefulness of each one to the other—to achieve idea transfers of its own. On the one hand, it is possible that the communications theorist may gain from the historian, who is trained in the handling of complex documentary evidence, suggesting new hypotheses which then can be submitted to rigorous tests. On the other hand, it is certain that the historian will acquire from the communications theorist analytical techniques and insights which will give order to the material he studies. It seems likely even that the theory of communication could bring about a revolution in some areas of historical interpretation comparable to the revolution it has wrought in communications technology.

The most spectacular progress in the study of communications has come in the area of pure information theory, the examination of physical message transfers from point to point.[4] Embedded in the terminology and analytical apparatus of this subject are concepts which are especially valuable in the more restricted study of the intercultural transfer of ideas. The most fundamental concept in information science is the simple notion of a communications system in which there is a linear flow of information from a source, through a transmitter, down a channel to a receiver and thence to an ultimate destination. A significant modification of this linear model for the process of the flows of intercultural ideas as well as for the flows of other messages is the concept of cybernetics developed by Norbert Wiener and associates.[5] Here a communications system is pictured as circular, with feedback from the destination affecting the continued flow from the source. The technical device called a servomechanism, which amplifies and transmits the cybernetic effect, has obvious analogies in social institutions. The concepts of entropy, meaning the degree of randomness or disorganization in a flow of information, and of noise, meaning the communication of useless information, are both directly applicable to the type of material which has been examined in the chapters above. The capacity of a noiseless channel, meaning the maximum rate at which useful information can be transmitted over a channel, the coding process, the disturbing effects of noise, and the use of redundancy to overcome uncertainty in communication are all factors which the historian in the same way as a communications technician should examine in any system he studies. The historian must be attentive to the equality of, and relationships among, the varieties of expression at the source in a transfer, the effectiveness of the channel, and the intelligibility and fidelity of the message. He may find it useful to make an estimate of the total quantity of "information" passed through a transfer system, meaning the potential volume of communication, contrasted with the actual meaningful signals communicated. No attempt can be made here to describe the full range of analytical tools in information theory which strike the present writers as valuable to the historian. Nor is a universal prescription proposed for historiography. Rather the general usefulness of information theory is suggested as a guide to historical understanding.

Social psychologists have viewed communication as one aspect of the process of social interaction, and consequently they have focused their studies on human rather than physical codes and networks.[6] They have drawn heavily on the mathematical theory of communication, especially the concepts of noise and feedback and control, substituting psychological barriers and distances for physical ones. But the psychologists have also introduced to the analysis of communication such distinctly novel and human considerations as environmental relationships and expectations. They have distinguished among the participants in communications by their type of role perception, task orientation, or other determinants of behavior. Special attention is given to two-person or small group interaction as a key to understanding the communication process, and networks among individuals in personal contact are found to be analogous to physical networks. Human characteristics are stressed by psychologists as vital determinants of communications networks, and the networks in turn are seen as determinants of social organization and performance. Psychologists have been specially interested in the concept of noise in human communications channels, both white noise or irrelevant information and coding noise or ambiguity of signals. The ability of human networks to filter out or compensate for noise and information distortion through redundancy and other techniques is found to be critical to their effectiveness and survival. Psychologists have not derived their concepts fully from the mathematical theory of communication, but they have gained valuable framework for analysis from a substantial degree of dependence. Their experience in this respect, as well as their discoveries, should be instructive to the historian.[7]

The linguistic approach to the study of communications has particular relevance to examinations of intercultural transfers. Analysis of speech is always important to an understanding of communications among articulate human beings, but it is crucial where two languages interact. Linguistics is concerned both with the signal system which lies at the base of the technology of communication and the human and social context in which the exchanges occur. The two basic divisions of linguistics, historical and descriptive, are relevant to the student of idea transfers. The first division may cast light on a special case under study; the second, in which is included linguistic geography, may lead to greater understanding of the transfer process itself. Modern linguists have been moving from the study of linguistic units and syntax to analyses of meaning or semantics. The study of non-verbal symbols, or more specifically kinesics—communication through body movements—may even be relevant to the historian of ideas. The crucial importance of linguistics to an understanding of culture contact is expressed in most extreme form in the so-called Whorfian hypothesis that patterns of language are fundamental determinants of culture, social forms, and personal behavior.[8]

The theory of communications has had a powerful impact upon a number of disciplines other than the three mentioned here, all of which may contribute to an understanding of intercultural transfers. In political science, Karl W. Deutsch and others have shown that communication is central to the formation of political units and that social and political problems can stem from communication difficulties such as "overload."[9] Economists concerned with economic development have focused specifically on the transfer of educational methods and technological thought.[10] Sociologists have looked at communications from a variety of perspectives;[11] for example, they have examined coding systems for their impact on social relations, and the effect of social stratification on the flow of messages. Cultural anthropologists have analyzed the impact of such factors as differences in perception on the success of cultural contact.[12] Students of journalism and mass media have made effective use of the theory of communication for a number of purposes which closely approach the tasks of the historian of ideas. In addition to using the concepts of entropy, channel capacity, redundancy, and noise, they have developed analogues in social theory to the physical notions of "systems coupling" through chain relationships, and "gatekeepers" as transmitters of messages.[13]

II

A conceptual framework for the historical analysis of idea transfer

From the brief survey of the various applications of communications presented in Section I, it should be clear that a complete theory of the intercultural transfer of ideas, susceptible to test and trustworthy for prediction, is still far off. The purpose of this section is to set forth a simple analytical framework which may guide future historical examinations of idea flows. It is hoped that with the approach implied in this framework greater knowledge of the transfer process and of significant historical incidents can be gained. If a single characteristic of idea transfers had to be given, it might well be "complexity." This model framework is designed to enable a historical investigator to see the phenomenon broken into its component parts—as they have been distinguished by communications theorists—and thereby advance toward greater understanding.

The main discrete elements in the process of intercultural transfer are these: (1) the source of an idea in one culture, (2) the agent through which the idea is transferred, and (3) the receiver of the idea in a second culture. These elements may be single individuals, but more often they are complex social institutions. An important objective in the historical analysis should be the discovery of whether the three elements in the transfer (or two, where no intermediary agent is involved) consciously enter into the process. A complication exists where an element is a plural entity, such as an entire community, because then conscious participation may be only partial for this single element. A cybernetic feedback, conscious or unconscious, also may be a characteristic of the transfer process.

The following diagram illustrates in simple outline form the essence of the conceptual framework needed for historical analysis of the transfer of ideas:

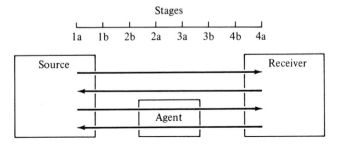

This diagram shows that the stages of transfer in one direction may be either two or four depending upon whether or not an agent or intermediary has an active role in the process. The stages also may occur with the individual elements participating wittingly (stages marked "a") or unwittingly (stages marked "b"). Arrows on the diagram indicate the location of potential stages in the transfer process and also the direction of idea flows. The possibility of cybernetic feedback is portrayed by a flow of ideas back from the receiver to the source.

Once the schematic framework for analysis of the transfer of ideas has been described, it is easier to identify the type of additional factors in the process which deserve the historian's attention. First, the characteristics of behavior of the principal participants must be examined using the tools of the psychologist. The role perceptions, goals, expectations, coding procedures, and interpersonal networks of the source, agent, and receiver should all be investigated for an understanding of the communication. If appropriate, the functions of "gatekeepers" (such as broadcasters or newspaper reporters) as filters of information should be assessed. Second, the historian must explore the flow of messages which make up the intercultural transfer and the channel through which the transfer occurs. He should ask such questions as, what is the channel capacity? what is the amount and type of noise in the system? what is the character of the messages which make up the flow? Here he may look to the linguist for aid.

Finally, the historian must examine the total social, economic, political, and cultural environment in which the transfer of ideas takes place. He must leave the guidance of the communications theorist and venture into grounds where his trained intuition—the historian's art—must be his main guide. In this part of his analysis, the historian may learn much from the economist, the sociologist, and the political scientist, in the same way as he learned from the communications theorist; but his borrowings, his selection of evidence, and his appraisals will remain a measure of his special skill.

For the historian who would venture into the intriguing and challenging field of intercultural transfers, the authors readily concede that the foregoing discussion may seem at once too simple and too complex. It must appear too simple in that it understates the difficulties the investigator is sure to encounter. The suggestions offered give little or no attention to the essential and incredibly intricate task of analyzing the source, the agent or agents along the line of transmission, and the receiver in their appropriate milieu. Nor, for that matter, is any real attention devoted to the problem of time. Transfers may often continue through extended periods, changing in character as the process goes on. This evasion is deliberate. The authors consciously trimmed away all but the barest essentials. It was their intention in doing so to induce more historians to consider their work on intercultural transfers in terms that would most readily lead to fruitful borrowings from the growing literature on the theory of communications. On the other hand, the authors were equally aware of the forbidding character that some of the mathematical studies on communications almost certainly present to many students of intercultural transfers. They will be content if they have managed to steer a middle course, encouraging a wider appreciation of what has already been written in a variety of disciplines without at the same time maknig these studies appear too formidable.

III

For further reading

The starting point for anyone concerned with the theory of information is Claude E. Shannon and Warren Weaver, *The Mathematical Theory of Communication* (Urbana, Ill., 1949). Even with the aid of Warren Weaver's chapters, however, non-mathematical readers will find this heavy going. A somewhat more accessible and highly readable introduction to the field is

John R. Pierce, *Symbols, Signals and Noise: The Nature and Process of Communication* (New York, 1961). For those wishing a briefer introduction there is George A. Miller, "What is Information Measurement?", *American Psychologist*, VIII (1953), 3–11. For another brief account of information theory and its application to a variety of discplines, see Brockway McMillan et al., *Current Trends in Information Theory* (Pittsburgh, 1953).

Several stimulating anthologies and collections of readings are available. Perhaps the best all-around volume for illustrating the remarkable range of applications of information theory is Alfred G. Smith, *Communication and Culture* (New York, 1966). Also useful are James H. Campbell and Hal W. Helper, eds., *Dimensions in Communication* (Belmont, Calif., 1965), and Wilbur L. Schramm, ed., *The Process and Effects of Mass Communication* (Urbana, Ill., 1954). Rather more tangential and less thoroughly related to the theory of information but also provocative is F. S. C. Northrop and H. H. Livingston, eds., *Cross-Cultural Understanding: Epistemology in Anthropology* (New York, 1964).

For those interested in pursuing the problem of model building in the transfer of ideas, a useful starting point is F. Craig Johnson and George R. Klave, "General Models of Communication Research: A Survey of Developments of a Decade," *Journal of Communication*, XI (1961), 13–26, 45. Historians and scholars ini the social sciences will be particularly interested in two articles by Karl W. Deutsch, "On Communication Models in the Social Sciences," *Public Opinion Quarterly*, XVI (1952), 356–380, and "Communication Theory and Social Science," *American Journal of Orthopsychiatry*, XXII (1952), 469–483. Also helpful is Irwin D. J. Bross, "Models," a chapter in his volume, *Design for Decision* (New York, 1953), reprinted in Campbell and Helper, above. Similarly useful is B. H. Westley and M. S. MacLean, Jr., "A Conceptual Model for Communications Research," *Journalism Quarterly*, XXXIV (1957), 31–38, reprinted in Alfred Smith, above.

NOTES

[1] A recent collection of readings, ranging over "the heart and core of human communication," is Alfred G. Smith, *Communication and Culture* (New York, 1966).

[2] Claude E. Shannon and Warren Weaver, *The Mathematical Theory of Communication* (Urbana, Ill., 1949), p. 95.

[3] Smith, *Communication and Culture*, p. 522.

[4] See, for example, John R. Pierce, *Symbols, Signals and Noise: The Nature and Process of Communication* (New York, 1961).

[5] Norbert Wiener, *Cybernetics, or Control and Communication in the Animal and the Machine* (New York, 1948).

[6] See, for example, Jurgen Ruesch and Gregory Bateson, *Communication: The Social Matrix of Psychology* (New York, 1951).

[7] See, for example, Fred Attneque, *Applications of Information Theory to Psychology* (New York, 1959), and Henry Quaster, *Information Theory in Psychology: Problems and Methods* (Glencoe, Ill., 1955).

[8] Joshua A. Fishman, "A Systematization of the Whorfian Hypothesis," in *Communication and Culture*, pp. 505–516. For a general treatment, see George A. Miller, *Language and Communication* (New York, 1951). See also John B. Carroll, "Com-

munication Theory, Linguistics, and Psycholinguistics," *Review of Educational Research*, XXVIII (1958), 79–88.

[9] Karl W. Deutsch, *The Nerves of Government: Models of Political Communication and Control* (London, 1963). See also L. W. Pye, ed., *Communications and Political Development* (Princeton, 1963), and Robert T. Oliver, *Culture and Communication* (Springfield, Ill., 1962).

[10] For example, see C. A. Anderson and M. J. Bowman, eds., *Education and Economic Development* (Chicago, 1965); and Zvi Giriliches, "Hybrid Corn: An Exploration in the Economics of Technological Change," *Econometrica*, XXV (1957), 501–522.

[11] See Pitirim A. Sorokin, *Sociological Theories of Today* (New York, 1966), esp. parts i and ii.

[12] See, for example, Donald T. Campbell, "Distinguishing Differences of Perception from Failures of Communication in Cross-cultural Studies," in F. S. C. Northrop and Helen H. Livingston, eds., *Cross-cultural Understanding: Epistemology in Anthropology* (New York, 1964). See also Leonard W. Doob, *Communication in Africa* (New Haven, 1961).

[13] See, for example, Wilbur Schramm, "Information Theory and Mass Communication," *Journalism Quarterly*, XXXII (1955), 131–146.

A TEAM-TEACHING APPROACH:
COMMUNICATION AND INTEGRATION
IN WESTERN EUROPE

Hanno Hardt and Brian Goodey

HANNO HARDT is an associate professor at the University of Iowa School of
Journalism. His interests in intercultural communication are related to his work on
historical and philosophical aspects of communication. He is a contributor to a
number of books and scholarly journals.

BRIAN GOODEY was born at Chelmsford, England, in 1941. He received a B.A. with
honors from Nottingham University and a Fulbright Fellowship to Indiana University where he received his M.A. in 1967. He was an assistant professor in the
Department of Geography at the University of North Dakota from 1967 to 1969
and since 1969 he has been a lecturer in urban studies at the Centre for Urban and
Regional Studies at the University of Birmingham. His major research interests
include social planning, environmental perception, and the process of new community
development. His most recent publication is Perception of the Environment,
published by the University of Birmingham in 1971.

How to share and apply findings in an interdisciplinary setting is
one of the major problems on campuses today. The rigid structure
of departmentalization still prevails—if only for administrative reasons—and
often stifles efforts to break down traditionally defined barriers between disciplines within the university.

However, this pattern has been challenged by a number of new fields, and
by specialists who have little regard for established boundaries but a great curiosity for areas of study that could help explain and solve problems in their
own fields.

Communication, in particular, defies departmentalization as it now exists in
the form of journalism schools and departments, since it overlaps a number of
disciplines. Geography, too, is a field that combines various socio-economic
and political elements of the environment and thus draws heavily on findings
from other disciplines.

Recognizing the advantages of a team-teaching approach, the authors decided upon a new method of teaching the regional geography of Western Europe by emphasizing the role of communication in contemporary European society; they hypothesized that communication is the key to integration, both
personal and political. Instead of getting lost in studies of the political or
economic significance of topographically delimited regions, students concentrated on an examination of the means by which forms of face-to-face and
mass communication could aid political and cultural integration in a spatial
context.

Reprinted with permission of Journalism Quarterly, 46 (Spring 1969), 114–122.

Within the seminar format of the course, both instructors presented position papers which drew from their respective disciplines. In outlining the development of communication an attempt was made to trace the impact of printing on the liberation of the individual, on the rise of nation-states and on inter-state perception. In addition, the forced migration of several million people after World War II with its sociological and psychological consequences, and the impacts of American policy on Western Europe, were considered the *sine qua non* of contemporary inter-European communication programs.

In approaching the geography of Western Europe, students were encouraged to understand aspects of state size and accessibility, steps taken toward European integration in the post-war period, and developments of inter-state linkages. Specific papers focused on such topics as the nature of trans-boundary interaction in Scandinavia, and the regional fragmentation of the British Isles.

As was to be expected, the course had several weaknesses as well as strengths. For example, most participants did not make the effort to establish a mental map of Western Europe during the early stages of the course, while previously, this had been the major role of regional geography courses. Although publications on European integration are profuse, there are few, if any, books that provide an adequate background to the pattern of Western European communication and interaction. Also, the lack of language skills among students probably meant an over-emphasis on English-language sources.

However, it can also be said that the presentation of geographical facts about a series of states within a sub-continent or continent has become an unacceptable method of geographical instruction at the university level. By focusing on important contemporary problems, the participants examined many of the "facts" whilst exploring the background to problems which must be solved in the contemporary world.

Participating instructors were forced to clarify their presentations. To the geographer, who has too often been concerned only with those spatial distributions which were clearly part of the landscape, the discussions of mass media functions underlined his need to examine the "invisible" elements. To the communication specialist, the discussion of regionalism, transportation and boundary concepts added to his understanding of these variables in the integration process. To students who imagined that the story of European integration might be told in the establishment of bridges and tunnels, the information on the diffusion of ideas was new and stimulating.

Participants in the seminar were required to select reading material from a wide range of sources and to present a paper. They were also required to read two books during the early part of the course, Richard Fagen's *Politics and Communication* (Boston: Little-Brown & Co., 1966) and Karl W. Deutsch's *Nationalism and Social Communication: An Inquiry into the Foundations of Nationality* (Cambridge, Mass.: The M.I.T. Press, 1962).

The course dealt with the more general problems of European integration during the first part of the semester and considered detailed area studies during the final weeks. The topic areas were selected according to the need for a coherent presentation of Western European Geography and communication.

Following is a synopsis of the major areas covered in the course, together with notes as to readings and sources used. The authors compiled a selected, 12-page, bibliography. There are obviously many other sources available; the ones listed in the reference section following the article were chosen to stimulate the reader and give an idea of the type of reading and lecture material available and utilized in class.

INTRODUCTORY STATEMENTS

1) Human communication: an overview

The discussion focused on many facets of human communication and how they could reflect and affect the existence of people organized in communities and states. Forms of nonverbal and verbal communication were compared in their role as conveyers of thought, meaning and experience. Various language communities and their influence on the cultural and social development in Western Europe were examined, including the impact of the English language after World War II. A description of channels of communication and their usefulness preceded the introduction of geographical material.

2) Integration: geographical comments

This presentation outlined the physical, and especially the social and political, geography of Western Europe and indicated how the course approach differed from that of earlier regional studies. The process of Western European integration since World War II was noted, including the existing problems between EEC and EFTA countries. Some of the physical linkages which are being developed in Western Europe were mentioned, including international railroad co-operation, the "E" road network, Alpine tunnels, internal waterway improvements, pipeline services, and tunnel/bridge links between Denmark and Sweden, England and France, and Italy and Sicily. The class examined the degree to which such physical developments indicated or encouraged integration.

3) Regions in Western Europe

"With the suggestion that a new system of regional divisions might provide the basis for a future, integrated Western Europe, this second geographical observation was devoted largely to the regional concept and to the many problems of regional definition; the French concepts of pays and circulation were introduced, and the paper examined the functional region and its appropriateness as a unit for areal-political organization. The stagnation of political units in Western Europe was contrasted with the rapid fluctuation of such internal divisions in Eastern Europe. The group discussed the importance of traditional ties and the rights of minority groups to be heard during integration debates. Finally Geraud's concept of L'Europe des Ethnies was considered and led to the more basic question of cultural trends.

4) Communications and culture

Particularly stressed were the importance of the phonetic alphabet in the development of Western culture and how language as a system of symbols is constantly changing under the impact of foreign thought and behavior. The presentation traced the influence of the Catholic church on early Europe, noted the growing awareness of qualitative differences between Western Europe and other parts of the world and indicated how printing aided in the rise of the individual and helped destroy the power of authoritarian rulers.

5) Politics and communication

Although it is almost impossible to separate cultural and political aspects of communication, an attempt was made to concentrate at this point on political communication in Western Europe. The discussion included a brief history of censorship and the philosophical environment in which ideas of free speech and freedom of the press prospered. Among the later developments were the rise of the party press and the use of mass media by totalitarian systems in Germany, Italy and Spain since the 1920s and 30s. Also examined was the cross-national flow of information during the post World War II period. It was recognized that differences existed not only among states but also within any given country.

6) Within-state differences

A discussion of within-state differences in Western Europe clarified the seeming conflict between contemporary moves towards a united Europe and the spasmodic voicing of nationalistic or localistic feelings by small groups of European dissenters. Within-nation differences fell into three categories—resources, population and development. It was suggested that such differences were often evident in problems and conflicts existing between core and periphery of states. The possibility of communication barriers between state capital and periphery was examined in a number of cases including Britain, Norway, and Finland. The bases of more severe within-nation differences were found in Belgium and Italy. Later discussion centered around the possibility of the eventual emergence of a United Europe, divided for local government purposes, into ethnically-based units.

7) Inter-state perception

Initial examples and problems of inter-state perception centered on the historical growth of national images and stereotypes, with illustrations taken from recent surveys and reports, and from earlier writers such as Erasmus, Tacitus and Dr. Johnson. Much of the subsequent work was devoted to an examination of assigned studies on national character in inter-state relations and included current perception research in political science, psychology and geography. The role of the mass media in the perpetuation of national images was discussed separately.

8) Mass media images among states

The investigation concentrated on the use of mass media for the portrayal of other peoples and for evaluations of prestige and character of neighboring states. Stereotypes were compared during time intervals of war and peace as were the types of media used for the dissemination of images. An appraisal of the contemporary scene gave electronic media, and particularly television, a good chance of bridging the gap between Western European nations.

9) Communication systems

The presentation featured the flow of news and information in Western Europe, the distribution of mass media facilities and their organizations. It dealt with economic and political aspects underlying mass media growth and emphasized the role of broadcasting as a unifying force. A brief historical review of radio broadcasting was followed by a more detailed analysis of use and content of mass media in several countries, and an evaluation of their role in the integration process. A separate paper was devoted to the means by which printed media and other goods were distributed.

The establishment of Eurovision, its operation and an appraisal of its future role in European cooperation, was discussed separately. Other topics included distribution systems of printed media in Western Europe, foreign language programming of Western European radio stations and informal channels provided by migratory workers and tourists.

10) European transporation systems

In an overview of transportation networks of Western Europe, areas of high network densities were contrasted with low density areas. Associated problems of within-state integration were emphasized and future transport plans were evaluated as contributions to subcontinental and continental integration. As in the previous papers on communication, considerable use was made of cartographic handouts and visual aids.

The discussion, then, turned to case studies where attempts were made to present—in detail—problems of one country or area.

CASE STUDIES

11) Communication and separatism

The possible bases for separatism in the United Kingdom were isolated in analysis of British minority party participation and support in the British General Electon of 1964, concentrating on the geographical distribution of support for nationalist parties in Scotland, Northern Ireland and Wales. In each case economic factors were suggested as reinforcing cultural desires for a degree of separation from London's authority. Also raised was the current issue of communication between local white and colored immigrant populations, including British press coverage of racial issues and the degree of press concentration in London.

12) Mass media hierarchy in Germany

The mass media development in Germany after World War II was used as a study of economic and political trends in a national system. It included democratization methods by the allied forces, problems of media ownership, legal and extra-legal restrictions and the role of broadcasting. Another facet covered media relations with local, state and federal governments and the degree to which consideration is given to international and, particularly, Western European affairs.

13) Interaction in Scandinavia

Whilst the first case studies were devoted to within-state differences in the United Kingdom and mass media differences in Germany, the following dealt with the state of international *cooperation* in border regions of Scandinavia. After a general examination of boundary interaction research in recent geographical literature, it turned to Danish-West German, Norwegian-Swedish and Finnish-Russian border areas. Economic stimuli to cross-boundary interaction were explained and suggestions offered as to other Western European boundaries where the lessening of the barrier effects might encourage economic activity. Finally, discussion turned to man's perception of local and international boundaries as barriers.

14) Political interaction

Based on selected readings an effort was made to evaluate the historical and economic roles played by the United Kingdom, France, and West Germany in European affairs. Also considered were the present state of political relations between the three possible state pairings, and the question of Britain's entry into the Common Market and the consequent demise of EFTA.

15) Localism in Southern Europe

The final geographical presentation attempted to make redress for a comparative neglect of Southern Europe. An introduction to the physical geography of the region was followed by exemplification of localisms which exist in Portugal, Spain and Italy. The traditional political behavior of these areas was also discussed. Within-state differences and poor transport and communication links were identified in Italy, where a superficial analysis of agricultural modernization served to locate barriers to innovation. Problems of integration within Italy, and of Italy's relations with more northerly areas of Europe received special attention.

16) Communication in Southern Europe

The paper supplemented the preceding presentation but also dealt with mass media status and performance in Spain, Portugal and Greece. It included a review of economic and political problems affecting the mass media, especially the press and how, if at all, integration into the Western European community could be achieved.

SUMMARY

As this was the first such experiment for all participants, a number of problems became evident during the course of the semester. But overall, student reaction to the approach seemed favorable and the instructors benefited considerably from the experience.

In the future it should be possible to prepare and present a more coherent course on this theme, or to apply the method to some other area of the world. Certainly, the integration theme might be applied to such regions as Southeast Asia, Africa, south of the Sahara or Latin America. The authors would be interested to hear of any similar undertakings along these lines.

REFERENCES CITED

(Numbers correspond to sections of the article)
1) There are a number of books and readers which supply a fair amount of introductory material. Among them are: Wilbur Schramm, The Process and Effects of Mass Communication (Urbana, 1966); Bernard Berelson and Morris Janowitz, Reader in Public Opinion and Propaganda (Urbana, Ill., 1966); Joseph T. Klapper, The Effects of Mass Communication (Glencoe, 1960); Carl I. Hovland, Irving L. Janis and Harold H. Kelley, Communication and Persuasion (New Haven, 1953); Wilbur Schramm, The Science of Human Communication (New York, 1963); Charles R. Wright, Mass Communication (New York, 1959).
2) For examples of the traditional method of regional presentation of Western Europe see, E. J. Monkhouse, A Regional Geography of Western Europe (London, 1959) and J. M. Houston, The Western Mediterranean World: An Introduction to its Regional Landscapes (London, 1964). There is a surplus of sources on European integration, for an introduction to both EEC and the more limited Nordic Association see Amitai Etzioni, Political Unification: A Comparative Study of Leaders and Forces (New York, 1965). For some general considerations of transportation, integration and interaction see Edward L. Ullman, "The Role of Transportation and the Bases of Interaction," in William L. Thomas Jr., ed., Man's Role in Changing the Face of the Earth (Chicago, 1956) pp. 862–80. For information on specific structures, see for example Deryck Abel, Channel Underground: A New Survey of the Channel Question (London, 1961) and Aloys A. Michel, "The Canalization of the Moselle and West European Integration," The Geographical Review, 52: 475–91 (October 1962).
3) For two recent discussions of the regional concept see Roger Minshull, Regional Geography: Theory and Practice (Chicago, 1967) and David Turnock, "The Region in Modern Geography," Geography, 52:374–83 (November 1967). Urban and functional regions in Western Europe are examined by Robert E. Dickinson, The City Region in Western Europe (London, 1967); for examples from Eastern Europe see Kazimierz Dziewonski and Stanislaw Lesczycki, "Geographical Studies of Economic Regions in Central-Eastern Europe," Przeglad Geograficyny, 32:115–25 (Supplement 1960). The inadequacy of contemporary internal areal-political organization in Western Europe is noted by Brian R. Goodey, "Recent Change in West Europe's Internal Political Geography," The North Dakota Quarterly, 35: 119–25 (Autumn 1967); an introduction to Europe's complex ethnic structure is provided by Guy Heraud, Peuples et langues d'Europe (Paris, 1968); see also the federalist journal, L'Europe en formation, published in Paris.
4) Besides a number of general philosophical and historical works the following books and articles are noteworthy on the subject of communication and culture: Robert T. Oliver, Culture and Communication (Springfield, Ill., 1962): Harold A. Innis, The Bias of Communication (Toronto, 1951); Alfred G. Smith, Communication

and Culture (New York, 1966); Edward Sapir, Culture, Language and Personality (Berkeley, 1964); Marshall McLuhan, The Gutenberg Galaxy (Toronto, 1962); Carl T. Rowan, "The Challenges of Cultural Communication," Journalism Quarterly, 40:428–88 (Summer 1963, Special Supplement).

5) Besides Fredrick Siebert et al., Four Theories of the Press (Urbana, 1956), a number of articles such as Raymond Nixon's "Freedom in the World's Press: A Fresh Appraisal with New Data," Journalism Quarterly, 42:3–14 (Winter 1965) and Vincent Farace and Lewis Donahew, "Mass Communications in National Social Systems: A Study of 43 Variables in 115 Countries," Journalism Quarterly, 42:253–61 (Spring 1965) and Karl Deutsch and Walter Isard, "Towards Western European Integration: An Interim Assessment," Journal of International Affairs, 16:89–101 (1962) were recommended. Leslie John Martin, International Propaganda: Its Legal and Diplomatic Control (Minneapolis, 1958) and George Codding Jr., Broadcasting Without Barriers (Paris, 1959) were also used for discussion of political communication within Western Europe.

6) The best source for discussion of recent within-state conflicts is undoubtedly the European newspaper or weekly journal. For a simple survey of such problems see Lewis M. Alexander, World Political Patterns (Chicago, 1963). Essays on the nature of within-nation differences and center-periphery relations are included in Richard L. Meritt and Stein Rokkan, eds., Comparing Nations: The Use of Quantitative Data in Cross-National Research (New Haven, 1966) and Erik Allardt and Yrjö Littunen, eds., Cleavages, Ideologies and Party Systems: Contributions to Comparative Political Sociology (Helsinki, 1964). For examples of within-nation differences see Geoffrey Moorhouse, Britain in the Sixties: The Other England (Harmondsworth, Middx., 1964) and Sergio Barzant, The Underdeveloped Areas Within the Common Market (Princeton, 1965); for a parallel study of EFTA see Regional Development Policies in EFTA (Geneva: EFTA 1965).

7) Amongst the studies examined were K. E. Boulding, The Image (Ann Arbor, 1956); Otto Klineberg, The Human Dimensions in International Relations (New York, 1965; H. C. J. Duijker and N. H. Frijda, National Character and National Stereotypes: A Trend Report Prepared for the International Union of Scientific Psychology (Amsterdam, 1960); Gunnar Myrdal, "Psychological Impediments to Effective International Co-operation," The Journal of Social Issues, Supplement No. 6:1–31 (1952). Geographical contributions to the study of perception are scattered; a good introduction is provided by Peter R. Gould, On Mental Maps (Michigan Inter-University Community of Mathematical Geographers, Discussion Paper No. 9, Ann Arbor, 1966).

8) Among articles used for this discussion were chapters in the International Press Institute's The Flow of the News (Zurich, 1953), Karl W. Deutsch et al., France, Germany and the Western Alliance (New York, 1967) and International Press Institute, As Others See Us (Zurich, 1954). Also used were Richard L. Merritt and Ellen B. Pirro, Press Attitudes to Arms Control in Four Countries, 1946–63 (New Haven, mimeographed) as well as data from Elizabeth Noelle and Erich P. Neumann (ed.), Jahrbuch der Offentlichen Meinung, 1958–64 (Allensbach und Bonn, 1965).

9) Typical of the kind of articles read were R. Vincent Farace, "Identifying Regional Systems in National Development Research," Journalism Quarterly, 43:753–60 (Fall 1966) and Llewellyn White and Robert D. Leigh, "Merchants of Words and Images," in Charles Steinberg (ed), Mass Media and Communication (New York, 1966). Other sources included Burton Paulu, Radio and Television Broadcasting on the European Continent (Minneapolis, 1967); E. Dofivat (ed), Handbuch der Auslandspresse (Bonn, 1960). The discussion of private broadcasting stations was based on a number of articles in the New York Times, Time, Newsweek and Saturday Review between 1961 and 1966; also: H. F. Van Panhuys et al., "Legal Aspects of Private Broadcasting, A Dutch Approach," American Journal of International Law, 60:303 (April 1966).

Besides the above mentioned book by Paulu other material used includes Wilson P. Dizard, *Television: A World View* (Syracuse, 1966); Donald K. Pollock and David L. Woods, "A Study in International Communication: Eurovision," *Journal of Broadcasting*, 2:99–117 (Spring 1959); Don R. Browne, "The Limits of the Limitless Medium—International Broadcasting," *Journalism Quarterly*, 42:82–86 (Winter 1965).

10) Material for this paper was drawn from several sources, including George Kish, "Transportation Within the European Economic Community: Problems and Policies," *The East Lakes Geographer*, 1:13–20 (November 1964); Margaret Axelrad, "Petroleum Pipelines in Western Europe," *The Professional Geographer*, 16:1–5 (July 1964); George Hoffman, "Toward Greater Integration in Europe: Transfer of Electric Power Across International Boundaries," *Journal of Geography*, 55:165–76 (April 1956); James Bird, "Seaports and the European Economic Community," *The Geographical Journal*, 133:302–27 (September 1967; *General Cargo Handling in Three EFTA Ports* (Geneva: EFTA, 1968); Michael Chisholm, "Must We All Live in Southeast England?: The Location of New Employment," *Geography*, 49:1–14 (January 1964).

11) Nationalist and other minority parties in the United Kingdom are discussed by George Thayer, *The British Political Fringe: A Profile* (London, 1965). Further sources on the spatial aspects of minority parties in the British Isles and elsewhere are to be found in Brian R. Goodey, *Geography and Elections: A Bibliography* (Grand Forks, N.D., in Press). On variations in economic development in the British Isles see, Bryan E. Coates and Eric M. Rawstron, "Regional Variations in Incomes," *Westminster Bank Review*, 28–46 (February 1965); *Regional Development in Britain* (Central Office of Information Reference Pamphlet No. 80, H.M.S.O., London, 1968); David Eversley, "North-south exaggerations," *New Society*, May 2, 1968, pp. 640–1; satirical but quite accurate is C. Northcote Parkinson, "Two Nations," *The Economist*, March 25, 1967, pp. 116–7.

12) Because of questions of accessibility and language proficiency, most sources are English-language publications, although much more detailed studies are available in German and were consulted by the author. *Gazette*, 5:1 (1959) is devoted to the German scene; other articles included John Gimbel, "The Spiegel Affair in Perspective," *Midwest Journal of Political Science*, 9:282–97 (August 1965); F. E. Nirsch, "How Free is the German Press," *Current History*, 44:226 (April 1963); Hanno Hardt, "Axel Caesar Springer: Dangers of Press Concentration in Germany," *Grassroots Editor*, 8:15–17 (Jan.–Feb. 1967); and a number of earlier articles in *Journalism Quarterly* covering the post-war period.

13) Two of the most significant recent studies of boundary effects have been J. Ross Mackay, "The Interactance Hypothesis and Boundaries in Canada: A Preliminary Study," *The Canadian Geographer*, No. 11:1–8 (1958) and Robert S. Yuill, *A Simulation Study of Barrier Effects in Spatial Diffusion Problems* (Michigan Inter-University Community of Mathematical Geographers, Discussion Paper No. 5, Ann Arbor, 1965). Current research into boundary effects is summarized by David R. Reynolds and M. L. McNulty, "Political Boundaries, Barrier Effects, and Space Perception," unpublished paper prepared for presentation to the Political Geography section of the Association of American Geographers, St. Louis, Easter 1967. The discussion of Scandinavian boundaries was based on diverse sources including Department of State and Office of Naval Research reports. See also Kaare Svalastoga and Preben Wolf, "A Town in Danish Borderland," *Danish Foreign Office Journal*, No. 50:36–9 (September 1964) and their book *En by ved graensen* (Copenhagen, 1963); *Alternative Permanent Links Between Denmark and Sweden* (Stockholm and Copenhagen, 1962) and Ronald A. Helin, "Finland Regains an Outlet to the Sea: The Saimaa Canal," *The Geographical Review*, 58:167–94 (April 1968).

14) Amongst the materials found to be of value in the discussion were Dorothy Pickles, *The Uneasy Entente: French Foreign Policy and Franco-British Misunderstandings* (London, 1966); Ronald Inglehart, "An End to European Integration?" *American*

Political Science Review, 61:91–105 (March 1967); Rodney Preece and Viggo Graf Blücher, "Do the Europeans Want Us?" *New Society*, Oct. 12, 1967, p. 523; Emile Beniot, *Europe at Sixes and Sevens: The Common Market, The Free Trade Association, and the United States* (New York, 1961); Norman J. G. Pounds, "France and the Resource Pattern of Western Europe," in Sydney Nettleton Fisher, ed., *France and the European Community* (Publications of the Graduate Institute of World Affairs of the Ohio State University, No. 4, Columbus, 1964) pp. 117–38.

15) Examples of localisms are afforded by J. A. Pitt-Rivers, *The People of the Sierra* (Chicago, 1961) and by Dan Stanislawski, "The Monchique of Southern Portugal," *The Geographical Review*, 52:37–55 (January 1962). Important aspects of local communication in traditional political life are examined by E. J. Hobsbawn, *Primitive Rebels* (New York, 1959); for a commentary on the economic effects of the Mafia in Sicily see Renée Rochefort, *Le Travail en Sicilie* (Paris, 1961); on the separatist activities of the Basques see Paul Barker, "The People of Guernica," *New Society*, Aug. 25, 1966, pp. 295–97. The discussion of regional variations in agricultural modernization in Italy was based on Giuseppe Medici, Ugo Sorbi and Antonio Castrataro, *Rolverizzazione e Frammentazione della Proprietà Fondiaria in Italia* (Milan, 1962), supported by information from Shepard B. Clough, *The Economic History of Modern Italy* (New York, 1964).

16) Articles dealing with problems of mass media operation in Southern Europe include Marvin Alisky, "Spain's Press and Broadcasting: Conformity and Censorship," Journalism Quarterly, 39:63–69 (Winter 1962); Anna M. Cornetta, "Italy's Disappearing Dailies," *Nieman Reports*, 15:28–32 (July/October 1962); Ignazio Weiss, "The Daily in Italy," *Gazette*, 4:251–60 (1958); also in that issue, pp. 232–48, Malcolm MacLean Jr. and Luca Pinna, "Mass Media in Scarperia"; MacLean and Pina, "Distances and News Interest: Scarpia, Italy," Journalism Quarterly, 35:36–48 (Winter 1958); Ronald H. Chilcote, "The Press in Latin America, Spain and Portugal," *Hispanic American Report* (special issue, 1963) also contains brief accounts of the press.

INTERNATIONAL COOPERATION IN TELECOMMUNICATION FOR EDUCATIONAL AND CULTURAL PURPOSES

Robert K. Woetzel

ROBERT K. WOETZEL was born in 1930. He attended Shanghai American School in China and received his B.A. at Columbia College in 1952. He received a Ph.D. at Oxford University in 1954 and his J.D. from Bonn University in 1959. Woetzel has served as a scholar at the Hague Academy of International Law, in the United States Army, as a legislative assistant for the United States House of Representatives during the Eighty-Fourth Congress, as the associate to the director of the Institute of International Law at Bonn University, as a staff member for the Center for the Study of Democratic Institutions, and as a consultant on arms control at the jet propulsion laboratory of the California Institute of Technology. He has taught at Fordham University, New York University, the University of West Indies in Trinidad, Harvard Divinity School, Immaculate Heart College, Seminary of the Immaculate Conception, Oxford University, and Boston College, where he is currently a professor of international politics and law. He has received fellowships and grants from Columbia University, Oxford University, Bonn University, the Ford Fund for Public Affairs Research, American Council of Learned Societies, the Von Humboldt Travel Fund, and Boston College University. He is the recipient of the Einstein Prize in American Diplomacy, the Stokes Prize in Political Theory, and the Curtis Gold Medal. His main area of research since 1960 has been international criminal law in the protection of human rights. His books include The Nuremberg Trials in International Law (London, 1960); Die International Kontrolle der hoeheren Luftschichten und des Weltraums ("The International Control of Space") (Bad Godesberg, 1960); The Philosophy of Freedom (New York, 1968; Allahabad, India, 1969); and Toward a Feasible International Court, with Julius Stone (New York, 1970). Woetzel and his wife have been involved in the Danforth Associates Program of the Danforth Foundation, and Professor Woetzel has served as chairman of several of its programs and conferences.

The relation between telecommunication and literacy is an established fact; Wilbur Schramm has written that "underdeveloped countries have underdeveloped communication systems, too." The new technologies of communication satellites make possible an expansion of facilities for telecommunication. Telstar and its successors open up new circuits for telephone, telegraph, radio, facsimile pictures, and television. Literacy is a condition *sine qua non* for social and economic development; information is an indispensable requirement for greater freedom and dignity for the world's people. Through radio and television in particular, it is possible to raise educa-

Reprinted with permission of *International Relations* (April 1968), pp. 355–363, 370.

tional and cultural standards; space technologies enable us to do this on a global scale. The American Early Bird and the Russian Molniya programs point the way to town-meets of the world, to seminars from country to country with direct participation of people around the globe, to universities of the air for peoples everywhere, with the resources and know-how of different countries pooled in concerted endeavours to raise the level of enlightenment and thereby standards of living; it is even possible to look forward to a continuing Venice Festival of the Air with the best products of different cultures channelled to individual receivers.

In the meantime, serious differences in arrangements for national and international telecommunication exist; differences that create political, economic, and ideological obstacles to effective international cooperation. This paper will concentrate on the television aspects of the problem of reconciling these different approaches. In the United States, educational television is decentralized; it follows the national educational pattern of localized operation and control. While the National Educational Television network groups together over a hundred local stations in a loose federation, control and planning by and large, take place on a local level. In England, the British Broadcasting Corporation began school broadcasts in 1924 and has steadily expanded its "enrichment" programs for classroom use. Similarly, Radiodiffusion Television Française and the Italian Telescuola or "television school" offer special incentives for education via television. In Germany, a network of locally controlled ETV stations has offered school broadcasts since the first ETV station, operated by Hessischer Rundfunk, began operations in September, 1964. Soviet television has experimented with both direct instructional and enrichment programs since 1962. In the same year a Chinese report indicated that stations in Peking, Tientsin, Canton, and Harbin were sponsoring "television universities" and the Shanghai station was offering university-level courses in chemistry and physics. The Japanese Nippon Hossi Kyokai network inaugurated the first station of a separate national education television network in 1958. The Japanese experience has been most successful offering courses for correspondence school students since 1959. By 1965 almost all Japanese schools were equipped with television receivers channeling programs from 46 educational television stations throughout Japan. With regard to educational television in the developing countries, the Jesuit sociologist Neil Hurley tells us that "Television's finest educational possibilities at present seem to be at those levels where as yet there is no pedagogical tradition: the training of the illiterate and the unskilled." Of Chile's "revolution in liberty" he writes that it will meet "its acid test in the area of the underprivileged, those who eagerly want to read and write, to learn a craft and vocational skills, who want to be incorporated into Twentieth Century life. It is precisely at this level where TV can leap the literacy barrier and barriers of space and time to carry light into the darkness of the lower classes and those in remote areas." In Colombia, the Alliance for Progress helped to finance an Italian Telescuola-type project. In Argentina, the Ministry of Education inaugurated the Telescuela Tecnica Argentina in April, 1963, aimed at students who were "drop-outs" or who lived in remote areas where there were no highschools. Mexico, Nigeria, the United Arab Republic, Iran, and other developing countries have also initiated ETV programs of one variety or another.

Methods of control and planning in the television industry differ from country to country. Public ownership prevails, of course, in the Socialist countries, while in the United States the commercial networks predominate although the newer forms like ETV, subscription or pay television, and ultra-high-frequency channel television are expanding. Recently, the President of the Ford Foundation, McGeorge Bundy, called for a communications satellite system, to be operated by a nonprofit private organisation, for the service of both commercial and noncommercial TV in the United States. Other plans have been submitted, notably by the Carnegie Commission on Educational Television, which would have significant effect on educational television in this country. The Communication Satellite Corporation, which is responsible for the international aspects of satellite communications, has also interested itself in this area. The question whether Comsat or a nonprofit organization should concern itself with the national aspects is being debated at the present time. What emerges from these discussions is that there are different models from which to choose, and this is especially true in the international community where different social and economic systems compete with each other. Joseph Charyk, President of the Communications Satellite Corporation, recognized this when he stated that the Communications Satellite Act of 1962 which established Comsat, "did not attempt to prescribe the *nature* or *form* of the international arrangements but left this responsibility to the President, the State Department and the Corporation" (italics mine). Public and private ownership features of telecommunications must be reconciled then, in order to produce a genuine international system.

The need for international cooperation in telecommunictaion for educational and cultural purposes was stressed in a resolution prepared by Gaston Berger and unanimously adopted by the General Conference of the United Nations Educational, Scientific and Cultural Organization in 1960 which drew attention to the *impossibility* of bringing about universal literacy without using space communication. The UNESCO Meeting of Experts on the Use of Space Communication by the Mass Media held in 1965 added that "Space communication should, in fact, make it possible to find solutions on a different scale from those of the past and give education new frontiers and new dimensions." Three teaching situations were described, corresponding to the three stages in technical development: (a) stationary point-to-point satellites transmitting messages received by ground broadcasting stations, which would broadcast them over their own wavelengths, reception being through the conventional channels —schools, television clubs, individual reception of broadcasts integrated in the normal programs; (b) stationary distribution satellites broadcasting messages received direct by specially equipped receiving stations, reception of the educational message being supervised and on a community basis (television schools); and (c) broadcasting satellites capable of sending messages direct to any individual or group receiver in their coverage zone, reception of the educational message being entirely free and unsupervised. Commenting on the future uses of telecommunication, Dr. Charyk has stated that "it will be possible for us to get a wide range of communications services right in our own homes, by merely pushing a button. Such services will include video-telephone, television, radio and facsimile units that can bring you the latest newspaper, or other important record. All kinds of shopping and banking services will be only a push button away. Centralized charging, billing and reporting will be routine." Satellites are multiversal and capable of transmitting all forms of communication—telephone, telegraph, radio, television, data and facsimile. They may service a limited area or a vast territory; they can be national, regional or global in configuration.

Some of the effects of this communications explosion on educational television have been outlined by the UNESCO Meeting of Experts: it will be possible to increase inter-school exchanges, in particular by means of telephone or television conversations, some of which might set an example like the Paris-Wisconsin Early Bird experiment; higher education by television on a world scale may be another result, using point-to-point inter-university communication by telephone or transmission of photographic material; in the developing countries, the "feeding of stations via communication satellites should make it possible to organize a system of common educational and cultural programs for use by all stations concerned; and general adult education programs designed for uniform cultural and linguistic zones would also be facilitated by the use of communication satellites. Science and technology can be advanced and cultural exchange aided through space communications. Marshal Shulman has commented that "as more people have had some direct contact with other countries, the effect has been to reduce the foreign quality of other cultures and systems." And Charles Frankel tells us that "the division of intellectuals into rival camps that are out of touch with each other is a principal cause of international misunderstandings and animosities." Hopefully, the dialogue via TV between persons in different countries will diminish such divisions; in the phrase of Marshall McLuhan, "the medium is the message."

The basic principles that must guide international cooperation in the field of telecommunication have been laid down in the Treaty on Principles Governing the Activities of States in the Exploration and Use of Outer Space, including the Moon and other Celestial Bodies. Article III provides that "States Parties to the Treaty shall carry on activities in the exploration and use of outer space, including the Moon and other celestial bodies, in accordance with international law. . . ." Article VI states that "States Parties to the Treaty shall bear international responsibility for national activities in outer space . . . whether such activities are carried on by governmental agencies or by non-governmental entities . . ." Conflicts are to be avoided through "appropriate international consultations" before proceeding with controversial activities or experiments, and activities are to be carried on by states "on a basis of equality," according to Articles IX and X respectively. These are some of the salient featuers of the Treaty which codifies much of the international law of outer space which has existed to this point.

The United States, the Soviet Union, and certain European countries have pioneered international organizations for transmission of television programs via space satellites. The countries of the world are gradually being drawn into these networks. Comsat has sponsored the International Telecommunications Satellite Consortium which was established by two international agreements first opened for signature on August 20, 1964. Any state which is a member of the International Telecommunication Union may join INTELSAT and well over fifty have done so already. According to Article III of the Agreement Establishing Interim Arrangements for a Global Commercial Communications Satellite System, "The space segment shall be owned in undivided shares by the signatories to the Special Agreement in proportion to their respective contributions to the costs of the design, development, construction and establishment of the space segment." Article V provides that "Each signatory to the Special Agreement or group of signatories to the Special Agreement represented on the Committee shall have a number of votes equal to its quota, or to their combined quotas, as the case may be." Accordingly, the United States segment amounts to over fifty per cent of the vote. Soviet officials criticized this arrangement; Ambassador Federenko has stated that "These steps were taken by the United States for the benefit of the selfish interests of a private corporation, Comsat, and those of the powerful monopolies standing behind it . . . pursuing for their own purposes the subordination of the whole field of international communications . . . to the hegemony of the United States." And Cheprov points out that the less developed countries would have little say in such an organization; the principles of equality and common use would be endangered thereby. In this connection, Resolution 2223 of the Twenty-first U.N. General Assembly declares that "space activities be carried out in such a manner that States may share in the adventure and the practical benefits of space exploration *regardless of the stage of their economic or scientific development*" (italics mine), and the UNESCO Meeting of Experts stressed the fact that the words "cultural exchange" "implied equal opportunities for all, and reciprocity, so as to avoid a predominance, in the space communications field, of any one culture over another."

Some of the fears of the Russians are echoed by European writers: Edmund Faller of Cologne referring to the INTELSAT quota system, states that "It appears to be undesirable to grant such a strong position to any single State." The Report submitted by the Committee on Space Questions to the Assembly of the Western European Union declares that it is "unacceptable that European countries should be totally dependent on American research and development. There is the question of television and telephone connections which both have a great political impact and require free use by the Western European countries." Article VII of a Special Agreement appended to the INTELSAT Agreement Establishing Interim Arrangements provides that "In considering whether an earth station should be permitted to utilize the space segment, the Committee shall take into account the technical characteristics of the station, the technical limitations on multiple access to satellites due to the existing state of the art, the effect of geographical distribution of earth stations on the efficiency of the services to be provided by the system, the recommended standards of the International Telegraph and Telephone Consultative Committee and the International Radio Consultative Committee of the International Telecommunication Union, and such general standards as the Committee may establish. . . ." And Article VIII states that ". . . In making allotments of satellite utilization the Committee shall give due consideration to the quotas of the signatories to be served by each earth station." The quota system of voting gives the United States greater power than the other states in deciding how allotments of satellite utilizaion are to be made: this it is feared may result in discrimination against members with smaller quotas.

The arrangements of INTELSAT are subject to re-examination by a conference to be convened by the United States in 1969 [which has since been held], where the members "shall seek to ensure that the definitive arrangements will be established at the earliest practicable date, with a view to their entry into force by 1st January 1970" (Article IX of the Agreement Establishing Interim Arrangements). In the meantime, the Soviet Union is developing an international communications system in cooperation with its allies, and on June 30, 1966 certain agreements were signed between the U.S.S.R. and France which anticipate further cooperation in this area between these two countries. The European Space Research Organization, the European Launcher Development Organization, and Conference on Satellite Communications are also proceeding to establish independent European space programs. In that connection, Jean Delorme, President of Eurospace, has commented that "Unless European countries want to become backward economies within fifty years, underdeveloped in comparison with the Big Two, they must lose no time in entering this laboratory of the future." And the Consultative Assembly of the Council of Europe, adopting a statement presented by its Cultural and Scientific Committee on April 20, 1966, has recommended the establishment of "a strong European organization which would have, subject to Ministerial and Parliamentary control, the authority to co-ordinate the European effort in space and the resources to make that effort effective." The statement envisages "a unified and joint European space policy."

These programs are not mutually exclusive. As Dr. Charyk has pointed out, an important feature of satellites is that "while they are international in dimension, they are also regional by nature. . . . (This) is particularly significant when assessing the nature of a domestic or regional satellite system." Different social and economic systems have not prevented cooperation between the National Aeronautics and Space Administration and the Soviet Academy of Sciences in the field of international telecommunication, in connection with Echo-2 and other experiments, not to speak of international cooperation in the assignment of frequencies which has been going on for a long time. The experience of the International Telecommunication Union may assist in gauging future possibilities for international cooperation. Certain problems arise, however, which have special relevance to space communications: the danger of broadcasting by "pirate stations" has led Jean Persin of the ITU Secretariat to conclude that "the regulation of space broadcasting should be studied as a matter of urgency at an international level and . . . pending a general agreement on the subject, it should be forbidden to establish and use broadcasting stations (sound broadcasting and television) on board space vehicles." And

Professor Hilding Eek of Stockholm states that "If only a few countries or some groups of allied countries had the capacity of launching high power communications satellites they would have in their hands a means of influencing opinion which, if used or suspected of being used in a monopolistic manner, could create international tension and misunderstanding." The Soviet writer G. Zhukov cites the Convention on the Use of Radio in the Interests of Peace of September 23, 1936, as a possible precedent for the right of a state to prevent harmful broadcasts that may instigate war (Article II). And Richard Gardner correctly points out that "Countries with no immediate prospect of carrying on space broadcasting fear that the United States and the Soviet Union may use this technology to send their people political or commercial messages that the governments do not like." He recommends that "In each case the receiving countries will determine what programs should be broadcast to their peoples, within the framework of agreements with the countries financing the hardware and perhaps with technical assistance from UNESCO and other international agencies."

According to Article 47 of the ITU Convention, members are obligated to avoid harmful interference, when frequencies are allocated and regulations of the ITU are otherwise complied with. Since judgments may differ on what constitutes abuse, provisions for arbitration of disputes may in the long run be more effective than "the right to jam" so-to-speak. In that connection the arbitration agreement of INTELSAT might provide a helpful model, without reference, of course, to the question of private ownership.

The problem of public versus private ownership need not stand in the way of international cooperation. As has been shown, such cooperation already exists between different systems, and as the Analysis of the Space Treaty by the Staff of the Senate Committee on Aeronautical and Space Sciences indicates, "the government would accept responsibility for the activities of NASA as well as those of the Communications Satellite Corporation. . . . Furthermore, the government would see that such activities conform to the treaty's provisions, and also authorize and continuously supervise the space activities of non-governmental entities. . . . The treaty also provides that an international organization as well as the states participating therein are responsible for compliance with the treaty." Whatever domestic arrangements exist, therefore, this does not prevent coordination of different programs by the states. The question is whether this should be done ad hoc and from case to case or if there should be a coordinating body, which may be either a new independent international organization, or a department or section of an existing or new international organization. Zhukov mentions the following alternatives for coordination: (a) directly between various systems of telecommunications by satellites; (b) through the International Telecommunication Union; and (c) through the establishment of a special agency for this purpose on a parity basis.

It is clear that in any convention establishing a global system of telecommunication, the one-nation-one-vote standard would be favoured by most states, especially those whose resources are limited, as compared to the quota system. The experience of UNESCO might be helpful in this regard: weighted voting was not necessary to make this organization an effective instrument in the promotion of educational and cultural programs. In fact, the dangers associated with propaganda and advertising might be diminished by ensuring an equal voice for all participants. This does not mean that national and regional programs could not adopt different formulas as long as the international broadcasts were not interfered with. The contribution by states to a genuine international system would not detract from their other efforts but complement them by making possible a dialogue different in *kind* and *scope*. Finally the International Law Association at a session on space law chaired by Professor Tunkin in Helsinki last September unanimously adopted a resolution presented by Dr. Pepin of France "to consider the usefulness that questions relating to the establishment and operation of telecommunications system (or systems) by satellites should be dealt with through an international organ. . . ."

I would like to suggest, therefore, that we use as a starting point for our discussion where the ILA left off: the possibility of creating an international organization which might be called the Space Educational, Scientific, and Cultural Organization, and which, ideally speaking, will take what is best from each national and regional communications system to give the most to all. SPESCO should be a specialized agency of the United Nations which will afford each partner an equal voice and be responsible for planning and programming transmissions via a global system to which nations may contribute much as they do now to the various specialized agencies. Programming, at the outset, would be largely confined to fulfilling educational needs *i.e.* literacy programs, agricultural training, hygiene methods, etc., and bridging cultural voids—providing a much needed outlet for creative talent from all lands. Propaganda and advertising would be barred. Disputes would be subject to arbitration, which would lessen the danger of interference. Nations will compete to provide the best educational and cultural fare they have to offer. Thus one day we may say with the Japanese child from a rural school:

Even if there were no television,
I will imitate the act of switching it on.
I will recall the time when we had television
Because it was like love itself.

THOUGHTS ON THE RELEVANCE
OF THE 'COMMUNICATION EXPLOSION'
TO THE FUTURE OF WORLD ORDER

Colin Cherry

COLIN CHERRY *is professor of telecommunications at the Imperial College of Science of the United Kingdom. His previous research has been involved with the psychological and social aspects of telecommunications, and he is currently interested in the values of communication technology for international relations and experimentation upon human conversation. He is the author of* On Human Communication *(1957) and numerous articles. He has lectured and broadcasted widely in the United Kingdom, Europe, and the United States.*

Since the end of the Second World War there has been a remarkable increase in our technical power for international communication, including such means as submarine cable and satellite telephony, Telex for the News Services and for business, and to enable the airways to operate, the airways themselves of course, international radio and T.V. programme sales—a whole complex of inter-related systems. The question to be raised here is: what are the real values of this fast-expanding technology for "world order" (a concept which I, personally, wish to distinguish sharply from that of "centralized world government")? Will these increasing powers help unite us or divide us, and why?

When speaking of this "explosive growth" of world communication it is essential to retain a sense of proportion. Most communication in this world is still within the borders of countries and, bearing population numbers in mind, "always" will be. This international traffic explosion, shipping apart, is almost wholly a post-Second World War phenomenon; although relatively small compared to inland traffic, it is of course of very great importance in two general ways: (a) *emotionally* (b) *practically* (i.e. organizationally). These two broad ways I would associate with the two facets of human existence—the personal and the social.

Four curves are shown here, Figs. (1) (2) and (3) and (4) to illustrate the very rapid growths being referred to as "explosive." Fig. (1) shows the total number of telephones in the world; most are capable of being connected. Such a curve, by itself, tells us very little however. It should be pointed out that most of these instruments are within the richer industrial countries.[1] Fig. (2) shows how the number of channels across the North Atlantic has increased since 1950 with the official predictions up to 1975. The world's busiest route, this alone carries no less than 80% of the world's inter-continental traffic. Fig. (3) shows another form of post-War "communication explosion"—the traffic

Reprinted with permission of International Relations (November 1969), pp. 541–549, 564.

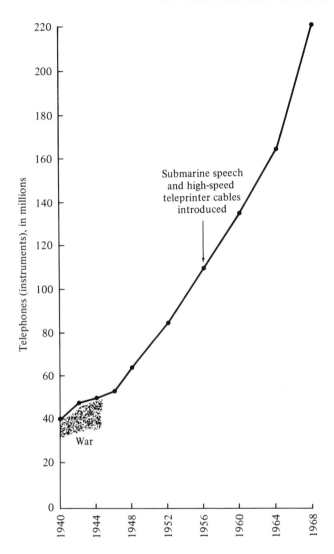

Figure 1. World Telephone Growth.

through London Airport, the world's busiest centre for international air traffic. Fig. (4) shows the growth of Telex traffic between the U.K. and the rest of the world.

So we might go on with endless illustrations, all approximating in shape to the exponential form, whose increasing steepness suggests that supply creates demand—as indeed is the case with most, if not all, technology. A system is invented and installed, and only then does the public come to see totally new ways of operating their affairs. And one of the characteristics of the post-War era has been the creation of international industries, of which the Airways and

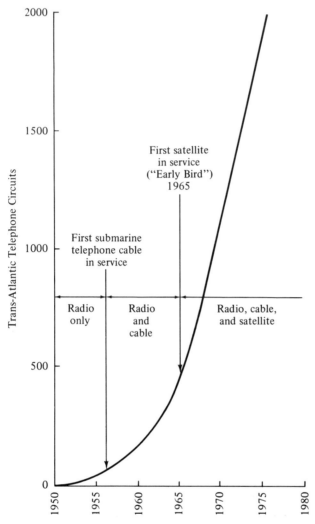

Figure 2. *Official prediction of telephone circuits on North Atlantic ("The Rome Plan")*.

News Services are the most globally extended examples. We are now also seeing the fumbling beginnings of international manufacturing industries, whilst we are all too painfully aware that our international affairs today are handicapped by the failure of one particular communication medium—an adequate international monetary system.

For that is what money really is, at rock bottom, a communication system. Its coins and notes are tokens of exchange, which can readily become numbers or words on paper accounts. In this communicative sense money is one form of "organizing power." All media of communication have this common element

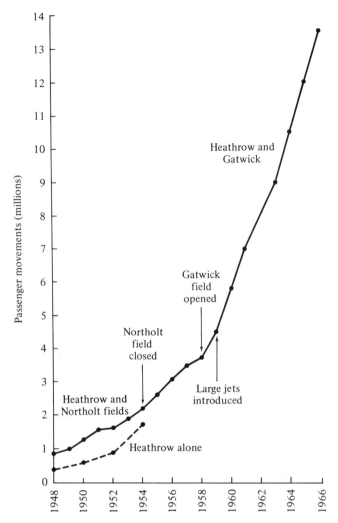

Figure 3. Civilian air passenger movements in London. Heathrow and Northolt fields opened in 1946. Figures were supplied by the British Airports Authority.

in their natures, that they offer "power to organize" various forms of social institution. The inventions of money, of telegraphy, of telephony, data-transmission, computers and all the media pouring in from the cornucopia of modern communication technology, all offer one essential thing—the power to relate one set of activities, at one place, to other sets at other places, i.e. to organize. In this sense, all may be thought of as extending the values of the principle of the division of labour, over whole countries and, increasingly, internationally.

Such academic definition is, of course, hardly realistic. Who owns and con-

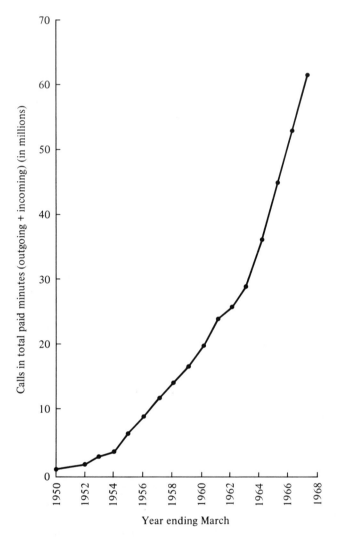

Figure 4. The "explosive" growth of international Telex traffic with the United Kingdom. With grateful acknowledgments to the Postmaster General.

trols these international media? And how do they organize or what do they organize? These are political questions. Fortunately, there has been a long and fairly happy history of international communication, starting with the Telegraphs, Telephones and Postal Services, a hundred years ago, which have evolved traditions of a very self-sustaining kind. This may not be so surprising if we remind ourselves that the word "communication" means "sharing." It is noteworthy that the very first Specialised Agency set up by the United Nations after their initiation was the International Telecommunication Union.

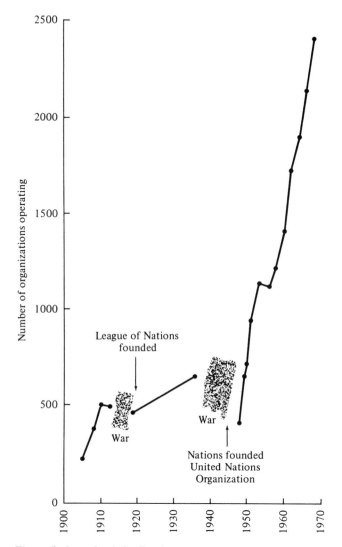

Figure 5. Growth of the listed international organizations (both governmental and non-governmental) since turn of the century.

Nevertheless, it is true to say that the technology of modern communication has been, and is, created in the so-called "advanced" countries; the knowledge and industrial potential largely exist there. But it is also true that these countries rely increasingly upon *international* communication to maintain their various institutions. Many of the "developing" countries have, as one of their most urgent present needs, greatly improved *internal* communication systems, as many U.N. Reports emphasise, to link together their various institutions and areas and to create a deeper understanding of nationhood. The U.N. Reports stress particularly their needs for better Press, radio, and even television and have set minimum targets. It is the values of the various media for "nation-building" that are emphasised—i.e. their power for organization. It is only too easy for us in the seemingly secure and wealthy nations, to take our nationhoods for granted, as a fact of Nature, and to confuse this concept with that of "nationalism," with misplaced scorn.

I have used the term: "developing country." What is the real difference between a developing and a "developed" country? I would argue that every distinction of value ultimately rests upon one thing—their different concepts of trust. I am not saying that the people of developing countries are not trustworthy people; far, far from it! Rather, that their trusts lie in individual persons whom they know as people, whereas the trusts of people like ourselves in "advanced," industrialized, societies lie in abstract institutions and their representatives, whom we may never know as persons. We trust "the Manager," "the Bank," "the Law," "the Accountant," . . . and all else rests upon such trusts. When these trusts fail us we are righteously angry. Today we hear a great deal about the need for "law and order." Law and Order? Of course we want law and order; but these are not primary causes; they are *consequential states of affairs*. It is really trust in institutions and trustworthy institutions that are the prime needs. Law and order follow as a result.

To return to the question of communication media and their true values, it seems to me that these values undoubtedly lie in the powers which all media possess for changing people's trusts—for better or worse. However, to say this may suggest to some readers that I refer to such things as "propaganda," "educational broadcasting" and other direct approaches to people's minds. Quite on the contrary. All media possess these two broad powers (a) the emotional (b) the organizational and it is to the latter that I refer. Briefly then, it is my belief that the real values to future world order that communication media may contribute will come, not from their power to attack other countries' faiths or traditions or to seek to make them "more like us," but almost wholly from their great powers for organization, giving the conceivable possibility of new forms of institution, especially international institutions. If international trust, and hence law and order, are ever to improve, this happy state of affairs can come about only by the successful creation of international institutions, including those of Law, which are actually seen to work. It will not arise from attacking national identities, or racial and cultural identities, from telling the Americans to stop being American and start being more like the Chinese, or hoping for some vague merger between the world's diversified political systems. The real values of the media are practical, not emotional, in the first place.

Such stress upon the practical values of international communication may suggest a steady move towards centralisation. It is certainly true to say that the building of roads, then of railways, telegraphs and other communication media has enabled centralised government to operate over increasingly larger areas with increasing effectiveness, and many there are who fear that this process will continue inevitably, with a loss of all forms of local government and local identity. At the same time, there are also many, perhaps the same people, who long for a world Government and for a shedding of our national autonomies. Is there not some curious contradiction here?

There is, of course. It partly arises from the belief that communication inevitably increases centralisation. Up to the present time in history, this has been largely true, but it is not inherent in the nature of communication; communication has exactly equal power for decentralization. Improved communication services can certainly strengthen central Government, but so they could local Government too, dealing with local affairs and there are many signs now, in Britain for example, that this is beginning to be realised. Even more important than this however, is the falsity of analogy between any kind of centralised "world Government" and a national Government. Under what particular political system would it operate? What unthinkable size of bureaucracy would it require? Furthermore, the analogy is false because national Governments exist to deal with those overall affairs of whole nations, especially as these relate in various ways (trade, defence, finance) to those of other nations. And with what "other worlds" would a centralized "world Government" deal? Mars? Outer Space? No, the analogy is plainly false.

However, to say this is not to despair. It rather requires us to examine again the nature of this apparent contradiction between our feelings for locality, for local identity, even for nationhood (where it is established) and our desires for a better "world order."

The contradiction can be resolved if we remember that we are never, any of us, members only of one community at one time. Thus, for certain purposes I think of myself as "British," for others as "English speaking," for others as "European," for others as a "university member," for others as a "food consumer," and so on. And all these purposes differ, to some extent or other. In other words what is "me," what I feel myself to be, is given by a host of institutions and communities with which I identify, on varied occasions.

If this be accepted, then there is no reason to see contradiction between movement towards a "world order" whilst preserving many, if not most, elements of national and smaller community identity, or even autonomy. The urgent thing is to distinguish these various elements which characterize our various communities.

The essential difference between the idea of a centralized "world Government" with concentrated power and that of a system of "world order" with dispersed power is that the latter involves identifying and separating out, in increasing numbers, those elements of international relations which are shared by differing groups of countries, the idea upon which the International Organizations have been built.

This brings me to the final post-War "explosion" to which I shall refer, and to my conclusion.

The first body of this new kind was set up at the Congress of Vienna (1814–15) and it aimed to deal with a communication medium—the free navigation of the rivers of Europe. From that time on during the 19th century the number of International Organizations grew increasingly rapidly as specific common interests became identified (see Fig. (5)) until the First World War saw the collapse, more or less, of the whole hopeful process. Between the Wars the International Organizations stagnated but the conditions after 1945 were very different and the "explosive" growth of the number of these Organizations during the past 25 years is something new on the international scene.

Only some 25 or so of all these Organizations come under the U.N.— mainly the Specialized Agencies and only about 10% of the total are intergovernmental bodies.[2] There are now some two and a half thousand of these Organizations, each dealing with specific, defined, interests common to a particular group of countries, which share those interests though operating under different political systems. They deal with many and varied aspects of life—of different trades, of law, of health, of fuels, of transport, of finance, of education—a host, each having a specific, defined, *function*.

There is some evidence to suggest that, before the Second World War, we may have been trying to operate international institutions of various kinds with grossly inadequate means for organizing them on global scale; that is, with inadequate communications. To my mind, one of the principal contributions which modern international telecommunication and transport will make to "world order" will come from the new and immense powers which they offer us to set up and run these Organizations, with their Secretariats, their widely separated members, and their needs for modern duplicating and data-transmission. They are world-wide organizations and could not exist upon the horse and the ship, as did the Roman Empire.

A number of writers upon international law have commented upon the steady improvement in its operation today.[3] This has not come about because Man has suddenly become a better animal! It has come about because international law has become increasingly clearly *defined*. It is the separation and clear *identification* of specific affairs, which are found to be of common interest to specific groups of countries, that will make for better "world order"—and our emotional attitudes to one another will then have some chance to follow along this pragmatic track. It is towards such dispersal of power among *functions*, rather than among nations, that I hope my own technology, that of Communication, will gradually lead.

I am aware that the comment has frequently been made that the title of the present world's major International Organization is designated *United Nations Organisation*, and, rightly, not "World Nation Organisation" or such as may be suggestive of wholesale destruction of national identities. It signifies a union —and there must be nations before there can be a union of them. Furthermore, there is no logical reason why they should all be united in the same ways for every purpose. The urgency is *to seek out and clearly define* these varied purposes in the multitude, for it is these that constitute our plural international relations.

NOTES

[1] About half being in the U.S.A. However the majority of their telephones are in private homes. Per hundred population, the number of telephones in the public sphere

(business, industry, Government) in Britain and the U.S.A. are nearly the same.

[2] They are listed with their constitutions, memberships, etc. in (a) "Yearbook of International Organizations," Sec. Gen., 1 Rue aux Laines, Bruxelles 1, and (b) *The Europa Yearbook*, London.

[3] e.g. Mangone, G. J. *A Short History of International Organizations*, New York, 1954.

INDEX OF NAMES

INDEX OF SUBJECTS

72 73 74 75 76   9 8 7 6 5 4 3 2 1